Rabah Saoud

Architectural Encounters: Islam and the West

Rabah Saoud

Architectural Encounters: Islam and the West

Noor Publishing

Imprint

Any brand names and product names mentioned in this book are subject to trademark, brand or patent protection and are trademarks or registered trademarks of their respective holders. The use of brand names, product names, common names, trade names, product descriptions etc. even without a particular marking in this work is in no way to be construed to mean that such names may be regarded as unrestricted in respect of trademark and brand protection legislation and could thus be used by anyone.

Cover image: Provided by the author

Publisher:
Noor Publishing
is a trademark of
International Book Market Service Ltd., member of OmniScriptum Publishing Group
17 Meldrum Street, Beau Bassin 71504, Mauritius

Printed at: see last page
ISBN: 978-3-330-85240-2

Zugl. / Approved by: كتابي

CONTENTS

ACKNOWLEDGMENTS AND CREDITS OF ILLUSTRATIONS

The present work is based on historical research conducted mostly in Manchester, UK. I am grateful to John Ryland Library of the University of Manchester for allowing me to use their valuable documents while I had an Alumni membership. I am indebted to all friends and colleagues who encouraged, helped or shared information with me, enabling me to research and publish this work. I am particularly grateful to my historian friend and colleague Dr. Salah Al-Jazairi (Zaimeche), who was behind my perseverance in finishing this tedious task.

In later stages, some other important people became involved. I am particularly thankful to Lujain Al-Mezaini, who kindly oversaw the freehand work, and Abeeha Awan for designing the book cover. My gratitude also extend to Enfal Ahmedoglu, Ibtihal Ahmedoglu and Zahra Cagırcı for their help on Turkish material. I am thankful to Amir Reza for his time and effort in helping me with the material of Iran.

Finally I am indebted with gratitude to the support and love of my family – My wife and children Adam, Yasmine and Hussam. They were all there for me and without them this accomplishment would not have been possible.

Photo Credits:
Lujain al-Meziani (all free hand drawings)
Abeeha Awan (Book cover image)
Enfal Ahmedoglu, Ibtihal Ahmedoglu and Zahra Cagirci (figure 39, figure 62, figure 63, figure 67)
Amir Reza (figure 38, figure 40, figure 41, figure 42, figure 46, figure 56, figure 57, figure 58, figure 59, figure 60, figure 61)
Noor AlNahar (figure 8, figure 9, figure 43)
Abdelmonem Mohamed (figure 18, figure 28, figure 29, figure 30, figure 31, figure 32, figure 44, figure 45, figure 90, figure 92)
Moataz Egbaria (Figure 16)
Ali Amor (figure 7, figure 10, figure 11, figure 12, figure 13, Figure 14, figure 75)
Ahmed Kadhimi (figure 17, figure 19, figure 106, figure 107)
Katharina Schachtner (figure 47, figure 48, figure 49, figure 50)
Glyn Willett (figure 65, figure 66, figure 68, figure 83)
Tom Nomad courtesy of amazing-world-in-free-stock-pictures-and-photos.com (figure 33, figure 34, figure 36, figure 37, figure 84, figure 85)
Silvjia Seres (Figure 23, Figure 24, Figure 35, figure 86, figure 139)
Habib M'henni at Wikimedia Commons (figure 26)
Meghana Hassan at My World (http://meghanahassan.blogspot.ae), (figure 51, figure 53, figure 54, figure 55)

PROLOGUE

Samuel P. Huntington, the chief protagonist of the strained relation between Islam and Christianity, for example, says the following: *"The relations between Islam and Christianity, both orthodox and western, have often been stormy. Each has been other's other."*[1] In his opinion, it is the fault of Islam, as he claims, *"Islam is the only civilisation which has put the survival of the west in doubt, and it has done that at least twice."*[2] For many Westerners, Islam is the religion of the sword, and since the events of the controversial 9/11/2001, it is seen as a religion of explosive belts and suicide bombers.

For Muslims these misconceptions are merely justifications for waging war on their countries, exploitation of their natural resources and enslaving their populations. The painful memories of the crusade and colonialism speak of western aggression and imperialism as well as Christian militancy. It is only in Islam where minorities, Jewish and Christian, survived with all their privileges and wealth intact. Despite the Israeli Muslim conflict over Palestine (Jerusalem), and Israel's attempts to force migration of Arab Jews into Israel, many of these still prefer to remain in their Muslim countries such as the Jews of Morocco, Tunisia and Yemen. Meanwhile, historians, Arabs and non-Arabs, always hailed Arab Christians for their Arab patriotism and always stood beside the Muslims to defend against the Christian aggression, not only at times of the crusades but also in modern days. These instances highlight the true character of Islam, which was never against Christianity but against the imperial greed of Christianised militants. Islam encouraged positive and friendly relationship with Christians and early Muslims took refuge with the wise king of Christian Abyssinia (Ethiopia).

The civilised and positive contact between Muslims and Westerners were more numerous and impressive than contacts of war and misfortunes. These were unfortunately either deliberately concealed or mistakenly ignored. There existed many instances of coexistence and cooperation, shared human values, traditions, vigorous commercial trading, and mutual cultural penetration within a mosaic of political rivalries and religious rhetoric. One of the few recently published books, which gives a groundbreaking account of such co-existence, is the edited work of John Tolan et al., Europe and the Islamic World: a History, Princeton University Press, 2012. The book puts beyond any doubt the common shared history between Europe and Islam, illustrating how ongoing cultural encounters have profoundly shaped both.[3] It simply argues that both are part of the same civilization.

The present book provides unique perspectives on Muslim-European cultural encounters, and architectural and artistic exchanges. The present volume is dedicated to the contribution of Muslim architecture to many aspects of European architecture particularly during the medieval period.

Notes

[1]Samuel. P Huntington, *the Clash of Civilisations and the Remaking of World Order, Simon and Schuster*, 1996, p. 209.

[2] Ibid. p. 210

[3] John Tolan, Henry Laurens and Gilles Veinstein (2012), '*Europe and the Islamic World: A History,*' Princeton University Press, 2012

CHAPTER ONE

General Setting and Introductory Notes

Concepts and Paradigms.

Although Muslim architecture has been investigated by both Muslims and non-Muslims, it is still omitted from mainstream architecture theories and many of the existing works are no more than curiosities undertaken by a group of sympathisers mainly Orientalists. The general conclusion the reader can draw from the existing literature is the striking shift in paradigm in which Muslim architecture is accepted or understood. In the first instance there is a deliberate silence as many of the relevant text books jump from the Byzantine architecture (4th and 6th century CE) to European Medieval architecture of the 11th century, known as Romanesque, neglecting a period of over five centuries in which Muslim architecture was flowering across many parts of Asia Minor, Africa and Southern Europe. For example, Porter[4] and Simpson[5], two key early reference works on History of architecture did not refer at all to Islamic architecture. The three-volume work of Simpson touched upon the architecture of most world cultures, including the Sassanians, but failed completely to refer to Muslim architecture. He jumped from Sassanian and Byzantine architecture to the Romanesque.

Indeed, there are views circulating in the West, which reject the islamisation of architecture arguing that the name "Islamic architecture" was used by Orientalists only to differentiate it from other types of architecture. The misconception of Islam's opposition to building and urbanisation that circulates among Western scholars was the basis for many of these claims.   For them the saying of the Prophet: *"Building is the most pointless of the undertaking that can endeavour the riches of a believer"*, or of the Quran in Surah 16, verse 80, *"And Allah has made for you in your homes an abode, and made for you out of the hides of the cattle (tents for) dwelling, which you find so light (and handy) when you travel and when you stay (in your travels)... "*, are all testimonies indicating the lack of any architectural or building tradition among the Arabs and Muslims. In addition to the nomadic lifestyle of the Arabs which encouraged the widespread use of the temporary shelter of tents. Much of the building heritage of what is called Muslim architecture came from Christian, Persian, or Indian origins[6] and Muslims only imitated and sometimes employed masons from these cultures. Hope[7], for example, provided a chapter on Islamic architecture entitled "Derivation of the Persian, Mohammedan, and Moorish architecture from that of Byzantium".   The title clearly demonstrates why Hope referred to Islamic architecture.

1

The answer to these claims involves three main arguments. Islam although it opposes the exaggeration of unnecessary spending, it has no objection to comfortable life or wealth as such, nor to the enjoyment of this worldly life. The hadith reported earlier speaks against excessive spending on building for the sake of pomposity and extravagance. If the building was for a lawful purpose, such as providing shelter for the needy, as a means of earning, providing housing for one's dependants, or the like, there is nothing in Islam against that. Deeds are judged according to the intentions, and every person shall have but that which they intended.[8] Allah has submitted all of his creation to the benefit of man, his favourite creature, but man has to use it within the boundary of Allah's law and guidance and therefore Muslims do not have to live miserably. Sources from Prophet's tradition asserted that he had worn rich clothes in festivities and was very fond of exquisite perfumes and essences. The Islamic saying: *"Strive for your earthly life as you live forever and strive for your hereafter as you will die tomorrow"* sums it all up.[9]

Islam has no objection to building and urbanisation; on the contrary, it requests the son of Adam to work and settle Earth if he is to fulfil his main divine purpose as Allah's entrusted servant (Caliph). The 14th century Muslim sociologist, Ibn Khaldun was the first to define man as an urban creature, this urbanity entails him, and the Muslim in particular, to dwell earth and make use of its bounties: *"It was He who raised you up from the earth and gave you means to dwell upon it"* (the Quran, 16:4).

In relation to building activity, we find indications in the Quran as well as in the tradition of the prophet Muhammad showing that the first builder was prophet Adam who, under the guidance of God (Allah), built the Kaaba[10], the first earthly building. After him, it was prophet Ibrahim and his son Ismail who rebuilt it after its collapse, some 800 years before prophet Suleiman built his famous temple which the West consider as the origin of architecture. The Quran also refers to building in a number of occasions. In Surah 66, verse 11, for example, the wife of the Pharaoh in her supplication says *"My Lord! build for me a home with You in Paradise, and save me from Fir'aun (Pharaoh) and his work, and save me from the unjust people"*. Reliable historic reports established that prophet Muhammed was also involved in the construction of his mosque as he carried bricks, and helped in the construction of dwellings of some of his followers. In one of his sayings, he stressed that *"for him who builds a mosque, God will build him a home in Paradise"*[11].

As for borrowing from other cultures, we find the argument endorsing the universal concept of the message of Islam. Islam's accommodation and tolerance to other cultures has been its strongest point: *"There is no difference between an Arab (Muslim) and a non-Arab except by Piety"*, declares the Prophet. *"Believers are but brothers"*, adds the Quran (49:10). In no other part of the world was the population so diversified but united than in the Muslim World. This is the secret of the success story of the Muslim art, architecture, science and technology during the middle Ages. Its expansion over a vast territory, spanning three continents, provided a cultural richness that played a significant role in the elaboration of Muslim art and architecture. Converts of Christian, Persian and Indian origins enthusiastically redefined their knowledge as well as their experience in the arts, industry and various accomplishments of their respective nations, conforming it to Islamic values and injecting it into their new world in the form of an outstanding innovation. Fletcher (1961) denied the blind imitation of Muslims of other cultures and admitted that: *"The Muslims were content to adopt each local style that they found, modifying it mainly in distinctive ornamental details, but also introducing several important new features of plan and structure"*[12].

On the other hand, early imitation or sometimes adaptation of non-Muslim buildings was deliberate, as these buildings were often communal centres for pagan societies. The early introduction of a completely alien architecture was not desirable as Islam remodelled existing traditions and built on them the new values and life systems. Therefore, these centres, which played prominent roles in misleading a particular community in ignorant pagan times, provided new enlightened rays of the new belief. The early use of churches in Syria and Spain, and temples in Persia and India is evidence of these attitudes, and according to Henry Saladin, the plan of the mosque was also derived from older Semitic sanctuaries[13]. Muslims have always maintained that Islam is a purification and renovation of God's (Allah) old religion dictated to previous prophets Ibrahim, Moses and Jesus. The building of mosques and the diffusion of the new architecture did not take place until Islam was strong in that community or region. This is evident in Spain and Sicily where Muslim architecture clearly showed no connection with existing Visigothic and Lombardic/Byzantine building cultures respectively. As Islam grew stronger and reached a high degree of economic and cultural prosperity, core architectural features, forms and techniques unique to Muslim buildings started to develop under the Umayyad Caliphs and their successors. The existence of these core features is a fundamental factor behind the Muslim identification, in similar way other elements unique to Christian or Japanese architecture would define their building style as such.

The Changing Paradigm of Muslim Architecture

In other instances, different concepts and meanings were applied to Muslim architecture, evolving through time and reflecting the changing relations between the East and West. At the beginning, Muslim architecture was denoted as *Saracenic*, a crusading name refusing to accept Islam as a divine religion[14]. Here, architecture was given a geographical identity connecting it with people of the East, *sharqiyun* as the Arabic origin of Saracenic indicates. The etymological root of the word 'Saracen', however, goes back to Abraham and his wife Sarah. Saracen means 'someone who is not from Sarah', reflecting the belief of medieval Christians that Arabs/Muslims hailed from Hagar, Abraham's slave wife. Early scholars such as Sir Christopher Wren, for example, talked of Saracenic architecture having influenced the Gothic architecture. Other examples include the works of Lane Poole Stanley and Hanbury Hankin who used the same name to denote Muslim art and architecture.[15] The majority of these early Anglo Saxon views treated Muslim architecture with the same dislike and rejection they retained for the Muslims. Ruskin wrote, *"You will find that the (Saracenic or Muslim) art whose end is pleasure only is pre-eminently the gift of cruel and savage nations, cruel in temper, savage in habits and conception; but that the (western) art which is especially dedicated to natural fact always indicates a peculiar gentleness and tenderness of mind".[16]*

A shift in paradigm can be noted in another category of works where authors narrowed the definition to only the followers of Muhammad, thus replacing Saracen with Mohammadan. Muslims strongly object to this definition as it insinuates that Islam is not God's message but a fabrication of Muhammad. One of the earliest authors to adopt this concept was the historian R.B. Smith[17] in his book "Mohammed and Mohammedanism", which was published in London in 1874. This was followed by Stanley Lane-Poole's 1894 publication of "the Mohammedan Dynasties. Architectural historians such as Martin Briggs and others[18] also applied this definition to Muslim architecture.[19]

Although these definitions are becoming less popular in recent times, they nonetheless dominated most of what was written about Islam, up to late 19th century. It was during this period that Europe saw the rise of orientalism and colonialism as it started discovering the Muslim world from a new. Following in the footsteps of the colonial armies, connoisseurs, travellers, missionaries and adventurers poured into various Muslim countries. As their work was published, substantial amount of information on the nature and character of Muslim life, art and architecture was made available. These developments incorporated for the first time the concept of Arabism, introduced mainly to undermine the Ottoman caliphate, the only Muslim power capable of defeating colonial plans of Europe, by "liberating" the Arabs from the "dominance" of the Turks. Such approach was successfully executed; Arab nationalism engaged the Turks, with the help of their colonial allies, considerably weakening the already "sick man of Europe" - as Turkey was called then. The works of French Arabists such as Pascal[20], Prisse d'Avennes[21], and more recently Glubb[22], Hayes[23] and Hutt[24] are typical examples of the new Arabic paradigm.

It is quite clear that limiting much of the achievement of Muslim civilisation to the Arab people of countries such as Egypt, Syria, Iraq and the Arabian Gulf is misleading and incorrect. The Arabism unfairly disregards the huge contribution of many races, which once formed the heart of the Muslim world, i.e., Persia, south East Asia, Anatolia, Turkey, and Africa. As the reader will discover in this book, many of the major accomplishments of Islam were attributed to other cultures rather than the Arabic. The use of the term "Islamic" Architecture is a more recent conviction as the Islamic taboo among Western intellectuals was defeated by the rise of modern liberalism. We saw a surge of a large number of books incorporating the Islamic title in various topics, including art and architecture. Here, the charm of Muslim architecture and art gained their due respect. In the opinion of Sir Banister Fletcher, the Muslim style had `reached peaks of accomplishment that rank high among man's achievements.'[25]

Generally, the work of this group of scholars can be grouped into three main categories in relation to their approach of study. The first team studied Muslim architecture in historical chronology underlying the main construction works carried by various dynasties and rulers. Such works include those of Creswell[26], Bloom & Blair, [27] Ettinghaussen and Grabar, [28] and many others. The chronological approach is most important in studying the historical evolution of various architectural elements, techniques, buildings, and decor. This undertaking seems to be the most appropriate to the theme of this book and subsequently it was adopted in the first chapter where the chronological study was limited to periods having the most critical/ influential innovations.

The second group of work adopted a geographical approach based on studying the architecture of localities highlighting the similarities and differences between various regions and countries of the Muslim world. Examples of such works include Marcais[29], Behrens,[30] Wilber,[31] Hattstein and Delius[32] and others. With the spread of Islam to various regions in Asia, Africa and Europe architects and designers had to adapt to a new geography, faced different challenges and consequently developed different solutions. They designed, arranged, and built structures to fit the new location, climate, resources and local cultures that were available. The main critique against this approach is that it does not provide a general picture of the architectural evolution and developments introduced throughout the history of Muslim civilisation, and more importantly, it ignores the influences coming from main centres of the Islamic culture, such as Damascus, Baghdad and Cordoba.

The third approach concentrated on building typologies that form the centre around which Muslim architecture evolved. Here, the notion of Islamic architecture has been associated with Muslim monuments such as mosques, palaces, and castles. Works of this scope include those of Mitchell et al.[33], Hillenbrand[34], Clevenot[35] and many others. It is obvious that this approach is more suitable for studies of the functional aspects of Muslim architecture, a very important element in understanding its meaning and formal properties. In its review of Muslim architecture, the book combines the functional approach with that of the chronological considering it to be the most suitable way of meeting the objectives and aims of the analysis of the evolution of Muslim architectural innovations.

Muslim or Islamic Architecture.

The second issue is terminological connected to the use of "Muslim" and "Islamic". The two words are theoretically interconnected but conceptually different. Muslim is a general word referring to religious and geographical setting of Islam. Muslim architecture is the building style of the countries of Muslim religion, a term which may include modern or old architecture practised in these countries and which may not be necessarily Islamic nor display any known features of Islamic architecture such as the arch, the dome, and stucco decoration. Similarly, we say today a Muslim city to refer to its location in the Muslim country rather than to its Islamic morphological features. The other disadvantage of using this concept is related to buildings of Muslim origin but not in the Muslim world as the case of Spain, Sicily, former USSR and other countries. More positively, one can define it as including the architecture of Muslim masons, architects, for or under Muslim patronage (government), or in a Muslim country.

Islamic architecture can be also misleading, as one may understand that it refers to the architecture of a particular religious (Islamist) group or that of a religious function while in reality it refers to the Islamic way of building as prescribed by the *Sharia* law. In this definition, we are not concerned with the location and actual function of the building but rather with its Islamic character in terms of design, form and décor, a definition that includes all types of building rather than only monuments. The main rule for this is Surah 9, verse 109 which states "*is it then he who laid the foundation of his building on piety to Allah and His good*

6

pleasure better, or he who laid the foundation on the brink of an undetermined precipice ready to crumble down, so that it crumbled to pieces with him into the Fire of Hell. And Allah guides not the unjust people. "[36]. This is as practical for the ordinary house, as it is for the mosque as well as the palace and other major architectural monuments.

Muslim Architectural Contribution

The other issue is whether Muslim architecture has played any role or exercised any influence on the architecture of other cultures, especially the European. Studies of civilisation as well as social theories have long established that societies interact and exchange experiences as well as goods. For example, Braudel in his Grammaire des civilisations[37] added the interaction element to the definition of civilisation arguing that although civilisation is attached to geography but: *"the establishment of spaces inhabited (by this civilisation) and frontiers which border them does not exclude the permeability of these frontiers in face of various journeys of cultural goods continually crossing through them."* He adds further, *"Each civilisation exports and receives cultural elements produced elsewhere"*. These elements can be a particular technique, a raw material, a craft or an industrial product. Although exchange can be in both directions, the scales are often dominated by the culturally strong and economically (or militarily) powerful, who creates and innovates while the poor and weak usually imitates. This is dramatically true in modern days where the developed world with its intellectual and industrial powers does most of the creating[38], while the Third World, including many Muslims, is trailing behind in the consumption and in the imitation of much of its material and cultural production. With globalisation, this phenomenon is increasingly gaining importance and the gap between the developed and the undeveloped is becoming wider reaffirming what is known as the culture of dependency.[39] We increasingly see the Third World, and Muslims, becoming dependent even in their lifestyle on the Western system. This is particularly articulated by those views promoting modernity. The spread of skyscrapers, modern housing, Western consumption products (such as cars, computers, fast food, Pop music, and jeans) and even the Western teaching and education systems in the Muslim world, all are but indicators of this exchange.

If one accepts the truth in this theory, then similar processes must have taken place in the middle ages, a time when the reverse situation was present. History tells us that Europe was in an unfavourable situation probably worse than that of the Muslim world today, and the only high civilisation existing was that of the Muslims. History also informs that there was mutual exchange between Europe and the Muslims, although not to the same extent as today. A similar process of imitation and adaptation to take place then but this time favouring the Muslims who were the source of innovation and creativity. In this respect, Western scholars acknowledge the leading role played by Muslims in the spread and development of science especially mathematics, geometry, optics, chemistry, medicine and astronomy. The European elite travelled and studied amongst the Muslims, acquiring their knowledge, and universities, such as Cordoba, were crowded with Christian and Jewish students.[40] The literary and philosophical production of Muslims exercised a powerful influence on their counterparts in Europe, especially in what is known as the "troubadour" poetry, which paved the way for an artistic and literary revival in Europe. In the domain of decorative arts, we also find Muslim hands at work in most areas.

In architecture, however, there is complete silence, sometimes compounded by deliberate concealment. The task of the present study is to establish, giving evidence where possible, the contribution of Muslim architecture to the development and rebirth of European architecture. The investigation is carried out in five main chapters. The first two are intended to establish the general historical setting and the underlying general conditions dominating the medieval world of the Muslims and Europeans. The aim is to provide an historical comparison between the achievements and contribution of each side and assess the motives and chances of exchange of ideas and techniques between the two societies. The central argument of the first chapter is that the Muslim civilisation was raised on the vestiges of the two old empires of the Greeks and Romans with additional contributions from the Persian (Sassanian) and Indian cultures. From this heritage, Muslims went on to make some of the most outstanding scientific and technological advances, which played a decisive influence on the architectural innovations. The nature and character of Muslim civilisation, which had reached its peak by the eleventh and twelfth centuries, a time when Europe was just coming out of the Dark Ages, permitted new inventions, theories and ideas to spill over to the rest of Europe, particularly from neighbouring Spain, Sicily and North Africa. The tolerance of Islam and its universal message encouraged the transmission and dissemination of knowledge to other cultures. There are numerous verses from the Quran, which condemn the concealment of knowledge and truth. For example, one verse warns those who hide information and truth of dire consequences: *"(Nor) those who are niggardly or enjoin niggardliness on others, or hide the bounties which Allah hath bestowed on them; for We have prepared, for those who resist Faith, a punishment that steeps them in contempt"* (the Quran, 4:37), and in another those who sell information and truth for money are also severely cautioned: *"Those who conceal Allah's revelations in the Book, and purchase for them a miserable profit, - they swallow into themselves naught but Fire; Allah will not address them on the Day of*

8

Resurrection. Nor purify them: Grievous will be their penalty" (the Quran, 2:174). Examples of such overflow are the use of Arabic numerals and other mathematical advances as well as numerous medical and philosophical ideas, which did not recognise geographical or cultural boundaries.

The second chapter argues that Europe, with its ancient history, experienced civilisation centuries before the birth of Islam, with the majority of its regions once belonging to either the Greek or the Roman empires. However, as it is commonly thought after the fall of the Roman Empire, in the fifth century, Europe entered a period of decline, lasting up to the 12ᵗʰ century, after which a sudden revival and awakening took place. The case put forward here is that the rise of Islam coincided with the long nap that Europe took during the Dark Ages. Europe was in desperate need for Muslim knowledge to start the much-needed cultural and scientific recovery, which it began towards the end of the eleventh century. These motives were far more important than the apparent Europe's enmity to Islam. The endeavour of this chapter is to establish the circumstantial evidence, which suggests that it was Europe's turn to build itself on the foundations of Medieval Islam.

The third chapter discusses the routes of the transfer of ideas, motifs and themes between the two cultures and the modalities of their cultural exchange. The central thrust here is to explore the role of those actors involved in the movement of ideas, items and equipment and to examine various ways the transfer took concentrating mainly on those which had the greatest impact on the transmission of art and building techniques and forms. This process is summarised in three main transfer areas where most of the contact took place. In the East, the Levant played a role essentially through trade, the crusades and pilgrimage. In neighbouring North Africa, the means were mainly trade, crusades, and visiting scholars, headed principally by Italian and French merchants and crusaders. Spain and Sicily constituted the third and most influential pole due to their geographic proximity to Europe and the presence of a large Christian-Jewish minority, which established strong bonds with Muslims and had a linguistic advantage as their majority spoke Arabic.

The fourth chapter sets out to investigate the circumstances and origins of the architectural recovery in Europe. First, it looks briefly at the general circumstances leading to the so-called architectural revival of the middle Ages, concluding that the general environment in Europe was not congenial to the development of any architectural innovation and particularly the highly elaborate Gothic style, which suggests an external influence. This will be theoretically examined in a brief review of the main theoretical framework dealing with the question of the origin of Gothic architecture. After this, there is a concise discussion on the predominant cultural and philosophical ideologies coinciding with the birth of the Gothic style in Europe. Here, once again, the Muslim influence can be established. This will be incorporated into another section, which concentrates on the main popular literary production, which emerged in Europe at that particular time. Its possible influence is examined and traced to its source, which is found to be also connected to the Muslims. Then the route, which facilitated the flow of Muslim architectural forms and ideas to Europe, is explored and evidence given. The three main ways in which such a transfer took place, namely through the Spanish (Andalusian), Sicilian and Crusader connections, are established. Finally, the processes, which led to the birth of Gothic, are followed up, explaining the ways and dates when various constructive elements of Gothic were incorporated in European architecture and establishing their Muslim origin.

The previous chapters should have demonstrated how the Muslims inspired most of the intellectual and artistic movements of Medieval Europe. Such influence will be traced in both Romanesque and Gothic styles, which dominated the period between the 11th and 15th centuries. These developments were the main ingredients behind the rebirth and awakening of Europe which reached its peak in the 15th century, marking the beginning of what is known as the Renaissance. This period will be the focus of a second stage of investigation, which is devoted to the assessment of the Muslim contribution to European art and architecture of this time. Following the analytical approach adopted previously, chapter five begins with establishing arguments for the continuous validity of Muslim architectural and artistic motifs for Europe in the Renaissance period and emphasising the prominent role of Muslim civilisation despite the emerging influence of Chinese art. Then, it looks at the processes which enabled Europeans to accumulate considerable amount of information on Muslim art and architecture. Later, the chapter discusses the ways and routes through which such information reached Europe, examining various possibilities based on historical accounts and documentation. After that, attention is paid to areas of influence where the contribution of Islam is evident and substantial, concentrating on Arabesque, textile, pottery, and architecture.

10

Notes

[4] Porter Arthur Kingsley (1909), '*Medieval Architecture, its Origins and Development*', Vol:1-2. Vol.1: Origins. Vol.2: Normandy and The Ile de France., The Baker and Taylor, New York.

[5] Simpson, F.M. (1913) '*A History of Architectural Development*', Longmans, Green & Co. London.

[6] Similar argument was also put forward against Muslim Science arguing that the role of Muslims was merely concentrated on the translation of Greek and Roman manuscripts.

[7] Hope, T. (1835) '*An Historical Essay on Architecture*', John Murray, London.

[8] As the Messenger of Allah (peace be upon him) said, "*Actions are only according to intentions, and every person shall have but that which they intended.*" Related by Al-Bukhari and Muslim in their two authentic or *Sahih* books of Hadith.

[9] This is a popular saying in the Muslim World, widely considered as an authentic saying from Prophet Mohammed, but recently scholars disputed its authenticity; see the Permanent Committee for Fatwa, Fatwa 269/3.

[10] The are two views in this matter: The first view emphasises that Adam (puh) was the one who built the Kaabah in Makkah arguing that the Quran referred to prophet Ibrahim (puh) and his son Ismail (puh) in the rebuilding activity suggesting that the Kaabah had existed before. The other view supports the theory of Ibrahim (puh) and Ismail (puh) to be the first builders translating the corresponding verse as building rather than rebuilding.

[11] There are numerous sayings about building and making use of earth.

[12] Fletcher, B (1961), '*A History of Architecture, on the Comparative Method*', the Athlon Press, London, 17th edition, p.1226.

[13] Saladin, H. (1899), '*La Grande Mosquée de Kairwan*', Paris.

[14] In Deutch Sarazin and Italian Saraceno.

[15] Lane-Poole (1886), '*Saracenic Art*', London, and E. H. Hankin (1925), '*The Drawing of Geometric Patterns in Saracenic Art*', Central Publication Branch, Calcutta, Government of India.

[16] Ruskin, John (1859), '*The Works of John Ruskin*', ed. E. T. Cook and A. Wedderburn, George Allen, 1903-1912, London

[17] Smith R.B. (1874), '*Mohammed and Mohammedanism*', Smith Elder, London.

[18] See for example, Shakespeare, John (1816), '*The History of the Mahometan Empire in Spain*', James Cavanah Murphy., T. Cadell and W. Davies, London

[19] Briggs, M.S. (1924), '*Muhammadan Architecture in Egypt and Palestine*', Clarendon Press, Oxford.

[20] La Cost Pascal (1837), '*Architecture Arabe ou Monuments du Kaire*', Paris.

[21] Prisse d'Avennes (1877), '*L'art Arabe d'Après les Monuments du Kaire; Depuis le VIIe Siècle Jusqu'à la fin du XVIIIe*', Morel, Paris.

[22] Glubb John (1963), '*The Empire of the Arabs*', Hodder & Stoughton, London

[23] John R. Hayes (ed.) (1983), '*The Genius of Arab Civilization*', MIT Press, USA and Westerham Press, UK.

[24] Hutt, A. (1984). "*Arab Architecture: Past and Present. An Exhibition Presented by The Arab-British Chamber of Commerce at the Royal Institute of British Architects*". *University of Durham, the Centre for Middle Eastern & Islamic Studies.*

[25] Sir Banister Fletcher (1975), '*A History of Architecture*': 18th edition, revised by J. C. Palmes: University of London, The Athlon press, 1975. p. 415.

[26] Creswell, K.A. (1958) '*A Short Account of Early Muslim Architecture*', Harmondsworth, Middlesex, Baltimore, Penguin Books.

[27] Bloom, J. & Blair, S. (1998), '*Islamic Arts*', Phaidon Press, London. and Blair, S. & Bloom, J. (1994), '*The Art and Architecture of Islam 1250-1800*', Yale University Press.

[28] Ettinghausen, R. and Grabar, O. (1987). '*The Art and Architecture of Islam 650-1250*', New Haven, Yale University Press, republished in 1994.

[29] Marçais, Georges, (1954), '*L'architecture Musulmane d'Occident : Tunisie, Algérie, Maroc, Espagne et Sicily*', Arts et métiers graphiques, Paris.

[30] Behrens-Abouseif, D. (1989), '*Islamic Architecture in Cairo*', the American University in Cairo Press.

[31] Wilber, Donald N. (1969), '*The Architecture of Islamic Iran*', Greenwood Press, New York.

[32] Hattstein Markus and Delius Peter (eds.) (2000), '*Islam: Art and Architecture*', Konemann, Cologne.

[33] Mitchell, G. et al. (eds.) (1978), '*Architecture of the Islamic World, its History and Social Meaning*', Thames and Hudson, London.

[34] Hillenbrand, R. (1994), '*Islamic Architecture Form, Function and Meaning*' Edinburgh University Press, Edinburgh.

[35] Clévenot, Dominique (2000), '*Splendours of Islam: Architecture, Decoration, and Design*'; photographs by Gérard Degeorge. New York: Vendome Press; Distributed in the USA and Canada by Rizzoli International Publications through St. Martin's Press.

[36] For more elaborate discussion of various rules of Sharia in building, consult Hakim.B. (1986) Hakim, B. (1986) '*Arabic Islamic Cities: Buildings and Planning Principles*', Kegan Paul, London.

[37] Braudel, F. (1987), '*Grammaire des Civilisations*', Arthaud, Falmmarion, Paris, p.45.

[38] Such creativity is economically driven and directed towards achieving more dominance.

[39] See for example, Amin, S. (1974) '*Accumulation on a World Scale: a Critique of the Theory of Underdevelopment*', 2 vols, Monthly Review Press, New York, and Frank, A.G. (1967), '*Capitalism and Underdevelopment in Latin America*', Pelican, London.

[40] In the same way as today's Muslim elite students travel European lands in pursuit of learning.

CHAPTER TWO

The Golden Age of Muslim Civilisation: Scientific and Architectural Achievements

Historical Introduction.

The rise of Muslim civilisation was the direct outcome of a number of unfolding socio-economic and intellectual circumstances, which reached their peak in the middle Ages. This was a time when the rest of the world, particularly Christian Europe, was engulfed in the ignorance and barbarity of what is known as the Dark Ages. It is widely acknowledged that the most striking feature of Islam had been its rapid expansion. Emerging between the great empires of Byzantium and Persia, within 80 years, from the Prophet's migration to Medina and his foundation of the first Mosque there, Islam reached North Africa and Spain and later other parts as far away as China (fig.1). This expansion was primarily sustained by the appealing nature of the Islamic message with its logical reasoning, social justice and promotion of good and forbidding of evil. The overwhelming power of this teaching is clearly seen in the devotion of new Muslims (converts) who played decisive roles in its proclamation and expansion. We find for example, North African Berbers leading the Islamisation of Spain as well as most of Africa. Similarly, the Persians led the way in carrying Islam to South and Central Asia.

A wide audience in the West sees the spread of Islam as achieved by conquest and force. Recently and after the attack against New York World Trade Centre and the Pentagon on 11th September 2001, the Muslims are increasingly being portrayed as barbarian killers who hate life. This does not reconcile with the Quran, which states: *"Let there be no compulsion in religion."*[41] (Quran, 2:256). Muslims talk of *"Futuhat"* which can be translated as "opening up lands and/or societies to Islam". This means that the spread of Islam was achieved mainly by peaceful means and force was used as a last resort only to deter those who interfered with it. The Quran outlined this declaring in one verse: *"and call on to the path of your Lord with wisdom and good argument"* (Quran, 16:125), and in another: *"Verily you (O Muhammad) guide not whom you like, but Allah guides whom He wills. And he knows best those who are guided."* (Quran, 28:56) In other words, the use of force was permitted only in self-defence. In most occasions, Muslims had to engage others, especially the Romans and Sassanians, because the latter were igniting rebellions and helping those opposing Islam.

This was the approach adopted during the great journey of Islam, which started with the prophet Mohammed fleeing with his companion Abu Bakr from Makkah, his dearest city, to Medina in 622 CE. Reaching Medina, the fugitive Prophet soon gathered hundreds of followers who enabled him to protect his faith and to return, eight years later, victorious to Makkah. His declaration of a general amnesty brought him respect and admiration from his enemies as well as his followers. Upon this noble behaviour, the Quran declares, *"We sent thee not, but as a Mercy for all creatures."* (Quran, 21:107). Scott, meanwhile, admires *with magnanimity unequalled in the annals of war, a general amnesty was proclaimed and but four persons, whose offences were considered unpardonable, suffered the penalty of death.*[42]

Though the Quran was fully revealed and no other Prophet or messenger will follow, it was left to the Muslims to choose the political authority of the head of state by election or selection. The elected heads of state are known as Caliphs[43]; they followed his example, and preserved the peaceful nature of Islam. In this respect, Scott observes that: *"The policy of Islam was more conciliatory than menacing. It preferred to inculcate its principles by argument rather than to provoke opposition by invective. It disclaimed the invention of new dogmas, but laboured to reconcile its tenets with those of its venerated predecessors. It discouraged proselytism (conversion) by violence."*[44] Consequently, the attacks made against Islam as a "violent religion" represent one of the biggest perjuries committed by Western scholars. O'Leary accused them, especially historians, of this as he concluded: *"History makes it clear however, that the legend of fanatical Muslims sweeping through the world and forcing Islam at the point of the sword upon conquered races is one of the most fantastically absurd myths that historians have ever repeated."*[45]

Lombard explained that one area where the appeal of Islam was decisive in the conversion of various cultures was its tendencies for democracy, justice, and cosmopolitanism[46]. These communities welcomed Islam as a liberator from the deteriorating conditions imposed by the long lasting injustice of the existing Roman, Byzantine and Sasanian empires. The essence of this change was outlined by the speech of Jaafar ibn Abi Talib (a companion and cousin of Prophet Muhammad), which he delivered to the Abyssinian court about the Islam: *"We were plunged in the dark meanders of ignorance and barbarism; we adored idols; we ate animals that had died of themselves; we committed hateful things; we wounded the love of our own relations, and violated the laws of hospitality. Ruled by our passions, we only recognised the law of the strongest, until God has chosen a man from our race, illustrious by his birth, for very long respected for his virtues. This Prophet had taught us to profess the unity of God, to reject the superstitions of our fathers, to despise Gods of stones and wood. He*

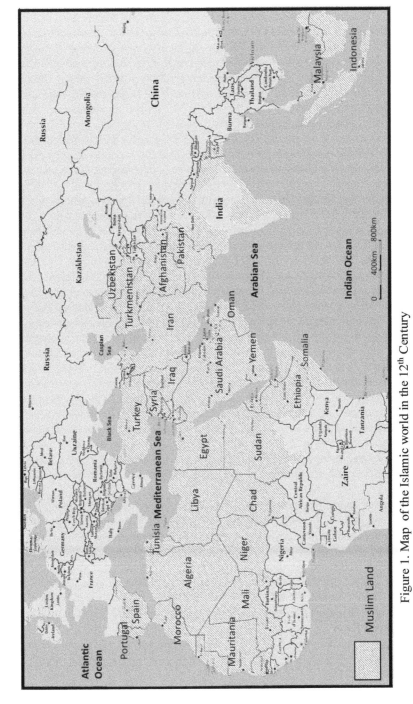

Figure 1. Map of the Islamic world in the 12th Century

commanded us to speak the truth, to be faithful to our trusts, to love our relations, and to protect our guests, to flee vice, to be kind and generous towards our parents and neighbours. He has forbidden us from despoiling women's honour, and from robbing orphans. He recommended us prayers, giving alms, and fasting. We have believed in his mission; we have respected the laws and the morale that he brought us on behalf of God. "[47] Indeed, in the opinion of James Michener, Islam made a great difference in terms of liberty: "*No other religion in history spread so rapidly as Islam...The West has widely believed that this surge of religion was made possible by the sword. But no modern scholar accepts that idea, and the Qur'an is explicit in support of the freedom of conscience.*"[48]

With this peaceful approach, Islam swiftly expanded through Arabia, Syria and Mesopotamia (633-7) and Egypt (639-42). North Africa followed suit in 709 CE enabling Islam to cross to the other side of the Mediterranean Sea, into Spain and Sicily (710 CE). In the East, Islam spread with the same speed through Persia (642 CE) the land of Sind (711 CE) and to Tashkent in 712 CE. Islam's considerable tolerance and accommodation of other scriptural religions, namely Christianity and Judaism, is demonstrated by the long presence of Christians in Syria, Lebanon and Egypt, and Jews in North Africa and Andalusia. They were often referred to as *dhimmis*, meaning people of the pact. The pact gave the non-Muslim minorities, including the people of the Book (Jews and Christians) a legal and religious status by which Muslim rulers are obliged to protect and guarantee their public and private rights. The dhimmis also enjoyed a large degree of freedom, living in accordance with their own laws and customs and subjected to the authority of their own leaders and judges. In the words of Glubb: "*the Muslims of the seventh century had abstained from persecution and had permitted Jews and Christians to practise their own laws and to elect their own judges. Yet nearly a thousand years later, people in Europe were still being tortured and burned alive for their faith. And in general, the Ottomans continued the policy of religious toleration which they had inherited from the Arabs.*"[49]

In harsher conditions, Islam imposed protection taxes, known as Jizyah, on well off dhimmis, while Muslim subjects had to pay Zakat. This tax is often misunderstood, seen as a penalty or tribute for not converting. Professor Arnold was one of the few who correctly studied and understood why the Jizyah was imposed: "*This tax was not imposed on the Christians as a penalty for their refusal to accept Muslim faith, but was paid by them in common with other dhimmis or non-Muslim subjects of the state whose religion preclude them from serving in the army, in return for the protection secured for them by the arms of the Musalmans.*"[50]

Professor Arnold used quotes from Muslim Army generals Khalid Ibn al-Walid and Abu Ubayda ibn al-Jarrah to demonstrate this truth. In his treaty with people of al-Hira (Iraq), Khalid was quoted by al-Tabari reassuring them: *"If we protect you, then Jizyah is due to us; but if we do not, then it is not due."* When the people of al-Hira contributed the sum agreed upon, they expressly mentioned that they paid this Jizyah on condition that *"the Muslims and their leader protect us from those who would oppress us, whether they be Muslims or others."*[51] Abu Ubayda ibn al-Jarrah also wrote to the governors of the conquered cities of Syria, ordering them to pay back all the Jizyah that had been collected from the cities, and wrote to the people saying, *"We give you back the money that we took: from you, as we have received news that a strong force is advancing against us. The agreement between us was that we should protect you, and since this is not now in our power, we return you all that we took. But if we are victorious we shall consider ourselves bound to you by the old terms of our agreement."*[52]

The Jizyah and Zakat were to maintain the social welfare and support the poor including non-Muslims. It was this tolerance, that despite his criticism and intolerance to Islam, Bernard Lewis admitted that *"Muslims were willing to tolerate significant differences in practice and even belief among themselves; they were also willing to concede a certain place in society to other, approved religions ... There is no equivalent to this tolerance in Christendom until the Wars of religion finally convinced Christians that it was time to live and let live. During the eight centuries that Muslims ruled part of the Iberian Peninsula, Christians and Jews remained and even flourished. The consequences of the Christian re-conquest, for Jews and Muslims alike, are well known."*[53]

The Making of Muslim Knowledge

The reasons behind the prominent position Muslims reached in the medieval world in the areas of art, science and technology continues to amaze most historians and civilisation experts. They attribute such an achievement to a number of factors. The first, and by far the most important, was the Muslims' inner desire to acquire knowledge, an ambition fostered by the teaching of Islam. Knowledge was made a primary quest of the Muslims as demonstrated by the request to read (learn) embodied in the first message the prophet Mohammed received. *"Read in the name of thy Lord Who has created all things, Who has created man of congealed blood. Read by your most beneficent Lord, Who taught man by the pen that which he didn't know"* (Quran, 96:1-5). In other numerous other verses the Quran establishes the power and position of the learned over the ignorant: *Say: (unto them, O Muhammad) Are those who know equal to those who know not? It is only men of understanding who will remember"* (Quran,

39:9). The authentic hadith emphasized further: *"Knowledge is a duty upon every Muslim male and female"*. Such a duty should accompany the Muslim throughout his or her life: *"Seek knowledge from the cradle to the grave"*, and wherever he settled: *"Seek knowledge even if in China."*

This message gave early Muslims the impetus to learn, first acquiring religious knowledge to enable them carry out the basic duties of worship and obedience to God. Those who excelled wondered at the discovery of God's marvels embodied in natural and metaphysical laws governing human and universal life. The Quran outlines the spiritual outcome of knowledge: *"Seest thou not that Allah sends down rain from the sky? With it, We then bring out produce of various colours. And in the mountains are tracts white and red, of various shades of colour, and black intense in hue. And so amongst men and crawling creatures and cattle, are they of various colours. Those truly fear Allah, among His Servants, who have knowledge: for Allah is Exalted in Might, Oft-Forgiving."* (Quran, 35:27-28). Therefore, knowledge, even of material forms, was another religious duty bestowed only on those well equipped. The Quran gives a clear message on this: *"O assembly of Jinns and Men, if you can penetrate regions of the heavens and the earth, then penetrate them! You will not penetrate them save with a power."* (Quran, 55:33). With that power (knowledge), the sky is not the limit for Muslims and humans in general.[54]

These directives were translated in society's general appeal to learning led by the Caliph and his court who were often people of literature and had considerable talent in the arts[55]. In the East for example, al- Ma'mun (r.813-833), exceeded the rest of the Caliphs in his intellectual attainment. In Spain, Abd-al-Rahman I (r.756-788) was an astronomer and a successful poet. Hisham I (r.788-796) and al-Hakem I (r.796-822) were distinguished scholars and critics of their time. The attainment of Abd-al-Rahman II (r.822-852) in Science, Philosophy and letters was compared to that of al- Ma'mun. Al-Hakem II (r.961-976) is said to have lost his eyesight because of his extensive reading. His library was so extensive that it overflowed the great building, which had been erected for it.[56] His most famous work was his book on the critical history of Andalusia.

The governors of provinces were of similar qualities and played a complementary role in the propagation and diffusion of knowledge. These learned leaders often offered generous encouragement to people of intellectual genius by the provision of substantial honours and rewards. Distinguished scholars whether Muslims, Jews or Christians received high social regard and were employed in prominent positions and enjoyed the confidence of the Caliph and the favour of the Emirs, patrons and dignitaries. These generous rewards attracted scholars and people of intellect from other nations and religions. The

18

result of this tolerance was the gathering of a rich knowledge and a gigantic research enterprise was established in Muslim capitals especially in Spain. Encouraged by the example of their leaders, the intellectual development of the mass of the population extended considerably.

The second factor involves the cultural and scientific knowledge that Muslims inherited from past civilisations. Unlike other religions, Islam paid great respect to pre-existing traditions and customs that did not interfere with its idealism. It had modelled them into a new way of life regulated by set of laws and rules already familiar to the Christian and Jewish worlds. These attitudes enriched the general cultural life and activated scientific and technological transfer from these civilisations to Muslims through the process of conversion to Islam.[57] The spread of Islam to the East and Mesopotamia (Egypt and Syria) and later to the lands of Sind and Northern India brought it in contact with the Greek and Indian Civilisations. Muslims also made contact with the Chinese civilisation in the course of their expansion into central Asia (Bukhara and Samarkand). These contacts opened the door for wider commercial, cultural and scientific exchange. Meanwhile, the advance of Islam into North Africa and Southern Europe brought it into contact with Roman and Greek heritage. The legacy of the cultural and scientific knowledge that the Muslims gathered from various cultures and regions undoubtedly made a remarkable impact on Muslim scientific development and technological advances, particularly in the 10th and 11th centuries.

The third element consists of the translation of various scientific and philosophical works into Arabic. The expansion of Islam over this vast area provided it with language diversity and capabilities, which played a decisive role in the translation activity. Newly converted Muslims often talked, in the presence of a wide audience of various ethnic origins and experiences, of their cultural and scientific background in animated debates that were usually organised in the main mosque. This gathering provided a referential element in the transmission of knowledge. Additionally, the quest of knowledge mentioned earlier, is not limited to local knowledge but also encourages learning from others. The result of all this was that a considerable translation activity took place, officially established by the Caliph Harun-al-Rashid (786-809) who acquired a large collection of Greek manuscripts from Byzantium and set up the library known as "*Khizanat al-Hikma*", Wisdom Wardrobe. In the reign of al-Ma'mun (813-833), the translation work expanded considerably by the setting of "*Bayt-al-Hikma*" (House of Wisdom) which was a much larger and more ambitious institutional undertaking[58]. Such was his enthusiasm that al- Ma'mun gave Hunayn a famous translator, its weight in gold for every volume he translated.

A number of translators excelled in this work including Ibn-al-Muqaffa' (d.756 CE), who was of Persian origin, and translated the book of fables "*Kalila wa Dimna*" from Pahlevi into Arabic and the biographies of Persian kings (*Sirat Muluk al-Ajam*). Al-Fazari (c.771 CE) translated the Hindu treatise on astronomy the "*Siddhanta*" (Sind Hind). He also compiled the Sassanid astronomical tables (*al-Zij*), and was the first Muslim to construct an astrolabe. The famous Hunayn Ibn Ishaq (809-874 CE), translated many Greek works on medicine, philosophy and mathematics, namely works of Aristotle and Galen. Thabet Ibn Qurra (825-901) translated, among numerous works, "*Archimedes*" and "*Apollonius*" of Parga who was famous in geometry and mechanics. He also translated "*Almagest*" of Ptolemy, "*Elements*" of Euclid as well as other works of Theodosius. Because of this hard work, an academic wealth was generated enriching Muslim libraries, which in Spain had reached up to 400,000 volumes by the time of the Caliph al-Hakem II (961-976). By the mid tenth century, most of the existing Greek and Hellenic works had been translated into Arabic. These efforts have undoubtedly contributed to the scientific attainment of Muslims, which reached its peak in the eleventh and twelfth centuries. Europeans substantially benefited from the advances the Muslims made in initiating the Renaissance.

Scientific and Technological Advances.

The factors outlined above enabled Muslims to lay the foundation of one of the world's most advanced intellectual revolution, producing most of the scientific and technological miracles of the Middle Ages. Muslim capitals such as Cordoba, Cairo, Damascus and Baghdad were the seats for scientific attainment, artistic and architectural magnificence, and the skilful adaptation of mechanical arts. For example, in Cordoba, there were 800 public schools attended by Muslims, Christians and Jews, while at one stage its university accommodated some eleven thousand students.[59] The application of these scientific achievements to industrial and mechanical production was the corner stone for various inventions, which secured the technological superiority of Muslims and delivered their convenience and social happiness for over 800 years. The Muslims introduced into Christian Europe the Arabic numerals, the tabulated observation of Babylon, and the discoveries of the Egyptian astronomers (Alexandria). They constructed the pendulum clock and the balance, terrestrial and celestial globes, astronomical instruments, and astrolabes. Their theoretical and experimental work expanded over a wide range of knowledge leading to numerous discoveries, which established the foundation of many aspects of modern science. Briffault beautifully summarised the contribution of Muslims in the following: "*it is highly probable that but for the Arabs modern European civilisation would never have arisen at all; it is absolutely certain that but for*

20

them would not have assumed that character which has enabled it to transcend all previous phases of evolution. For although there is not a single aspect of European growth in which the decisive influence of Islamic culture is not traceable, nowhere is it so clear and momentous as in the genesis of that power which constitutes the permanent distinctive force of the modern world, and the supreme source of its victory, natural science and the scientific spirit....What we call science arose in Europe as a result of a new spirit of inquiry, of new methods of investigation, of the development of mathematics in a form unknown to the Greeks. That spirit and those methods were introduced into the European world by the Arabs"[60]*. And if it "had not been for the fall of Cordoba and the sack of Baghdad and Ray at the hands of foreign invaders in the 12th and 13th centuries, Europe would not have had to wait three centuries to see the dawn of its scientific renaissance"*[61]

In literature, for example, poetry was the central point around which revolved the intellectual life of the Muslims especially in Spain. Arabs always viewed poetry with the highest respect; a pre-Islamic tradition gave celebrated poems a great honour by hanging them in the sanctuary of the Kaaba (al-Muaalakate). Poetry was so popular among Muslims that rhyming writing was used in most private correspondence and in scientific and religious publications. The majority of medieval Muslim manuscripts were written in this style, and it was reported that the passport given to Ibn-Khaldun (1332-1395) by Mohammed V., Caliph of Granada (r.1354-1359 and 1362-1391), was written in rhyme[62]. Renowned poets of Muslim Spain include; Abul-Hasan (d.1095), Ibn-Zaydun (1003-1071), and Abbas-Ibn-Ahnaf (748-808) who were famous for the beauty of their love poetry (*El-Ghazal*), Ibn-Chafadscha (1058-1139), for his martial arts poetry, Ali Ibn Musa Ibn-Said (13TH century) for his bacchanalian poetry, Ibn-Ammar (1031-1086) for his poetry of satires, and Abul-Beka (1204-1285) and Ibn-al-Khatib (d.1374) for their descriptive poetry. In folk poetry, Muqaddam Ibn Mu'afi Al Oabri (d. 912 C.E.) from the town of Oabra, in Cordoba province, was the inventor of the Muwashahat, a post- classical form of Arab poetry arranged in stanzas and with free prosody. The poet Abu Bakr Mohammad Ibn Oazman Al Qurtubi (d.1114 C.E.) invented another form called 'Zajal', which he used to sing in the market place accompanied by instruments and singers. It is to be noticed that both the Muwashah and the Zajal are similar; however, the al-Muwashah is purely Arabic save its epilogue, which was in Spanish or Spanish vernacular. Zajal on the other hand was in colloquial dialect with some Spanish words. This Spanish folk song with its epilogue and Zajal later on influenced the poetry that emerged in southern Europe at the end of the 11th century. Roving singers known as troubadours in northern Spain used this new style. It is also said that the songs, known as 'villancico' and sung by the Spanish people during Christmas festivities, were Andalusian Zajal. Recently Rosalind expressed the significance of Muslim literature to Europeans in the following: "*Whatever the 'shape' of the tale, however, the East is consistently characterised as the original home of narrative fiction and such fiction is always 'fabular'. It carries a veiled message for it consumers; it seeks to 'move' them in terms of their response, prompting some change, ethical, political, or emotional.*" [63]

Muslims can be considered, without exaggeration, as the founders of the science of history not only for their momentous work but also for the methods and techniques they developed in studying or writing about it. The all-time greatest was Abd al-Rhman Ibn Khaldun whose work al-Muqaddimah reached an unprecedented fame[64]. Numerous European scholars named him, as the founder of the sciences of history and sociology. Hitti observes on him: "*The fame of Ibn Khaldun rests on his Muqaddamah, an introduction to history. In it he presented for the first time a theory of historical development which takes due cognizance of the physical facts of climate and geography as well as of moral and spiritual forces. As one who endeavoured to find and formulate laws of national progress and decay, Ibn Khaldun may be considered the discoverer- as himself claimed- of the true scope and nature of history or at least the real founder of social science. No Arab writer, indeed no European, had ever before taken a view of history a once so comprehensive and philosophic. By the consensus of all critical opinion Ibn Khaldun, who died in 1406, was the greatest historical philosopher Islam produced and one of the greatest of all time.*"[65]

Among well-known historians is Ibn al-Assaker (Syria, d.1176) who is credited for the works: instructive history of the first inventors of the arts and the history of Damascus "*Tarikh Dimashq*". Al-Firdausi (Iran, 940-1020) became famous for his *Shah Nameh*" or "Book of Kings." Ibn Jubayr (Andalusia, 12th century), also an explorer, wrote about Sicily and the Norman rule there. Yaqut al-Hamawi (Syria, 1179-1229) distinguished for his history of the crusades wrote two encyclopaedic works: *Mu'jam al-buldan* (dictionary of countries) and *Mu'jam al-Udaba* (dictionary of men of letters).[66] Ibn-al-Khatib (Andalusia, 1313- 1374) wrote the famous work "The Universal Library". The list goes on for at least another dozen historians. According to Scott, in the Muslim world, especially in Spain, every town had its annalist and every province its chronicler[67].

The Muslims also made invaluable contribution to geographical knowledge. Geography was a natural interest nurtured by the physical expansion of the Islamic World involving various lands with different topographic, climatic, and ethnic characteristics. Long distance travel was a common activity dictated by at least three factors; the yearly ritual of pilgrimage (Haj), trade exchange and learning as previously indicated. The free movement and trade were highly practiced, as Muslim countries did not have political boundaries until introduced by the European colonialism. Travellers, traders and scholars could usually go wherever they wished without fear. The twelfth century Muslim historian, Abu al-Fida,[68] for example, counted 60 Muslim geographers who lived before the 13th century[69]. The large area they covered and the multidisciplinary approach they adopted enabled them to correct many of their predecessors, especially the Greek geographers. Muslim geographers dwelt on many branches of geography, including traditional descriptions of lands and regions, mapping, geodesy, and maritime exploration. They did not only produce written material but also maps, and represented them in models[70]. Famous geographers included; Ahmed Ibn Fadlan (Baghdad, 10th century) who travelled and wrote about Northern Europe, and Scandinavia; Ibn-Jubair (12th century) who described Sicily and the countries of the Orient, Ibn-Battutah (Morocco, 1304-1368/70) whose travels lasted 24 years and Abu Abdullah al-Bakri (Andalusia, 1014-1094) who was the author of a geographical dictionary.

However, the most prominent of all was al-Idrisi (Morocco, 1099-1165) whose work marked a significant development in the history of science. In addition to valuable historic information, his descriptions of many aspects of the earth are still valid today. His maps were of an unprecedented accuracy and provided the main reference source for other geographers for a period exceeding three hundred years. The celestial and terrestrial spheres he made for King Roger of Palermo was about six feet in diameter, and weighed four hundred and fifty pounds[71]. Piri Reis (Turkey, 1465-1554) was a maritime explorer who wrote *Kitab-i-Bahriye*, famously known as the Book of Sea Lore and made an accurate map of the world in 1528-29, where he located accurately America some 21 years after Columbus reached the 'New World'.

In philosophy, Muslim scholars tackled questions relating to the origin, destiny, and the soul. They commented on ancient philosophers such as Pythagoras, Heraclitus, Socrates, Empedocles, Aristotle, and Plato. Works of al-Ghazali (Khorasan, 1058-1128) obtained wide acceptance and influenced many leading European scholars, including Dante. Ibn Hazm (Cordoba, 994-1064) studied the ethics and boundaries of sciences and classified them. Al-Farabi, or Alpharabius, (Iraq (870-950) discussed reasoning and logic portraying that it is unable to comprehend the absolute and the infinite. The works of Ibn-Rushd (Averroes) (Andalusia, 1128-1198), all times famous philosopher, touched upon wide spectrum disciplines, theology, philosophy, jurisprudence, and medicine and were leading references (particularly his commentaries on Aristotle) to most Muslim and Jewish as well as Christian scholars. Other philosophers included Ibn-Bajja or Avempa in Latin (Andalusia, d.1138), Ibn-Tufayl (Andalusia, d.1185) and Ikhwan al-Safa, or Brothers of Purity (Iraq, c.983), all of whom are traceable in Western texts.

In science, Muslims made unprecedented contributions to the development of many branches and fields. Carra de Vaux observed: *"The Arabs have really achieved great things in science; they taught the use of ciphers, although they did not invent them, and thus became the founders of the arithmetic of everyday life; they made algebra and exact science and developed it considerably and laid the foundation of analytical geometry; they were indisputably the founders of plane and spherical trigonometry which, properly speaking, did not exist among the Greeks"*[72] Indeed they examined the effect of gravity and narrowly missed ascertaining its principles. They were the first to establish the cosmic nature of the aerolite (not a missile of Divine wrath). They discussed the force of capillary attraction, and calculated the height of the atmosphere (although they were only slightly out), and had noted its diminished weight at a distance from the earth. As early as the tenth century, they developed many ideas explaining the nature and causes of many geological phenomena such as soil erosion and surface topography. Muslim laboratories in Spain and Baghdad developed the sciences of chemistry and pharmacy. Their anatomical research established the scientific and experimental basis of medicine and surgery. In mathematics, they were the first to establish with accuracy the length of the year and the first to introduce, to Europe, Arabic numerals and the decimal system. The trio al-Khwarizmi (Khwarizm, 780 - 850), al-Karaji (also known as al-Karkhi), (Iraq, 953-1029) and Umar al-Khyyam (Iran, 1048-1122) made the foundations of what is known today as mathematics. Al-Kindi (Iraq, 801-873 C.E.), pioneered the advances made in algebra and opened the door for most of modern scientific development. Meanwhile, The Banu Musa Brothers (Iraq, 9th century) and later al-Jazari (Turkey, 1179/1180 C.E.) led a technological revolution by the advances they made in the construction of clocks (fig.2), automated technical equipment and water raising machines.[73] Modern trigonometry owes a great deal to the Muslims. Al-Karaji generated formulae solving cubic equations and in his treatise, described not only the application of geometry and algebra to hydrology but also the instruments used by master well diggers and canal builders. He was the first to point out the intriguing properties of triangular arrays of numbers.[74] Ibn-Yunis made formulae for tangents and secants and invented the pierced *gnomon* for the determination of time and latitude, and observation of the sun. Much of this work was illustrated and explained in numerous manuscripts that now lie in libraries in Oxford, Dublin, Paris, Leiden and Istanbul.[75]

The Muslims considerably advanced astronomy, for example, by tabulating the movements of the stars[76], and discovering the third lunar inequality of 45", some 650 years before Tycho Brahe. Abd al-Rahman al-Sufi (Iran, 903-986), who compiled an illustrated catalogue of stars, based upon his own observations, and was the first to mark the nebula of Andromeda in his atlas[77]. Al-Zarkal (Andalusia, 1029-1087) was the first to propose the substitution of the elliptical orbit to correct the errors of the Ptolemaic system long before Copernicus and Kepler. He wrote the *Toledan Tables* and invented a universal astrolabe known as *al-Safiha*. Abu al-Wafa al-Buzjani (Iraq, 940-998) wrote "*Almagest*", an astronomical treatise that made significant advances on that of Ptolemy[78]. For his part, Ibn-Sina (Avicenna) (Uzbekistan, 980-1037) catalogued some 1022 stars, while Ibn-Abi-Thalta studied the movements of the heavenly bodies for 30 years[79], and Ibn Rushd (Averroes) (Andalusia, 1126-1198) studied the motion of Mercury, and observed spots on the sun (fig.3).

Muslim astronomy was, indeed, vital for European astronomers who had inherited little scientific knowledge, particularly in this subject. Lindberg outlined how important Muslim astronomical works were: "*While Latin scholars were doing what they could with their limited heritage, their Islamic counterparts succeeded in recovering a substantial portion of the Greek astronomical corpus. This body of material had been preserved and, indeed, improved and extended in Islam, and it was by acquiring Islamic astronomical works and Greek astronomical works preserved in Arabic that the Latin world would finally achieve a high level of astronomical knowledge*"[80]. Hodgson went further as he explicitly observed, "*for a time Muslim astronomers, building not only on their own Babylonian and Greek but also on Sanskrit developments, were teachers of astronomers everywhere from the Latin West to China.*"[81]

Optics in the middle Ages was wholly a Muslim science. The Greek works were very limited, mainly based on two opposed theories. Aristotle, Galen and their followers who thought the vision was carried out through something entering the eyes representative of the object, championed 'Intromission'. The 'emission' theory of Euclid and Ptolemy and their followers, explained it as occurring when rays emanate from the eyes and are intercepted by visual objects. "*Such an inclusive and broadly based discipline had not always existed, nor did it ever attract large numbers of adherents. It came into existence largely through the efforts of Ibn al-Haitham (known to the Latin world as Alhazen or Alhacen) and appeared in the West in the thirteenth century under the aegis of Roger Bacon.*"[82]

Figure **2** Al-Jazari (Turkey, 1179/1180 C.E.) led a technological revolution showing here the elephant clock reconstructed in Ibn Battuta Shopping Mall, Dubai 2006.

Figure 3. Statue of Ibn Rushd (Averroes) in Cordoba, Spain

Al-Hasan Ibn al-Haitham (Al-Hazen, Syria, 965-1039) made numerous discoveries, which greatly influenced the development of this science. First and for most, he resolved the problems of the intromission theory of Aristotle and Galen, by explaining physical contact between the object and observer through the intromitted rays, and through its visual cone explained the perception of shape and accounted for the laws of perspective. He determined the cause of twilight; estimated the density of the atmosphere and its height[83]. He explained by the principle of refraction the reasons, which make celestial bodies visible when they are below the horizon providing an early contribution to Snell's law. Ibn al-Haitham (Al-Hazen) also corrected the prevailing theory that rays of light proceed from the eye to the object seen surpassing his predecessors. He was also the first to discover the camera obscura.

Muslims carried out laborious research in botany and their success was translated into one of the most advanced agricultural revolutions of the middle Ages.[84] At the request of the Caliph, Abd al-Rahman III (r. 912-961) "*Dioscorides*", or *De material medica*, was translated into Arabic in the 10th century. The Caliph received the manuscript from the Byzantine Emperor Romanos in 948 CE[85]. Muslim botanists later discovered more than 2000 varieties of plants and a number of books were published dealing with various aspects and varieties of plants, describing the circulation of the sap, variety of soils and explaining which is good for planting, its properties and qualities.[86] It is not surprising that the first royal botanical gardens of Europe opened first in Toledo, Spain, and later in Seville. The Spanish botanical school, in particular "*reached its Zenith with the two pharmaco-botanists al-Ghafiqi (12th century) and Ibn al-Baytar (c.1190-1249).*"[87] The most distinguished botanists include Abu Hanifa al-Dinawari (Andalusia, d.895 A.D) who wrote extensively on botany and made numerous classification of plants and their benefit to humans or animals. The German Silberberg studied his work, which contained the descriptions of about 400 plants, in his thesis in Breslau in 1908[88]. Ibn-al-Baytar (of Malaga) drew and preserved various species of plants he encountered on his journeys in Andalusia and the Orient. Ibn Bassal (Andalusia, d.1085) writing in Toledo, between 1075-80, referred to over 100 plants in his encyclopaedic book untitled, *Kitab al-Filaha*, or the Book of Agriculture[89]. This was succeeded by another list made by Ibn al-Awwam[90] in his book also untitled "*Kitab al-Filaha*" or The Book of Agriculture, which dates from 1180, was translated into Spanish in 1802 and into English in the same century. The manuscript contained more plants than any other book, in fact "*more numerous than those which were cultivated by the Greeks and the Romans*"[91]. According to Loudon, the book listed some 157 plants of which 81 were not known in the Palladius (ca 380CE) the classical flora book. This was in time when best list of plants in Europe, which was compiled by Macer Floridus (late 11th century), did not exceed 77 plants of which 12 were imported herbal drugs. Harvey observes:

"The great importance of Ibn Bassal lies in the survival of the masterly handbook on agriculture and gardening, both16cientific and practical, which he dedicated to his royal master al-Ma'mun. The Arabic text has been rediscovered in our own time, as well as an incomplete Castilian translation made c. 1300. The book is thoroughly modern in tone and starts with a discussion of water supply, soils, manures and the choice of ground and its preparation."[92]

In chemistry, their work resulted in unprecedented advances particularly in pharmaceuticals.[93] Muslims were the first to advocate the oxidation of metals and the possible generation of gases. Jabber Ibn-Hayyan (Iraq, d.803), known as Geber, is famous for his discovery of nitric acid, his reference to the generation of gases by heat, and his discussion to the changes undergone by substances. The second most influential figure is Abu Bakr al-Razy (Iran, 865-925), known as Rhazes. His work Secret of Secrets was a huge encyclopaedia, which classified natural substances into earthly, vegetable and animal. The most interesting part of this work is the section, which describes his various experiments, the materials used, and the apparatus needed. These were the first examples showing the development of a laboratory in the modern sense. Their research bore many fruits leading to the discovery of many chemicals and made use of them. *"They made and named most of the common chemicals that we use in the school laboratory today. They also discovered petroleum, which they used in a special burner, like the Bunsen burner, for their experiments. They linked mathematics, chemistry and medicine so that future scientists would know the importance of taking measurements, to distil and purify chemicals, and to use small quantities for making new medicines."*[94]

One of the key discoveries, which had great impact on our lives, is the distillation process, which among the many things it brought us was perfume. Muslim Chemical laboratories also produced the Naft, the oily substance that became the main source of energy for the world of today. The literary meaning of Chemistry comes from the Arabic word *al-Kimya*, or *Kimya, which* was first used in French as *"La Chimie"*. Later it was wrongly applied by some biased Western scholars to mean *Alchemy*, first used in 1362[95] and gradually was transformed to mean the work of sorcery accusing Muslim chemists of indulging in sorcery rather than chemistry.

Medicine had a long tradition among Muslims, the art of healing and relieving pain is considered the summit of the "good deed". The Prophet attended the sick and advised on health matters and the importance of hygiene. Among his sayings, one can incorporate the Hadith narrated by the companion Anas ibn Mas'ud: *"Verily, Allah has not let any malady occur without providing its remedy. Therefore seek medical treatment for your illnesses."* (Reported by

Nasa'i, Ibn Majah, and al-Hakim.), and his saying *"Diet is the principle of cure, and intemperance the source of all physical ills"*. Thus, the medical profession gained greater respect, above all other professions, and greater efforts were made to develop its techniques, leading to some monumental discoveries that transformed the history of this science. Major developments were made by the schools of Baghdad, Cairo, Damascus, and particularly Andalusia[96]. The Muslims were the first to perform the lithotomic operation, and medical science owes the operation of tracheotomy and the original description of pericarditis to Ibn-Zuhr (Avenzoar) (Andalusia, 1091-1161). Another crucial invention was the new technique developed by al-Mosuli to remove cataract by the use of hollow needle, which sucks it completely. Muslims physician performed huge number of treatments that previously were considered as untreated illnesses caused by satanic interference. The middle Ages witnessed a large number of Muslim pioneers in medicine and surgery[97], who produced an enormous amount of valuable medical information. Ibn Al-Nafis (Damascus, 1210-1288 CE) explained the basic principles of the pulmonary circulation (fig.4), over three hundred years before Sir William Harvey of Kent, England, who is wrongly credited with this discovery.

The book of al-Razi (Rhazes) (Iran, 864-930) on the diseases of children was the first on such a topic. His book *"The Continent"* together with *"The Canon"* of Ibn Sina (Avicenna) (Uzbekistan, 980-1037) and the *"Meliki"* of Ali-Ibn-Abbas al-Majusi (Haly Abbes) (Iran, 930-994) represent scientific reference material, which established the principles of modern medical practice. The works of Ibn al-Haitham and Ali-Ibn-Issa also enjoyed a worldwide reputation. Meanwhile, Abul Kassim al-Zahrawi (Abucasis) (Andalusia, 936-1013), Ibn Rushd (Averroes) (Andalusia, 1126-1198) and Ibn Zuhr are considered the originators of modern surgery[98]. Al-Zahrawi, a tenth century Andalusian surgeon revolutionised surgery and developed over 200 surgical tools, which he carefully designed and accompanied them with a manual detailing how to make and how and when to use (fig.5).

The wealth of medical research led inevitably to the appearance of the first hospital in history, which was founded in Baghdad. The advances made in chemical and botanical research produced pharmacology, a completely new and separate science that resulted in substantial increase in curative medicines and drugs. Proper hospitals were established to cater for the ill. The botanical works of al-Tighnari and Ibn al-Wafid, who were also physicians, were very influential in this respect. Al-Biruni (Iran, 973-1048 C.E.) and his *"Kitab al-Saidana"* (Materia Medica) was another influential work. Medical colleges, hospitals and laboratories spread all over the Muslim lands representing an innovation that was exported later to Christian Europe via Salerno, Palermo and Montpellier. The fame of these

Figure 4. Page of Ibn Nafis Manuscript, *Sharh Tashreeh al-Qanun,* p.93, Jumaa al-Majid Centre for Culture and Heritage, Dubai, copy obtained from microfilm, from the Department of Manuscripts, Section Conservation, Storage and Photography.

schools attracted students of every nation particularly the Jews and Christians. The historian Scott noted that in the 11th century, there were more than 6000 students of medicine in the schools of Baghdad alone. By the 12th century, pharmacies were also established in all principal towns of the Muslim World. In Cordoba, historic sources indicate that there were about 50 public hospitals and a large number of private surgeries.[99]

From the above it is clear that the contribution of Muslim civilisation in all aspects of intellectual life was considerable, and one wonders whether present day technological and scientific advances would have proceeded at the speed and form they did if it was not for the strong foundations laid by the Muslims. The importance of the Muslim influence can be better appreciated if one remembers that the apogee of this wonderful civilisation was close to Europe in Spain, North Africa and in the East near the Christian Holy Land. These events also unfolded at a time when the rest of the world, and Europe in particular, was in the intellectual obscurity of the period famously called the Dark Ages. Bertrand Russell (1948) admitted what Europe owes to the Muslims: *"Our use of the phrase 'The Dark Ages' to cover the period from 699 to 1000 marks our undue concentration on Western Europe ... From India to Spain, the brilliant civilisation of Islam flourished. What was lost to Christendom at this time was not lost to civilisation, but quite the contrary ... To us it seems that West-European civilisation is civilisation, but this is a narrow view."*[100]

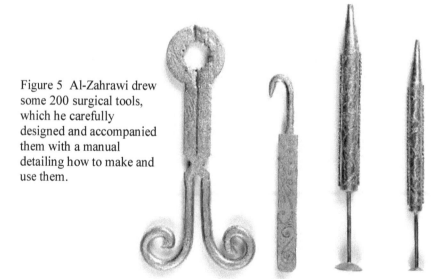

Figure 5 Al-Zahrawi drew some 200 surgical tools, which he carefully designed and accompanied them with a manual detailing how to make and use them.

32

Muslim Architectural Achievement

The intellectual creativity discussed in the previous chapter had a direct impact on the productivity and expansion of the artistic and architectural production of the Muslim world, which despite the diversity of these origins retained a unique identity. Muslim architecture has encompassed a wide range of religious and secular buildings and styles extending over a period of more than fourteen hundred years. Generally, the features of this architecture were developed through a process of skilful adaptation of the inherited building knowledge, foreign influences and outstanding innovation. However, to appreciate these developments one has to follow the chronological order of this evolution.

Architecture of Early Islam (622-661)

Architecture during the early years of the Muslim World (between 622 and 661) was characterised by simplicity and humbleness. This was due to the infancy of the state, which was still concentrating its forces on fighting surrounding hostile tribes, and its slender economic resources were exhausted in providing adequate defence. Furthermore, the devotion of these early faithful and their aspiration for the hereafter made an extravagant and luxurious lifestyle repulsive. It was a matter of priorities. Furthermore, since the Muslim faith excluded the veneration of relics or any saintly hierarchies and any intervention of priests between the believer and God, there was no need for artistic representation of these elements and Muslims needed to invent a new approach fitting in line with the general guidelines of Islam. This required stability, wealth and time. Architectural sophistication came about later as intellectual and economic prosperity created a demand for more elaborate forms and arts compatible with the enlightened vision of Islam.

The first Muslim building erected was the Prophet's mosque at Medina (622), the year of his flight from Makkah.[101] Despite its simplicity, it contained the first embryonic plan of the mosque, a large courtyard comprising a sheltered space (portico) made from hardened clay bricks and a flat roof of compacted mud and palm branches providing a sanctuary for congregational prayers and a shelter for the homeless followers (Muhajirun), and finally rooms for the Prophets' household. This structure remained the centre of the social, cultural and political life of the Muslim community for over 30 years. The mosque saw many extensions and alterations, but the Umayyad Caliph al-Walid ibn 'Abdulmalik, or shortly al-Walid I (705-715 CE.) was the first to completely rebuilt it in 706CE (fig.6).

The transfer of the seat of government from Medina to Kufa by Ali (the fourth caliph) in 657 CE, brought substantial changes and resulted in unprecedented architectural and building activities. The Medina lost its prestigious status becoming a provincial town, and its role slowly changing into a predominantly religious one. Meanwhile, this transfer had set a precedent that was repeated throughout Muslim history. The change of capital every time a new Caliph (ruler) came to power slowly led to the diffusion of luxurious and rich tastes and practices in Muslim life. The simple mosque soon became complex with the first modification appearing at the time of Saad ibn al-Waqqas. Descending from an aristocratic Makkan family (from Makkah), this Prophet's companion built the Kufa Mosque, after defeating the Persians, and annexed his residence, known as Dar al-Imara (638), to it from the back. The mosque, however, was raised on marble columns imported from Persia, and enclosed by a trench. This building was so elaborate that it was reported the Caliph Omar was unhappy with it and that he ordered it burned down[102]. Historical sources have established that the only furniture the mosque of this period had was the *"Minbar"* which was first introduced by the Prophet himself in the form of a step (chair) which he used so that the numerous faithful could see and hear him during his *Khutba* ceremony. This is attested by a number of *Hadith* narrators who referred to the *Minbar* such as the *Hadith* narrated by Abu Huraira that the Prophet said: *between my house and my pulpit there is a garden from amongst the gardens of Paradise, and my Minbar (pulpit) is over my Hawd (plot)".* However, Briggs (1931) thought Amr Ibn-al-Aas was the first to introduce the *Minbar,* in the Mosque he built in Egypt[103]. As for the origins, he thought they were Arabian derived from the chair used by the judge in ancient Arabia.[104]

Muslim Architecture under Umayyad Patronage (661-750)

The arrival of Mua'wiya to the throne of the Caliphate initiated the Umayyad dynasty, a period known for its architectural achievement. The relative security and peace that followed the turbulent first few years after the death of Ali and the war the Umayyad led against his family and sons' al-Hassan and al-Hussein, in addition to the new wealth, generated by the annexation of Iraq, Iran and Syria to Islam, were all factors favourable for artistic and architectural activity to develop. Signs of this change were felt in religious as well as secular buildings. In the former, it is to the Umayyad that the development of the major architectural components of the mosque is attributed. Mua'wiya introduced the *minaret* while he carried out some enlargement works to Amr mosque (built in 641-2) in Egypt (Fustat) in 673. He equipped it with four minarets for the call for prayer. This innovation, according to Creswell[105], was copied from Syrian Christian practice. However, Michell related it to the Egyptian light tower.[106]

Moreover, according to Ibn Khaldun (1967), Mua'wiya was also responsible for the introduction of the *maqsura*, because of an attempt made on his life by the Kharijite[107] (outlawed group). In decorative terms, the Mosque employed floral and vegetal representation embedded in an urban landscape, which adorned the façade. Such décor recalls that found in the Dome of the Rock indicating the possibility of the influence of Syrian tradition on both works rather than Byzantine origins as many Westerners have claimed.

By the time al-Walid I became Caliph in 705 AD, the Prophet's Mosque was becoming unfit to receive the large crowds of the faithful so al-Walid I decided (in 707-709) to enlarge it. He used the four minarets and introduced the *mihrab*, a semi-circular prayer niche in the centre of the *Qibla* wall (the direction of the Kaaba (the sacred building in Makkah) to which Muslims turn in ritual prayers), which according to al-Samhudi was the work of Coptic artisans. The origin of the *mihrab* had many explanations, which chiefly linked it to the apsidal form in Christian architecture. Havell for example associated the *mihrab* with the niche forms found in Buddhist temples,[108] while Rivoira maintained that the origin comes from the apses of Christian churches.[109] In Islam, the mihrab was a symbol of orientation (in the mosque, as well as in any other Muslim building) indicating the direction of the qibla and emphasising its sanctity. The Quran defines this orientation; Sura 2 Ayah 145, states that 'And *now We will turn you indeed towards a qibla which shall please you. So turn your face [in prayer] toward the Sanctified Mosque, and ye [o Muslims] wheresoever ye find yourselves, turn your faces [likewise] toward it'*. This rule is also applied to domestic and secular buildings, we find in private houses bedrooms, and bathrooms are deliberately disoriented as a mark of respect. This leads us to raise an issue that confuses many non-Muslims who think that Muslims attach special regard to the *mihrab* like the Christians do to the *Altar*. The sanctity of the *mihrab* does not come from the shape per see but from the direction it indicates (qibla), in other words Kaabah (the black cubic house in Makkah). This meaning had been clearly expressed in Turkey where they included some fragments of stones of the Kaabah in *mihrab* of Sokollu Mehmet Pasa mosque at Kadirga in Istanbul as well as the representation of Kaabah underneath the arch of the *mihrab* in some Ottoman Rugs.[110] Furthermore, there are other hypothesis, which one cannot ignore. The Quran explicitly spoke of the *mihrab* in Surah 3, Ayah 39 referring to prophet Zakariya being praying in front of a *mihrab* when he was promised the son Yahia, "*Then the angels called to him as he stood praying in the sanctuary (mihrab): that Allah gives the good news of Yahiya verifying a word from Allah, and honorable and chaste and a prophet from among the good ones*" (Quran: 3:39). In Ayah 37 of the same Surah, Maryam (Mary) is the one described as praying in the *mihrab* "*whenever Zakariya entered the sanctuary (mihrab) to (see) her, he found with her food.*" The *mihrab* here was translated

35

as sanctuary rather than the niche. The meaning of niche is also introduced in Surah 24, Ayah 35: *"Allah is the light of the heavens and the earth, a likeness of His light is as a niche in which is a lamp, the lamp is in a glass, (and) the glass as it were a brightly shining star, lit from a blessed olive oil- tree, neither eastern nor western, the oil whereof gives light though fire touch it not- light upon light – Allah guides to His light whom he pleases"*. The word niche here became a symbol of Allah's light and having it in front of the faithful was an element in helping them achieve the devotion and sincerity required for the prayers. Traditionally Muslims use candles and lanterns reflecting the divine description and later this was expressed in the use of this lamp under the arch of the *mihrab* in most prayer rugs and carpets.

The splendour of Umayyad architecture is better experienced in the Dome of the Rock[111], the architectural jewel of Islam and the Great Mosque of Damascus, its masterpiece. According to an inscription found on the building, the Caliph Abd-el-Malik built the Dome of the Rock in 691-692 (fig.7). The dome forms the heart of the complex of al-Haram Ash-Sharif and covers the rock "al-Sakhra" (in Arabic) from where prophet Muhammed ascended to heaven accompanied by the Archangel Gabriel. The significance of this building can be seen at numerous levels. The geometrical pattern of both plan and elevation, and the relation between dome, arches and columns, all create a sense of harmony and unity greatly emphasised by the rich décor of polychrome marble and colourful mosaics. The octagonal shape is interpreted by Muslims as to stand for the eight angels carrying the Divine Throne as described in the Quran[112]: *"And the angels will be on its sides, and eight will, that Day, bear the Throne of thy Lord above them"*. (Quran: 69:17). The dome is the oldest in Muslim architecture made of double shell; a wooden internal cupola succeeded by a gilded metal external shell. Its lobbed form was a source of inspiration for many European buildings including the domes of St. Marco at Venice. The octagonal building consists of two sets of colonnades and an octagonal exterior wall. The central colonnade made of four piers and twelve columns support a rounded drum pierced with grilled windows for lighting. The most interesting aspect of these colonnades is their gently pointed outline (gently), the first prototype to be ever built.

In decorative terms, the building caught the attention of numerous scholars who tried to decipher its symbolic significance and classify its artistic style. Numerous conflicting opinions were produced with the majority claiming a Roman or Byzantine decent. The most recent and outstanding work is that of Grabar who gave it a more realistic interpretation suggesting a combination of Persian and Byzantine influences[113]. In this building, Muslims, however, made their first eight-pointed star pattern, which became an essential component of

Figure 6 Medina Mosque, showing the original mosque of the Prophet, the green dome designates the grave of the Prophet and next to him his companions Abu Bakr and Omar.

.
Figure 7 the Dome of the Rock was built between 691 and 692 AD.

later Islamic geometrical art.[114] It was here also that they applied calligraphy to architectural decoration for the first time.[115] The beauty of the Dome of the Rock has a worldwide reputation, which challenged all prejudices against Muslim architecture.

When Islam entered Damascus, Syria, Muslims and Christians shared an old derelict temple, which the Christians, at the hands of Theodose (379-395) transformed into a church named St. John the Baptist. A famous treaty concluded between the Christians and the Muslim army commander Khalid Ibn al-Walid and lasted for well over half a century established this partnership. It was not until the time of Caliph al-Walid I (r. 705-715), a renowned Umayyad patron of great architectural projects, i.e., the reconstruction of mosques of Medina and al-Aqsa, decided to build a separate mosque for the Muslims to accommodate their growing numbers. After long negotiations, al-Walid I (705-715 CE.) bought the derelict site and converted it into the Great Umayyad Mosque between 706 and 715CE.

The mosque layout is rectangular with a large courtyard surrounded by galleries of horseshoe arches (fig.8). The Muslim origin of the horseshoe arch is therefore very factual according to many scholars including Leclerc, Rivoira and Dieulafoy, who believe the Moors introduced the horseshoe arch to Spain. This fact contradicts those views, which suggest that Muslims developed it from the examples left by the Visigoth in Spain[116]. Muslims reached Spain only in 726, more than a decade after the construction of this Mosque[117]. Three small domed polygonal structures were distributed there; the oldest and most important of these is the treasury (Bayt al-Mal), which was erected in the western side of the courtyard by Caliph al-Mahdi, in 778CE, to accommodate the treasury. The other two are the ablution fountain in the centre and the dome of the clocks in the eastern side. The prayer hall, the sanctuary (136 meters long and 37 meters) occupies the southern part of the site, containing three longitudinal aisles, which stretches from east to west parallel to the qibla wall. The nave (known locally as El-Majaz), which is in the form of transept, runs north from the main gate (which opens to the courtyard) to the qibla wall at the mihrab crossing perpendicularly the qibla aisles in a T shape. At the contact with the mihrab area, the nave is adorned with a great dome (about thirty meters high) symbolically representing the Dome of the sky. This space configuration was also adopted in North Africa in al-Kairawan Mosque (Tunisia) (836) and later in mosques of Samara (Iraq) al-Mutawwakil Mosque (848/849) and Abu-Dullaf (860). There are six large horseshoe diaphragm arches, which define the nave aisle running across the isles parallel to the qibla (fig.9). This is not the first use of diaphragm arches in Islam as it is found in desert castles Qasr al-Kharanah (Jordan 710) and Qusair Amra (Jordan around 715).

38

The rectangular open courtyard based plan reflects the inspiration of the Prophet's Mosque in Medina, which was later reinstated in Kufa. This plan is a continuation of Arab plan that was used in Yemeni temples as well as in pre-Islam Kaaba. In contrast, the plans of Christian, Hellenic and Roman temples have a covered scheme. The use of porticoes on the three sides of the courtyard was also a precedent employed in the Prophet's Mosque. After their experience with the covered plan in Al-Aqsa mosque in Palestine, thought to be derived from the basilican church, the Umayyads returned to the open plan. Among other architectural merits of the mosque include the accentuation of the main nave leading to the mihrab equipped with a large dome, which also appeared in al-Aqsa Mosque, one of the fundamental elements of the mosque plan introduced by the Umayyads and later became an essential feature of Mosque architecture. The introduction of *maqsura* by Mua'wiya set also a precedent, which later became part of the mosque furniture. The method employed in the roof of Damascus Mosque (and in al-Aqsa) which consists of parallel steep roofs running from east to west, and crossed by the roof of the nave running from north to south is another arrangement introduced by the Umayyads and had no Christian precedent. The Umayyad Mosque represents also the first instance of the adoption of the square minaret, which later spread particularly in North Africa and Andalusia. Some historians believe that the European square steeple, which appears in their churches, was an adaptation of this Umayyad and other Muslim minarets[118]. Golvyn summarised the merits of the Mosque design in the following: *"In summary, this plan appears to us revolutionary. Its spatial arrangements had no precedent in Christian architecture. But it is inspired very much from earlier works of Medina (especially the Prophet's Mosque)... From the antiquity prelobe, the plan maintained the (external) frame, but all the remaining features are innovative except from a few details (such as doors, arcaded aisles, nave leading to mihrab) which appear to be borrowed from a well-defined local (Syrian) architecture. The remarkable balance of the building mass and various elements do indeed honour the architect who knew how to meet the needs of the new architectural spirit."*[119]

In their domestic and social life, the Umayyad Caliphs and princes lived a rural (Badiya) life in palace complexes pursuing their favourite hobbies of hunting, fishing, riding competitions and gardening. For this purpose, they built a series of fortresses protected by strong walls and containing all the amenities necessary to sustain their luxurious lifestyles. Among these complexes are Qasr al-Kharanah (Jordan 710) (fig.10), Qusayr Amra (Jordan around 715), Qasr al-Qastal (Jordan 720–744, Khirbat al-Mafjar (Jordan 743-744), and Meshatta (Jordan 750).

In these palaces, the Umayyads showed considerable architectural and decorative talent. In terms of design, a complex layout containing audience halls, baths, domestic apartments for both males and females, mosques, courtyards, stables and garden enclosures was developed reflecting their luxurious standard of living and their political and tribal power.[120] The structural aspects of these palaces show an elaborate use of the vaulting system involving the dome and barrel vaults. The most interesting structural aspect found in some of these palaces is the use of diaphragm arches to support the vaults found in Qasr al-Kharanah (Jordan 710), Qusayr Amra (Jordan around 715), Qasr al-Qastal 720–744. According to Bier[121] and Urcie[122], this is the first time such a technique is used.

Qasr El-Kharana is a two storey square fort (36.5x35.5m) with strong walls supported by circular towers raised at corners. Loopholes were fitted around the building for added defence. These loopholes allowed a bowman to fire on the enemy while protecting him from returning fire. An inscription dates the building back to 710 CE. The palace was built with small stones or rubble covered in mortar (a Persian technique), Creswell though it was Sassanid building built before the Umayyads. The entrance leads into a ribbed long hall supported with transverse arches sprung from walls without columns or pillars. This lead to a central courtyard, which is bordered by two levels comprising a number of rooms and halls. The rooms on the second floor contain the most important decorative details consisting of stucco mouldings, sculpted plaster roundels, and both closed and open arcades. In the southern side of the palace, there is a small room with crossed vaulted ceiling, comprising lozenge coffers. A number of vaulted cells, with transverse arches, used as barns surround the square courtyard, which has two staircases leading to the second floor rooms, also vaulted and supported with transverse arches resting on three colonnets reminiscent of an earlier Sarvistan palace in Iran, an Umayyad palace wrongly attributed to Sassanid time.[123] Another striking feature is found in a unique square room (3.5x3.9m), on the southern side, consisting of a vaulted ceiling, supported by two arches crossed perpendicularly dividing the vault into four square sections containing four coffers (fig.11). The transverse arches supporting the vault was sprung from the walls. This is the first known cross-ribbed vaulting. In later times, this system was introduced in Córdoba Great Mosque and Bab Mardum Mosque in Toledo (999).

Figure 8 The Great Umayyad Mosque between 706 and 715 CE.

Figure 9 The nave aisle running across the isles parallel to the qibla, defined by six large horseshoe diaphragm arches, here showing one of these diaphragm arches.

41

Figure 10 Qasr al-Kharanah (Jordan 710), showing the castle form.

Figure 11 Ceiling of Qasr al-Kharanah, room 61 showing supporting crossed ribs

Qusayr Amra was regarded as a small palace by the Umayyad standards (Qusayr in Arabic means small palace). Caliph al-Walid I (705-715 CE.) built the palace with three sections, comprising an audience hall, baths, and water cistern. The audience hall measures 8.5x7.5m, consists of three aisles covered with barrel vaults and separated by two gently pointed transverse arches bearing small wall to reach vault levels (fig.12). This was the second trial of construction of the pointed arch, which reached its full development under the Abbasids in Cistern of Ramla commissioned in 789 CE by the Abbasid Caliph Harun al-Rashid. The first use of slightly pointed arches were in the Dome of the Rock (between 688 and 691 CE) at the inner colonnade surrounding the Sacred Rock. The second system of vaulting consists of a cross vaulted room which was used as the warm room (tepidarium). The hot room (caldarium) is covered with a large dome with pendentives and has four windows for lighting. The apodyterium (changing room) is a barrel- vaulted room. Qusayr Amra is particularly famed for its frescoes, which cover much of the walls and ceilings of the palace. The paintings are the most extensive examples to survive. They depict a variety of subjects including astronomical representations in the caldarium; signs of the zodiac coupled with illustrations of the primary constellations found in the northern hemisphere. Another important painting depicts a dignitary, possibly the caliph, who sits under a canopy of fabric encircled by birds and monsters. To the south, another depiction shows six lavishly robed figures, the Byzantium emperor, the Persian Shah, the Ethiopian Negus, and Roderick the Visigothic king, the emperor of China and the Khan of the Turks. The frescoes symbolize the dominance of Islamic caliph over these once kings. Other painted subjects include hunting scenes, athletic activity, and mythological images (fig.13).

In decorative terms, these palaces gathered the most exquisite forms of architectural décor extending from mosaic floors (al-Mafjar), to walls tinted with decorated tiles and stucco which consisted of geometrical and vegetal representation (Meshatta). Perhaps the most influential of these are the six lobed (pointed) rosettes and octagons, which appeared in Khirbat al-Mafjar and reappeared in Meshatta. In the first instance, the centre of the circular window consists of a six-pointed star allowing void areas for the aeration (fig.14). In Meshatta, the centre of the circle has an eight leaves rosette. In al-Kairawan Mosque, however, we have the earliest complete example of a rosette window appearing on the square base of the dome (fig.15). Here lobes were inserted in the circle of the window just as they appear on European churches of the 13th century. These together with the circular window found in Meshatta are precursors to European prototypes, and must have been behind the inspiration, via crusaders, to develop the famous Gothic rose window.[124] Khirbat al-Mafjar and Qusayr Amra also represent instances where humans and animals were issued in the Umayyad decorative art.

Figure 12 In Qusayr Amra, the audience hall measures 8.5x7.5m, consists of three aisles covered with barrel vaults and separated by two gently pointed transverse arches bearing small wall to reach vault levels.

Figure 13 Other painted subjects include hunting scenes, athletic activity, and mythological images

Figure 14 In Khirbat al-Mafjar, the centre of the circular window consists of an octagon transformed into six-pointed star allowing void areas for the aeration

Figure 15 In al-Kairawan Mosque; however, we have the earliest complete example of a rosette window appearing on the square base of the dome

Muslim Architecture under the Abbasid Patronage: (750-892)

The arrival of the Abbasids to the throne of the Caliphate introduced upheaval in the socio-economic and political life of the Muslim world. This period is renowned for the establishment of the Muslims intellectual base as Abbasid Emirs nurtured education and learning and founded numerous libraries such as the famous "*Khizanat-al-Hikma*" (Wisdom Wardrobe) and "*Bayt-al-Hikma*" (House of Wisdom). Translation work reached its zenith as Muslims embarked on an unprecedented intellectual mission, starting with a learning process based on acquiring existing knowledge from other cultures.

In political terms, the Abbasids' connection with Persia broke the traditional link with Syria, giving the former more influence in shaping various aspects of Muslim life. Persia contributed militarily to the succession of the Abbasids especially under the leadership of Abu Muslim later al-Ma'mun[125] who led the coup d'état against his brother al-Amin (in 813 CE) from his residence in Merv (Persia). Under these circumstances, we can see why the Muslim capital was moved from Damascus to Baghdad nearer to Persia. Furthermore, the strategic location of Baghdad in the middle of rich and populated Mesopotamia and at a crossroads of the ancient trade routes between Africa, Asia and Europe, was also a decisive factor in its choice as the new capital. The result of this was a concentration of wealth in this city providing an opportunity for the Abbasid Caliph to develop lavish tastes and lifestyles, which reached its peak under Harun Al-Rashid. This was so impressive that the Abbasids' religious and political rival in Byzantium tried to emulate such elegance. Historical sources reveal that in 830 CE a Byzantine envoy went to Baghdad where he was so impressed by the splendour of Abbasid architecture that on his return to Constantinople he persuaded the Emperor Theophilos (829-842) to build a palace, in Bryas (now Maltepe), exactly like the ones he had seen.[126] Ziryab (789-857), the famous musician who spread high culture in Cordoba, setting the standard of dress, table manners, protocol, etiquette and even the coiffures of men and women was an Abbasid migrant from Baghdad.

Meanwhile, the impact of the new "Pax Persia" resulted in the adoption of Persian and Sassanid royal architecture leaving strong traces on the character of princely palaces and buildings and later extending to the general art of this period. The building mania of the Abbasids took on a new dimension in the construction of mosques, as reflected in their size and character. Unlike the Umayyads who continued the stone tradition of Syria, the Abbasids adopted the Mesopotamian tradition of construction with mud and baked brick, often arranged in a decorative manner or carved and moulded with geometric and vegetal designs.

The earliest major work of the Abbasids was the rebuilding of al-Aqsa. The mosque was originally built by Omar (the second Caliph) in 634, but extended and improved upon by a number of Umayyad Caliphs especially al-Walid I (705-715 CE.). After its destruction by the earthquake of 747-748, the Abbasid Caliph al-Mahdi (775-785) rebuilt it in 780 and according to Creswell,[127] the mosque retains this plan to present times.[128] The major Abbasid addition was the introduction of the arcaded portico in the northern, western and southern side to protect the faithful from winter rain and summer heat as well as sheltering the poor and travellers. The other feature introduced by the Abbasids was the unusual shape of its plan by running the aisles of the sanctuary from North to South parallel to the central nave and intersecting them with the qibla in the mihrab area forming a T shape seen earlier in the Umayyad mosque of Damascus.

The al-Aqsa mosque is renowned as the second example, after Ukhaidir palace (see below), for the systematic use of the pointed arch (fig. 16). It is also famous for its connection with the transfer of this arch to Europe. Historic sources indicate that during the first crusade of 1099, and after the fall of Palestine to the crusaders, crusading leaders held their first meeting in the Dome of the Rock Mosque. This was to settle their differences and intimidate the defeated Muslims. Those leaders who were interested in architecture could not escape noticing the beauty of the pointed arcades of both the Dome of the Rock and al-Aqsa, which they brought back with them when they returned to Europe.[129]

The next major Abbasid building was the central mosque of Al-Mutawakkil (Samara) which was erected between 848 and 849 (some 140 years after the Umayyad Mosque in Damascus)) and was, until recently, considered the world's largest,[130] with an area of 109 acres and containing some 25 aisles or "riwaqs" separated by octagonal piers supporting the teakwood beamed roof. The uniqueness of this mosque is revealed in a new design and architectural techniques showing a great deal of ingenuity and innovation.[131] The helical minaret al-Malwiya, as it became known, consisted of a spiral tower, which in an unprecedented fashion, stood on its own on the north side outside the enclosure wall (fig.17). A number of windows were carefully placed in the enclosure and spanned by cinqfoil arches. This is the first appearance of this motif which soon afterwards reached Muslim Cordoba and from there entered Europe where it became a predominant feature in Gothic architecture. The substitution of antique columns to carry arcades with brick piers in al-Mutawwakil Mosque was also the first recorded instance at least 150 years before its adoption in Europe. These columns were octagonal in form on a square base, and have four circular or octagonal marble shafts joined with metal dowels and had bell shaped capitals.

These features were re-employed by al-Mutawakkil in his second most important mosque, Abu Dulaf (Samara, 860/61) and later by Ibn Tulun Mosque in Cairo (876 CE). This was the first employment of piers outside Samara as well as the systematic use of pointed arches, which had become more popular by then. This was at least two and a half centuries before it was introduced to Europe. Rice admitted this as he announced, *"The pointed arch had already been used in Syria, but in the mosque of Ibn Tulun we have one of the earliest examples of its use on an extensive scale, some centuries before it was exploited in the West by the Gothic architects"*[132]. Moreover, according to the same theory, Ibn Tulun Mosque was the means through which the pier was transmitted to Europe.

The other important feature, in Ibn Tulun Mosque, is decorative and connected to the use of an advanced (to Samara) combination of geometrical and floral patterns (Arabesque) on the architrave of its arcades, which in the opinion of Richmond (1926) is also the earliest example found[133]. Later, this feature became a prominent theme in most Muslim decorative art. Other innovations included the introduction of ornamental battlements, which crowned the external walls (fig. 18) which later became a prototype of Gothic pierced and crested parapets[134]. The transfer of these motifs to Europe according to Ibn Tulun's theory took place through the strong links the Fatimids had during the 11th century with Amalfitan and Venetian traders who often visited Cairo and this monument.

Among the palaces built by Abbasid Caliphs and Emirs that attracted wide interest is a fortified living complex containing halls, courtyards, living apartments and a mosque, known as Ukhaidir Palace in Iraq (fig.19). The palace, built between 774-775 CE by Isa ibn Musa[135] some 75 miles Southwest of Baghdad, was a masterpiece of architectural innovation, which had a long lasting impact on the development of architecture. The architects and masons of Ukhaidir first introduced a new elaborate technique based on the construction of elliptical (pointed) barrel vaults with bricks in a similar technique to building a wall and therefore considerably improved the way vaults were built.[136] The old tradition consisted of the use of a mixture of mortar and small stones and debris laid out on wooden base. Such a method required a lot of wood not available in this arid region and building took a considerable time to finish, as masons had to wait for the vault to dry in order to move the scaffolding to another part of the building. This new technique, likely to have been introduced through Persian and Mesopotamian Muslims, provided solutions to these problems. Further elaboration of the vault construction technique was made in the palace's mosque,

Figure 16 The al-Aqsa mosque is renowned as the second example, after Ukhaidir palace, for the systematic use of the pointed arch.

Figure 17 The helical minaret al-Malwiya, as it became known, consisted of a spiral tower, which in an unprecedented fashion, stood on its own on the north side outside the enclosure wall.

Figure 18 Ornamental battlements, crowning the external walls that later became a prototype of Gothic pierced and crested parapets

using flattened arches to support the brick vault, a technique that became known later as ribbed vaulting.[137] According to Marcais (1954), this method was also employed in Medinat Al-Zahra (10th century) in Andalusia.[138] This achievement provided the foundations for the rise of Gothic architecture in Europe.

Another innovation in Ukhaidir was the introduction of the first fluted dome, which appeared at the crossing beyond the main entrance and which later was adopted in al-Kairawan mosque. Finally, Ukhaidir elaborated the defensive technique found in Raqqa[139] by introducing what is known as *chemin de ronde*[140] along the ramparts. The introduction of arrow slits in its walls enabled defence against attackers. Meanwhile, the four gates, each consisting of a chamber with an inner wall and an outer portcullis, which could be lowered in case of assault, trapping the attackers inside, provided another defensive architectural technique, again transmitted to Europe through the crusaders.

Muslim Architecture of the Andalusian Caliphate (756-1500)

The arrival of Abd-al-Rahman I (r.756-788) to Spain in 756 brought security and prosperity to Spain as well as North Africa. It became a fertile environment for the growth of agricultural and industrial production. Trade opportunities increased substantially resulting in the accumulation of considerable wealth. With their personel interest in science and arts, the Caliphs gave great impetus to intellectual prosperity in al-Andalus. Within this intellectual environment and scientific attainment, artists, masons and architects pushed human creativity to its limits producing some of the artistic wonders of the Muslim world.

As is customary with Muslim Caliphs, the first important building of the Andalusian architecture was the Mosque. In Andalusia (Muslim Spain), the Great Mosque of Cordoba was founded by Abd-Al-Rahman I in 787. Its construction continued for a number of years as each succeeding Caliph added his contribution to the mosque in the form of restoration and extension, yet the building still preserved its unity and harmony as if one single person built it (fig.20).

In terms of architectural and ornamental innovation, the Cordoba mosque introduced several features and techniques that became part of late Muslim architecture particularly in North Africa. The mosque introduced a fascinating technique in extending the height of short columns to achieve a standard height of space (roof and ceiling). In the first instance, the design of Abd-Al-Rahman I used super-imposed arcades of round arches while in Al-Kairawan Mosque (in 836) this was achieved by stretching up the arch to the desired height. In 961,

Figure 19 Ukhaidir Palace in Iraq

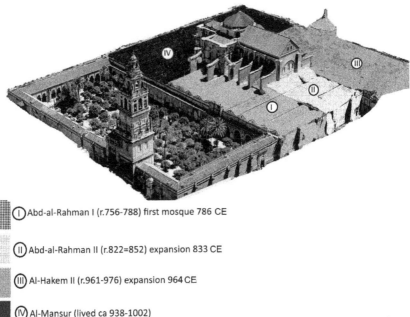

Ⓘ Abd-al-Rahman I (r.756-788) first mosque 786 CE

Ⓘ Abd-al-Rahman II (r.822=852) expansion 833 CE

Ⓘ Al-Hakem II (r.961-976) expansion 964 CE

Ⓘ Al-Mansur (lived ca 938-1002) expansion 987 CE

Figure 20. Mosque of Cordoba construction continued for a number of years

53

and under Al-Hakem II, a third technique was introduced in the maqsura of Cordoba Great Mosque by using the super-imposed trefoil intersecting arches which added more decorative touch to this technique. Meanwhile, the substantial use of both horseshoe and polylobed arches in Cordoba was a source of inspiration for Europeans.

The next development was the use of ribbed domes. It was used in the maqsura (erected between 961-968 CE). This fashion consisted of adding ribs to the vault of the dome to give support to the structure as well as provide a fascinating internal decorative technique in the form of a rose formed by interlacing arches (ribs) (fig.21). After this experiment in Cordoba, the use of these ribbed domes extended in Andalusia. It was eventually employed in the majority of buildings including the famous Mosque of Bab Mardum built in 1000. Muslims progressively mastered this style and produced remarkable domes such as those found in Kutubia Mosque (1162) in Morocco. In the Great Mosque of Telemcen (Algeria, 1135), a twelve pointed star ribbed dome decorated the ceiling in front of the mihrab. In Masjid –i-Jami of Isfahan (Iran), the southern dome built by Nizam al-Mulk[141] (1018-1092), also incorporated ribs supporting the structure. The popularity of the style also extended to churches in Christian parts of Andalusia and then to Europe where the majority of domes adopted the Cordoban approach. Some academics, such as Lambert, Male, and Choisy are firmly of the opinion that this Cordoban technique was the origin of the ribbed vaulting of the Gothic style.

Another remarkable feature of this Mosque is its use of red and white coloured bricks. The first use of such polychromy was in the Dome of the Rock where an alternation of black and white was introduced. Its use in Cordoba, especially in the voussoirs of the arches produced a delightful atmosphere emphasising structural unity and aesthetic continuity. European visitors of the 9th and 10th centuries could not resist its overwhelming beauty and wasted no time in introducing it in their buildings.

The other influential Andalusian building is Bab Mardum Mosque, built in Toledo between 999 and 1000, according to an inscription found on its façade. The mosque is thought to be a private institution as reflected by its relatively small size (26.4 square feet) and its pavilion type form[142]. Its significance is in its contribution to early gothic architecture. Marcais (1954) found a link between Bab Mardum, the mosque of Casa de las Tornerias (Toledo 12th century), and Abu Fatata Mosque (Tunisia), while Creswell[143] extended this link to include the Ribat of Sussa (Tunisia, 821) and Mosque of Masjid-I-Tarikh at Balkh (early 9th century).[144] These buildings have one common plan consisting of square shape subdivided into square compartments. In Bab Mardum, Casa de las Tornerias and

Balkh, there are nine chambers covered with domes. In Bab Mardum, the technique introduced in these domes is very revealing, with the insertion of supporting ribs intersecting each other in a similar fashion to that of Cordoba. The ribs of the central dome were arranged in a star form crowning the structure and externally the dome was raised slightly above the rest of the roof. The whole structure is supported by four centred columns which also define its nine bays and above them horseshoe arches were placed.

In one of these domes, the ribs intersect at 90° in the centre of the dome, a basic form of the quadripartite ribbed vaults of early Gothic architecture, which appeared in late 12th century (fig.22). Lambert (1958) firmly believed that the ribs of Bab Mardum must have been the inspiration of the Gothic ribs[145]. Alfonso VI conquered Toledo in 1085[146] and the Mosque was immediately converted into a Christian church under the name of Cristo de la Luz. Direct imitation was undertaken in the second half of the 12th century in the construction of Casa de las Tornerias (also in Toledo) under the Christian rule. Meanwhile, the first quadripartite vault appeared in St. Dennis in 1144.

One cannot discuss Muslim Spain without referring to the famous al-Hambra Palace in Granada. Its origins are still under debate as most scholars date it to 13th century Granada, but there are indications, which suggest it was first built in the 11th century,[147] a significant time for both Muslim and European architecture. The palace complex briefly consists of a series of apartments, halls and courts organised in a delightful interconnected setting of hierarchy. The palace is an architectural masterpiece in every term. The successions of spaces are clearly defined by boundaries and each space contains identical features enhancing its identity as well as its function. The visual effect reaches its peak through careful combinations of colour, light and pattern. The structure is cleverly disguised by continuous work of stucco, muqarnas and faience covering the entire walls, floors and ceilings. The composition of courts, gardens and water meantime expressed the Muslim views of paradise and its eternality reward for those who strive to reach it. The Pool of the Court of Myrtle is one example representing this paradise through the display of water, another "river" extending to the eastern side of the Palace (fig.23)

Honey, one of the prestigious drinks of paradise, is symbolised by the honeycomb vault of the Hall of the Abencerages, the world's most fascinating vault (fig.24). Here the interlocking of small squinches of lozenge shapes which project from the walls produced a cell very similar to the honeycomb organised in an eight-pointed star. The drum of the star carries 16 windows, two for each side of the star, allowing in an enormous amount of light (dazzles the eye). The four rivers of paradise are represented by the four streams, which run from the central fountain of the Court of Lions to supply the rest of the numerous springs of the palace. The Pool of the Court of Myrtle is another "river" extending to the eastern side of the Palace. The golden stucco and calligraphic ornament covering the walls as they appear in the Hall of Ambassadors may refer to the golden jewellery and silky dresses the believer is promised.[148]

The impact of Alhambra in disseminating Muslim Moorish style was substantial. Rich and wealthy Europeans who heard about or visited it could not resist the idea of reproducing elements in their own buildings. Owen Jones (1809-1874) had a fascination with Muslim architecture in general and Alhambra's Court of Lions in particular was behind his creation of "Alhambra Court: at the Crystal Palace at Sydenham.[149] The Alhambra style of ornamental and internal decoration invaded most European houses especially in Victorian England.[150]

Muslim Architecture under the Fatimid Patronage (909-1171)

The Fatimid Caliphate ruled Egypt, North Africa and managed to control the Holy Lands in Makkah, Medina and Palestine (Jerusalem) but failed to take Baghdad. Claiming descent from Fatima al-Zahra, the daughter of the beloved prophet Muhammad, they revolted against the dying authority of the Abbasids in North Africa under the leadership of the founder Ubaid Allah al-Mahdi. Ubaid Allah established al-Mahdiya in Tunisia as his capital in 921 CE. His son and successor al-Mansur (r.946-53) moved the capital to al-Mansuriya, south of al-Kairawan, to undermine the Abbasid power in this old city and establish firmly the Fatimid Caliphate. His successor al-Mu'izz Lidin Allah (r.953-75) was more ambitious having eyes on Egypt, which he conquered in 972 CE with the help of his Sicilian commander Jawhar. They founded al-Qahira, The Victorious, or Cairo in 973 CE, which they made the new capital.

The Fatimid left a considerable intellectual and artistic heritage highly admired by historians and collectors, the most glorious was in Egypt. Under their rule, Egypt produced some of the highly respected scholars such as al-Mosili (10th century), a genius eye-surgeon who carried out the first cataract removal operation.[151] Ibn al-Haitham (or al-Hazen, 965-1039), originally from Syria, produced Kitab al-Manazir in which he developed his theories of optics as noted in earlier chapter.[152] Finally yet importantly, Nasir Khusaro (1003-1088) was a celebrated poet, philosopher and traveller, originally from Iran, who also thrived in the Fatimid court.

Figure 21 The maqsura, built between 961-968 CE

Figure 22, The ribs of the domes of the maqsurah intersect to form a star, a basic form of the quadripartite ribbed vaults of early Gothic architecture, which appeared in late 12th century.

57

Figure 23 The Pool of the Court of Myrtle is another "river" extending to the eastern side of the Palac

Figure 24 The honeycomb vault of the Hall of the Abencerages, the world's most fascinating vault

Fatimid minor arts are well renowned in various media and forms; in ivories, rock crystals, ceramics, woodcarvings, textiles, or metal works. Among the decorative themes used were arabesque designs, animals, epigraphic bands, and human figures, which were drawn, carved, or painted with distinctive reality not familiar in previous Islamic periods. A peculiar motif consisting of long eared hare became particularly identified with Fatimid art largely depicted in tin glazed and luster pottery. Rock and crystal products were produced of high quality, predominantly decorated with birds, animals and scrolls. One of these crystal vessels, a water jug, found its way to the treasury of St. Mark Cathedral in Venice. Metalwork in the form of incense burners, aquamaniles and other vessels were also popular. The bronze griffin, which was made in 11th century and preserved in the Campo Santo at Pisa, Italy, is a good example showing the high quality of Fatimid skills. In textile industry, the textiles that the Fatimid made reached worldwide reputation and numerous pieces of their silk and embroideries (tiraz), in silver or gold embroidery, were among the exquisite products bought. One of these pieces is found in Vauclause, France, and known as "the veil of St. Anne."[153] The cloth bears an inscription dating it to 1096/7 from Damietta.[154]

In architecture, the Fatimids introduced a few changes and additional features mostly reflecting the cultural trends of their Shiite doctrine and the domains they ruled. Apart from a few literary descriptions, little is known about their palaces which unfortunately did not survive, but their splendour and talent is evident form the remains of their work in a few shrines, mosques and gates which had a long lasting influence on subsequent periods. The Fatimids faced challenges from the Abbasids who were recognised by an important section of the Muslim population to be the real and true Caliph of all Muslims, which the Fatimids were also claiming. They also faced Byzantine threats across the Mediterranean, especially in Sicily. This rivalry was reflected in their palaces and mosques, which were designed of a greater magnificence decorated with delicate arabesque and rare birds and animals, and animated by beautiful fountains and water pools adding an atmosphere of freshness and coolness to the air. A summary of their architectural contributions would encompass four main elements. First, the use of projected portals in both religious and secular buildings marked a distinctive feature from previous works. The extensive use of the keel arch was another successful innovation in a region dominated by the horseshoe arch. The Fatimids also introduced the Mashhad, or tomb, a type of building usually known in Persia to accommodate relics of important people. The last feature the Fatimids introduced was decorative using muqarnas and Kufic inscriptions promoting the Shiite beliefs, and the use of joggled voussoirs.

Fatimid Architecture in North Africa

The first Fatimid construction projects involved the foundation of two capital cities of al-Mahdiya, and al-Mansuriya. Sadly, nothing remains of the latter but from al-Mahdiya there are two preserved structures, which can provide an idea about the architecture of this period. The first is a gatehouse, called Skifa al-Kahla (obscured entrance), a 33 meters long and 5 meters wide entrance that once reinforced the defences of the city. The gate consisted of a large horseshoe arch flanked by two robust bastions, which the Ottomans renovated in the sixteenth century (fig.25).[155] The second structure is the Great Mosque, first built in 916 CE but restored on the model of its original form in the 1960's. The influence of al-Kairawan mosque is quite visible; the layout with nine aisles running perpendicular to the qibla wall and a transverse aisle parallel to it (T plan), the doubling of supports in the central aisle, and the arcades surrounding the court are all indices of this influence[156]. The mosque has two interesting features, its projecting portal and the absence of a minaret. The portal is a tripartite structure, consisting of a large central arched opening, flanked on each side by two shallow niches, one above the other (fig. 26). George Marcais thought late-antique triumphal arches found in many parts of Tunisia inspired this gate.[157] As to its function, some historians claimed the character of the portal provided the Fatimid court with setting for ceremonial activities.[158] However, in the absence of any supporting testimonial records, such suggestion is difficult to sustain.

Another Fatimid significant building in North Africa was the complex of al-Qala' of Beni Hammad built in 1007, in Eastern Algeria. The Hammadids, like the Zirids, belonged to an influential Berber tribe of North Africa, known as Sanhaja[159]. They became vassals of the Fatimids ruling North Africa for them after their conquest of Egypt. The al-Qala' complex consisted of a Great Mosque, gardens and a number of prestigious palaces. According to Paul Blanchet[160] and General de Beylié[161] who were the first to conduct excavations on the site, the mosque consisted of a large rectangular prayer room of typical North African T plan made of thirteen aisles arranged perpendicular to the qibla wall. The most important element of the mosque, however, is its minaret, which is the only remaining structure of the whole town. Set at the end of the courtyard opposite the Qibla wall, in similar fashion to that found in the Great Mosque of al-Kairawan, the minaret remains one of the largest minarets of the period, 25 meters high, consisting of six sections of equal size. The southern façade incorporates a peculiar decoration, a tri-partite design inspired form the portal of al-Mahdiya Great Mosque (fig. 27). The decorative scheme is made of a central deep arched niche running from the base to the top section, flanked by long deep scalloped niches, one at each side, running along the height of the third and fourth sections of the minaret and topped by two sets of arched windows.

Figure 25 Skifa al-Kahla (obscured entrance), a 33 meters long and 5 meters wide entrance that once reinforced the defences of the city.

Figure 26 The portal of al-Mahdiya Mosque is a tripartite structure, consisting of a large central arched opening, flanked on each side by two shallow niches,, one above the other

Figure 27 al-Qala' of Beni Hammad built in 1007, in Eastern Algeria.

The tripartite scheme, especially the use of narrow deep niches seems to dominate much of the surface decoration of the region during this period. Already noted in al-Mahdiya, we find it in the royal palaces of the Qala', especially in the al-Manar and al-Bahr Palaces. Some sources traced its first appearance to the external decoration of facades of pre-historic palace of Warka (Uruk) in Mesopotamia[162]. Others related it to the palace of Firozabad (224 CE) in Iran where similar niches decorated the whole height of the facades.[163] The form and size of the minaret of Qala' and its decorative scheme could have influenced some of the Romanesque and Gothic towers in Europe. Its resemblance to many towers such as those of St. Abbondio church in Italy (1063-1095), Abbey aux Hommes at St. Ettiene (1066-1160), St Martin in Spain (12th century), and St. Edmund at Bury in England (1120) must be brought to attention, which will be discussed in detail in chapter 5.

Fatimid Architecture in Egypt

Most of the remaining Fatimid buildings are essentially mosques, mostly in the traditional hypostyle form with a cloister. The main distinguishing features include the use of projected roofs and portals of the central aisle, which is usually perpendicular to the mihrab. The introduction of domes over the bay of the mihrab was another feature the Fatimid consistently repeated. In almost all their important mosques the mihrab was *"always enhanced architecturally either by a dome above it or by a transept (al-Azhar and al-Hakim have both), or by a widening of the aisle adjacent to the qibla wall (al-Akmar mosque), or the aisle perpendicular to it (al-Salih Tala'i mosque)."*[164]

The al-Azhar or the Splendid Mosque[165] was founded by al-Mu'iz at the centre of his capital al-Qahira (972CE). His successor al-'Aziz (975-996) upgraded it into a theological school in 988 CE, playing a central role in Muslim education besides al-Hakim and al-Mustansir universities[166]. The plan of the mosque has evolved from numerous alterations, which were carried out by enthusiastic rulers who desired to mark their legacy with this prestigious theological school. The oldest part of the mosque is the original prayer hall (sanctuary) showing some similarities to Ibn Tulun Mosque. It is made of five aisles parallel to the old qibla wall with the central nave (transept) cutting through them in the middle and running from the court in the west to the old qibla wall in the east, a reminder of the North African T plan mosques, ie.al-Kairawan. The nave was made wider than the other aisles to emphasise the connection with the mihrab and its arcades were carried on coupled columns, culminating on either end in a bay carrying a dome as in al-Kairawan.

Another important feature worth mentioning here is the "keel" arch or so-called Persian arch used extensively in portico and arcade (fig.28). While most historians agreed the Persian origin of this form of arch, Rivoira[167] had wrongly considered the al-Azhar example to be the earliest and thus the Persian arch was actually invented by the Fatimid architects. It was developed from a combination of the pointed horseshoe arches of Ibn-Tulun with the high imposts of the al-Kairawan arcades and the "cyma reversa" arch used in India[168]. Another feature of al-Azhar that found its way to Europe was the triangular cresting, which decorates the top of the roof. Together with those of Ibn Tulun and al-Hakim mosques, these battlements provided a prototype for Gothic pierced and crested parapets that were constructed in Medieval Europe, particularly those found in Palermo Cathedral, built in 1185 CE, and Cromer Church of Norfolk (England, 15th century).

The second most important building is al-Hakim mosque was built by al-Hakim Bi Amrillah (the ruler by the orders of God) during his reign (990-1012). It was built following the tradition established by Ibn Tulun and al-Azhar mosques, emulating the building forms and techniques of the former and the spatial configuration of the latter. Al-Hakim reutilized the plan of al-Azhar mosque with a five aisled prayer hall (sanctuary) and arcaded porticoes (fig. 29). The central nave in front of the mihrab was enlarged and raised higher above the roof accentuating its importance and was pierced with clerestory windows as in al-Aqsa Mosque in Palestine (Jerusalem). The mihrab itself was defined by a semicircular dome raised on squinches and standing at the centre of two corner domes of similar design. The arches supporting the arcades of the sanctuary (prayer hall) as well as the portico were built in Tulunid fashion pointed and carried on robust masonry piers with engaged columns at the corners.

Other Works

Towards the end of the 11th century, the Fatimids faced several security problems, arising from internal disputes, Byzantine threats and the crusaders. Their chief work during these troubled times was the Mosque of al-Aqmar, built in 1125. Its hypostyle plan consists of five aisles but the most interesting part of the mosque is the hugely ornamented façade, which represented a novelty not known before, especially in Egypt. The elaborated stone carvings in the form of muqarnas, medallion in the tympanum and blind ribbed niches marked a new era in stone architecture (fig.30). The monumental entrance is tripartite structure, a reminder of al-Mahdiya Mosque, with the central part being a large Persian archway decorated with joggled lintel above which a medallion in the tympanum with calligraphic inscriptions was inserted. Flanking the portal are two long blind arches carrying projections of muqarnas and above them blind scalloped niches. Both Caroline Williams[169] and Doris Behrens-Abouseif[170] read these features as elements of ceremonial expression of the triumph of Shi'ism.

As expected the other major work concentrated on reinforcing the structural defences of the city, especially its walls. The enceinte was supported by three renowned gates, Bab al-Futuh (1087) (fig.31) and Bab al-Nasr (1087) (fig.32) in the northern side and Bab Zuwaila (1091) in the south. The three gates were built by Badr al-Jamali (d.1094), an Armenian Muslim who was made a vizier by al-Mustansir billah (Imploring the help of God) (r.1036-1094) for restoring peace and security. Each of the three gates is flanked by two towers, square in the case of the Bab el-Nasr, and round in the other two. The quality of these gateways was observed by Rice "*the fine stone masonry, the pointed arches, the elaborate voussoirs and the defensive conception of these structures all represent developments which were to follow in Romanesque and Gothic architecture a generation or so later.*"[171] The presence of the joggled voussoirs of the lintels in the three gates is very interesting as it is among the first examples in Islam. Under the Mamluks, joggled arches became very popular, used in gates, doorways and even mihrabs, often with elaborated polychromy of white and black colours.

The final element of Fatimid architecture was the spread of memorial monuments, tombs and funerary mosques, a feature that was explained by the veneration of Shiite doctrine to the high clergy (imams) and the descendants of Ali, the second Caliph and cousin and son in law of Prophet Muhammad. The Mashhad has a Persian Seljuk (below) origin, literally meaning 'places of witnessing'. The Fatimid adopted this tradition after al-Mu'izz had the remains of his ancestors brought form North Africa and buried them near his palace in a Mashhad. According to Williams, although the Fatimids occasionally venerated their imam's ancestors they did not practice the cult of the dead.[172] Williams blames Badr al-Jamali who introduced this cult. Badr recovered the head of al-Hussein and brought it to Cairo, founded Mashhad of al-Hussein at Ascalon and restored Mashhad of Sayyida Nafissa, a saintly woman.[173] In 1085, he built a funerary mosque that became known as al-Juyushi, a corruption of his military title *Emir al-Juyush* or Chief Commander. The mosque surprisingly did not contain a tomb but the calligraphic inscription found there refers to it as Mashhad, suggesting it was intended as a commemoration of restoration of order for the Caliph al-Mustansir after decades of strife and turmoil.[174] The Mashhad/mosque has a few distinctive features. In addition to its small size, it has a peculiar minaret over the main entrance, which incorporates a cornice made of muqarnas believed to be the oldest in Egypt.[175] It has been suggested that this

Figure 28 the "keel" arch or so-called Persian arch in al-Azhar

Figure 29 Al-Hakim reutilized the plan of al-Azhar mosque with a five aisled prayer hall (sanctuary) and arcaded porticoes

Figure 30 Mosque of al-Aqmar, built in 1125.

Figure 31 Bab al-Futuh (1087)

Figure 32 Bab al-Nasr (1087)

motif was transferred from Persia through Badr al-Jamali while the square shaft of the minaret is believed to be of Syrian inspiration. 176 The minaret consists of four sections rising narrower towards the top. The first section is tall and square topped with muqarnas cornice, a second narrower square section tops it up followed by an octagon gallery and then a tall bulbous dome.

Muslim Architecture in Sicily (827-1194)

The first contact Sicily had with the Muslim world was during the ninth century when the Abbasid appointed Aghlabid rulers of North Africa landed in Sicily in 827 CE, taking it from the Byzantines, the major enemy of the Abbasids in the East. Later their successors, the Fatimids, assumed the ruling of Sicily until its final fall to the Norman rule in 1072 CE.[177] The Muslim legacy in Sicily has generally received only a small fraction of the attention given to its neighbouring Spain, probably because of a comparatively shorter period of Muslim rule there, and the systematic destruction of Muslim remains in the island. Historians and travellers of the time such as Ibn Hawqal: in 972-973 and Ibn Jubair (1145-1217), wrote about the marvels of Sicily, especially its capital city *Bal'harm* or Palermo, which became the largest of Sicilian cities outshining the old Byzantine capital of Syracuse on the Ionian coast.[178] Over the two centuries of Muslim rule, "*every aspect of Sicilian society was drastically altered --from cuisine to religion to language. Architecture was also influenced. Today, it's easy to point to the "Norman-Arab" style which led to the design of churches that looked like mosques*"[179] This prosperity reached its apogee under the rule of the Kalbid dynasty (948-1052 CE), who were very trusted by the Fatimid rulers that they gave them considerable independence to rule the island. Sicily developed a vital trade route, as it became a node in the commercial activity around the Mediterranean Basin connecting between European Muslims and those of North Africa and the East.[180]

Muslim Architectural Legacy in Sicily

The Fatimids imprints are also found in many aspects of Sicilian, and Italian, art and architecture. In contrast to the large number of important Fatimid pieces of gold and silver artefacts scattered in south Italy, Muslim palaces, mosques, baths, mills and gardens once engraved the Sicilian landscape are all but wiped out. From Palermo, the city once described by Ibn Hawqal in 973 as "the city of the 300 mosques", no single mosque remains. Taking advantage of the internal disputes between various corrupt Arab princes and nobles, the Normans successfully occupied the island in 1061 CE. The new rulers, however, chose to retain much of the Muslim administration and artistic traditions, after experiencing the Muslim high civilisation they found in Sicily. Norman rulers, especially Roger II (ruled 1130-1154), and William II (ruled 1166-1189), played an important role in integrating Muslim art and architecture into Sicilian and European art and architecture. One of the features they admired most were the polychrome, intersecting arches, which they used widely[181]. The contribution of Sicily in the transmission of many architectural and art themes to Europe is well documented and will be discussed in full details in chapter five.

Norman Churches

Examples of such interaction are churches of San Giovanni degli Eremiti, or St. John of the Hermits and San Cataldo church built in 1161 CE. The three churches have many common features including; external appearance consisting of baked brick surfaces decorated with blind arches, red onion shaped domes resembling that of Mashhad al-Juyushi, Cairo 1085, and square towers built in sections and topped with an open gallery. Originally, a mosque transformed between 1132 and 1148[182], San Giovanni degli Eremiti, or St. John of the Hermits (fig.33) still maintains the Muslim T shaped plan and the cloister[183]. In the opinion of Symonds *"San Giovanni degli Eremiti, with its low white rounded domes, is nothing more or less than a little mosque adapted to the rites of Christians"*[184]. In another instance, the transmission of the onion dome from the square plan to the circular one was achieved by means of semi-circular squinches closely resembling the scheme at al-Azhar Mosque (Cairo) and Qala Beni Hammad.[185]

George of Antioch, an admiral who served the Emir of Tunis, founded la Martorana, also known as Santa Maria dell'Ammiraglio. Its foundation charter, written in Arabic and Greek, dates the building to 1143 CE (fig.34). On the exterior, the church is decorated with a set of recessed niches and a frieze of Pseudo- Kufic inscription written in Greek and runs along the top of the exterior walls[186]; both bear a derivation from North African Islamic tradition. Ibn Jubayr in his praise of the church indicated the existence of carved Arabesque decoration on its main door. Historic sources indicate that the elaborate pair of carved wooden doors, in the south façade of the western extension were carved by local craftsmen, recalling the Fatimids of North Africa who made the splendid ceiling of Roger's own Palace Chapel, Capella Palatina.[187] The use of *"pointed arches, the way of basing the cupola upon a square, the exterior inscription forming a frieze, are to be found in the Saracen edifice."*[188] The roof structure and ceiling of the nave of the chapel are the work of Muslims, decorated with paintings of oriental style illustrating Eastern legends and fables.[189] The wooden beams at the base of the dome bear a painted inscription in Arabic translating a Greek Hymn.[190] The form of the church and the mosaics are the only two Byzantine elements.

The Capella Palatina was built by King Roger II in the Palazzo Reale and consecrated in 1140. Apart from its shape of a Latin cross, the chapel is regarded as the inspiration of many of the features of Martorana church described above; the recessed pointed arches, bulbous domes, and the mosaics. The combination of Byzantine and Muslim work is clearly visible, Byzantine mosaics adorning the walls of the chapel and Muslim style ceiling crowning the chapel (fig.35). *"The ceiling of the naves is not vaulted, but of wood, and that of the principal nave is entirely Arabian and fashioned and ornamented in that Saracenic manner called by architects, the honeycomb ornament. The centre is composed of a series of large roses or stars, with pendants between each, and on the edges of these compartments, are inscriptions in Cuphic (Kufic) characters, associating Mohammedan recollections with Christian temple."*[191]This honeycomb decoration consists of muqaranas growing from the wall and in the middle two rows of coffered eight angle stars enclosing rosettes. Other Muslim features are the pointed arch and an Arabic inscription, which appears on a handle of the chancel door.

Norman Palaces

The Normans also employed Muslims to build them luxurious palaces imitating the Abbasids' and Fatimids'. The objective was to create *Jannat al-Ardh* or Paradise of Earth, which was planned on an immense park extending to the southeast of Palermo in which most of these palaces, kiosks and fountains were concentrated.[192]   However, in the account of Ibn Jubair, palaces were built everywhere in Palermo appearing *"like pearls on a young girl's necklace."*[193] One of the most prestigious palaces was La Ziza or al-Aziza Palace, built 1166/80, which shows the extent of Muslim identity adopted by these Norman rulers.

The construction of La Ziza Palace was initiated by William I, nicknamed William the Bad (r.1154-1166) and completed by his successor William the Good (1144-89) in 1180, as a summer residence in the centre of the Genoardo park in Palermo, the former capital of Muslim Sicily. Built with a rectangular plan in the form of a high tower comprising three floors the palace was equipped with three facades adorned with blind arches incorporating tiers of windows and a frieze inscription. The interior of the palace was ordered symmetrically greatly resembling the palatial configuration developed earlier by the Beni Hammad in Ashir and Qala'. *"The continuation of the palatial style found at Ashir and the Qal'a of the Beni Hammad may most conveniently be traced in the following century in Sicily, where the Norman kings delighted in palaces that were at least as much Islamic as Western."*[194]

Figure 33 San Giovanni degli Eremiti, or St. John of the Hermits

Figure 34 la Martorana, or Santa
Maria dell 'Ammiraglio, had its
foundation charter written in Arabic
and Greek, dating the building to
1143 CE.

Figure 35 The Capella Palatina was built by King Roger II in the Palazzo Reale and consecrated in 1140. Apart from its shape of a Latin cross, the chapel is regarded as the inspiration of many of the features of Martorana church described above; the recessed pointed arches, bulbous domes, and the mosaics. The combination of Byzantine and Muslim work is clearly visible, Byzantine mosaics adorning the walls of the chapel and Muslim style ceiling crowning the chapel.

Representing the principal feature of the palace, the hall consists of a central *iwan* rising to the height of two stories. Two lateral niches covered with muqarnas were added casting a majestic atmosphere on the room, similar to that found in Muslim reception halls especially of North Africa. The use of coupled colonnettes on inward corners of the room as well as on its entrance is a Hammadid theme that was employed largely in the Dar Al-Bahr of the Qala'.[195]

The back wall of the hall holds one of the most famous and beautiful features. It consists of a large niche of muqarnas ornamented with a set of mosaics in the form of roundels incorporating figures of affronted archers in the central roundel and peacocks on either side of a date palm, which "*seem to mirror in a more durable medium the textiles which might once have graced the walls of these Norman palaces.*"[196] The archers aiming arrows at a tree of different nature may be a depiction of the Tree of Paradise on which the archers (bowmen of the king) are hoping to find their mark.[197] Beneath these mosaics is a fountain fitted with *shadirwan* or *salsabil* from which water flows down into a stream along a marble canal the length of the pavement of the hall connecting with three square fish pools before being emptied into a large reservoir that rested immediately before the palace (fig. 36). Sources indicate that the reservoir was fitted with a central island on which a pleasure pavilion was built on the model of the cistern of al-Kairawan (860-62) and Raqqada. Al-Bakri reported that in al-Kairawan there was a pavilion with four doors which the Emir Ziadat Allah III used to make regular pleasure visits in his boat, 'the glider'[198]. The *shadirwan* is a slanted, pebbled or chevroned slab, form stone or marble, fitted in an angular form below the fountain allowing water gurgles to pour down bubbling to a channel to be collected in a central fountain. The whole scheme has a decorative as well as environmental purpose creating a nice cool breeze in the palace. This beautiful display of water became a Norman fashion reappeared in a number of their palaces including Cuba Palace and Uscibene (fig.37).

Figure 36 La Ziza Palace, Palermo (1154-1180), showing the *shadirwan or salsabil* fountain and the muqarnas above

Figure 37 La Cuba Palace (Palermo, 1180) and Uscibene Palace (both attributed to the reign of Roger II, ruled 1130-1154), here showing details of the muqarnas in la Cuba.

Muslim Architecture under the Seljuk Patronage (1038-1327)

Herdsmen descending from a Turkish tribe called Ghuz, the Seljuk people converted from old Shamanism, the central Asian religion, to Islam in the tenth century. They were the first Turkish dynasty to rule the Muslim World reviving the dying Caliphate. Their arrival introduced a fresh inspiration marked by their religious devotion and strong leadership. Their rule quickly expanded to Persia, Azerbaijan and Mesopotamia entering Abbasid Baghdad in 1055, then Fatimid Syria and Palestine. They defeated the Byzantines in the battle of Manzikert in 1071 and managed to hold and pacify eastern and central Asia Minor.

In cultural and religious terms, this period saw the rise of mysticism known as Sufism. In scientific and intellectual life, names such as al-Ghazali (1038-1111), in theology, and Umar Al-Khayam in poetry were some of the most renowned scholars of this era. In artistic and architectural production, Grabar considered this period, as the second epoch of Islamic classicism, reviving the great works of the Ummayads and the Abbasids. The variety and quality of its ornaments and the inventiveness of its architectural techniques and forms brought a new breath of inspiration to Muslim architects and masons worldwide. Such creativity can be seen in the size of its monuments especially in Persia, Anatolia and Muslim Asia Minor. This period is also renowned for the spread of two unique building complexes, the caravanserais, which denoted the Seljuk's enthusiasm to trade and commerce, and the madrassa, which reflected their desire to promote learning. This engendered prosperity and produced the desired intellectual and artistic revival for architectural and decorative activities.

Although coming from Anatolia, the Seljuks adapted the general character of Islamic architecture in all their buildings was partly due to the employment of Arab and Iranian architects and masons. This was in addition to the religious devotion of Seljuk leaders, who identified more with the community of Islam rather than with their geographical origin. Meanwhile, the cultural amalgam, resulting from the contact of the Seljuks with Persians and central Asians, enriched their architecture and introduced a number of new features, techniques and building types. The first of these was the use of both stone and brick, the former extensively used in Rum (Anatolia) while the latter was chiefly used in Iran. This dual use of material and the advanced technical methods employed in the construction in load-bearing systems and vaults show the influence of local environments and building cultures.[199]

In building types, the Seljuk made considerable changes to the traditional hypostyle mosque. The development of the iwan plan revolutionised the form and function of the mosque, and later introduced new types of buildings, the *Madrassas*, the *hospitals* and the *caravansaries,* which spread in Anatolia, Syria and Iran respectively. The iwan plan, according to Godard[200] was derived from the plan of houses of Khorasan.[201] This was first applied in the madrassa, and then transmitted to the Mosque and later even to secular buildings and palaces. The Sassanid used also the iwan as a vestibule leading to the main domed ceremonial hall.[202]   Scerrato added a new formula arguing that the iwans were mainly developed to serve a number of functions including, prayer, teaching, lodging of teachers and students, keeping books and as a reading library as well as a number of charitable activities in stopping points on the pilgrimage routes intended to serve the ill and the needy.[203]

The first mosque to adopt the four-iwan plan was the Friday mosque of Isfahan (Masjid-I-Jami) which was originally built by the Abbasids in the 9th century. The Seljuk Caliph, Nizam al-Mulk (1029-1092) made some additions including the construction of a large brick dome, in front of the mihrab, in the old hall on its Abbasid cylindrical piers imitating Umayyad and Abbasid mosques. Historical sources indicate that Nizam al-Mulk copied the Umayyad Great mosque of Damascus, which he had visited in 1086.[204]   His political rival, Taj al-Mulk built (between 1088/89) a great domed pavilion, at the opposite end on the axis of the mihrab and the southern dome of Nizam al-Mulk. The dome consisted of similar formal elements of its sister to the south in terms of the hemispheric shape, the eight tripartite squinches, as well as the brick construction techniques.   However, it *"attained a perfection seldom equalled and never surpassed"*.[205] This perfection is particularly seen in the verticality expressed by the alignment of the decorated blind panels of the walls and the squinches and windows above them. In the words of Hoag *"he (the architect of Taj Al-Mulk) achieved a structural consonance and a hierarchy of ordered parts not again approached until the High Gothic of thirteen century Europe."*[206] The four iwans were believed to have been erected after the fire of 1121/1122, in which both domes escaped damage[207] (fig.38).

In addition to these developments made in the form, function and character of the mosque, the Seljuk expanded the use of madrassa, which, according to Van Berchem, first appeared in Khorasan early 10th century as an adaptation of the teacher's house to receive students. In the middle of 11th century, the madrassa was adopted by the Seljuk Emir Nizam -al-Mulk to become a public domain under his control, an inspiration from the Ghasnavids rulers of Persia who used it for teaching theology. The oldest madrassa was founded by Nizam-al-Mulk in Baghdad in 1067 (but no trace remains). Evidence from the madrassas that survived, (built between 1080 and 1092) at Kharghird in Khorasan; show the use of four-iwan plan[208]. However, Hattstein & Delius referred to another madrassa known as the Khoja Mashhad Madrassa (south of Tajikistan) as the oldest madrassa discovered dating back to between the 9th and 11th centuries.[209]

The best surviving examples of madrassas are those found in Anatolia, with their Iranian character including the use of the iwan and the double minaret framing the portal. As in mosques, Anatolia converted the courtyard into a central domed area connecting to a number of chambers (rooms) which provided classes for students. These arrangements can be seen in the famous Karatay Madrassa in Konya founded (1251-1252) by Jelaleddin Karatay, a vizier of Sultan Izzeddin Keykavus. Here the courtyard was covered with a huge dome perforated to admit light, transforming it into a central area equipped with a pool for ablution. The iwan is located on the west while the portal, which falls out of axis with the iwan, is framed by the *pishtaq* and decorated with Syrian inspired knot design, latticework, and polychromy as well as with the classic Seljuk muqarnas. Another building resembling Karatay, especially in the treatment of the dome, is Ince Minare Madrassa (Konya 1265). Ince Minare does not substantially differ from Karatay but more famous for its portal which represents one of the most opulent works of Seljuk architecture and decoration with its *thuluth Naskhi* type of calligraphy presented like a tapestry motif incorporating some vegetal (leaf and fruit) motifs. The whole composition created a baroque effect (fig.39), a style that later appeared in Europe in the 17th century.

The other building type spread by the Seljuk was the caravanserais, also known as *khans* or *hans* (Anatolia) or *ribat*.[210] These were charitable foundations providing travellers with three days of free shelter, food and entertainment (in some cases) as part of the charitable work emphasised by Islam towards travellers (*Ibn al-Sabil*). They were set up at regular intervals of about 30km, along important trade routes in Asia Minor. Physically, these structures consisted of a courtyard pierced with iwans and along its walls rooms were arranged according to their function as lodgings, depots, guardrooms and stables. This organisation is found in Rabat-i-Malik, a typical early Seljuk caravanserai in Iran, which was built between 1078-1079 by Sultan Nasr[211] on the road between Bukhara and Samarkand. The structure resembled the Abbasid desert palaces with a square plan guarded by strong walls, which were buttressed by a number of semicircular towers. Later, this plan was altered leading to the emergence of two separate functional sections as in the case of Rabat Sharaf caravanserai built between 1114-1115 on the road between Nishapur and Merv (fig.40), and Akcha Qala

(11th century) about 80km north east of Merv. Both structures had two separate courtyards arranged on a longitudinal axis with similar design principles to the four-iwan mosque and the madrassa. The first courtyard contained depots and stables while the second seemed to be reserved for accommodation.[212]

These spatial arrangements were also retained in most of caravanserai in Anatolia, which also contained two main sections, the first being evolving into a barrel-vaulted hall used for sleeping arrangements. In some *khans* or *hans*, as in Sultan Han near Kayseri, this hall took the form of a basilica with an axial monumental portal (representing the central nave) opening into the second section of the building. This is the Sahn, a courtyard surrounded by one or two storey arcades comprising a number of rooms accommodating bathing services, storage, and stables as well as the staff working in the *han* such as physicians, cooks, and musicians. Seljuk caravanserais in Anatolia often had in the centre of their court a freestanding Masjid, "Kiosk" mosque. As with most Muslim buildings, these were often provided with high quality architecture and décor, which reached its highest standards in the mosque and portal.

Another building type that saw considerable development under Seljuk patronage was the mausoleum. This type of building evolved from early funerary monuments first erected to honour the Umayyad rulers in the 8th century. However, under the Seljuk it took on new dimension, housing the remains of important people not only rulers but also religious scholars (suffis). Their spread was particularly due to the expansion of Sufism, which was widely practised in Persia as well as Anatolia and Asia Minor. Seljuk mausoleums display great diversity of forms involving the octagonal, cylindrical (also called tower) and square shapes topped with a dome (mainly Persia) or conical roof (especially in Anatolia). These monuments can be found freestanding in cemeteries, or attached to particular buildings connected with the deceased such as mosques or madrassas. Here, architecture reached its highest refinement and beauty. Because of the religious, social or political importance of the people buried in these tombs, the mausoleums were often highly decorated with symbolic designs depicting paradise awaiting the soul of the founder, and large amount of calligraphic inscriptions from the Quran connected with death and paradise. Sometimes the good deeds and the moral life of the deceased were also expressed.

Figure 38 Friday Mosque of Isfahan (Masjid-I-Jami) was originally built by the Abbasids in the 9th century; the four iwans were believed to have been erected after the fire of 1121/1122, in which both domes escaped damage

Figure 39 Ince Minare Madrassa (Konya, 1265), the whole composition created a baroque effect

Figure 40   Rabat Sharaf caravanserai, built between 1114-1115 on the road between Nishapur and Merv

Figure 41 Shams al-Maali Qabus (978-1012) mausoleum consists of a cylinder supported by 10 buttresses planned by rotating a square five times within a circle, and had a conical roof

Figure 42 The tomb of Sultan Ismail (built before 943 CE), the Samanid ruler of Bukhara.

In central Asia and Persia, the earliest Seljuk tombs were cylindrical or tower type. This seems to be derived from earlier tower tombs of the area especially that of celebrated Gunbad-i-Qabus at Gurgan, Iran (1007). This monument was built for Shams al-Maali Qabus (978-1012) and consists of a cylinder supported by 10 buttresses planned by rotating a square five times within a circle[213], and had a conical roof (fig.41). Such features appeared also in Tughril tomb at Rayy, (1139-1140 near Tahran) with the latter having more muqarnas decoration and a more impressive *Pishtag* doorway. As for the square mausoleums, historians have established that the Seljuk derived this type from existing examples especially the tomb of Ismail, the Samanid ruler at Bukhara. According to an inscription, this was built before 943 CE with a square plan supported by semi-circular buttresses at the corners and a domed roof with dogteeth décor and four small projections (domelets) which were placed at the corners of the roof (fig.42). However, the tomb is famous for its brick decoration, which exceeded in quality and richness those found in the Abbasid Baghdad Gate at Raqqa (775) and the Great Mosque of Samarra. Examples derived from this tomb include the Gunbad-i-Surkh (1147-1148) at Maragha (west Persia) which developed a similar square plan, semi-circular corner buttresses and domed roof and the tomb of Sultan Sanjar at Merv (around 1157).

Muslim Architecture under Ayyubid and Mamluk Patronage (1171-1571)

The Ayyubid were descendants of a family of Kurdish emirs who ruled Syria and Egypt between 1176 and 1250. They joined the court of Imad al-Din Zangi (r.1127-1146) in Aleppo and later raised to chief viziers during the reign of his son Nûr al-Dîn Zangi who ruled Aleppo and Damascus between 1146 and 1174, a period that saw considerable tension with the crusades. Nûr al-Dîn built a strong army for liberating Palestine and expelling crusaders from the remaining Muslim land. A token of his dedication to this cause was a wooden *minbar*, which he commissioned for the Al-Aqsa mosque after its liberation. In 1969, a fanatic Jew set fire to the mosque and destroyed this historic *minbar*. Nûr al-Dîn choose Salah al-Din, or Saladin (1138-1193), the son of Najm al-Din Ayyub, to be his right arm and the right leader for his army and diplomacy overseas, especially after the death of his uncle Assad al-Din Shirkuh, the general commander of the army, in 1169.

Indeed Salah al-Din managed to protect Egypt against the crusades and became the vizier of the last Fatimid Caliph al-Adhid (r. 1160-1171). After the death of al-Adhid he became the emir of Egypt, the long dream of uniting Egypt with Syria became within his grasps. The death of Nûr al-Dîn in 1175, however, created another hurdle as Nûr al-Dîn's 11-year-old son, al-Salah Ismail (1163-1181) who had been installed as ruler of Aleppo refused to adhere to this unity and Salah al-Din had to take control by force first over Damascus, Aleppo and then northern Syria and Mesopotamia in a war lasting over 10 years. Once the desired unification of the Muslim realm (Syria-Egypt) was achieved, Salah al-Din moved swiftly to Jerusalem where he defeated the crusaders at Hittin in 1187 driving them out of Jerusalem in a legendary protocol. He spared their lives and gave them free passage contrasting their infamous slaughter of the population of the city when they occupied it in 1099. Salah al-Din al-Ayyubi was later declared the supreme leader of the Muslim world setting up the Ayyubid dynasty, which lasted a little over a century. Following his death, the Ayyubid reign was divided between his relatives ending up with al-Kamil (1218-1238) ruling in Cairo and Damascus, while Aleppo and Hums became independent sultanates ruled by other Ayyubid emirs. In 1260, the Mongol Ilkhanids put an end to their rule in Damascus and Aleppo.

In Cairo the Ayyubid rule was weakened considerably, especially under Emir, al-Salih Najm al-Din (r.1240-1249), they decided to recruit a number of loyal Turkish slaves into their service. They resided in military garrisons in two main camps; those whose camp was near the river Nile (called Bahr al-Nile) were called Mamluk Bahri, mostly from Qipchaq Turkic origin, from southern Russia. Others were housed in a camp near the citadel or al-Burj of Salah al-Din thus became known as Mamluk Burji mostly of Caucasian Circassian origin. The Mamluk were trained as cavalry soldiers following the orders of *furusiyya*, knighthood order, which imposed a code of conduct that included certain values such as courage, honour and generosity as well as military skills tactics and horsemanship. They gradually gained the trust of the ruling family and raised to high-ranking military officers and powerful administrators.

The death of Sultan al-Salih in 1249 coincided with the launch of the sixth crusade in which the French King Louis IX took Damietta and advanced down the Nile threatening Cairo. The throne went to Turanshah, also known as al-Malik al-Ashraf, a young and inexperienced son of al-Salih. The Mamluk conspired, with his stepmother Shajarat al-Dur, his assassination and organised the defence of the city. They defeated Louis IX at al- Mansura, capturing him and many of his forces. The knight Aybeck married Shajarat al-Dur and thus became the first Mamluk Sultan (r. 1250-1257). The uncertainty of early years following the Mamluk takeover troubled with the threat of the Mongols must have caused considerable difficulties as Egypt started preparing for war once more. The Mamluk Sultan Saif al-Din Qutuz who replaced Aybek in 1259 decided not to repeat the Abbasid mistake of reaching for peace with the enemy in Baghdad and gathered a strong army capable of defeating the Mongols. His commander Baybars (r.1260-1277) defeated them in 1260, at *Ayn Jalut* in Palestine, becoming a great hero with a reputation equal to that of Salah al-Din. This reputation enabled him later to become the Sultan of Egypt.

The Mamluk history in Egypt has been closely identified with significant revival of art and culture as witnessed by the many monuments they built in Cairo, Damascus and Jerusalem. Sultan Qalawun, for example, left behind a great selection of monuments including the masterpieces: the Maristan (hospital) and Madrassa of Cairo. His son Sultan al-Nasir Muhammad built some thirty mosques, in addition to monasteries, baths, and schools. Mamluk art has gained world reputation especially in the quality of their delicate metalwork, pottery and textile. The Ottomans ended the Mamluk reign in 1517.

The historical and political events surrounding the rise and rule of Ayyubid (1171-1250) and Mamluk (1250-1571) dynasties were determinant factors in shaping their architecture. Having a non-Arab origin, these rulers established their legitimacy through their relentless fighting against the crusaders and Mongols, and through a deliberate expansion of architectural projects of religious and charitable natures. The need to fight the spread of the Shi'ism doctrine brought by the Fatimids was another factor influencing the character of their art and buildings, which in general adapted the Fatimid themes and motifs to the Sunni identity.[214] Without discarding these political motives, the religious zeal of the Ayyubid was another motivator. As mentioned above, Nûr al-Dîn Zangi started this Sunni passion, becoming renowned in Muslim circles for his promotion of moral unity of Islam and his support for religious orthodoxy. The Ayyubid architecture can thus be regarded as a kind of "monumentalizing piety" through the spread of madrassas, mosques and khanqas.[215]

The successful unification of a large section of the Muslim realm under one Ayyubid banner led to developing building techniques largely from integrating influences from the Fatimid and Seljuk legacies. One of the characters identifying Ayyubid and Mamaluk facades was the exaggerated size of the portal, often in the form of an arch topped with muqarnas conch. In late Mamluk rule the gateway assumed the form of a tri-lobed shouldered arch also topped with muqarnas and flanked by a floral relief as found in the mosque of Sultan al-Mua'yad Salih (1415-1420). The iwan, a Persian and Seljuk feature, was employed everywhere. Mamluk domes are mostly of the bulbous type some of which are fluted or ribbed i.e. Qubba of Yunus al-Dawadar (1382), which echoes the Iranian Ilkhanid domes and prefigures the Timurid's of Samarkand. Others were highly decorated with geometrical patterning as seen in the complex of Sultan Qaytbay (1472-74). The use of muqarnas corbelling for the dome transition was another feature employed first in Aleppo madrassas of Ayyubid Syria and then Mamluk Egypt,[216] suggesting a Syrian influence although the Fatimids used muqarnas before in other areas of decorations. Their minarets were also distinctive, consisting of a three-tiered octagonal structure with added balconies separating between the sections.

In decoration, one of their key decorative schemes was the use of the so-called *ablaq*, literally "piebald", which consists of two contrasting shades of stone, black and white or white and pink limestones. It is an earlier technique known in Byzantine architecture, produced for instance in Ibn Wardan palace near Hims in Syria (ca.561-66 CE), and first in Islam in the northern wall of the Umayyad mosque. Thus, Syrian artists must have been the source of its introduction to Egypt. It was in Syria also where the first stone muqarnas portal was made, in Mashhad al Dikka built in 1189, during the reign of Al-Zahir Ghazi[217], although the first stone muqarnas vault was made at al-Aziza Palace in Palermo (1166). Bichromed marble was also used in alternating black and white. Sometimes an interlaced stone or marble relief ornamentation was employed for the decoration of the spandrels and frame of arches of portals and mihrabs, forming a knot or medallion above the keystone, a feature that became very popular in late Mamluk architecture.

Military Works

To face up to the crusaders' threat, most early works of the Ayyubid understandably concentrated on strengthening city defences, i.e. walls, castles and forts. Salah al-Din strengthened the enceinte protecting Cairo and Fustat and reinforcing it with a citadel that still bears his name. Unfortunately he did not live long enough to enjoy his residence in it but instead it went to his successor al-Malik al Kamil (d.1238) who made it a royal accommodation and it remained so until the nineteenth century. This marked a distinguishable shift from the traditional *dar al-Imara*, which was usually located, adjacent to the central mosque or suburban royal palaces found in Abbasid Samarra. The citadel type of royal palace (residence) was first initiated in Aleppo where it occurred in the middle of the eleventh century.[218]

Other citadels were built in key locations such as Qal'at Rabad at Ajlun in Jordan and Qal'at Nimrud at Banyas in Syria, but the most celebrated Ayyubid citadel was that of Aleppo (fig. 43). Looking both majestic and bold above a 40 meters high mound, this citadel is considered as one of the most spectacular and best preserved Muslim fortress. Originally a site of an old Roman fortress, it was rebuilt first during the Hamdanid rule of Aleppo, by Sayf al-Dawlah (944-967). On numerous occasions, Byzantine raids caused partial or total destruction of the citadel and each time the locals and Muslim leaders carried out the repairs. Nûr al-Dîn Zangi (1147-1174) put an end to the Byzantine threats on the city and carried out a considerable restoration and reinforcement works in 1172. Ibn Jubayr who saw it in 1185 described it as being famous and impregnable.[219] Al-Malik Al-Zahir Ghazi (1186-1216) made substantial works and extensions most of which make the current form of the complex. The plan reveals a large complex comprising an amalgamation of all what the royal or princial life needs; audience halls for the reception of dignitaries and embassies, throne room, residential quarters from palaces, baths and mosques for religious activities, and military installations including arsenal, prisons, granaries and open space for training and parade of the army. The most important feature is the concentric plan, a clear development from Crusade and Christian square keeps. Ayyubid round towers impressed upon the crusaders the need to leave out projecting angles because they provided for flanking fire. The other defensive instrument used in Aleppo castle was a series of machicolations supported by corbels, which break the surface of its external walls. The third device was the use of loopholes, which are arrow slits in fortified walls used as early as second century BC to protect Syracuse and later in the fortifications of Rome. Muslims improved and popularised their use in many instances such as Palace of Ukhaidir, and Ribat Sussa. The first recorded use of them in England was in London in 1130.[220] The Barbican is a fourth defensive element used in Ayyubid citadels including Aleppo. It is a walled passage added to the entrance of a castle in front of the main defensive wall. It has been defined by Turner as *"Projecting defensive position to protect a town or castle gate, or placed at the head of a fixed bridge or drawbridge."*[221] The device delayed the enemy's entrance into the castle and gave the defenders more opportunities to hold up the attackers by forcing them into a small space. The enemy could then be attacked from above and the sides. In no other building, the combination of impressive architectural forms and great artwork with a wide variety of defensive provisions was so successful than in this edifice. These features effectively protected the citadel, which was stormed many times but only once successfully by Timur Leng.[222]

Religious and Charitable Works

The threat of Shi'ism was the second preoccupation of the Ayyubid. They expanded the construction of madrassas and shrines for Sunni imams (called Khanqas) in both Syria and Egypt to restore the Sunni doctrine and abolish all signs of the Fatimid Shi'ism, a mixed expression of both power and piety[223]. Some scholars describe the Ayyubid and Mamluk architecture as the Sunni revival, considering the large number of schools and charitable complexes they erected.[224] It was also the event behind the transportation of Madrassa from the Muslim East, Syria and Iraq, to Egypt and the Western side of Islam. Ayyubid and Mamluk architecture is said to have been the outcome of the trio, patrons, waqf and women. Lacking the religious or political legitimacy, the emirs, and influential leaders patronised architecture and relentless military campaigns against the crusades and Mongols to establish this legitimacy. The war effort must have consumed a large portion of the state's budget, as they had to pay, in addition to military expenses, substantial budget on strengthening and repairing defences, gates and castles. This explains the reason behind Nûr al-Dîn Zanqi's foundation of the *waqf*, an endowment deed where princes and dignitaries endowed land and charitable structures both for pious and social reasons[225]. *Awqaf* (plural of *waqf*) financed the construction and the running of religious and social buildings such as mosques, fountains, madrassas, hospitals and mausoleums. Women were the third agent of the construction work, a tradition that was set by their Fatimid predecessors. According to Humphreys, Ayyubid women, in Damascus for example, participated with nearly one-third of the constructions made.[226] Dayfa Khatun, the widow of al-Malik al-Zahir Ghazi, for example, built khanqah al-Farafra and the madrassa al- Firdaws. Ismat Al-Din Khatun, the wife of Nûr al-Dîn built Madrasa Khatuniya and Khanqah known by her name. Sitt al-Sham Zumurrud Khatun, sister of Salah al-Din, founded Madrasa of Husamiyya and al- Shamiyya and her sister Rabi'a Khatun founded Madrasa Sahibiyya or Madrasat al-Sahiba.[227]

In Aleppo, the Ayyubid were conscious to build madrassas at earnest, probably because of the geographical proximity to al-Nizamiya madrassa of Baghdad (1067). Nûr al-Dîn found them instrumental in bringing people back to their religion and cultural roots, an essential step towards awakening and uniting them to fight the crusades. For this purpose, he built several madrassas including al-Muqaddamiya (without a trace), al-Hallabiya (1148) and al-Shuaibiya (1150) in Aleppo. Al-Shuaibiya was built on the site of the first mosque in Aleppo, which was built by the companion Abu Ubayda ibn al-Jarrah near Bab Antakya or Antioch gate. According to some sources, the Ayyubid and Mamluk built a staggering fourteen madrassas in Aleppo.[228] Salah al-Din (1174-1193) founded five madrassas in Cairo alone. The most architecturally revered madrassas are

Figure 43 Ayyubid Citadel of Aleppo, originally a site of an old Roman fortress, it was rebuilt first during the Hamdanid rule of Aleppo, by Sayf al-Dawlah (944-967), Nûr al-Dîn Zangi (1147-1174) and Al-Malik Al-Zahir Ghazi (1186-1216) both carried some substantial work for the citadel.

without a doubt Madrassa al-Firdaws in Aleppo and al-Salihiyya in Cairo. The widow of Sultan al-Zahir, Daifa Khatun founded Al-Firdaws Madrassa, or school of Paradise, between 1235 and 1241. It was arranged around a rectangular courtyard flanked on three sides by arcades carried on marble columns crowned with a variety of muqarnas capitals. They are the earliest muqarnas capitals known so far, spreading later to other parts of the Muslim world and as far as north Anatolia. It is established that the Muslim introduced muqarnas to Anatolia following its conquest in 11th century, *"and examples were executed in wood, stucco and stone following precedents from neighbouring Iran and Syria."*[229] Tabbaa and Turner also believe that the early use of stone muqarnas was concomitant with the development of the vigorous stereotomic tradition in Aleppo that began in the last quarter of the 12th century.[230] The mihrab of the mosque itself is considered as one of the best examples of Ayyubid prayer niches made of polychrome marble arranged in vertical panels in lower sections and at the sides. An interlaced pattern framed the niche and ended at the crest with a distinctive knot that became a famous Syrian motif greatly influencing the Mamluk architectural decoration and later spreading to Anatolia.

Al-Salihiyya was commissioned by Sultan al-Salih Najm al-Din Ayyub (r. 1240-1249), the Grandson of Salah al-Din, in 1243 to teach the four Islamic schools of law, the first of its kind as earlier madrassas were dedicated to teach only one, either Maliki, Hanbali, Hanafi, or Shafi'. Al-Mustansiriyya in Baghdad (1233) was perhaps the model as it taught the four branches. It was designed as a complex consisting of two self-contained wings, parallel in plan but separated by a public passage. Each section comprised a courtyard, onto which two opposing vaulted iwans were opened, with the larger one being oriented towards Makkah. According to al-Miqrizi, each iwan served as a teaching place of one of the four Sunni theological schools. After the completion of the complex and death of Sultan al-Salih, his wife Shajarat al-Durr added his mausoleum (1250), introducing what was to become a Mamluk mausoleum formula: a tomb adjoining a theological school. The most interesting element of the mausoleum was the transitional zone, which had the earliest example of a Cairene three-tiered brick muqarnas squinch. The mihrab is also known to be the earliest example incorporating black and white polychrome marble lining in Egypt.[231] The minaret stood at the passage way separating the two wings and considered the only fully preserved minaret of the Ayyubid period in Egypt. It is made of brick and curiously designed in the *mabkhara,* or incense burner style, a term first used for this type of minaret by the Orientalist Richard Burton, recalling the tradition of Fatimid Caliph al-Hakim who burned incense in his minarets to perfume the mosque. Creswell followed the genesis of this style concluding that it was first initiated at al-Jayyushi minaret, which had the same elements but topped with a square section. The other development was made in the minaret of the mausoleum of Fatimid prince Abu al-Ghadanfar, built in 1157. The minaret here consists of a tall square shaft carrying an octagonal second storey pierced with lobed-arched openings and surmounted by an octagonal section or helmet in the shape of *mabkhara* decorated with "a little fluting".[232] In the example of al-Salihiya similar features were employed but "*the lantern has become much more elaborate, thanks to the additions of stalactites.*"[233] Other important features of the madrassa include chamfered corners (only extant on the west corner of the mausoleum) and recesses surmounted by keel-arched, fluted shells which are all part of Fatimid heritage.[234] The monument is considered a showcase of architectural and institutional transition between the Fatimid and Mamluk complexes. Indeed, during the Mamluk period, this madrasa served as the supreme judicial tribune of the State and most of Mamluk complexes were greatly inspired by it.

Ayyubid and Mamluk Hospitals

The first hospitals built in Islam were inspirations of the Byzantine *nosocomia* such was the case of Damascus hospital, built by al-Walid I (705-715 CE.). Later hospitals were subject to modification and evolution as Muslims debated modified designs and functions in an attempt to bring them up to their cultural and temporal needs. Al-Razi (865-925), for example, wrote a book on the indispensable characteristics of a hospital entitled '*Kitab fi sifat al bimaristan*', or the Book on the characteristics of the hospital. The Abbasid rulers, Harun al-Rashid and Ibn Tulun, built a few more providing free treatment and care. "*These hospitals were not only a place for clinical care of the patients, but also for educating medical students, for interchanging scientific knowledge and developing medicine.*"[235] Ayyubid hospitals were distinguishable marking speedy evolution from previous ones. The most important of these was al-Nuri hospital of Damascus, denoting its founder Nûr al-Dîn Zangi who commissioned it in 1156. On this hospital, the 13th century medical historian, Ibn abi Usaybi'ah wrote: "*When Nûr al-Dîn built the Grand Bimaristan he appointed as the director Abul Majd al-Bahilli. This physician went regularly to the hospital to care for the patients, to examine them and to give the necessary orders to the attendants and servants who worked under his direction. After that this physician went to the citadel to examine the dignitaries and the noblemen that were ill*". The *bimaristan*, or *maristan*, was both a health institution providing treatment to patients as well as a medical school serving the public for over seven centuries. It was not until the beginning of the 20th century when it was replaced by the modern University Hospital. Among the eminent physicians, the Nuri *bimaristan* produced was Ibn Al-Nafis (1210-1288) who discovered the lesser pulmonary circulation (see above fig.4). The hospital is believed to have initiated the first known medical record keeping in history. The most interesting architectural piece of the building is the portal, which is located on the western side of the building. Its projected structure displayed eastern skills in both stone and brickwork. Like the rest of the building, the gate is made of stone, pierced in the centre by a large arch that is crowned with stucco and brick muqarnas. Below are a set of multifoil niches running above an antique pediment spanning the doorway, which is made of a solid wooden core wrapped with a layer of copper that is attached with copper nails set in geometric patterns.

Al-Nuri hospital became the model for other hospitals, including al-Nasiri hospital built by Salah al-Din in Cairo and since then a close link existed between the medical centres of Syria and Egypt for several centuries. The most notable hospital in Egypt was the al-Mansuri, built by al-Mansur Qalawun in the 13th century on the site of an old Fatimid palace. Sources indicate that Qalawun (1279-1290), while still a prince, fell ill during an expedition he led to Syria. He was treated at al-Nuri hospital where he was so impressed by the quality of services provided there. He vowed to build a similar one at his home city, Cairo. The hospital had different wards specified for various illnesses and separate sections devoted to each gender. It also possessed lecture halls, a library, a mosque and separate administrative quarters.

Mausoleums or Qubbas

The Ayyubid and Mamluk called mausoleums *qubbas*, literally meaning dome (over the tomb). Unlike the Seljuk isolated mausoleums, these were generally incorporated within larger complexes comprising a monastery mosque and madrassa, mostly consisting of masonry cubic base topped with a dome of muqarnas or its transition was achieved by a muqaranas. A puzzling question must be raised here; why did they build such structures although the Sunni doctrine does not encourage the veneration of the dead as well as raising building on their tombs? The answer could be explained by their desire to counter the Shi'ite mausoleums, which they could neither destroy nor ignore. First, the qubba was built and then other buildings were added to it in the hope that the charitable functions of these adjacent structures will benefit the dead person and bring him heavenly rewards.[236] The sultan al-Kamil commissioned the first qubba to accommodate the grave of Imam al-Shafii', a descendant of the Prophet's uncle, abu Talib and one of the four Sunni imams who came to Egypt in the 9th century.[237] Unfortunately, little is left of the Ayyubid works as the mausoleum was subject to many restorations as recent as 1772 involving the repairs made by the Ottoman 'Ali Bey al Kabir.

93

The Mamluks continued in this tradition. Sultan Qalawun (r. 1280–90) built a funerary complex consisting of a mausoleum, madrassa and a hospital (*bimaristan*), between 1284 and 1285 (fig. 44).   The chief work of art of the complex is the mausoleum, which is a typical square domed structure, but unlike other occasions where the dome is supported by muqarnas transition section, Qalawun's dome is raised on four colossal columns and four massive piers imitating the octagon of the Dome of the Rock.   The tomb chamber is magnificently decorated with a variety of themes including woodwork, inlaid marble and on pillars supporting the dome. Under the dome and at the centre of the chamber is a *mashrabiya* or a wooden screen enclosing the cenotaphs of Sultan Qalawun and his son al-Nasir Muhammad. The qibla wall is pierced with a niche that is embedded with turquoise stones and coloured marble. The facade and dome incorporate Gothic shaped windows, a clear inspiration of Crusader architecture, which Qalawun must have become familiar with during his military campaigns in Syria. Qalawun's complex greatly influenced other Mamluk works including the complex of his grandson Sultan Hassan (ruled 1356-1361) (fig.45), and on the works of Burji Mamluks, especially Sultan Qaitbay (1486-1496) and al-Ghuri (1501-1516). Qaitbay was in particular influential for his love of arts and literature bringing new and fresh breath into architecture. It was during his reign, that the holy mosques of Makkah and Medina were extensively restored. His building complex at Cairo was completed in 1474, distinguished for its exquisite masonry, which is displayed in various parts of the building, especially in the carved work of the portal, minaret and dome.

Figure 44 Sultan Qalawun (r. 1280–90) built a funerary complex consisting of
a mausoleum, madrassa and a hospital (*bimaristan*), between 1284 and 1285

Figure 45 Sultan Hassan (ruled 1356-1361) Complex.

Muslim Architecture under the Timurid Patronage (1370-1506)

After the death of Genghis Khan, the supreme leader (Great Khan) of the Turko Mongolian peoples, his four sons inherited the empire and subdivided it between themselves according to Mongol custom, each controlling a territory or an *ulus*. Ugedei, the third son succeeded his father as the Great Khan, and later passed it to his son Mongke (1251-1260). Mongke commissioned his brother Hulagu to re-conquer the Genghis' territories and expand into Persia and the Islamic world. The weakening and partial collapse of the Seljuk dynasty in the eastern parts of the Muslim World in mid-13ᵗʰ century eased the mission of Hulagu, who sacked most of these regions devastating Persia, Syria and the Seljuk territory and followed it by the famous destruction of Baghdad city in 1258. Hulagu's army could have moved westward towards Egypt and the Maghreb if it was not for the Mamluk, especially Baybars, who defeated them in Ain Jalut in 1260 and put an end to their expansion. The land they conquered became under the direct rule of the Ilkhanids, a short-lived Mongol dynasty that derived its name from Hulagu, who received in 1261 the title of Ilkhan, a local khan under the authority of the Great Genghis Khan. Because of their tribal and nomadic character, these new rulers gave little impetus to the development of architecture. Their legacy consisted merely of a few buildings culminating at the mausoleum of Uljaitu (r. between 1304-1316) at Sultaniya in Iran (fig.46).

The Ilkhanid world fell apart after the death of Uljaitu's son in 1335 as various provinces and territories broke away only to be reunited once again by the Timurid, descendants of the famous Timur or Tamerlane, a corruption of the Persian name Timur i Leng which means Timur the Lame while the word Timur is Turkish for "iron". Timur (1336-1405) rose to power when Genghis' second son Chagatay (1227-1241) became in control of territories of Central Asia and north of Transoxiana, the region of present-day Samarkand. By the death of Chagatay, his kingdom was defragmented between his sons into smaller territories. Timur was able to move into this power vacuum and slowly made his fortunes when he generated some loyal followers, especially after entering in alliance with an influential Emir Hussein who resided in Balkh. Timur married the Emir's sister and the two formed a team expanding their influence over the old Genghis Empire.²³⁸ After defeating all his enemies, Timur turned against his brother in law Emir Hussein and took his seat in Balkh, crowning himself as the sole ruler of Transoxiana in 1369 and establishing his capital at Samarkand. From there he moved swiftly across the area adding to his domain the regions of Khwarazm (modern-day Turkmenistan), Khorasan (northern Afghanistan), Persia, Syria and Baghdad, and all lands which had formerly been part of the

Figure 46 Sultaniya Mausoleum in Iran, between 1302–12

Mongol Empire. He also conquered India in 1398 where he was proclaimed the Emperor of Hindustan. Stories of the atrocities he committed made his fame as *"one long story of war, butchery and brutality unsurpassed until the present century."*[239] After his death in 1405, his sons could not keep the empire together and subsequently disintegrated into small kingdoms often engaged in internal strife and dispute.[240]

Timurid Architecture

Historians agree Timur was as a great builder as a destroyer, accounts reported that he gathered artists, artisans, scientists and literati from the regions he conquered and brought them to Samarkand to create his royal capital that "will dominate the world". His sons and other rulers, who succeeded him, were people of letters and art lovers; among the many distinguished arts the Timurid mastered were manuscript illumination and illustration. The school of Herat, their capital after the death of Timulane, saw the apogee of Persian and Timurid painting. The influence of the Silk Road trade is understandably visible, as the Timurid incorporated many Chinese decorative motifs in their visual arts. Chinese painting was particularly influential. Timurid achievements in other luxury arts included metalwork and jade carving. This cultural efflorescence was particularly fostered in the courts of distinguished emirs such as; Shah Rukh (1409-1447), an art loving prince, his son Ulugh Beg, a famous astronomer and man of letters, and Hussein Baiqara (r. 1470–1506), the last Timurid ruler. Ulugh Beg became more distinguished as an educational and scientific scholar than did as a ruler, and under his reign, Samarkand became the scientific and educational centre of the late medieval world.

Timurid women were also active patrons of art and architecture, a tradition which evolved from Fatimid and Ayyubid times and continued after the Timurid into their immediate successors, the Shaibanid, Safavid, Mughals (Mongols) and the Ottomans,. For example, Gawhar Shad, Shah Rukh's wife, built a magnificent mosque at Mashhad (1405-1418) and a mosque-madrasah-mausoleum complex in Herat (1417-1437), albeit mostly destroyed because of war and earthquakes over the last two centuries.

Timur adopted his architecture to his "limitless" power and overwhelming achievement, thus Samarkand deserved unprecedented magnificence, which only gigantic works, colossal buildings and extra grandeur can achieve. The city and his architecture were to radiate around the four corners of his rule and perhaps beyond. Within this paradigm Timurid's imprint on architecture spread over a vast region, extending from Afghanistan, Iran and up to the Soviet Union, displayed in a variety of monumental buildings distinguished for their ribbed bulbous domes, sparkling coloured tiles, rich stucco, and innovative vaulting techniques. Their successful adaptation of all architectural elements in a sophisticated decorative scheme was unique. The exquisite muqarnas disguised their brick vaulting and domes. The gigantic portals in the form of freestanding iwans added to the magnitude of buildings and expressed the greatness of the empire. The large and richly decorated bulbous domes raised on substantially high drums emphasised the mass of the building and its symbolic significance. The decorative mantle covered their buildings in dazzling coloured tiles sometimes combined with glazed coloured bricks arranged in geometrical designs.

As well as architecture, the Timurid treated their cities and urban spaces with the same vigour and greatness. The creation of an elaborate layout based on the open square system was an innovation that exceeded the realms of the Roman *Agora* or the Muslim *Maydan*. The symbolic impression created by Rajestan Square with its monumental grouping and royal connection emphasised the power and achievements of the rulers and brought city life and function in line with their veneration. Such metaphor was explicitly expressed in the portal of Aq Saray Palace (White Palace), which Timur, himself, built in his home city of Ahahr-i-Sabz (ca. 1379–96) which displays the following statement *"if you doubt our power, just take a look at our buildings."*[241] The palace has unfortunately long vanished apart from small remains of the colossal portal. Timur's splendour, however, can be seen in two other buildings, which survived in good conditions, Bibi Khanum Mosque and Gur-i-Mir Mausoleum.

In the congregational mosque of Bibi Khanum, built between 1399- 1404, after his favourite wife, Saray Mulk Khanum, the daughter of Chagatay Khan, Timur set the general guidelines of his dynasty's architecture, which adopted Iranian and Seljuk architecture as culminated in the Masjid-i-Jami of Isfahan. The mosque was organised in a four-iwan plan, which was to become the principal layout of major Timurid monuments. It was unusually equipped with eight minarets, four of them at the corners of the building and two for each iwan including the portal. Since then it became a regular practice to engage the minarets to either side of the portal[242]. The main central dome covers the prayer hall and characterised by its projecting ribs polychrome tiles of beautiful designs (fig.47). Smaller domes supported on piers were distributed on the courtyard galleries as they did in Masjid-i-Jami of Isfahan. It is reported that Timur built it after returning from India using some 95 Indian elephants to haul construction materials from the quarries. When completed the mosque was *"one of the most colossal monuments ever built in the Islamic world."*[243]

Timur's greatest building, however, was the Gur-i Mir Mausoleum, or the Tomb of the Emir, which was originally to house the body of his favourite grandson, Muhammad Sultan (1375-1403), who died of wounds after the battle of Ankara in 1403[244]. A Spanish ambassador, Clavijo (1403-6), at Timur's court reported that when Timur returned from an expedition and found the tomb completed he thought it was too low, ordered it to be demolished, and gave the workers ten days to rectify their work.[245] The mausoleum later became the burial centre for Timur and his descendants including Shah Rukh and Ulugh Beg. Ulugh Beg commissioned the front portal, an inscription relate its architect to Mohammed Ibn Mahmud al-Isfahani in 1434.[246]The monument consists principally of a square room with deep axial bays decorated with panelling of luxurious onyx and painted ornaments, ending with a projected portal used as entrances for four sides of the external octagon shape of the mausoleum. At the centre are eight commemorative slabs with the names of Timur, his sons, ministers, and saints who were buried there. The ceiling is a splendid 26 meters high internal dome resting on a tall drum, which was rebuilt and redecorated in the 1950's with gilded papier-mâché relief work. On the exterior, the dome is 37 meter high, made of a bulbous or melon shaped shell stabilised with some 64 ribs covered with square and oblong blue glazed bricks forming lozenge grids (fig. 48). The drum appears like a long neck supporting the dome, covered with blue and glazed bricks arranged in similar decorative patterns of the dome. Around its base, however, the drum is adorned with a large band of a white-lettered calligraphy in Kufic script evoking the immortality of the Almighty God. The inscription is written in the so-called *hazarbaf* or *banna'i* technique, which consisted of glazed bricks, white in this case, arranged in the Arabic script shapes.[247] The technique is employed everywhere including secular Timurid buildings. Dani et al. attributed this extensive use of Arabic calligraphy to the Timurid veneration of Sufism, as the inscriptions are mostly part of Sufi prayer or remembrance ritual, *dhikr*. The Timurid who did not speak Arabic venerated the script, as it is the language of the Quran and Hadith.

Figure 47 Bibi Khanum Mosque, built between 1399- 1404

Figure 48 Gur-i Mir
Mausoleum, or the
Tomb of the Emir, built
by Timur and was
completed in 1404

Commentators agreed that the high drums and the double dome scheme, made of internal and higher external dome welded together by a set of radiating spokes geared upon a hub of masonry, were the main instruments behind the resistance of these buildings to the numerous earth quakes that devastated the region.[248] In the mausoleum he built, between 1389 and 1399, for Khoja Ahmed Yassawi, Timur first introduced the featured dome and drum. A certain Haji Husayn an architect from Shiraz built the mausoleum, which encompassed a mosque, a *khanqa* or monastery and a library. The double dome schemes was, according to Jairazbhoy, derived from Damascus, brought by the workmen and artists brought by Timur.[249] In relation to its influence, sources indicate that Gur-i-Mir mausoleum was an inspiration for other Timurid works, especially the mausoleum complex of Shah-i-Zinda in Samarkand (built between 1370 and 1435) (fig.49). The mausoleum also sent a wave of inspiration around the Muslim world especially in India and Persia. India's Mughal dynasty was partially Timurid as most of its rulers were descendants of Timur. Accounts related that in the 1620s Emperor Jahangir (1605-1627) entertained a Samarkand author, inquiring about the Gur-i Mir, and promising to pay for its maintenance and running costs.[250] This ancestral tomb inspired major Mughal monuments including the distinguished mausoleums of Humayyun and Taj Mahal. In Iran, Masjid-i-Shah in Isfahan represents the culmination of Timurid influence.

Other reputable Timurid works are the madrassa and observatory of Ulugh Beg. Being a scholar, it was characteristic of Ulugh Beg (1394-1449) to build madrassas and other educational institutions. At least three of his madrassas of nearly identical features are still standing today in Samarkand (1417-1420), Bukhara (1418), and Gishduwan (1437). His passion for learning and education is explicitly expressed by the inscription of a relevant hadith of Prophet Muhammad, which he ordered to be written on the madrassa of Bukhara: "*To acquire knowledge is the duty of every Muslim.*"[251]

The Samarkand Madrassa was implanted at the Registan Square, together with two more recently built ones; the Shir Dar madrassa constructed as an imitation of Ulugh Beg's madrasah (1417 to 1422) and the Tilla Kari madrassa built between 1646 and 1659. Thus, the square was transformed into an education centre from which knowledge radiates in the whole Timurid Empire and Asia. Ulugh Beg Madrassa building was described as "*unique in its complexity and its ambitiousness. It ranks among the best work of this period.*"[252] It is a four iwan rectangular structure dominated by its huge 34.7-metre tall portal, typical of Timurid architecture, which opens onto the Registan Square. Four cylindrical minarets were fitted, one at each of its four corners, with the pair of the portal considerably higher than the rest. The flanking of either side of the portal with minarets had a precursor in Bibi Khanum mosque as mentioned above. The rooms are distributed on two floors and organised around a courtyard, along with deep axial iwans making it a classic example of the Central Asian madrassa.

Ulugh Beg's passion for astronomy manifested in a three-storey observatory which the architect Ali Kushji built for solar, lunar and planetary observations in North of Samarkand, between 1428-1429. This was neither the first nor the last Muslim observatory to be constructed; two observatories were built in 8th century, during the reign of Caliph Al-Ma'mûn (r. 786-833) at al- Shammasiyya quarter in Baghdad and on Mount Qasiyun in Damascus.[253] These were followed by Maragha observatory built for Nasir al-Din al-Tusi (1201-1274) by Hulagu (1217-1265) in 1258 south of Tabriz in Iran[254]. In 16th century, Taqi al-Din built an observatory in Istanbul, which was financed by Sultan Murad III.

Based on the descriptions provided by historian Abd al-Razzak Samarkandi (1413-1482), Samarkand observatory was a three storey circular monumental building of 48 meters in diameter, the plan of which shows a resemblance to Maragha observatory. It was equipped with three gigantic astronomical instruments that dictated the building's structure and layout. The first was a huge masonry sextant that was placed along the north-south axis and unearthed by Russian archaeologist Vladimir Viatkin in 1908. It is thought to be as high as the dome of Hagia Sophia Mosque in Istanbul, about 50 metres (180 feet) high, running through the building's centre; it consisted of a trench of about two metres wide, with steps marked in degrees, which contained the gigantic curve of the sextant (fig.50). A concave wall was built perpendicular to the sextant along the east-west axis to act as a solar clock (*i'itidal*) reflecting the shadows casted by sextant as the sun moves. The third instrument was a quadrant sector, with the roof, and possibly the piers of the arcades, being marked with bronze plates serving as an azimuthal circle to assist in sighting heavenly bodies. The main use of these instruments was to determine the basics of astronomy, such as the length of the tropical year and with it, Ulugh Beg compiled his famous astronomical tables. He successfully achieved unprecedented accurate calculations suggesting, for example, the stellar year to be 365 days, 6 hours, 10 minutes and 8 seconds, remarkably only 62 seconds more than the present estimation.

The central sextant divided the observatory into two sections; the northern section contained rooms of cruciform plan while the southern section had rectangular rooms. Service rooms formed the ground floor and contained detailed decoration incorporating, "*the nine celestial orbits (aflak), and the shapes (ashkal) of the nine heavenly spheres, and the degrees, minutes, seconds, and*

Figure 49 Shah-i-Zinda (the Living Prince) complex, in Samarkand built between 1370 and 1435

Figure 50 The architect Ali Kushji built the observatory for Ulug Beg in North of Samarkand (1428-1429).

tenths of seconds, of the epicycles; the seven planets (aflak-i tadawir) and pictures (suwar) of the fixed stars, the image (hay'at) of the terrestrial globe, pictures (suwar) of the climes with mountains, seas, and deserts and related things..."[255]

Muslim Architecture under the Indian Caliphate (1030-1857)

As noted previously the expansion of Islam into various regions of the East, North Africa and central Asia was associated with a systematic exchange between the newly acquired religion and local traditions. This exchange extended to India, a region renowned for its cultural and artistic heritage about which the Muslims had long known and extending beyond the translation of *"Siddhanta"* as noted above to the Indian numerals.[256] India had a complex structured society, which developed a wealthy culture, philosophies and intellectualism from the religions of Hinduism and Jainism. Nevertheless, its overall impact remains limited, in comparison to other regions, especially Mesopotamia and Persia, due to Islam's late arrival to India whose innovations were far behind the attainment of 12th century Islam. This was clearly the case for architecture where despite the exquisite quality of the Hindu heritage, local masons and artists *"during this long period had neither invented, improved methods nor acquired any scientific building procedure, their technique having remained static through persistent isolation."*[257]

The first contact Islam had with India was in the 8th century when the Indus territory came under the influence of the Umayyad and Abbasid Caliphates. Under the Umayyad, Muslims reached the Sind (Pakistan) between 711-712 CE, annexing the area to the commercial centres of Damascus and Baghdad. They set up a number of centres along the coast including the Bengal Bay. The real breakthrough, however, came in the mid-12th century when the Punjab became a Muslim province administered by the Ghaznavids of Afghanistan, who gradually persuaded the remaining parts of India to embrace Islam. By the end of the 12th century, Delhi became the capital of the Muslim Sultanate of India, which lasted well over four centuries and involved a number of dynasties,[258] which established a number of succeeding independent sultanates. The remains of the extensive buildings of these states from mosques, tombs, palaces and forts, express both their prosperity and their investment in great building projects. Similar processes took place in the provinces,[259] which seceded from the central authority of Delhi, leading to the dissemination of Muslim buildings and architecture to all parts of the Indian subcontinent.

Islam not only injected new blood, but also brought "*innovations gained from other lands, fresh principles and practices which had proved effective under all conditions*"[260]. Enlightened Muslim rulers invested in vital water-works such as canals, dams, artificial lakes, step-wells and underground water-channels, works which revolutionised agriculture and food production. In industry, they contributed to the introduction, spread and prosperity of the industries that many Indian cities became renowned for, for instance, so Farrukhabad became renowned for printing, Firozabad for glass wares, Khurja and Siwan for pottery, Mirzapur for carpets, Moradabad for brass ware, and Sahranpur for wood-carving. Not only did India enjoy a trade surplus but also experienced an expansion of urban life and culture which activated a considerable building activity as large-scale projects were undertaken everywhere. Meanwhile, this cultural and economic prosperity made the region a focus attracting masons, architects and skilled artisans from the rest of the Muslim lands, which by this time had entered a period of decline and conflicts, connected mainly to the crusades and the Tatar invasions.

Before the arrival of Islam, the achievement of India's architecture was based on the post-and-beam system, which was applied, mainly in massive blocks of stone, in the construction of both Buddhist and Hindu temples. The Buddhist architecture evolved from the stupa, a large hemispherical mound modelled on ancient funerary mounds. It is usually surrounded by a stone fence known as the *vedika*, and topped by a smaller enclosure, the *harmika*, containing the casket for the relics of the Buddha, with rails on top of the stupa. Other forms of Buddhist temples are rock-cut monastic foundations such as those of Ajanta and Ellora. The Hindu temples were built with large stones and consisted of a garba-griha or the womb chamber, a small room with a circumambulation passage, forming the central focus housing the deity of the temple.[261] The roof is usually a tall pyramidal tower consisting of several progressively smaller storeys. These temples were covered in a sculptured array of icons and sculptures of Hindu deities accompanied with a number of decorative themes that also conformed to the Hindu teaching.

Muslim artists were behind much of the greatest successes of the medieval architecture of this region, which became known as the Indo-Muslim architecture. The substitution of traditionally favoured Buddhist or Hindu sculpture based art with Islamic ornamental flavour was the first sign of change taking place. Above all, Muslims introduced the technique of cementing, the mortar of which allowed the joining of stones, thus ending the old practice of placing one free stone on another. Another major change was the replacement of the beam with the arch. This revolutionised the static understanding of local masons from that of tackling a simple vertical pressure (seen in most Budhist temples) to scientific and mechanical formulae applied to deal with other forms of thrust such as the oblique or lateral, and to resist the forces of stress and strain thus providing greater strength and stability. The other impact was formal, creating a complete change of building sky- line from the traditional flat and pyramidal roofs (*sikhara*), to the use of the bulbous dome and minarets. Another contribution was the introduction of a variety of building typologies from mosques, tombs, madrassas, to secular buildings such as palaces, forts, bridges, dams and domestic buildings, ending the predominance of Budhist temples, the unique building type known to India before Islam.

The stylistic development of Islamic architecture in India has been divided into three main phases, involving the sultanates of Delhi, the architecture of independent provinces, and the great achievements of the Mughals. The greatest architectural works of these periods reflect numerous inspirations but the Persian influence is fundamental as Muslim India employed Persian artists and imported Persian poets and writers. Indeed some art historians considered Indian Muslim architecture a regional derivative of Persian architecture and art. The Islamisation of India coincided with the Seljuk Caliphate in Persia, reaching its turning point after its great attainments of the 11th and 12th centuries, when numerous architectural wonders were produced. A good example of this influence is the complex of Qutb Minar, (Delhi, c.1197), built by the Slave king Qutb ad-Din Aybak, consisting of Quawwat al-Islam Mosque (the mosque of the Might of Islam) and the minaret famously known as Qutb Minar which was added two years later (fig.51). Constructed on the raised platform of an old ruined Hindu temple site, the mosque, the first to be built in India, was based on a hypostyle plan consisting of a central courtyard surrounded by arcades raised by a number of superimposed columns (two or three small columns on top of each other) to achieve the desired height. This is another method of raising short columns to achieve crown height, different from those employed in the mosque of Cordoba[262] and Al-Kairawan.[263] While the flat roof supported on the beams carried by the columns is a Hindu tradition, the style of the façade, which is in the form of a tall free-standing screen flanked by two small and a central wide ogee arches emphasizing the direction of the qibla, is definitely Persian, resembling the mosques of Isfahan. Its Persian carvings were made in low-relief bands of *naskhi* inscriptions, spiral floral designs and lotus patterns. Its geometrical decoration, a common feature of Islamic architecture, combined with arabesque was blended with local Hindu tradition, in the form of geometric roundels in the spandrels, to produce the Indian *Jaali*. Although the general form of the minaret resembles that of Jam (Afghanistan), erected by the sultan Ghiyas al-Din Muhammed (1163-1203), the inclusion of muqarnas balconies is a Seljuk Iranian feature. Another edifice bearing early Persian influence is the Arhai-din-

Ka-Jhompera Mosque, built at Ajmer (1200-1206). The mosque, built in the record time of twelve and half days, as the name indicates, comprised a central *iwan* surmounted by two minarets. In 1229, a screen façade with seven ogee arches was added to the Qibla side imitating the tradition set at the Quawwat al-Islam Mosque of Delhi.

After the sacking of Delhi by Timur's army in 1399, the Sultanate lost control over the many provinces that constituted the vast land of India. These provinces declared independence leading to the rise of many smaller states all across India. Taking the place of the Samanid of Central Asia, the Timurid promoted arts and learning, giving rise to two of the most important urban centres of the medieval world in that region, Samarkand and Bukhara, and exercising considerable influence on the Muslim world, including India, in numerous aspects especially in astronomy, mathematics, art and architecture. Under their rule (15th 16th centuries) and following the fall of the Seljuk Caliphate, the Indian sub-continent became more susceptible to the influence of central Asia. Tile work in dazzling green, blue and turquoise developed in Afghanistan, Samarkand, Bukhara and other Central Asian centres to decorate numerous mosques, palaces and gateways in the Punjab and in the Deccan (Bijapur). Another key feature of this influence was the replacement of the pointed arch with the four-centred arch (known as the Tudor or ogee arch). This was introduced to solve the spanning of wide spaces, which did not allow the use of the ordinary pointed arch.

Typical of this era is the Atala Jami Mosque, Jaunpur, 1408 (fig.52). This was the first mosque to be built after the independence of this state from Delhi and the establishment of the Sharqi dynasty under the leadership of Shams Al-Din Ibrahim (1402-1440). The mosque illustrates a unique architectural development that evolved during this period. The expansion of the *pishtaq* facade to such a monumental dimension, up to 23 m high, that the projecting portal (*pishtaq*) became the dominant feature comparable to the Egyptian propylon.[264] This gigantic façade was also reproduced in Jami Masjid of 1470. The Persianisation of Indian art was accentuated under the Mughal rule. It was traced in miniature paintings, an art which was essentially first developed by the Mughals, under King Akbar. This school of painting, the first of its kind in the Islamic world produced much of the best-known Muslim painting. Persians had also greatly influenced the design, styles and decoration of textiles and carpets.

The Mughal Caliphate, in India, began with a prince named Babur, a descendant of both Chingiz Khan and Timur, who defeated the last Lodi emperor in 1526, establishing the Mughals domination of northern India for the next 250 years. With their Timurid ancestry, the Mughals drew their styles and designs from the Timurid models and employed architects and artists of that region. Historical sources, for example, indicate that the chief architect of Sultan Akbar (1542-1605) was a certain Yusuf, a favourite pupil of the famous Ottoman architect Khoja Mi'mar Sinan (1489-1588). He was responsible for building most of the splendour of Lahore, Delhi and Agra.[265] The major endeavour of King Akbar, who succeeded to the throne of his grandfather Babur, was the foundation of a new city of Fatehpur Sikri, some 25 miles west of Agra, in 1571. Following similar design principals to those found in Isfahan, the city consisted of homogenous red buildings built of the famous Indian red sandstone[266] and contained within strong ramparts. Like any Muslim city, the main building was the congregational Friday mosque with its hypostyle plan and a courtyard surrounded by arcades. The main feature of interest, however, was the Buland Darwaza, a monumental portal on the south wall leading to the palace at Fatehpur Sikri (fig.53). The gateway is a lofty structure in the form of an *iwan* with a massive central ogee arch and a flat roof topped by a number of small turrets, known as *chhattri*, raised on columns and themselves topped with small domes. The other contribution of King Akbar was the construction of a monumental garden mausoleum for his father Humayum at Delhi (fig.54), a tradition that established some of the greatest works of the Islamic-Indo architecture such as the Tomb of Akbar, at Sikandra (1614) and the Taj Mahal.

Mughal architecture reached its apogee during the reign of Jahangir (1605-1627) and Shah Jahan (1628-1658), whose masterpiece, the Taj Mahal, is the ultimate expression of Mughal architecture (fig.55). This world landmark was built in memory of the favourite wife of Shah Jahan, Mumtaz Mahal, who died prematurely in 1631. The bereaved emperor gathered architects and artisans from all over the Islamic world to construct a tomb worthy of holding such a memory. The overall character displays the great integration of architectural elements of Islamic Asia, incorporating Iranian features such as the octagonal shape, the *iwan* and *pishtaq*, Indian features such as the bulbous dome, the *chhattri* and Central Asian features such as the four detached robust cylindrical minarets. All were blended in wonderful geometrical relationships hardly containable within a building.

The whole edifice, overlooking the Jumna River, is set within a large garden divided by a number of water channels, a feature developed under Jahangir. This creates a unique visual impact, greatly emphasised by the white marble covering the entire construction, which contrasts with the red sandstone of the adjacent structures, the two royal pavilions, the mosque and the visitors' lodging. The plan is an elaboration of Humayun mausoleum (1562-71) consisting of four corner chambers and axial corridors leading to the central focal point, the central chamber accommodating the tomb. Further emphasis on this room is expressed

Figure 51 Qutb Minar, Delhi, c.1197

Figure 52 Atala Jami Mosque, Jaunpur, 1408, shows the expansion of the *pishtaq* facade to a monumental dimension, up to 23 m high.

Figure 53 Buland Darwaza, built in 1601 A.D. by Akbar to commemorate his victory over Gujarat.

Figure 54 Humayum Mausoleum, Delhi (1562-71)

Figure 55 The Taj Mahal, between 1631 and 1648 is the ultimate expression of Mughal architecture

by the height and size of its dome set on a high drum behind the raised central iwans. The design and the general setting within the huge garden in front of the river Jumna, and the majestic decoration carefully executed on the highly polished marble walls, is no less than one of the many palaces of paradise described in the Quran and by the authentic hadith, which awaits the soul of the Muslim believer. In wanting to reward the soul of his beloved with such a palace on earth, Shah Jahan created an architectural masterpiece that stole the hearts of those who visited it. Its traces are found in many high profile buildings in major European countries including the Royal Pavilion at Brighton in England.

Architecture under the Safavid Patronage (1501-1722)

The aftermath of the Mongol devastation of the Muslim land, and its destruction of the central religious authority and legitimacy that existed in the Abbasid or Ayyubid Dynasties, gave rise to many local and regional authorities which filled the spiritual and social vacuum. This coincided with an expansion of the Sufi order in many areas of central and East Asia, of which a renowned Sheikh Safi (1252-1334) founded a Sufi sect, al-Safawiyya, in his town Ardabil, in Kurdustan Iran[267]. This religious network gained considerable influence infiltrating among the masses around areas of Kurdustan, Azerbijan and Iran. In the 15th century, the order underwent a considerable change: adopting a militant Shii't doctrine. Its new leader Sheikh Junaid (1447-1460) recruited local tribesmen and some Turkish soldiers to defend his cause. His son and successor, Haidar (1460-1488), created a complete army from the Turkmen and tribesmen who became known as the Qizilbash, or red heads, because of the distinctive red turbans of twelve folds representing the twelve imams which they wore. Like the Mamluk, the Qizilbash army became powerful taking key administrative and economic positions. The Safavid state is often described as mamlikat-i-qizilbash, the Kingdom of qizilbash, or dawlat-i- qizilbash, meaning the State of qizilbash.[268]

Safavid Art and Architecture

The Safavid rulers were mostly men of religious and literary abilities; Shah Ismail, the founder of the dynasty, was a poet and great calligrapher in both Persian and Turkish languages. It is reported that he penned a self-valorising verse; "*I am Feyredun, Khosrow, Alexander, Jesus, Zahak. My mother Fatima, my father .Ali: I too am one of the Twelve Imams.*"[269] His sons Tahmasp and Sam Mirza were also poets, the first also being a painter and a ruler while the second was compiler of an anthology of contemporary poetry, including his father's.[270] Shah Abbas II was also known to be a poet. Under such highly cultured rulers, art and architecture substantially flourished and attained levels of excellence.[271] Iranian miniature, already established by the Timurids in Shiraz and other parts of Iran, flourished under the Safavid, especially during their rule from Tabriz and Isfahan. At Tabriz, school rose great names of Persian miniature such as Bihzad and his disciples whose influence extended to Turkish and Mughal Indian miniature schools. In Isfahan, school Riza Abbasi (1565–1635) was its greatest miniature artist as well as calligrapher. Using traditional forms and materials, he painted handsome youth and beautiful landscapes. One of the greatest miniature works that is still preserved in good condition is the famous *Shahnameh-yi Shah Tahmasp*. Originally commissioned by Shah Ismail, the manuscript became eponymous for his son Tahmasp, under whose rule the majority of the editing of the book took place. The book contained a staggering 742 folios from which an unprecedented 258 leaves contain full-page miniature paintings.[272]

Shah Abbas I or the Great (1587-1629), went a step further as he promoted the arts and artisanal production such as pottery and carpets for commercial purposes, destined for export to European markets[273]. Under his reign carpet export and the silk trade became the main sources of income and wealth for Iran. The production took on a wholesale dimension as manufacturers were receiving orders from European consumers. Carpet making became a professional art requiring designers to draw patterns first on paper before translating it into woven designs[274]. Persian artisans from Tabriz, Kashan, Isfahan and Kerman produced eye dazzling and mesmeric designs, ranging from medallion centred carpets, and mihrab and vase carpets to 'personalised' carpets bearing the coat of arms of a number of European rulers including King Sigismund III (1566-1632) of Poland.

The Safavid ruled over Persia and a small area bordering it, a region with great Sassanid, Islamic and Anatolian architectural heritage. The Abbasid, Seljuk and Timurid had elaborated a distinguished Islamic Persian style, which consisted essentially of a mixture of motifs from the three traditions. The Safavid maintained most features of this style adopting the four-iwan plan as the main organisational framework for most of their buildings, with each iwan having a rectangular frame covered with muqarnas work and predominantly blue tiles of delicate geometrical and vegetal patterns. Similar intricate tile designs were applied to their bulbous domes. The reign of Shah Abbas added new heights of quality and brilliance, in the words of Pope: "*Abbas initiated a new period in Persian architecture in which the rich, sensationally coloured and imaginative details developed by his predecessors became unified into serene and meaningful ensembles of immense scale and grandeur.*"[275]

Most of early Safavid Architecture in Tabriz and Qazvin did not survive. The earliest important building that survived, however, is a mausoleum built for the founder of the Safawy order, Sheikh Safi at Ardabil. This simple building was later transformed into shrine with each Safavid leader adding more structures, turning it into a large complex containing the tombs of Safi, Shah Ismail, some emirs and other dignitaries and their children, a library, a Quran recitation hall or Dar al-Huffaz, and a Hadith recitation hall or Dar al-Hadith. Shah Tahmasp (1524-76) built, in his capital Qazvin, a palace known as Ayvan-i-Chihil Sutun, which, according to Chardin, was designed by a Turkish architect[276]. Sources also reported that the Shah himself drew one or two paintings of the palace, including the one about the life of Prophet Joseph.[277] The most important buildings, however, are those resulting from the works of Shah Abbas in Isfahan.[278]

When Shah 'Abbas the Great moved his capital to Isfahan he wanted it to be a capital of Islam and of the world. He envisaged that the city plan should be based on a centrepiece development in the form of a large rectangular plaza or *maydan*, known as the Maydan-e-Shah or Imam's Square. The square was adopted in earlier occasions in Muslim cities and in the East in general, in many forms. The so-called *al-Rahba* or *Maydan* were known at Firozabad in Iran, in Nishapur (as the Review Ground), Aleppo (as Maydan al-Akhdar), Damascus (as Al-Maydan) and of course Samarkand (as Registan Square)[279]. However, none of the above matched the size of Isfahan square, which stretched over 1700 feet long and 500 feet wide. It was originally destined for ceremonies and sports competitions, especially polo games as witnessed by the original goal posts from Shah Abbas' polo grounds, which are still in place today at the far ends of the square. In 1602, however, "*it was redeveloped for commercial purposes, with two storeys of shops around the perimeter, which were let at low rents to attract reluctant merchants from the old city centre. The long modular facades, originally decorated with polychrome glazed tiles, are broken only by the monumental entrances to four buildings.*"[280] Surrounded on all four sides by long walls, the square is framed by a monumental building on each side, the Imam Mosque in the south, the Mosque of Sheikh Lutfullah (between 1617-19) in the east, the Ali Qapu Palace (residence of Shah Abbas I, built at end of 16th century) in the west and the entrance of the great Bazaar in the north (fig. 56). The square was listed by UNESCO as a world heritage site and still continues to be a popular destination for both local and foreign tourists.

115

Located in the southern side of the maydan, the Masjid-i Imam, formerly Masjid-i-shah or Shah Mosque is perhaps one of the finest Safavid structures in Isfahan, completed in 1602. The most distinguished features of the mosque are its great harmonious proportions and striking symmetry, which made it, according to Pope *"the culmination of a thousand years of mosque building in Persia."*[281] It is set at a 45 degrees angle to its portal and the axis of the square due to the Qibla orientation. This awkward arrangement necessitated the inclusion of an oblique corridor between the portal and the mosque, a feature that first appeared in Sheikh Lutfallah Mosque. The main portal is a large arch, 27 meters high, pierced in a rectangular frame and flanked by two slender cylindrical minarets (fig.57). The interior consists of a four-iwan plan opened into the central courtyard, with each iwan being followed by a chamber covered with a large slightly pointed bulbous dome raised on high drums closely resembling Timurid mosques, namely Bibi Khanum mosque. The largest dome, behind the main portal, was also built in Timurid tradition with a double shell, the outer shell being about 45 feet higher than the inner one. Decoration is lavishly displayed in all aspects of the building. Complex patterns of muqarnas cover the vaulted areas, with the most splendid scheme displayed at the great portal in the form of a tiers muqarnas hood covered with enamelled faience mosaics (fig.58). A complex decorative mantle consisting of multi-coloured glazed tiles of both organic and geometric designs and panels and bands of calligraphy adorn the surfaces of the mosque.

The earliest building of the square was the mosque of Sheikh Lutfallah (built in 1617-1619 and restored in 1954 -1956). Shah Abbas built it in honour of his father in law, a great Lebanese theologian and scholar: Sheikh Lutfallah Maisi al-Amili. As in the Shah Mosque, while the entrance and facade were on axis with the maydan on the eastern side, the structure stood behind at a 45 degrees angle to correctly face the Qibla. As a result of this angular position an oblique corridor for access between the portal and the interior of the mosque was created. The plan consists of an unusual large central doomed hall without courtyard or minaret, features that suggest the possibility of it being used as a mausoleum or private mosque or chapel as some argued.[282] Another character unique to this mosque is the decoration, which was executed in two distinctive colours, blazing blue in the facade and portal and tan or yellow background in remaining surfaces including the dome. The facade and portal, however, were predominantly in blue mostly from a 20th century restoration. The prayer hall is covered with a huge dome made in a single shell and supported by a high drum set on eight pointed arches. A series of grilled windows were pierced on the drum, carefully distributing light around the edge of the dome to accentuate its cove shape and glitter the space with various colours and shapes of its brilliant decorative scheme. The pattern consists of tiers of concentric ellipses drawn in turquoise

Figure 56 The Mosque of Sheikh Lutfullah, built between 1617-1619 in Isfahan

Figure 57 The Masjid-i Imam, formerly Masjid-i-shah or Shah Mosque, completed in 1602

117

Figure 58 Masjid-i Imam great portal in the form of a tiers muqarnas hood covered with enamelled faience mosaics

Figure 59 Sheikh Lutfallah mosque, the ellipses or medallions are decorated with delicate white floral motifs of arabesque, which play against the blue monochrome ground.

colour, which grow, in size with the curve of the dome. The ellipses or medallions are decorated with delicate white floral motifs of arabesque, which play against the blue monochrome ground (fig.59). The Qibla wall is pierced with a mihrab (prayer niche) decorated with mosaic tiles and stalactites, all of a highest artistic value. The name of the architect Mohammad Reza (son of Master Hussein the builder of Isfahan) was written on two tablets inserted in the mihrab wall. Ali Reza Abbassi executed the calligraphy work.[283]

The third building on Maydan-i-Shah is the garden palace of Ali Qapu. This type of architecture is an ancient tradition going back to the times of Achaemenid Persians (559 BC–330 BC) and Sassanids (226–651), and central East Asian regions. In Islam, the Fatimid developed sophisticated garden palaces, mostly during the course of the 11th century. Their palaces were set in the midst of artificial water pools and lakes, in similar fashion to that described in al-Qala' of Beni Hammad and Sicily.

The al-Nasrid employed the scheme in al-Hambra and other Andalusian palaces in Saragossa and Seville. The Mughals designed the Chahar Bagh and many garden palaces and mausoleums culminating at the Taj Mahal. The Safavid continued in this old tradition beginning from Shah Abbas who built a palace, which he named Ali Qapu or the High Gate, no doubt intended to leave a lasting impression symbolising the power and authority of the dynasty, and Shah Abbas in particular (fig.60). The palace was placed in front of a royal garden known as Naqsh-i-Jahan, or the Image of the World. The most interesting parts of the building are found in the upper floor where the royal rest rooms are. The *talar*, a terraced veranda or logia with a flat roof supported by wooden columns overlooking the square provided an ideal setting for the Shah to review his 40,000 cavalry twice a year, and for royal audience to watch the games of polo, which took place in the square[284]. According to Jairazbhoy, Shah Abbas must have been inspired by *"the wooden tower (alkushk) in the esplanade outside the city of Bishdagh from which the Uzbeg Sultan witnessed archery exercises"*[285]. The murals of the veranda were covered with colourful paintings, depicting naturalistic scenes, animals including peacocks and gazelles, as well as "moon-faced darlings."[286]

Other palaces of the above style included Chihil Sutun, built in 1647 built by Shah Abbas II (1642-1666) and reconstructed after a fire in 1706, and Hasht Behesht palace built by Shah Suleiman (ruled 1667-1694). Chihil Sutun is an open pavilion enclosed in a garden aligned with the axis of the west of Maydan-i-Shah. It was largely rebuilt after a fire incident in 1706, at which time a *talar* with 20 columns was added at the front. The name Chihil Sutun, which literally translated as forty columns, refers to the reflecting pool, which doubled the number of its 20 columns. At the back there is the main audience hall, a large room covered with three domes and opened to the outside through shallow porches from the four sides. The walls of this hall contain historical paintings; according to Chardin, they represented Abbas the Great's battles against the Uzbeks.[287]

Another area the Safavid reached distinction was in the construction of bridges, a tradition that was mastered before them by the Seljuk in Persia and Anatolia. The Safavid skills and brilliance culminated in two particular bridges, Si-o-Seh Pol and Pol-i-Khwaju (spelled Khaju). Allahvardi Khan, a general of Shah Abbas I (or the Great), built the first bridge around 1602, with thirty-three arches. Shah Abbas II commissioned Pol-i-Khwaju completed in 1650. Both bridges consist of two-storey structure aligned across Zayahde River and fitted with rooms and pavilions, which allow pedestrians and passers-by to stop and enjoy the views of the river. High walls shelter the passage from the wind and hazardous falls. Pedestrian access to Khwaju Bridge is provided through the arcades on the sides while projected octagonal pavilions were erected at the centre of the bridge providing vantage points on both lower and upper floors for the pleasurable views around (fig.61). Khwaju Bridge has another distinguishing feature from Se-i-Seh Pole as it is designed as a bridge-dam acting as a regulator of the water flow in the river as it is fitted with sluice gates under the archways, which can be closed and opened at any time.

Muslim Architecture Under Ottoman Patronage (1326-1922)

By the end of the 12th century, the Islamic world had lost its power, prestige and prosperity, through internal fighting and fragmentation into small states, lacking any cultural and religious purpose. These conditions encouraged its enemies who wasted no time in attacking it from various fronts. The invasion of the Tartar from the East resulted in widespread destruction. Like locusts, they did not leave any building standing, any green leaf alive and any book of knowledge without putting it to the fire. The saga of the destruction of Mutassim's Baghdad is clear evidence of the evil violence of these invaders. Spanish Christians invaded Islam from the north and west and progressed slowly into Andalusia until they reached the famous Gibraltar and then crossed into Morocco and Western Algeria. They would have infiltrated inwards towards the rest of the Muslim World had it not been for the Ottoman army, the only and newly emerging Muslim power. The intervention of the Ottomans to defend North Africa opened up the process of Ottoman succession to the throne of the old Caliphate in most parts of Muslim land. This Muslim integration, in addition to the Ottoman expansion,[288] particularly in Eastern Europe - Greece, the Balkans and Hungary - was an incentive for artistic and architectural revival following the destruction and

Figure 60 Ali Qapu or the High Gate (end of 16th century), no doubt intended to leave a lasting impression symbolising the power and authority of the dynasty, and Shah Abbas in particular.

Figure 61 Khwaju Bridge, Isfahan 1650

decline brought about by the Tartar invasion. Once again, Islamic arts and culture were the focal point of attraction for wealthy European elite who not only collected a large number of these items but also initiated a process of the imitation and adoption of Islamic motifs. The influence of the Ottomans on Europe will be the focus of Chapter 6.

Early Ottomans, in the 14th and 15th centuries adopted the architectural and artistic vestiges of their Seljuk predecessors. However, they soon developed their own architectural style, which appeared especially in mosques. The mosque evolved from the traditionally horizontal space to a vertical structure rising into the sky. This was achieved firstly by giving the pillars greater height, which added an unprecedented grandeur to the space, and secondly, by the adoption of the domed roof, which was arranged in a number of small domes rising progressively like steps towards the main dome of the central nave. The attempt to re-organise the internal space of the mosque is also evident. The cupola in the front of the mihrab was substantially enlarged allowing greater span and giving the area more centrality. In these conditions, infinity is expressed through verticality and hence the dome became the dominating skyline of Muslim mosques, probably influenced by Hagia Sofia as suggested by many Western academics.

Furthermore, this mosque stressed another important symbol involving the oneness of God, conceptualised by Al-Tawhid, which forms the essence of Muslim faith. The perfect centralisation of the space under the main dome affirmed its unity and confirmed the symbol of one God. In the view of Davies[289] (1982, p.127): *"The interior is then one unit to be perceived in its entirety at a single view. Its reality is not to be found in the domes and arcades but in the cavities they define. Plenitude of space ... majestic space ... continuous space ... tawhid (the consciousness of divine Unity) made visible."*

Such an attempt was first seen in Manisa Mosque (1566 built by Ishak Celebi). In Ulu Cami Mosque of Bursa (1396-1400), the architect devised 12 pillars for the support of the total span of the space and its roof, which was arranged in 20 equal bays (squares), covered with 20 cupolas (fig.62). In another step, the number of these piers was reduced to a minimum of four piers producing nine bays with nine cupolas as seen in Eski Cami Mosque of Edirne (1403). Greater span was achieved as the intervals between these pillars increased substantially. The architect of the mosque of Orhan Bey in Bursa (1399) tried another technique by following the enormous cupolas of the front of mihrab with another one of similar size behind it.

This feature was replicated in a number of Ottoman mosques including Yesil Cami of Bursa (1412-1413). The mosque was founded by Mehmet I (1403-1421) and known as the Green Mosque, a complex site that included a bath, a tomb, and a madrassa. Typical of Ottoman mosques, Yesil Cami was dominated by its domes, which provided the roof for most of the interior space. The Mosque consists of three main domed sections, the qibla iwan, the nave, and the minaret section. The fame of the Mosque is derived from the Persian-made blue and green tiles decorating its walls, which were made by artisans from Tabriz city.[290] The general decor and ornamentation of the mosque evokes that of Hall of the Ambassadors at Alhambra. It is a mixture of both late Seljuk and early Ottoman art as seen in the style of its entrance, which clearly emphasised the Seljuk tradition of extensive use of muqarnas. These cupolas later increased in size and number first in Bayzid II Mosque in Istanbul (1501-1506) built by Kheyruddin and then at Suleimaniya Mosque (1549-1557), built by the famous Khoja Mi'mar Sinan (1489-1588), the chief architect of 16th century Ottomans, for his patron Sultan Suleiman the Magnificent[291] (fig.63). The second feature of the Ottoman mosque is the pointed slender minaret, which differs greatly from the rest of the Muslim world.

This was also the time renowned for the spread of the so-called *Kulliye* complexes. A building complex consisting of a mosque, a hospital, a school (*madrassa*), and a public kitchen (*'imarat*), these *Kulliyes* had a great impact on the development of the Ottoman city, especially Istanbul. In addition to palace complexes, they created new urban environments, known locally as *mahalle* or district. By making them functional centres of the neighbourhoods, Sinan used these *Kulliye* as "*the chief device of Ottoman city-making,*"[292] At first, they accommodated their own populations, administration and services, but later served as a nucleus for "sprawling" neighbourhoods.

Figure 62 Ulu Cami Mosque, Bursa (1396-1400)

Figure 63 Suleimaniya Mosque (1549-1557), built by the famous Khoja Mi'mar Sinan (1489-1588) the chief architect of 16th century Ottomans

124

Notes

[41] The full verse reads as follows: "*Let there be no compulsion in religion: Truth stands out clear from Error: whoever rejects evil and believes in Allah hath grasped the most trustworthy handhold, that never breaks. And Allah heareth and knoweth all things*".

[42] Scott S.P. (1904), '*History of the Moorish Empire in Europe*'; 3 volumes; J.B. Lippincott Company, 1904. p.90.

[43] Prophet Mohammed died in 632, two years after the conquest of Makkah.

[44] Scott, S. P. (1904) 'op. cit. p.95.

[45] O'Leary de Lacy (1923), '*Islam at the Crossroads: a Brief Survey of the Present Position and Problems*', Kegan Paul, London, p.8.

[46] Lombard, Maurice (1971), '*L'Islam Dans sa Première Grandeur*', VIIIe-XIe siècle' Flammarion, Paris.

[47] Le Bon G. (1884), '*La Civilisation des Arabes*', IMAG, Syracuse, Italy, p.68

[48] Michener, James, A. (1955), '*Islam-the Misunderstood Religion*', Readers' Digest, vol. LXVI (May, 1955), pp.67-75

[49] Sir John Glubb (1969), '*A Short History of the Arab Peoples*'; Hodder and Stoughton, p. 251.

[50] Arnold T. W. (1965), '*the Preaching of Islam: A History of the Propagation of the Muslim Faith*', Muhammad Ashraf Publications Lahore, Pakistan, p.61, first published by Coustable, Westminster in 1896. See also S. Lane Poole (1898), '*Review of Books*', in Justin Winsor, Samuel Rawson Gardiner, Reginald Lane Poole, John Goronwy Edwards, Mandell Creighton (eds.), English Historical Review, vol.13, Longman: 756-758, at p. 757.

[51] Ibid.

[52] Ibid.

[53] Lewis, B. (1995), '*Cultures in Conflict: Christians, Muslims, and Jews in the Age of Discovery* ', Oxford University press; pp. 16-7.

[54] M. Bucaille (1981), '*The Bible, The Quran and Science*', translated from the French by A.D. Pannell and the Author; 3rd edition, Seghers Publishers, Paris gives a detailed account on the relationship between Islam, learning and science.

[55] Briffault speaks of the role of the Muslim caliphs in spreading learning, see Briffault, R. (1928), '*The Making of Humanity*', George Allen and Unwin Ltd, London, p. 188.

[56] Scott, S. P. (1904), '*History of the Moorish Empire in Europe*', op cit. p.429.

[57] See Hill, D.R. (1993), '*Islamic Science and Engineering*', Edinburgh University Press. England.

[58] Hill, D.R. (1993), 'Islamic *Science and Engineering*' p.11.

[59] Scott, S. P. (1904) '*History of the Moorish Empire in Europe*', op cit.p.446

[60] Briffault, R.(1928), '*The Making of Humanity*', George Allen and Unwin Ltd, London, pp.190-191

[61]Nordenstreng Kaarle, Schiller Herbert I.(1993), '*Beyond National Sovereignty: international communication in the 1990s*',Praeger/Greenwood, p.400

[62] Scott, S. P. (1904) '*History of the Moorish Empire in Europe*', op cit. p.226.

[63] Ballaster Rosalind (2005), '*Fabulous Orients: Fictions of the East in England, 1662-1785*', Oxford University Press, p.58.

[64] Ibn Khaldoun (1967), '*The Muqaddimah: An Introduction to History*' trans. by F. Rosenthal, 2nd edition (1967), Routledge and Kegan Paul, London.

[65] Hitti, P.K. (1996), '*The Arabs: a Short History*', Regnery Gateway Publishers, p.181.

[66] His work was edited and translated in Yaqut, Jacut's Geographisches Worterbuch, ed. F. Wustenfeld. 6 vols. Leipzig, 1866-70.

[67] Scott, S. P. (1904) '*History of the Moorish Empire in Europe*', op cit.

[68] Abulfeda is Isma'iI ibn 'Imad-ud-Din (1273-1331), a Muslim Historian and Geographer Born at Damascus.

[69] Abulfeda Isma'il (1273-1331), *'Annales Muslemici Arabice et Latine'*, 5 volumes, edited and Translated by J. J. Reiske, edited by J. G. C. Adler, Hafniae, 1789-1794, Copenhagen.

[70] Scott, S. P. (1904) *'History of the Moorish Empire in Europe'*, op cit. p.460

[71] Ibid., p.461.

[72] Carra de Vaux, Baron, (1931) *"Astronomy and Mathematics,"* in Arnold and Guillaume, eds., The Legacy of Islam, (1st ed. 1931), Oxford University Press. pp. 376—397, at 376

[73] Hill, D.R. (1994), *'Arabic fine technology'*, in, The Arab Influence in Medieval Europe, ed. D. Agius, and R. Hitchcock, Ithaca Press, Reading, pp. 25-43.

[74] Berggren, J. L. (1983), *'The Correspondence of Abu Sahl al-Kuhl and Abu Ishaq al- Sabl: A translation with Commentaries"* Journal of the History of Arabic Science 7, PP.39-124

[75] See lyon

[76] Wickens, G. M. (1976), *'The Middle East as a world centre of science and medicine'*, in, Introduction to Islamic Civilisation, edited by R.M. Savory, Cambridge University Press, Cambridge, pp. 111-18.

[77] Kenneth Glyn Jones, (1968), *'The Search for the Nebulae, part I'*, Journal of the British Astronomical Association, Vol. 78, No. 4, pp. 256-267.

[78] His book also entitled *"Almagest"*.

[79] Scott, S. P. (1904), *'History of the Moorish Empire in Europe'*, op cit. p.477

[80] Lindberg David C. (1980), *'Science in the Middle Ages'*, University of Chicago Press, pp.308-309

[81] Hodgson Marshall G. S., Burke Edmund (1993), **'Rethinking World History: Essays on Europe, Islam, and World History'**, Cambridge University Press, p.119

[82] Lindberg David C. (1980), *'Science in the Middle Ages'*, op., cit. p.338

[83] For more on Muslim science see Roshdi Rached (ed.1996), op cit and Sardar. Z (ed. 1984), *'The Touch of Midas; Science, values, and environment in Islam and the West'*. Manchester University Press; on Ibn Al-Haytham see chapter, Science and technology in Islam: the underlying value system, pp. 66-90.

[84] Watson, A.M (1983), *'Agricultural Innovation in the Early Islamic World'*, Cambridge University Press.

[85] Glick, F. Thomas, Livesey, J. Steven, Wallis faith (2005), *'Medical Science, Technology and Medicine: An Encyclopaedia'*, Routledge, p.97.

[86] See Roshdi Rashed (ed.1996), *'Encyclopaedia of The History of Arabic Science'*, op cit. vol, 3, pp. 813-52

[87] Glick, F. Thomas, Livesey, J. Steven and Wallis faith (2005), *'Medical Science, Technology and Medicine: An Encyclopaedia'*, Routledge, p.97.

[88] Silberberg, B. (1910), *'Das Pflanzenbuch des Abu Hanifa Ahmed ibn da'ud al-Dinawari. Ein Beitrag zur Geschichte der Botanik bei den Arabern,'* dissertation, Breslau, published in part in *Zeitschrift für Assyriologie* 24 (1910): 225-65; 25 (1911): 38-88.

[89] Ibn Bassal: *'Kitab al-Filaha'*, or *'Book of Agriculture'*. 1955 edition of this manuscript is available at Cambridge University Library (www.lib.cam.ac.uk/University/Libraries).

[90] Ibn al-Awwam: *'Kitab al-Filaha,'* or *'The Book of Agriculture'*. A 19th century edition of this manuscript is kept by Cambridge University Library (www.lib.cam.ac.uk/University/Libraries).

[91] Loudon, J.C. (1822), *'An Encyclopaedia of Gardening'*, 3rd Edition (1825), volume 9, p.63, quoted in Harvey J.H. (1992), *'Gardens Plants of Moorish Spain: A Fresh Look'*, Garden History, vol.20, No.1., pp.71-82.

[92] Harvey John H. (1975), *'Gardening Books and Plant Lists of Moorish Spain'*, Garden History, Vol. 3, No.2, pp. 10-21.

[93] Mathe, J. (1980), *'The Civilisation of Islam'*, Tr. David Macrae, Crescent Books, New York.

[94] Solomon Joan (2000), *'Chemistry'*, Nelson Thornas publishers, p.15

[95] Taylor, W. (1933), *'Arabic Words in English'*, Society, Vol.38, the Clarendo Press, pp.567- 599, at.p.573

[96] Hamarneh, Sami Khalaf, (1975), *'Catalogue of Arabic Manuscripts on Medicine and Pharmacy at the British Library'*, History of Arabic medicine and pharmacy; no.3, The Publishing House of the Egyptian University [Dār al-Nashr lil-Jamiāt al-Misriyah], Cairo.

[97] The list is still long but one can include; Hunein-Ibn-Ishak, Abu-Yusuf-al-Kindi, Thabit-Ibn-Qora, Ibn-Bothan, Ibn-Sina, Abu-Bekr-Mohammed (of Persia), Ibn-al-Haitham, Al-Hazen, Abul-mena-Ibn-Naso (of Egypt), Ibn-al-Mathran, Ibn-al-Dakhnar, Ibn-Khalifa, Abd-al-Atif, Jamal-al-Dine (of Syria), Ibn-al-Jezzar, and Edrisi. Non-Muslim physicians of the Islamic Empire included Constantinus Africanus, Bakhtichous, Masues, and Serapions.

[98] Other physicians such as Arib-Ibn-Said-al-Khatib wrote on gynecology and obstetrics. Ibn-Wafed (of Toledo) in 10th century spent 20 years writing his book on the general practice of medicine. Ibn-Zoher (of Seville) was the first to point to the role of parasites in the production of scabies, and he was the first to prescribe sculpture as a remedy. Mohammed-Ibn-Quassum wrote on the diseases of the eye, and Salah-din-Ibn-Yusuf published works on the anatomy of the eye and the theories of vision. Mohammed al-Tamimi wrote on tumors and hernia, and Dawud-al-Agrebi wrote on fumigation, collyriums, and hemostatics.

[99] Scott, S. P. (1904) *'History of the Moorish Empire in Europe'*, op cit. p.517.

[100] Russell, Bertrand, 1872-1970. *'History of Western Philosophy'*, 2nd ed. (2000), Routledge, London, p.419.

[101] Marking the first year of Hijra, the new Islamic Calendar.

[102] Gibb H. A. R, et al. (1979), *'Encyclopaedia of Islam'*, Brill, Luzac Leiden ; London : Vol.4, pp.29-30.

[103] Briggs, M.S. (1931), 'Architecture', in T. and A. Guillaume, eds., *The Legacy of Islam*, Oxford University Press, p.158.

[104] Briggs, M.S. (1924), *'Muhammadan Architecture in Egypt and Palestine'*, the Clarendon Press, Oxford.

[105] Creswell ,K.A.C. (1958) *'A Short Account of Early Muslim Architecture'*, Penguin Books, London. p.14.

[106] Michell, M. et al. (eds.) (1978), *'Architecture of the Islamic World'*, Thames and Hudson, London, p.143.

[107] Ibn Khaldun (1967) *'The Muqadimah'*, translated from the Arabic by F. Rosenthal, edited by Dawood, N.J., Princeton pub.

[108] Havell, E. B. (Ernest Binfield), (1913), *'Indian Architecture: its Psychology, Structure, and History From the First Muhammadan Invasion to the Present Day'*, J. Murray, London, p.5.

[109] Rivoira, G. T. (Giovanni Teresio), (1918), *'Moslem Architecture: Its Origins and Development'*, translated from the Italian by G. Mc. Rushforth, Oxford University Press, London.

[110] Michell, M. et al. (eds.) (1978), op cit. p.173.

[111] The story of the building had been widely repeated that Abd-al-Malik constructed it to rival Makkah, which was at the hands of his enemy Ibn-Zubayr so that pilgrims would go there instead and subsequently would endorse his power and legitimacy. Although it has been established that Ibn Zubayr rebuilt Kaabah (between 683-692) as the Prophet had said it was at the time of Ibrahim (puh), it is not known that Abdel-Malik had issued any call for any change of pilgrimage direction. The most acceptable view is that Abd-al-Malik might have wanted to match Ibn Zubayr's devotion to Islam by building the Dome of The Rock to cover the Sacred Rock or *"Sakhra"* which is also connected to the prophet Mohammed. The symbolic significance was also suggested that the building's main objective was to celebrate the victory of Islam over other religions especially Judaism and Christianity, which had deep roots in Palestine.

[112] Wijdan Ali (2000), *'The Arab Contribution to Islamic Art'*, the American University in Cairo Press, p. 26.

127

[113] Grabar, O. (1959), *'The Umayyad Dome of the Rock in Jerusalem'*, Ars Orientalis, vol.3, pp.39-62.

[114] Wijdan Ali (2000), *'The Arab Contribution to Islamic Art'*, the American University in Cairo Press, p. 26.

[115] Ibid., p.26

[116] Lamperez y Romea (1930), *'Historia de la Arquitectura Cristiana en la Edad Media Según el Estudio de los Elementos y los Monuments*, Espasa-Calpe, Madrid, Spain.

[117] Briggs, M.S. (1924), op cit. p.42.

[118] Mason William, (1827), ' *The Works of Thomas Gray: Collated From the Various Editions; With Memoirs of his Life and Writings'*, published by J. F, Dove, London, p.188.

[119] Golvyn, L. (1971), *'Essai sur l'Architecture Religieuse Musulmane'*, Tome 2, l'Art Religieux des Umayyades de Syrie', Klioncksiek, p.153, translated from French.

[120] Michell, M. et al. (eds.) (1978), op cit.pp.76-77.

[121] Bier, L. (1979), *'The "Sasanian Palace" Near Sarvistan'*, New York University, Graduate School

[122] Urice S.K. (1987), *'Qasr Kharana in the Transjordan'*, American School of Oriental Research, Durham, N.C.

[123] Bier, L. (1986), *'Sarvistan: A Study in Early Iranian Architecture'*, Pennsylvania State University Press, pp28-50

[124] Otto von Simson (1956), *'The Gothic Cathedral, Origins of Gothic Architecture and the Medieval Concept of Order'*, Princeton University Press, USA. (3rd ed. 1988), p.220, plate 44.

[125] Al- Ma'mun's mother was also a Persian.

[126] M. Hattstein and P. Delius (eds.), *'Islam Art and Architecture'*, Konemann, Cologne, p.95.

[127] Creswell ,K.A.C. (1958), *'A Short Account of Early Muslim Architecture'*, Penguin Books, London, pp.207-210.

[128] There were other additions and modifications carried out in successive periods. Al Aqsa is the second of the three holiest mosques in Islam after the Kaaba and Medinah. The platform upon which it is constructed is referred to in the Quran and it is the location from where the ascension of prophet Muhammed took place. Al-Muqaddisi (10th century) gives a technical description of Al-Aqsa as follows: *"the mosque had a building lofty central nave leading to the mihrab and covered by a trussed timber roof. The nave had a width measured by 15 places of worshippers. In front of the mihrab, the space was covered by a great dome of bigger diameter than today's and had four minarets projecting high in the sky."* (Richmond, 1926)

[129] Lethaby, W.R. (1904), *'Medieval Art From the Peace of the Church to the Eve of the Renaissance'*, Duckworth &Co, London, Charles Scribner's Sons, New York, Vol.4, pp100-111.

[130] Today the largest mosque is The Mosque of Hassan II of Casablanca, Morocco (1992)

[131] Creswell ,K.A.C. (1958), op cit.p. 359.

[132] Rice, D.T. (1979) *'Islamic Art'*, Thames & Hudson, Norwich, p.45.

[133] Richmond, Ernest Tatham (1926), *'Moslem Architecture, 623 to 1516: Some Causes and Consequences'*, The Royal Asiatic Society, London, p.59.

[134] Briggs, M.S. (1924), op cit.

[135] A nephew of the Caliph Almansour who was exiled due to a dispute about the succession to the throne.

[136] Jairazbhoy, R.A. (1972), *'An Outline of Islamic Architecture'*, Asia Publishing House, Bombay, London and New York.p.58.

[137] Ibid. p.59.

[138] Marcais, G. (1954), *'l'Architecture Musulmane d'Occident'*, Arts et Metiers Graphiques, Paris, p.139.

[139] A town founded by the Caliph Almansur before 770. It is worth noting that the Abbassids founded numerous cities including the famous Baghdad with its round plan (762), Al-Rafiqqa (772), and Samarra (836).

[140] Small alley that is located on the projection of the wall of a fortress; it is located behind the battlements and once served the movement of men.

[141] This is confirmed by an inscription found in the collar of the large dome over the mihrab stating that it was built for Malik Shah by order of his Minister. Among the many features introduced by Nizam al-Mulk was a large brick dome in front of the mihrab in imitation of the Umayyad mosques. Sources reported that Nizam al-Mulk visited the Great Umayyad Mosque at Damascus in 1086 and on his return, he ordered the construction of the dome. This was also the first recorded example of the adoption of the Mihrab dome in iwan plan although the use of such a dome in traditional hypostyle plan was widespread in Umayyad and Abbasid architecture.

[142] Hoag, J.D. (1987) *'Islamic Architecture'*, Faber & Faber, London.

[143] Creswell ,K.A.C. (1958) `*A Short Account of Early Muslim Architecture'*, Penguin Books, London.p. 351.

[144] Marcais, G. (1954), op.cit. p.24.

[145] Lambert, E. (1927), '*L 'art Hispano Mauresque et l'Art Roman* ', Hesperis, vol.7.pp.29-43, at p.40.

[146] The first Mass was held there on 25th May 1085.

[147] Bargebuhr, F.P. (1968), '*The Alhambra, a Cycle of Studies on the Eleventh Century in Moorish Spain*', Walter de Gruyter & Co., Berlin.

[148] Grabar, Oleg (1978), '*The Alhambra*', Harvard University Press, Cambridge, Mass.

[149] Darby, M. (1983), `*The Islamic Perspective, an Aspect of British Architecture and Design in the 19th Century*', Leighton House Gallery, London.

[150] The position of Al-Hambra in the European mind can be demonstrated in the writing of Victor Hugo in his "Les Orientales".
L'Ahambra! L'Ahambra! Palais que les génies
Ont dore comme un rêve et rempli d'harmonies;
Forteresse aux créneaux, festonnes et croulants,
Ou l'on entend la nuit de magiques syllabes,
Quand la lune, à travers les milles arceaux arabes
Serme les murs de trèfles blancs!

[151] He compiled "al-Muntakhab fi ilm al-Ayn wa Mudawatiha bi'l Adwiya wal Hadid", or the Book of Choices in the Treatment of Eye Diseases.

[152] Among his popular manuscripts is: "*Kitab al-Manazir*", or Treatise on Optics,

[153] Elsberg H. A.; Guest R. (1936), '*The Veil of Saint Anne* ', The Burlington Magazine for Connoisseurs, Vol. 68, No. 396, pp. 140+ 144-145+ 147.

[154] Rice, D.T. (1973), '*Islamic Art* ', Thames and Hudson, reprinted in 1993, pp.95-96.

[155] Lezine Alexandre (1965), '*Mahdiya: Recherches d'Archéologie Islamique*, Paris, , pp. 24-38

[156] Bloom M. Jonathan (1985), '*The Origins of Fatimid Art* ', Muqarnas, Vol. 3. pp. 20-38.

[157] Georges Marcais, (1954), '*L'Architecture Musulmane d'Occident* ', Paris, pp. 106 ff.

[158] Lezine Alexandre, (1967), '*Notes d'Archéologie Ifriqiyenne, IV: Mahdiya, Quelques Précisions sur la 'Ville' des Premiers Fatimides,* ', Revue des Études Islamiques, Vol.35, p.90.

[159] The Zirids, headed by Ziri Ibn Munad, founded the capital of their State in Ashir, east of Algiers, in 935 CE. The Hammadids, headed by Hammad, founded their capital, al-Qala' or the fortress on the Hodna hills, about 50 kilometres south of Ashir.

[160] Blanchet, P. (1889), '*La Kalaa des Beni-Hammad* ', Recueil de la Société Archéologique de Constantine', Cezayir, s.97-176.and Blanchet, P. (1904), 'Description des monuments de la Kalaa des Beni-Hammâd, Nowelles Notices de Missions Scientifiques, XVII, Paris, pp. 1-21

[161] Beylié, G. L. de, (1909), '*Le Kalaa des Beni-Hammad, une Capitale Berbère de l'Afrique du Nord au XIe Siècle* ', Paris.

[162] Saladin, H. (1905), '*Deuxième Note sur les Monuments Arabes de la Kalaa des Beni Hammad* ', Bulleting Archéologique, p.189

[163] Dieulafoy (1889), '*l'Art Antique de la Perse* ', Vol.4, Paris, plates 9, 10 and 11.

[164] Abouseif Doris Behrens- (1989), '*Islamic Architecture in Cairo: an Introduction*', Brill Publishers, p.10.

[165] Others connected it to Fatima al-Zahra, the daughter of the beloved prophet Muhammed.

[166] Hill, D. (1976), '*Islamic Architecture in North Africa*', Faber and Faber, London, p.76.

[167] Rivoira G. T. (1919), '*Moslem Architecture*', translated by G. Men. Rushforth. London. 1919.

[168] Briggs, S. Martin (1920), '*The Fatimite Architecture of Cairo (A.D.969-1171)*', in The Burlington Magazine for Connoisseurs, Vol.37, N0.210, pp.137-139 and 142-147.

[169] Caroline Williams, (1983), "*The Cult of the Alid Saints in the Fatimid Monuments of Cairo: Part One: The Mosque of al-Aqmar*', Muqarnas, vol. 1, pp. 37-54.

[170] Doris Behrens Abouseif, ((1992), 'The *Facade of the Aqmar Mosque in the Context of Fatimid Ceremonial*', Muqarnas, vol. 9, pp. 29-38.

[171] Rice, D.T. (1973), '*Islamic Art*', Thames and Hudson, reprinted in 1993, p.89

[172] Williams Caroline (1985), '*The Cult of 'Alid Saints in the Fatimid Monuments of Cairo, Part II: The Mausolea*', in Muqarnas: An Annual on Islamic Art and Architecture', vol.3., pp.39-6o, at p.57

[173] Ibid.

[174] Ettinghausen Richard Oleg Grabar (1987), '*The Art and Architecture of Islam: 650-1250*', Yale University Press.

[175] Berchem, Max van. (1978). '*Une Mosquée du Temps des Fatimites au Caire. Notes sur le Gami el Goyushi*. Opera Minora I. Editions Slatkine. Geneva, pp.61-75.

[176] Ibid., pp.61-75.

[177] Udovitch A.L. (1980), '*Islamic Sicily*', in Dictionary of the Middle Ages; Charles Scribners' Son, New York, Vol. 11, p.263.

[178] For some of their quotes see Breckenridge J. D. (1975), '*The two Sicilies*', in S. Feber (ed.), *Islam and the Medieval West*; A Loan Exhibition at the University Art Gallery; State University of New York, p. 43.

[179] Carlo Trabia (2005), '*Kanats of Sicily*', Best of Sicily Magazine, see http://www.bestofsicily.com/mag/art154.htm

[180] Udovitch, A.L. (1980), '*Islamic Sicily*', op cit; p.262.

[181] Goss, V.P. (1986) '*Western Architecture and the World of Islam in the 12th Century*', in V.P. Goss and Borstein (eds.), pp.361-375.

[182] Kleinhenz Christopher (2004), '*Medieval Italy: An Encyclopaedia*', Routledge, p.840

[183] Chisholm Hugh (1910), '*The Encyclopaedia Britannica*', The Encyclopædia Britannica Co. Vol.1, p.395

[184] Symonds John Addington (1910), '*Sketches and Studies in Italy and Greece*', John Murray, London, p. 318

[185] Marcais, G. (1954), '*l'Architecture Musulmane d'Occident*', Arts et métiers Graphiques, Paris, p.125 and figure 84, p.124.

[186] For the text of the frieze, see Lavagnini, B. (1987), '*L'Epigramma e il Committente*', Dumbarton Oaks Papers vol.41, pp. 339-50.

[187] Kitzinger Ernst and Curcic Slobodan (1990), '*The Mosaics of St. Mary's of the Admiral in Palermo*', Dumbarton Oaks Studies 27, Washington, 35 ff.

[188] Knight, H.G. (1839), '*The Normans in Sicily*', The Dublin Review, Vol.7, C. Dolman, London, p.121-138, at p.132

[189] Breckenridge J. D. (1975), '*The Two Sicilies*', op cit; p. 53.

[190] Ibid., p.53.

[191] Knight, H.G. (1839), *The Normans in Sicily*', op.cit. at p.132

[192] Michell, George (ed). (1980), '*Architecture of the Islamic World: Its History and Social Meaning*', Thames and Hudson, London, p.222

[193] Quoted in M. Hattstein and P. Delius (eds.) (2000), '*Islam Art and Architecture*', Konemann, Cologne, p.161.

[194] Hillenbrand, R.(1994), '*Islamic Architecture; Form, Function and Meaning*', Edinburgh University Press, p.441

[195] Marcais, G. (1954), '*l'Architecture Musulmane d'Occident*', op cit. p122.

[196] Ibid.p.122

[197] Jairazbhoy, R.A. (1972), '*An Outline of Islamic Architecture*', Asia Publishing House, Bombay, London and New York., p.120

[198] Al- Bakri (1068), '*Description de l'Afrique Septentrionale*', translation of de Slane, 1913, Alger, Paris, p.60.

[199] See Michell, M. et al. (eds.) (1978), op cit. pp.112-143.

[200] Godard, A. (1965) '*the Art of Iran*', Allen & Unwin, New York, p.279, 282.

[201] Initially in Parthian Assur Palace (2nd century C.E.)

[202] Godard, A. (1965) op cit.

[203] Scerrato Umberto (1980), '*Islam, Monuments of Civilisation*', The Reader's Digest Association Ltd., London, p.73.

[204] M. Hattstein and P. Delius (eds.) (2000), '*Islam Art and Architecture*', Konemann, Cologne, p.368.

[205] Hoag, J.D. (1987) '*Islamic Architecture*', Faber & Faber, London.p.95.

[206] Ibid.

[207] According to Scerrato (1980), op. cit. the fire took place between 1120-1121.

[208] Ibid. p.72.

[209] M. Hattstein and P. Delius (eds.) (2000), '*Islam Art and Architecture*', Konemann, Cologne, p.354.

[210] This is different from Ribat in North Africa, which refers to a theological boarding college for volunteer fighters.

[211] The Qarakhanid ruler (1068-1080) and the son in law of Sultan Alp Arslan.

[212] Hoag, J.D. (1987) '*Islamic Architecture*', Faber & Faber, London.p.98

[213] Ibid, p.92.

[214] Humphreys R. Stephen (1972), 'the *Expressive Intent of the Mamluk Architecture of Cairo: A Preliminary Essay*', Studia Islamica, No. 35. pp. 69-119.

[215] Priscilla P. SOUCEK (2000), '*Monumentalizing Piety: Religious Practices and Mamluk Architecture*', Islamic Area Studies Group 5, Report on the 6th Seminar of Group the Institute of Fine Arts, New York University. http://www.l.u-tokyo.ac.jp/IAS/HP-e2/eventreports/45urbanspaceHY.html, accessed 30/05/2015.

[216] Tabbaa Yasser (1997), '*Construction of Power and Piety in Medieval Aleppo*', Pennsylvania State University Press, p 149.

[217] Ibid. p. 145.

[218] Tabaa Yasser (1993), '*Circles of Power: Palace, Citadel, and City in Ayyubid Aleppo*', Ars Orientalis, Vol.23, pp. 181-191.

[219] Goulton, G.G. (1930), '*Crusades, Commerce and Adventure*', Nelson, London p. 117.

[220] Briggs M. S. (1931), '*Architecture*', in in T. Arnold, and A Guillaume, (eds.), The Legacy of Islam, Oxford University Press, first edition, pp 155-79, at p.168

[221] Turner Jane (1996), '*The Dictionary of Art*' Grove Publishing, p.545

[222] Lynn Teo Simarski (1987), '*The Lure of Aleppo*', ARAMCO, Vol.38, Number 4, pp.34-40

[223] Tabbaa Yasser (1997), '*Construction of Power and Piety in Medieval Aleppo*', Pennsylvania State University Press.

[224] See Tabaa Yasser (2001), '*The Transformation of Islamic Art During the Sunni Revival*', University of Washington Press, also Humphreys R. Stephen (1972), 'The Expressive Intent of the Mamluk Architecture of Cairo: A Preliminary Essay', Studia Islamica, No. 35, pp. 69-119.

[225] Tabbaa, Yasser (1982), '*The Architectural Patronage of Nûr al-Dîn*', Thesis (Ph.D), New York University.

[226] Humphreys R. Stephen (1994), '*Women as Patrons of Religious Architecture in Ayyubid Damascus*', Muqarnas, Vol. 11. (1994), pp. 35-54.

[227] Ibid., pp.49-50

[228] Dodge B. (1962), '*Muslim Education in Medieval Times*', The Middle East Institute, Washington, D.C., p. 23.

[229] Turner Jane (ed. 1996), '*The Dictionary of Art*', Macmillan Publishers, London, p.323

[230] Tabaa Yasser (2001), '*The Transformation of Islamic Art During the Sunni Revival*', University of Washington Press, p.152, and Turner Jane (ed. 1996), '*The Dictionary of Art*', Macmillan Publishers, London, p.323

[231] Scerrato, U (1972), '*Islam, Monument of Civilisation*' Reader's Digest Association, p.85

[232] Creswell K. A. C. (1926), '*The Evolution of the Minaret, with Special Reference to Egypt-II*', The Burlington Magazine for Connoisseurs, Vol. 48, No. 278, pp. 252+256-259, at p.257

[233] Creswell K. A. C. (1926), 'op., cit. p.257

[234] Creswell, K.A.C. (1959). '*The Muslim Architecture of Egypt*', vol. II. Clarendon Press, Oxford, reprinted by Hacker Art Books, New York, 1978.

[235] Gorini, R. (2002), '*Attention and Care to the Madness During the Islamic Middle Age Syria*', JISHIM, vol.2, pp.40-42, at p.40

[236] Working by the hadith of prophet Muhammed which narrates: "*When a person dies, the opportunity of gaining more rewards ends except for these three: perpetual charity (*or Sadaqa Jariyah*), knowledge from which there is a benefit, or a pious child supplicating to Allah for him.*"

[237] The four imams are: Imam Malik founder of the Maliki School, Imam Al Shafi founder of the Shafi'i School, Imam Abu Hanifa founder of the Hanafit School, and Imam Ahmad Ibn Hambal founder of the Hambalit School.

[238] Aḥmad ibn Muḥammad Ibn Arabshāh, (1936), '*Tamerlane, Or Timur, the Great Amir*', translated by J. H. Sanders, Luzac & co., London, p.3

[239] Wilfrid Blunt, (1973), '*The Golden Road to Samarkand*', Hamish Hamilton, (London), p.138.

[240] Jackson P., and Lokhart Laurence (1986), '*The Cambridge History of Iran*', Cambridge University Press.

[241] Chmelnizkij, S. (2000), '*Central Asia: The Timurids, the Shaybanids, and the Khan Princedoms*', Hattstein, M. And Delius, P. (eds.), Islam Art and Architecture, Konemann, p.406-451, at p.417.

[242] Ratiya S. E. (1950), '*The Mechet' Bibi Khanum at Samarcand*', (in Russian) Moscow, 1950 cited in Jairazbhoy, R.A. (1972), 'An Outline of Islamic Architecture', op.cit. p. 271

[243] Golombek, Lisa and Wilber Donald (1988), '*The Timurid Architecture of Iran and Turan*, Vol. 1, Princeton: Princeton University Press, p.255

[244] Jackson Peter, Lockhart Laurence (1986), op.cit. p.83

[245] Guy le Strange (ed.1928), '*Clavijo, Embassy to Tamerlane 1403-1406*', Harper New York and London.

[246] Michell G. (1978), '*Architecture of the Islamic World*', Thames and Hudson, p.262.

[247] Dani, A.H. et al. (1999), '*History of Civilizations of Central Asia*', Motilal Banarsidass Publishing, p.349.

[248] For details see Limongelli M. D. (1921), '*la Stabilité de la Coupole au Mausolée de Tamerlan a Samarcande*', in Bulletin de I 'Institut d' Égypte, vol. IV, pp. 77-92, Also Chmelnizkij, S. (2000), op cit. p.420.

[249] Jairazbhoy, R.A. (1972), op., cit. p.268

[250] Sanjay Subrahmanyam (2014), '*Early Modern Circulation and the Question of 'Patriotism' Between India and Central Asia*', in Green N. ed. (2014) 'Writing Travel in Central Asian History', Indiana University Press, Bloomington and Indianapolis, pp.43-67, at p.62

[251] Jairazbhoy, R.A. (1972), op., cit. p.272

[252] Golombek and Wilber (1988), op. cit. Vol. 1, p.263.

[253] Al-Hassani S.T.S., E. Woodcock and R. Saoud (2006), '*Muslim Heritage in Our World*', Foundation for Science, technology and Civilisation publishing, pp.286-289. Also Sayili, A.

(1980), 'the Observatory in Islam', pp. 53-56. the International symposium on the Observatories in Islam 19-23 September 1977 (ed. M. Dizer), Istanbul 1980, pp. 21-32

[254] See Golombek, Lisa and Donald Wilber. (1988), '*The Timurid Architecture of Iran and Turan*'. Princeton: Princeton University Press, pp.265-266.

[255] Cited in Barthold V. V. (1958), '*Four Studies on the History of Central Asia*', tr. V. and T. Minorsky, vol. 2, Leiden, p. 132, and in Golombek and Wiber, Vol. 1, 266f.

[256] There are those who suggested that Arabic numerals are derived from the Indian ones.

[257] Brown, P. (1968) '*Indian Architecture (Islamic Period)*', Taraporevala's Treasure House of Books. Bombay, p.1.

[258] Including: the Slave Kings period 1206 90, Khalji period 1290 1320, Tughluq period 1320 98, Sayyid period 1414- 51, Lodi period 1451-1526.

[259] Leading to the establishment of a number of independent provincial sultanates such as: Bengal 1336-1576, Kashmir 1346-1589 , Deccan 1347-152, Gujarat 1391-1583, Jaunpur 1394-1479, Malwar 1401-1531, Bijapur 1490-1686, Suri period 1540-55, Mughal period 1526-1858.

[260] Brown, P. (1968), op.cit. pp.1-2.

[261] For more on Indian architecture see Hardy Adam (1995), '*Indian Temple Architecture: Form and Transformation: The Karnata Dravida Tradition 7th to 13th.*', Abhinav Publications.

[262] In the Great Mosque of Cordoba, architects superimposed a whole series of semi-circular multifoil arcades.

[263] In the case of the Great Mosque of Kairawan, an extra stone was added on top of the column.

[264] Michell, M. et al. (eds.) (1978), op. cit., p.271.

[265] See Goodwin Godfrey (1987), '*A History of Ottoman Architecture*", Thames and Hudson, London.

[266] Bloom, J. & Blair, S. (1998), '*Islamic Arts*', Phaidon Press, London, p.322.

[267] Jackson Peter, Lockhart Laurence (1986), '*The Cambridge History of Iran*', Cambridge University Press, pp.190-250

[268] Savory R. (2007), '*Iran under the Safavid*', Cambridge University Press, p.34

[269] Thackston, W. M. (1988), '*The Diwan of Khatai: Pictures for the Poetry of Shah Ismail*', Asian Art, p. 37, quoted in Abolala Soudovar (1992), 'Art of the Persian Courts', Rizzoli International Publications, New York, p.147.

[270] Donzel, E.J. Van, (1994), '*Islamic Desk Reference*', Brill Academic Publishers, p. 393

[271] Scerrato, U. (1976), '*Islam: Monuments of Civilisation*', the Reader's Digest Association Ltd., London, p.114.

[272] Blair Sheila S. and Bloom Jonathon M. (1997), '*Islamic Arts*', Phaidon Press, Hong Kong, p. 338.

[273] Blair, S. & Bloom, J. (2000), '*Islamic Carpets*', M.Hattstein & P. Delius eds, Islam: Art and Architecture, Konemann, Cologne, pp.530-533.

[274] Ibid., p.532.

[275] Pope, Aurthur Upham (1965), '*Persian Architecture*', George Braziller Inc., New York, p.207.

[276] Chardin Chevalier (1686), '*Journal du Voyage du Chevalier Chardin en Perse et aux Indes Orientales, par la Mer Noire et par la Colchide*', Moses Pitt, London, p.388

[277] Sarre Fredrick (1924), '*Ardabil, Grabmoschee des Schech Safi*', Berlin Translation Sedigheh Khansari Mousavi and Minorsky, V. *(ed.1959), 'Calligraphers and Painters, a Treatise by Qadi Ahmad, Son of Mir-Munshi*', tr. V. Minorsky, Freer Gallery of Art, Washington DC. p. 182

[278] Pope, Aurthur Upham (1965), op. cit. p. 207.

[279] See Jairazbhoy, R.A. (1972), '*An Outline of Islamic Architecture*', op. cit. p.277.

[280] Blair, Sheila S. and Jonathan M. Bloom (1994), '*The Art and Architecture of Islam 1250-1800*', Yale University Press, New Haven, p.185

[281] Pope, Aurthur Upham (1965), op. cit. p. 210

[282] Blair, S. And Bloom, S. (2000), '*Architecture (of the Safavids)*', in M. Hattstein and P.Delius (eds.), Islam Art and Architecture, Konemann, pp.504-519, at p.512.

[283] Ibid., p.512

[284] Manucci Niccolao (ed.1907), '*Storia do Mogor*', translated by William Irvine, John Murray, London, vol. I, p. 30

[285] Jairazbhoy R.A. (1972), op.cit. p. 277

[286] Ibid. p.277

[287] Chardin Chevalier (1686), '*Journal du Voyage du Chevalier Chardin en Perse et aux Indes Orientales, par la Mer Noire et par la Colchide*', Moses Pitt, London Vol.7, p. 378 and vol.10, pp. 468f. Cited in Jairazbhoy R.A. (1972), op.cit. p. 278.

[288] The succession of the Ottomans to the Caliphate in the 14th century was at the hands of their founder Othman (d.1326) and reached its apogee in the 16th century.

[289] Davies, J.G. (1982), '*Temples. Churches and Mosques*', Pilgrim Press, New York, p.127

[290] Hoag, J.D (1968), '*Western Islamic Architecture*', Studio Vista, London. p.42.

[291] His built legacy exceeds 477 buildings; see *The Encyclopaedia of Islam*, (1997), volume 6, Brill, Leyden, p.629.

[292] Kostof, S. (1995). '*A History of World Architecture*', Oxford University Press, Oxford, p.457.

CHAPTER 3

Europe in the Middle Ages

General Background to European Christian Civilisation

Like other cultures, European culture and civilisation went through many phases of development, displaying the evolution process of civilisation theorised by Ibn Khaldun[293] (14th century). The Greek civilisation dominated the classical phase, extending over a wide area encompassing Southern Europe, the Middle East and the Mediterranean Basin including North Africa. This phase was renowned for many theoretical and philosophical achievements, with its greatest contribution being the development of logical methods for studying and explaining various natural phenomena such as the nature of things, understanding the being, goodness, truth, the best state, law and justice and so on. Among the most well known scholars from this era one can name, Isocrates (436-338BC), Plato (427-348BC) and Aristotle (384-322BC).

These achievements were translated in the Grecian approach to art and architecture. The explanation of the nature of the senses and the being of the individual were particularly influential introducing, for the first time, a systematic understanding of aesthetics leading to a greater inclusion of this theme in their artwork. The other effect was the gradual use of natural themes in art, to which some historians attribute the origins of Western representational art. Meanwhile, the promotion of the individual being as a social and economic unity made architecture more attached to the individual taste than at any time before. Principles of rationality, order and quality (goodness) were transmitted in various architectural projects. Consequently, buildings became more determined by a degree of mathematical proportions and aesthetic delights.

The major work of Greek architecture is undoubtedly the Temple, a building of religious and cultural importance where all creativity was displayed. Historians generally accept that the temple itself consisted of three main architectural components. The first was a space, composed of rows of columns, which formed the central area where people carried out their ritual worship of the gods. The columns belonged to three architectural orders; the *Doric* column from Doria, Greece, the *Ionic* from Ionia in southwestern coast of Anatolia, Turkey, and the *Corinthian* from Corinth in southwest of Athens, Greece. Each order consisted of a column, sometimes a base on which it stood, and a lintel called entablature. The characteristics of these columns range from the plain, coarse, robust to the most decorated, smooth, and slender. The proportions of the orders and their mouldings and carvings were developed over a period, starting massive around the sixth and seventh century and becoming more slender and refined in later periods. The Romans later added two more types of columns, the Tuscan from Tuscany (Italy) and the Composite, which is a combination of the Greek Ionic and Corinthian columns[294]. These five categories, which together represent the columns chiefly used in Europe, are widely known as the Five Orders of Architecture, and European architecture was based upon them.

The entablature, the second architectural component of the Greek temple, consists of the beams laid on top of the columns to carry the roof. These beams comprise three horizontal sections; the *architrave*, a plane section coming immediately above the column; the *frieze, a* middle section made of a horizontal band, sometimes decorated with carvings and running above the architrave; and above the frieze, the *Cornice*, a section made of mouldings situated just below the roof. The third component is the *pediment*, a triangular form at the end of the pitched roof and known for the sculpture and stucco- work adorning its western and eastern sides. One of the best-known temples is the Temple of Zeus at Olympia (470 and 450 BC).

In terms of decoration, the Greeks drew many of their motifs from earlier civilisations including the Egyptians, Assyrians and Minoans. The most commonly used forms were based on plant and animal motifs, introduced in the frieze and the cornice of the building in the form of mouldings or sculptures of carved marble. The most common plant motifs included the *acanthus* leaf, which was widely used in Corinthian capitals. The *anthemion* or honeysuckle was largely used as a moulding decoration, known as *cyma recta,* sometimes accompanied with a band of egg and dart or leaf and dart and its moulding known as *cyma reversa*, bead and reel often formed a narrow band at the bottom or top of the main moulding decoration. The scroll was widely used for Ionic capitals. Animal forms had religious significance and they were used as friezes or sculpture decorating the pediment or the frieze section of the temple. The most widely used animals were lions, bulls and sphinxes, all of which were expressions of power and might. Human sculptures were generally nude and used in two forms, in a freestanding state representing Greek gods or as part of a religious or war scene involving animals and chariots.

The Roman Tradition

After the Greeks, came the Romans who continued in the path of the classical tradition, taking much of their learning from the Greek heritage, concentrating, however, more on practical aspects of the Greek scientific and philosophical thought. In religion, the Romans maintained many of the Greek religious practises but adopting Latin names to their gods and imposed their pagan state religion on conquered societies, which put them into conflict with local populations. In the first century of the Common Era, Christianity emerged through the teachings of Prophet Issa (Jesus) who was sent as a messenger to revive the worship of the Almighty God, after the spread of paganism imposed by the Romans. Christians first faced persecution by the Jews who also incited the Romans against them[295]. According to the New Testament, Jesus' crucifixion was authorized by Roman authorities but demanded by the leading Jews and carried out by Roman soldiers. The New Testament also records that St.Paul was imprisoned on several occasions and that he was executed in Rome. After these early years, the Romans generally tolerated Christians until the times of Nero who subjected them to persecution blaming them for the fire of Rome[296]. The struggle of Christians culminated under the rule of Diocletian and Galerius at the end of the third and beginning of the fourth century[297], when the Emperor Constantine (c.306-337) converted to Christianity and consequently Rome officially adopted this religion. The first Christian church, The Holy Sepulchre, was consecrated in 335, supposedly on the site of what is traditionally believed to be the tomb of Prophet Issa (Jesus,).[298]

Towards the Middle of the 4th century C.E, and after the foundation of Constantinople in 330 by Constantine I (c. AD 274-337), the Roman Empire was split into a prosperous east, where Byzantium became the rising empire benefiting from the concentration of wealth and ideas. A declining west where a weakening Rome became more and more marginalized losing much of its world influence. Constantinople soon overshadowed Rome becoming the largest and most prosperous European city of the middle Ages, the centre of the glories and luxuries of the Byzantine Empire, especially in the 5th century under Theodosius II.

The Romans in general drew their science and education from Greek sources, especially the works of Plato and Isocrates[299].The Greek centres of Athens and Alexandria continued to be poles of attraction for Roman students who wanted further scientific investigation in various disciplines. Students were taught art and philosophy, and equipped to contribute to the political and juridical debate in the Senate. Scientific subjects such as arithmetic, geometry and astronomy were also part of the Roman curriculum. The education system, however, neglected science and medicine and favoured the upper class of free men while women and slaves were excluded from it. For example, among the renowned scholars from the Roman period one can refer to Galen (129-200 CE) in medicine, and Hypatia (c.370 - 415 CE) in philosophy and mathematics; the former was Greek from Pergamum and the latter studied the Greek tradition of Alexandria. Marcus Vitruvius Pollio (70-20 BCE) the author of *De Architectura*, is claimed to be the main source of Roman construction and the revival of the classical orders in Italian Renaissance architecture. The Roman real contribution was in practical sciences especially in technology, navigation, building harbours, roads, stone drainage ditches, bridges, aqueducts and war machines.[300]

In art and architecture, the Romans adopted the Greek forms with significant improvement. In representational arts, the depiction of natural objects and human sculpture and portrait, especially of emperors and powerful elite exceeded that of Greek sculpture. The temple with its columns, entablatures, and triangular pediment was adapted to Roman gods and given the central position in the Forum, approximate to the political, economic and social activities[301]. The Romans excelled in wall construction and diversified their building materials introducing brick, stones, as well as marble into their constructions[302]. However, the most significant invention was concrete, which greatly influenced the course of Roman architecture. The Romans made their concrete from mixing a number of ingredients including the volcanic ash known as *pozzuolana* and lime[303]. Two types of brick were produced; sun dried was naturally made and kiln burnt was industrially produced in production centres. The brick was later widely used for the construction of walls, columns and vaults. These innovations, in addition to their practical knowledge in construction, allowed them to introduce the arch but they hesitated to use it fully, as a load bearing structure that can be used in structural as well as decorative aspects. The semi-circular form of arch required a simple geometrical knowledge and *"facilitated cutting of the voussoirs and construction of the timber centering on which the arch was erected"*[304]. This arch revolutionised classical architecture, as the Romans developed the dome by spinning it from about its centre and constructed the barrel vault (also known as tunnel vault) which was widely used in tunnel roofing since the third century BC[305]. In a third stage, from the intersection of two-barrel vaults, the Romans developed the groin vault. In all cases, little use was made of trigonometry; reliance was mainly on rectangular grids.[306]

The domes and vaults were largely produced through centring which involved pouring the concrete mixed with brick and travertine fragments onto wooden scaffolding that was kept in place long enough for the concrete to dry before being moved to another section of the dome or vault[307]. Sometimes, in large areas, piers subdivided the vaults into square compartments or bays. In later times of the empire, the Romans, particularly in Syria and Nimes, began constructing vaults from stones. The dome construction was limited and consisted mainly of hemispheric shape.

The Romans also introduced the robust pier, as an alternative method of supporting arches and vaults. However, due to their massive size the supporting piers obscured much of the interior space. In general, the use of these elements remained limited to aqueducts and other works of utility while buildings continued to use the lintel, a fact that shows the Roman struggle with static problems and indicates their limited scientific understanding of it[308]. Thus, they continued to rely in their construction on robust structures and walls to support the roof. Dearmer (1921) valued Roman architecture in the following: "*Roman architecture fails between two incompatible principles-that of the lintel which takes pressure direct and that of the arch which spreads it: Its columns and entablatures are therefore usually only a veneer. Roman ornament, also, is seldom free from heaviness and vulgarity; Roman domes and vaults are giant lids of concrete.*"[309]

In terms of building typology, the Romans used a variety of buildings to meet their needs. The most prestigious of these were the temples, which were built, in rectangular forms resembling the Greek. Examples of these are the Maison Carrée of Nimes, (France, c.16 BCE) and Temple of Fortuna Virilis, Forum Boarium, Rome (100-40 BCE) (fig.64). There are also a few examples of Roman circular temples such as the famous Pantheon (Rome, 120 C.E). This edifice, built by the Emperor Hadrian, consisted of two main sections; the portico, a square structure comprising 16 Corinthian columns carrying the entablature and the pediment and the circular cella, a hall covered with a huge dome of over 142 feet, one of the largest domes ever constructed in the Roman Empire[310] (fig.65). The hemispherical dome was made of brick and concrete with inserted panels of coffers, a decorative tradition that was used subsequently in the fourth century C.E. in the vaults of the Basilica of Constantine (c. 306-312 C.E) [311]. Despite this attempt to develop dome construction, it remains very timid as the dome of the Pantheon was set upon circular walls making its construction straightforward.

139

Figure 64 Temple of Fortuna Virilis, Forum Boarium, Rome (100-40 BCE)

Figure 65 The Pantheon, Rome (120 C.E).

The most important Roman secular building is the basilica, a Greek word meaning 'kingly' or royal hall of justice and a centre for commercial exchange usually located at the centre of a town near the forum[312]. The building is famous for its rectangular plan, generally twice as long as wide with an apse at one, or sometimes, at both ends. The roof, whether wooden or vaulted, was raised on two rows of columns or piers dividing the hall into a larger central area and two narrower side aisles. These design features were later adapted to the Christian church. The most well known basilica is the Basilica of Constantine construction of which was started in 308 CE by Emperor Maxentius and completed by Constantine.

Baths were another building type that was institutionalised by the Romans. They were building complexes consisting of a number of vaulted chambers or rooms. The *Caldarium* was the hot steam room containing small compartments with hot water baths where bathers proceeded first to wash before being rubbed and scrubbed by servants. The *Frigidarium* was a cool room containing the so- called cold plunge pool where the bather took a plunge to cool down before the Greek tradition, but striving to translate concepts of Christian belief such as reincarnation, salvation, and sacrifice.

By the late 5th century, Rome had fallen to pagan Barbarians, Germanic peoples who like locusts, ravaged most of Europe. This marked the end of the Roman and western classical civilisation. Europe entered what is widely known as the Dark Ages, a period dominated by the being to the complex[313]. Bathing in these centres was subject for a fee quite reasonable for most free Roman males[314]. Other Roman buildings included the theatre and the amphitheatre, the circus, triumphal arches and victory columns, massaged and oiled. The *Tepidarium* was a medium heated room where visitors could sit and relax. In some instances, other sections such as the changing room (Apodyterium), reading room and sports arena were added as well as many engineering works such as bridges and aqueducts, all of which employed the semi-circular arch.

In ornament and decoration, the Romans continued in the Greek tradition using their motifs although the Grecian were more refined and superior in quality. Forms such as acanthus foliage, scrolls and anthemion were widely used, although there were some slight changes e.g. the use of a more rounded acanthus plant rather than the spikier one favoured by the Greeks. The Greek moulding and sculptural traditions were also maintained throughout the Roman Empire. In internal decoration, the Romans relied heavily on mosaic and marble works, generally formed coloured compositions of human, animal or landscape representations. Very little has survived of paintings, mostly in the fresco used to adorn the interiors of private homes. There is consensus that the Romans were content to imitate the Greek tradition: *"Roman art is an appendix to the art history of Greece. It originated little in painting, and was content to perpetuate the traditions of Greece in an imitative way. What was worse, it copied the degeneracy of Greece by following the degenerate Hellenistic paintings."*[315] The largest collection of surviving frescoes has been found in Pompeii, in Campania, the region around Naples, a region that was buried intact under the eruption of volcano of Mount Vesuvius in 79 CE[316]. The wall ornamentation of Roman villas and houses consisted of paintings made of fresco of architectural, landscape and figural representations, exclusively secular and having almost no religious purpose.

These architectural techniques were transmitted all over the Roman Empire stretching around the Mediterranean basin including Syria and North Africa as far north as England. Roman cities were famous for their grid plan organised around the Forum[317], a large open space surrounded by civic buildings, which provided a focal point for commerce and public life. Two main axial avenues, the Cardo and the Decumannus Maximus subdivided the grid.[318]

The Roman Emperor's profession of Christianity took place in the fourth century C.E, at a time when much of their power had collapsed forcing them to accept the increasingly popular religion[319]. The church filled the spiritual and - to a certain extent- political vacuum enabling it to increase substantially its power leading to the appearance of a new form of religious buildings developed in an attempt to distance itself from old pagan religions and their temples. Much building activity had been in the erection of churches to a design adapted from Roman basilicas and law courts as noted previously[320]. The basilica was equipped with two or four rows of columns set along the axis to provide three or five aisles, the central one was to become known as the nave while the eastern end was usually apsidal. The ceiling was generally flat and made mostly from wood. Later on there were many additions to this basic plan with functional sections such as a western narthex and a separate baptistery. The western narthex was no more than a portico built across the whole façade providing an area for visitors who do not wish to enter the church. With its circular plan, the baptistery was introduced into the church, usually adjacent to larger churches, for the practice of baptism[321]. These early churches are mostly found in Italy and they were subject to later rebuilding and alteration. The examples of these include Santa Maria degli Angeli (Rome, 306 C.E.) (fig.66), Santa Maria Magiore, built 432-40, of which only some of the interior retains the original features, San Paolo Fuori le Mura, built 380, which was entirely destroyed in 1823 and rebuilt after that and San Lorenzo Fuori le Mura, built 432-578 which was destroyed during World War II and completely rebuilt.

Roman architectural achievement in Europe ended in the fifth century, but continued for some time in the East under the Byzantines. The Byzantine Empire was raised on the ashes of the declining imperial Roman state in the west. From the capital Constantinople (Istanbul today), the Byzantines Empire was stretched to the Balkans, Asia Minor, Syria, and Palestine, Egypt and as far as North Africa. With such geographical magnitude, this Christian Empire had frontiers with the Arabs and the Islamic Caliphate, and the Sassanians, with whom it had military conflict lasting for years in an attempt to subdue and dominate them. The Byzantines reached their golden period during the reign of emperor Justinian (r. 527-65 CE), just before the beginning of Islam. Like their Roman counterparts, their art and architecture were greatly influenced by classical heritage that some academics spoke of the "Renaissance" of classical arts[322].

Perhaps, the most important structural development made by the Byzantines was in dome construction, which they set over a square plan rather than a circular one. The method was achieved by first using squinches, which were built at the corners of the square providing an octagonal base for the dome. The squinches were used much earlier in Sassanian architecture, in Palace of Ardeshir, also known as Fire Temple, at Gur[323] or Firozabad, constructed ca. 250 C.E by King Ardeshir the founder of the Sassanian dynasty[324]. At a later stage, the Byzantines replaced these squinches with pendentives, which "were normally constructed of brick with some solid backing to resist the subsequent outward thrust".[325] The semicircular profile dominated the shape of domes, arches and other vaults, which were also mostly built of brick.[326]These techniques made dome construction easier and enabled the building of larger sized domes.

The greatest achievement of Byzantine architecture was Hagia Sophia, Santa Sofia or Divine Wisdom, built between (c. 532 - 537) by Justinian (fig.67). Its huge yet delicate dome was built with bricks and mortar using the pendentive method. This building showed that Byzantine architects and artists had learnt the lesson from the eastern tradition of dome construction.[327] Their Sassanians neighbours constructed domes particularly over their temples and palaces giving them astrological or mystical significance mirroring the cosmic sky. The best and earliest surviving dome is that of the throne room of Palace of Ardeshir mentioned above. Three of the royal rooms of the palace were domed, the throne room is majestic, almost 10 m high crowned with a huge dome built with stones set in mortar and covered by stucco. However, Hagia Sophia marks not the beginning of the golden chapter of Western architecture but its end. Byzantine designers and artisans clearly wanted to close it with such a spectacular edifice as if they sensed the approach of the sweeping darkness of the Dark Ages.

Figure 66 Santa Maria degli Angeli, Rome (306 C.E.)

Figure 67 Hagia Sophia, also known as Santa Sofia or Divine Wisdom, built between (c. 532 - 537) by Justinian

144

Most of the building, whether in walls or domes and vaults, was done in brick in Egypt, Greece and Italy and stone in Syria, Armenia, and Southern France. While the exterior of Byzantine churches remained simple, the interior received careful treatment. Windows were kept small to keep the interior cool and dark for worship, darkness was considered as helping contemplation. The reduction in the size of windows also allowed greater space for walls to be covered with mosaic and painting depicting Bible stories and figures of saints[328]. Byzantine art was fundamentally based on the incorporation of Christian themes into Greek humanism and naturalism. Together, these concepts symbolised and reflected divinity. Man and nature were seen as the image of the divine. This new figurative art was not seeking the aesthetic per se, as in the Greek tradition, but striving to translate concepts of Christian belief such as reincarnation, salvation, and sacrifice.

By the late 5th century, Rome had fallen to pagan Barbarians, Germanic peoples who like locusts, ravaged most of Europe. This marked the end of the Roman and western classical civilisation. Europe entered what is widely known as the Dark Ages, a period dominated by the fragmentation and disintegration of the countries and regions once made the Roman Empire. The Barbaric experience and continuous wars between powerful warlords, knights and barons resulted in the spread of small monarchies and priest-hoods based principally on an agrarian feudal system[329]. These conditions *"formed an ideal medium for the growth of bodies of retainers, and particularly of bodies of armed retainers. Those who felt the need of protection would look for it to their more powerful neighbours, and such protection would involve in return the acceptance of some form of service. The magnates on their side, whether from a desire to play a conspicuous part in political affairs or from the hope of profiting by the political disorder and of establishing or increasing their own power and wealth, needed the services of men who were personally attached to them and whom they could use in private warfare. In extreme case, free men might be prepared to become the slaves of powerful protectors, or the latter might create their own soldiery by arming their slaves."[330]* Some, like Reynolds[331] object to this interpretation denying the existence of slavery[332], but one cannot underestimate the conditions, which make a free man placing *"himself under the protection and at the service of another free man, while maintaining his own free status."[333]* Meanwhile as one would imagine such a bond or deal could not be carried out without any kind of submission ("homage") or allegiance. On their turn, the lords took vassals who adhered to their service; *"they seem always to have been fighting-men par excellence and, as such, to have ranked far above ordinary peasants"[334]*, and in return for their services and allegiance they were awarded with estates and other benefices.

This system of land ownership and control, which characterised the Medieval European economy, played a part in producing deterioration in the living conditions of the European populace and the general degradation of learning and arts. While the few lords acquired most of the land and lived in manor houses, usually fortified castles, the majority of the populations became peasants working the land in return for food and protection and living in simple houses clustered around the gardens and stables of their lord. To make the cluster self-contained, a church and a mill were added giving it the form of an independent village managed and protected by the aristocrat. Ideas of individual rights emphasised by the Greek philosophy, had been replaced by the domination and intimidation of whole populations often endorsed and maintained by the church.

The populations abandoned sophisticated urban life in favour of simple farming in the countryside, quickly losing many of the technical and industrial skills, which once thrived under the Romans. With the depopulation of European cities and the loss of technical skills building activity halted and classical architecture, and its five Orders, was totally lost. Apart from the persistence of a very limited classical style in areas colonised by the Romans and used mainly by the rich, there was a general spread of a variety of local styles consisting mainly of vernacular forms adapted to local geographical and environmental conditions. In northern areas, for example, where wood was available in abundance; the medieval carpenter became the chief builder during this period, erecting wooden houses, churches, and workshops. The shallow pitched roof spread by the Roman colonists, and found mainly in the Mediterranean region, was replaced by the steeply pitched roofs to correspond with the heavy rain and snow fall of the Northern regions. It was often made with local building materials such as thatch, clay tiles, or wooden shingles. Stone building became very rare and relied on small stones and debris. Later, half-timbered buildings were erected consisting mainly of a wooden frame of large timbers connected together with mortise and tenon joints, made by carpenters and filled with daub and brickwork called nogging (seen also in many English timbered cottages).

In the eastern parts of the Roman Empire, in Constantinople, a similar situation was reported. After the early years of the empire when the emperors supported and financed liberal arts as well as public education, by the 7th century such support ceased and education became a luxury attained only by rich individuals who could afford to pay private tutors[335]. Another indicator of the decline of the Byzantine civilisation is the stagnation of intellectual and artistic life, since the 7th century, reflecting the collapse of existing education sources and the lack of innovation and cultural production. Most of what came down from this period were merely writings defending Christianity against the emerging Islam. This can be clearly seen in the writings of John of Damascus (c.750) whose endeavour was to stop the penetration of Muslim ideas, themes and motifs, especially against the hierarchy and iconography, into Christianity. The issue of iconography became so important that it was debated in the Second Council of Nicaea (787), leading to the adoption of standard norms for the depiction of Christ and the saints in church decoration. It designated particular parts of the building to particular personages accompanied by standard iconographic accoutrements and inscriptions. Such measures had a great impact on the character of Byzantine art of the remaining periods[336]. Another aspect showing the decline of the Byzantine culture in this period (between 7th and 9th centuries) was their imitation of Muslim cultural fashions. *"Borrowings from the Muslims are noticeable in this period include the use of prayer rugs, the wearing of turbans by men, the sequestering of women in their own domestic quarters, and the veiling in public"*[337]. Stronger Muslim influence came under the Caliph Harun Al-Rashid, when imitation of Muslim themes extended to palace building as noted in the previous chapter. Later in the 11th century Byzantine scholars adopted Arabic numerals, Muslim astronomy, and mathematics[338].

The Beginning

In the 8th century during the reign of Charlemagne[339], timid efforts were made to revive Europe's cultural and artistic heritage. Muslim influence was felt throughout the whole Carolingian Empire as Charlemagne tried to emulate and compete with Baghdad and Cordoba (fig.68). He too assembled at his court scholars, poets, theologians and teachers from the provinces, and even from Spain and England[340]. He also established schools and wave of learning swept through the Frankish Empire[341.] This revival was chiefly master-minded by three influential scholars; Theodolfus (d.821), Claudius (d.c.839) and Agobardus (d.840), all of whom had contacts with Muslim learning as they were Goths born or educated in Spain or Southern France. The three pioneers were behind the rise of the spiritual reform as they spoke against the "worship" of images and relics, a doctrine, which was generally adopted by the Spanish church, influenced by Muslim teaching of iconoclasm against images and their use. Haines wrote about this issue and asserted that: *"The great Iconoclastic reform, which arose in the East, undoubtedly received its originating impulse from the Moslems. In 719, the Khalif destroyed all images in Syria. His example was followed in 730 by the Eastern Emperor, Leo the Isaurian. He is said to have been persuaded to this measure by a man named Bezer, who had been some years in captivity among the Saracens. In 754, the great council of Constantinople condemned images. Unfortunately, neither the great patriarchates nor the Pope were represented, and so this council never obtained-the sanction of all Christendom; and its decrees were reversed in 787 at the Council of Nicæa. In 790 appeared the Libri Carolini, in which we rejoice to find our English Alcuin helping Charles the Great to make a powerful and reasonable protest against the worship of images. In 794, this protest was upheld by the German Council of Frankfurt. But the Pope, and his militia, the monks, made a strenuous opposition to any reform in this quarter, and the recognition of images became part and parcel of Roman Catholic Christianity.*"[342]

Theodolfus, Bishop of Orléans (South France),[343] a learnt scholar, theologian and a poet, was born in Muslim Spain[344]. Charlemagne sent him to Narbonne and Provence as *missus dominicus*, or envoy of the Lord, with the aim of developing learning and establishing schools. "*After Theodolfus had developed and improved the schools, Charlemagne, and later Hugh Capet* (King of France, founder of the Capetian dynasty), *sent thither their eldest sons as pupils. These institutions were at the height of their fame from the eleventh century to the middle of the thirteenth. Their influence spread as far as Italy and England whence students came to them*"[345]. He wrote *Libri Carolini* in which he attacked the practice of paying religious honour to images as idolatry[346]. His knowledge of Muslims does not stop at his birthplace but must have extended to his studies. He showed this acquaintance when he wrote describing the bribes the Frankish judges used to get from people trying to influence them: "*The people eagerly offered gifts, thinking that, if they gave, whatever they wanted would be done... One offered both crystal and gems from the east if I should contrive to get possession of another's fields. Another brought a large number of fine golden coins which were struck with Arabic letters and characters, and coins of white silver imprinted with Roman stamp, if only he might procure a farm, a land, a house.*"[347]

Claudius, as Bishop of Turin, was born and bred in Muslim Spain. He was a leading scholar in the court of King Louis the Pious (reigned 814 to 840), the son and successor of Charlemagne, in Chasseneuil near Poitiers (France)[348]. His literary achievement was in writing a commentary on Genesis at the request of King Louis himself and he taught at Ebreuil in Auvergne, a southern French region close to Spain known for its connections with Andalusian Muslims. Like Theodolfus, Claudius was famous for attacking the church for a number of excesses, especially the worship of images, relics, pilgrimage to Rome, intercession of the saints, and the adoration of the cross and other visible symbols of Christ's life[349]. Claudius was accused by his opponents of admiring Islam and according to Haines "*Of the relations of Claudius to the Saracens we have the direct statement of one of his opponents, who said that the Jews praised him, and called him the wisest among the Christians; and that he on his side highly commended them _and the Saracens.*"[350]

Agobardus or Agobar was born somewhere in Spain, sometime in year 769, a year after the Muslims lost Narbonne[351] He too found a respectable place at the court of Charlemagne. He led a crusade against the worship of images, witchcraft, superstition, and ascription of tempests to magic sources.[352] He is thought to have angered by the conversion of bishop Bodo (born c. 814) to Judaism that he spoke critically of the Jews accusing them of converting Christians and selling them as slaves to Arabs in Spain.[353] Bodo was the palace deacon to Louis the Pious when he converted and migrated to live in Muslim Saragossa under the name of Eleazar.[354]

The Abbasid relations with the Carolingian Empire started with Pepin III, the father of Charlemagne, who was approached by the Abbasid Caliph Jaafar al-Masur to help them against the Umayyads in Spain who established their state in Cordoba after losing it in Baghdad. A witness of these relations was the ambassadorial mission Pepin III sent to Baghdad in 765 CE[355]. Charlemagne did not only maintain this relationship but developed it further through various ambassadorial missions and gifts exchanged between him and Harun al-Rashid (786-809 CE); also, known in Western circles as Aaron the Just. For example, among the items the ambassadorial delegation of Harun al-Rashid at the end of 8th century presented Charlemagne with an Oliphant[356] which became known as Oliphant of Charlemagne, now kept in the treasury at Aachen[357]. It was this Oliphant that Roland blew when he was fatally wounded in the battle against the "Saracens" according to the epic Songs of Roland[358]. Harun also gifted him an elephant, known as Abu al-Abbas[359], which according to the Frankish Annals died at Luppenheim on Luneburg Heath as Charlemagne took him with him into this battle. The famous clepsydra, water clock, which struck the hours and had moving figures was another present of Harun al-Rashid. The event was reported by Eginhard *sub anno* 806[360]. Another delegation arrived from Baghdad with a musical organ, which is thought to have been brought by a certain Jaafar in 807 CE.[361] The organ was not the only musical instrument to reach the Frankish Kingdom. According to some sources, Pepin III and Charlemagne introduced a number of Muslim musical instruments with which they developed and expanded the use of the type of church music, known as "Gregorian chant", into Europe. Schlesinger[362] is adamant that these instruments came from Spain or Sicily. She pointed out that the instruments portrayed in the Evangelarium of St. Medard (8th century) and the Lothair, Aureum and Labeo Notker Psalters (9th & 10th centuries) were all Oriental instruments derived from the Egyptian or older

Asiatic civilisation and disseminated into Europe mainly through the Muslims. Historians also relate that the beginning of the 800s saw the first translation of Arabic works, carried out at the monastery of Santa Maria de Ripoll (Spain). The Mozarabic monks sent their translations north to the abbeys of Cluny and St. Gall.

There is also evidence that these relations extended to include trade. According to the Italian historian Giosuè Musca, Charlemagne sent "Frisian" cloths to Baghdad to correct a "balance-of-payments" problem caused by western tastes for 'Abbasid silks, rock crystal, and other luxury objects[363]. The Swedish historian and numismatist Sture Bolin made further elaboration on the subject. After studying a large number of coins that had hoarded by the Vikings in Scandinavia and Russia, he concluded that without Muhammad's trade there could be no Charlemagne, contrary to the views of Pierenne[364]: *"an examination of the hoards from Carolingian times will show fairly directly how close the connections were between the Frankish and Arab worlds."*[365] What reached us from Muslim coins during the Carolingian Empire is only a fraction of what was exchanged in the Frankish kingdom because most of them were either melted by the church or simply used in other commodities. In his study, which was presented as a scholarship thesis in the 1930's, Sture demonstrated that not only the design, weight and value of Charlemagne's coin were determined by contemporary Islamic silver coinage but coin reforms were also based on an Islamic model[366]. On his part, Maurice Lombard showed how Muslim gold reached Europe in exchange of timber, fur and minerals concluding that it was due to this trade relationship between Islam and Europe that the economic revival of Europe came about[367]. Hitti reached similar conclusion as he confirmed, *"Arab money was in use in the Christian kingdoms of the north, which foe nearly four hundred years had no coinage other than Arabic or French.*[368]"

Another piece of evidence relates to King Offa, Charlemagne's contemporary, who exchanged letters with Charlemagne and exchanged ambassadors with the Caliph of Baghdad, all indicative of the existence of trade and political relations between Europe and the early Muslim Caliphate. Further evidence of these relations and the influence of Muslims are the copies, which King Offa made of a Dinar, struck in 774 by Caliph Al-Mansur of Baghdad and dated 157 in the Hijri Calendar. A unique example in the British Museum of a gold mancus (that is, 30d) of Offa shows that the coin was made by an European die-cutter who got the Arabic inscription on the coin's obverse side upside-down when inserting Offa's name; errors an Arabic craftsman would have avoided.

Figure 68 Charlemagne's Palatine Chapel at Aachen (790-805 CE), a marvel of Carolingian Europe shows a great similarity to the Dome of the Rock. The interior of the central space, organised in an eight-sided octagon covered with a dome raised on eight black and white polychrome arches and decorated with plant motifs and a band of calligraphy, is a clear adaptation of the interior space surrounding the Rock in the Dome of the Rock.

By the approach of the millennium, the achievements of Charlemagne were forfeited as Europe entered a period of anxiety and uncertainty. It was haunted by the predictions of the supposedly inevitable apocalypse and the end of the world. These beliefs hindered any revival especially in building activities, as they were considered futile and populations were engaged in saving themselves from this doom by giving up their belongings to their saviour, the Church and its ally the aristocracy. Perhaps the burning down in three hours of Charlemagne's wooden bridge across the River Rhine at Mainz, which took him ten years to build,[369] summarises the fate of the Carolingian revival.

The cultural and intellectual stagnation was rightly described by Colish: "*Beset by new Magyar and Viking invasions and the replacement of central by localised institutions, tenth century intellectuals could do little but tread water until political and economic life became more stable.*"[370] In the late 900s, in a time when Muslim Spain contained more than 70 public libraries and at least 17 universities, Europe did not have a single public library and only two universities[371]. Another element, which created great obstacles in Europe's return to Greek knowledge, was the substitution of the Greek language with the Latin, which made Greek texts and books inaccessible to students. Indeed, the Greek language "*ceased to be cultivated in the West; and this circumstance is of some importance in the history of astronomy* (as well as other sciences); *for we have seen that this science was almost completely neglected in Italy (and Europe): those who wished to cultivate it were necessarily obliged to have recourse to Greek authors... during the middle ages, the little learning that existed in Western Europe was confined entirely to a knowledge of the Latin language: the works of Ptolemy* (and other classical scholars) *were a sealed book for the few learned men (if they may deserve the name) of those days.*"[372]

The Revival of the 11th -12th Centuries

By the beginning of the 11th century, Europeans had discovered the error of the Millennium predictions and subsequently a new desire and approach to life were sought. Their rulers understood that the new approach must be established on firm scientific knowledge rather than mythology, giving a new breath to the revival of Europe. Europe slowly entered a period of relative stability enabling some kind of cultural recovery; France was under Capetian rule,[373] Germany and Italy under the Ottonians[374] and England under the Anglo-Saxons. First, there was the reform of monastic life under the leadership of the monastery of Cluny, which was founded in 909 with a new governance structure for monasticism.[375] One of the most important aspects of the Cluniac order was the promotion of the pilgrimage to Santiago Compostella in Northern Spain, close to the border with Muslim al-Andalus. Cluny began the process of erecting priories all over Europe and transmitting its principles and its style of liturgical art and music. There are many indications, which suggest that the reform of Cluny was closely connected with the influence of Muslim al-Andalus. The monastery is located in southern France strategically situated between Muslim Sicily and al-Andalus. Because of this proximity, considerable cultural exchange was established between the two worlds of Islam and Christianity[376]. There are at least two pieces of evidence suggesting such a connection; the Arabic numerals found in Pseudo-Odo of Cluny tract entitled "*Regulae Domni Oddonis super abacum*"[377], and the use of a number of Muslim architectural and decorative elements, such as the pointed arch, corbels, and arabesque in the building of the church (see next chapter).

Second, Europe launched a crusade for learning and the lands of Islam became the pole of destination for European students and scholars. This coincided with the establishment of the Ottonian empire in Germany under which literature and arts grew significantly so that some historians speak of the Ottonian renaissance. Among the leaders of this revival, we find the distinguished Gerbert of Aurillac (940-1003) who played a leading role in the introduction of scientific thought in Europe. He reinvented the teaching curriculum of the cathedral school giving particular emphasis to logic and reflective thinking. He was the first to introduce instruments into the teaching of arithmetic, astrology and geometry[378]. He was also behind the introduction of abacus[379] and Arabic numerals[380] into Europe, which he used in calculation and the astrolabe in astronomical research, were particularly influential. A former pupil of Gerbert named Bernelius (c.990) employed Arabic numerals in his work "*Cita et vera divisio monochordi in diatonico genere*".[381]

Colish (1997) established the Muslim origin of Gerbert's innovations indicating that: "*In Gerbert's case we see new material added to the curriculum thanks to his importation of scientific advances from Muslim Spain*"[382]. Gerbert studied at an early stage under the direction of Bishop Atto of Vich, some 60 km north of Barcelona[383], and probably also at the nearby Monastry of Santa Maria de Ripoll in the tenth century.[384] Later he undertook parts of his studies, if not all of them, in the Muslim world, in the universities of Cordoba[385] (al-Andalus) and al-Qarawiyyin in Fez[386] (Morocco). He is also known to have travelled in al-Andalus and worked for a Muslim patron from whom he was accused, by a Christian legend, of stealing a book of magic and seducing his daughter[387]. On his return in 969, Gerbert made a pilgrimage to Rome with the Count Borrell and the bishop of Vic who introduced him to Pope John XIII (965-971) and the emperor Otto I (r.962-973), who was visiting the area[388]. The pope persuaded Otto, king of Germany (Ottonian dynasty) to employ Gerbert as tutor for his son and grandson, the future Otto II (r.973-983) and Otto III (r.983-1002). He later taught at Rheims and in Ravenna before being named Pope Sylvester II by Otto III of Germany. That is how Muslim science and art entered the court of the Ottonians making a clear impact on the development of these subjects in their kingdom.

Gerbert's influence extended to France and the rest of Europe. He taught the famous Fulbert (c.970-1028) at Rheims as well as Adalboldus (d.1027) and Bernelius (c.990). Fulbert or Fulbertus founded the famous school at Chartres in France, which drew students from all over Europe but especially from England, Germany and Italy. Thus, Muslim learning was present in Chartres through Fulbert and others as well as through the presence of many Muslim books, belonging to Thierry of Chartres, in its library[389]. Further evidence was traced in the work of William of Conches (ca.1080-1154), another principal teacher at Charters who wrote a treatise "Philosophia" or Philosophia Dragmaticon on astronomy and physiology. His borrowing from Arabic sources was observed by Prioreschi who confirmed "*The most important innovation by William in his Philosophia and in his annotations to the Timaeus was the use of texts that had recently been translated from Arabic, largely by Constantinus Africanus, namely the Isagoge and the Pantegni*"[390]

Third as medieval Christendom confronted Islam in military crusades in Spain and the Holy Land greater contact was directly established between the two cultures. As Muslims were pushed south from Poitiers and back beyond the Pyrenees, treasures left behind them from various original Arabic works of science and philosophy as well as translations of Greek works were claimed by the Franks. The fall of many Muslim held territories such as Sicily (1060) in Italy, Toledo (1085) in Spain and Jerusalem (1099) in the East to the Christians was the turning point for the fortunes of Europe. There is a consensus among historians that the fall of the city of Toledo, with one of the finest libraries in Islam, was particularly important. Among the first occupiers were Christian monks who confiscated all the content of its many libraries and employed Jewish and Muslim scholars to translate Arab and Arab translated works into Latin. Sources indicate a number of Christian translation centres spread in south Europe. The Spanish were key players Christian intellectuals and clerics of Castile, Asturia, Aragon and Navarra had direct access to the treasures of cultural centres of al-Andalus, especially after the Reconquista of Toledo (1085), Saragosaa (1118), Bajadoz (1228), Huela (1248), and Seville(1248) which opened up the Muslim Arab learning centres.[391] They established translation centres in Tarazona in Aragon, in Toledo under Raymond Lull, in Seville by Alfonso X and Barcelona and Catalona (Ripoll). The Italians and Germans established their translation centre in Sicily at the court of Frederick II. The French established their translation centre in Cluny under the leadership of Peter the Venerable, the Abbot of Cluny, (1094-1156) who was assisted by a mysterious Muslim named Muhammed.[392] French cultural centres like Perpignan, Narbonne, Nimes and Toulouse also were active in the translation from Arabic into old French language, namely the vernacular Langue d'Oc, and later formed transmission belts of Arabic learning[393]. The English did not have a translation centre until 13th century when Arabic language was, according to Tytler Patrick Fraser, one of the fashionable subject taught at Oxford.[394] English scholars, however, journeyed between these translations centres. The English monarchy publically supported the translation effort when Edward I invited Raymond Lull to visit England. In this way, Arabic learning and science reached major centres of Europe, sparking the European 11th and 12-century intellectual revival.

Among the translators, one can mention the Italian Gerard of Cremona (1114-1187), who was one of the most influential scholars responsible for popularising Arabic learning in Europe. He spent more than fifty years in al-Andalus, mostly in Cordoba devoting himself to the pursuit of Arabic learning. Historic sources reported that he knew or met there visiting scholars including the English Daniel of Morley, and Spanish John of Seville. Gerard translated more than sixty Arabic works including the Canon of Ibn Sina, Liber Trium Fratrum of Banu Musa, Almagest of Ptolemy, Liber Azaragui de Ccirurgia from al-Tasrif of Al-Zahrawi, De Scientis of al-Farabi and many others.

On the role of Gerard of Cremona Briffault wrote: *"....was the most industrious among the popularizers of Arab literature, he spent fifty years fifty years at Cordova and brought forth no less than sixty translations, among which the Almagest, and the Astronomy of al-Haitham."*[395] Most of these gigantic works reached European teaching institutions establishing the foundations of most of their curricula. *"The evolution of the university curriculum during the thirteenth and fourteenth centuries reveals the slow but sure penetration of many of Gerard's translations, which nourished the awakened interests in natural science until the end of the Middle Ages."*[396] His works Haskins reckoned that: *"More of Arabic science in general passed into Western Europe at the hands of Gerard of Cremona than in any other way"*[397].

Michael Scott (ca. 1175-1232) learnt Arabic at Oxford and then went to Paris and Padua before joining Toledo in 1207. There were rumours that he met Averroes in Cordoba, *"It is not improbable that the reputation which Michael brought into Spain, assisted by a congenial passion for the same studies, may have led to a meeting between Averroes and the Scottish philosopher...it is difficult to believe that Michael should have left Toledo without visiting the most learned scholar of the most learned university in the country."*[398] His reputation as a wizard was based on his knowledge of the philosophy and science, the astronomy, alchemy.[399] Michael Scott joined the translation centre at the Court of Emperor Frederick II, where he worked on numerous projects including the astronomical treatise of al-Bitruji *On the Sphere*, and Ibn Sina *de animalibus*. He left Frederick for Germany where he worked on the dissemination of his Arabic based knowledge before returning to his native country England to be received at the court of King Edward I.[400]

In addition to these examples Hermann of Carinthia, Hugh of Santalla, Mark of Toledo, Burgandia of Pisa Robert of Chester (1140) John of Seville Sacrobosto (1200-1236). By the end of the 12th century, much of the Arab and ancient heritage was again available to the Latin West. Europe before rediscovering its Greek heritage discovered the Muslim (Arabic) heritage first. The translation work "*descended on the barren scientific soil of Europe. The effect was that of a fertilising rain*[401]" Many of these works were unfortunately claimed by their translators as their own and therefore the extent of the influence of Arabic learning goes well beyond what was established above. Ibn Abdun, a writer of the period wrote, "*Books of science ought not to be sold to Jews or Christians, except those that treat of their own religion. Indeed, they translate books of science and attribute authorship to their coreligionists or to their bishops, when they are the work of Muslims*" [402]

The Rise of Scholasticism

The results of frequent waves of scholars visiting Cordoba and other Muslim universities as well as the voluminous books captured through various crusades started to appear as early as the 11th century, which saw the first signs of intellectual rebirth. The process of change started in ecclesiastical institutions, which were under enormous pressures from the rational thinking presented by the philosophy of Ibn Sina (Avicenna), Ibn Rushd (Averroes) and Al-Ghazali (Algazel). Seeing the popularity of these works among scholars and some of its clergy, the church at first condemned and banned them[403], provoking it to seek rational solutions for Christian doctrines to defend them against Islam. Despite the intellectual development this step created, adequate answers to stop the rise of the numerous difficult questions Muslim philosophy raised for the Christians were hard to find, and the defeat of the church was inevitable. At the end, the idea became to Christianise such works to solve the problem "*and effect a reconciliation between philosophy and theology, between reason and faith, by providing that scientific system which theology had been seeking since the early ages of the Church. To do this it was necessary to get back to the primitive text, then to purge the authentic thought of Aristotle of its pagan errors ... In this last task the Arab commentators could be utilized.*"[404] Therefore, much of these explanations followed the Muslim lead and sometimes used similar arguments. Such imitation started with Peter Abelard (1079-1142) whose efforts had been to fit the new science and logic, filtering in from Muslim sources, with the Christian belief, especially in issues relating to the incarnation and the trinity[405]. His tragic condemnation shows the struggle for acceptance of the new ideas, "*the tragedy of Abelard was that of a sincere seeker for a new apologetic to fit the new science and logic which was filtering in from Jewish and Muslim sources*"[406]. Abelard found no refuge except with his friend, Peter the Venerable, he too pursued similar endeavour to defend rationally Christianity. He even studied Islam and made a translation of the Quran in an attempt to find faults.[407]

157

Hermann the Dalmatian (1110-1154) studied in Chartres with his English friend Robert of Ketton at the hands of Thierry of Chartres where he acquired basics of philosophy. After Chartres, he travelled with Ketton to the Orient to Constantinople and Damascus where they discovered Muslim science. Around 1138 the pair returned to Toledo (Spain), where they studied astronomy based on Arabic texts and later joined the translation school of Peter the Venerable (Petrus Venerabilis) whom they met in 1142.[408] Hermann's legacy was fifteen works that were *"of vital importance for the systematic study and advancement of natural science in the West. His original work of exceptional significance is De esentiis (1143) in which he offered an original synthesis of Arabic Aristotelianism and Platonism of the Chartres school of philosophy. He translated Euclid's Elements, Ptolemy's Planisphe- re, Abu Ma'Shar's A General Introduction to Astronomy, Koran, and some other Islamic religious manuscripts."*[409]

A century later, we can still trace the Muslim influence on European scholastics. Albert the Great, or Albertus Magnus (ca.1200-1280), who familiarized himself with all the works of the Arabs and Jews[410], constantly refers in his works to a number of Muslim authors. The influence of Avicenna is quite visible in his De Animalibus that one writer commented, *"Similarly, in his zoological treatise De Animalibus, which is based on Aristotle and Avicenna, Albert made many new observations and gave detailed descriptions of all the fish, birds, animals, and insects which he had encountered on his journeying on foot through Germany, France and Italy."*[411] Avicenna's work was made available in Latin in 1200, fifteen years later, copies of these translations appeared in the universities of Paris and Oxford.[412]

His pupil Thomas Aquinas (1224-1273) followed his footsteps in pursuing Muslim approaches and explanations. He affirms this as he justifies borrowing from the Muslims defending it by quoting St. Augustine who says, *"If those who are called philosophers said by chance anything that was and is consistent with our faith, we must claim it from them as unjust possessors"*[413]. Professor Ghazanfar found strong evidence that Aquinas economic thought discussed in his Summa Theologica evolved from his use and contacts with Arabic sources and al-Ghazali's thought, which was made available in a Latin translation of his work Ihya Ulum al-Din made before 1150[414] while Hammond thought he derived it from al-Farabi.[415]This Muslim connection brought him condemnation at first but later he was reconciled with his enemies to become one of the Doctors of the Western church.[416].

The examples of these above scholars are not unique in showing the interaction between Islamic philosophy and ideas and a section of European scholars who learnt about Islam from a distance without having direct contact with its civilisation. For those scholars who did have some direct contacts with Islam the influence was deeper. This is how Benedictine Adelard of Bath (1075-1160), who toured Salerno and Sicily during the Norman rule, Syria and the Crusader state in the Levant and Spain before returning to England,[417] summarised the lesson he learnt from his Muslim teachers: "*I was taught by my Arab masters to be led only by reason*". This at a time when European scholars "*were taught to follow the halter of the captured image of ancient authority*", that is the authority of the church[418]. He was resolute on introducing this reason into his country and Europe, bringing with him, according to Briffault, from Cordoba a large collection of books and much doctrine, which he and his nephew actively spread abroad in France and England.[419]

His compatriot Roger Bacon (1214-1294) condemned Europe for ignorance because it could not properly understand Arabic science. He is credited with being the father of modern experimental science in Europe, but Briffault reiterated the real contribution of Bacon, ''*Neither Roger Bacon nor later namesake has any title to be credited with having introduced the experimental method. Roger Bacon was no more than one of apostles of Muslim Science and Method to Christian Europe; and he never wearied of declaring that knowledge of Arabic and Arabic Sciences was for his contemporaries the only way to true knowledge. Discussion as to who was the originator of the experimental method...are part of the colossal misinterpretation of the origins of European civilization. The experimental method of Arabs was by Bacon's time widespread and eagerly cultivated throughout Europe.*''[420] Dressed as an Arab, Bacon travelled through various learning centres of Muslim Spain. He returned first to Paris to teach natural philosophy.[421]

The list of scholars having similar indebtedness to Islam goes beyond those few singled out above[422], but their stories establish beyond any doubt that the establishment of rational scholasticism was made under the pressures and influence of Islam rationalism, especially Averroism, which rocked the whole of Europe, starting first in Paris then to the universities of Padua and Bologna[423]. The outcome was that *"These developments created a climate of opinion in the scientific community that made it possible for scientists to do more than make discoveries along the line of their Muslim or Greek predecessors."*[424]

The Rise of Universities and other Learning Institutions

The scholarly priorities launched, since the 12th century, led to the emergence of a new kind of scholastic literature and pedagogical approaches. These developments necessitated new institutional structures gradually shifting creativity from the traditional monastic to cathedral schools. Unlike the former, which were limited to students of the particular order, cathedral schools enjoyed an international reputation drawing students from all over Europe. They also produced independent liberal thinkers, who surpassed the monastic scholars in their intellectual.[425] In the words of Walsh: *"To the Arabs we owe the foundation of a series of institutions for the higher learning."*[426]

One of the leading institutions was Chartres, a French cathedral school, which acquired a distinguished reputation, especially under the leadership of the chancellor Thierry, paving the way for the foundations of the renaissance[427]. Charters in the twelfth century had numerous Arabic books including medical treatises[428]as well as many of the translations made by the translating school of Toledo. French priests who accompanied French knights and crusaders were the first to lay hands on Arab manuscripts of the Toledo library and made translations of others. *"They were the first to turn the military victories into intellectual use. So the schools of France –in Charters first, then in Paris- benefited from the work of those Spanish translators and their libraries welcomed the new books"*[429]

The connection between cathedral school of Chartres and Islamic learning has been also related to its chancellor Thierry of Chartres in the 1140's. He taught his students a new revolutionary concept based on the compatibility of the scientific approach with the story of creation in the Bible, in other words religion no longer contradicted science. This shows how courageous Thierry was despite his outraged critics. In his support, Goldstein writes, *"Someday Thierry will be recognised as one of the true founders of Western science"*[430]. This emerging European scientific spirit found answers in Muslim books, which Thierry was ambitious to collect. While chancellor he is known to have commissioned the translation of Arabic books and incorporated numerous volumes into his personal library, Library of the Seven Libreral Arts.[431]

Benedict of Norcia founded the famous Monte Cassino cathedral school in 529 CE. The abbey gained its reputation as an intellectual focal point, situated at the crossroads of the European, Greek, and Arabic cultures,[432] under the direction of Abbot Desiderius between 1058 and 1087. Since then *"it played an important role in the history of Western culture in general and of medicine in particular."*[433] This was directly attributed to the migration of the famous scholar Constantinus Africanus (1010-1087). A Tunisian physician and scholar who was either a

Christian, from North African Christian communities, or converted from Islam[434] During his monastic years, Constantinus completed numerous translations of Arabic medical texts into Latin, more than 26 major works,[435] many of which went to become principal text books read in most European universities in years to come. Constantinus and his work were also behind Salerno and its reputation as a European centre for medical science. According to legend, Salerno medical school was founded by four masters; a Saracen Adela or Abdellah, a Jewish Rabbi Elinus or Ilyas, a Greek Pontus and a native of Salerno, each of whom lectured in his native language.[436] In addition to his teaching, his writings and translations were *"used for the teaching and study of medicine until well into the sixteenth century, that is, for about half a millennium."*[437] On other hand, they contributed to most of the works that appeared in Europe during much of the 12th and 13th centuries. His *Antidotorium*, for example, was a source of many of the prescriptions found in the Salernitan *Antidotarium Nicolai*. Another medical work known as the Viaticum circulated widely throughout Europe's academic institutions. It became a seminal work in almost all European medical curricula, and it remained the most widely read source until a translation of the Avicenna's Canon in the sixteenth century.[438] Thus, the theory linking the rise of Salerno school to Monte Cassino and Constantinus Africanus is well founded, as the school is no more than eighty miles away from the cathedral.[439]

The cathedral schools gave way to universities towards the end of the 12th century, although they were not granted recognised charters until the late 13th century. Paris established its first university in 1200 to be followed by other regions leading to the emergence of Oxford, Montpellier, Salerno and Bologna. The appearance of faculties such as medicine, arts and theology in particular reflects the stream of ideas coming from Muslim sources[440]. In chapter four Goldstein describes how the rich store of ancient manuscripts discovered by the Arabs became available through military conquest in Spain, just as the West was ready to receive them. Such a statement gives us only one side of the truth, as one cannot imagine crusaders selecting ancient "classic" manuscripts and rejecting original Muslim works.

One authority having much to say on the development of European universities and learning in general, was Julian Ribera y Tarrago whose work Disertaciones Y Opusculos[441] represents a leader in the subject. Makdisi[442] who studied the work outlined a number of important facts about the influence of Muslim universities on European ones. There are a number of features, which connected the rise of European universities to the Muslims. The first element is the swiftness in which these universities appeared and propagated, and the absence of any gradual transformation of the organisation of studies and much of these early universities appeared in France, Italy and Spain, areas in proximity to al-

Andalus. The second factor is related to the administrative and organisational nature of these universities, which displayed, in many cases, contrasting tendencies duality as if they were following a system of two distinct civilisations; the Muslim system and old Christian one. Finally, education credentials adopted by these universities had no precedent in earlier traditions but were prevalent in the Muslim educational institutions where it has been known and used for three or four centuries in that form.

There are at least two examples demonstrating that Muslim universities served as models for the rising universities in Europe. King Alfonso VIII (1155-1214) of Castile, who issued, in 1175, a Christian coin with Arabic script, copying the coins of the recently conquered Emirs of Murcia, founded the University of Palencia in Spain in 1208 C.E. King Alfonso, in imitation of Prince Abd Allah, called himself "Prince of the Catholics" and invoked the assistance of God[443]. The Pope was named "Imam of the Catholics"[444]. Finally, the verses quoted from the Bible imitated the use of Qur'anic verses on the Islamic coin. Such coins were called morabetinos or maravedis, the name in Spanish of the gold dinars of the Almoravids (al-Murabitun).[445]

The second example involves the universities built by Emperor Frederick II (1194-1250), who was nick named the "second of the two baptised sultans of the Sicilian throne"[446], the first being King Roger II (ruled 1130-1154). Frederick II received some of his education at the hands of the Muslims,[447] became a friend of sultans of Egypt, Tunisia and Syria, had at his court the Cordoban scholar and Arabic translator Michael Scot and another scholar translator from Antioch, Theodore the Philosopher. Frederick II is also known to have cared for Averroes two children.[448] Because of this, Pope Innocent III at the Council of Lyon, attributed Frederick's own heresy to his association with heretics while to Frederick II they were simply scholars and learned men. It was Frederick II who built the university of Naples in 1224 C.E, then Messina and Padua remodelling them from Muslim universities and equipping them with a considerable collection of Arabic and translated books. He also re-established the old medical school of Salerno. Salerno, Europe's earliest University, was established around the tenth century formerly a Medical School,[449] owing its foundation to "*its southern Italian location and its proximity to Muslim medicine,*"[450] as well as to the three scholars mentioned earlier. As already noted above, the North African scholar Constantine the African (c. 1020-1087) had taught at the school and by his translation of medical works from Arabic had helped disseminate Arabic learning and reintroduce Greek medicine to Christian Europe. The university reached its highest apogee at the end of the twelfth century, under the dedication of Emperor Frederick II, who was renowned for his Arabism.

Montpellier, in southern France, in proximity to Muslim Spain, also had an emphasis on medicine mostly from Muslim sources in addition to astronomy and law and if Muslims had nothing to do with its foundation, they certainly had some influence on its medical reputation "*Its location close to Muslim Spain also explains its medical eminence*" says Colish[451]. This location proximity resulted in a large presence of learned Muslims, Mozarabs[452] and, above all, Jews with Islamic learning.[453]

French universities, Paris in particular, were generally over stated for their influence on the rise of Oxford University, which itself gave birth to Cambridge, the first two English Universities. The seed idea, however, can be attributed to Muslims and the English scholars returning from Cordoba. Sources indicate that the origins of Oxford University go back to the school first established King Henry I (c.1068-1135), who was a literary man and fond of Oxfordshire. In 1114, he built a hunting place at Woodstock, and in 1130, he finished his Palace of Beaumont[454]. Henry I grew fond of courtly scholars that he summed them at his service, among them was Abelard of Bath (1080-1160) who after returning from his journey in the East, Syria and Antioch, and Spain was employed at the King's Exchequer.[455] Adelard soon was followed by Daniel of Morley (c.1140-c.1210), who was not satisfied with what he learnt in Paris he decided to travel into Spain to collect books and perfect himself in mathematics[456]. In Toledo, he was involved in translation work before returning to England equipped with Muslim books and learning to teach at Oxford.[457] Although neither there are nor does historical record show that Adelard and Morley were involved in the foundation of Oxford but they must have influenced the emergence of the idea of the university or behind its foundation in 1220[458].

The Rise of the New Church Building: 11th-13th Centuries Europe (The Romanesque and Gothic)

The impact of all the above events on European architecture was overwhelming. After more than five centuries (from 500-1000) of stagnation and decline following the collapse of the Roman Empire, suddenly, at the start of the eleventh century, European art began to flourish, coinciding with the beginning of the Muslim inspired intellectual development described in the above section. Becoming the educational, intellectual as well as the spiritual source for a largely illiterate population, the church received gifts, contributions and endowments enabling it to accumulate substantial wealth most of which was spent on building new churches. In other cases, the building was associated with feudal and royal patrons who dedicated countless churches and priories as part of their alliance and allegiance. Above all, the church emphasised its role as a refuge against all sorts of danger especially from the worlds of spirits and devils. Such a role could be read from the architectural decoration of this period where much of church art- work emphasises the element of fear. Romanesque churches incorporated strange sculptures of monsters, devils, dragons and terrifying animals and humans. Therefore, the style of the new churches expressed hope and salvation, which were expressed in the verticality phenomenon. The revival of the style of Roman basilica and the use of the semi-circular arches, as well as the large size, were elements in asserting this authority.

One of the most important structural developments of the Romanesque era was the vault. The wholesale barbarian burning of the customary wooden made churches was behind the adoption of vaulting and the use of brick and stone in the construction. In countries of southern France and Italy, the dome was adopted for the crossing and in other instances, a tower was added to carry the bell, which indicated worship time or served as a warning from danger.[459] Towards the end of the 11th century, ribs, in the form of arches --of brick or stone- were added to support the barrel vault. These features had been in use in the Islamic world since the eighth century and in the southern European region, in the architectural splendours of al-Andalus, Sicily and North Africa. It has been acknowledged that such developments were not coincidental but followed a pattern of systematic borrowing covering not only science and technology as illustrated above, but extending to all aspects of life including art and architecture. Further evidence is that the Romanesque style first emerged in southern Europe, Italy and France, countries sharing boundaries with Muslim Spain and Sicily. This theory will be elaborated in the following sections.

The Romanesque style was spread through the *monastic orders*, the dominant religious power of the time. Orders competed against each other physically as well spiritually, owning and erecting large number of churches and priories, often transcending frontiers and borders. The Benedictine order and the reformed Benedictine rule of Cluny had followers all over Europe, and their churches were built in the same manner as the mother church. The orders also promoted pilgrimages by acquiring relics of saints for their churches, a system which ensured the visits of thousands of people every season and brought wealth to the churches visited. One of the most important pilgrimage sites is the church of Saint James at Santiago de Compostela in North West Spain, which is believed to contain the remains of the apostle, St. James. Pilgrims travelling to these sites spread the elements of the Romanesque style as they travelled and hundreds of churches were built along the pilgrimage routes offering spiritual guidance, accommodation and general rest and care to pilgrims.

The Romanesque style continued to define most European architecture, especially religious architecture, until the 13th century when early traces of the Gothic style emerged in France. The beginning of the 11th century was marked by the ultimate dominance of the church, especially after the unification of the western church, under the leadership of Rome. The 11th century also brought life again to European cities, a number of thriving cities emerged such as Amalfi, and Venice reached highest positions in the urban hierarchy due to their economic and cultural growth Historians clearly demonstrated that these towns had the greatest contacts with the Muslim world, especially North Africa.

European architects and masons made giant steps forward in both understanding the rules of static and load bearing as well as the technology of building. The introduction of piers, the pointed arch and rib vaulting as structural solutions to deal with the problems of the support of thrust and the achievement of considerable height and span were the achievements of the period. Instead of using columns of limited height and spanning the space between them with beams, as commonly used in the Greek and Roman traditions, the Gothic masons built piers as high as they wished and ran thin ribs up from one pier, across the space, to the one on the other side. The space between these ribs was filled with non-load bearing masonry, revolutionising Romanesque vaulting. To lighten this vast interior, large windows of stained glass were incorporated into these high walls, transforming the pre-Romanesque and Romanesque notion of worship in darkness. Light became a sign of the Divine and its presence therefore an aid to contemplation, a concept developed by Muslims at least a century before. However, this feature caused weakened the walls, which then had to be supported by flying buttresses, another structural invention which transmitting the thrust from the wall to the ground. These developments gave the church its highest physical domination on the built landscape. Meanwhile, Gothic art shifted from the sculpture of fear to the depiction of Bible and Gospel stories, which appeared as paintings covering the walls and in stained glass windows and as carvings incorporating human figures on portals and porches[460]. During the 14th and 15th centuries, the rise of wealthy merchants who commissioned domestic buildings played a part in expanding the Gothic style beyond religious buildings. Scholars have established the Muslim influence on the emergence and execution of Gothic architecture. The employment of elements such as the pointed arch and the ribbed vaulting, were both developed in Muslim architectural centuries before as noted in previous chapter. This issue will be fully discussed in the next chapter.

Notes

[293] Ibn Khaldun (1967), '*The Muqadimah*', translated from the Arabic by F.Rosenthal, edited by Dawood, N.J., Princeton pub.

[294] For more on when and how these columns were developed see Dan Cruickhank (edt.) (1996), '*Banister Fletcher's A History of Architecture*', 20th Edition, Architectural Press, pp.115-120.

[295] Krauss, S. (1996), '*The Jewish-Christian Controversy from the Earliest Times to 1789*', Vol.1, edited and revised by William Horbury, Tubingen, Mohr Siebeck, p.11.

[296] Gibbon reckons that the Jews set the fire in Rome and blamed Christians for it. See Edward Gibbon (1862), '*History of The Decline and Fall of The Roman Empire*', John Murray, London, Vol. 2, pp.233-234.

[297] Edward Gibbon (1862), op.cit. pp.268-273.

[298] Muslims believe that Jesus was saved and raised by the almighty God to the heavens. The Quran explains the event explicitly in the following:
The event also is a preparation for his return to Earth as

[299] Chambers Mortimer (1958), '*Greek and Roman History*', Service Centre for Teachers of History, Washington, p.8

[300] Mortimer (1958), op.cit. p.8

[301] Contrary to the Greeks who had it on top of hills and mountains.

[302] Kirby, R.S., Withington, S., Darling, A.B and Kilgam, F.G. (1956), '*Engineering in History*', McGraw Hill, New York, Toronto, London, reprinted by Dover Publications in 1990, p.61.

[303] Ibid., p.62.

[304] Dan Cruickhank (ed.) (1996), '*Banister Fletcher's A History of Architecture*', 20th Edition, Architectural Press, p.197.

[305] Sear, F (1983), '*Roman Architecture*', Cornell University Press, p.18

[306] Kirby, R.S., Withington, S., Darling, A.B and Kilgam, F.G. (1956),op, cit. p.79

[307] Sear, F (1983), '*Roman Architecture*', Cornell University Press, p.80

[308] Dearmer, P. (1921), '*Art*', in F.J.C. Hearnshaw (ed.), '*Medieval Contributions to Modern Civilisation*', Dawson of Pall Mall, London, pp.149-173, p.161.

[309] Dearmer, P. (1921) op cit. p.161-162.

[310] The next in size are St. Peter's at Rome of 140 feet, and Florence Cathedral of 137.5 feet. For more see Yarwood, Doreen, (1974), '*The Architecture of Europe*', Chancellor Press, Hong Kong, p.50.

[311] This tradition apparently came down from similar patterns the Romans made earlier in timber roofed ceilings in the form of sunken panels or coffers.

[312] Sear, F (1983), '*Roman Architecture*', Cornell University Press, p.22

[313] Fikret Yegül (1992), '*Baths and Bathing in Classical Antiquity*' The Architectural History Foundation, New York.

[314] Ibid., p.30

[315] Van dyke, J.C (1909), '*A Text Book of the History of Painting*', Longman Greens and Co., London, Calcutta and Bombay, p.52

[316] The Metropolitan Museum of Art Bulletin (1988), '*Painting in Rome and Pompeii*', in The Metropolitan Museum of Art Bulletin, New Series, Vo.45, No.3, (Winter, 1987-1988), pp.3-16, at p.4

[317] Mumford, L. (1966), '*The City in History*' Penguin Books, Harmondsworth, UK.

[318] Owens, E., J. (1992), '*The City in the Greek and Roman World*', Routledge, London.

[319] Since early third century, people throughout the collapsing Roman Empire embraced Christianity, which increasingly adopted "popular" elements of pagan practices, see Wilson Brian C. and Lewis Nancy D.(2002), '*The Pocket Idiot's Guide to Christianity*', Alpha Books, p.30

[320] There are other examples, which show the church's attempts at adapting the circular Roman mausoleum as in the case of San. Costanza, built c. 320-50 and San. Stefano Rotondo.

[321] In earlier times, two or three baptisteries of circular plan were built in every town receiving Christian converters, See Yarwood Doreen (1974), op cit. p.82.

[322] Cormack Robin (2000), *'Byzantine Art'*, Oxford University Press, p.23

[323] Gur means in Persian, grave, remained the name of this ancient city until 9th century when King Adhud ad-Dowleh Dailami, who frequently resided there, changed its name into Firozabad.

[324] Stevens Roger Sir (1979), *'The Land of the Great Sophy'*, Eyre Methuen, p.262

[325] Dan Cruickhank (ed.) (1996), *'Banister Fletcher's A History of Architecture'*, 20th Edition, Architectural Press, p.201.

[326] Ibid, p.201

[327] Reuther, Oscar (1938), *'Sāsānian Architecture. A. History'*, in Arthur Upham Pope and Phyllis Ackerman eds., Survey of Persian Art, vol.II, reprint Oxford University Press London, pp. 493-537.

[328] Yarwood Doreen (1974), op cit. p.87.

[329] For the warfare, origins of feudalism see Stephenson Carl, (1956) *'Mediaeval Feudalism'*, Cornell University Press.

[330] Ganshof Francois-Louis, (1996), *'Feudalism'*, University of Toronto Press, pp.3-4

[331] Reynolds Susan (1994), *'Fiefs and Vassals: the Medieval Evidence Reinterpreted'*, Oxford University Press, Oxford.

[332], Vassal and Fiefs

[333] Gansho Franðcois-Louis, (1996), o-p.cit. p.4

[334] Stephenson Carl, (1956) *'Mediaeval Feudalism'*, Cornell University Press, p.9

[335] Colish, M.L (1997) *'Medieval Foundations of the Western Intellectual Tradition, 400-1400'*, Yale University Press, New Heaven and London.

[336] Ibid., p.125.

[337] Ibid., p.125.

[338] Ibid. p.126.

[339] Charles the Great or Charlemagne (742-814) was the grandson Charles Martel (686-741) who defeated the Muslims at Tours in 732. Charlemagne became king of the Franks in 771 and was crowned emperor over most of Western Europe on Christmas day, 800, in Rome, leading to the foundation of the Carolingian empire.

[340] Heinrich Fichtenau, (1976), *'The Carolingian Empire'*, University of Torento Press, p.82

[341] Campbell, D. (1926), *'Arabian Medicine in the Middle Ages'*, Cambridge University Press, vol.1, p.111-12.

[342] Haines Charles Reginald (1889), *'Christianity and Islam in Spain (756-1031)'*, Kegan Paul, Trench & Co., London, p.131.

[343] And several abbeys, notably of Fleury (Saint-Benoit-sur-Loire)

[344] Freeman Ann (1992), *'Theodulf of Orléans: A Visigoth at Charlemagne's Court'*, in Jacques Fontaine and Christine Pellistrandi eds., L'Europe héritière de l'Espagne wisigothique, Collection de la Casa de Velázquez n° 35, Madrid, pp.185-193-94

[345] Herbermann Charles George (1913), *'The Catholic Encyclopaedia'*, The Encyclopaedia Press, p.319

[346] Freeman Ann (1957), *'Theodulf of Orleans and the Libri Carolini'*, Speculum, Vol. 32, No. 4. pp. 663-705.

[347] Versus Teudulfi, lines 166-82, trans. Nikolai Alexandrenko, (1970), *'The Poetry of Theodulf of Orléans: A Translation and Critical Study,"* Ph.D. Dissertation, Tulane University, p. 166, quoted in Bowman Jeffrey Alan (2004), *'Shifting Landmarks: property, proof, and dispute in Catalonia around the year 1000'*, Cornell University Press, pp.87-88.

[348] Gorman, M. (1997), *'The Commentary o Genesis of Claudius of Turin and Biblical Studies under Louis the Pious'*, Speculum, Vol.72, No.2, pp.279-329.

[349] Waddington George (2004), '*A History of the Church, from the Earliest Ages to the Reformation*', 1st published in 1833, Kessinger Publishing, p.268.

[350] Haines Charles Reginald (1889), '*Christianity and Islam in Spain (756-1031)*', Kegan Paul, Trench & Co., London, p.131

[351] Cabaniss Allen (1953), '*Agobard of Lyons: Churchman and Critic*', Syracuse University Press, p.2

[352] He wrote a treatise untitled Against the Silly Opinion of the Mob About Hail and Thunder, See Cabaniss Allen (1953), op., cit. and Cabaniss, A.J. (1951), '*Agobard of Lyons*', Speculum, Vol.26, No1, pp.50-76.

[353] For more on this issue see Cabaniss, A.J. (1951), op.cit.at p.61.

[354] Graetz Heinrich Hirsch (1949), '*History of the Jews*', Jewish Publication Society of America, Philadelphia, Volume 3, pp.168-169.

[355] Richard Hodges, David Whitehouse (1983), op cit. p.120

[356] A delicately carved horn made of ivory.

[357] Shalem Avinoam (2004), '*The Oliphant: Islamic Objects in Historical Context*', Brill, pp.94-95.

[358] Ibid., p.5 Shalem Avinoam (2004),

[359] Gérard Chandè ed. (1989), '*Le merveilleux et la Magie dans la Littérature: Acte du Colloque de Caen*', 31August 2nd September, Redopi, Amsterdam and Atlanta, p.106

[360] Spargo John Webster (2004), '*Virgil the Necromancer: Studies in Virgilian Legends*', Kessinger Publishing, p.131.

[361] Mahmoud Raghib (1929), '*Descriptions d'Orgues Données par Quelques Anciens Auteurs Turcs*', Revue de musicologie, Volume 10, No.30, pp. 99-104.

[362] Schlesinger, Kathleen (1910), '*The Instruments of the Modern Orchestra*', Vol. 1 Modern Orchestral Instruments'; Vol. 2 the Precursors of the Violin Family, Charles Schribner, New York. p.329, 342, 371,374, 398, 399, 420.

[363] Musca G. (1963), '*Carlo Magno ed Harun alRashid*', Dedalo, Bari, pp.108-15

[364] Pirenne claimed that it was Muslim advance and destruction of Western civilisation and Roman Empire that gave chance to the rise of Charlemagne. See Pirenne Henri (1939), '*Mohammed and Charlemagne*', London.

[365] Sture Bolin (1952), '*Mohammed, Charlemagne and Ruric*', Scandinavian Economic History Review, Vol.1. pp.5-39 Quoted in Richard Hodges, David Whitehouse (1983), 'Mohammed, Charlemagne and the Origins of Europe: Archaeology and the Pirenne Thesis', Cornell University Press, p.6

[366] See Richard Hodges, David Whitehouse (1983), '*Mohammed, Charlemagne and the Origins of Europe: Archaeology and the Pirenne Thesis*', Cornell University Press, p.7

[367] Lombard Maurice (1947), '*L'Or Musluman du VII au XI Siècles, Les Bases Monetaires d'Une Suprematie Economique*', Annales, ESC e, pp.143-60, cited in Richard Hodges, David Whitehouse (1983), op cit. p.8

[368] Hitti, P.K (1996), '*The Arabs: A Short History*', Regnery Gateway publishing, Washington, p.172.

[369] Kirby, R.S et al. (1956), op cit. p. 107.

[370] Colish, M.L. (1997), op cit. p.160,

[371] Trend, J.B. (1931), 'Spain *and Portugal*', in T. Arnold et al. (eds.1931), The Legacy of Islam, Oxford University Press.pp.1-39, at p.9.

[372] The Society for the Diffusion of Useful Knowledge (1939), '*Library of Useful Knowledge*', Vol.III, Philosophy, Baldwin and Cradock, Paternoster-Row, London, p.37.

[373] Descending from dynasty of Capet, which controlled the area around Paris.

[374] Referring to the reign of Otto I, crowned emperor in Rome in 962, and his son and grandson (also named Otto).

[375] Conant, Kenneth John (1968), '*Cluny: les Églises et la Maison du Chef d'Ordre*', Impr. Protat Frères Mâcon, Paris.

[376] Male, E (1928) `Art et Artistes du Moyen Age', Librairie Armand Colin, Paris.

[377] Farmer, H.G. (1970), `Historical Facts for the Arabian Musical Influence', Georg OlmVarlag, Hildesheim, New York, p.185.

[378] Roland Allen (1892), `Gerbert, Pope Silvester II', the English Historical Review, Vol. 7, No. 28. (Oct., 1892), pp. 625-668.

[379] According to Weissenborn the English chronicler, William of Malmesbury (c. 1150) wrote "Abacum certe primus a Saracenis rapiens regulas dedit"; that that Gerbert learned the use of the abacus from the Arabs. See Weissenborn, H. (1888), `Gerbert: Beiträge zur Kenntniss der Mathematik des Mittelalters', Berlin, p. 236.

[380] See also Thomas F. Glick, Steven John Livesey, and Faith Wallis (eds.) (2005), `Medieval Science, Technology, and Medicine: An Encyclopaedia', Routledge, p.47

[381] Farmer, H.G. (1970), op cit. p.185.

[382] Colish, M.L. (1997), op cit. p.164.

[383] Wolff Philippe (1968), `The Cultural Awakening', Pantheon Books, p.173

[384] Dunlop, D. (1952), `A Christian Mission to Muslim Spain in the Eleventh Century', in al-Andalus, Vol.17, pp.259-310, at p.260.

[385] According to an eleventh century writer, Adhemar of Chabannais: Causa Sophiae Prirno Franciam, dein Cordobam lustrans. Bouquet, x. 146, A. See Roland Allen (1892), `Gerbert, Pope Silvester II', the English Historical Review, Vol. 7, No. 28. (Oct., 1892), pp. 625-668, atp.628.

[386] Landu Rom (1967), `Afrique Mauresque', Albin Michel, Paris, p.97.

[387] Briffault Robert (1928), `the Making of Humanity', George Unwin and Allen, London, p.173

[388] Otto I is known to have had good relation with the Muslims. Historic records show that he sent at least two embassies to Andalusia. John of Gorze a learned and loyal monk, and John of Lorraine, later Abbot of Gorze in Metz in Lorraine were sent to the Andalusian capital, Cordoba, in 953-4. The aim of this embassy was in answer to Caliph al-Nasir's letter sent previously, as well as to learn the extent of Andalusian intellectual and scientific progress, in the hope of gaining from it.

[389] Colish, M.L. (1997), op cit.

[390] Prioreschi P. (2001), `A History of Medicine', vol.5, Horatius Press, Omaha, p.183,184.

[391] Lindberg D.C. (1980), `Science in the Middle Ages', University of Cicago Press, p.63

[392] Kritzeck, J. (1964), `Peter the Venerable and Islam', Princeton University Press, pp.57-58, no.31

[393] Baeck Louis (1994) `The Mediterranean Tradition in Economic thought', Routledge, p.119

[394] Tytler Patrick Fraser (1831), `Lives of Scottish Worthies', vol.1, John Murray, London, p.98

[395] Ibid. Briffault R. (1928), op.cit. p.199

[396] Lemay Richard (1978), `Gerard of Cremona', Dictionary of Scientific Biography, volume 15, pp. 173-92.

[397] Haskins C.H. (1927), `Studies in the History of Medieval Science', Harvard University Press, Cambridge Mass., 2nd Edition, p.15.

[398] Tytler Patrick Fraser (1831), `Lives of Scottish Worthies', op, cit. p.99, 101.

[399] Conder, C.R. (1886), `Syrian Stone Iore', R.Bentley and Son, p.370

[400] Patrick Fraser (1831), `Lives of Scottish Worthies', op, cit. p.117

[401] Meyerhof, M. (1931), `Science and Medecine', in T. Arnold et al. (eds.1931), The Legacy of Islam, Oxford University Press.pp.311-355, at p.351.

[402] O'Callaghan, J.F. (1983), `A History of Medieval Spain', Cornell University Press, p.313.

[403] Spirituality Today Autumn (1987), `Albert the Great by Sr. M. Albert Hughes, O.P. The Mission of St. Albert and St. Thomas', Vol. 39 Supplement, chapter 8.

[404] Ibid. chapter 8

[405] Sweetman, J.W. (1955), `Islam and Christian Theology', Lutterworth Press, part 2, vol.1, p.71.

[406] Ibid. p.71

[407] Ibid. p.71

[408] Kutlesa Stipe (2004), *'Croatian Philosophers I: Hermann of Dalmatia (1110-1154)'*, in Prolegomena vol.3, Number 1, pp.57-70, at p. 58

[409] Ibid.p.58

[410] Spirituality Today, Autumn (1987),*'Albert the Great by M. Albert Hughes, O.P Doctor Universalis'*, Vol. 39, Supplement chapter 8.

[411] Spirituality Today, Autumn (1987),*'Albert the Great by M. Albert Hughes, O.P Doctor Universalis'*, Vol. 39, Supplement chapter 6.

[412] Jonathan Wolff and M. W. F. Stone (eds.), (2000), *'The Proper Ambition of Science'*, Routledge p.29.

[413] *Summa Theologiae* (ST, I. Q.84, a5), quoted in Spirituality Today, Autumn (1987),*'Albert the Great by M. Albert Hughes, O.P Doctor Universalis'*, Vol. 39, Supplement chapter 8.

[414] Ghazanfar S.M. and Lowry S.T (2003), *'Medieval Islamic Economic Thought: Filling the Great Gap in European Economics'*, Routledge.

[415] Hommon, R. (1947), *'The Philosophy of Alfarabi and its Influence on Medieval Thought'*, Hobson Press, New York, p.55)

[416] *Summa Theologiae* (ST, I. Q.84, a5), quoted in Spirituality Today, Autumn (1987),*'Albert the Great* by M. Albert Hughes, O.P Doctor Universalis', Vol. 39, Supplement chapter 8. Ibid.

[417] Chisholm Hugh (ed.) (1910), *'The Encyclopædia Britannica: A Dictionary of Arts, Sciences, Literature and Gener.al Information'*, The Cambridge University Press, Vol.29, p.189

[418] Quoted in Tina Stiefel (1989), *'The Intellectual Revolution in Twelfth Century Europe'*; St. Martin's Press, N.Y., pp.71, 80.

[419] Briffault Robert (1928), *'the Making of Humanity'*, George Unwin and Allen, London, p.199

[420] Ibid., p.190.

[421] Lyons, J. (2010), *'The House of Wisdom How the Arabs Transformed Western Civilization'*, Bloomsbury Press, New York, Berlin and London.

[422] and other names such as Robert Grosseteste, Alexander of Hales, St. Bonaventura, Marsilius of Padua, Richard of Middleton, Nicholas Oresme, Joannes Buridanus, Siger of Brabant, John Peckham, Henry of Gant, William of Occham, Walter Burley, William of Auvergne, Dante Algheri, Blaise Pascal, Gerbert (later Pope Sylvester II), Alexander of Hales, Raymund Lull, Nicholas Oresme, Johannes Buridanus, Copernicus, and Kepler.

[423] Dearmer, P. (1921) *'Art'*, ed. Hearnshaw, F.J.C., Medieval Contributions to Modern Civilisation, Dawson of Pall Mall, London, pp.149-173.

[424] Colish, M.L. (1997), op cit. p.325.

[425] Ibid. p.266.

[426] Walsh James, J. (1911), *'Old Time Makers of Medicine'*, Fordham University Press, New York, p.65

[427] Goldstein, T. (1988), `Dawn of Modern Science', Houghton Mufflin, Boston, p.76

[428] Association of America Victorian Literature Group (1903), *'Modern Philology'*, , University of Chicago, vol.1., p.97

[429] Duby, Georges, (1981), *'The Age of the Cathedrals: Art and Society, 980-1420'*, University of Chicago Press, pp.116-17

[430] Goldstein, T. (1988), `Dawn of Modern Science', op.cit. p.77.

[431] Peter Linehan, Janet Laughland Nelson, (2001), *'The Medieval Word'*, Routledge, p.114

[432] Wack, Mary Frances (1990), *'Lovesickness in the Middle Ages: The Viaticum and its Commentaries'*, University of Pennsylvania Press, Philadelphia.

[433] Prioreschi P. (2001), *'A History of Medicine'*, vol.5 Horatius Press, Omaha, p.188.

[434] Jacquart, D. (1996), *'The Influence of Arabic Medicine in the Medieval West'*, in Roshdi Rashed (ed.), Encyclopaedia of the History of Arabic Science, Routledge, 3 vols., vol.3, pp.963-984.

[435] Meyerhof, M. (1931), *'Science and Medecine'*, in T. Arnold et al. (eds.1931), The Legacy of Islam, Oxford University Press.pp.311-355, at p.191

[436] Walsh James, J. (1911), '*Old Time Makers of Medicine*', Fordham University Press, New York, p.68

[437] Meyerhof, M. (1931, op.cit. at p.198

[438] Wack, Mary Frances (1990), '*Lovesickness in the Middle Ages: The Viaticum and its Commentaries*', University of Pennsylvania Press, Philadelphia

[439] Hastings Rashdall (1936), '*The Universities of Europe in the Middle Ages*', Clarendon Press, p.80.

[440] Ralph McInern (1963), '*A History of Western Philosophy*', University of Notre Dame Press, Indiana, USA.

[441] Ribera, J (1928), '*Disertaciones Y Opusculos*', 2 vols. Madrid.

[442] George Makdisi (1980), '*On the Origin and Development of the College in Islam and the West*, in Islam and the Medieval West, ed. Khalil I. Semaan, State University of New York Press/Albany. 1980.

[443] Wijdan Ali (1999), '*The Arab Contribution to Islamic Art: From the Seventh to the Fifteenth Centuries*', The American University in Cairo Press, p.120.

[444] Glick, T. F. (2005), '*Islamic and Chrsitain Spain in the Early Middle Ages*', Brill Academic Publishers, p.135.

[445] An 11th century dynasty that ruled Morocco, Western Algeria, and al-Andalus.

[446] Haskins, C.H. (1922), '*Science at the Court of the Emperor Frederick II*', The American Historical Review, Vol. 27, N0.4, pp.669-694, at p. 670

[447] He was taught logic by a Sicilian Muslim while on crusade, See Haskins, C.H. (1922), op. cit. p.674

[448] Professor Charles Burnett (1999), '*The "Sons of Averroes with the Emperor Frederick*" and the Transmission of the Philosophical Works by Ibn Rushd', in G. Endress and J. A. Aertsen with the assistance of K. Braun (eds.), *Averroes and the Aristotelian Tradition: Sources, Constitution and Reception of the Philosophy of Ibn Rushd (1126–1198)*, Leiden, 1999, pp. 259–99.

[449] Walsh, J.J. (1911), '*Old Time Makers of Medicine*', Fordham University Press, New York, p.141.

[450] Colish, M.L. (1997), op cit. p.269.

[451] Colish, M.L. (1997), op cit. p.270.

[452] Christians living in areas under Muslim control.

[453] W.M. Watt: *The Influence of Islam on Medieval Europe*, Edinburgh University Press, 1972. pp. 66-7.

[454] Holland, T.E. (1891), '*The Origin of the University of Oxford*', The English Historical review, Vol.6, No.22, pp.238-249

[455] Cochrane, L. (1994), '*Adelard of Bath, the first English Scientist*', British Museum Press.

[456] Drane Augusta Theodosia (1910), '*Christian Schools and Scholars: Or, Sketches of Education from the Christian Era to the Council of Trent*', G. E. Stechert & co.p. 55.

[457] See Burnett C (1994), '*The Introduction of Arabic Learning into British Schools*, in Charles Edwin Buttenworth, Blake Andree Kessel, The Introduction of Arabic Philosophy Into Europe, Brill, pp.40-53

[458] Southern, R.W. (1984), '*From School to University*', in J.I. Catto (ed.), The Early Oxford School, vol.1, of T.H. Aston (ed.), The History of the University of Oxford, Clarendon Press, Oxford, pp.1-36

[459] Yarwood Doreen (1974), op cit. p.135.

[460] Ibid., p.134.

CHAPTER FOUR

Cultural Encounters and Transfer of Knowledge Between the Muslim East and Christian West.

The wide gap in scientific, philosophical and technological development between the Muslim World and Christian Europe in the Middle Ages resulted in a gradual flow of knowledge between the two societies. This process was due to two main factors. The saturation of knowledge in the Muslim world triggered a "natural" diffusion process worldwide, particularly into Europe. This is related to the global -human- dimension of the Islamic message that was clearly established in the Quran and the Prophet's sayings. The second factor is connected with the European endeavour to improve their worsening conditions. This quest reached its peak in the 11th century when major contact with the Muslims took place during the First Crusade, which enabled Western Europe to discover the cultural wonders of the Muslims. Furthermore, the new crusading ideology, which had swept over Christian Europe, encouraged such knowledge for missionary purposes. An example of this is the strategic thinking of King Alfonso the Wise of Castile (1252-1284)), who established the Toledo school, after the city's capture from the Muslims in 1085. The exploitation of Muslim libraries and translators in his mission for learning was a key element in the setting up of the school. In general terms, Elisseeff classified the borrowing from Muslims into two main categories.[461] Formal transfer involved the direct imitation of particular forms, techniques or physical items. The other was conceptual or ideological borrowing including ideas, themes and other philosophical and theological concepts that were used to develop principles of Christian ideology Figure 69 summarises this process by showing three main areas where most of the contact between the two cultures took place. In the East, the role the Levant played was essentially through trade, the crusades, and pilgrimage. In neighbouring North Africa, the means were mainly trade, crusades, and visits of Scholars (fig.69). Many of these contacts were headed by Italian and French merchants and crusaders. Spain and Sicily were the third and most influential area due to their geographic proximity and the presence of a large Christian-Jewish minority, which established strong bonds with Muslims as well as crossing the language barrier.

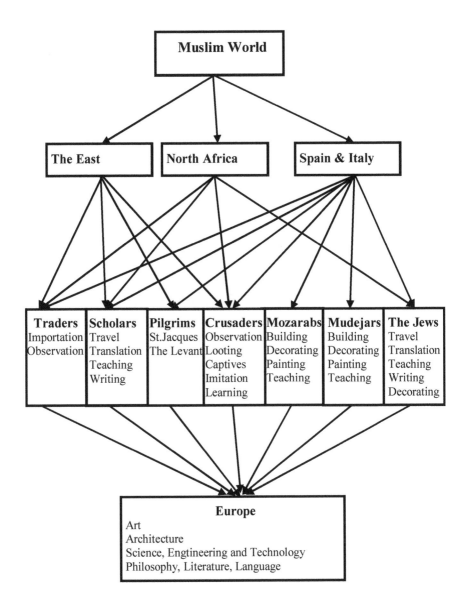

Figure 69 The main transfer routes of Muslim Knowledge

The Role of Traders

After the fall of the Roman Empire, trade collapsed in Europe and other Roman dependents regions in Africa and Asia. As a result, economic prosperity and standard of living in these areas received a severe blow. When Islam spread in west and central Asia, North Africa and Southern Europe in Spain and Sicily trade flourished once more. Muslim traders transported goods to and from various regions of the extensive Muslim Caliphate. Some of them maintained the trade tradition of their Arab ancestors through winter and summer caravans which trotted between Yemen, Abyssinia, Syria and Mesopotamia. Muslims revived the old Silk Road enabling goods to travel from China and India to as far as North Africa and Spain through Alexandria and Cairo. Europe was left out of this trade boom until about 8th century when Charlemagne managed for a while to unite parts of the European realm and built trade contacts with Harun al-Rashid in Baghdad as noted in previous chapter. The invasion of Barbarians; the Magyars and Vikings sent the achievements of Charlemagne in the drains. In the words of Professor Walbank: *"With the collapse of the imperial state* (Carolingian Empire*), that large section of the economy which depended on it simply disappeared. The residue- small artisans and traders in towns, local markets, itinerant craftsmen, the villages around the manor or the monastery, and, for the rich, an irregular trade in luxuries from all parts of the Mediterranean- was left as the economic foundation of the new states of medieval Europe."*[462] The Feudalism transformed Europe's states into private dominions centred in castles and fortifications, which were described by Anderson as prisons for the rural population.[463]

During the 10 and 11th centuries few cities of southern Europe bordering the Mediterranean assumed most of the trade activity. Italian cities such as Naples, Venice, Pisa and Genoa and French port of Marseille traded principally with Muslims, following the old Roman trade route involving North Africa (or the Maghreb) and Egypt. With their naval and military powers, the three Italian states secured trade bases in many Islamic ports including Andalusia and North Africa while Venice acquired special status in Byzantium. Following the first crusade, the three states established trade bases at ports in Syria and Palestine. French southern trade centres established strong links with Muslim Spain and North Africa. A series of trade treatises established *Funduqs*, hotel like buildings lodging merchants and traders, in North Africa and Egypt. Mas de Latrie, who studied these treatises, showed that Marseille concluded a trade treaty with the king of Morocco in 1138 and had privileges and possessions in the Orient[464]. The region also accommodated a large section of Jewish minorities who kept contacts with European Jews allowing the flow of goods and ideas on both sides of the

Mediterranean. The regions of Marseille, Montpellier, Provence and Languedoc maintained close cultural and political contacts with Northern Spain and North Africa. These provinces were often held as lordships by kings of Aragon; exchanges were frequent, O'Callaghan confirms that: *"Throughout the medieval era communication was constant between Catalonia in the northeast and Languedoc and Provence in southern France."*[465]

Egypt was an important port channelling most of eastern commodities to European cities, especially the Italian ones. Stern uncovered a Fatimid document, which reported the frequent visits of Italian and Genoese merchants[466]. The Maghreb or North Africa played similar role for commodities coming from Africa, especially the gold of Timbuktu in Mali and Sijilmassa (perished town) in Morocco. Port cities along the Mediterranean coast like al-Mahdiya in Tunisia, Bougie in Algeria and Ceuta in Morocco were the main hubs for European merchants and gold traders during most of the eleventh century. It was during this period that trade reached its peak that some states like Genoa and Pisa engaged in a war to establish trade counters at al-Mahdiya.[467] A rare evidence, known as Genizah documents, was unearthed in a Jewish synagogue in al-Fustat, Egypt, containing letters, bills and documents about commercial businesses and dealings. For example, among other documents, a letter written in Alexandria in 11th century refers to the arrival of ten Sicilian ships each carrying five hundred people.[468] Mas de Latrie documented a number of trade agreements between Almoravids of North Africa and south European states counting more than seven agreements during the second half of the 12th century alone[469]. More importantly, in 1133 a delegation of Almoravid dignitaries went to Pisa and signed a major agreement there.[470]

Europeans also traded with Muslims of the East through Constantinople. The Christian and Jewish minorities in Syria, Palestine and Iraq played an active role in stimulating trade and cross- cultural exchange,[471] Abulafia explained the role of Constantinople as follows: *"there were annually companies of Syrians in Constantinople who had conveyed Syrian stuffs and Indian goods imported through Iraq by road across Asia Minor. A mosque was maintained in the city for the use of Muslim visitors."*[472] The Turkish port of Antalya provided another trade counter for Europeans, especially Venetian merchants. In 1205, Tuscany occupied briefly the port in an attempt of securing permanent access to Anatolian Seljuk and Persian goods.[473] The Seljuk capital Konya grew into another important commercial and exchange centre between Muslims and Christians through Constantinople.[474]

It was this booming trade business and the gold coming from the Muslims, whether in the form of raw material or as gold coins, which flourished the economy of southern European countries. For this reason, Europe invaded many parts of the Mediterranean waters under Muslim control, capturing Islands of Sardinia in 1022, Corsica in 1091, and Sicily in 1058-1090. The continent guaranteed more access to the sea, slowly building its maritime power. The new easier and cheaper maritime transport permitted an unprecedented expansion of trade with the East.[475]   Europe religiously orchestrated the first crusade (1099) sending a proportion of its population to Jerusalem, to the mysterious, rich and developed East. Merchants accompanied various Crusader expeditions to set up new markets while Venetian and Genoese forces conquered seaports in the Levant to secure bases for their import and export activities. Crusaders also established trading quarters in cities of Tyre and Acre[476]. Everybody, especially Italians merchants, enriched himself through the importation of various Muslim goods to the European consumer. Knights and cavalry orders became themselves increasingly involved in trade and banking, quickly losing the crusade its religious perspective.[477] The crusaders discovered many new goods, styles and fashions that they had never known before, including large amount of agricultural products, textiles, ceramics and artefacts. For this reason, Steven Runciman painfully remarked: *"the crusades were launched to save Eastern Christendom from the Moslems. When they ended the whole of Eastern Christendom was under Moslem rule"*[478] As to their role in the transmission of architectural knowledge, the crusades were instrumental in the importation of many Muslim motifs and a full discussion is provided below.

After the final defeat of the crusaders and Acre returned to the Muslims in 1291, the Pope issued a general embargo against Muslim goods (Mamluk Syria and Egypt). Some Europeans merchants relocated in Cyprus while the Genoese and Venetians discovered the trans-Asian trade which was accessible from the black sea and the Mediterranean port of Legatso in Armenia. Europe established access to Anatolia and Persia, a region that was then ruled by the Mongols. Mongol silk and spices of the Silk Road were the main imports to European markets. This situation continued until the fall of the Mongols by mid-14th century. Following the decline of the Mongols the black sea and Asian trade became dangerous due to the instability of the region. Venice persuaded the Pope to lift the embargo and Italian trade resumed with Mamluks in late 1340s'[479]. Italian merchants from Sicily traded for gold with Tunis and Aragonese merchants traded for wool and animal skins with Algiers. In general, the period between thirteenth and fifteenth century was categorized, by consensus of scholars, as a period of trade revolution. The wealth and experience brought by the crusades initiated economic and social dynamism as the power of the Feudal system started fading away. The many years of isolation between European states were replaced by greater contact and considerable trade exchange between various regions. This coincided with the prosperity of Mamluk arts and economies in Syria and Egypt, with craftsmen producing elaborate works in textile, embroideries, ceramics, gilt and enamelled glass and metal wares, furniture and jewellery. During this period, Europe also saw the first signs of recovery and Renaissance. Building and art projects spread in countries such as Italy, France, Spain and England. The consumption of new ideas, luxury goods and sophisticated lifestyle was all time record high. At this crucial time Venice was playing a dual role between East and West, the gateway to the Orient and the "bazaar of Europe," controlling the Mediterranean and, with it, the flow of Near Eastern goods, ideas, and influence. This role involved, according to Stefano Carboni, nine centuries of commerce between Venice and *La Serenissima*[480] and the Islamic world. Wood, metal, grain, furs and leathers from northern Europe were shipped from Venetian docks to Islamic lands in the Near East and North Africa. Venice imported refined Islamic luxury goods: Turkish velvets, Egyptian glass, carpets and Syrian brass work of a quality that matched and exceeded the finest of Europe.[481] Genoa exported to Egypt among other things shields known as *janawiya*, as well as woods and ships.

The question about the impact of Muslim trade on the rise and development of these projects is thus very relevant. First indices of the deep influence of trade with the Muslims are found in the many words of Arabic origin in most European languages. Commonly used words such as Muslin, Damask, Fustian and Baldachin which are types of textile originally made and imported from Mosul in Iraq, Damascus in Syria, Fustat (old Cairo) in Egypt and Baghdad respectively. In silk industry, we find words such as attabi, taffeta fabric made of silk and cotton originally produced in Attabiya, a district of Baghdad, *isfahani* and *jurjani* silks, respectively named after the city of Isfahan in Persia, and the province of Jurjan, southeast of the Caspian Sea. Other words such as gauze (from Gaza in Palestine), cotton (from qutn) and satin (from Zaytun) which denote types of woven fabrics have also Arabic origins.[482] Other vocabulary words such as musk, camphor, saffron, cinnamon, caraway, balsam and ginger are all of Arabic origin identifying incense and spice trade. The list of such words is endless including rebec (from rabab), naker (from naqqara), anafil (from al-nafir), adufe (from al-duf), albogon (from al-buq), atambel (from al-timbel), Exabeda (from al-sababa), and panderete (from bandair) which are musical instruments taken from Arabic names.

With trade came concepts such as commercial, financial and legal institutions and logistics. One of such instruments is the so-called *commenda* contract, which was, according to Cizakca, no more than the Islamic *mudaraba* contract transferred to Europe as more complex forms of partnership between European and Muslim merchants developed.[483] The two contracts are strikingly similar, both involve two partners; one invests capital and the second employs it. While profits are shared, any loss is the liability of the investor. Before him Udovitch went in the same direction as he established firmly the Muslim origin of *commenda* and later discovered a *commenda*, contract made in fifteenth century between a Venetian and an Arab merchant in Alexandria, clearly providing the method by which the transfer took place.[484] Udovitch also showed how Muslims developed, years before Europe, bills of exchange, or *suftaja*, letters of credit or *hawala*, which allowed a merchant to advance or transfer a sum of money to a business associate at some distant place[485], and private bank, or *ma'una*. Last but not least, the cheque, or *Saqq*, which both Udovitch and Karmers believe to be '*functionally and etymologically the origin of our modern cheques.*"[486] European commercial vocabulary also preserved many other Arabic words such as tariff (from ta'rif), traffic (from tafriq), risk (from rizk), tare (from tarah), calibre (from qalib), magazine (from makhazin), and douane (from divan). This can only "*signals the profound cultural impact if centuries of trade with the Islamic world. Arabic words, at first used self-consciously, gradually became naturalized until their origin was no longer recognized.*"[487]

The contribution of trade to the transfer of Muslim knowledge and skills has been traced by Abulafia[488] in the valuable items and artefacts brought by these traders. European merchants conducting the trade and travelling between various Muslim provinces had developed an interest and attraction to Muslim civilisation and in particular, luxury items especially the arts. The wealthy indulged themselves by importing luxury items and exotic objects. A fourteenth century Florentine merchant wrote: "*Really all Christendom could be supplied for a year with the merchandise of Damascus...There are such rich and noble and delicate works of every kind that if you had money in the bone of your leg, without fail you would break it to buy of these things.*"[489] Cochrane talked of the trade in books which were sold like any other items.[490]

Architectural features of Muslim buildings also formed part of the knowledge transmitted by trade. This subject recently gained the interest of a few scholars who identified some kind of comparison and interchange between Islamic and European arts. Two of the most recently and comprehensively published studies have indeed established strong links between medieval European trade and the spread of many Muslim themes and motifs. Debora Howard's richly illustrated book established without a doubt that European merchants imported more than material goods from the East but also a wealth of visual ideas and information about Muslim art, architecture and culture in general.[491]Concentrating on Venice, Howard showed how for a period of three hundred years (1100-1500) Venetian merchants gained deep insight into Islamic art and architecture through their many contacts with Muslim partners and their many visits to the East. One way Venetian traders learnt about Muslim architecture was through the buildings they lodged. First instance was in purpose built buildings such as *Funduqs* or *foundaci* in Italian, which were hotel like residences built by local merchants or bought by European embassies, royals or noble merchants to accommodate their compatriots. Second means was in converted buildings belonging to locals or bought by Europeans, an example of these was a merchant who reported staying at a converted mosque in Acre.[492] The third way was in houses of Muslim or eastern friends where traders were directly exposed to Muslim architecture. In most cases, they developed good relationship with local Muslim or Christian merchants who could guide them through Muslim culture as well as architecture. The information acquired from various experiences was not only transmitted through scattered drawings, diagrams, and portable objects, but, more elusively and perhaps more importantly, through travellers' writings, oral narratives, and memories. [493] Howard convincingly demonstrated the impact of Muslim architecture and art on Venetian and Italian works which she summarised in three levels; on the organization of the urban space of Venice, on its religious architecture as in the icon of St Marco, and on its secular buildings and palaces namely the Palazzo Ducale (See chapter 6).

In a recent publication, Rosamond Mack traced the influence of oriental motifs, imagery and craftsmanship on Italian artists and craftsmen[494]. Her findings are exceptionally revealing of the magnitude of the influence of Muslim trade on European and Italian art and the complex cultural and aesthetic interchanges between the two cultures. Unlike Howard who dealt with all possible ways of transmission, Mack concentrated particularly on the influence of luxury goods imported from the Muslim East, which she found making a strong and lasting impression on Italian artistic taste and production during the late Middle Ages and early Renaissance. The great age of Italian artistic development from about 1300 to1600 coincided with the peak of Italian trade with Islamic lands. In addition to the wealth it produced, which was invested for both artistic patronage and consumption of luxurious goods, Islamic luxury goods and products sold in Italian and European markets directly influenced the artistic development and production there. During this period, superior Islamic luxury goods served as models for developing Italian works of art. Mack thought the influential models arrived in regular commerce rather than as booty of war or diplomatic gifts.

Through Venice, Genoa and Pisa, Italy and Europe established trade relations with the Muslim world as early as 829 CE, the year when two Venetian merchants stole the remains of St. Mark from Alexandria and transported it to Saint Marco.[495] Indeed Stefano Carboni revealed that some of the earliest Islamic objects to arrive in Venice were through trade destined for churches and church treasuries, which suggests they were highly prized[496]. Around year 1000, the importation of Andalusian and North African ceramics was wide spread in North and central Italy when many of the so-called *bacini*, mainly bowls, were used in architectural decoration, such as the 12th century Tunisian ceramics found on the facade of Saint Miniato (end of 12th century). This colourful lustre glazed ceramics served as substitute for expensive marble and mosaic inlay decoration of facades and towers of churches[497]. In this way a variety of Islamic glass, rock crystal, carpets, textiles, and metalwork were put to use in Venetian ecclesiastical settings. Other important items of early presence in Venice were medieval Islamic scientific instruments and illustrated manuscripts, which were far more advanced than anything available in Europe was at the time. Venetians enthusiastically acquired and translated into Latin famous Islamic texts, like Avicenna's *Canon*, helping them to spawn their own medical and technological advancements.[498]

The process of transmission, as set by Mack, started with goods brought by Venetian, Genoese and Pisan merchants into Italian markets. Market demand for these items was quickly established and more imports were sought. Encouraged by this increasing demand local artists started imitating these luxury goods and later competed with highly esteemed imports when consumer demand and their own means were sufficient. In a third stage, Italian and local artisans assimilated foreign patterns and designs into local ones producing hybrid types slowly leading to their independence of foreign models. This model seems to apply to ceramics, glass works, silk weaving and leather and inlaid metalwork production. In carpet making, however, local artisans did not try to imitate, reproduce or compete with Muslim carpets because they were considered as work of art for themselves. Italian painters of 15th and 16th centuries proved how these carpets were both valued and appreciated in Europe. Rich and aristocratic families choose often to be portrayed standing or kneeling on or sitting on these expensive carpets to display their status and power (see chapter 6). Mack outlines: *"Oriental carpets made too profound an impression on Italian taste to allow a new industry much leeway for competition. By the time the representation of carpets in paintings went out of fashion in Italy, Oriental carpets had acquired a unique position in Western material culture that persists to this day."*[499]

The Role of Scholars

What the Arabs added to pre-existing scientific and artistic knowledge eventually reached its climax during the period extending between tenth and twelfth centuries, at time when Europe was just coming out of its long nap of the Dark Ages as indicated in the previous chapter. Muslim universities and madrassas lectured their students on advanced theories on mathematics, astronomy, logic and medicine. They had the period's state of the art administrative and accreditation system, lecture halls, discussion classes and voluminous libraries. Admission was open to everybody regardless of his origin or religion, a mixed student community was created from old and young, Muslim and non-Muslims. European counterparts belonged to the church and the admission of students was reserved to those who took holy orders and accepted to become part of the clergy. The teaching activity followed an out dated curriculum based principally on a very limited number of Greek and Roman resources.

Students who aspired for new advanced learning practices and free and liberal intellectualism had to seek alternatives in Muslim universities and schools, sometimes even encouraged by wealthy nobles and unsatisfied clergymen. European scholars were attracted to this pole of knowledge and undertook journeys to the Muslim lands despite the hardship of travel in those days. They travelled from one Muslim area to another, from Sicily and Spain, to North Africa and the Middle East, meeting Muslim scholars, collecting books and manuscripts, and recording what they saw, encountered and learnt. After quenching their thirst after knowledge directly from Muslim sources, they strongly thought of its transfer to their home lands in Europe, just like non-European students today try to transmit European learning and technology to their countries in the third world including Muslim countries. Some scholars, like the French Gerbert of Aurillac (930-1003) who was "*a man of great talent and very superior to the age in which he lived, found himself obliged to attend the Moorish universities in Spain, to acquire some knowledge of mathematics and astronomy, which it was impossible at that time to study in any Christian country.*"[500] He brought from Spanish Muslims the fundamentals of astronomy and mathematics, and "*taught his astonished pupils from terrestrial celestial globes.*"[501] He is credited of introducing the decimal notation, the abacus, the astrolabe and the algorism.[502]

Many aspiring scholars followed the steps of Gerbert; apart from the list of scholars provided in previous chapter, one can list the Spanish Arnold of Villeneuve[503] (d.1245-1311) from Valencia and his compatriot Raymond Lull (1232-1315), the friend of Roger Bacon (1214-94 CE.), who studied in Spain and taught at Montpellier. The Italian Campanus of Navara (1220-1296) studied mathematics at Cordoba and taught in Vienna[504]. The Englishman Daniel de Morlay (c.1140-1210) went to Cordoba to learn mathematics and astronomy and lectured at Oxford where he also published the fruits of his studies[505]. Michael Scot (1175-1232) repeatedly visited Cordoba for the sole purpose of obtaining manuscripts and making translations. Other scholars who had contacts with Islamic learning but not confirmed to have studied or travelled in Muslim Lands include; the Swiss Herman the Cripple (1013-1054), Alexander of Halle (1245 CE.), the Italian Pietro of Abano (1250-1320 CE.); and the Englishmen Robert Grosseteste (1255 CE.) and Roger Bacon who taught Arabic and Arabic science at Oxford, as advocated in his *opus majus* (Great Work) of 1267, to study philosophy in the original languages instead of unreliable translations. Briffault exclaimed:[506] *"The influx of students into Spain and the activity of translators went on till the last days of the Khalifate."* As they returned home, these scholars were instrumental in igniting the torch of learning and rational thinking. Campbell proclaimed his conviction that *"The impulse of this intellectual activity was derived, in the main, from the Arabian writers and Albertus Magnus and Roger Bacon were the eminent types of Arabo-Scholastics of the period who derived the basis of their learning from Arabian sources."*[507]

The books these scholars published and the teachings they practised undoubtedly played a major role in the spread of rational and intellectual thought, which is the main source of artistic activity. The influence of Muslim thinkers on *Dante's* work, Europe's most celebrated revolutionary artist, particularly in the `Divine Comedy' is clear evidence of the contribution of Islam to Europe's renaissance[508]. Although, evidence for such claims have been widely provided in scientific, theological and philosophical aspects, in art and architecture, however, such evidence is hard to find as most of the material evidence in buildings has disappeared through demolition or decay with only ruins remaining. However, the experience the scholars had in Muslim cities, streets, colleges, universities and in their accommodation in Muslim houses must have left some impressions on their sentiments and memories. The fame of the Muslim Capital, Cordoba, penetrated as far as distant Germany where a Saxon nun named Hrosvitha (flourished 2nd half of 10th century) described it as 'The Jewel of the World", in a poem she wrote about the death of the Mozarab Pelagius (d.925):

" Corduba famosa locuples de nomine dicta,
inclyta deliciis, rebus quoque splendida cunctis,
Maxime septenis sophiae repleta fluentis,
Necnon perpetuis semper praeclara triumphis[509]

Hrosvitha also mentions Abd al-Rahman III saying: *"Abdrahemen dictus, regni splendore superbus."*[510] Such detailed knowledge proves that she was there at the time and shows how the great social and cultural progress of Cordoba excited universal admiration particularly amongst European travellers.

Historic sources indicate, for example, that Constantinus Africanus and his Saracen translation aide and student known under a Latin name of Johannes Saracenus were staying at Monte Cassino when Desiderius rebuilt it in 1071. This Saracenus was no more than the famous Johannes Afflacius, the scholar who according to Houtsma and van Donzel was a Persian converted from Islam.[511] Constantinus dedicated five of his translations to Afflacius, who in turn was responsible for the translation and writing of many treaties including *The Liber de hereos morbo* [512] It is inadmissible that they did not give some building advice to Desiderius, who was close friend of Constantinus. They could, therefore, be the source of the introduction of pointed arches there for the first time in Christian Europe outside Sicily as will be argued in next chapter. The importation of illuminated manuscripts of various architectural details was another source of the transmission of motifs to Europe. Christian and Muslim books could be easily acquired in the Muslim market. Debora Howard provided details about the influence of some Muslim illuminations, especially *maqamat al-Hariri* on the mosaics of north atrium in San Marco.[513] Islamic bookbindings displayed a variety of themes including cusped and pointed arches, medallions and Arabesque which could explain the appearance of many forms of European arches and decorations.[514]

Cochrane offered another example; the contribution of the most distinguished European scholar; Adelard of Bath.[515] She did not rule out the possibility of Adelard having played another role in the transfer of Muslim architectural and building techniques to the West. Given Adelard's interest in measurements, practical geometry and proportion he must have been attracted to Muslim architecture during his travels in Spain, North Africa and Syria. Although, he left no evidence of this, one cannot rule out the possibility of him passing on what he had learnt from Muslim architecture to his architect and mason friends[516]. The coincidence in the timing between Adelard's return to England and the construction of the Fontenay Abbey in 1118 which had strong similarities with a mosque at Bitlis in Anatolia that Adelard visited on his journey. It is well known that Adelard travelled through France as he studied and taught at Laon and Tours[517]. The other coincidence involved Queen Matilda (1102 –1167), the wife of King Henry I, who commissioned the construction of a bridge with an unusual structure, across the river Lea at Stratford. Cochrane thought it would have been the use, for the first time, of pointed arches that gave the bridge such an unusual shape.[518] This also coincided with Adelard's return who witnessed the repair works of Misis bridge in Anatolia after its destruction in the earthquake of 1114. According to Harvey, the bridge was repaired using pointed arches replacing the rounded ones of the original bridge, which dated from the time of Justinian.[519]

The second major contribution of Adelard is his translation of numerous Arab works on mathematics and geometry, particularly his translation (with other scholars) of the Arabic version of Euclid's Famous work `Elements'.[520]Cochrane pointed out how the development of Gothic architecture coincided with the return of Adelard of Bath from the East and his translation of Euclid. Stone representations of the Liberal Arts at Chartres prove that Thierry of Chartres used Adelard's Euclid to confirm his architectural designs for the rebuilding after the fire of 1145. In addition to the translations of Gerard of Cremona and Herman of Carinthia or Hermannus Dalmat, Muslim mathematics gave inspiration of the static qualities of the equilateral triangle, already tested in their architecture, and inspired the practical geometry (construction geometry) of Gothic Europe. Both Harvey[521] and Boorke[522] admitted that the spread of mathematical and geometrical knowledge revolutionised Western architecture. Such knowledge allowed a greater accuracy in the setting of building foundations and enabled masons to erect buildings of greater span, and loftier height. Such developments speeded up the transition from the rounded Romanesque arch to the pointed Gothic arch.

The final argument connecting Adelard to the diffusion of Muslim architectural forms and building techniques is related to the manuscript known as `Mappae Clavicula'. The manuscript was translated as the `little Key to drawing' exists in three formats; a fragment dates from the early 9th century, an extended manuscript from the tenth century and a nearly complete version dating from twelfth century. The manuscript contained information on methods of naval warfare used by the Muslims and other military instructions. More importantly, it included descriptions of Moorish Arabic methods of buildings with oil and pitch, in addition to information on the weight of gold and silver and some fountain tricks. The Phillips version is of particular relevance as it introduced an `orthagonium', an Arab instrument constructed from a right-angled triangle used for the measurement of heights. It also incorporated many Arabic terms. The manuscript contained many details of advanced architectural techniques, which Adelard added but wrongly attributed to Vitruvius by some scholars.[523] Chapters 101, 102 &103 of the manuscript described the method of building bridges. They also provided instructions on the correct depth of foundations for all structures with arches, including bridge arches. It also indicated that if vaulting or arches were involved, the foundations should be as deep as the height of the wall without the arch. In other chapters, the manuscript dealt with techniques of building in water and other building methods, showing a deliberate interest in the dissemination of such knowledge in Europe. Cochrane attributed the manuscript to Adelard, based on her discovery of a 13th century Royal Collection which attributed this work to Adelard of Bath.[524] The English Royal Library list of manuscripts includes a work untitled: Liber magistri Adalardi Bathoniensis qui dicitur Mappae Clavicula. Cochrane is not the sole scholar with this view, George Sarton,[525] Edward Grant,[526] Alastain Crombie ,[527] Judith Field,[528] and many others endorsed it. The presence of many Arabic and English words in the manuscript is another indicator that Adelard wrote or edited this document. However, the issue of the authorship of the manuscript is of secondary importance to its existence as an evidence of the transfer of architectural and building techniques. What has been said here about Adelard can also be said about other Western scholars (e.g. Roger Bacon and Gerard of Cremona) who played a major role in the transfer activity to various levels.

The Role of Pilgrims and Travellers.

The main concern in this section is to trace the route of Christian pilgrims visiting holy sites in Muslim lands. The first pilgrimage route was to the Holy Land Jerusalem, a long tradition which was strengthened in the Middle Ages, towards the 10th century, and still maintained today. Despite continuous disputes with Muslims, Christian pilgrims were never interrupted in their journey and were granted freedom to cross Muslim lands.[529] Historical sources indicate that pilgrimage was interrupted only once - in 1009 - during the reign of the Fatimid Caliph Al-Hakim, who in one of his mental crisis also banned Muslims from pilgrimage to Makkah and from fasting Ramadan.[530] The pilgrims were often people who had the means and could afford the cost and sustain the hardship of the journey. Their convoys often included a considerable number from various sects, classes and professions.[531] The event was organised by the church in the form of group travel, granting every pilgrim a *Licentia Romani Pontificis.* The license assured the pilgrim him a three-year security of home and property, against civil and criminal suits during his absence, a recommendation letter granted by his diocesan bishop guarantying for him the hospitality of charitable hostelries and religious houses on the road, and access to special facilities for borrowing money.[532]

Egypt, in addition to Jerusalem, was an important destination to most pilgrims. Besides being on the main route of the pilgrimage, half way between Europe and the Levant, it has a biblical connection and was the setting of many events of the Old Testament. Egypt has also the ancient heritage of the Egyptians, the Romans and the Greeks which attracted European pilgrims. Other pilgrims crossed to Jaffa in Venetian or Genoese ships. The pilgrims' influx increased substantially after the establishment of the Latin Kingdom of Jerusalem. Pilgrims and travellers such as Burchard of Strasburg travelled from Cairo to Damascus as Ambassador to Salah al-Din (or Saladin) in 1175-76 reported on Muslim culture and the animals of Egypt.[533] The twelfth century legend Prester John described the wonders of the East.[534] Jewish pilgrims and travellers form Spain, France, Italy and Germany wrote about what they saw in their trips including the description of holy shrines. Benjamin of Tudela, for example, left Spain at the end of the twelfth century to Jerusalem visiting many towns and sites including the Umayyad Mosque at Damascus. He also wrote about the grave of Ali, the fifth Caliph and cousin of the Prophet Mohammed.[535] Vincent of Beauvais (1190 – 1264) wrote about the history of the Mongols in his *Speculum Maius*[536]. Jean de Joinville (1224-1317) biographer of Louis IX reported an expedition to determine the source of the river Nile. Christian missionaries and embassies worked closely with the Mongols also reported details of the wonders of the East. Other work was produced on Egypt, Jacques de Vitry (c. 1160/70 –1240) and Oliver of Paderborn (ca. 1170-1227) who took part in the fifth crusade in the thirteenth century wrote about Egypt and the churches of Nubia and Ethiopia.[537] Franciscan and Dominican missionaries were founded all across the East. They travelled unrestricted across large parts of the Levant and some of them produced written details of their experience including descriptions of buildings, towns and markets. The English John Mandeville (flourished 14th century) who did his pilgrimage on an armchair provided a description of the Levant in 1322. His book "the Book of Sir John Mandevile"[538] was very popular until the mid-seventeenth century and was translated into many languages.[539] Another armchair pilgrim was Margery Kempe (c. 1373-1438), from Lynn in Norfolk, who published a book about her experience and the shrines she visited. John of Wurzburg, a 12th century German patriotic priest visited the Holy Land (between 1160 and 1170) and wrote about his trip and his experience there. He mentions details about Jerusalem, the Al-Aqsa Mosque which was then stables for the crusaders, estimating that it contained more than two thousand horses or fifteen hundred camels[540] Another German pilgrim; Theoderich, also referred to the stable and palaces and other buildings in Jerusalem (ca.1172). Ludolf von Sudheim who travelled between 1336 and1341 published his experiences as well as descriptions of shrines of Jerusalem around 1468. His compatriot Hans Tucher travelled between 1479 and 1480 to the Holy Land and published his travel book in 1482 which consisted of three major parts; Jerusalem, Sinai and Cairo. Italian Franciscan pilgrims, such as James of Verona (ca 1335) and Niccolo da Poggibonsi (ca 1345-1350), wrote about their experiences and journeys giving detailed accounts of the Eastern Muslim culture, religion, dress, practices and buildings.[541] It was from these accounts that Pilgrimage geography was born.

As emerged from these written and other non-written accounts, this route provided pilgrims and Europeans at home with an insight into the various artistic, scientific and philosophical developments of the Muslim World of the East. Architectural and building techniques, in particular, would have been easy to grasp, as they required only observation and admiration. It is widely acknowledged that the decorative motifs of the so-called perpendicular style of Gothic were inspired by Muslim architecture and transmitted by the pilgrims. Sources indicate that artist pilgrims Simon Simeon (also known as Fitzsimeon) and Hugh the Illuminator, Irish Franciscans, went to the Holy Land in 1323, through Egypt and Alexandria. Simon left an account of the journey "*Itinerarium Symonis Semeonis Ab Hybernia Ad Terram Sanctam*," where he provides a description of the lighthouse of Alexandria.[542] Harvey reckoned Simon must have seen the Mausoleum of Mustafa Pasha (1267-1273) in Cairo, which had Muslim perpendicular style decoration, which the two artists admired and later introduced to the UK.[543] The manuscript was given to Simon Bozoun the prior of Norwich cathedral in 1344-1352, who collected other books, totalling 31 volumes including a Quran, which were all gifted to the library of Norwich.[544]

The second pilgrimage was to Santiago de Compostela in the north-west, which the Spanish claim to hold the relics of the Saint James, an Apostle of Jesus. The impact of this route is far more important, it was at home in Europe and at the edges of the Muslim western Caliphate in al-Andalus (fig.70). Far Greater numbers of pilgrims converged to Compostela and often returned to their homeland in the same year. The first pilgrim known to reach Compostela from France was bishop Gottschalk of Le Puy in 951.[545] The trip usually went through numerous territories and involved visiting many shrines and churches in both ways. A pilgrimage itinerary of Robert the Pious of France which he undertook in 1019-1020 shows that he visited the following pilgrim stations; St. Stephen at

Bourges (11th century and rebuilt after 1195), shrines of St Maiolus at Souveigny, St Mary or Notre-Dame cathedral of Le Puy (first half of the 12th century), St. Julian of Brioude (1180), St. Gilles in Provence (12 century), St Saturninus (St Sernin) at Toulouse (1077-1119), and Ste Foy at Conques.[546]

Like the case of the pilgrimage to the Holy Land, there are no figures for the numbers of Compostela pilgrims but scattered reports of some key events indicate they must have been numerous. For example, in 1120 when a fire broke out in Vezelay church 1127 pilgrims lost their lives.[547] In England records and documents show that *"thousands of English pilgrims are mentioned in safe conducts, letters of protection, ships' licences, confirmation of wills, payments of civil servants' salaries, inquisitions post mortem and other documents."*[548] After the marriage of Edward I, in 1254, with Eleanor of Castile, sister of Alfonso el Sabio, English pilgrims had better protection and their numbers grown rapidly that worried the French who persuaded later king Enrique II not to allow any English pilgrim without obtaining the French King permission.[549] In the fifteenth century, records show, for example, 916 licenses were granted in 1428 and 2460 in 1434.[550]

The Compostela provided a meeting point between the Muslims of Spain and European Christians, especially the French. As well as being geographically closest to al-Andalus, the French were also involved in repeated crusades against Muslim areas of Spain. Lambert[551] counted that the Franks carried out more than thirteen crusading expeditions on al-Andalus between 1018 and 1148. Male noted the presence of French monks at Cordoba as early as 9th century and Cluny, the abbey, had priories all over Spain including Aragon, Castile and Leon.[552] For this reason, he did not rule out the importation by the French of some Muslim building techniques and forms during the development of their Gothic style. In particular, he suggested that the development of structural techniques such as vaults and ribs provided the foundations for the Gothic style. In Lambert's opinion, this route introduced the Roman art to Spain in pre-Islamic times through the Franks and in the Middle Ages; it transmitted Islamic art and motifs from Spain to France. The pilgrimage route, famously known as 'the Franks Route or the Route of Saint Jacques", was supplied with many stop stations mostly Mozarab churches and monasteries renowned for their numerous Muslim motifs. Watkin admitted *"Muslim influence flowed back along the pilgrimage routes from Spain into France, as can be seen in the remarkably Moorish looking twelfth century cathedral of Le Puy in the Auvergne* (fig.71), *which even has Kufic inscriptions on its wooden doors. At the cloister of Santo Somingo de Silos (c.1085-1100)* (fig.72), *which contains some of the most famous architectural sculpture in Spain, the arabesque capitals are of Islamic inspiration"*[553] The

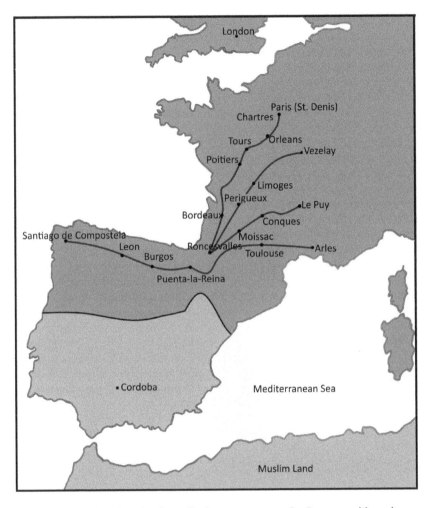

Figure 70 Map showing the four pilgrimage routes to St. Jacques with main
stop stations

cathedral of le Puy was inspirational for most of the religious buildings of the region and south France, seen in examples such as Saint Michel d'Aiguilhe, (tenth and twelfth century) (fig.73) and Église Saint Vosy 12th century. It came as no surprise that the French Romanesque was developed along the pilgrimage route in the central and southern parts of the country, regions on proximity to Spain; Burgundy, Aquitaine, Auvergne, Poitou and Provence are all regions once occupied by the Muslims and continued to be influenced by them. They are located on the pilgrimage south and eastern routes connecting Santiago with the Alpes and Italy. Other important churches rose along other routes between the eleventh century and twelfth centuries; St. Martin at Tours (after 997), St. Martial at Limoges, Ste Foy at Conques (1087-1130), and St. Sernin at Toulouse (1077-1119). Hardly anything remains today of the original character of thee churches as most of them were renovated like St. Sernin or completely rebuilt like St. Martin at Tours. They were built with spacious nave, with five aisles, to accommodate pilgrims and liturgies. Among the uniting elements of these churches were the substitution of tall clerestories and wooden ceilings with stone barrel vaulting resting on single storey triforium galleries[554]. Other features included some of the Romanesque principal characteristics such as the ambulatories, compound piers and radiating chapels containing relics of saints to be shown to pilgrims. Normandy in the North was also a Romanesque region connected with the Normans and the northern pilgrimage route. Sarton noted: *"Pilgrims were especially numerous because it was now a well-established custom in Christendom to start on pilgrimage to obtain indulgences or the remission of sins. So many were the pilgrims that hospices were built to accommodate them, on the Alpine and Pyrenean passes. The influence of these pilgrims cannot be overestimated. The pilgrimage roads stand in the same relation to the intellectual and artistic development of Christendom as the commercial roads to its economic organisation."*[555]

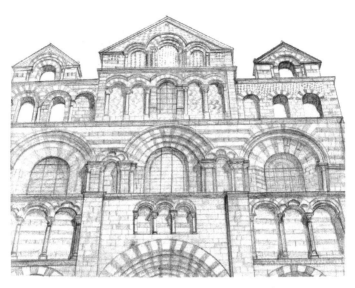

Figure 71 Cathedral of Notre Dame Le Puy (Auvergne 12th century), is perhaps the most "Muslim" Ecclesiastic building in France, with features such the horseshoe and the trefoil arches and alternating colours of the voussoirs.

Figure 72 the cloister of Santo Somingo de Silos (c.1085-1100)

Figure 73 The façade of Saint Michel d'Aiguilhe the chapel dates from the 12th century showing the influence of the Cathedral of Notre Dame de Puy, the main entrance adorned with a trefoil arch accompagned with intricate arabesque.

The Role of the Crusaders

The sweeping spread of Islam put it into geographical contact with the Christian lands of Constantinople in the East and Spain, France and Italy in the west. Christian Europe conceived its overwhelming success as a real threat. Hostilities between Muslims and Christians were inevitable and culminated in the Crusades, which was a strategic action aimed to defeat the Muslims, re-Christianise the world and to establish the claimed Latin Kingdom of Jerusalem.[556] Economic considerations were also involved. The need to open up trade routes to Syria, India and South-East Asia for Venetian and Genoese traders was also a contributing factor. The assistance the rising sea powers of the Venetian and Genoese states provided various crusader expeditions, especially the early ones, is clear evidence of their commercial intentions. The establishment of trading quarters in Syria, Tyre and in Acre after the Christian recapture of Jerusalem is another evidence of the economic influence. Riley Smith developed more economic reasons suggesting that the corrupt Feudal system resulted in increasing scarcity of land, which made families choose the crusading warrior path for their young sons. Discovering most of the crusaders were not heads of household or elder sons; Riley concluded that the families must have decided to designate the eldest son, the sole heir, to go crusading. This was to save themselves from financial disasters, hoping that they could perish or make financial gains in the East. [557] Others suggested that the church enjoyed a substantial economic benefit from the crusades. Its huge landed wealth of the eleventh century needed to find markets for its products overseas. Through the crusaders, the church secured its control on the pilgrimage, a source of great wealth[558]. Political motives were also involved sources indicate that the Crusades sent troublesome elements and contentious knights outside Europe enabling their monarchs to consolidate their control much more easily. The spoiling of Constantinople in the fourth crusade, and the colonisation of the Americas by the Spanish and Portuguese, and later the British and French colonisation of Africa and parts of Asia are clear indicators of the economic aims of the crusades.[559]

The importance of the crusades and their role in the transfer of Muslim building knowledge can be summarised in three main areas. The first of these relates to the duration of the hostilities with their various expeditions.[560] The first stages of the crusades were merely French expansions into Spain, Sicily, the Holy Land and England. Painter provided a societal analysis of these expansions. French warlords sought to colonise other parts rather than compete local feudal powers: *"The removal of the most adventurous and warlike members of the feudal class made less bitter the competition for French fiefs."*[561] The Hauteville brothers of Normandy, Robert Guiscard (1015-1085) and Roger Bosso (1031-1101), invaded Sicily and established their Norman Kingdom. The younger and illegitimate children of the ducal house of Brittany supported William the Conqueror (1028-1087), the illegitimate son of Robert of Normandy, who invaded England in 1066.

The crusades against Muslims of Spain lasted over 600 years as Spanish Christian and French warriors never ceased to attack Muslims whenever chances occurred. Towards the middle of the eleventh century, the old skirmishes along the borders became serious invasions as armies of Northern Spanish kingdoms and France joined efforts and became more organised. Indeed the first town to fall was Barbastro in 1064 under the deadly attacks of the Norman, French and Italian crusaders.[562] It was here where the first atrocities of systematic killing of Muslim civilians started. The crusader broke the surrender terms and killed as many as they could and enslaved more than 6,000 Muslims who were sent as presents to various kings of Europe. Alfonso VI of Castile added to the misery of the Muslims by conquering Toledo in 1085 and the troops of al-Cid managed to conquer Valencia. If it was not for Almoravids who crossed from North Africa with fresh troops and armament, the Christians could have over run the whole al-Anadalus. They were finally defeated at Las Navas de Tolosa in 1212 and since then rapid loss of Muslim territories in al-Andalus became inevitable.

In Normandy, Robert Guiscard and his brother Roger left as chief robbers looking for opportunities until they reached Messina, which they took in 1060, and a year later landed in Sicily in 1061. In 1091, Roger established his full control on the Island making it a Norman Kingdom. The Normans later went to threaten North Africa and attacked cities of Tunis, Sfax, al-Mahdiya, Monastir, Sussa and Annaba (Bona).[563] With the fall of so many Muslim cities into their hands, Crusader countries; France, Italy and Spain inhaled from Muslim intellectual and artistic treasures, especially the libraries of Toledo and Palermo which became the main sources of European scholastic. In the next chapter, the impact of Spain and Sicily on the transfer of architectural and artistic knowledge will be discussed in full details.

The bounties and treasures, especially books and libraries, looted by crusaders in Spain and Sicily opened European lust for the exotic treasures of the East. The looting of the East extended from 1095 to 1291, stretching from the first successful campaign in early 11th century to the fall of Jerusalem in 1098 and the final departure of crusaders in 1291. In 1095, at Clermont in France, Pope Urban II preached for the first crusade claiming to release the Holy Sepulchre and the Holy Lands from the Saracens. The campaign was headed by the key players of the European crusade (Portugal, Toledo and Sicily). The list included

Godfrey of Bouillon (c.1061-1100) and his brothers Eustace (1058-1125) and Baldwin (1058/64-1118)- sons of the Duke of Lower Lorraine-, Raymond IV of Saint-Gilles (1041-1105), Count Raymond of Toulouse who had already fought the Muslims in Spain. There was also Count Stephen of Blois (c.1097-1154), and Bohemond (c.1057-1111), Hugh the Great (1050-1102), Count of Vermandois son of French King Henry I and brother of Philip I. The team also included Robert, Duke of Normandy, son of William the Conqueror King of England, and Marcus Bohemond (c.1057-1111), Prince of Toranto and son of the Norman King Robert Guiscard who invaded Sicily with his brother Roger. The Levant or what became known as "the land that flew in milk and honey" consisted of Palestine, parts of Lebanon, Syria and southeastern Turkey. It was divided into the four Crusader States of Antioch under Bohemond, Edessa under Baldwin, Tripoli under the Count Raymond of Toulouse and Jerusalem under Godfrey of Bouillon (fig.74). The fall of these cities, and Jerusalem in particular, was followed by well-documented acts of terror and butchery as almost every inhabitant of the city was killed. Muslims, Jews, and even a few of the Palestinian Christians were all massacred. Gibbon observed: *"They indulged themselves seven days in a promiscuous massacre; and 70,000 Moslems were put to the sword"*.[564] Consequently, the local population of Jerusalem was significantly reduced and was replaced by European settlers. The Latin Kingdome lasted nearly a hundred years from the fall of Jerusalem in 1098 until its liberation by Salah al-Din in 1187.

The Second Crusade took place between 1145-49, as a reaction against the liberation of Zangi to Edessa in 1144. Zangi also united Aleppo and Mosul and was growing in strength. St Bernard of Clairvaux preached the crusade giving the leadership to Kings Louis VII and Conrad who collected what they could from French and German armies. Like its predecessor, this crusade also involved a desire to expand the borders of Christianity in the Iberian peninsula and the Holy Land. Crusaders gained Portugal and retook Lisbon from the Muslims in 1147. In Spain they took, between 1145 and 1149, Almeria, Tortosa and Lleida. In the East they failed to win any major victories, both kings returned to their countries without any result.

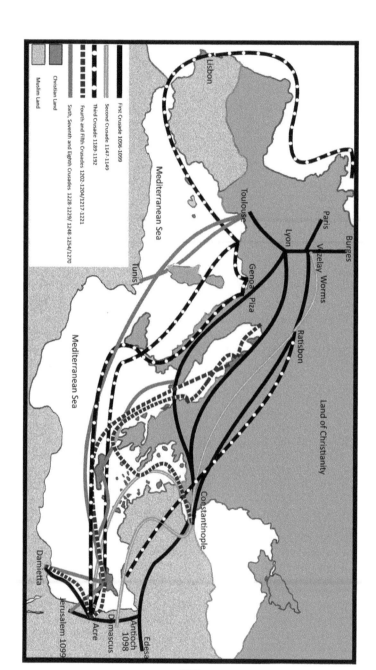

Figure 74. Map of the Crusades

196

The third crusade was an attempt to retake Jerusalem which Salah al-Din had liberated following his victory at Hittin in 1187. Pope Gregory VII rushed to gather his knights and called for a crusade to liberate Palestine once more. The English King Richard the Lion Heart and Philip August, also known as Philip II, King of France answered his call. On their way, Richard captured Cyprus from Byzantium in 1191. The crusades captured Acre and the port city of Jaffa. King Philip returned to France in 1191 while Richard succeeded in making a deal with Salah al-Din signing a treaty that allowed unarmed Christian pilgrims to make pilgrimages to the Holy Land (Jerusalem), while it remained under Muslim control. Richard was captured in his way back by his enemy Duke Leopold but was ransomed.

Five more unsuccessful crusades were organised. The repetition of these campaigns, with each one lasting a number of years and months, provided great opportunities for the Christians to marvel the achievement of Muslims, particularly in building works and military techniques. The crusades culminated by the establishment of the so-called "Latin Kingdom" of Jerusalem in 1099, which encompassed Palestine, parts of Syria, Acre, Lebanon and looking eastwards towards Mosul and Baghdad and Cairo. The Latin Kingdom established regular trade with Europe transforming occupied Syrian ports into trading quarters for Venetian and Genoese cities as mentioned above. In this way, Europe[565] came to the East and despite initial hostilities; it established direct contacts with the Muslim civilisation. As evidence and stories of the Muslim East were spread by the returning crusaders, more enthusiasts were attracted for further missions.

The second element in the importance of the crusade includes the size and background of the crusaders. Historic sources reported that each campaign involved several thousands of people consisting of traders, masons, clergymen, teachers, students, nobles and royalties. The armies were made up of a large number of horse riders, knights and a hoard of populations marching on foot. The moderate figures put forward by Gibbon show that the army of the first crusade alone contained 100,000 horseback and 600,000 pilgrims who could carry arms marched to Jerusalem.[566] They were later joined by more pilgrims who accompanied Hugh the Great and Stephen of Chartres: in two columns: 260,000 persons in first column and 60,000 horses and 100,000 foot in second column.[567] More people followed during the remaining crusades totalling well above one million and a half according to moderate figures of Gibbon (table 1 below). In the second crusade, for example, Bernard of Clairvaux was content for his success in recruiting most of the population of Europe as he proudly declared that cities and castles were emptied of their inhabitants.[568] Unlike in

Table 1. The Crusades periods, populations and leaders

Period and Date	Leaders	Population	
		Horses	Foot
1095- 1187 First Crusade	Godfrey of Bouillon and his brother s Eustace and Baldwin , Count Raymond of Toulouse, Count Stephen of Blois (c.1097-1154), and Bohemond (c.1057-1111)	100,000 60,000 (more troops rode in 1101, with Hugh the Great and Stephen of Chartres) 5,000 (rode with Bohemond to Ottoman Anatolia and Syria)	600,000 360,000 40,000
1147-1149 Second Crusade (Damascus)	King Louis VII (1120-1180) of France and King Conrad III (1093-1152) of Germany	140,000	400,000
1189- 1192, Third Crusade	Frederick Barbarossa (c.1123-1190), Richard I (or the Lion Heart) 1157-1199) , Philp Agustus of France	2000	80,000
1203-1204 Fourth Crusade, to Constantinople	Thibaud de Champagne (1201-1253)	Not Applicable to Constantinople	NA
1218-1221 Fifth Crusade to Egypt	Andrew II (1175-1235) King of Hungary and Casimir , Duke of Pomerania	Not Available	200,000 (Franks)
1227-1229 Sixth Crusade	Frederick II (1194-1250)	Not Available	NA
1249-1254 Seventh Crusade	Louis IX (1215-1270)	Not Available	Na
1269-1272 Eighth Crusade	Louis IX King of France Edward I (1239-1307) of England	Not Available	NA
Totals		+232,000	+1,640,000

most nineteenth-twentieth- century colonial situations, the crusade settlers did not come from a single motherland but included almost all European countries; French, Italians, Spanish, German, Armenians, etc.... Historical studies have showed that great numbers of Crusaders have settled in cities they conquered, the Normans in Sicily, Spanish, Frankish and Anglo Flemish crusaders in al-Andalus,[569] and Frankish and Italians in the Levant.

The settlers were often given land and property and made new and better life than the one they left in Europe. Ronnie Ellenblum thought that the crusades were part of a more general process of migration in contemporary Europe.[570] Europeans in general and rural populations in particular were in severe hardship suffering from the burden of the Feudal system and the backward state of Europe as noted previously. Scores of warriors, pilgrims, settlers, merchants, and artists converged on the Muslim land. The Levant, like Portugal, Spain and Sicily, offered an ideal place for those looking for better fortunes. Ellenblum observed: *"heterogeneous societies, consisting of settlers who had arrived from distant places, were created."*[571] The Latin Kingdom became part of Europe, its colony in the east and its battleground against the Muslims. The Muslim world was exposed to a wider Christian society, which would have ultimately resulted in wider scale learning and imitation.

The third major factor connected with crusaders involves the captives and prisoners of war. The Muslims imprisoned a large number of Christians during their continuous wars along the French borders with Spain and Italian borders in Sicily and Northern Italy. These captives served their masters and lived in their buildings, walked in their streets and served their study and leisure needs. Other captives who converted into Islam acquired greater access to Muslim knowledge. The return of these captives to Europe after being ransomed or exchanged with Muslim prisoners had a strong impact on the diffusion of Muslim philosophical, scientific and artistic knowledge. They were also responsible for much of Christian understanding about Islam and Muslims.[572]

The Christian recapture of many cities in Spain and Sicily also resulted in the enslaving of Muslim prisoners. In European, slave markets such as Arles, Montpellier, Narbonne, Antibes, and Nice these Muslim slaves were often sold to various parts of the continent. The Genoese, Pisan, Florentine and Venetian fleet and merchants also traded in slaves. The captives were put in the service of their Christian masters. Ibn Jubayr reported that he saw many Muslim captives, many of them were from al-Maghrib, doing hard labour; women became slaves for crusade families doing much of the cooking and other housework, farmers were forced to work on their lands, builders, and artisans to build their castles[573].

He also recounts how a Maghribi prisoner form Annaba (Bona in Algeria) was ransomed by Muslims and freed but later converted to Christianity and lived among the crusaders.[574] Sources indicate Saphet Castle contained more than 400 slaves and 820 staff which were usually conducting labour and office work. Some of these slaves *"may well have been the same Muslim prisoners of war used in its original construction."*[575] Historical records revealed that crusader household furnishing in the Holy Land followed that of the Muslim custom, sitting on rugs or mats, and on benches and tables when eating a meal. Arab artists ornamented many of the rich houses of the upper class of crusaders.[576] At tyre and Acre, glass and clay pottery and textiles were manufactured. According to al-Idrisi, Tiberias (or Tabaria) was a beautiful town famed for the production of mats called Samaniyah.[577] When Richard the Lion heart ordered the massacre of the Muslim hostages at Acre in 1191, he spared only one man, who `was notable and strong enough to be of use in building castles'.[578] In 1263, the Templars and Hospitallers refused the offer of Sultan Baybars to exchange Christian with Muslim slaves because the latter were all artisans and hiring other artisans would be very expensive.[579]

Crusaders also employed skilled Muslim and Arab physicians and rejected theirs. In one occasion, William of Tyre criticised the Latin princes who preferred Jewish and Muslim physicians to Latins[580]. Some of the prisoners were brought to Europe. Their skills were widely used in building, decoration, and other artistic works. Because of their numbers, the impact of Spanish Muslim captives exceeded that of those from the East. Lambert[581] noted that in just one event - the capture of Menorca - more than 1287 Muslims were sold as slaves. Most of the inhabitants who could not afford to pay the often high ransom were enslaved. Later, the seizure of the whole of Andalusia resulted in the whole population known as Mudejars being either enslaved or deported by the year 1500. The role of the Mudejars is overwhelming and therefore will be discussed separately.

The impact of crusades in the transfer of Muslim know how to Europe has been widely recognised. A few sceptics, however, refuse to accept this truth arguing that crusaders were in general illiterate fanatics who did not care about art and learning: *"The Latin Kingdom of Jerusalem was a rude military settlement, without the impulse, or at any rate without the time, for the creation of any achievements of civilisation."*[582] Haskins took the same view suggesting that crusaders played surprisingly little role in the transmission of Arabic science if compared to Spain and Sicily.[583] Barker agreed with him arguing that their role has been exaggerated.[584] This could be true for the first generation of crusaders but their continuous contact with Muslims, as revealed by the numerous stories of their encounters, have indeed transformed many of them into civilised individuals, who became later the transmitters of learning and skills, although not in the magnitude of Spain and Sicily. Norman Housley noted: *"Although there is much that is contested in the history of crusading, one advance that has been made in the course of the last half century would probably be disputed by nobody: that the crusade played a central rather a peripheral role in the development of medieval Europe. Directly or indirectly, they affected the lives of most who lived in the twelfth and thirteenth centuries, and of many during the late Middle Ages"*[585] This conclusion was also reached half a century ago by Herr who linked the whole European development of the middle ages to them and their contact with the Muslims.[586]

Crusaders kept contacts with their motherland and exchanged gifts, goods, soldiers, ammunition and talents. The flow of ideas and motifs which accompanied this exchange was enormous and mainly in one way, from Islam to Europe. Oleg Grabar noted: *"the Crusades hardly mattered in the artistic life of the Muslim world. Matters are far more complicated when one turns to the reflection of Islamic forms in Western art. They are complicated because the range of these reflections is much wider."*[587] This is true as the influence of crusades on Muslim architecture is merely limited mostly to the adoption of few techniques such as cushion-shaped voussoirs and folded cross vaults which are found in Mamluk architecture in Jerusalem and Syria.[588] Muslim influence, however, is noted in almost all aspects of the intellectual, economic and artistic life. In medicine, for example, Mitchell Piers wrote: *"it can never be known how medicine in the medieval period would have evolved without the effects of the crusades, a sentence in which the word medicine could be replaced by many others."*[589] One example may suffice to explain how contacts with Muslim medicine were made. The physician and philosopher Muwaffaq al-Din Ya'qub ben Siqlab (1160-1228), who was a *Maqdissi* from Jerusalem born in 1160, was known to the crusaders as 'the Antioch philosopher'. He practiced with another physician, Shaykh Abu Mansur, under the crusade rule. Muawffaq later moved to Damascus after Salah al-Din conquest of Karak des Chevaliers castle between 1187 and 1188.[590]

A moving storey was revealed by Usama Ibn al-Munqidh when he described how his extensive library was pillaged, along with other treasure, in 1145 despite a safe passage promised by King Baldwin III of Jerusalem. The library and the treasure was being transported by ship along the Syrian coast when the vessel carrying them was driven ashore near Acre and its contents plundered by Baldwin in person. The estimated number of his books was no less than 4000 volumes which Usama commented on their loss grieved him as no other experience in the course of a long life.[591] A similar storey happened to the library of Banu Ammar, a literate family living in Tripoli, Lebanon. After selecting the books they liked, the crusaders set fire to his library and its content.[592] According to Cochrane, Adelard of Bath was present at the scene and might have chosen a few himself.[593] Another evidence of direct transmission of books from East to West is reported in a letter from a certain Raban Ata, Catholicus of Armenia, to Pope Innocent IV in 1247 in which he mentions that he is sending two books together with the letter.[594]

Accounts of the life of crusaders in Palestine and Syria show a continuous interaction and good relations, especially at peace times, with the Muslims and Arab Christians. Numerous were the times when crusaders, especially the Franks, had to deal with their Muslims subject and neighbours in a variety of circumstances. Indeed, Usama Ibn al-Muqidh revealed many instances of these contacts. In 1151, for example, Mujeer al-Din Abaq, the governor (or *atabeg*) of Damascus, granted permission for a number of soldiers of Baldwin III to visit the bazaars of the city to buy what they needed.[595] In another occasion al-Salih Ismail, Emir and ruler of Damascus, in 1240, authorised similar permission to the Franks.[596] In his article, Attiya showed that many crusader leaders and dignitaries knew Arabic.[597] William of Tyre was well acquainted with Arabic, known for his work *Historia* and translation of *Historia orientalium principum* of Arab historian, Said ibn al-Batrick (Eutychius). Reynald, lord of Sidon and Beaufort, `was a learned man, who knew Arabic and was well-versed in Arabic history and literature. He employed a Muslim to teach him, and he frequently visited the Sultan (Saladin), to debate with him about his religion.*[598] A certain Simon was knowledgeable in Arabic and worked as a scribe and interpreter for the Hospitallers. The list does not end here "*many others knew enough of the language to deal with natives. Franks adopted native dress, ate native food, employed native physicians, and married Syrian, Armenian or convert-Muslim women.*"[599] Ibn Jubayr also reported that custom officers at Acre were Franks who wrote and spoke Arabic well. He pointed that most of the administrators of the crusade states were bilingual.[600] The authorities or rayses[601] of towns and villages and the dragomans and the scribes, who worked as intermediaries between the Frankish governments and their Arab subjects, spoke Arabic well and some of them were Muslims or oriental Christians.[602] Crusaders employed *muhtasib* in Tyre and in Syria. Godfrey of Bouillon established the "*Cour des Syriens*" (or Syrian Court) ruled by Muslim law between the locals (Muslims) while crusaders had their own Latin law and jurists.[603]

Crusader artists and masons had similar intercourse with the Muslims. Some of them went to the east looking for the exotic while others were invited to carry out works at crusading buildings. During his visit of 1120, count Fulk of Anjou brought with him a number of artists who might have been behind the decoration of the Church of the Ascension. The ivory covers of the so called "Queen Melisande's Psalter', now in the British Museum, thought to be the work of a "Syrian trained in a Byzantine school," [604] show how deep was the influence of Muslim art. The book covers were decorated in predominantly Muslim style combined with some Byzantine embellishments. The interaction of crusader artists and patrons with Arab Christian artists was in most cases fruitful resulting in the realisation of many great rebuilding and redecorating projects in the Latin Kingdom. The Syrian participation in the project of Bethlehem, between 1167 and 1169, to redecorate the Church of the Nativity sponsored by King Amaury I was noted by many historians. It was the Syrian Basilius, who was behind the mosaic works of the angles in the nave of the church.[605] This interaction also promoted cross-cultural understanding and enabled other local artists to participate in crusader art, which Folda rightly defined as *"one that meshes the traditions of the Latin West and the Greek and Islamic East."*[606]

In relation to crusader architecture in the East, historians connected it to French Romanesque and classic Byzantine works. Muslim influence was disputed although traces of Muslim influence can be found everywhere. In the Holy Sepulchre among the Muslim fingerprints one can include the use of pointed arch, the roofs of the transepts and the ambulatory were flat following Palestinian practice, and eight pointed windows are found on the dome over the crossing. George Wigley thought crusade architecture was the encounter of Crusader Romanesque architecture with the *ogival* Arab architecture. He also accepts the presence of Arabesque in their ornamentation and architecture.[607] Emmanuel Guillaume Rey (1837-1916)[608] put forward a theory dividing Crusade architecture into the school of Hospitallers, which according to him was mainly inspired by Byzantine architecture with heavily fortified entrances and inner courtyards. Castles of this order are Crac des Chevaliers or Kilaat al-Hisn and the Margat or Margab castle. The school of Templars was instead influenced by Muslim architecture; the plan followed Muslim fortresses with shallow loopholes and machicolation. Examples of Templars' castles include Tortosa or Tartus castle, Castle Blanc or Safita and Chateau Pelerin or Atlit, which had a polygonal chapel likely modelled upon the Dome of the Rock.[609] The third type of crusade castles is a combination of the two styles examples of which are Saone, Beaufort and Shaubak.

According to Strzygowski, Jerusalem under the crusaders saw a synthesis of Hellenistic, Arab and Romanesque motives.[610] He commented on the artist who made the *mihrab* of the Dome of the Rock which he thought to belong to the Tomb of Baldwin: "*a Western artist who was thoroughly informed in the entire field of the Orient and had created a unique style, equally exotic for us in Europe and for the Orientals.... a Western artist who, stimulated by observations in the field of Iranian-Byzantine and Syrian-Armenian art, elaborated his own style.*"[611] From these fragments, he hypothesised that Gothic might have been introduced in the East, in the Latin Kingdom, before Europe. Strzygowski concluded his remarks with the following recommendation: "*What will my honourable colleagues say when I invite them to accept the idea that something like the later Italian Renaissance was produced in Jerusalem out of the close of the Romanesque style as early as the twelfth century to thirteenth century under the influence of the art of the local environment?*"[612]Indeed if one compares the conditions of Italy and France, where the seeds of architectural Renaissance were first planted, with those at the Levant a remarkable similarity can be traced. They both had strong contact with the Muslims, the former in both Spain and Sicily which made them "a melting pot" of art from all countries[613], while the latter encompassed the heart of the Muslim Caliphate and eastern civilisation in Syria, Lebanon and Palestine, a region which is also a crossroad between Asia and the Mediterranean.

Harvey pointed out that many crusaders remained after the war and witnessed or were even employed in the rebuilding activity to repair the damages and destruction.[614] They subsequently imitated these techniques in their own buildings. An example of this was Eudes de Montreuil who accompanied Louis IX and worked in Jeffa and Cyprus, between 1248 and1254.[615] Among other French artists, who worked in the Holy Land, one can mention Philipe Chinard (c.1230) who worked in Cyprus and later in Apulia for Frederick II, Master Assut and Garnier de Cordes who worked for Alphonse of Poitier and brother of Louis IX in 1268. Nevertheless, these reported numbers remain small compared to the size of projects carried out in the Latin Kingdom. Emmanuel Enlart believed the Christians adopted a learning process from Eastern artists, whether Syrians, Byzantine, Armenian, Copts or Arabs, either by observation and by lessons. They were also assisted by Muslim slaves or prisoners, many of whom could have been instructed and taught to adapt their art to the Crusade style by their Christian masters[616]. One of these was a Jordanian mason who left his mark "Jordanis me fecit" on the tower of the Holy Sepulchre.[617] Setton thought that it was the local Arabs, Muslims and Christians, who did the work and the crusaders only supervised them: *"We can only infer from the buildings themselves and the probability of events that western master masons presided over local workmen who themselves had a long tradition of mason's craft behind them."*[618]

Crusaders abandoned the Byzantine models of fortification and adopted Muslim ones after experiencing the toughness of Muslim strongholds in their many attempts to besiege and capture them. In many cases the captured castles and palaces provided architectural details; Boase emphasised this as he wondered about the influence of an old Muslim castle on the Crack des Chevalliers or Hisn al-Akrad: *"The Castle of the Kurds which represented the original Arab fortification on the site of the Crac, was taken during the first crusade and was permanently occupied by Tancred in 1110."*[619] The Hospitallers rebuilt it in 1142, transforming it into the famous Fortress of the Crac. It is hard to tell how the old fortification influenced the reconstruction but also difficult to ignore it. Among the signs of influence is the use of machicolations which replaced the wooden galleries previously employed in Christian fortifications. These consisted of closely spaced bold brackets (corbels) carrying projecting parapets. Between each pair of machicolation is an opening, closed with a trap door designed for throwing hot oil or water, arrows, stones and other things on the enemy as he attempted to climb the walls or open the gates of the fortification. From the Crack, they were later transmitted to Europe, appearing first at Niort, near Poitier built by Henry II about 1160.[620] Syria and Poitou were closely related and therefore one can understand how they reached that part of France. Machicolations then spread all over Europe appearing in Chatillon (1186), Norwich (1187), and Winchester (1193).[621] Boase thought Chateau Gaillard, built by Richard the Lion Heart in Vexin, in 1193, was inspired by Crac des Chevalliers, but Richard had never seen it suggesting he might have brought builders from the East, or he might have seen another building resembling it.

The crusaders learnt many other military defensive elements which are fully discussed in next chapter, including the use of multiple circular towers. These techniques effectively reduced dead angles which protected the enemy.[622] They also learnt and adopted a number of defensive and other military tactics adopted by the Muslims they besieged.[623] The admiration of crusaders for the art and forms of Muslim building was further demonstrated by the Conte of Flanders, Philippe of Alsace, who built his Palace de Grand (Ghent-Gravensteen Castle) immediately after his return from an expedition to Palestine at the time of Salah al-Din (1176-1178). Much of the character of this palace expressed the Syrian and eastern building inspiration.[624] Another feature which was imported into Europe was the public bath or '*Hamman*'. This had existed in Europe during

Roman times, but Christians rediscovered it in Syria and Jerusalem during the crusades.[625] Boase extended Muslim influence to domed structures as in the baptistery at Giblet which incorporated rosettes and zig-zag designs, the rotunda of the Ascension and the octagon of the Temple Baptistery and the Temple of Jesus which *"show the feeling for local forms, the small domes tombs of Islam."*[626]

The conclusion reached by Grabar sums up the role of the Crusades: *"There is simple exoticism of imported forms and techniques, as with so many textiles, bronzes, or ivories reused for relics or for the ornamentation of churches and ecclesiastical vestments, with the construction of a very Syrian Islamic mausoleum for the Norman prince Bohemond, or with the random initiation of the Arabic script found all over medieval art and especially in textiles. There may well have been subtler impacts, as the memory of the Hoy Land may well have affected the architecture of late Romanesque cloisters. Altogether, at this mini level, the presence of Islamic forms was greater in the West than that of Western forms in the Islamic world, that presence is only partly to be related to the crusades."*[627]

The Role of Mozarabs or the Christian Minorities

The *Mozarabs* a nickname adopted for Spanish Christians who lived in al-Andalus within the Muslim society, originated from the Arabic *Musta'arab*, which literally means arabised in both language and lifestyle. They consisted of a large section Spanish (Visigoth) Christians as well as Arab Christian migrants from the Near East, who were mostly talented artisans and professionals; physicians, translators and masons[628]. The Mozarabs included also Christian minorities who migrated to al-Andalus from northern parts of Spain and beyond the Pyrenees who were attracted by the wealth, civilisation and prosperity of the Muslim Caliphate[629]. These Christians were regarded as members of the community with the usual status prescribed by Islamic law. Relations between Muslims and Christian communities were generally on good terms and only when the Christians opposed the authority of the Islamic rule that clashes and problems started. In the second half of the ninth century, for example, several attacks against the Caliphate of Cordoba were orchestrated by the Church to slow down the rate of voluntary Christian conversion to Islam. One of these was the event of so called "martyrs of Cordoba" where some Christian fanatics sought martyrdom by publically insulting Islam and the Caliph, leading to Muslim reprisals, which resulted in the departure of a great number of Mozarabs, among them artists, scholars, builders and architects, to the Christian North.[630]

The Mozarab concept indicates that these Christians were bearers of the Islamic culture and knowledge. This can be traced in the evidence provided by the `Indiculus Luminosus`[631] written in 9th century by Alvaro of Cordoba, also known as Paulus Albarus, who described the Arabic culture of his fellow Christian as he wrote: *"My fellow Christians delight in the poems and romances of the Arabs. They study the works of Muhammadan theologians and philosophers, not in order to refute them, but to acquire a correct and elegant Arabic style. Where today can a layman be found who reads the Latin commentaries on Holy Scriptures? Who is there that studies the Gospels, the Prophets, the Apostles? Alas, the young Christians who are most conspicuous for their talents have no knowledge of any literature or language save the Arabic; they read and study with avidity Arabian books; they amass whole libraries of them at a vast cost, and they everywhere sing the praises of the Arabian world..."*[632] Indeed, the Mozarabs lost contact with their Latin tongue so much so that a Latin glossary known as Glossarium Latino Arabicum was written in 12th century to help them in their Latin.[633]

Other Christians formed the so called al-Muwalladun, or the adopted Christians who were taken by Muslim families and individuals although having some Christian blood; such as the children of inter marriage between Muslims and non-Muslims. Among the most famous and powerful Muwalladun were the Banu Qasi, who descended from Fortun, the son of Count Castius, who converted to Islam in 8th century.[634] Large populations of al-Muwalladun existed in major cities of al-Andlaus, in Toledo, Cordoba, Seville, and Merida and in other parts of the peninsula.

The Mozarabs excelled in building, and produced some impressive monuments as will be illustrated shortly. In addition, they provided a direct link between Muslims and the rest of Europe. Through their continuing contact with other Christians of Spain and Europe, they managed to provide the latter with valuable knowledge about developments taking place in the Muslim World. The exchange of visits and inter marriages certainly played a complementary role in this process. They played role in the translation of Arabic manuscripts into Latin or Romance, for example, the translation of al-Khawarizmi's manuscript on arithmetic and Mashallah's treatise on the astrolabe which were translated in the monastery of Ripol in the mid 10th century.[635] The Mozarabs formed the backbone of the translation centre of Toledo set by Archbishop Raymond, in Spanish Raimundo. Their chief translator was, of course, John of Seville who was the son of a Mozarabic count named Sisnando Davidiz.[636]

The chief contribution of the *Mozarabs* in the transfer of art of building and its technology is connected to the numerous buildings they erected in Christian Spain and Portugal, especially the so known as Mozarabic churches. They travelled between various regions and particularly to the North, to Aragon, Castile, Catalonia, Navarre and the Asturias, as well as parts of Portugal.[637] As they settled there, a considerable number of churches and monasteries spread around that area, particularly in the northern provinces of high-Aragon, the Asturias and in the north west of Portugal and Galicia[638]. These included; San Salvador of Tevara which was built near Zamora at the end of the ninth century, San Facundo of Sahagun built between Leon and Palencia, in 935, San Cebrian de Mazote in 916, Santiago de Penalba between 931-937 and San Martin de Castaneda in 921 in Leon, San Miguel de Escalada built in 913 in South east of Leon, Santa Maria of Lebena built in 930 in Santander, San Pedro of Cardena in old Castile (founded in 902 CE), Suso Monastery in San Millán de la Cogolla in Castile (10th century), Santa Maria de Melque 9th century, in Toledo, and San Juan of Pena (920 CE) in high-Aragon, San Miguel de Celnova in Galicia (founded in 936 CE), San Pedro de Lourosa near Coimbra in Portugal (912 CE), Abbey of San Michel or San Miquel de Cuxa in Roussillon ((974-12th centuries), and San pere de Roda (10th century) in the Catalan Pyrenees and Santa Maria de Ripol in Cataluna (9th-12th centuries).

In the opinion of Lambert, these buildings, showed the ability of these Christians to incorporate Muslim art and architecture into Christian culture and theology. Much of their work reveals the Muslim fingerprints. Among the many Muslim features these churches incorporated, Gomez listed the horseshoe arch, elongated and joined together with voussoirs, windows with geometric lattice-work or in paired horseshoe arches, and the panel or *Ijmiz* around the arches, flat doors, cupolas with egg and leaf ornaments and arris[639]reminiscent of the Mosque of Cordoba. Other features included the use of bricks, Corinthian capitals in fine limestone, friezes with geometric designs and plant themes with birds pecking at grapes or figures of facing quadrupeds, porticos of columns and the general use of arcades[640]. At the church of Santa María de Bamba in Valladolid (10th-12th centuries), the Mozarabs reproduced patterns from Islamic textiles consisting of lozenge border frames surrounding a crisscrossed design of roundels containing geometric and animal motifs. The imitation of Cordoba intersecting ribbed vaults, first introduced in the extension (961-6) of the mosque of Córdoba by al-Hakam II (also known as al-Mustansir and ruled between 961–76), which appeared in most churches and monasteries at the end of the tenth and in the eleventh centuries as in the Monastery of Suso in San Millán de la Cogolla (Rioja) and the church of San Baudelio de Berlanga de Duero (Soria, 984 CE)). Through these churches and mobile Mozarabic artists, this type of ribbed vaulting reached southern France as in the Abbey of San Miquel or St. Michel de Cuxa (974-12th century) and Hospital Saint Blaise (12th century). As will be demonstrated in the next chapter, this imitation formed the initial stage of the development of European ribbed vaulting which later became responsible for the emergence of the Gothic style.

Muslim military architecture also provided first- hand lessons for Mozarabic castles and fortresses. Castles of great design and construction skills such as San Esteban de Gormaz, built in 956 and the castle known as Tarifa, de Banos de la Encina, ca 960, both built by caliph Al Hakam II were indeed very influential.[641] Mozarab artisans worked for Christian kings and built for them fortresses based on the Muslim prototypes. Glick reported that the defences of tenth century Zamora were built by Mozarabic masons (*alarifes*), from Toledo.[642] Durant noted that when Alfonso VI of Castile (1073-1108) captured Segovia from the Muslims he built there a castle-fortress on the plan of Alcazar of Toledo.[643] The abundance of Arabic terms which relate to various parts constituting a castle, and found in the Castilian Middle Age fortification vocabulary such as el-adarve from al-Darb meaning narrow path, acitara, from al-sitarah meaning curtain wall used for thick front wall, and atalaya, meaning watch tower.[644]

In other cases Arabic names often exclusively appeared in the inscriptions left on these works, in some instances, the Arabic name came after the Latin one. The case of the church of Sts. Justa and Rufina in Toledo is not unique. A memorial flagstone embedded in the pavement to the right of the entrance of the church in which the year 1156 was inscribed incorporated Latin and Arabic inscriptions. The Latin text consisted of the name Michael Semeno and a Christian phrase: *In nomine domini nostri Jesu Christi*, translated as in the name of our Lord Jesus Christ. Next to the Latin text, it was written in Arabic Miqa'il ibn Samanuh, followed by *basmalah* which says: *Bismillah al-Rahmani al-Rahim*, translated as "In the name of Allah, the Merciful the Compassionate"[645]. The use of *basmalah* appears in almost most Latin Mozarabic documents including the Gospels in the Arabic translation made from the old Latin version by the Mozarabic Ishaq ibn Balashk.[646] The extent of the influence can still be felt today in the use of numerous Arabic words and phrases in the Spanish language as already noted above.[647]

The *Mozarabs* also transferred the art of Muslim building art through their works of art. One of their most renowned works were miniatures which Lambert noted that many of them as well as paintings produced in the period of between ninth and thirteenth centuries, had portrayed Muslim architecture in their churches, chapels and other painted buildings.[648] He particularly referred to manuscripts

209

dealing with `Commentaries on the End of the World` which numbered 23 manuscripts. A manuscript in the Archivo Nacional de Madrid, dated in 970 CE and produced by Magius Arxipictor and his student Elmeterius, illustrated work on a monastery which appeared with arched openings and decorated walls, all of which imitated the horseshoe arch, geometric Arabesque decor, strong colours, and some had Arabic inscriptions (calligraphy). Among the masters of miniature, one can refer to Beatus who worked at the monastery of Liébana and produced around 786 CE a commentary of the Apocalypse of St. John the Evangelist, a certain Magio or Maius and Magius of the monastery of San Miguel de Escalada and Florencio of San Isidor de Leon. Historians, such as Lambert, revealed strong influence of this Hispano-Arabic art on artistic movements elsewhere in Europe. The schools of learning founded under the reign of Alfonso VI of León and Castile, between 1065–1109, at Toledo which attracted scholars from all over Europe and as far England and Scotland, provided the point of contact enabling the transmission of Muslim motifs, through Mozarabic art, to Europe, especially during the Romanesque and Gothic periods. From this, it is clear that the *Mozarabs* had been involved in a cross-cultural transfer of the building skills which they had gained from their Muslim friends. This was in addition to the oral transfer of building knowledge as well as their involvement in the translation of scientific, philosophical and theological books.

The Role of Mudejars and Other Muslim Minorities

The`al-*Mudejjanin*', or *Mudejars* is a Hispano-Arab name for the Muslims who lived under subjugation of the Christian rule after the re-conquest. The earliest Muslims to become Mudejars were those whose territories were conquered by Christians in the eleventh century; in cities such Toledo which became under the control of the Kingdom of Castile in 1085, Huesca in Aragon in 1096 and Tudela in Navarre in 1119. Once under the Christian domain these communities were blended in the Christian fabric, talking their language and most of them either willingly or by force taken many aspects of the Christian lifestyle.

The Mudejar provided another means for the transfer of Muslim knowledge, culture and arts. Despite their enmity to the Muslims and Moors, Christian rulers of Spain respected their superior culture and continued employing them for most of the administrative and cultural needs. This royal respect of Islamic culture and knowledge contributed to more rapid and easy assimilation. The political alliances through marriages between Muslim princes and those of Castile and Aragon were frequent. Alfonso VI, the conqueror of Toledo for example married Zaida, the daughter of Emir of Seville, and his capital resembled the seat of a

210

Muslim court. The fashion later spread to private life as Christians dressed in Arabic Moorish dress and the rising Roman language of Castile was enriched by a large number of Arabic words. The influence of the Mudejar culture was immense and reached its climax during the rule of Alfonso X or the Wise (reigned 1252–84).

As a prince and of governor of Murcia, Alfonso X built a college for the famed Muslim scholar and educationalist Muhammad al-Riquti, originally from Ricote who remained in the town after its conquest by Castile in 1266, where he lectured to Moors, Jews and Christians.[649] Alfonso also patronised the translation work and the transmission of Muslim knowledge. Among his translations was *Kalila wa Dimna* from Arabic into Castilian, which became influential on Western literature, notably on the Roman de Renart, on Boccaccio's Decameron, and on the Fables of La Fontaine. Other translations from Arabic included philosophical and spiritual works of *Bocados de Oro and Poridad de de las Poridades*. Based also on Arabic sources Alfonso produced *Grand e general Estoria.*[650] Above all, Alfonso's most famous artistic and literary work, the *Cantigas de Santa María* - available at Madrid, Escorial, Bib. Monasterio S Lorenzo, MS. J.b.2 – was produced from Arabic sources and the Mudejars played a significant role in the paintings.

Most of the Mudejars continued, with little disturbance, in their professions. Before 1158, Abd Allah ibn Sahloh, for example, had taught mathematics and philosophy to Moors and Christians at Baeza.[651] The foundation of Latin and Arabic College at Seville was based on Muslim teachers lecturing on medicine and science side by side. Toledo translation centre, under the Archbishop Raymond, included the Encyclopedia of Aristotle with commentaries of al-Kindi (alkindus), al-Farabi (alfarabius) Ibn Sina (Avicenna), al-Ghazali (Algazel) and Ibn Rushd (Avirroes). The centre also translated from Arabic the works of Euclid, Prolemy, Galen and Hippocrates with Arabic comments of al-Battani (Albatenius), Ibn Sina, Ibn Rushd, al-Razi (Rhazis) and al-Bitruji (Alpetragius). These were translated into the Romance language of Castile with the help of Mudejars and Jews, and later by Christians into Latin and distributed all over the Christendom.

Lambert noted that the Christian rulers who took over from the Muslims were particularly attracted to their predecessors' luxurious art and they called for best artists of the *Mudejars* all over Spain and commissioned them to build palaces as rich as those vacated by the Muslims. He added: `*The (Christian) rulers and influential personalities instructed the building of luxurious palaces where they could create the rich decoration, noisy fountains, and comfortable baths of those*

211

Andalusian rulers. In some cases, they even attempted to reproduce in their religious buildings the splendour of the mosques they inherited and offered to Christ.' [652] A historical source, Leon of Rosmithal, a European traveler also known as Baron of Bohemia, described how women of the nobility dressed in Islamic fashion and people ate Arabic style food when visited some important lords in Burgos in 1466. Rosmithal also reported that King Henry IV of Castile surrounded himself with Muslims and Jews and that he ate, drank and dressed in the Muslim manner. [653]

The Mudejars were great builders and were treated so by their Christian patrons. They monopolised specialities such as brick building, plaster sculpturing, ceiling decoration, carpentry and ceramic industry[654]. The Spanish proverb: *"qui tienna Moro tienna d'oro"* meaning who holds a Moor holds gold, perhaps explains the value of this community.[655] Because of their skills and talents, they undertook, sometimes forced to, most of the building activity in Spain after the defeat of Muslim rule. When Ferdinand III of Castile (ruled 1217–52) conquered Cordoba in 1236, Mudejar masons and carpenters were made to work for a specified period every year on sacred structures and in return for their tax exemption.[656] They were also involved in teaching this profession to a considerable number of Christians. Their work gave Spanish architecture and buildings their renowned Moorish style. Córdoba's Mudejars reproduced the famed vaults with interlaced ribs at the Great Mosque for churches in Toledo, Soria, Navarra and Saragossa, as well as at the hospital of San Blaise, near Oloron, and Havarrens in southern France as will be demonstrated in next chapter.[657] Similarly Seville's conquest in 1248, gave the Christians access to the great monuments of Almohads, the last rulers of Cordoba and Seville (12TH century). The famous Giralda provided a model for many *Mudéjar* towers produced in churches such as Omnium Sanctorum built in mid 13th century on the ruins of an old mosque, San Marcos also built on the site of an old mosque in late 14th century but reconstructed in 1470, and Santa Catalina built in 14th century. Seville Islamic domes were also reproduced in many chapels and churches as in the chapel of the Magdalena, the Piedad de San Marina (1693) and the narrow Quinta of San Pablo.

The Mudejars spread a new finer version of Almohads style through Spain. They soon established it as a complete new delicate art that was later adopted by other Spanish ethnic builders; Christians and Jews. The style dominated Spanish architecture until the end of the 16th century.[658] For their Christian patrons, the Mudejars built churches, towers and palaces which often displayed Muslim construction techniques, motifs and decoration, although structurally might have appeared in Romanesque or Gothic style. The employment of horseshoe and trefoil arches, the ribbed cupolas of exquisite design, and the muqarnas were

212

some of the most popular elements of the Mudejar style. The decorated tower-minarets, porticoed patios, exquisite baths and gardens designed in Muslim fashion with two water channels crossing at the centre were other features the Mudejars employed in Christian palaces and churches. In decoration flowing Arabesque, carved woods, decorated stucco, and glazed tiles and ornamental metals formed essential ingredients of their decorative scheme in most of these buildings. The Mudejars excelled, particularly, in coffered ceilings and coloured tiles, an art which was a continuation of the Muslim art in Granada and North Africa. This can be found in Toledo in numerous tombs such as the tomb of Fernand Gudiel (made in 1278), as well as in the chapel of Saint Eugene.[659] They even worked in private houses such as the Infantado palace at Guadalajara. The popularity of Mudejar art during the period that followed the reconquest indicates that Christian monarchs and clergy must have admired the mosques, palaces, towers and mansions which they gained from Muslim cities and villages.

It comes as no surprise that most of the churches built during the period of the Reconquista, especially between 12th and 15th centuries, were of Mudejar style. In Toldeo, the church of San Román, rebuilt in 1221, displayed the same brickwork technique, horseshoe arches with polychromed voussoirs alternately painted in red and white in the Cordoban fashion, and Arabic and Latin calligraphic inscriptions surrounded a number of figural paintings. At the west end, multifoil arch decorates the wall above a framed arch which stood at the middle in the mihrab fashion. On the exterior, blind multifoil arches decorate the apse and a huge Mudejar tower with two bell openings at the top level very much resembling Muslim minarets. The church of Santiago del Arrabal, Toledo, (12th century), was once a mosque but rebuilt as a Christian church with brick and coursed masonry after the Christian reconquest. The façade is a remarkable reproduction of the façade of the Great Mosque of Cordoba; framed section in the wall incorporating a horseshoe entrance decorated with multifoil arch, followed by two sections of intersecting blind arches. The minaret of the original mosque was preserved and toppled with a Mudejar belfry. The church kept the square plan of the mosque but adopted the pointed arches instead of the original horseshoe ones. Among the treasures the church still keep is a beautiful 14th-century Mudejar plasterwork pulpit.

Mudejar features can be found in many other churches all over Spain; as in San Bartolomé (restored early 14th century), Church of San Tirso (12th century) and San Lorenzo (c. 1200) both at Sahagun in Leon. In Las Huelgas, there was San Tomé, in Toledo, San Juan de Los Reyes after 1504 with its famed ceiling made in Mudejar atesonado, as well as Hospital de Santa Cruz, Alcala de Henares, San Ildefonso Chapel, all in Toledo. The greatest concentration of Mudejar work is, however, found in Aragon, which was named a World Heritage Site by UNESCO in 2001. One of its greatest buildings is San Martin (1315) famous for its tower and the use of baked brick and glazed ceramics in repeating geometrical patterns. Other important Mudejad buildings include San Pedro, El Salvador (built in 1257 and restored in 1993) with its interlocking geometric pattern in low relief fired brick work, cathedrals of Santa María de Mediavilla, Santa María in Calatayud, Santa Tecla in Cervera de la Canada, Santa María in Tobed, Palace of Al-Jafaria, Church of San Pablo, and La Seo Cathedral in Zaragoza.

The influence of King Pedro or Pierre the Cruel[660] (1350-69) in the spread and development of the Mudejar art is of particular importance. His attraction to and respect for Muslim art exceeded that of all other rulers. He had good relations with Mohammed V, the Muslim ruler of Granada at that time, and his financial minister was a Mudejar named Samuel Halevi Aboulafia[661]. Pedro the Cruel is known to have encouraged the spread of Mudejar building art, and according to Lambert, his minister set up a Mudejar art school during his reign. The Mudejars and Granada Muslims also built a royal palace for him in Seville, Alcazar (Arabic for Palace) in about 1354. The principal features of the palace are its Arabic façade. The Hall of Ambassadors and its cupola dominate the rest of the building. The walls were all covered with beautiful *azulejos* (glazed tiles) and geometric decorations. The influence of Alhambra and Alcázar of Seville was behind the proliferation of splendid palaces of lavish reception halls in 14th-century Spain, such as the Taller del Moro, the Casa de Mesa and the hall of the Corral de Don Diego. Such attitudes resulted in another revival of Muslim architecture, this time under Christian rule, which penetrated deeply into Spain and Portugal. A survey undertaken by Lambert[662] of the main churches and monasteries of that time revealed the spread of Muslim minarets which served as towers all over Spain from Toledo,[663] to Castile[664] and Aragon.[665] Another area where the Mudejars were involved in practicing their architecture was synagogues. One of their best buildings was Santa Maria la Blanca in Toledo which was built in 1180 and converted into a church later. It is a good example of Mudejar work in Christian soil, for non-Muslim or Christian use. The use of brick and horseshoe arches supported on pillars and topped with vegetal decorated capitals are characteristics of the Almohad and Mudejar architecture. El-Transito built by Samuel Halevi in 1356, was another synagogue featuring Nasrid style polychrome stucco work, muqarnas, multifoil arches and panelled ceiling with Hebrew calligraphy arranged in Arabic fashion.

Many instances from the end of the fourteenth century show that Mudejar artisans worked on Spanish gothic buildings; Henry Terrace revealed that the chapel of the gothic Cathedral of Toledo was built by two Muslims.[666] Mudejar art and architecture were blended into Gothic giving Spain its distinctive style as found in San Julian, San Isidore, Santa Lucia, Santa Marina, San Marcos, San Esteban and others. Torres Balbas who studied this style revealed that these works were mostly made not by Mudejars, but by descendants of foreign artists, French, Burgundians, Flemish and Germans who migrated to Spain. This shows how much this art has penetrated in Spain and Europe.[667]

During the Renaissance, Mudejar art did not loose its appeal and was mixed with the building style of this period. Example of this include the palace of Peñaranda de Duero (Burgos), the chapel of San Ildefonso (1510) and the Paraninfo (Great Hall; 1518–19) at the university in Alcala de Henares, the palace of Cárdenas de Ocaña (Toledo) and the Casa de Pilatos. By the 19th century, the Mudejar style still going strong by the rise of the so called the Neo-Mudejar style, a movement which employed Mudejar features, especially the horseshoe arches and the use of abstract shaped brick ornamentations for the façades in the construction of modern buildings, as seen in bull fight rings across Spain, Portugal and Latin America. Among the neo-Mudejar buildings one can list Gran Teatro Falla in Cadiz, Las Ventas bullring in Madrid, Church of Santa Cruz, Madrid, Church of La Paloma, Madrid, Train Station in Toledo, Post Office in Zaragoza, and Campo Pequeno bullring in Lisbon in Portugal.

We may also wonder about those Mudejars who left Spain and travelled into Europe. Could they have been involved in the development of Medieval Western architecture, particularly the Gothic style? From the Italian experience, it seems very likely. The recapture of Palermo, Sicily and other parts of Muslim Italy, in eleventh century, was followed by an extensive   use of Muslim captives in the construction of Italian buildings was as extensive as in Spain. The Norman kings were particularly favorable to Muslim art and architecture. At the court of Kings such as Roger II and Frederick II, there were many Arab scholars including geographers, doctors, philosophers, poets and architects. The Muslims built numerous monuments for these kings. The most celebrated one was San Giovanni degli Eremiti with its Muslim dome built on the site of a former mosque in Sicily[668], Capella Palatina was built in 1132, the church of the Martorana in 1136, La Ziza in 1154, and La Cuba in 1180. In the opinion of Barker, the integration of Muslim captives into the Norman kingdom produced a mixed culture that was capable of influencing the west.[669]

Scott[670] gave the Italian connection an unprecedented role in the development of European building techniques and architecture. The Normans spread Italian and Mediterranean forms with their conquests in Europe. His thesis was based on the argument that the Normans were not the original influential element in Italian architecture as widely suggested, but rather the opposite. The Normans developed their architectural forms and typologies from southern Italy. Scott wrote: '....the so-called Norman architecture in Sicily having so much more affinity to Italian forms rather than to French Norman, and it accounts for the Saracen East.'[671] The movement of Mudejar and other Muslim artisans and builders between Sicily and other parts of the Norman realm must have contributed to the sudden expansion of many ambitious architectural programme in northern France and in England as concluded by Harvey.[672] Scott suggested that the Romanesque style was formed by the marriage of north Christian Italy and southern (Saracen) Sicily. He then traced the origins of the rounded arch in France and Normandy in particular, revealing that the first rounded arch was introduced into Normandy by St. Guillaume, Abbot of St. Benigne in Dijon. St. Guillaume de Volpiano was a Lombard, born in 961 in Santa Giulia in Italy, who travelled to France and to Cluny under the leadership of Abbot Saint Mayeul. He built a monastery dedicated to St. Benigne in Dijon and was personally involved in the design and building of the Abbey.[673] However, the construction work did not start until the design had been sent to Italy to be commented upon by renowned masons, architects, artists, scientists and other people of building knowledge. St.Guillaume was later invited by Richard II, Duke of Normandy to found monasteries and erect other monuments. This clearly shows how the round arch, at least, and much of early Norman architecture found its way to Europe. After the Norman conquest of Sicily, the Sicilian Muslim forms and ornaments once more remodelled Norman architecture. Captive Muslim masons often followed their Norman masters into areas they conquered in Europe, one of these many captives was a certain Lalys who was taken by his master Richard de Grandville to England where he designed the abbey of Neath in Glamorgan in 1129.[674] Another historian Dulaure, in his Histoire de Paris, revealed that that Muslim architects were active in the French soil, including the city of Paris where they assisted in the construction of St Nicolas des Champs in Paris (ca 1119).[675]

The Role of the Jews

It was under the Muslim rule, whether in the East, North Africa or al-Andalus, that the Jews reached a status not experienced in any other part of the Medieval world. In al-Andalus in particular: *"No other Jewish community produced as many Jews who achieved positions of status and even power in the non-Jewish world; and no other Jewish community produced such an extensive literary culture reflecting the deep impact of an intellectual life shared with non-Jews."*[676] Their greatest fame was between the tenth thirteenth century, coinciding with the period of the apogee of Muslim civilisation. The high level of education and the prominence they reached was due to the tolerance Muslims bestowed on them, entrusting them with important administrative and political positions as well as giving them unlimited access to education and resources. These conditions permitted them to produce their golden age with significant development of the Hebrew art and intellectual talents. In the opinion of Erwin Rosenthal, this age was unique for the Jews: *"The Talmudic age apart, there is perhaps no more formative or positive period in our long and chequered history than that under the empire of Islam from the Mediterranean the Indian Ocean"*[677]

Among their scholars who achieved distinction one can cite Ibn Zoher (Avenzoar) (1094-1162), a famous physician and surgeon, Hasdai-Ben-Shaprut (915-ca.970), a Rabbi who wrote a commentary on the botanical treatise of Dioscorides, Rabbi Judah who was well acquainted with both Arabic and Hebrew literature, Joseph translated, in 1006, the Talmud for Caliph Hischem I,[678] and Manasseh ben-Baruch who compiled a critical lexicon, A *Colossal Monument of Patience and Erudition.* Other pioneer scholars included Isaac Ben-Chanan translator of the complete works of Aristotle into Hebrew, Isaac Alphes codifier of the laws of the Talmud, Samuel Ben-Alarif minister of Habous (religious property endowment also called Waqf) in Granada, Isaac Ben- Baruch a great mathematician, Judas Levi man of Hebrew literature, Ben Chia astronomer, Isaac Latef and Benjamin of Tudela both geographers, Charizi physician and Solomon Ben-Gabirol a poet and philosopher who lived in Saragossa in 1070 CE.[679] The most renowned of these, however, is Moses-Ben-Maimon (Maimonides) from Cordoba who wrote "The Guide of Lost Spirits" a Hebrew masterpiece. He also wrote about 14 works in medicine and a famous commentary on Hippocrates. He was also knowledgeable on the doctrines of Christianity and in literature; he was named The Eagle of Jewish Literature, the Guide of the Rabbis and The light of the Occident. The liberal character of his thoughts and his rejection of the idea of the eternity of matter had substantial impact on progress and reforms in the West. He visited Fez, Montpellier, Cairo, Baghdad, Jerusalem, and was the Court physician of Salah al-Din. His works were translated into Latin and studied by Christians and diffused throughout the south of France where they played an important part in the promotion of the Albigensian heresy. Aben Ezra, who lived in Toledo in 1147 and produced works in mathematics, philosophy and astronomy, and Solomon Ben-David-Halevi were other prominent scholars. In public and civic domains among the highly influential Jews, one can mention Hasday ben Shaprut, a physician in the court of Abd al-Rahman III .who had also important diplomatic and financial responsibilities. Ismail ibn Naghrila (993-1056), or Samuel the Nagid, was a military general and a scholar very accomplished in poetry and became the second man of the Zirid state of Granada in charge of Granada's foreign affairs.[680] Historical records show that when the central Umayyad authority collapsed in Cordoba in 1031 and the establishment of what is known as the *Ta'ifa* rule, a number of small kingdoms ruled by authoritative families or individuals, particular rise of Jewish dignitaries in various courts of al-Andalus. Among the many names *Ta'ifa* courts employed, a certain Abraham in Granada, Ishaq ibn Hasday and Abu Fadl ben Hasday in Saragossa and Abraham ben Muhajir in Seville. For a number of reasons the *Ta'ifa* rulers, who were mostly weak, illegitimate and ruled over small political realms, relied on these Jews in diplomacy, finance and public administration. The Jews did not pose potential risk for the *Ta'ifa* kings or princes as they were not power contenders as did fellow Muslims. The Jews were also safer than Christians who were feared because of their allegiance and loyalty to their neighbouring Christian armies and states.[681]

The Jews also occupied important positions in European courts, after the Christian conquest eminent Jews served in the royal courts of various kingdoms. In Castile for example Joseph Ferrizuel, known as "Cidellus" served under Alfonso VI (ca 1040-1109). Samuel Levi was the treasurer of Pedro the Cruel (1334-1369); and Isaac ben Sadok, known as Don Caq de la Maleha, worked under Alfonso X (1221-1284). In Aragon, Sheshet Benveniste served under Alfonso II (1152-1196) and Pedro II (1174-1213)[682]. Jewish physicians were employed at the courts of other Spanish and Portuguese kings such as Henry III (1379-1406), Juan II of Castile (1405-1454), Jaime I of Aragon (1208-1276), Duarte (1391-1438) and Juan I of Portugal (1357-1433). Jewish Courtiers were desirable in Christian kingdoms "*as the bearers and mediators of the culture of prestige among the far less sophisticated knights and clerics of the Christian kingdoms.*"[683]

The intimate relations the Spanish Jews maintained with Jewish communities scattered throughout Europe particularly in France, Portugal and Italy resulted in the diffusion of the Iberian Muslim knowledge deep into Europe. Jewish mobility along the Mediterranean shores and other extensive areas in Europe was decisive in the transmission of many Islamic motifs. Jews merchants were trotting numerous countries buying and selling before returning to their homes. The Jewish role in the trade with Europe was emphasised by Genizah documents. Written by Fustat Jews the document contained countless letters and documents about various Jewish merchants who traded with Italy, Sicily, Spain and Bougie on Algerian coast. A typical Jew merchant was Nahray ben Nissim (fl.1045-96) who traded in precious stones also exported flax from Egypt to Sicily and Tunisia, imported silk from Sicily and Spain, brought lacquer, indigo and brazil wood from the far East and exported them westwards[684]. The itinerary of Benjamin of Tudela, a Spanish merchant, in one of his travels he undertook between 1165-1167 he travelled through Catalonia, south France, Italy, Greece, the Archipelago, Rhodes, Cyprus, Cilicia, Syria, Palestine, and Persia and when returning he passed by Indian Ocean, Yemen, Egypt, Sicily and Castile.[685]

The Jews and their networks in South France and Spain played a key role in the trade and cultural exchange on both sides of the Pyrenees, North France and in the Rhineland cities of Speyer, Worms and Mainz which had active Jewish minorities. Under Almohads, some of the Jews migrated to regions of southern France and Provence where they played significant role in mediating *"the peculiar Anadalusi Jewish intellectual life and style to a new community innocent of Arabic."*[686] Among the key advantages they had was the use common language shared between them. From their extensive travel they became acquainted with various languages especially, Arabic, Latin and local dialects which enabled them to establish good contacts. They succeeded in organising a good system of exchange throughout much of Europe through their knowledge of the Muslim trade system, such as credit letters and cheques and money lending. They managed to secure free and safe trade, Louis the Pious (ruled 814-840) granted them extensive trade privileges that contemporary cleric, Agobard of Lyons (d.840), protested to him to end it.[687] Due to their financial and administrative skills (which they practised in al-Andalus), the Jews succeeded in making themselves indispensable to the Christian community, enabling them to further expand their network. There is at least one example, among many, of Abraham Ibn Ezra (1089-1164) who was born in Toledo and studied in Cordoba and Granada. He was a renowned scholar and a doctor translated al-Biruni's commentary on Khwarizmi's Tables and travelled into Egypt, Palestine and Arabia. He moved from Spain to Rouen where his influence, particularly on French biblical exegesis was extensive.[688]

The Jews were instrumental in the translation of Arabic manuscripts into Latin due to their acquaintance with both these two languages. The catalogue of Bartholoccius listed some 4000 Jewish scholars, from Spain, Italy and France, who attained distinction in the Middle Ages.[689] Those of Spanish origin were predominant. The translation centre established in Toledo used them as interpreters. All Arabic treatises of practical or scientific value were translated into Hebrew and Romance or Latin. Farragut, a Jew, who studied at Salerno and Montpellier, translated the "Continent" of al-Razi or Rhazes and dedicated it to Charles of Anjou, brother of Louis IX, King of France. It was also in France, in Norbonne, that most of the Arabic philosophical texts were translated[690]. Among the great translators are members of Ibn Tibbon and Kimchi families who after migrating from Spain to South France they established an intellectual and a translation nucleus there. The Kimchi family, Joseph (1105-1170) and his sons Moses (d.1190) and David (d.1235) *"brought with them the Spanish tradition of grammar, lexicography and philosophical learning."*[691] Ibn Tibbon family, moved from Granada to the town of Lunel in the south of France.[692] Their father Judah ben Saul knew Arabic and Hebrew. He became renowned as the father of translators as three generations including, son Samuel Ibn Tibbon (1150-1239), grandson Moses ibn Tibbon and great grandson Jacob Ibn tibbon (1236-1304) of this family worked as translators of Arabic learning[693]. Moses ibn Tibbon, who also practiced medicine at Montpellier, translated from Arabic numerous medical works including those of al-Maimonides including *Regimen Sanitatis*, of Hippocrates *Aphorisms* based on Arabic and Hunain Ibn Ishaq *Masa'il fi al-tib* or *al Mudkhal ila al-tib* as well as *Kitab taqasim al-'ilal and Kitab al-aqrabadin* of al-Razi, and Ibn al-Jazzar's treatise *Zad al-Musafirwa-qut al-badir*.[694] Jacob Anatoli (1194-1256) was the son in law of Samuel Ibn Tibbon worked for Emperor Frederick II translation centre at Naples and translated Averroes' work and Aristotle's book on logic from Arabic as well as other astronomical Arabic work.[695] Other famous translators included; Abraham bar Chiya (d.1136), Kalonymos ben Kalonymos (1286-1337) who translated Jabir's treatise on poisons, *Kitab al-amud fi usul al-tibb of Ali ibn Ridwan,* and other works of al-Kindi and al-Farabi.[696] Isaa ben Pulqar (flourished 1307-1330) translated the book on philosophy, *maqasid al-falasifa,* of al-Ghazali in 1307. Shem Tob Ibn Ishaq and Meshullam ben Jonah each made a translation of medical book of *al-Tasrif li man Ajazaan al-Taalif* of al-Zahrawi or Abulcasis.[697] Draper summarised their contribution as follows: *"Throughout the middle ages they were the physicians and bankers of Europe. Of all men they saw the course of human affairs from the most elevated point of view. Among the special sciences they became proficient in mathematics and astronomy; they composed the tables of Alfonso, and were the cause of the voyage of De Gama. They distinguished themselves greatly in light literature. From the tenth to the fourteenth century their literature was the first in Europe. They were to be found in the courts of princes as physicians, or as treasurers managing the public finances.*"[698]

Petrus Alphonsi, formerly Moses Sepharadi (1062 – 1110), a Spanish Jew who was born, lived and studied in Muslim ruled Huesca and Zaragoza. When the Christians took these two cities in 1097 and 1118 respectively he converted to Christianity in 1106 and migrated to North France and England where he transmitted his Muslim based learning. In England he worked as royal physician of King Henry I from 1112 to 1120. His work "*the Disciplina Clericalis*" which he wrote in Arabic in Huesca in 11th century was translated into Latin and is said to occupy "*a very important position on the caravan route of the transference of oriental tales to the West*"[699] Arabic exempla from *the Disciplina Clericalis* also reached Iceland[700]. Joseph Kaspi (b.1280) was another Jewish scholar but from Languedoc region in France. He travelled the Muslim Lands in search for learning, including Egypt, Spain and Fez of which he said: "*I am live in the great city of Valencia. If the Quickener of the dead grant me life, I will again traverse the whole of Aragon and Spain. I will cross to Fez, for I have heard that it is a seat of learning*"[701] Ettinghausen showed the mobility of trade and Jews was paralleled by the movement of artisans who influenced the diffusion of traditions and techniques, especially in minor arts such as pottery and bookbinding.[702] Jews were also employed as couriers not only between various Muslim Emirs but also as messengers between the Muslim Caliphate and European crowns. The conclusion is that the translation of Arabic works into Hebrew made them available to non-Arabic speaking Jews in Europe who translated them into Latin and other local dialects, thus becoming part of its cultural heritage.

The Jews cultivated Islamic style architecture, even after the Christian conquest. Synagogues built under the Christian authority such as those mentioned above in Cordoba and Toledo continued to be in Islamic character. According to Dodds, the Jews maintained this tradition because it was distinct from the Christians their prosecutors.[703] They even employed Arabic script in Cordoba synagogues while in Toledo they combined it with Hebrew. Some connected the presence of Arabic scripts and calligraphy to Arab or Muslim artisans but Dodds thought it was the Jews who preferred to use Arabic and considered it as a sign that they regarded it as their own architecture. Wexler suggested that the Jews preferred to keep a separate identity in Europe even if it had to be in an Islamic dress.[704] This leads us to believe that the Jews identified themselves with Arabic and Islam more than Christianity during the Middle Ages and continue to do so in present time. "*Insulted, plundered, hated and despised by all Christian nations, banished from*

England by Edward I, and from France by Charles VI, they found in the Spanish Moors rulers who, in addition to that measure of tolerance which is always produced by a high intellectual culture, were probably not without a special sympathy for a race whose pure monotheism formed a marked contrast to the scarcely disguised polytheism of the Spanish Catholics; and Jewish learning and Jewish genius contributed very largely to that bright but transient civilization which radiated from Toledo and Cordova and exercised so salutary an influence upon the belief of Europe."[705]

Ashtor Eliyahu, a Jewish historian, endorsed Dodds views highlighting the Arabic/Islamic cultural roots of the Jews as he observed: "*The profound influence of Arabic literature is conspicuous in the ennobled type of Jew found in many of their works who is both loyal to the heritage of his forebears and permeated with the general culture.*"[706]The use of Islamic and oriental architecture in synagogues continued across much of late 19th and early 20th century. After the expulsion of the Jews from Spain in 1492 and Portugal in 1496, they were dispersed all over Europe into France, England, and Netherlands. Some of them migrated to Provence where they played a role in mediating "*the peculiar Anadalusi Jewish intellectual life and style to a new community innocent of Arabic.*"[707] Jews built synagogues wherever they went. Al-Andalus furnished the technique as well as the regulations. In one event, for example, Maimonides (1135-1204) permitted the portrayal of animals in synagogues but not humans[708].

Through the Jews, Muslims were instrumental in awakening the spirit, which inspired the Renaissance and the intellectual development of Europe. The impact of the Jews on changing the mentality of Europeans was clearly recognised by the church, which influenced King Ferdinand to issue an expulsion order in 1483 against both Muslims and Jews of the peninsula. This measure resulted in further dispersal of the Jews and subsequently further dissemination of Muslim heritage. This can only illustrate that Christians of the Middle Ages had many opportunities to learn from much needed Muslim ideas. This was considerably facilitated by the universality of the Islamic message, which forbids concealing knowledge and makes sharing it amongst all humans a duty. Despite hostilities, Christians were enabled, by numerous means, to share the secrets of the development of the Muslim world. Therefore, Islam made a decisive and substantial contribution to the development of the European Middle Ages and "Renaissance". Scott remarks "*A vast interval of time divides the ages of Abd-al-Rahman I and Luther; the cities of Cordova and Worms are separated by many hundred leagues; but the inherent ideas of personal liberty and private right recognised on the banks of the Guadalquivir ultimately prevailed in the centre of Germany, once the most unlettered of countries.*"[709]

Notes

[461] Elisseeff, N. (1986), '*Les Echanges Culturels entre le Monde Musulman et les Croises a époque de Nuraldin ben Zanki (1174)*, in V.P. Goss, and C.V. Borstein, (eds.), the meeting of the two worlds, Medieval Institute Publications, Michigan, pp.39-52.

[462] Walbank, F.W. (1987), '*Trade and Industry Under the Later Roman Empire in the West*', in M. M. Postan and Edward Miller, eds. Cambridge Economic History of Europe, Cambridge University Press, 2nd edition, vol.2,.pp. 74-131, at p.131

[463] Anderson, P (1978), '*Passages from Antiquity to Feudalism*' Verso, London, p. 142

464 De Mas Latrie, M.L. (1975), '*Traites de Paix et de Commerce, et Documents Divers, Concernant les Relations des Chrétiens avec les Arabes de l'Afrique Septentrionale au Moyen Age*', Burt Franklin, New York, Originally published in Paris. 1866, p. 117

[465] O'Callaghan, J.F. (1983), '*A History of Medieval Spain in Western Civilisation*', Cornell University Press, Washington, p.25.

[466] Stern, S.M. (1956), '*An Original Document From the Fatimid Chancery Concerning Italian Merchants*', Studi Orientalistici in Onore di G. Levi dell Vida, Vol.2, Rome, pp.529-38 cited in Abulafia (1987) op. cit. p,421

[467] Abulafia David (1987), '*Asia, Africa and the Trade of Medieval Europe*', in M. M. Postan and Edward Miller, eds. 'Cambridge Economic History of Europe', Cambridge University Press, 2nd edition, vol.2, pp.402-472, at p. 463

[468] Abulafia David (1987), '*Asia, Africa and the Trade of Medieval Europe*', op.cit. p. 426

[469] De Mas Latrie M.L. (1866), '*Traites de Paix et de Commerce, et Documents Divers, Concernant les Relations des Chrétiens avec les Arabes de l'Afrique Septentrionale au Moyen Age*', Burt Franklin, New York, Originally published in Paris, Vol 1; p.xv.

[470] Ibid.

[471] Curtin, P.D. (1984), '*Cross-cultural Trade in World History*', Cambridge.

[472] Abulafia David (1987), '*Asia, Africa and the Trade of Medieval Europe*', op cit. p.142.

[473] Ibid., p.456.

[474] Ibid., p.456

[475] Atiya, S. (1962), '*Crusade, Commerce and Culture*', Oxford University Press. London.

[476] Abulafia, D. (1994), '*The Role of Trade in Muslim-Christian Contact during the Middle Ages*', in Agius, D.A. and Hitchcock, R. (eds.), The Arab Influence in Medieval Europe', Thaca Press, Reading, pp.1-24.

[477] Savory, R. (1976), '*Introduction to Islamic Civilisation*', Cambridge University Press, p.132.

[478] Runciman Steven (1987), '*A History of the Crusades*', Cambridge University Press, Vol.3, p.469

[479] Lopez, R.S. (1987), '*The Trade of Medieval Europe: the South*', in M. M. Postan and Edward Miller, eds., Cambridge Economic History of Europe, Cambridge University Press, 2nd edition, vol.2,.pp. 305-400, at p.352, 387.

[480] a name for the Republic of Venice, from the title Serenissimo literally meaning 'the most/very serene'

[481] Stefano Carboni (2007), '*Venice and the Islamic World, 827-1797*', Yale University Press.

[482] Kramers, J.H. (1931), '*Geography and Commerce*', in T. Arnold, and A Guillaume, (eds.), the Legacy of Islam, Oxford University Press, pp.79-107, at p.104.

[483] Cizakca Murat (1996), '*A Comparative Evolution of Business Partnerships: the Islamic World and Europe, with Specific Reference to the Ottoman Archives*', E.J. Brill, Leiden

[484] Udovitch, A.L. (1962), '*At the Origins of the Western Commenda: Islam, Israel, Byzantium?*', in Speculum, vol.37, pp.198-207, at p.198 and Udovitch, A.L. (1970), '*Partnership and Profit in Medieval Islam*', Princeton University Press.

[485] Udovitch, A.L. (1989), '*Trade*', in the Dictionary of the Middle Ages', J.R.Strayer Editor in Chief, Charles Scribner's Sons, New York, Vol. 12, pp. 105-8p. 106

[486] Udovitch A.L.*1989), '*Trade*', in the *Dictionary of the Middle Ages*; op cit. p. 106 and Kramers, J.H. (1931), '*Geography and Commerce*', T. Arnold, and A Guillaume,. (eds.), the Legacy of Islam, Oxford University Press, pp.79-107, at p.105.

[487] Howard Debora (2000), '*Venice and the East*', Yale University Press, p.36.

[488] Abulafia, D. (1994), '*The Role of Trade in Muslim-Christian Contact During the Middle Ages*', op.cit.

[489] Bellorini Theophilius and Hoade Eugene trans. (1948), '*Visit to the Holy Places of Egypt, Ainai, Palestine, and Syria in 1384 by Frescobaldi, Gussi, and Sigoli*', Jerusalem, pp.183-182. Quoted in Mack R.E.(2002 'Bazaar to piazza: Islamic Trade and Italian Art: 1300-1600'University of California Press, p.1

[490] Cochrane, L. (1994), '*Adelard of Bath, the first English Scientist*', British Museum Press. p.29, 33.

[491] Howard Debora (2000), '*Venice an d the East*', Yale University Press

[492] Howard Debora (2000), '*Venice an d the East*', Yale University Press, p.35

[493] See Howard Debora (2000), '*Venice an d the East*', op.cit. chapter 2, pp.43-64

[494] Mack R.E. (2002), '*Bazaar to piazza: Islamic Trade and Italian Art: 1300-1600*', University of California Press.

[495] Ibid.

[496] Stefano Carboni (2007), '*Venice and the Islamic World, 827-1797*', Yale University Press.

[497] Mack R.E.(2002 '*Bazaar to piazza: Islamic Trade and Italian Art: 1300-1600*', University of California Press., p.3

[498] Stefano Carboni (2007), '*Venice and the Islamic World, 827-1797*', Yale University Press, p.154

[499] Mack R.E.(2002 '*Bazaar to piazza: Islamic Trade and Italian Art: 1300-1600*', University of California Press, p.93

[500] The Society for the Diffusion of Useful Knowledge (1939), '*Library of Useful Knowledge*', Vol.III, Philosophy, Baldwin and Cradock, Paternoster-Row, London, p.37.

[501] Briffault Robert (1928), '*the Making of Humanity*', George Unwin and Allen, London, p.198.

[502] Stock, B. (1978), '*Science, Technology and Economic Progress in the Early Middle Ages*', in D.C Lindberg ed. Science in the Middle Ages, The University of Chicago Press, Chicago and London, pp.1-51, .p.37

[503] He is known to have taken the positions of Avicenna and al-Razi (Rhazes) of whom he wrote in his manuscript: "*This little book on the purpose of physicians is based on the teaching of several authors, i.e. Galen and certain Arabs Rhazes, a man of clear thought, prompt in his work, decisive in judgement and trustworthy in experiment*" quoted in Jacquart, D. (1996), '*The influence of Arabic Medicine in the Medieval West*', in Roshdi Rashed (ed.), Encyclopaedia of the History of Arabic Science, Routledge, 3 vols., vol.3, pp.963-984.

[504] Briffault Robert (1928), '*the Making of Humanity*', George Unwin and Allen, London, p.199

[505] Ibid. Briffault R. (1928), op.cit. p.199

[506] Briffault R. (1919), '*The Making of Humanity*', George Unwin and Allen, London, p.199

[507] Campbell, D. (2001), '*Arabian Medicine and its Influence on the Middle Ages*', Routledge, London, vol.1, p.143, first published in 1926 by Keegan Paul,

[508] See Asin Palacios (1919), '*la Sccatalogia Musulmane en la Divina Comedia*', Translated by Sunderland, H. (1926), '*Islam and the Divine Comedy*', Cass, London.

[509] Barack Karl August (1858), '*Die Werke der Hrotsvitha*', Bauer u Raspe, Nurnberg, p.65, also quoted in Dunlop D. M (1958), '*Arabic Science in the West*', Pakistan Historical Society, p.26

[510] Ibid.p.26.

[511] Houtsma, M.Th., Van Donzel, E. (1993), '*E.J. Brill's First Encyclopaedia of Islam, 1913-1936*', Brill, p.48, originally published as The Encyclopaedia of Islam, a Dictionary of the Geography, Ethnology and Biography of the Muhammadan Peoples, by E.J. Brill and Luzac & CO, 1927.

[512] Some, like Walsh, suggested he was surnamed the Saracen because he was originally a Muslim like Africanus or came from the Muslim land, see Walsh James, J. (1911), '*Old Time Makers of Medicine*', Fordham University Press, New York, p.81.

[513] See Howard Debora (2000), p, cit. pp. 85-87 and p.93

[514] Howard Debora (2000), p, cit. p144.

[515] Cochrane, L. (1994), op cit.

[516] Ibid., p.36.

[517] Chisholm Hugh (ed.) (1910), '*The Encyclopaedia Britannica: A Dictionary of Arts, Sciences, Literature and General Information*', The Cambridge University Press, Vol.29, p.189

[518] Cochrane, L. (1994), op cit. p.65.

[519] Harvey John Hooper (1968), '*The Origin of Gothic Architecture*', in Antiquaries Journal, Vol.48, pp.91-94.

[520] Murdoch, J. (1968), '*The Medieval Euclid: Silent Aspects of the Translations of the Elements by Adelard of Bath and Campanus of Novara*', 12eme Congrés International d'Histoire des Sciences, Colloques (Revue de Synthese), 3eme Serie, No. 49-52, Paris, pp.67-94.

[521] Harvey John Hooper (1968), op cit.

[522] Boorke, Christopher, (1969), '*the Twelfth Century Renaissance*', Thames & Hudson, London, pp.102, 103.

[523] Cyril Stanley Smith; John G. Hawthorne (1974), '*Mappae Clavicula: A Little Key to the World of Medieval Techniques*', Transactions of the American Philosophical Society, New Ser., Vol. 64, No. 4. pp. 1-128.

[524] Cochrane, L. (1994), op cit. p.37.

[525] Sarton G. (1927, '*Introduction to the History of Science*', Williams & Williams Company, p.534

[526] Grant, E. (1974), '*A Source Book in Medieval Science*', Harvard University Press, p.809

[527] Crombie, A. (1967)), '*Medieval and Early Modern Science*', Harvard University Pressp.176

[528] Field Judith Veronica (2005), '*Piero Della Francesca: A Mathematician's Art*', Yale University Press, p.256.

[529] Atiya, S. (1962), op cit.

[530] Atiya, S. (1962), op cit.

[531] Atiya, S. (1962), op cit. named some of these people. These included Royalty such as Judith, the duchess of Bavaria and the sister of Emperor Otto I who visited Jerusalem in 970, the Counts of Ardeche, Vienne, Verdun, Arcy, Auhalt, and Gorizia. Members of the Church Hierarchy included the Bishop of Olivola in 920, St. Conrad, Bishop of Conatarce who visited Jerusalem three times, St. John, bishop of Parma, visited six times, the Abbots of Saint Cybar, Flavigny, Aurillac, Saint Aubin d'Angers, and of Montier-en Der.

[532] Hazard, H.W and Setton, K.M eds. (1977), '*A History of the Crusades: The Art and Architecture of the Crusader States*', vol.4, Madison, p.39

[533] Rosamund Allen (2004), '*Eastward Bound: Travel and Travellers, 1050-1550*', Manchester University Press, p.5

[534] Ibid, p.5

[535] Weber Elka (2004), '*Sharing the Sites: Medieval Jewish Travellers to the Land of Israel*', in Allen Rosamund (ed.), Eastward Bound: Travel and Travellers, 1050-155, Manchester University Press, pp.35-52.

[536] Rosamund Allen (2004), '*Eastward Bound: Travel and Travellers, 1050-1550*', op cit. p.5

[537] Ibid. p.5

[538] John Mandeville (1953), '*Mandeville's Travels*', ed. Malcolm Letts, Vol. II, Hakluyt Society, London, p.294

[539] Rosamund Allen (2004), '*Eastward Bound: Travel and Travellers, 1050-155*', Manchester University Press, p.9

[540] Kollek Teddy and Pearlman Moshe (1970), '*Pilgrims to the Holy Land: the Story of Pilgrimage through the Ages*', Harper and Row, p.107

[541] Rosamund Allen (2004), '*Eastward Bound: Travel and Travellers, 1050-155*', Manchester University Press, p.7

[542] Curl James Setevens (2005), '*The Egyptian Revival: Ancient Egypt as the Inspiration for Design Motifs in the West*', Routledge, p.61

[543] Harvey John Hooper (1972), '*The Medieval Architect*', Wayland, p.239

[544] Atherton Ian (1996), '*Norwich Cathedral: Church, City, and Diocese, 1096-1996*', Continuum International Publishing, p.248.

[545] Webb, D. (2001), '*Pilgrims and Pilgrimage in the Medieval West*', I.B. Tauris, p.17

[546] Webb, D. (2001), '*Pilgrims and Pilgrimage in the Medieval West,*' op., cit. p.18

[547] Miles, M.R. (2005), '*The Word Made Flesh: A History of Christian Thought*', Blackwell publishing, p.156

[548] Lomax, D.W. (1985), '*The First English Pilgrims to Santiago de Compostela*', in Henry Mayr-Harting and R.I. Moore eds. 'Studies in Medieval History Presented to R.H.C. Davis', Continuum International Publishing Group, pp.165-176, at p.165.

[549] Erasmus Desiderius and Nichols John Gough (1849), '*Pilgrimages to Saint Mary of Walsingham and Saint Thomas of Canterbury*', John Bowyer Nichols and Son, London, p.77

[550] Ibid., p.78

[551] Lambert, E. (1958), '*Art Musulman et Art Chrétien dans la Péninsule Ibérique*', Éditions Privat, Paris.

[552] Male, E. (1924), '*Art et Artistes du Moyen Age*', Librairie Armand Colin, Paris.

[553] Watkin D. (2000), '*A History of Western Architecture*', op.cit. p.143

[554] Watkin D. (2000), '*A History of Western Architecture*', Lawrence King Publishing, p.134

[555] Sarton, G. (1955), '*Introduction to the History of Science*', Vol.2, The Carnegie Institute of Washington, p.893

[556] Barker, E. (1931), '*The Crusades*', in Arnold, T. and Guillaume, A. (eds.), the legacy of Islam, Oxford University Press, pp.40-78.

[557] Riley Smith Jonathan (2002), '*Early Crusaders to the East and the Costs of Crusading, 1095-1130*', in Thomas F. Madden (ed.), The Crusades: The Essential readings, Blackwell, Publishing, pp. 155-171.

[558] Richard J. And Birrell, J. (1999), '*The Crusades, C.1071-c.1291*', Cambridge University Press, p.26

[559] Brundage, J. A. (1964), 'the *Crusades: Motives and Achievements*', Lexington, Mass.

[560] However, the idea might have persisted longer. Barker (1931), for example, considers Heraclius as the first crusader. Colonisation of Muslim countries in the 18th and 19th was another considered, not only by the Muslims but also by Christians, as another crusade (see, for example, Vallensi, 1977).

[561] Painter Sidney (1957), '*French Chivalry: Chivalric Ideas and Practices in Medieval France*', Cornell University Press, p.8

[562] Nicolle David (1988), '*El-Cid and the Reconquista, 1050-1492*', Osprey Publishing, p.11

[563] Gibbon, E. (1860), '*The History of the Decline and Fall of the Roman Empire*', , Harper & Brothers, New York, p.532

[564] Gibbon, E. (1860), '*The History of the Decline and Fall of the Roman Empire*', op., cit. p.555

[565] Christianity has never left the East. Christians continued to prosper under Muslim rule.

[566] Gibbon, E. (1860), '*The History of the Decline and Fall of the Roman Empire*', , Harper &Brothers, New York, p.549

[567] Ibid... p.557

[568] Ibid. p.559

[569] Ellenblum, R. (1998), 'Frankish Rural Settlement in the Latin Kingdom of Jerusalem', ambridge

[570] Ibid.

[571] Ibid. p.78

[572] Atiya, S, (1962), op cit.

[573] Ibn Jubayr (2003), 'The Travels of Ibn Jubayr', op. cit. p.322,323

[574] Ibid. p.323

[575] De constructione castri Saphet, p.381-82, cited in Molin Kristian (2001), 'Unknown Crusader castle', Continuum International Publishing Group, p.287

[576] Hatem Anouar (1932), 'Les Poèmes épiques des Croisades: Genèse, historicité, localisation. Essai sur l'activité littéraire dans les colonies franques de Syrie au Moyen Age', Paul Geuthner Paris, p.297

[577] Al-Idrisi, Trans. Le Starnge Palestine under the Moslems, pp.338-339

[578] Baha al-Din Ibn Shaddad (1964), 'al Nawadir al-sultaniyha wa'l-mahasin al-yusufiyah', ed. Gamal El Din El Shayyal, Cairo, p.174

[579] Les Gestes des Chiprois (1906), in Recueil des Historiens des Croisades (RHC), Documents Arméniens, vol. II, Paris, pp.653-1012, at p.756.

[580] William of Tyre, (1986), 'Chronicon', ed. R.B.C. Huygens, 2 vols, Corpus Christianorum, Continuatio Mediaevalis 63-63A, Turnhout,. p.859.

[581] Harvey John Hooper (1973), op cit. p. 16, also see Lambert, E. (1958), op cit.

[582] Barker Ernest. (1931), 'Crusades', IN T. Arnold, and A Guillaume,. (eds.), the Legacy of Islam, Oxford University Press, pp.40-77, at p.54.

[583] Haskins, C.H. (1925), 'Arabic Science in Western Europe', Isis, vol.7, No..3, pp.478-485, at p.481.

[584] Barker, E. (1931), op cit.

[585] Housley Norman (2006), 'Contesting the Crusades', Blackwell Publishing, p.144

[586] See Herr, F. (1962), 'the Medieval World- Europe 1100-1350', translated from German by Sandheimer, J., Weidenfield & Nicholson, London.

[587] Grabar, O. (2006), 'Early Visual culture, 1100-1800', op.cit. p.369.

[588] Peterson, A. (1996), 'Dictionary of Islamic Architecture', Routledge, p.231

[589] Mitchell, P.D. (2004), 'Medicine in the Crusade. Warfare, Wounds and the Medieval Surgeon', Cambridge University Press, Cambridge, p.218.

[590] Kohlberg E. and Kedar B.Z. (1988), 'A Melikite Physician in Frankish Jerusalem and Ayyubid Damascus: Muwaffaq al-Din Ya'qub b. Siqlab', Asian and African Studies, vol.22, pp.113-26.

[591] Beddie James S. (1933), 'Some Notices of Books in the East in the Period of the Crusades', Speculum, Vol. 8, No.2, pp. 240-242.

[592] Ibn al-Furat, quoted in Eche, Y. (1967), 'Les Bibliothèques Arabes, Publiques et Semi Publiques en Mésopotamie, en Syrie et en Égypte au Moyen Age', Institut Français, Damascus, p.120-21

[593] Cochrane, L. (1994), 'Adelard of Bath, the first English Scientist', British Museum Press, p.33

[594] The text in Latin is: "... Misimus autem vobis per manus dictorum fratrum, nuntiorum vestrorum, libellum, quem attulimus de pectore Orientis, scilicet de terra Sin, et libellum alium de fide ex parte archiepiscopi N esibini, cui subscripserunt alii duo archiepiscopi et tres episcopi. . . .", see Beddie James S. (1933), 'Some Notices of Books in the East in the Period of the Crusades', op.cit.

[595] Ibn al-Qalanisi (1983), 'Dhal Tarikh Dimashq', or Continuation of History of Damascus, ed. S. Zakkar, Damaascus, p.487, cited in Attiya Hussein M. (1999), 'Knowledge of Arabic in the Crusader States in the twelfth and thirteenth centuries', Journal of Medieval History, vol.25, issue 3, pp.203-213.

[596] Al-Maqrisi (1934), 'Kitab al-Suluk ii Maarifat Duwal al-Mulauk', ed. M.M. Ziada, vol. 1, Cairo, p. 304. cited in Attiya Hussein M. (1999), 'Knowledge of Arabic in the Crusader States in the twelfth and thirteenth centuries', op.cit. en.7

[597] Attiya, Hussein M. (1999), '*Knowledge of Arabic in the Crusader States in the Twelfth and Thirteenth Centuries.*' Journal of Medieval History 25:3, pp. 203-13.

[598] Baha al-Din Ibn Shaddad (1964), '*al Nawadir al-Sultaniyha wa'l-Mahasin al-Yusufiyah*', ed. Gamal El Din El Shayyal, Cairo, p, 97,98. Quoted in Attiya Hussein M. (1999), 'Knowledge of Arabic in the Crusader States in the twelfth and thirteenth centuries', op.cit. p.205

[599] Dickson Gary (1998), '*Crusades*', in The New Encyclopaedia Britannica, pp.827- 838, at p.833.

[600] Ibn Jubayr (2003), '*The Travels of Ibn Jubayr*', ed. and transl. by Roland Broadhurst, Goodword publishers, India, p.317

[601] Comes from Arabic ra'is, medieval title given to a person who had authority over a professional or religious corporation.

[602] Riley-Smith (1972), `*Some lesser officials in Latin Syria*', 11, 13, 15, 16, 22, 23; Prawer, *The Latin Kingdom of Jerusalem* (London,), 367-9. The English Historical Review, Vol. 87, No. 342. (Jan., 1972), pp. 1-26.

[603] Ibid.,p.2

[604] Runciman, Steve (2002, '*A History of the Crusades: The Kingdom of Acre and the Later Crusades*', vol.3, first printed 1954, Cambridge University Press, New York, p.384.

[605] Simon Jonathan and Riley Smith Christopher (1997), '*The Oxford Illustrated History of the Crusades*', Oxford University Press, p.148

[606] Folda Jaroslav (2005), '*Crusader Art in the Holy Land, From the Third crusade to the Fall of Acre, 1187-1291*', Cambridge University Press, p.i

[607] Wigley, George J. (1856), '*Archaeological Studies in Jerusalem*', C. Dolman, London.

[608] Rey Emmanel G. (1871), '*Architecture Militaire des Croisés en Syrie et dans l'ile de Chypre*', Collection de Documents Inédits sur l'Histoire en France, Série 1., Histoire Politique, Paris Imprimerie Nationale.

[609] Hazard, H.W and Setton, K.M eds. (1977), '*A history of the Crusades: The Art and Architecture of the Crusader States*', vol.4, Madison, p.74

[610] Strzygowski, J. (1936), '*Ruins of Tombs of the Latin Kings on the Haram in Jerusalem*', Speculum, Vol.11. No.4, pp.499-508

[611] Ibid., p.504.

[612] Ibid., p.508

[613] Ibid, p.508

[614] Harvey John Hooper (1968), op cit.

[615] Harvey John Hooper (1973), '*the Master builders*', Thames and Hudson, London, p.40.

[616] Enlart Camille (1925-28), '*Les Monuments des Croisés dans le Royaume de Jérusalem: Architecture Religieuse et Civile*', 2 volumes, Bibliothèque Archéologique et Historique, vols.8 and 9, Paris. Cited in Folda Jaroslav (2005), 'Crusader Art in the Holy Land, From the Third crusade to the Fall of Acre, 1187-1291', op.cit. p.8

[617] Hazard, H.W and Setton, K.M eds. (1977), '*A history of the Crusades: The Art and Architecture of the Crusader States*', op.cit. p.74

[618] Ibid.,p.74

[619] Boase, T.S.R. (1938), '*The Arts in the Latin Kingdom of Jerusalem*', Journal of the Warburg Institute, Vol.2, No.1, pp1-21, at p.17

[620] Ibid

[621] Creswell, K.A.C. (1924), op cit.

[622] Deschamps, P. (1939), '*Les Châteaux des Croises en Terre Sainte*', B.A.H.T, xxxiv, Ganthmer, Paris.

[623] Creswell, K.A.C. (1924), '*Bulletin de l'Institut Français d'Archéologie Orientale*', Vol xxiii, Cairo.

[624] Elisseeff, N. (1986), op cit.

[625] Elisseeff, N. (1986), op cit.

[626] Boase, T.S.R. (1938), *'The Arts in the Latin Kingdom of Jerusalem'*, Journal of the Warburg Institute, Vol.2, No.1, pp1-21

[627] Grabar, O. (2006), *'Early Visual Culture, 1100-1800'*, op.cit. p.369.

[628] Vernet, J. (1979), *'Los Médicos Andaluces en el 'Libro de las Generaciones de Médicos' de Ibn Yulyul'*, in Estudios Sobre Historia de la Ciencia Medieval, Barcelona Bellaterra, pp.445-62.

[629] De Plaza Mikel (1992), *'Mozarabs: An Emblematic Christian Minority'*, in Salma Khadra Jayyusi, ed. The Legacy of Muslim Spain, Brill, pp. 149-70

[630] Southern, R.W. (1962), *'Western Views of Islam in the Middle Ages'*. 20 ff, Cambridge, Mass.

[631] Agius, D.A. and Hitchcock, R. (1994), *'The Arab Influence in Medieval Europe'*, Thaca Press, Reading, pp.1-24.

[632] Paulus Albarus, Indiculus Luminosus., quoted in Dozy Reinhart (1913), *'Spanish Islam: A History of the Muslims in Spain'*, Translation Stokes Francis Griffin, International Scholarly Book Services, Portland, p.268 for his Jewish origins see Allen Cabaniss (1953) *'Paulus Albarus of Muslim Cordova', in Church History*, Vol. 22, No. 2, pp. 99-112.

[633] Burman,Thomas, E. (1994), *'Religious Polemic'*, op cit. p.18

[634] O'Callaghan, Joseph, F. (1975), *'A History of Medieval Spain'*, Cornell University Press, p.112

[635] They are still preserved in a manuscript MS 225 of the monastery of Ripoll and found in the Archives of the Crown of Aragon. See Gomez Margarita Lopez (1992), *'the Mozarabs: Worthy Bearers of Islamic Culture'*, in Salma Khadra Jayyusi, ed. The Legacy of Muslim Spain, Brill, pp. 171-175, at.p.172.

[636] Gomez Margarita Lopez (1992), *'The Mozarabs: Worthy Bearers of Islamic Culture'*, op.cit. p.173

[637] Lambert, E. (1958), op cit. p.107.

[638] Gomez Margarita Lopez (1992), *'The Mozarabs: Worthy Bearers of Islamic Culture'*, in Salma Khadra Jayyusi, ed. The Legacy of Muslim Spain, Brill, pp. 171-175

[639] The sharp edge where two surfaces meet at an angle

[640] Gomez Margarita Lopez (1992), *'The Mozarabs: Worthy Bearers of Islamic Culture'*, op.cit. p.171-72

[641] Goodwin, Godfrey. (1990), *'Islamic Spain'*. London: Penguin Group, 121.

642 Glick T. (2005), *'Islamic and Christian Spain'*; Brill, p. 273.

[643] Durant W. The Age; op cit; p. 892.

644 Torres L. Balbas, (1947), ' *Los Adarves de las Ciudades Hispano-Musulmanas'*, in al-Andalus; XII, pp. 164-93.

[645] Burman,Thomas, E. (1994), *'Religious Polemic and the intellectual History of the Mozarabs'*, c. 1050-1200', Brill, p.13

[646] Ibid., p.16

[647] see Atiya, S. (1962), op cit.

[648] Lambert, E. (1958), op cit. p.116.

[649] Al-Maqqarri, Anaectes, vol,II, p.510

[650] Palacios Miguel Asin (1968), *'Islam and the Divine Comedy'*, Routledge, p.245

[651] Ibid., p.245

[652] Lambert, E. (1958), op cit. p.121.

[653] Arie Rachel (1991), *'Singular and Plural: the Heritage of al-Andalus - Spain Under the Moors - Al-Andalus: Where Three Worlds Met'*, in Unesco Courier, Volume XLIV, number 12, pp.15-19, at p.19

[654] Terrace, H. (1958), *'Islam d'Espagne; une Rencontre de l'Orient et de l'Occident'*, Librairie Plon, Paris, p.179.

[655] Ibid.

[656] Scott, S.P. (1904), '*History of the Moorish Empire in Europe*', Vol II; op cit; p. 569.

[657] Bloom Jonathan M. and Blair Sheila s.(2009), '*The Grove Encyclopaedia of Islamic Art and Architecture*', Oxford University Press, p.8

[658] Harvey, L.P. (1992), '*The Mudejars*', in Salma Khadra Jayyusi, ed. The Legacy of Muslim Spain, Brill, pp. 176-187

[659] Lambert, E. (1958), op cit.

[660] Named so for the number of assassinations and his hard-handed crushing of rebellions in Castile.

[661] Most probably a Jewish Mudejar.

[662] see Lambert, E. (1958), op cit. pp.119-130.

[663] Such as in the church of San Bartolome.

[664] Such as in the church of Sahagan in Leon.

[665] Such as in the cathedrals of Tarazona, Teruel and Saragossa.

[666] Terrace, H. (1958), '*Islam d'Espagne; une rencontre de l'Orient et de l'Occident*', Librairie Plon, Paris, p.188.

[667] Torres Balbas, L. (1949), '*Arte Almohade, Arte Nazari, Arte Mudejar*', Plus Ultra editorial, Madrid

[668] Herr, F.(1962), op cit.

[669] Barker, E. (1931), '*The Crusades*', in Arnold, T. and Guillaume, A. (eds.), the Legacy of Islam, Oxford University Press, pp.40-78. At pp.53-548.

[670] Scott Leader. (1899), '*Cathedral Builders: the Story of a Great Masonic Guild*', 2nd edition, Sampson Low, Marstar & Company, London.

[671] Ibid., p.130.

[672] Harvey J. (1985), '*The Development of Architecture*', in J. Evans ed., the Flowering of the Middle Ages; Thames and Hudson, pp. 85-105.

[673] Scott Leader (1899), '*Cathedral Builders: the Story of a Great Masonic Guild*', op.cit.. p.122.

[674] Cochrane, L. (1994), '*Adelard of Bath, the first English Scientist*', British Museum Press, p.66.

[675] Dulaure Jacques-Antoine (1854), '*Histoire de Paris*', P.H.Krabbe, Librairie-Editeur, Paris, p.262.

[676] Scheindlin Raymond P. (1992), '*The Jews in Muslim Spain*', in Salma Khadra Jayyusi, ed. The Legacy of Muslim Spain, Brill, pp. 188-200, at p. 188

[677] Rosenthal Erwin (1961), '*Judaism and Islam*', , Thomas Yoseloff, London, quoted in Sheikh Mohammad Iqbal (1979) Realms of Peace, Idarah-i Adabiyat-i Delli, Delhi, p.154

[678] The Bible Cyclopedia, or Illustrations of the Civil and Natural History of the Sacred Writings by Reference to the-Manners Customs Rites Traditions Antiquities and Literature of Eastern Nations, John W. Parker West Strand, London volume 1, 1841, p.695

[679] The Bible Cyclopedia, op.cit. p.695

[680] Scheindlin Raymond P. (1992), '*The Jews in Muslim Spain*', op cit. p.189

[681] Ibid, p.191

[682] Ibid, p196

[683] Ibid. p.196

[684] Abulafia David (1987), '*Asia, Africa and the Trade of Medieval Europe*', op.cit. p. 427

[685] See Asher Adolf ed. (1841), '*The Itinerary of Rabbi Benjamin of Tudela*', Vol. II, Adolf Asher and Company, London and Berlin, and Menache Sophia (1996), 'Communication in the Jewish Diaspora: The Pre-Modern World', Brill, p.53

[686] Scheindlin Raymond P. (1992). '*The Jews in Muslim Spain*', op cit. p.195

[687] Cohen Jeremy (1999), '*Living Letters of the Law: Ideas of the Jew in Medieval Christianity*', University of California Press, p.119

[688] Signer, M. A. (1995), '*Bible, Jewish Interpretation of*, , in William Westcott Kibler, Grover A. Zinn eds., Medieval France: An Encyclopaedia, Routledge, pp.123-26, at p.125

[689] Scott, S.P. (1904), '*History of the Moorish Empire in Europe*', J. B. Lippincott Company, Vol.3, p.161.

[690] Signer, M. A. (1995), '*Bible, Jewish Interpretation of*', op.cit. .124
[691] Ibid., p.125
[692] Braver Rabbi Hirsch (1930), '*Great Figures and Events in Jewish History*', Vol. I, Bloch Publishing Company, p.233
[693] Ibid.
[694] Barkai Ron (1998), '*A History of Jewish Gynaecological texts in the Middle Ages*', Brill, p.35, 36.
[695] Ibid., p.238
[696] Al-Djazairi S. (2005), '*The Hidden Debt to Islamic Civilisation*', Bayt al-Hikma Press, p.174
[697] Ibid., p.176
[698] Draper J.W. (1910), '*History of Conflict Between Science and Religion*', 25th Edition, Kegan Paul, London, p.187.
[699] Hermes Eberhard (ed.) (1977), '*The Introduction to The Disciplina Clericalis of Petrus Alfonsi*', Translation to English by P.R. Quarrie, Berkeley and Los Angeles, p.8 Quoted by Brinner Wiliam M. (1997), Popular literature in Medieval Jewish Arabic', in Norman Golb ed. Judaeo-Arabic Studies: Proceedings of the Founding Conference of the Society, Harwood Academic Publishers, pp.59-72, at p.71
[700] Kalinke Marianne E. (1990), '*Bridal-Quest Romance in Medieval Iceland*', Cornell University Press, p.107
[701] Abrahams Israel ed. (1926), '*Tsaya'ot ge'one Yi'srael*', ha-Hevrah ha-Yehudit le-hotsa'át sefarim asherbe-Amerika, p.131.
[702] Ettinghausen, R. (1959), '*Near Eastern Book Covers and Their Influence on European Bindings*', Ars Orientalis, vol.3, pp.113-31.
[703] Dodds, J. D. (1992), '*Mudejar Tradition and the Synagogues of Medieval Spain: Cultural Identity and Cultural Hegemony*', in Vivian Mann, Thomas Glick and Jerrilynn Dodds (eds), Convivencia: Jews, Muslims and Christians in medieval Spain, George Braziller in association with the Jewish Museum, New York, pp.113-31, at p.122
[704] Wexler, p. (1996), '*The Non-Jeaish Oridins of the Sephardic Jews*', Suny Press, New York, p.197.
[705] Lecky William Edward Hartpole (1866), '*History of the Rise and Influence of the Spirit of Rationalism in Europe*', Vol. II, Appleton and Company, Boradway, New York, p.265-67
[706] Ashtor Eliyahu (1973), '*The Jews of Moslem Spain*', 3 vols. Jewish Publication Society, Philadelphia, p.7
[707] Scheindlin Raymond P. (1992), '*The Jews in Muslim Spain*', op cit. p.195
[708] Krinsky C.H. (1996), '*Synagogues of Europe: Architecture, History, Meaning*', Dover Publications, p.45.
[709] Scott, S. P. (1904), '*History of the Moorish Empire in Europe*', J. B. Lippincott Company, Vol.3, p.170.

231

CHAPTER FIVE

The Contribution of Muslims to European Art and Architecture in the Medieval Period

Violet le Duc[710] defines architecture as the art of making beautiful buildings. Such an art has been generally perceived to require a high level of skills, a good knowledge of science particularly mathematics and geometry and substantial ability of imagination. These qualities develop through a process of learning that is greatly influenced by the general intellectual tone of the society as a whole. Primitive structures despite their degree of complexity are still considered simple and non- elaborate, reflecting the general intellectual limitations of their societies. Highly complex buildings did not appear until science produced a better understanding of statics and a wide variety of improved building material. This has been illustrated in previous chapters where building and architectural achievement of the Muslims in the middle Ages was in parallel to their scientific and artistic development. Similarly, the general decline of Europe in the Dark Ages was paralleled by the general decline of architecture and building activity as violent periods of barbarism not only reduced the chances of architectural development but also caused the destruction of what was standing. However, in the mid-12th century unprecedented architectural activity took place resulting in the birth of what is known as the Gothic style. Western scholars tell us that Medieval European architecture was derived from Western roots whether it was Nordic "genius", or Roman or Byzantine heritage combined with the talent of the Medieval European man. The contribution of Muslims is paramount yet this has been largely ignored. Muslim architects, unfortunately, seem to accept these claims with little questioning.

General Circumstances and External Influence on the Medieval European Architectural Revival.

There is a consensus among art historians that after the fall of Rome, art and architecture in Europe declined significantly. As outlined in chapter three, this was due to a number of factors mostly connected to the general intellectual and cultural stagnation of the continent. After the fall of Rome, Europe entered a period of chaos. The dying authority of the Roman Empire and the invasion of Barbarians sapped much of the strength of the continent and resulted in massive destruction. The English monarch, King Edgar (c.943-975), provided a summary on the condition of buildings then as he wrote in his charter to the Abbey of Malmesbury in 974 AD: "*All the monastries of my realm to the sight are nothing but worm-eaten and rotten timber and boards.*"[711] The transfer of authority from Rome to the Byzantine capital of Constantinople expressed the declining state of Europe and further undermined its political and economic life. What was left of Christian architecture was amalgamated with Greek and Asiatic elements producing its all time achievement in Hagia Sofia. Harvey stressed that "*it would be vain to seek among the Franks, Goths, Anglo-Saxons and Scandinavians for any capacity for organisation on the grand scale. The greatest cathedrals, monasteries or palaces are insignificant when compared with the ruins of the Romans or even the earliest of the magnificent buildings of the resurgent eleventh century*"[712]. It was not until the 11th century when Cluniac monks led a reformation movement that the redemption of Europe was accomplished. The church was freed from secular domination, established its supreme power as a religious, social and economic authority, surpassing the imperial authority. This was later reinforced in the 12th century by the spreading Cistercian movement.

The other fundamental change transforming Europe was the emergence of nation states, which had a profound impact on the political, socio-economic and cultural spheres. The powerful influence of the church on the sovereigns of these states resulted in the rise of large-scale ecclesiastical constructions celebrating both the power of the church and the ruler. The manifestation of these emerging conditions can be seen in the grandeur in which buildings such as St. Martin at Tours (1000-1040), Saint-Benigne at Dijon (1001-10081); Santiago de Compostela (begun 1074) and Cluny (1088-1121) were built. The technical origin of this revolution we are told to have been derived from the work of Vitruvius Pollio (circa 100 BCE) which contained architectural information and some aspects of building activity. To say such a revival was derived only from this work is far from reality. Harvey dismissed such claims pointing out that Gothic architecture was based on the use of proportion derived from a source not related to Vitruvius. European medieval masons and architects had their experiments among the Saracens, he suggested.[713]

He also criticised the idea, popularised by some scholars[714] of the role of the Masons' guilds and Stonemasons lodges, known as *comacini*[715] that existed in the Lombard kingdom.[716] In addition to the lack of substantiated proof, Harvey dismissed the idea that these masons travelled in groups producing such buildings all over Europe[717]. He insisted that they worked singly and that any chance of group collaboration was very remote except possibly in the form of

233

small partnerships. Other scholars (mainly northern Europeans) came up with a theory suggesting that Barbarians from the North were responsible. In their attempt to imitate the forest and its high trees, they introduced this high span building tradition. As we shall see later, such a theory has been widely discredited. In general, conditions in Europe were not favourable to the development of any artistic or architectural talent save a few limited attempts. The external origin, therefore, becomes paramount. Harvey confirms, "*This sudden revolution in technique bears all the marks of external impact, and could not have been the result of a slow evolution in traditional skills. There can be no mere coincidence in the fact that exactly such skills had existed among the stonemason of the Near East for centuries, and at this very date the great campaign known (inaccurately) as the first Crusade had just taken place.*"[718] Lethaby found the Christian borrowing from the East to be long standing going back to the Romans, but from the Muslims it was exceptional. He declares, "*There is much more of the East in Gothic, in its structure and fibre, than is outwardly visible.*"[719] He adds "*It is not generally realised in how large a degree the Persian, Egypto-Sarecenic and Moorish forms are members of one common art with Gothic.*"[720] Rome not only acquired the rich and various forms of the Hellenistic art of Syria and Egypt and Asia Minor, but Egyptian art has long refreshed Roman arts. However, "*The East came to the west through Byzantine rule in Italy, by relations with the German Empire and by the Muslim occupation of Sicily and Spain. The most living and potent of all was the last, and indeed it seems to have been almost a possibility that we should have to name this age from the Caliphs instead from Charlemagne.*"[721]

After long years of enclosed self-preservation, and a preoccupation with internal fighting which resulted in the evaporation of any intellectual or artistic ideas essential to national prosperity and development, Europe by the 11th century was becoming receptive to Muslim and eastern culture. The influence exerted by pilgrims, missionaries, embassies, trading and military contacts in changing the old negative perception of Muslim high civilisation is decisive. Furthermore, this was the apogee of Muslim culture. They produced renowned scientists, thinkers, and excellent works of arts as well as a great number of architectural masterpieces in many lands especially in the areas bordering Europe - Spain, Italy and North Africa. Therefore, it is inconceivable that Europeans developed this "well timed" architectural revival in complete isolation from the impact of this neighbouring development. In fact, as we shall see, a great number of scholars emphasise that the first impetus towards a new architectural style in Europe was very much connected to the defeat of the Muslims in Spain and Sicily. The beginning of this building activity and the appearance of the so-called Romanesque style came at a time coinciding with the capture of Sicily by the Normans in 1042 followed by the capture of Barbastro in the north east of Spain in 1064 by the Normans and the French. Among the spoils of victory were a large number of Muslim prisoners who were distributed among European nations. At Barbastro, for example, the French share of the booty included thousands of Muslim prisoners, Rome received 1500 and Constantinople 7000 Muslims[722]. The reader may guess how many masons, craftsmen, and artists were among these prisoners. Harvey endorses this stating that: "*It is probably no coincidence that the 11th century developments which are associated with the rise of the fully Romanesque style were contemporary with the first of a series of waves of political action in which the West undertook a counter-campaign against the Muslims, both in Spain and in the Holy Land. ...Successful forays resulted in the capture of Saracens, many of whom were artists and craftsmen; but even apart from this, the penetration of the South by relatively barbarous northerners such as the Normans, provided a glimpse of the comforts of higher civilisation. There was a direct incentive to emulate such relative luxury in the northern homeland, and in spite of the climatic difficulties a successful transfer was accomplished.*"[723] One of these captives as already mentioned was Lalys who designed the abbey of Neath in Glamorgan in 1129. It took only fifty years after the promotion of Lalys to become the architect of Henry I (c.1068-1135) that the first English schools of Gothic appeared.[724]

Moreover, the connection between the Normans and the spread of this architectural inspiration to Europe particularly Northern France and England is well documented. English writers, for example, relate much of the English architectural heritage to the Norman occupation in 1066. Yet history also shows us how before their occupation of Sicily, these Norman dukes terrorised Europe and erased any signs of civilisation. Descending from the Norse and Vikings, they conquered Normandy and later spread southwards towards Italy and Sicily causing much destruction and slaughter.[725] The contact that Normans made with Muslim civilisation in Sicily has subdued their barbarity and sophisticated their organisation and they were converted into great builders rather than destroyers. The Normans later played a leading part in civilising Europe. Harvey rightly admitted the impact of the contact between the Normans and Muslims as he declared, "*the re-activizing of Europe into a dynamic age stemmed from the cultural explosion which took place when the Normans and the East came into direct contact.*"[726] Porter approved this role but he attributed it to the influence of Lombardy as he wrote, "*Normandy perceived and imitated the architectural progress of nations even far removed from her own borders. At this time, there*

235

was no other country in Europe that for architectural attainment could compare with Lombardy. Therefore, it was to Lombardy that the Normans turned for inspiration for their own buildings."[727] Porter defies Western historians who clearly established that the lands of high civilisation of that time were in Sicily, Spain and the rest of Muslim land. How could Lombard architecture reach such a position and sophistication? Cantu (1829) described it as, "*The early Lombard architecture was not an order, nor a system, as much as a delirium. Balance and symmetry utterly disregarded no harmony of composition or taste, shameful neglect in form proportion; in place of the perfect classic design, which satisfies the eye, they substituted incoherent and useless parts, with frequently the weak placed to support the strong, in defiance of all laws of static. Columns-which used to be composed of a base, shaft and capital, in just proportions, supporting a well-adapted architrave or frieze more or less fitly adorned, and a cornice which only added beauty ad strength- were exchanged for certain colonnettes, either too short or too slight, knotted, spiral and grouped so as to torture the eye, and above the disproportioned and inharmonious abacus of the capitals were placed the arches, which in good style should rest on the architrave.*"[728]

Muslim Sources of Medieval European Architecture

It is surprising to find that European scholars have been debating the issue of Muslim influence for quite some time, although in the last century or so they resolved to rule out any significant Muslim sources for the origins of the medieval architectural revival. They accepted the unsatisfactory answers that were offered, and the subject was quietly put aside, greatly helped by the absence of any Muslim challenge. In this work, we try to revive this issue, aiming to shed light on new developments and raising questions that may lead us closer to the truth.

The academic dispute over the role played by Muslim art and architecture in Medieval European architecture has been mainly centred on Muslim sources of the Gothic style, which marked the major architectural development taking place in Europe from the late 12th century to the Renaissance. Here we find theories to be divided into two main groups: Early theories that occupied much of the 17th and 18th centuries condemned the Gothic style and expressed their dissatisfaction. In this case, Gothic was considered foreign to Europe and as a Muslim style originating in the East, and spread by the Moors and Andalusians. Medieval

Europe lacked the taste for arts and copied this art blindly from the Muslims. These views also considered the pointed arch as the most important element in Gothic architecture, and finding out its origins will determine the origins of Gothic as a whole.

The second group of theories emphasised the European and Christian origins of Gothic. This was mainly derived by favourable 19th century attitudes towards this architectural style. Among this group of scholars, Gothic is considered a work of genius and should be highly appreciated and valued. Theoretical assumptions, automatically, shifted towards emphasising the European and Christian origins. These attitudes are typical of those found in most theories of science where the Muslim contribution is deliberately ignored or understated. Even at the present time, such attitudes are still expressed where the Western is considered good and the foreign is considered bad. Currently, the pointed arch, of which the Muslim origins were firmly established, is considered less decisive in the development of the Gothic style. Greater importance is attributed to the emergence of ribbed vaulting and particularly the quadripartite vault.

Negative Gothic and the Muslim Origin.

Historical sources, particularly the momentous work of Frankl: the Gothic, published in 1960 by Princetone University Press[729], reveal that the first to point to the influence of Muslim arts and architecture on Gothic is Florent Le Comte (died 1712) who was a sculptor and painter. In his work, he differentiated between older Gothic buildings, which are remarkable for their size and solidity, and the "modern" ones, which exceeded in artistic work and delicacy. He talked of the Muslim "*Saracenic*" way of building such as in Granada, Seville and Toledo in Spain, and the Greek way which is a mixture of Antique taste "*Gout Antique*" and Arabesque "*Gout Arabesque*" as in Saint Marco in Venice.[730]

Later, Christopher Wren (1632-1723), firmly established the so called the "*Saracenic Theory*" as he affirmed the Muslim origin of Gothic.[731] Wren was an important mathematician, an expert in theories of natural science, a renowned architect and the son of a clergyman. His views on the Gothic were somewhat better than that of his predecessors although he publically criticised particular Gothic forms and elements. For instance, he criticised flying buttresses, which he thought should be concealed as their exposure not was not ornamentally attractive and statically weak since their exposure to the weather and their corrosion resulted in the collapse of the vaults. He also thought that pinnacles were useless and had no ornamental value, while the very high roof cannot be durable as the lead is likely to slip[732]. In relation to origin, Wren states his argument in the following: "*This we now call Gothic manner of architecture, though the Goths were rather destroyers than builders' I think it should with more reason be called the Saracen style, for these people wanted neither arts nor learning: and after we in the West lost both, we borrowed again from them, out of their Arabic books, what they with great diligence had transformed from the Greeks.*"[733] In his opinion, the crusaders were the source as they brought with them ideas and descriptions of these Muslim architectural forms. After this, "*The Saracen mode of building, seen in the East, soon spread over Europe, and particularly in France, the fashions of which nation we affected to imitate in all ages, even when we were at enmity with it.*"[734] Frankish knights and nobles must have encountered the pointed arch in Jerusalem during in the first crusade (1099). Their fascination with such forms resulted in them imitating them at home in Europe when they returned.

Similar attitudes were expressed by Francois de Salignac de la Motte Fénelon (1651-1715), archbishop of Cambrai and tutor to Prince Louis de Bourgogne (the eldest son of Louis XIV). In his works *Lettre sur les occupations de l'Academie Francaise*, he clearly promotes Greek architecture which is more Christian than Gothic which originates from the Muslims.[735] He wrote: "*The inventors of the architecture that is called Gothic and that is, so they say, a product of the Arabs doubtless thought that they had surpassed the Greek architects. A Greek edifice has no sort of ornament which only serves to adorn the work; the parts necessary for support and shelter, such as the columns and the entablature, appeal to us because of their proportion; everything is simple, everything is measured, everything is intended only for use, one sees neither boldness nor caprice that could impress the eye; the proportions are just, that nothing is restricted to satisfying true reason. In contrast to this, the Gothic architect raises on very slender piers an enormous vault that ascends to the clouds; one expects that it will all collapse, but it endures for many centuries; it is all full of windows, roses, and pinnacles; the stone seems to have been cut out like cardboard, everything is in light, everything is in the air. It is not natural that the first Gothic architects flattered themselves that they had surpassed Greek simplicity by their vain refinement answer.*"[736] In another document, *Dialogue on Eloquence*, which is in the form of a dialogue between himself and another person, Fénelon outlines, "*This architecture, which we call Gothic, came down to us from the Arabs; their type of mind, very lively and understained by rules or culture, could not do otherwise than plunge into false subtleties. Thence comes poor taste in all things.*"[737]

238

Francois Blondel the Younger (1683-1748) in his influential work *Grande Encyclopedie* adopted the views of both Wren and Fenelon. For him *"The Goths destroyed the most beautiful buildings of antiquity, and architecture was reduced to such a barbarous state that the architects lost all sense of proper proportions. From these abuses was developed a new manner of building, which was Gothic, and which lasted until Charlemagne undertook to restore antiquity again."*[738] For him Europe and France in particular saw two distinctive architectural styles. The "Gothic" which was introduced under the rule of the Goths is characterised by its weightiness. Clearly here, the use of Gothic does not refer to Gothic style but rather to buildings built under the rule of the Goths chiefly in Italy, which were carried out before the reign of Charlemagne. This is the "Romanesque" style. The "Arabic" style is characterised by its delicacy, lightness, and over-ornamentation. This is the "Gothic" style, which he called in another document (*Architecture Francoise*) "modern." It was brought from the south by the Arabs and the Moors: *"The second Gothic architecture known as modern lasted approximately from the 11th century to the reign of Francois first, and has a different origin attributed to the Moors and Arabs who had in architecture the same taste in their poetry. Both of these are equipped with overflowing ornaments, which go beyond nature. These are distinguished from the Goths through their excessive hardiesse of height of its buildings as well as the abundance of its delicate and bizarre ornaments. In order to uncover this truth one must study those who saw or described Spanish Mosques and Cathedrals that were built by the Moors. We will find that it was from the region of these peoples that this architecture spread to Europe. Literature flourished among the Arabs when their Empire was the most powerful, and they were cultured in philosophy, mathematics, and medicine. Their attainment in science nurtured the love for science in regions they occupied around Spain, and all over Europe their books were read, their philosophy and architecture were renowned. As a result many churches were built in the Moorish taste even without correcting what was more suitable for hot countries than for regions with a temperate climate. This manner of building lasted up to the end of the 15th century, an example of this is the Amiens Cathedral."*[739]

Bishop William Warburton (1698-1779) emphasised the influence of Muslims but provided a new theory as to the way such influence spread to Europe (See Appendix 2). He identified two styles[740]. The first architectural style was developed under the rule of the Saxons and he called it the Saxon style. The Templars introduced it to Europe borrowing models from Palestine. This is an imitation of the Holly Spulchure, hence of Greek and Byzantine origins. The second style is Norman, which was spread by the Goths, after they had conquered

239

Spain where they found a mature architecture. Warburton must have been referring to the European conquest of Andalusian lands, especially Toledo, since he could not have meant the Goths (Visigoths) who, as some scholars maintain, occupied Spain in the 6th century before the arrival of Muslims. His theory was later taken up by Arthur Schopenhauer (1788-1860) who adopted Warburton's views considering that the Gothic is of Muslim origin spread by the Spanish Goths into Europe. He also declared his preference for classical architecture. According to him, architectural beauty comes from the struggle between heaviness and rigidity, which has never been better achieved than in the column and entablature of antiquity. Such perfection of this could only be carried out in southern climate while in the North Gothic is impaired by its climate. He further states, "*I hardly need to remind the reader that in regard to all these architectural reflections I had in mind solely the ancient style of building and not the so-called Gothic, which, of Saracenic origin, was introduced to the rest of Europe by the Goths in Spain. Perhaps the latter, too, cannot be denied a certain beauty in its way; but when it undertakes to claim equal rank with the former, that is barbarous presumption that cannot be permitted.*"[741]

The Russian Nikolay Gogol (1809-1852) provided a chronological study of European and Christian architecture from primitive styles to Roman and Byzantine architecture. In relation to Gothic, he provided three definitions. The first is the "*rough Gothic*" which generally means "*Romanesque*" style[742]. The second is "*Gothic-Arabic*" which Gogol applied to the style of early Gothic that spread around the 12th century. The third is the Gothic style proper, which he called matured Gothic. In terms of origin, he puts forward a different theory suggesting that Byzantine lands that came under Muslim control lost its native architectural style and adopted Muslim style. Byzantine migrants brought this style into Europe and "corrupted" European architecture. He wrote, "*A number of inhabitants of the Byzantine Empire fled the vicious capital when it was taken by the Mohammedans and subsequently ruined the taste of the Europeans and their colossal architecture. The Byzantines had long since lost their Attic taste and had not even retained their native Byzantine taste. They brought only miserable remnants of their degenerate style to Europe.*"[743]

Jacques Germain Soufflot (1713-1780) took the view of Blondel as he described the Church of Notre Dame in Dijon as a work of Gothic architecture, modern or Arabic[744]. He stressed that the pointed Gothic arches have more strength than round arches, but they are not so graceful. James Anderson (1739-1808) disagreed with him in the static role of the pointed arch.[745] He considered this arch to be the weakest with the lateral thrust, which diminishes more the steeper the arch, becomes. Anderson distinguished between "*Old Gothic*" which uses Roman round arches, and Saracenic "*Modern*", which employs the pointed arch.

August Wilhelm Von Schlegel (1767-1845) developed the Saracenic theory further as he introduced India. The Muslims "Saracens" of India developed this style. In dealing with the origin of Gothic, he stated, "*Its proper name is Saracen, in India. Its character falsified in Italy. In its pure state in Germany, France, and England, whether it has any artistic value at all, since it is so absolutely opposed to the Greeks?*"[746] Thus, Gothic was derived from Muslim India rather than from Spain. The striking similarity between architecture of Indian temples and Mosques and Gothic architecture is very noticeable. Schlegel considered such architecture as of Gothic type and the use of Ornamental foliage in Gothic as Oriental. However, he did not explain how this style spread into Europe.

In his Sentimental Journey through Normandy, Odard (1847) did not refer to the origin of Gothic, but confirmed the Muslim invention of the pointed arch as he wrote, "*there is no instance of that arch in Europe except among the Saracens of Sicily and Spain....*"[747] He added later, "*this is the opinion held by men whom the verdant bye-paths and flowery fields of theory never allured from the high road of clear authentic fact. Such men as Lord Aberdeen[748] and Mr. Knight[749]. Their researches have fully established for the pointed arch a Saracenic origin. I have already dwelt so long upon this subject that I will only refer to the writings of these gentlemen for evidence, which is conclusive on the point. They trace the birth and growth of the pointed arch in the Saracenic buildings in Egypt, at Kairoan, in Sicily, in Spain, in Persia, in short, wherever they went, the Saracens carried with them this favourite form. It was in universal use among them at a time when it was not in existence elsewhere. The Crusaders were struck with this new form when they visited the East. They brought back the idea to Europe, and the eastern workmen who accompanied them, or found their way westward at that time, were the means of securing it general adoption, till, at last, it gave the character to a new style.*"[750]

Spengler Oswald (1880-1936) provided a systematic analytical survey of the history of world's architecture. In his examination of Gothic architecture, he connected both Romanesque and Gothic art and architecture to Muslims. He termed Romanesque architecture as "*late Arabian*", while he called Gothic as "*Arab Gothic*". He included the facades of cathedrals of Burgundy and Provence and Strasbourg Cathedral in the late Arabian style. In setting up his argument, Oswald wrote, "*It is true that all cultures, with the exception of the Egyptian and perhaps the Chinese, have been under the tutelage of older cultural impressions: foreign elements appear in each of the worlds of forms. The Faustian soul of Gothic, already moved to reverence by the Arabian origin of Christianity, turned to the rich treasures of late Arabian art. The Arabesque of an undeniably southern, I might say Arabian Gothic are spun over the facades of the cathedrals of Burgundy and Provence, dominate the language of Strasbourg Cathedral with a stone magic, and everywhere-in statues and portals, in cloth designs, carvings, metalwork, and by no means least, in the intricate figures of Scholastic thought and one of the loftiest symbols of the west, the saga of the Holy Grail... More than once the pointed arch threatens to burst its restraining line and transform itself into the horseshoe arch of Moorish-Norman structures.*"[751]

From the above it appears clearly that there is a strong case of Muslim influence on the emergence of Gothic. The adoption of key Muslim features such as the pointed arch, the polilobed arch, Arabesque and a number of other ornamental motifs, were fundamental constituents of this new style. However, recent critics of these theories switched the subject of central element in the development of Gothic to the so-called ribbed vault, especially the quadripartite vault. The argument is that the decisive step in the invention of Gothic was not, the pointed arch but the ribbed vault. Their main argument is that the first ribs appeared in Durham in 1098, just before the first crusade[752]. Thus, the Gothic style had nothing to do with the Muslims. However, as we shall see, the rib vaulting was a Muslim invention and had been widely used in the Muslim world since the 8th and 9th centuries.

Positive Gothic and the Western Origins

By the turn of the 18th century, the acceptance and admiration of Gothic grew and consequently investigation into its origin concentrated on European side. Here we find a considerable prejudice as academics started promoting their own countries, each one claiming Gothic to be the invention of his own nation. Friedrich Seesselberg, for example, sees that blue-eyed and blond-haired people could only produce such an art[753]. Other scholars such as Worringer[754] and Haupt[755] continued in the race theory. However, we shall not go further in this discussion as this has been widely discredited; we concentrate instead on those views, which provide an objective explanation. From these we find the first to deny any relation of Muslims with Gothic was Thomas Gray (1716-1771). He put forward a different hypothesis suggesting that Gothic originated from the pointed arch, but that it was not the product of Muslim influence: "*I do not see anything* (Gothic in Muslim architecture) *but the slender spires that serve for steeples, which may perhaps be borrowed from the Saracen minarets on their mosques.*"[756] In his theory, the pointed arch arose accidentally from the experience of intersecting round arches[757]. Nobody has taken up this theory and the first people to intersect arches were the Muslims of Cordoba.

John Milner (1752-1826) put forward another argument based on historical chronology suggesting that Gothic originated in Britain with the Normans who introduced it there[758]. He emphasised that Gothic architecture was derived from the pointed arch. However, for the origins of pointed arch he took the view of Gray suggesting that it did not come from the Muslims "*Saracens*" but was discovered by the Anglo-Normans accidentally as a product of intersecting semicircles, first in the choir of Winchester and then in 1132 in the church of St. Cross. Such theory was also rejected right way and did not go further.

Meanwhile, Christien Ludwig Stieglitz (1756-1836) sided with the Germans arguing that the Muslims had nothing to do with Gothic since the style has high roofs and massive towers while the Muslims had domes and slender minarets[759]. For the pointed arch, he gave a surprising origin saying that it is the property of the Germans who passed it to the Muslims. As for the question of how Gothic came to being, Steglitz related it to the "*romantic spirit*" which spread in Germany (in the 13th century). Such an enlightened spirit inspired poets, incited heroic and knightly deeds and gave a nobler impulse for architects' imagination leading to the birth of Gothic[760]. We let Johan Wolfgang von Goethe (1749-1832) answer these claims: "*To me the strangest part of all this is the German patriotism that would like to represent this obviously Saracenic plant as having sprung from its soil. Yet on the whole the epoch in which this taste in architecture spread from South to North still remains most remarkable.*"[761]

Later, Alexandre de Laborde (1773-1842) promoted the French origin claiming that Gothic was a product of France[762]. He distinguished three medieval styles of architecture in France. The first is the Romanesque with completely round arches, also called Saxon or Lombard. The "*Style Ogivique*" as he called it, uses pointed arches. The third style is that of the Renaissance. The Gothic style was introduced to France and Europe through the crusaders whose experience in the East provided them with spirit for reform. Gothic did not come suddenly but it was developed through the processes of gradual change and improvements. Starting from the Romanesque style, architects each time made some refinements, added more precision, light and grace into buildings until it was perfected. This perfection, it is maintained by most scholars, was achieved in France, in the Ile de France, in buildings such as St. Denis and Chartres. The pointed arch is the first major element of Gothic, architects developed it from wooden construction imitating their lightness in stone building. The *quadripartite vault* is the second most important element, which together with the pointed arch produced the graceful facades and enabled the reduction of the weight of the building by permitting the use of lighter material. The extension of the use of the pointed arch to windows, doors and all other parts of the building was due to its usefulness in reducing weight and strength in statics. The pointed arch minimized lateral thrust, permitted the construction of thinner vaults, and saved material.

This idea of the progressive development of Gothic, enhanced by the rise of Darwin's theory of evolution, provided the corner stone for the next generation of scholars, starting with George Saunders (1762-1839). Saunders adopted this approach arguing that the vaulting is the principal element of Gothic as it allowed the spanning of such large spaces[763]. He described the groins (whether arches or vaults) as the weakest part of the structure. Medieval architects used groined vaulting in their smaller work but when they desired to use this system in churches of large span, they needed to strengthen the weaker parts. They started by placing arched ribs in the transverse direction of the vaulting, later they added diagonal ribs under the intersections of the cross vaulting to provide additional strength. Later for aesthetic reasons, the transverse arched ribs were moulded to correspond with the diagonal ribs. In relation to the curves of the arches, he thought that the ribs were constructed after the cell of the vaulting had been built. The reason for placing ribs underneath and filling the space between the rib and the groin lines of the vault cell was to strengthen these lines. In some structures where reinforcement was not needed the ribs were not used; an example of this is the transept of Winchester Cathedral (1079-1093). He also put forward a theory about the origins of stilted, pointed, horseshoe and groined arches. In a rectangular plan, the diagonal arches of half a circle will be higher than the longitudinal ones and these in turn higher than the transverse arches. To achieve level height, stilting of the arch was introduced, in other words having the horns of the semi-circle continued downwards in perpendicular lines to the same base as the others. Sometimes, this is achieved by the continuation of the arch itself, which results in the formation of the horseshoe arch. The introduction of the pointed arch across the narrow side of the vault bay also provided the solution.[764]

Arcisse de Caumont (1801-1873) sees the origin of Gothic to be based on the pointed arch, which is derived from the Orient. His theory is that Gothic has three main sources, native French, Roman recollection, and an Oriental taste.[765] He propounds that the idea came from the crusaders; the religious enthusiasm that was created by the Crusades, the wealth collected by the church, the decline and deterioration of religious buildings, and the population increase, which all led to the need for building new churches that reflected these new factors. *"How else to explain they say, the great revolution which took place in the art of building Will it be believed is an architect of France, England or Germany invented the style Gothic, and that despite the difficulty of communications, despite the tendency to follow the ordinary old routines, all architects in Europe have agreed to adopt the new forms roughly the same time or will be assumed that several architects have spontaneously created Gothic architecture in the various countries of Europe This assumption would be even less likely than the first .. It is much more natural to think that the Overflow of the European population in the East, which also produces a general improvement in the arts and sciences was as the cause of the change which took place in architecture. The Crusaders of all parties parts of Europe reported in their respective homelands what they had seen, they wanted to trace the image as the gothic architecture was introduced in Western Europe, about the time of the Crusades."*[766]

Violet le Duc (1814-1879) rejects the Muslim origin of the Gothic. He sees Gothic as a French style that represented a local taste.[767] The pointed arch was used for two main reasons. It provided more solidity and was statically more advantageous. Builders had learnt from the collapse of pre-Gothic buildings (Romanesque) that had vaults with round arches. The other reason is geometrical, as discussed by Sanders, and related to narrow (rectangular) vault fields where pointed arches could be employed on the narrow side in order to obtain the same crown height as over the wide side, as well as the same level as the intersection of the diagonals. In his opinion, the real inventive element in Gothic was the solution to the question of vaulting of the basilica, which represented a major problem for early architecture.

Joseph Quicherat (1814-1882) gave the rib the first position in the development of Gothic instead of the pointed arch. This rib was not originated in the Muslim world but in the West in North of France (Ile de France). In one of his texts, he wrote, *"The quadripartite ribbed vault is without exaggeration the generating element without which this architecture would not have found its laws or its physiognomy, or attained the originality that we see."*[768] In these terms, other elements of Gothic such as the pointed arch, buttresses and piers are descendants of the rib. Yet, in considering the whole Gothic epoch, the rib becomes no longer an indispensable characteristic as long as one or more of its descendent are present. This was probably influenced by the spread of ideas of evolution influenced by Darwin's work on the Origin of Species.

Harvey contested the French claims for Gothic arguing that the role of Paris and French Kings in the development and spread of Gothic was accidental.[769] The Gothic art, wherever it was originated, became concentrated around Paris, in the Ile de France, by virtue of the movement of scholars to the teaching of Abelard and others at the schools of Notre Dame. The origin instead is connected to the pointed arch, which Christian did not discover before the 11th century because of the lack of contact with the Muslims, then due to Europe preservation. It was not until the end of the 11th century, when such contacts were greatly established. This was mainly due to Norman conquest of Sicily, between 1060 and 1090, where they must have observed it there. Additionally, the crusade occupation of Jerusalem in 1099, in which the Normans played an important role, provided another contact point. Harvey noted that the first appearance of the pointed arch in the Christian world came after the establishment of the Norman Kingdom in Sicily. The Gothic art and its cultural movement followed the expansion of the Normans, spreading into England, Germany and Scandinavia.

Other theorists searched in Scandinavia for Gothic origins. They conjectured that Gothic is derived from wooden constructions of the barbarians. In this respect, Louis Courajod (1841-1896) states: *"Without the barbarian carpentry there would probably never have been a Gothic art."*[770] The Goths in their stone building imitated wooden building of the Gauls in Scandinavia. Their argument is essentially based on support elements such as buttresses, piers and shafts, which they describe as wooden support used by carpenters, translated into stone by masons. Costenoble (1769-1837) explains how the pointed arch was derived indirectly from wooden construction. At first, it was invented from inclining two beams toward each other in the formation of roofs. This was imitated in stone and when curves replaced the straight lines, the pointed arch was born.[771]

Also connected with wood is another group of theorists who developed what is known as the Forest Theory. Joris Karl Huysmans (1848-1907) attested that man imitated much of the forest. Element such as pointed arches and nave were taken from the organisation of rows of trees and the intersection of their higher branches gave the idea of arched vaults and nave[772]. Francois Rene Chateubriand (1768-1848) added further arguments to the forest theory. Germans used to worship their Gods under trees and when they became Christians, they wanted to translate this forest environment into their new worship. Evidence of this is the tree, which represented the God of fertility, was baptised and adapted in the Roman Christian doctrines for the Christmas tree.[773] In Chateubriand's views, all architecture is derived from human imitation of Mother Nature expression in the forest. He continued: *"Forests were the first temples of God, and in forests men grasped their first idea of architecture. This art had to vary according to climates. The Greeks shaped the elegant Corinthian column, with its capital of leaves, on the model of the palm. The enormous piers of the ancient Egyptian style represent the sycamore, the Oriental fig, the banana tree, and most of the gigantic trees of Africa and the forest of the Gauls passed in their turn into the temples of our fathers, and our oak forests have thus preserved their sacred origin. These vaults incised with leaves, these socles that support the walls and end brusquely like broken tree trunks, the coolness of the vaults, the shadow of the sanctuary, the dark aisles, the secret passages, the low doors, all of this evokes in a Gothic church the labyrinths of the forests...The Christian architect, not satisfied with building forests, wanted, as it were, to imitate their murmurs, and by the help of the organ and suspended bronze he has associated with the Gothic temple the noise of the winds and the thunder that rolls through the depth of the forest."*[774] The forest theory has been widely discredited as fantasy not based on any truth.

Another school of thought relates everything in Gothic to Christian belief. This type of architecture was developed as the understanding of various elements of the Christian religion. The verticalism, which is the essence of Christian architecture, represents the resurrection. Architectural features of the church depicted various mystical and philosophical Christian ideas. Such provisions are fully discussed in the next section. However, critics reject such claims insisting on the rationality of the style. Wren and Violet le Duc, for example, provided another explanation for the reasoning behind the exaggerated height of Gothic construction. This is based on the pillar, which gains in stability if it is vertically weighted.[775]

The Cultural Sources of Gothic

In addition to the elements of construction, that Gothic style introduced, such as the cross-ribbed vault, the pointed arch, and flying buttresses, the main decisive feature of Gothic is its widespread incorporation of light for artistic and formal ends and the promotion of greater relationship between function and form. In terms of light, the piercing of external walls by continuous rows of windows introduced the so-called transparent wall allowing greater light into all corners of the buildings. This architectural adaptation reflected a new mystical development of the idea of light that spread at the time promoting a particular meaning of light. Robert Grosseteste (1175-1253), Bishop of Lincoln, who was influenced by Muslim thinking and particularly those of al-Ghazali (Algazel) and al-Kindi[776], sees light as the mediator between bodiless and bodily substances, a spiritual body, and calls it an embodied spirit.[777]

This philosophical trend linked aesthetics and beauty to light giving it a significant meaning in art and usage. Beauty was seen in its relation to God; beautiful things should reflect their origin in God, in other words as his manifestation. Light, on the one hand, is the origin of life, and creation was an act of illumination, all beings would vanish without light. On the other hand, light was perceived as the radiant truth that illuminates darkness. This new aesthetic taste was reflected in the preference of the decorative arts of the time for glittering objects, shiny materials, and polished surfaces. Gothic architecture, therefore, was connected to mysticism with the structure, form and decoration being directed towards inducing contemplation and improving the religious state of mind of worshippers. Gothic mysticism found the light of stained glass to be one of the most convincing form of symbols. The more people became aware of the meaning of light and its impact on the soul, the larger they made the windows and the larger the windows became the more sophistication and variation of glass paintings were introduced to produce the maximum impact on the worshippers[778]. This is in contrast to early times when darkness was seen as the proper environment for meditation and contemplation.

In terms of form and function, the Gothic style used the pattern produced by the structural elements, the vault ribs and supporting shafts and the general form as aesthetic and artistic impression. In Romanesque art painted or stucco ornaments and mosaics were not only a compensation for poor work, but also served to invoke within the faithful a mystical experience with the celestial vision created by the internal decor making a heavenly sanctuary. The symbolic significance is conveyed by the monumental presentation of Christ. In the Gothic age the builder became the main artist, the independence that existed between form and function vanished, as form, and function became inter-dependent. *"The Gothic architecture was created in response to a powerful demand for an architecture particularly attuned to religious experience"*[779]. Inspired by the Book of Revelation, the church became a representation of the Heavenly City. Such a paradigm was introduced in the miniature known as Liber Floridus from St Bertin (c.1120) which depicted *"Jerusalem Celestis"* as a medieval cathedral. Here the twenty-four thrones stood in a circle round about the throne of God. From this, according to this theory, the circular form of the church was derived while the choirs corresponded to these thrones gradually incorporating the idea of the Holy City and the Heavenly Jerusalem. The basilica, for example, corresponded to the city gate, the nave and aisles to the street and market hall, the windows of the clerestory to the upper stories of the walls of the houses, the roof to the sky, the presbytery to the throne room of the ruler. Hence, the church form and plan symbolically represented Jerusalem.[780]

The other major development taking place in Europe was the rise of the mystical tradition which spread in 12th century France, led by the Cistercian movement under the leadership of St. Bernard of Clairvaux (1090-1153). His views in art and architecture, expressed in his "Apologia ad Guillelmum", were very influential on general thought. He denounced the Romanesque imagery and sculpture that occupied most of the church decor at that time, and attacked the luxury of Cluny that made it incompatible with the spirit of monastic humility and charity, in his views. The crude imagery of early architecture deriving from painting and sculpture had no purpose, and was inadequate and confusing. The experience of the divine truth comes from the mystical perception and spiritual contemplation in which the world of the senses has no place. St. Bernard, therefore, exercised a strong influence on developing a new approach to art and architecture. His commission of a number of churches and Cistercian abbeys, including the construction of his own abbey at Clairvaux (1135-1145) in which he was fully involved, further consolidates his contribution. St. Bernard's inspiration came from his visit to Monte Cassino, which was the intermediary by which Muslim forms, especially the pointed arch, were transmitted to Europe (see next section). However, French historian Lambert (1931) emphasised the influence of Cluniac architecture, which was subject to Muslim influence, on the Cistercian[781]. By 1130, the date of publication of Bernard's work, a new approach to art emerged. The abandonment of the representational arts paved the way for the perfection of construction and architectural proportion of Gothic age. The spread of many Muslim architectural features in European countries, which represented the first architectural departure from the Romanesque style and their later widespread use in Gothic, was mainly due to the spread of Cluniac and Cistercian thought in the 11th and 12th centuries.[782]

The impact of Muslim philosophy and theology on 12th century European thought has already been discussed, but here we refer especially to Al-Ghazali (1058-1111). His book *Tahafut Alfalasifa* was translated into Latin, widely circulated in Europe and. His second book, *Mishkatu Al-Anwar,* was wholly devoted to his mystical experience and involved many ideas about the divine meaning of light that resembled very much those circulating in 12th century Europe and outlined above. In this book, Al-Ghazali sees God as *"Allah is the Sun and besides the Sun there is only the Sun's light"*[783]. This is very much related to what was revealed in numerous verses of the Quran, which dealt with the mystical meaning of light and its connection with God. In Surah 24 Verse 35, for example, the Quran explains, *"Allah is the Light of the heavens and the earth"* (24:35). Some Muslim scholars thought the interpretation of this verse is manifested in the extensive use of light around the *mihrab* area either through numerous windows or through artificial chandeliers. The *mihrab* itself is considered as the source of light and often appears in Muslim works of art (particularly rugs) carrying the chandelier. Allah is also *"the First and the Last, the Most High and the Most Near. And He is the All-Knower of everything"* (57:3) and *"he for whom Allah has not given light, for him there is no light"* (24:40). We know that Peter the Venerable, Abbot of Cluny, had the Quran and other important religious works translated for him[784]. We know also that he offered at least the translation of the Quran to St. Bernard and they often exchanged letters where Peter talked about Islamic thought he had discovered and how false they were in his opinions. As this relationship demonstrates, Muslim mysticism was known among 12th century monks.

250

The other area of cultural influence was the rise of scholasticism. It is well accepted that each intellectual and cultural period demands scholarly manpower, which in its turn defines and determines the broader intellectual fields and characteristics of that period. The development of theology and metaphysics that the Muslims debated and developed in neighbouring Spain and North Africa certainly had its impact on theological reformation and metaphysical thoughts of the middle Ages. Architecture and other forms of art reflected this achievement in the form of symbolism that started to take shape in various European artistic and cultural productions. The Gothic architecture reached the peak of symbolism and employed sophisticated formal systems to express these theological and metaphysical developments. Another feature of intellectual development in the middle Ages was the lack of specialism and the wide and universally acquired knowledge. Distinguished scholars often attained a simultaneous distinction in philosophy, medicine, astronomy and literature. Architects of Gothic must have had similar universal knowledge to enable them to transmit this scholasticism via their artwork. The influence of Muslim intellect on Gothic culture is better explained by its influence on European scholars such as Dante (1265-1321), Adelard of Bath, Thomas Aquinas and many others. Both Thomas Aquinas and Hugh of St. Victor for example, who studied in Cordoba, considered beauty to be based on two main criteria involving perfect proportion and luminosity. This is very much the view of Al-Ghazali and the connection established in the previous chapter between these two philosophers would suffice to explain the influence of Muslim mysticism and philosophy. Simson (1988) considered the role played by Chartres in much of this metaphysical as well as rational thinking of Medieval Europe to be fundamental[785]. As we have seen in chapter 3, leading Chartres scholars such as Adelard of Bath, John of Salisbury and others acquired their knowledge from Andalusia. Thierry who was in charge of the school had a collection of Arabic books including a translation made by Herman.

Poetic and scientific literature of that time was the main source of Gothic as architecture and poetry are analogously constructed art expressed in different media. Dante's Divine Comedy was a typical example of Gothic culture, providing a general understanding of the intellectual and spiritual thought of the time. Dante was the Christian spirit of his time, his description of his journey under the guidance of his friend Virgil, then of Beatrice, through Hell, his ascent of the mountain of Purgatory to the spheres of the planets and up to the seven heavens is a spiritual and mystical experience with no European or Christian precedent. It provided spiritual, astronomical, metaphysical and mystical material for much of Gothic art and architecture[786]. Yet much of Dante's ideas were based on Muslim sources, particularly the direct parallel story of Prophet Mohammed's Ascension to Heaven. The Spanish Miguel Asin Palacios produced comparable passages from the Divine comedy and the story of the Prophet's Journey.[787]

In order to evoke sentiments of devotion and convey the divine presence, the Gothic builder relied on the aesthetic role of proportion and number. The rising interest and importance of mathematics and particularly geometry that was promoted by the Chartres School spread a new artistic phenomenon that attempted to link metaphysics of religion with mathematics and numbers. In the 12th century, Thierry of Chartres, for example, attempted to find the artistic side in the divine creation using geometry and mathematics. To explain the Trinity, he represented it with equilateral triangle, which reflects the equality of the three persons. The impact of these developments introduced a new understanding of art and beauty, which now reflected the ultimate harmony, which the blessed will enjoy in the other world[788]. This was the real beauty of the Gothic age rather than the image of man that was the centre of the artistic thought of early times. Harmony is a natural law that is derived from perfect proportions (geometry) and therefore for the building to be beautiful and stable it had to be built according to these natural geometrical laws. In these terms, the builder as an artist did not provide illusions and images of the divine world but applied the laws that order heaven and earth. This was the start of the rationality that later resulted in the Renaissance. This reminds us of the mystical approach towards art and beauty that was adopted by Muslims and widely disseminated in the 10th and 11th centuries at the hands of Al-Ghazali and Ibn-Al-Arabi. Meanwhile, such rationality was highly developed at that time in the Muslim world and particularly in Spain. Muslims introduced the use of the cypher (0) by which decimal fractions, rational and irrational, become possible. These Muslim ciphers, as well as the new `Algorithm', reached the architects of the Gothic period through the Latin translation of Al-Khwarizmi's *Algebra* treatise, written around 825, which was first made available by Adelard of Bath in 1126[789] and later Robert de Chester in 1144.[790] Adelard also translated the Arabic version of Euclid's *Element* with Arabic commentaries in 1120, which introduced a substantial amount of geometrical knowledge into Europe.

A further connecting point to Muslim geometry was the chapels of the Knight Templars, an order founded by nine French knights in Jerusalem in e1118, following the First Crusade. The chapels they built had a centralised form, derived from the Dome of the Rock. This form of church later spread in the west. The circular Temple Church in London was derived from these and was built in 1185. The rotunda, which is late Norman, and the Gothic choir (built in 1240) have a number of common features; they are both subject to the same geometric system[791]. Western scholars insist that this rationality descended to Europe and France in particular from the Greeks, especially Plato and Vitruvius. Nevertheless, one has to ask why this perfect timing? Why did not the French rediscover Plato earlier or later?

The application of this aesthetic and spiritual trend in building art, particularly by the reforming Cistercian order had its direct influence on the rise of Gothic. Both Bilson[792] and Bony[793], for example, linked the appearance of the world's first rib vaulting in England to the establishment of Cistercian order in England in 1128. Bilson sees the simultaneous emergence of the Cistercian order and Gothic style as revealing the connection between the moral order and the architectural order. Male held that the Cluniac and Cistercians employed elements such as the pointed arch and buttresses long before their adoption in the Ile de France where the birth of Gothic is believed to have taken place.[794]

The other cultural element of the Gothic era was the Crusades. The declaration of "holy wars" against Muslims under the pretext of freeing the Holy Sepulchre was not entirely a religious movement but had powerful political aims that were growing in strength during the period of the crusades between 1096 and 1291. The chief protagonists of this were the Popes, the princes of Europe and the emperor of Byzantium, and the commercial city-states of Genoa, Pisa and Venice. The struggle for power between the first three was the chief motivator. The conflict between papal authority and the monarchies has not been more tense than in these times. The rise of rebellious scholars, most of whom had been in contact with Muslim scholasticism, who questioned the divine authority of the Papacy and preached a more direct worship of God, also threatened the position of the Pope and his clergy. The crusaders were the major political factor behind much of Gothic culture. They gave birth to the concept of church militant whose role is the conquest of evil, the Muslims. The Cistercians, Cluniac and Benedictines were among the orders who believed their first goal was militancy in order to reach the position of church triumphant. Within this spirit, clerics collected large sums of money, received gifts and volunteers for the construction of the great cathedrals that transmitted this idealism. From church militant rose other militant orders of the Knights Templars, Hospitaliers and the Teutonic Knights who played an important role in the construction as much in the fighting. Viewed from this angle, the Crusades delayed the European Renaissance by enabling the clergy to regain their grip on power.[795] In addition to the above, a more direct influence of the Crusades on the development of Gothic was made through the architectural specimens that the crusaders brought from the East. The most important of these is the pointed arch, which was borrowed from mosques such as Al-Aqsa and Ibn Tulun and spread throughout France after the first crusade. After the brutal massacre of Muslims, the crusaders held their council meeting in the Dome of the Rock and surely would not fail to notice the pointed arch in the area. Furthermore, in 1104 King Baldwin I moved to live in Al Aqsa Mosque, calling it the *Templum Salomonis (Temple of Solomon)*, and it was there where Boldwin II accommodated the Templars (set up in 1119), from which their name came[796]. The Dome of the Rock was made into church, *Templum Domini*, or the Lord's Temple.[797] Many Europeans associate the fundamental idea of the Crusades with the pointed arches of Al-Aqsa and see the birth of Gothic as a divine reward for their victory over Islam in the crusades (fig.75).

As noted in chapter three, the 12th century was also the age of pilgrimage. The most celebrated pilgrimage was that to Santiago de Compostela in Northwestern Spain. The pilgrimage route crossed most of French territory and its contribution to the transfer of Muslim motifs and knowledge was decisive. The popularity of pilgrimage during this period transformed these roads into arteries full of activity. The churches located on these arteries, Cluny in particular, became the centres of the spiritual life of France and Europe attracting large crowds of pilgrims from all over Europe, a fame which gave them not only economic prosperity but also political and economic power. It is highly likely that when they returned home pilgrims imitated the artistic and architectural features of the holy places. Figure 70 shows the four main routes that pilgrims from all over Europe, took to get to Santiago de Compostela. These routes developed a network of stop stations that later became important churches not only to France but also to the rest of the Christian world. Lambert found Muslim features, such as the multifoil arches, dominating much of Romanesque architecture of South West France and Aquitaine, in scores of churches such as that of Saintonge and of l'Angoumois, at Echebrune, at Rioux, at Thouars, Chalais, Montmoreau, Plassac, Mouthiers, and le-Dorat-Haute-Vienne (fig.76)[798]. The multifoil arches can also be found in Britain in churches such as Tintern Abbey a former Cistercian church from the 12th century (fig.77). Important churches such as Ste Foy at Conques (1050-

Figure 75 AlAqsa Mosque, the crusade façade twelfth century

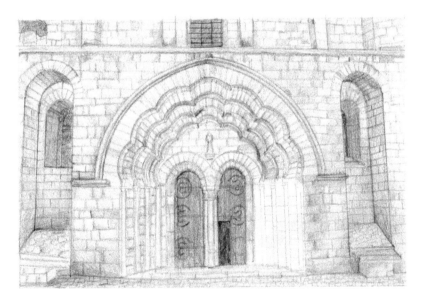

Figure 76 Portal of the Collégiale Saint Pierre in Liens de Le Dorat in Haute-Vienne

Figure 77
Archway in Tintern
Abbey a former
cistercian church from
the 12th century

1120), St Sernin at Toulouse (ca.1096), St Philbert at Tournus (c.950-1120), and Ste Madeleine at Vezelay (1104-1132) led the new building movement in Europe. The architectural features that were adopted from the Muslims and travelled along the pilgrimage route represented the main characteristics of this new style. The use of transverse arches, barrel ribbed vaults, piers and towers in addition to the enormous size and verticality set the first step towards the architectural achievement of Gothic.

The Role of Medieval Poets and their Architectural Fantasies

It has been argued in previous chapters that Muslim literature and art exercised a decisive influence on the poetry of medieval Europe. Muslims ideas filled the artistic mind of artists and poets, musicians and painters. Lethaby described the literary and artistic production of Europe then as "*Not only does a similar regard for things oriental appear in many of the Romances, but they themselves seem to be largely of an eastern character*"[799]. This influence is best demonstrated by various linguistic arrangements as well as Muslim elements treated by various poets. Thousands of legends and stories about the Muslims of Spain, their citadels, villas and princes were produced and spread throughout most of Europe. Among the names given to Granada for example were *Court of the Universe, Throne of Andalous, Mother of Peoples, Pomegranate of Rubies, Diadem and Roses,* and *City of Cities.*"[800] Detailed architectural descriptions of a number of Muslim Mosques and palaces were incorporated into many of the medieval poems that spread all over Europe.

The linguistic, literary and poetical developments in France during the 11th and 12th centuries took place in regions of Languedoc and Provence. During much of the middle Ages, this region was an integral part of Iberian kingdoms, first under Muslim control in eighth and parts of ninth centuries then part of Spanish Christian states. There are still a few reminder of Muslim influence in this region, for example names such as Castelmaur (Castle of the Moors) and Castelsarrasin (Castle of the Saracens), the medical School at Montpellier which was influenced by Muslims as seen previously, and Muslim coinage which was used for centuries alongside that of the Counts of Toulouse. Finally, there is the greatest legacy of the troubadours and their popular poetry, music and song. Consequently, we find a considerable reference to Muslim art and architecture as well as other aspects of civilisation. In the *Pelerinage de Charlemagne* song, which was dated to 1150, there is considerable description of Muslim lands and edifices. The poem told the story of Harun-al-Rashid and his journey to Basra with his knights including the description of buildings even those of India and the imperial Palace of Constantinople. It also described the fictional journey of Charlemagne to Jerusalem through Burgundy, Lorraine, Bavaria, Italy and Greece[801]. In one instance, the poet described the reception of Charlemagne by King Hugo, the Byzantine Emperor, in the great hall of his palace. In the domed hall all, the furniture is made of gold. Finished with an azure blue border, the walls are covered with paintings of all the animals of the earth, all the birds of the air, and all the fishes and reptiles of the waters. The vault is supported by one pier adorned with niello work on silver. Along the wall are a hundred pilasters of marble with gold inlays. In front of each of them stood two bronze figures of children with ivory horns at their lips. French scholar Gaston Paris thought such a hall would have been the *chrysotriclinium,* a Byzantine palace[802]. However, excavations have shown no connection with the *chrysotriclinium.* Art historians dismissed the existence of such a dome that rested on a central column as having been invented by the author who wanted to present something extraordinary to his readers. Others suggested that returning pilgrims related what marvels were to be found in foreign parts. No such a domed hall is known to have existed in Constantinople. The poet could have been influenced by *Triconchos,* the palace built by the Byzantine Emperor Theopilus (829-842) which was a throne room with walls encrusted with coloured marbles, columns of Phrygian marble and a golden ceiling. The walls were adorned with mosaics. In the hall called Magnaura where the reception took place, a plane tree of gold shaded the throne, on its branch sat golden birds. At the foot of the throne crouched lions, at its sides were griffins. The birds sang, the lions arose, waved their tails and roared. Diehl (1925) traced the splendour in the palace of Theophilos to buildings of Harun-al-Rashid (766-809) in Baghdad, a contemporary of Charlemagne[803] (see the Muslim architecture under the Abbasid Patronage, chapter 2).

However, a Hebrew poem of Ibn Gabriol (1021-1058) described Alhambra Palace in Granada, thus dating it to the eleventh century, which raises the possibility that it provided the descriptive material for the imaginary palace of the Pelerinage de Charlemagne.[804] This poem was read throughout France and Europe at a time when Abbot Suger was rebuilding the church of St.Denis (Paris), the first Gothic building. The connection of the *Pelerinage de Charlemagne* and the *Chanson de Geste* with St Denis is revealing[805]. The *Pelerinage de Charlemagne,* with its descriptions outlined above, claimed that Charlemagne himself started the journey to Jerusalem from St. Denis[806]. The *Chanson de Geste,* which narrate legendary incidents about Charlemagne and Roland and their crusade against the Muslims, was composed in the mid twelfth century. The epic claimed that Charlemagne returned from the Crusade in Spain to St. Denis. These poems were contemporaries with Suger and the *Chanson de Geste* was inserted in the French edition of the *Chronicles of St. Denis*."[807]

Another relevant epic is The *Roman de Trois* (1160), composed by the poet Benoit de Saint-Maure near Tours. This contained descriptions of at least three buildings, but the most important one was that of Chambre *de beaute*, which was depicted as a room containing pillars in its four corners each one of amber, jasper, onyx and garnet. On these four pillars, four figures stood two maidens and two youths. The first maiden held a mirror while the second danced. One youth played on twelve musical instruments, and strewed the floor with fresh flowers. The second youth provided each person present in the room with particular advice on how to conduct himself. Sohring wondered if these marvels existed and suggested, "*even though we have to think in this case of the Orient and not of the countries of the West.*"[808]

In 1164, the epic of *Eracle Eneas* was published showing great admiration of Oriental architecture and art. The main architectural description contained was that of the throne of "*Cosdroe*" (Khusroes the Persian King), which Heraclius the Byzantine King destroyed after his victory. The description reveals that the throne was a tabernacle with a domed vault and mentions a trefoil arch[809]. It was followed by the *Letter of Prester John* of 1165, which was made from the legend of an Indian priest of a Nestorian community who went to Byzantium in 1122 and narrated fabulous things about India. The description of the palace of the Indian king mainly contains a description of the roof, which is described as made of cedar and covered with ivory. The rest of the story described the furniture and social life of the king.

The quadripartite vault was described in the *Roman d'Alexandre* (1170) by Lambert li Tors and Alexandre de Bernay. The description referred particularly to the tomb of the Emir of Babylon as having four inside arches, which support all the weight. It did not refer explicitly to the vault or ribs as it used arches. This could mean either wall arches, or two diagonal ribs and two ridge ribs. However, it raised the idea that vaulting and arches are ancient in the Orient[810]. Similarly, the Romance of *Floire et Blanchefor,* thought to have been published after 1170, spoke of the true East-West relations that never ceased to exist even in troubled times. It told the tale of the infidel (Muslim) prince and his Christian ladylove, which is partly set in Baghdad. The tomb of Blancheflor rises in the shade of a tree before a cathedral. Verse 555 refers to a trefoil arch[811].

The ever popular story of the Grail was also linked to Muslim and eastern sources. The description of the Temple of Grail appeared in the epic poems of *Parzival (Percival) and Titurel* written by Wolfram von Eschenbach. The old French epic of *Percival ou le Conte du Graal* written by Chrétien de Troyes between 1180 and 1191 is thought to be the earliest on the subject although the origins of the legend of the Grail is far older. The Grail is supposed to be a sacred vessel or the stone, from which the vessel was made, which is supposed to have divine powers. According to the story, the stone came from heaven, before the creation of the world, when some of the angels rebelled against God and crowned Lucifer as their leader. When St. Michael threw Lucifer out of heaven into hell, he struck the crown with his lance and a stone fell down into Paradise. Adam found the stone and took it with him after he was expelled from Paradise to earth. He kept it in a cave where he and Eve lived and later buried.[812] This grave was thought to be at the centre of earth and the place where Christ was supposedly crucified. The dripping blood of Christ is supposed to have fallen upon Adam (in his grave), baptised him and redeemed him from sin. Some of the blood was collected in the vessel from the Last Supper, which was the property of Joseph of Arimathea. The epic states that Titurel was 50 years old when he was made king of the Grail. He was the grandson of Senabor, and became the keeper of the Grail. The legend states that at the age of four hundred[813], Titurel started the construction of the temple on mountain Monserrat near Barcelona. The description relates that the temple had a circular plan with seventy-two choirs on its periphery and a choir on the east twice as wide. Around this central edifice runs a ring shaped platform reached by circular steps. In the middle, there is a tower. The roof is of gold and made with ribbed vaults, which are carried on bronze columns. The ribs are embellished with pearls and coral and the surface of the vaults are covered with sapphires (this calls to mind the Ukhaidar palace). In the middle vault, in the tower, the ribbed vaulting has a keystone decorated with a lamb holding the cross. The walls are covered with mosaics. Along the partition walls of the seventy-two choirs are stalls of aloe wood. Above these wooden stalls, the wall is decorated with a blind gallery of columns and arches. The corners of the choirs have twisted columns ornamented with figures of dwarfs and strange creatures. In each choir, is an altar of sapphire, above it is a ciborium provided with a mechanism by means of which a dove brings an angel down from the vault during Mass and afterwards bears him aloft again. An elaborate clock with a gold sun and a silver moon announces the seven canonical hours. The Grail is placed in a tabernacle in the middle of the space. From outside, the structure looked like a big crown and over each two chapels rises a six-storey tower with each storey having three windows. This makes the roof totalling thirty-six towers, which are covered with gold. In short, this poem refers to most of Gothic elements such as ribbed vaults with keystones, polygonal chapels, painted windows and towers pierced with many windows and with interior spiral staircase and the absence of a crypt. Rothlisberger believes that all the elements of the Gothic style were already present in the Romanesque style such as stained glass, octagonal choirs, diagonal ribs with keystones and so on.[814] However, many disputed the idea of the polygonal choir being Romanesque as the main change during the 12th century was the abandoning of round choirs, corresponding to the diagonal, which was initiated by the diagonal rib.

In relation to its origin, Wolfram refers to his source as a poet named Kyot, a Provencal, who in turn took his story from an Arabic manuscript, which he found in Toledo.[815] According to Resie, *"the author of this manuscript was colled Flegetanis, who descended in genealogy from a mother's side of king Solomon. His father was a Saracen father who brought him up in the religion of Mahomet"*[816] This Flegetan is no more than a Latin corruption of *Felek daneh*, an Arab astronomer[817]. Others provided different explanations suggesting it meant "knowledgeable in the sky"[818], i.e. Astronomer, but the more acceptable view is that a corruption of *Felek Thani* which means the Second Sky, a title of an Arabic manuscript on Astronomy describing a "second sky or sphere" and written by Thabit Ibn Qurra.[819] Bezold thought it had a Syrian origin, and in 1883 published a German translation of the Syrian text[820]. Warton gave more details about the eastern origin of the epic as he wrote, *"The truth of this is supported by the internal evidence. The scene for the most part is not only laid in the East, but a large proportion of the names are of decidedly Oriental origin. The Saracen are always spoken of with consideration; Christian knights unhesitatingly enrol themselves under the banner of the Caliph; no trace of religious animosities is to be found between the followers of the Crescent and the Cross; and the Arabic appellations of the seven names are thus distinctly enumerated..."*[821] The existence of mechanical machines certainly refers to the highly elaborate Muslim machines of that time.[822] The name Percival comes from Parcifal, which is taken from Arabic "Parse or Parseh Fal", poor dummling who appears to have been the hero of an Eastern tale of a wonderful cup.[823]

Other scholars suggested that this epic was greatly influenced by the *Chanson de Charlemagne*, which again points to Arabic origin. The knights of Monsalvasch who trained themselves in arms to fight Muslims were stimulated by Muslim fantasies that go back to Harun-al-Rashid's architects or those of Alhambra. The Dome of the Rock has been also suggested to be the source of the epic, particularly in its reference to the rock *lapsit exillis*, the stone from which the knights of the Grail are supposed to live[824]. It is thought that this rock had a Biblical origins or a meteorite but it emerged to be the Rock in Jerusalem for which the shrine Dome of the Rock was built: "*Before we go any further, let us say that it is possible to explain lapsit exillis not as a chime of meanings, not as a reference to Biblical or legendary stones, but as the name given at that time to one individual stone of great sanctity: lapsit exiliens as a garbled rendering of lapis lapsus exiliens, which might be the Latin translation of Idrisi's "falling stone," i.e., the Rock in the Templum Domini (Dome of the Rock, Kubbet es-Sakhra) in Jerusalem. It was (and is) supposed to be suspended in the air, because it had wanted to follow the Prophet on his ascent to Heaven, but had been held down by the Angel Gabriel. Since Idrisi wrote his Geography for Roger II of Sicily (1154), knowledge of this peculiar stone which was also considered to be the point nearest to Heaven, might very well have reached Wolfram.*"[825]

The Oriental style appears evident in much of the splendour attributed to the temple. The form and splendours described in these epics certainly existed in Muslim lands. The character of the Caliphs and their palaces in Baghdad, Spain and North Africa was influential in many aspects of Muslim cultural and literary production, which have been proved a decisive influence in many aspects of European literary and artistic production. The Muslim philosophy of life and its concepts relating to God, heaven, hell and paradise have had its strongest impact on the development of such ideas in Europe. However, if the dating is accurate, one cannot rule out the influence of gothic buildings that existed at the time of the writing of the poem.

The last epic we consider here is that of Willehalm, also written by the German Wolfram von Eschenbach circa 1210. Willehalm deals with a legendary battle with the Saracens at Aliscans (near Arles). The storey in short is about Willehalm (St William, Wilhelm, and Guillaume) who was taken prisoner by the Saracens, and has escaped with Arabele, the daughter of the Saracen King Terramer. Arabele is baptized in the name Giburc and is married to Willehalm. The poem makes her a sort of a saint who sacrificed her family at home (the Saracen family) and her new family with Willehalm. The Saracens decided to avenge and recover their daughter, at first battle, Willehalm's forces were annihilated and his nephew Vivianz, a model of knightly valour, is killed. Willehalm and Giburc later build their strength, took the Saracens to another battle of Aliscans, which they won.[826] Helen Adolf studied the architectural descriptions and came to the following conclusion: " *the ground plan of the Willehalm, reveals that, contrary to the oblong shape in the case of Parzizial, nave and transept are here of equal length. One could call it then an octagon or a rotunda -which might be of interest in view of the similar ground plan of Templum Domini (Dome of the Rock) of the Templar churches.*"[827]

The Routes of Architectural Transfer

Chapter Four provided a detailed analysis of the major means by which architectural and artistic as well as technological transfer between Islam and the West could have taken place. Here we concentrate solely on how various Muslim architectural elements reached Europe, especially those connected with Gothic, in an attempt to establish a clearer understanding on the nature of the exchange and influence of Muslims in the area of architecture. Such an endeavour is not as simple or as straight forward as in subjects of science, philosophy and literature where historians have convincingly confirmed the important contribution of Muslims. In architecture finding similar concrete evidence is difficult as the violence of medieval times resulting from the continuous attacks of the crusades and various infighting, had destroyed a great proportion of Muslim buildings, echoing Scott "*the architecture of no other people has suffered such complete and systematic annihilation*"[828]. On the other hand much of this medieval architectural vestige, whether in Europe or in the land of Islam, was subject to substantial alteration and renovation greatly affecting its historic authenticity.

The Spanish Encounter

The borrowing from Muslim architecture started with the Mozarabic monks migrating from Cordoba bringing with them Muslim methods of building, forms and motifs as well as ideas of high culture to Northern Spanish regions, such as Aragon and Asturias, still under Christian rule[829]. The previous chapter discussed in details the role of Mozarabs in the spread of Muslim motifs across Spain and the Pyrenees. They erected Moorish style buildings wherever they went. For Example, the monks from Cordoba built San Miguel de Escalada in 913 near Leon, which among the features it had were the melon shaped domes and the horseshoe arches (see fig.78). The horseshoe arch was also illustrated by

Mozarabs in their illuminated manuscripts such as the one made by Beatus of Liébana mentioned previously, which had an impact on western art. San Cebrian de Mazote was founded in 921, also by Mozarab Cordoban monks, reveals similar planning, structural and decorative elements to that of St Miguel de Escalada, with a basilica of horseshoe arches, tripartite choir and horseshoe shaped apses (fig.79).

Most historians, including Trend, emphasised that through Spain Islam exercised the greatest impact on Europe compared to other factors including crusades.[830] In addition to the role of Mozarabs, the continuous crusades against Andalusia were the second major means by which Muslim motifs were transmitted to Europe. During the 11th and 12th centuries crusades against Spain multiplied and most of these were led by the French. These repetitive clashes must have played a role in the artistic and cultural exchange. In some cases, the French occupied a town for some period before being taken back by the Muslims. Barbastro for example was conquered by the French in 1064, was retaken by Muslims in 1065 before losing it again to the French in 1101. Eleventh century European revival also coincided with the successive fall of numerous Muslim towns, Toledo in 1085, Huesca in 1096, Barbastro 1101, Tudele 1114, Saragossa 1118, and Tarazona 1119. After the capture, migrating French monks, soldiers, merchants and artists colonised the north of the Andalusian Caliphate and formed quarters in cities particularly in Pamplona, Tudela, Saragossa, Salamanca, and Toledo. Mosques were given as priories to French cathedrals and churches. Ste Foy of Conques (fig.80) for example was promised the best Mosque in Barbastro by King Pierre I of Aragon.[831] A reminder of this connection is the presence of a Kufic writing, which decorate the bottom of dress of the angel with the horn, who is flying over Tartarus. The Kufic script refers to two concepts 'al naeem" or Bliss of paradise, and "al hamd" or Glory to God.[832] "This is a formula ...used here in direct relation with the central topic of the tympanum. The word al-Hamd ("Glory to God") adapts so well to the topic of the Last Judgement on the tympanum of Sainte-Foy in Conques, that it is no longer possible to attribute this inscription a simple decorative value. Its author, the Master of the tympanum, or less probably a member of his team, was fully aware of what he was engraving at the bottom of the angel's dress. Did he come from Mozarabic Spain? The question may arise."[833] The "Book of Miracles" of Sainte Foy also refers to a certain Jean Ferré, a converted Saracen, from Syria, who was imprisoned in 10th century, near Damascus and was liberated by Sainte Foy. In reconnaissance, he converted to Christianity and ended up serving at Conques.[834]

Figure 78 San Miguel de Escalada, Leon, Spain 913, showing the horseshoe arch.

Figure 79 San Cebrian de Mazote was founded in 921, also by Mozarab Cordoban monks

265

Figure 80 St. Foy (Saint Faith) of Conques (1050-1120), showing distinctive Muslim architectural elements in its towers, was is an important pilgrimage church on the route to Santiago de Compostela in Northern Spain promised the best Mosque in Barbastro by King Pierre of Aragon.

Figure 81 St.Sernin of Toulouse (ca.1096)

After the fall of Huesca in 1096, the archbishop of Bordeaux and the bishops of Oloron and Lescar officially dedicated its mosques to Christ. Mosques of other conquered towns such as the Great Mosque of Valencia followed suite. French churches such as Saint Martin de Seez, St. Pierre de Moissac, St.Sernin of Toulouse (fig.81), St Pons of Thomieres (c.1170), Saint Gilles de Gard (9th century), Saint Ruf d'Avignon (11th century), Saint Victor de Marseille (11th century, rebuilt in 12 and 13th centuries), all were actively involved in these crusaders and received as rewards mosques in Spain as priories.

By the turn of the 12th century, because of the strength and various successes of Christian crusades, in addition to the religious enthusiasm that spread throughout Europe, pilgrimage to Compostella increased substantially. Meanwhile, Cluny became the sole organiser of this event and its priories (mostly Mozarabic churches) along the pilgrimage route formed the main stop stations for pilgrims. On his pilgrimage to Compostella, Godescalc, the bishop of le Puy, stayed at the Monastery of Albelda where he made a copy of the manuscript of the workshop of Albelda. Lambert noted this strong link: "*It is therefore certain that since the middle of the 11th century, because of the holy war and the pilgrimage, the Medieval French knew Spain and the Hispano-Muslim art better than it is usually thought.*"[835] Therefore, Cluny played an intermediary role between Muslim Spain and Christian Europe in most of the artistic and cultural interaction.

The Role of Cluny

The connection of Cluny to Spain was deeply rooted. By the second half of 11th century, Cluniac houses stretched across the Pyrenees into Northern Spain, and Cluniac monks had a strong presence in that region. Links of Cluny extended to involve contacts with influential people and princes such as Ferdinando who used to pay 1000 *Mithqal* gold per year to Cluny[836]. Alfonso IV, his son and King of Leon-Castile married Constance, the niece of Saint Hugh the abbot of Cluny. His generosity to Cluny increased substantially and with his contribution, Hugh built the Abbey Church of Cluny. "*the Clunisian economy was dependent upon the continued flow of gold from Al-Andalus via the King of Leon-Castille to Burgundy. When the Almoravids cut off the supply it was more than Abbot Hugh's building operations that were threatened. Clunisian finances were dealt a blow from which it took the abbey half a century to recover.*"[837]

The 11th century witnessed Cluny leading the Christian world against the Muslims. It organised the pilgrimage to Santiago de Compostella (Saint Jacques la Compostelle in French) and had rest stations along the way between France and Spain. The Spanish crusade was one of its main functions. It continuously furnished armies attacking Muslims whenever the opportunity arose. Due to the leadership, they showed against the Muslims, French from the region of Cluny (e.g. Henri de Bourgogne) were promoted to the throne of Portugal and Castile. After the capture of Toledo in 1085, Cluniac monks had the upper hand. The following year (1086) a monk from Cluny named Bernard, a native of Perigord in France was made the first archbishop of the reconstituted Primatial See of Toledo. He was the person who confiscated the Mosque of Toledo and converted it into a Cathedral despite the promise given to the Muslims by King Alfonso IV to safeguard it. He also converted a large number of mosques in the surrounding villages into churches. Bernard imported clergy from France and particularly from the Cluniac order, and most churches of Castile and northern Spain were occupied by his protégés[838]. In 1124, another Frenchman called Raymond succeeded him. It is natural that such contacts must have had direct influence on European architectural and cultural movement at that time. There is a direct connection between the fall of Toledo at the hands of Alphonso IV in 1085 and the construction of the Abbey of Cluny. Alphonso was a close friend of Abbot Saint Hugh (of Cluny), and to his joy, Saint Hugh visited Toledo twice. He is known to have founded the Church at Cluny three years later, in 1088, probably to celebrate this victory. Male, (1928) suggested that doubtless some of the clergy and architects from Cluny must have seen the existing mosques of Toledo, and before the destruction of others, imitated some of their forms and decorations at Cluny. Additionally, Hugh also visited Monte Cassino in Italy, which was built with pointed arches.

This Cluniac relationship explains how Muslim features were transmitted to Charité sur Loire, for example. La Charité was one of the main priories of Cluny, founded in the year 1059 by Cluniac monks as a halting-place on the pilgrim route to Santiago de Compostella. The priory soon *"became one of the largest and richest of the Cluniac houses called the "fille ainée de Cluny," not because of its date of foundation but because of its importance in the hierarchy, it quickly grew to have two hundred monks, and dependencies scattered from Asia Minor to Portugal and England."*[839] The use of trefoil arches and the half circle main gate enclosed in the decorated rectangular frame bear testament to the Muslim influence. The latter feature is widely used in Isfahan, in the Mosque of Cordoba and in Fez. It appears that the horizontal side of the frame (rectangle) is exactly tangent in relation to the half circle of the gate, as it is in the case of Muslim monuments with this feature. The polylobed form of arch appeared in the Abbasside Caliphate, in Samara, and widely in North Africa and Andalusia. In la Charité sur Loir they appear at all levels on the tower bell, as well as on the tower, which stands at the crossing of the transept, as well as surrounding the apse (*chevet in French*) (fig.82)[840]. This leaves no doubt that some of the architects and people in charge of the construction of the church visited Toledo at some time. It is known that Henri de Bourgogne gave the monastery of Charité a priory in the Braga region recaptured from the Muslims. It is certain that its architects could have visited the other side of the Pyrenees and Toledo. The thesis of Male is that at the fall of Toledo, Spanish and other Christian crusaders knew nothing of arts and construction, and consequently the Muslims of Toledo (Mudejars) continued to be in charge of constructions and built early churches in the same style and decor as Mosques. Mudejar art continued to be dominant in Spain as well as Europe until the 15th century when the Muslims were deported in masses. Trend (1931) outlined the contribution of Cordoba to European architecture in the following: " *the most original contribution of Cordoba to architecture was the system of vaulting based on intersecting arches and visible intersecting ribs, a system which attacks the main problem of architecture- that of covering space with a roof- in much the same way as the system of gothic vaulting which was developed two centuries later.*"[841]

The role of Cluny in the transmission of Muslim motifs can be explained by the position of Cluny in the Western world. The claim of Voilet le Duc that Cluny is *"the mother of the Western Civilisation"*[842] gives us an idea on the role it played in the spread of these features over the whole continent. The spread of the Cluniac order was followed by a large scale dissemination of the new architectural approach. It had over 1500 priories stretched all over Europe; for example in England alone, it had 30 houses. The abbey itself accommodated up to 1200 monks in its dormitories, thousands of worshippers and in its twin Guesthouses could cater for 40 noblemen and noblewomen. The abbey also had 12 bathhouses fed with running water from a hidden conduit. Such an installation was not known in Europe and could be only derived from Muslim palaces in Spain. Male called it the greatest creation of the middle Ages.[843]. As visitors and pilgrims, Masons and architects visited such a massive undertaking. One of these was Gislebert, a mason and sculptor, who trained at Cluny, then supervised work at Vezelay and Autun Cathedrals. He signed the tympanum of the western portal of Saint Lazarus Cathedral at Autun. His floruit was between (1115-1140) at the very time the pointed arch of Autun appeared in the West.[844]

Figure 81 la Charité sur Loire, Bourgogne (1059 CE), lobed and sinqfoil arches

The Sicilian Encounter

While scholars have agreed that Spain was the route of transmission of rib vaulting, the horseshoe and trefoil arches, and many other features. Sicily has been linked to the movement of the pointed arch. We shall see that Sicily played an equally important role although it has not received similar acknowledgement. Collaboration and contacts between Sicily and Spain were always strong. For instance, Abu-Laith, a Sicilian educated architect and engineer, was known to have helped in the building of the 12th century mosque of Seville[845].In Sicily contact with the Muslims was nearly as tense and effective as it was in Spain and the level of development reached, under the Muslims, was also equal to that of Spain. The University of Palermo was a pole of attraction for scholars to nearly the same degree as the University of Cordoba. Salerno had an important trading position due to its coastal location, which rivalled that of Amalfi. It represented a cultural crossroads, one of its manifestations being the foundation of Salerno School of Medicine in the second half of the 9th century, making it the first European University. The School was founded by four scholars, a Muslim, a Jew, a Latin (Christian), and a Greek[846]. Constantinus Africanus, a Christian Arab from Tunis was the intermediary and transmitter of Muslim medicine to this School and from there onward to Europe.

The annexation of Sicily to Muslim domain in 827 CE was followed by numerous skirmishes caused by continuous infiltration of Christian warriors from Northern regions of Italy and France before peace reigned. In their reprisals, Muslims, in many occasions, followed the infiltrators to their regions capturing the port of Bari in 841 and dominating the entire coast as far as Provence and Marseille. Muslim forages reached Rome in 846 CE[847], and in one incident, in 884 AD; they pillaged the abbey of Monte Cassino. In 972, the Muslims run through St Bernard Pass between Mont Blanc and the Matterhorn and imprisoned Abbot Mayeul of Cluny[848]. According to Mann, Muslims were allowed to remain on Monte Moro, in the Alps between Italy and Switzerland, if they use their power to keep away the rivals of the Italian King from returning that land[849]. Nevertheless, they were expelled from Cote d'Azur in (975) and later they lost Sardinia (1020) and Corsica (1091). The booty gained by the Italian warriors included building artefacts as well as precious art items. For example, on one occasion the fleet of Pisa attacked al-Mahdiya, the capital of the Fatimid in Tunisia and carried off with them Fatimid columns used to build Pisa Cathedral [850](see fig.83).

Meanwhile, the fall of Sicily in the hands opened the door for Christians and Italians in particular, to experience the Muslim civilisation of the Eastern Mediterranean. At first, Sicily continued to prosper under the Normans just as in Muslim times. Roger II (1130-1154), for example, used the Muslim *Hijri* calendar (AH), made Arabic his official language (used in documents and administration), and even called his chief minister Emir of Emirs (Archonte of Archontes)[851]. His grandson William the Good (1166-1189), or William II, was known to be an authority on Arabic poetry and under his reign, according to Dante, Italian poetry was born. Frederick II (1197-1250), the founder of the University of Naples, was so fond of Muslims that he was accused of being a Muslim. His statue in Palazzo Reale at Naples (1888) presented him in embroidered robe with Arabic writing, and the hilt of his sword with the star and crescent insignia, which is a clear indication to his "Islamisation". For the above reasons kings of Sicily "*were, not without good ground, accused of being more Muslim than Christian*"[852]. They played an important role in integrating Muslim art and architecture in the Sicilian and European arts. In his building of Lucera castle, Frederick II for example, imported Islamic builders, while others suggested that they were Muslims who rebelled and brought from Sicily to Puglia. The castle had many Islamic features including the octagonal shape and the barbican[853]. Hitti, in his 'History of the Arabs', sums up this influence of Sicily and Frederick II as follows: "*This almost modern spirit of investigation, experimentation and research which characterized the court of Frederick marks the beginning of the Italian Renaissance. Italian poetry, letters and music began to blossom under Provencal and Arabic influence. On the whole, Sicily as a transmitter of Muslim culture might claim for itself a place next in importance to Spain and higher than that of Syria in the period of the Crusades.*"[854] The Normans later played a leading part in civilising Europe. Harvey rightly admitted the impact of the contact between the Normans and Muslims as he declared, "*the re-activating of Europe into a dynamic age stemmed from the cultural explosion which took place when the Normans and the East came into direct contact* (in Sicily)."[855] It was no surprise that European architectural renaissance took place in Normandy, the birthplace of Gothic architecture.

Against this background, one can understand the connection between Muslim art and architecture and Norman architecture, which gave birth to the so called 'Arabo-Norman style as "*virtually all monuments, the cathedrals, the palaces and castles built under the Normans were Arab in the sense that the craftsmen were Arab, as were the architects*"[856]. Arab architects and artists worked side by side with Byzantines under the direction of the Norman patrons to produce a distinctive style. This recalls similar processes, which led to the rise of the Mudejar style in Spain. Chapter two highlighted the Muslim features of key Norman buildings. The extensive use of Arabic calligraphy in St. John of the Lepers, in Martorama Church, and in Capella Palatina, the pointed arch and the muqarnas in Capella Palatine (fig.84), are clear signs left by Arab artisans and masons. In the Church of San Cataldo (Palermo, 1161) the battlements are pierced and forked and have their surface carved with a low foliage design resembling those of al-Hakim Mosque in Cairo, the windows covered with mashrabiyah (carved stucco) and its domes of onion shaped form (fig.85). In Palermo Cathedral (1185), the architect employed crests in a similar shape to those found in Ibn Tulun Mosque and the west minaret of al-Hakim mosque (fig.86). At Cifalu Cathedral (1131-1148), the twin towers resemble those of Kutubiya Mosque (Morocco), and above the entrance, there are intersecting pointed arches in a similar style to those found in Cordoba Mosque. In the Church of St. Giovanni Degli Eremiti (St. John of the Hermits) (Palermo, 1132) among its Islamic features are the cloister and onion domes.[857]In another instance, the transmission of the dome from the square plan to the circular was achieved in a way similar to those described in Muslim domes, especially at A-Azhar Mosque (Cairo), by using the semi-circular squinch at the angles of the square. The Palace Ziza, or al-Aziza (Palermo, 1166-1180) and the Cuba Palace (Palermo, 1180) are other Muslim edifices, which were built under the Norman rule full of Muslim features.

Sicily was the intermediary for the transmission of many Muslim motifs including the pointed arch. Conant established the Sicilian connection as follows[858]. Inspired by their experience of Muslim architecture, Amalfitan builders brought the pointed arch during the reconstruction of Monte Cassino (1066-1071) by Abbot Desiderius.[859] In his account of the building, Leo of Ostia has described these arches, especially those in the porches and the nave, as being *fornices spiculos*, meaning slightly pointed. The historian Lynn White Jr. endorsed this theory as he traced the

Figure 83 Piza Cathedral (1063 to 1350) built with Fatimid columns taken from al-Mehdiya, Tunisia.

Figure 84 Capella Palatina chapel (Italy, 1144), details of Muslim inspired internal decor

pointed arch to Buddhist India in the second century C.E.[860] According to him, it was transmitted to Persia and then to Syria and Egypt. In year 1000, it was transmitted to Amalfi through the existing commercial and trade ties with Egypt. The pointed arch was used first in the porch of the Abbey of Monte Cassino in 1071[861]. Hill has dismissed the Indian origin of the pointed arch and its passage to Syria and Egypt through Sassanid Iran,[862] but he accepts the way it was transmitted to Europe. This challenges the idea widely accepted in Europe that Gothic architecture was an invention of European architects in their efforts to overcome the static problems of Romanesque vaulting.

The Amalfitan thesis is well understood once we realise the contact they had with Muslims. Amalfi, before 1135, was a major trading centre in the Mediterranean, and had very strong trade links with Spain, North Africa, Syria, and Egypt where they had colonies in Alexandria and Cairo. Furthermore, Amalfi and Salerno were the only two European cities where minted gold coin was produced - often with Arabic inscriptions[863]. Amalfi Cathedral (1208) shows the close ties between Amalfi and Muslim art and architecture (fig.87). However, the cloister of Paradise with its intersecting pointed arches was built by Giulio di Stefano in 1104 although others suggest that it dates from 1266-1268.[864] Amalfitans played a prominent role in the transmission of the pointed arch as well as other Muslim techniques of construction of the 11th century to Italy and then Europe.

Furthermore, while building work was being carried out at Monte Cassino, the Tunisian Christian scholar, Constantinus Africanus, arrived there to retire and spend the rest of his life there. He died at Monte Cassino a year after the dedication of the monastery. A physician and a distinguished scholar in mathematics, science and theology, Constantinus Africanus would undoubtedly have commented or advised on building from his vast experience of Muslim building techniques and forms in Muslim Fatimid North Africa. According to Meyerhof[865], Constantinus had an assistant monk nicknamed "the Saracen" who helped him in translating Arabic books. He is also accredited for the introduction of the *bimaristan*, hospital system into Salerno.[866]

As outlined in the second chapter and above, Muslim masons continued to be the master builders under the Norman rule of Sicily. The use of pointed arches in their palaces and mosques as well as in Norman churches and palaces is certain. According to Bony, the Normans adopted the pointed arch from the island and soon spread it to Normandy and France after their conquests of the island in the 1060s and 1070s.[867]

As for the transfer into Europe, Desiderius who was the abbot of Monte Cassino between 1058 and 1087 was closely associated with Maurus of Amalfi. Maurus and his son Pantaleon brought the bronze gates from Constantinople to Monte Cassino (around 1066).[868] Constantinus Africanus dedicated his *Pantegni* to Desiderius, and Alfanus of Salerno, a friend of Constantinus who worked on the translation of Greek Medecine and celebrated in a song Desiderius' new buildings[869]. Francis Newton noted that Monte Cassino was connected with the Normans in many aspects[870]. He highlighted that it was Norman princes, Richard of Capua and Robert Guiscard (1015-1085), who sponsored Constantinus after meeting him in Salerno.[871]Guiscard is also known to have sent his son Bohemond to be hospitalised in Salerno for a battle wound.[872]William the Conqueror is thought to have visited the hospital for the same purpose[873] Norman princes also shared with Desiderius "*an interest in the cultural products of their Arabic neighbours in and of themselves.*"[874] Guiscard is known to have acquired the "*duas cortinas Arabicas, que pendant supra chorum*" which he later gave to Monte Cassino as shown in the list of gifts of monastery.[875] These were hanged in a prominent place, above the choir serving as "*a reminder of the openness to cultural diversity in the Cassinese sensibility under this abbot.*"[876] It appears that cities of the gulf of Salerno had enjoyed an energetic trade with the Maghreb for two centuries before Desiderius.[877]Francis Newton added: "*Furthermore, the explicit testimony of Amatus, a monk of Monte Cassino and contemporary of Desiderius and Constantine, links artisans of the Islamic world with the building of the church in which the continue were hung, and specifically the mosaic floor*"[878]

The other theory relates that abbey librarian, named, Leo of Ostia noted in his contemporary account of the renovation, Desiderius sent envoys to Constantinople to hire artists. Conant and others have suggested that the possibility of Muslims being brought with these artists is very strong. The migration of Muslim masons, artists and engineers into Christian land was common. Many Muslim prisoners of war, during the Crusades and the Christian *Reconquista* of Muslim Spain, ended up in France, Rome and Constantinople, as observed by John H. Harvey earlier. Under the leadership of Desiderius, Monte Cassino lived its golden, later becoming a popular pilgrimage centre second only to Rome after the visit of Pope Victor III. St Hugh of Semur, the Abbot of Cluny, visited Monte Cassino in 1083, five years before the beginning of work on the third Church of Cluny (1088-1095), known to historians as Cluny III and continued after his death until 1130—the year of Suger's visit. While most of Cluny III is gone, some pieces survived, including several 30-meter- high (nearly 100') pointed arches that played a crucial role in the story of the arch's journey from East to West (fig.88)

In 1130, King Louis VI sent Abbot Suger to Cluny Abbey, just five years before work began at St. Denis. Conant revealed that the new church of Cluny used some 150 pointed arches lining the nave, side aisles and transept[879]. The impact could not have been less than stunning. Catenary vaulting was also used on extensive scale.[880] Other features include the polygonal dome of the tower, use of polyfoil cusps framing the triforium arches[881], and the rectangular frame enclosing the arch of the gate (1109-1115)[882]. Suger understood engineering and knew what he was doing, he was one of the most educated and intelligent men of his time. He transferred what he saw and learnt in Cluny to his engineers who built St Denis, considered the first Gothic building by consensus of scholars. Suger's design introduced for the first time in a church the three elements of Gothic architecture; pointed arches the flying buttresses and the ribbed vaulting. The flying buttresses gave the arches greater strength enabling them to support still more weight while the ribbed vaulting, another Muslim innovation, provided greater support to the vaults of the nave. The ribbed vaulting was introduced in Durham cathedral, about half a century before, but it is at St Denis where the trio- act together to produce the Gothic. The result was stunning new features, soaring ceilings, and gravity-defying curtain walls. Sunlight streaming through these stained windows and curtain walls shining the vast interior. Suger created this new church, giving these features symbolic and theological roles in his overall architectural scheme. The church and Christianity submerge from its old dark and dull atmosphere to new shining mood. Light served a mystical purpose in similar way height served to attain the heavens and embrace them. Light mysticism as mentioned previously was disseminated through the works of Purity Bothers and the Quran, which resembles light to Divine light and reserved a special chapter entitled Light (chapter 24). How much Suger knew about this mysticism, no one knows.

Figure 85 Church of San Cataldo (Palermo, 1161) showing Muslim influence.

Figure 86 Palermo Cathedral (1185), is more "Muslim" than Christian.

Figure 87 Amalfi cathedral (13th century), showing arcade resembling al -Jafria Palace, Spain 11th century

Figure 88 Cluny III, some sections survived, including several 30-meter-high pointed arches that played a crucial role in the story of the arch's journey from East to West

The adoption by Cluny and Monte Cassino of forms and motifs of "pagan and infidel" Muslims encouraged the rest of Christian Europe to adopt these forms leading to their rapid spread across much of France, especially the south. This new architecture introduced by the two most influential churches in Europe was also seen as part of their reform activity. Subsequently, pointed arches appeared in other monuments built between 1075-1100 such as Saint Angelo in Formis, La Cava, and Minuto above Amalfi and later appeared in Autun Cathedral (1120-1132) and then St Denis (1140), then to the whole of Europe[883]. In the middle Ages, Italy with its Christian North and Muslim South provided a Mediterranean crossroad for over four centuries and had a significant impact on the revival of Dark Age Europe.

The influence of Sicily was due to the close ties between the Normans of the south and those across the English Channel. In one instance, in 1098 the Archbishop of Canterbury was in Italy and tried to Christianise Muslim mercenaries of Roger I in their stay in Italy. The development of the English Romanesque style was undertaken under the reign of Norman kings. This connection was maintained by succeeding Norman English monarchs. King Henry II. (ruled 1154-1189) for example, who was also the Duke of Normandy, Aquitaine and Gascony, married his daughters to Spanish and Sicilian monarchs; Matilda to Henry the Lion of Saxony; Eleanor to King Alfonso VIII of Castile; and Joanna to King William of Sicily. Under his reign, England played a significant role in the crusades sending money and fighters, Henry II himself had the intention of going but never made it. The returning crusaders brought with them ideas, artefacts, and prisoners; among whom was the future mother of Thomas Becket, the Archbishop of Canterbury and the king companion for some time before their great rift, which ended with Thomas being executed. King Richard I, or the Lion Heart, (1157-1199) who was also the Duke of Aquitaine (1168) and Poitiers (1172) led the third crusade campaigning in Sicily, Cyprus and the Levant. Stories between him and Salah al-Deen, or Saladin, reveal astonishing courteous treatment and cultural exchange. Later, Edward I (1239-1307) who made contacts with Muslim Spain through his marriage to queen Eleanor of Castile and with the Muslim East through his crusading experience where he *was so impressed by the concentric castles of the east that he built a number in England in this way.*[884] Some of the castles in question were Carnarvon Begun 1283, Conway between 1283 and 1289, and Beaumaris begun 1295 CE (fig.89). Edward also established good contacts with Persia, which was under the Mongol occupation. In one of the missions Edward sent to Persia for the purpose of ambassadorial exchange with the Mongols, his allies against the Muslims, which was led by Geoffrey Langley in 1292 and lasted a year, among the delegation was Robertus Sculptor who is thought to have brought with him a number of features closely resembling those of Persia. One of these is the ogee arch, also known as the Gothic arch, a feature that became popular in England, Venice and France. In this arch, the curve is formed in the shape of two 'S' shapes facing each other, used mostly for decoration. The arch was first developed in Muslim India and later reached Europe and England becoming popular especially in early 14th century. Such contacts are also commemorated in the English folklore by the Morris dance (Morisco). These dances were used on festival occasions, especially during May games when dancers wore costumes of personalities such as Robin Hood, Maid Marian and Friar Tuck, attaching bells to their arms and legs, and have streamers fastened to their sleeves, and handkerchiefs in their hands.[885]

St Mary Redcliffe at Bristol, for example, has a hexagon plan in its north porch and the profile of the doorway is suggestive of eastern contacts. The possibilities that the ogee curve provided for unifying the dissociated circles of geometrical tracery patterns and resulted in the development of what is known as decorated or flamboyant style. This was exploited in decoration, which dominated most of the Gothic before being driven out by the perpendicular style derived from Muslim perpendicular decoration. This is found in Cairo in the Mausoleum of Mustafa Pasha (1269-1273). Harvey thought that pilgrims and artists visiting Egypt in that period, including Simon Simeon and Hugh the Illuminator, both Irish who visited the Holy Land in 1323, were responsible for the transfer[886]. Another Muslim feature was the Tudor arch, also known as the four cantered arch, which was popular during the reign of the Tudors in the 16th century, particularly under the reigns of the monarchs Henry VII and VIII. The four-centred arch has been considered peculiar to England; but it was common enough in Flanders at the same time it was in England[887] The adoption of Tudor architecture of the star polygon plan as in Windsor, in the Tower of Henry VII and in the windows of Henry VII's Chapel, and the turrets of Wolsey's great gate at Oxford (now Tom Tower) was another manifestation of the crusade contacts.[888]

The Crusader Encounter

Circumstantial evidence has been established by Boase in the priory church of Le Wast, near Boulogne[889]. This church was founded by Ida the saintly mother of Godfrey of Bouillon and Baldwin I, after the departure of her eldest son (Eustace) for Jerusalem in 1100. The church was completed before 1109. Unfortunately, only the nave now remains. All its arches were pointed and on the doorway was jagged cusp decoration modelled on the Muslim pattern similar to that of Bab al-Futuh Gate in Cairo (see fig.90). A connection can be established through the crusading embassy, led by Pierre le Chambrier, which spent ten months in Cairo between 1095 and 1096, where they would have seen the pointed arch of Ibn Tulun and other Fatimid mosques, as well as the Gate of Bab al-Futuh.[890] Some of the arches of le Wast were built on a keystone, a common practice in Muslim buildings while in the West at that time arches were built without keystones. Christian Crusaders first used keystones in their buildings in Syria and Jerusalem before they transmitted them to Europe. The entrance gate is adorned with chevron and dogtooth patterns around the arch. The other feature of le Wast is its ribbed vaults which were thought to have been borrowed from Al-Andalus[891], while its zigzag voussoirs must reflect the Abbasid Al-Aqsa Mosque portal which had become the Temple of Solomon as mentioned previously[892].

The Anatolian thesis put forward by Harvey and Cochrane, discussed in the second chapter, suggests Crusaders connection. The Crusaders employed in their buildings Anatolian masons, and in some cases, the slave workers accompanied their new masters when they returned to Europe. Such was the case of Lalys previously mentioned. One can also argue the case of those European masons and artists who were involved in the crusades. They undoubtedly had opportunities not only to observe the character of existing buildings, but also to witness new building activity. In periods of peace, local builders repaired and rebuilt their damaged buildings. Sources also indicate that some Muslims masons worked for the crusaders while Christian masons also had to earn their living especially at times of peace and some of them were hired by Muslims to help in repair or in new constructions. French crusading artists, such as Philippe Chinard, c.1230, Master Assaut and Garnier de Cordes and Eudes de Montreuil are a few examples of many others who trained themselves in the East and returned to Europe where they were selected for big projects. Eudes de Montreuil, for example, is thought to have been the builder of the choir of Beauvais (1247-1272).

Crusades and the Transfer of Muslim Military Architecture

It has been strongly suggested that the Crusades were the main source for most of the development in Medieval European military architecture. Crusading Christians had opportunities to imitate Muslim military architecture. Architectural features of Muslim castles in Syria and Jerusalem enabled them to withstand the attacking Christians despite the superiority in ammunition and manpower of the Christians, thus providing crusaders with a practical experience. The military cities of Baghdad and Samara provided another source of applied military architecture and design. Christian military towers consisted of square keeps protected reinforced occasionally with a tower. The introduction of the rounded tower was a Muslim innovation. In their fight against Salah al-din, or Saladin, which led to their defeat in Hattin (1187), crusaders learnt that the lack of projecting angles facilitated flanking fire. The adoption of round towers and concentric walls was more advantageous and consequently was adopted by crusaders when they returned home to Europe. The first was Saone in 1120. The name barbican used for an outer gateway is taken from Arabic-Persian *Barbar Khanah* meaning "house on the wall" or *Bab-khanah* meaning "towered gateway."

Another feature was the introduction of machicolations, described by Briggs as an arrangement of bold brackets or corbels, and closely placed, carrying a projecting parapet. It is used to protect the entrance by throwing boiling water or oil, arrows, and other weapon down onto the enemy.[893] Machicolations superseded wooden galleries known as *bourdes*, which were used for the same purpose. They appeared first in Qasr al -Hair near Rusafa in Syria dating from 729. It has been suggested that their use was derived from early Ghassanid tower dated 559 near the Qasr, Caliph Hisham incorporated them his Qasr -al-Hair al-Gharbi Palace[894]. Those in Europe started with Chateau Gaillard (1184) , Châtillon (1186), Norwich castle (1187) and Winchester castle (1193). The Crusaders borrowed the idea and the connection was established through King Edward I who employed them, in addition to the concentric plan, for his castles, which he built after returning from the crusades as, mentioned above. Richard the Lion Heart also used them at Chateau Gaillard. Later they became very elaborate. According to Briggs, the other feature borrowed from Muslim architecture, from Egypt and Syria, was what he termed as "the right angled" or "crooked" entrance[895]. This technique prevented the enemy who reached the gateway from seeing or shooting through it into the courtyard. This technique was first used in the 8th century in the city of Baghdad as well as at the citadel of Salah al-Din at

Aleppo (built 1176). The other feature was the loopholes (arrow slits) which were used to allow bowmen (standing or kneeling) to fire their arrows. These were introduced first in London in 1130.[896] The origin of these features goes back to 215 BC where they were used in Syracuse on the advice of Archimedes. They were later used in the fortifications of Rome.[897] Muslims revived their use in Susa (c.821) in Tunisia (fig. 91) and Palace of Ukhaidar (720-800) in Iraq. Other features introduced include the use of various military techniques such as the crossbow weapon, the use of carrier pigeon for transportation of military communications, and to heraldic signs.

Muslim Motifs for the Gothic Style

In order to determine the Muslim contribution to the emergence of the Gothic style, one has to follow the processes of its development. This implies the consideration of the various elements of construction and examination of their modification and adaptation that led to the rise of the style. Once more, we find differing opinions on what constitutes the Gothic, but these generally involve the following.

The Pier

Ancient civilisations mainly relied on the use of columns to support the roof and walls of their constructions. The Greeks and the Romans were particular master of this technique but with the eclipse of these civilisations, the technique of column quarrying was lost and subsequent people, namely Byzantines and Muslims had to rely on re-using Roman columns on a number of occasions. According to Braun, the persistent use of the classical column by the Romans as a means of supporting the main walls of aisled buildings was the major defect of ecclesiastical building style.[898] It hampered its development for two main reasons. The first is that the column had a limited size (length) and consequently did not allow architects and masons to achieve great height in their buildings. The second constraint was the use of second hand columns from ruined structures, due to the above reasons, which presented a handicap in supporting greater span and weight. Muslims seem to have understood these problems and consequently adopted the pier as a replacement. There were other reasons influencing such decision, especially the shortage of columns as Muslim constructions stretched over a large area. The cost and effort involved in the transport of these columns was also another motivator for the adoption of the pier. This was revealed in Ibn Tulun

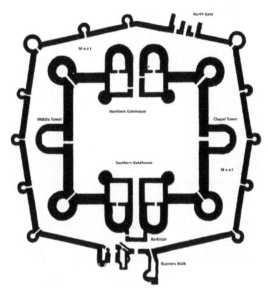

Figure 89 Beaumaris castle built in 1295 by King Edward I (1239-1307) after returning from the crusades; the plan and the barbican are both Muslim features.

Figure 90 Bab-Al-Futouh, Cairo (1087–1092) was an inspiration for le Wast.

285

Mosque, which was planned to include some 300 columns. However, the shortage of columns forced Ibn Tulun to accept the advice of his masons and employ the pier instead (fig.92). The Abbasid in Samarra made the first example of Muslim adoption of the pier. Ibn Tulun was also inspirational in the introduction of and development of battlements in Europe as shown in fig. 93. Europeans did not realise the drawbacks of the column until the 10th century. There is no clear indication where and when the first European pier appeared. The earliest suggestion was in Saint Eustorgio in Milan (c.900).   The claim that Europe borrowed the pier from Byzantine Constantinople cannot be accepted although Byzantine masons are known to have used the pier. If this allegation was true, the pier would have appeared earlier. As we shall see later, Europe's major borrowing of artistic and architectural forms and motifs during the tenth century was from the Muslims.

Transverse and Pointed Arches

The next development was the adoption of transverse arches over the aisles. These were semi-circular arches thrown from each pier of the arcade to the wall of the aisle. To support the connecting point, at which the arch sprung from the pier, a flat pilaster was added to the pier. Again, no clear evidence has been established to explain how and why these arches have evolved, and the earliest records connect them to Saint Eustorgio. Later these transverse arches were thrown over the nave, providing greater safety and durability. The first recorded example is found in the church of St. Felice e Fortunato at Vicenza (985). This feature represents a fundamental structural step in the process of development of Gothic. They led to the adoption of ribbed vaulting which progressively enabled the vaulting of the nave and evolving the compound. The pier abandoned the single or cylindrical shape and became compound with an engaged member carrying up to the spring of the transverse arch.

So how did Medieval European masons discover such usage? It is widely known that the use of the arch in architecture formed an essential part of early civilisations. The Egyptians and the Greeks used lintels, but the Romans and later the Byzantines adopted the semi-circular arch. However, Muslims mastered its use and design well than any other nation. Scott related the Muslims love of the arch to their love of the palm tree[899]. They imitated the curve of its graceful branches in their constructions leading to this wide variety they introduced. Nonetheless, one cannot ignore their skills and deep knowledge of geometry and

Figure 91 Loopholes Muslims revived their use in Susa (Tunisia c.821), here can be seen in walls and battlements of the Entrance.

Figure 92 With Ibn Tulun Mosque the pier replaced the column, notice also the battlements used

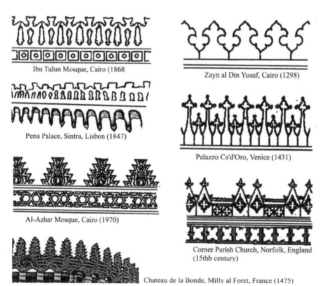

Ibn Tulun Mosque, Cairo (1868

Zayn al Din Yusuf, Cairo (1298)

Pena Palace, Sintra, Lisbon (1847)

Palazzo Ca'd'Oro, Venice (1431)

Al-Azhar Mosque, Cairo (1970)

Corner Parish Church, Norfolk, England (15thb century)

Chateau de la Bonde, Milly al Foret, France (1475)

Figure 93 Similarities of battlements in Muslim Buildings and European ones.

288

laws of static. As mentioned in the second chapter Muslims, especially in the 10th and 11th centuries, made fascinating discoveries and contributions in the development of the science of geometry. The arch was first employed for structural and functional purposes but progressively it was also used for decorative means. Structurally speaking in the simplest arch the thrust is exerted by the weight of the masonry and any other superimposed loads above the arch as well as sideways (horizontally) by the cumulative wedge action of the voussoirs. These characteristics reduced the thrust on a few points, which allowed lighter walls and vaults and permitted huge savings in material. Supports can be provided at either end of the arch extending laterally in the vertical plane of the arch forming what is known as buttresses. The saying "the arch stands as the load chain hangs" says it all.

The first Muslim adaptation and modification of arch design was the invention of the horseshoe type. This was first employed in the Umayyad Great Mosque of Damascus. The horseshoe had the advantage of allowing more height than the classical (semi-circular) arch as well as better aesthetic and decorative use. There is a suggestion that the horseshoe form was derived from the symbolic use of primitive ages where it represented a superstitious emblem for many societies. The use of the horseshoe in North Africa against the evil eye is still maintained to the present days, and they are often placed in front of their doors. Similar symbolic use is observed in India and many other parts of the world[900]. Nevertheless, Muslims used this curved form to develop their ultra-semi-circular arch, around which the whole of Muslim architecture evolved. The horseshoe arch provided a greater advantage in the centring technique at the time of its construction. In normal arches, the centring can be supported from three possible areas, from the ground, or upon the slight projection afforded by the impost, or the abacus of a capital. In the horseshoe arch, the lower parts of the curve can carry the centring.[901] Meanwhile, the introduction of the horseshoe into Cordoba (fig.94) established the route for its transmission to Europe through the Christian refugees of the Asturian mountains who used it in their churches.[902] (fig.95).

The second major development that took place in the 11th century Europe was its adoption of the transverse and later the pointed arch. The transverse arch is a structural self-standing arch placed across the vault (thrown from side to side), dividing it into bays. It usually projects down from the surface of the vault. As noted above, the Muslims used the diaphragm arch which is a transverse arch thrown from a wall to a wall partitioning the roof into sections (a wall was usually built on top of it to create a level horizontal top). According to historians like Urice, the Umayyads were the first to use this arch in Qsar al-Kharanah (710 AD), in Jordan[903]. Here most rooms had transferal diaphragm arches. Others like Arce claimed that the arch was developed in Persia first, in Ashur at Parthian Palace[904] (Reuther 1938)[905] and at the Taq-i-iwan in Khark (Khuzestan)[906], and at Sarvistan Palace[907] before being used by the Umayyad. However, Bier and more recently Urcie rebuffed the claims of Dieulafoy and Reuther first questioning the reconstruction made by both saying that it lacks any archaeological evidence.[908]

Bier also rejected their dating of Sarvistan Palace, which he thought to belong to early Umayyad period. Urcie accepts the Umayyad dating suggested by Bier, but he also thinks Taq-i-iwan in Khark belongs to the Seljuk or later periods rather than Sassanian period as suggested by Bier[909]. Godard[910] also had raised similar doubts about the reconstruction of Taq-i-iwan. This leaves the introduction of the diaphragm arch and its use under the tunnel vault to the Umayyad architects. This is supported by the wide spread of its use, in numerous buildings such as; Tariq Khana mosque (Damghan early 8th century)[911], Qusayr 'Amra (Jordan around 715), Umayyad Palace at Amman Citadel (Jordan, 730), Khirbat Hamman Sark (Jordan, 725), the Palace of al-Qastal (Jordan first half of the eighth-century), in Qsar al-Kharanah (Jordan, 710) (fig.96), in Qsar Hallabat mosque (Jordan early eighth-century) and Ukhaidir Palace (720-800). In buildings such as the mosques of Damascus and Cordoba, the diaphragm arches were placed in parallel rows, defining regular bays, each of them covered independently by wooden trusses. The first European use of diaphragm arch under the vault was introduced four centuries later, attributed to Church of Saint Philibert, Tournous, (consecrated 1120) (fig. 97). There is no clear evidence on how and when this arch was transmitted to Europe where it is considered the first step revolutionising the way churches were built. The use of the transverse arch over the nave not only provided greater safety and durability but also gave the final shape of the nave especially in terms of height and roof. This feature represents a fundamental structural step in the process of development of Gothic. It led to the adoption of ribbed vaulting which progressively enabled the vaulting of the nave and evolving the compound.

Figure 94 Cordoba Great Mosque 756-796, part of the façade showing the horseshoe arch of the entrance, the trefoil arch above the windows, and the battlements similar to those of Al-Azhar, and the use of "Ijmiz" on the door.

Figure 95 the Christian refugees of the Asturian mountains used the horseshoe in their churches, here showing the Polylobed entrance with "*ijmiz*" at Santiago De Penalba (Castile, Spain).

Figure 96 Qsar al-Kharanah (Jordan, 710) showing the transversal arches intersecting to provide support for the vaulted ceiling.

Figure 97 The first European use of diaphragm arch under the vault was introduced four centuries later, attributed to Church of Saint Philibert, Tournous, (consecrated 1120)

The origins of the pointed arch were already mentioned above in numerous occasions. The earliest use of this arch was traced to Umayyad period in the Dome of the Rock (between 688 and 691 CE) and two Umayyad desert castles built in Jordan; Qasr al-Kharanah (built in 710) and Qusayr 'Amra, (built in 715). In the former building, the gently pointed was employed for the inner arcade surrounding the Rock. In the latter examples, the pointed arch was used as a transverse arch also with a gentle form. The pointed arch was used as much an aesthetic device as structural one. In later Umayyad period as well as under the Abbasids the arch took its final more pointed form. The sturdy Semi-circular (rounded) arches were useful, used before Islam by the Romans in bridges, aqueducts, triumphal arches, colossus and other constructions. However, because they direct the weight they support outward, toward the walls, they weaken with height. The higher the arch, the thicker the walls need to be, resulting in thick impractical and expensive walls. Pointed arches, however, direct the thrust of weight downward, toward the ground, allowing for much thinner, higher walls. In geometry, the semi-circular arch is drawn from a single centre; pointed arches are composed of two different arches drawn from two different centres crossing over each other. The distance between the centres determines the angle at which the two sides meet at the arch's apex—its "pointiness." The transfer of the pointed arch from the Muslims, already discussed above, was made through many channels as discussed earlier; These include Amalfitan traders, scholars like Constantinus Africanus, and crusader returning from the East, who introduced knowledge of the pointed arch to Europe.

The semi-circular vaulting paused some static problems in the coverage of such a large and irregular plan (fig.98 a, b & c). The pointed arch resolved the difficulty of achieving level crowns in the arches of the vault allowing the vault to become suitable for any ground plan (fig.99 a & b). In this area, we find Muslims have employed a variety of techniques to tackle the question of height. In addition to the use of the pointed arch, the method employed in al-Kairawan Mosque is revealing. Here, in order to gain a crown level of height, masons raised the arcade of narrow areas above the arcade of other areas as shown in fig.100. In the Great Mosque of Cordoba, a more impressive method combining between intersecting arches and building a second arcade on top of a first lower level arcade was introduced (see fig.101). These clearly show genius as well as the rational method in addressing various architectural problems. The other feature is the Muslim technique of construction of these arches which reveals that in an area short of wood, masons had to first construct the bottom layer with minimum centring (fig.102) a technique which was later adopted in vaulting through the use of ribs.

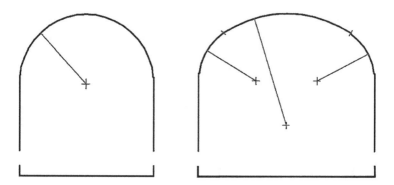

Figure 98 (a) Round arch is used in a square bay, if the bay is wider the arch can only be struck from 3 centres which flattens and weakens it considerably.

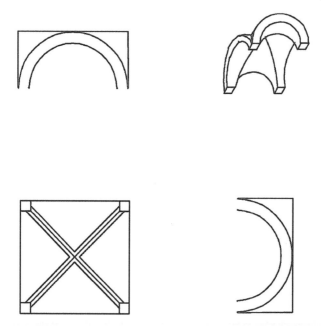

Figure 98 (b) The round arch in a square bay can be used in a groin vault which will take four equal arches.

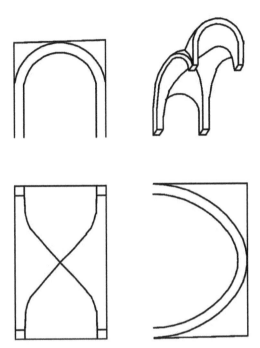

Figure 98 (c) The problem caused by rectangular bay and the use of round arches in vaulting. In order to reach crown level, the arch of the longer side of the bay will be flattened and consequently weakened.

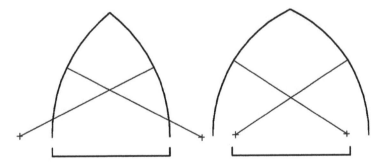

Figure 99 (a) The use of pointed arch however can be struck from centres falling within the arch span which makes it structurally strong.

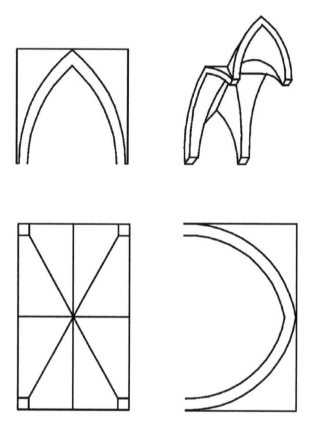

Figure 99 (b) The use of pointed arch in the rectangular bay provides the answer.

Figure 100 Method of attaining height in al-Kairawan Mosque (836) by stretching up the arch to the desired height.

Figure 101 Method of attaining height in Cordoba (Spain, 785 CE) by using super-imposed arcade of round arches.

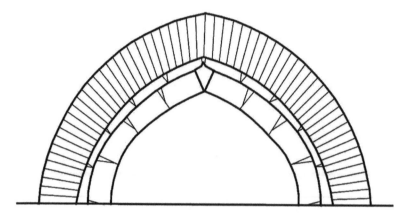

Figure 102 The construction of the arch without centring by using a lower layer, a technique which has similar use in ribbed vaulting.

Vaulting

Vaulting as a technique to cover space goes back to the Romans who used it widely in their military tunnels and food depots. The simplest type of vaulting was the cylindrical barrel vault. The main disadvantage of these vaults was the inability to provide for space to insert windows to allow in light and their inability to achieve any considerable height. These disadvantages come from the nature of the thrust, which is concentrated on both sides of the vault (fig.103). To overcome this, a thick wall had to be introduced to support this thrust and provide stability of the vault. Consequently, any increase in the height of building would require a proportional increase in the thickness of the walls, which is both costly and ugly. Meanwhile, any window piercing could not be done without endangering the whole structure, as the supporting wall will be considerably weakened. In early middle Ages, Europe preferred construction in wood as Europe lost the inherited Roman skill of masonry construction and wood was a cheap and readily available building material. This reliance on wood construction proved very costly as Europe endured a savage burning of its churches at the hands of the Vikings during the ninth century. It was not until Europe experienced the Muslim masonry buildings of Spain and Sicily that masons and patrons started thinking of building in stone that could be better defended. Stone was used for walls as well as in the vaulting, but because of the lack of skills and understanding of statics these "early" churches were often constructed with robust walls with minimum height and light. This architectural handicap had its influence on the nature of worship during the eighth and ninth centuries, had to be done in darkness, which was regarded as a condition helping contemplation.

The next development in vaulting was the adoption of the groin vault. According to architectural historians, the groin vault was also used by the Romans but in its simplest forms. This was achieved from the intersection of two semi-circular barrel vaults of equal radius. In a church, a number of these vaults were built along the side aisle providing the span continuity, and each cross vault defined a bay of the vaulting in the form of a square supported at its four corners with thick and heavy piers. This resulted in the division of the aisles into small squares. Builders did not dare to build these vaults over the nave as they were constrained by its height and span. [912]. The date at which such developments took place is not known, but the earliest examples are found in Normandy dating back to around 1050. The main problems encountered with these vaults were in the weakness of the groins. Being diagonals (over the bay square), groins constitute the longest spans of the bay thus bearing the main thrust coming from the two vaults (being also the intersection lines of the two vaults) (fig.104). Another problem was connected with the elliptical form of the groins, which is formed by the horizontal projection of the semi-circular boundary arches of the barrel vaults. Its weakness as load bearing necessitated deeper abutments and limited the height. The replacement of this weaker elliptical diagonal with stronger semi-circular arch produced the dome vault allowing greater height.

The next step was the adoption of ribbed vaulting. Ribs were developed in the Romanesque period from the transverse arches of continuous barrel vaulting in the form of semi-circular underlying arches[913]. The ribs provided support to the weakest points of the vault particularly in the groins and the crown areas (fig.105). They allowed thinning of the cells, thus also the piers and walls. They facilitated the erection of vaults and provided the builder with security during the hardening of the mortar. They also provided a saving in wood. As mentioned earlier, a number of theories were proposed to explain the origin and the manner in which the cross vaults were invented.

Violet le Duc[914] provided a different explanation saying that the transverse arches were elastic and could therefore deform, in the case of any movement of the foundation or settling of the walls or piers, and find their new form. This translates the Arabic saying, "vaults never sleep" which was later applied to arches. Having discovered the elasticity of the transverse arch, medieval architects attempted to design the vault with a similar elastic character. To see how these changes took place, one has to look at how the vault was constructed. Pre-Gothic Romanesque style vaults were made with rubble, which was poured into wooden scaffolding that retained the mortar in place until dry. This method consumed a lot of wood and caused delays, as masons had to wait for the vault to dry before moving the scaffolding to another area. The first attempt to solve this problem was to replace the wooden centring with stones that would be kept in place and carry the fragile groins. This was not satisfactory and a new method was developed. Long diagonal arches (ribs), called in French "*Arcs-ogives*" *or* "*Nervure*", were built to carry the four triangular cells of the groined vault and make them independent of each other. With these new techniques, both the rib (arch) and vault are elastic. Furthermore, Violet le Duc claimed from his observations, that the ribs were not connected to the vault itself thus allowing the arch to move without pulling the vault and the vault to settle without breaking the rib that carries it. The vaults or the triangles between the ribs were constructed with small stones in similar way the construction of a wall up to its third. After that, stones were laid down on a movable base (cerce), which is pushed ahead as the work advanced. Other element of the statics are pinnacles and buttresses. The weight of the pinnacles gives the pier the stability necessary to support the thrust of the flying buttresses. That means if the pinnacles were to be removed the flying buttresses would give way and the nave vaults would collapse. Therefore, the more the piers are weighed down vertically by a superstructure, the thinner they can be made. Therefore, all Gothic elements were developed as part of functional approach. However, the concentration of Violet le Duc on statics and technical causes to explain the origin of Gothic was attacked in his lifetime and later. The question of what gave rise to the rib was still unanswered. If the Gothic architect and mason could not predict the static characteristics described by Violet le Duc, how did he come to think of it?

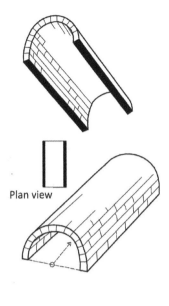

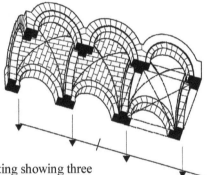

Plan view

Figure 103 Simple semi-circular barrel vault showing the thrust distributed along the two sides, and therefore buttressing must be done along the entire length of the vault producing thick walls.

Figure 104 Simple groin vaulting showing three bays. Here the thrust is concentrated in the four corners of the bay and support can be provided at these three points through the pier.

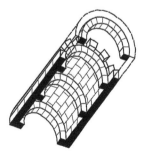

Figure 105 The use of ribs in simple barrel vault.

301

Among those who attacked le Duc's theory was Porter[915] who suggested that the ribs had a technical value for the execution of the vaults and were invented as a device to economise wood. The desire to dispense with the wooden structures that medieval architects used in their scaffolding was the main motive. In his words: *"Rib vaults therefore were invented in Lombardy as a simple device to economise wood. They were adopted by French builders for the same purpose. The same desire to dispose with temporary wooden substructures governed the development of architecture during the entire transitional period, and eventually lead to the birth of Gothic."*[916]. The saving on wood is achieved in the same way as described by Violet le Duc in the hand building of the vault cells and the use of a movable base (cerce).

Since wood was plentiful in the North, Porter suggested that rib vaults were invented in Lombardy in Italy where wood was relatively scarce. They appeared first sometime around 1040 in San Pietro di Civate, Sannazzaro Sezia (1040) and other buildings namely Saint Ambrogio of Milan (c.1060). Later, French builders adopted the idea then spread it to Europe. Nevertheless, why did French and Northern builders adopt this measure when they still had cheap and abundant sources of wood that they continued to use in roofing until the present time? Historically speaking, the first fully developed ribbed vaults were traced in Normandy, and England in Durham Cathedral, 1098, but Porter maintained that the Normans had acquired them from Lombardy at St. Ambrogio.[917] Other historians believe Normandy, which provided St.Ambrogio with the germ of this vaulting. However, Lethaby raised an uncertainty as he wrote, *"It seems that the evidence we are compelled to suppose that Saint Ambrogio derived its scheme of construction from Normandy. It may be that the origin of the vault is to be sought even in England; but there are many reasons for thinking that the seed idea, like so many others, came from the East."*[918] However, the chief criticism was related to the use of the movable base (cerce) with the ribbed vault. This cerce can be used in the same manner in groined vaults built of masonry, such as domes, just as in ribbed vaults. To set up a cerce, therefore, does not need a rib and wooden centring can be used just as well. Consequently, how can we say that the cerce gave birth to the rib?

Further problems facing these theories is related to the accurate dating of such buildings. St. Ambrogio, for example, turned out to be dated from 1128 and not as previously thought 1060. Furthermore, if Lombardy was the source of the ribbed vault why did they abandon its use in the 12th century? Lambert expressed his dismay of the explanations offered so far: *"It is not well explained how the great resurrection took place in the first half of the 11th century, in a period when Western architecture was generally still very mediocre."*[919]

Others maintain that the first ribbed vault appeared in Frejus (Province in France). If this is true, then the argument of the lack of wood as the primary reason for the development of ribbed vaults, which led to the development of Gothic, cannot be sustained. Historic sources indicate that the Muslims of Provence were known to work on the product of the cork tree[920], and to this day, these lands are known as the Forêt des Maures near Frejus. In fact, many names of places in the region still bear witness the Muslim presence; Puy Maure and Mont Maure, near Gap, the Col de Maure near Chateau Dauphin, and the whole county of Maurienne in the region of Savoie.[921] Provence region was also closely connected with Arabic poetry and literature through the troubadours, as explained in the previous chapter, and its cities and schools were connected with the Muslim science of Spain[922]. This would explain the appearance of the first ribbed vaults in that region before anywhere else. However, Lambert[923] traced the appearance of these ribbed vaults in Northern France in the lower hall of the north tower of the Cathedral of Bayeux (1060-1080), and upper hall of the tower porch in the Church of St. Ours at Loches (after 1086).

As outlined above, eevidence shows that the earliest development of rib vaulting in Muslim lands where numerous techniques were developed to provide support for the vaulting. The earliest instance of rib vaulting were traced to Umayyad buildings, particularly in their palaces. The diaphragm arch provided an early attempt to support the vault in Qsar Hallabat, Qusayr Amra, and Qsar al-Qastal. The transverse arch (without a wall bearing) was also employed under vaults, found in Qasr al-Kharanah, Ukhaidir Palace, al-Mahdiya Mosque and Ribat of Soussa. In Abbasid Palace of Ukhaidar (720-800)[924], the use of transverse arches and groin vault, which occurs eight times in the Palace, some of which had arches of support showed that Muslims had the first hand in this issue. The vaults of the main hall of Ukhaidar (fig.106) and its mosque (fig.107) can be a convincing argument. Further proof, is the system of vault support provided in the Ribat of Susa (821-822), which consists of a stone transverse arch sprung from the side wall below the vault (fig.108 (a) & (b)).

Ibn Idhari[925] in his description of Medinat Al-Zahra in Spain (strated in 940 AD) revealed that the Emir Abdellah had constructed a covered passageway leading from his residence (palace) to the mosque, allowing him to visit the mosque without being seen. This passageway was covered with a vault supported by ribs. Dozzy (1848) and Fagnan (1901) translated Ibn Idhari's wording "*sabatan maq'udan ala hamia*" as "voute reposant sur des arcs doubleaux"[926], meaning that the vault was laying (supported by) on transversal arches similar to that of the Ribat of Sussa. Velazquez has confirmed the existence of such a passage.[927] This revelation provides a more convincing explanation how these Muslim ribs appeared in France and later spread to Europe, greatly influencing the cross vault of the nave of St Sernin at Toulouse (ca.1096) (fig.109), St. Mary la Madeleine at Vezelay (1104-1132) (fig.110), and Fontenay Abbey (1139-1147). Vezelay transverse arches of the nave echo the pattern of the mosque of Cordoba (polychromy)[928]. The suggested route for the transfer in this case is European, and particularly French, contacts with Andalusia andNorth Africa. The Spanish connection discussed above has illustrated the strategic relations between France and Spain.

Another vaulting system, also copied from Muslims is found in the cistern of Ramla (Palestine), built by Harun Al-Rashid in 789. The cistern is constructed of pointed arcades carried on cruciform piers of masonry and covered with six-barrel vaults reinforced with walls carried on diaphragm arches[929]. Similar arrangements were employed in Sussa, in its two main mosques, Bu Fatata (834-841) and the Great Mosque (850-851). The similarity between this technique and that employed in Notre Dame d'Orcival is striking (compare fig.111 and 112). In this instance, we find both North African and Crusader connections to be the means of transfer.

The third technique is revealing and found in Qasr al-Kharanah, where Umayyad architects produced the germ of the quadripartite vault. As outlined previously in page 30, the vaulting system was used systematically throughout the whole palace, which consists of two floors with nine halls and 60 rooms. All rooms and most of the halls were barrel vaulted and their ceiling was supported by transverse arches sprung from three collonets or piers. Four of the halls on the upper floor their transverse arches were sprung from the walls. The square room on the southern side, as discussed previously, is barrel vaulted and its vault is supported by two arches crossed perpendicularly each other, dividing the roof into four bays covered by coffers (fig.96). The supporting arches were sprung from the walls.

Figure 106 The pointed barrel vault of the Great hall of Ukhaidar

Figure 107 Ukhaidir Mosque (Iraq) showing the use of arches (more decorative) for vault support.

Figure 108 (a)
Original vaulting in the Ribat of Sussa (Entrance hall), Tunisia. The barrel vault is supported with tranversal arch supported on column on one side and unsupported on the other side.

Figure 108 (b)
Original vaulting in the Ribat of Sussa (prayer hall), Tunisia. The tranversal arch here is not supported on columns

Figure 109 The Nave of St. Sernin, a pilgrim station, used vault support developed in Ukhaidir and Sussa Ribat

Figure 110 St.Madeline at Vezelay, (France, 1104-1132) another imitation of Muslim vault support.

Figure 111 Ramla Cistern showing another vault support technique developed by Muslims as early as the 8th century, Jerusalem, using a diaphragm arch.

Figure 112 The Diaphragm arch of the transept of Notre Dame d'Orcival (1166), Auveregne

The third technique is revealing and found in Qasr al-Kharanah, where Umayyad architects produced the germ of the quadripartite vault. As outlined previously in page 30, the vaulting system was used systematically throughout the whole palace, which consists of two floors with nine halls and 60 rooms. All rooms and most of the halls were barrel vaulted and their ceiling was supported by transverse arches sprung from three collonets or piers. Four of the halls on the upper floor their transverse arches were sprung from the walls. The square room on the southern side, as discussed previously, is barrel vaulted and its vault is supported by two arches crossed perpendicularly each other, dividing the roof into four bays covered by coffers (fig.96). The supporting arches were sprung from the walls.

The fourth vaulting system appeared in Cordoba and Toledo representing the connecting point that was acknowledged by a number of impartial Western scholars. The central argument is that the ribs of Cordoba had inspired European architects and their masters to adopt them first in the Romanesque movement and later in Gothic. Choisy (1899), a leading French authority on architecture (1841-1909), who sees the history of Gothic to be connected to the history of ribs and flying buttresses, was the first to make the connection between the ribs of Cordoba and the evolution of European ribs. In his opinion, the Muslims knew ribbed vaults more than hundred and fifty years before they appeared in Christian churches. He called them "*voutes sur nervures*" and cited the example of the ribbed dome of the Great Mosque of Cordoba (fig.113). He also found similar arrangements in Armenia where they were first used in a church named *Akhpat*. However, it was later established that this church dates from 1183, considerably more recent than Choisy thought[930]. On a number of occasions Lambert (see 1925 Gazette des Beaux Arts Sept-Oct, 1933 Revue Archeologique, and 1937 Bulletin de l'Office International des Instituts d'Archeologie, and 1939 Recherches, Vol.1) also stressed how the rib was derived from Cordoba and Andalusia in general. Pope (1933, and 1938-1939) and Godard (1949) traced these ribs to Persia. Godard highlighted the long Persian tradition in vault building, which he traced to the Sassanid period. Such techniques were used at the time of the Muslim Caliphate and are still used today especially among villagers. Pope found the origin of the rib in the Mosque of "*Masjid i Jami*" of Isfahan. In his opinion, the dome of the Mosque attests the derivation of the European rib. This was constructed with bricks supported by long slender intersecting arches composed of one single line of bricks. The lack of wood in this region is quite understandably the reason behind the invention of such a method. Harvey found similarity between the intersecting ribbed vault with

Figure 113 Ribbed domes in Maqsura of the Great Mosque of Cordoba, Spain

310

octagonal oculus at the Prior's Kitchen in Durham (1366) and that at the Masjid-i-Jami of Isfahan.[931] However, other scholars remain sceptical, as the dating of the dome is controversial. The Mosque was first built in the 8th century but further enlargement and modifications made in the 10th, 12th and in 17th century. The dome itself, according to Marcais[932], is dated to the first half of the 11th century. Nevertheless, how the ribs got to Cordoba remains a mystery.

Lambert[933] put forward a thesis on the development of intersecting arched vaulted domes, which represent the closest structural form to Gothic ribbed vaults. He took the view of Rivoira[934] who traced the first ribbed dome to the al-Kairawan Mosque (864). The dome here is made of 24 "*fuseaux*" radiating around the centre and separated by circular centre (fig.114). The minaret built by Abd Al-Rahman III in 950 for the Mosque of Cordoba to replace the old small minaret erected by Hisham I is the second example. From the ruins of this minaret that survived the alterations executed after the conversion of the Mosque into a Cathedral, a complete vault covering the bay was recovered intact. A study has shown the bay was composed of pointed barrel vaults "*berceau outrepassé*", transversely supported in the middle by a horseshoe arch diaphragm. This shows the Muslim use of the rib and arch diaphragm under barrel vaults as well as domes and arched vault of the cloister, which sets a precedent for the use of intersecting ribs in later buildings. These provide reference points for the origins and development of ribbed vaults in the Medieval West.

In fact, the germ of the quadripartite vault can be seen more clearly in the Mosque of Bab Mardum in Toledo. Two Muslim architects named Musa ibn Ali and Saada built it (between 1098-1000). Renowned for its trefoil-profiled windows, blind intersecting arches and the brickwork of its facade, Bab Mardum Mosque also represents a unique example of a well-developed technique of rib vaulting. In his study of the Mosque, which he thought was intact and unaltered when he saw it, Street[935] revealed a striking example of ribbed vaulting. He described the mosque as a square composed of nine small compartments covered with nine different ribbed cupolas (domes) (fig.115). Each dome is a little vault with intersecting ribs thrown in the most fantastic way across each other and varied in each compartment(fig.116). The intersecting arches of the ribs are quite evident. Similar vaulting was used in another mosque, which was later transformed into a house named Las Tornerias (980) (fig.117). It had nine ribbed domes combining a variety of ribs and dominated by the central vault, in addition to the use of a combination of polychrome horseshoe and trefoil arches. In three instances, the domes were made of arches intersecting in the centre forming a cross in exactly the same manner, as the quadripartite vaults are constructed. Lambert commented on the resemblance of these ribbed vaults to those adopted in Gothic in the following[936]: *"It is worth noting that these arches, which in two ribs "travées" carrying the cupola are made of a pair intersecting at the keystone at a right angle, exactly in the same fashion as they do in the Gothic ribs of the square plan. The Arab architects, therefore, knew and employed in their vaults, since the end of the 10th century, not only the same principle of the rib, but also the system of crossed arches, a system which became later known in France as the quadripartite vaulting."[937]*

Further evidence can be found in the Aghlabid dome of Zaytouna Mosque (853-865), Tunisia and in the dome of the Great Mosque of Telemcen (Algeria 1135) (fig.118). George Marcais was the first to point to this feature. At Zaytouna, the dome is made of 20 ribs set at equal intervals from the edge and meeting together in the centre. The dome of Telemcen, however, is made out of twelve intersecting arches, which leave a circular centre at the centre of the dome decorated with stalactite. A similar example is also found in the minaret of Kutubia mosque in Morocco, a Mosque contemporary to that of Telemcen.

The spread of these features to all parts of Andalusia speaks of their familiarity among Muslims, and so we find similar ribbed domes in the chapel of Belen, in Santa Fe, and in Aljafria palace (Saragossa). They soon reached Christian Northern Spain in places such as Suso Monastery in San Millán de la Cogolla (fig.119), San Baudelio de Berlanga of Duoro (984) in Soria, both in Castile. These places are all located on the pilgrimage route of St. Jacques where the cross intersecting arches form the ribs of the Mozarabic churches such as Almazan church in Castile (fig.120), Torres del Rio in Navarre, in the French Pyrenees such as Saint Croix d'Oloron and the hospital Saint Blaise (fig.121). They are also found at the Templar church at Segonia and chapter house at Salamanca (12th. century)[938]. At San Miguel de Celarona (founded in 936 CE), the ribs of the dome are even simpler composed of two ribs intersecting in the middle, producing the quadripartite Vault (fig.122). Lambert affirms his opinion in the following[939]: *"To judge from these curious churches of San Baudelio de Berlanga et de San Millan de la Cogolla, there is no doubt that at the end of the 10th and along the 11th century the ribbed vault had become a widely known technique in the hispano-moorish art, and this was not only in the mosques, but also in the churches even those located on the routes of the Pilgrimage of Saint Jacques where a large number of French pilgrims and monks went past."[940]*

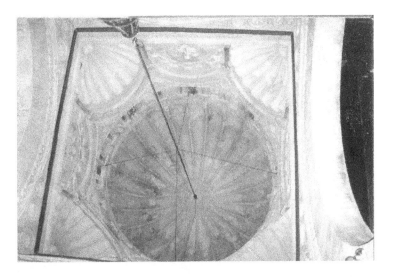

Figure 114 The dome of al-Kairawan Mosque (820-836) is made of 24 *"fuseaux"* radiating around the centre and separated by circular

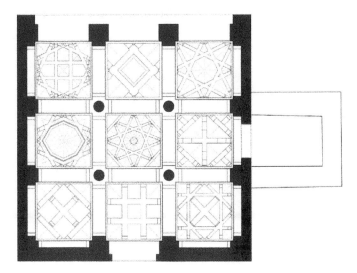

Figure 115 Plan of Bab Mardum mosque and its ribbed domes (Toledo, 999)

313

Figure 116 Six examples of ribbed domes of Bab Mardum. The two bottom
ones show the intersection of the ribs in the centre of the dome in similar
technique to that employed in the quadripartite vault of the Gothic style

314

Figure 117 Riibbed dome in Mesquita las Tornerias, a sister mosque to Bab Mardum, built around the same time At present it houses the "Center Foundation of Promotion of the Crafts"

Figure 118
Dome of Great Mosque of Telemcen, Algeria (1136).

San Baudelio de Berlanga (11th century) is more like a mosque than a church so that Bevan (1938) and Lamperez (1920) described it as the most "Mohammedan" building of the Mozarabs. This church consists of a chamber (26 feet long and 23 feet wide) covered with a large vault supported by eight ribs, which sprung from a cylindrical pillar in the middle of the room. These ribs have the form of graceful curves attached to each corner of the room above small shell corner niches and decorated in the middle with Muslim type modillions. The whole structure looks like a giant palm tree holding the roof (fig.123). Among other features, San Baudel is equipped with horseshoe arches and ornaments that included a Kufic inscription praising Allah (God)[941]. Dodds[942] explained such rich imitation of Muslim features to the improvement of relations between Mozarabs and Muslims at the time of Abd-al-Rahman III as well as the great cultural and artistic achievement of his reign. The capture of the Toledan mosques including Bab Mardum must have provided lessons for European artists and architects, particularly the French who were closely connected to this town after its fall. I t is worth noting that, such ribs do not appear in churches such as those of the Leon region, which were built before the Mosque of Cordoba.

The Plan

The plan of the Medieval European church was developed through a process of metamorphosis very much under the influence of the plan of Muslim mosques. The first impact was the rejection of the circular forms of the Romanesque in favour of rectangular ones. The introduction of the pointed arch symbolised the re-awakening of Europe and its acceptance of new ideas. It was seen as a rebellion against the old Europe and its circular arch and dome in favour of polygonal shapes[943]. There is strong evidence, which suggests that the influence of the mosque plan on Medieval European churches, especially in buildings erected by the Mozarabs of Asturia, after they had migrated from Cordoba in the 10th century. Particular reference has been made by Morino[944] to the similarity between the mosques of Bab Mardum and Las Tornerias and Santa Maria de Lebena founded (924-960). The square plan of this church, which was subdivided into square chambers defined by curtain arcade walls, translated Muslim principles of space and circulation as generally found in mosques. Such principles emphasise the lateral procession of worshippers to the internal centre of worship (compare fig.124 and 125). Similar planning arrangements can be found in other Mozarabic churches such as Santa Maria de Wamba (fig.126).

Figure 119 At Suso Monastery in San Millán de la Cogolla (10th century CE), the intersection of ribs was made simple producing what might be called "eight partite vault".

Figure 120 Cordoban and Toledan type ribbed dome of St.Miguel Almazan (11th century)

Figure 121 In the transept of St.Blaise, France, Cordoban and Toledan ribbed domes were also imitated

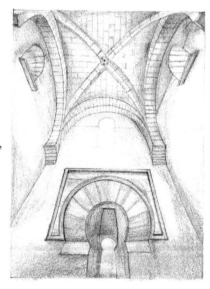

Figure 122 At San Miguel de Celarona (founded in 936 CE), Spain, the ribs of the dome are even simpler composed of two ribs intersecting in the middle, producing the Quadri-partite Vault, Notice also the Cordoban mihrab featured door.

318

Figure 123 At San Baudelieu de Berlanga, Spain, the whole roof is covered with one dome carried on ribs springing from a central pier in the form of a palm tree.

319

The contribution of these Mozarabic churches to Romanesque development has been emphasised by Spanish scholars such as Dodds. Such contribution was due to the architectural superiority of these churches, stemming from its Muslim connection. Dodds maintains that *"the Iberian Peninsula's contact with Islam becomes the unique quality that only Spain can contribute to the development of a European style, but this is diffused, Christianised through the medium of non-Islamic architectural styles: Mozarabic and Asturian."*[945] Not all French scholars object to such claims Gailliard at least, called Mozarabic architecture as *"the richest field of experience for pre-Romanesque art"*[946] Therefore, one can establish an idea how the round plan was replaced by the rectangular or the square plan.

Furthermore, the Muslim horseshoe form of the arch was also adopted in a number of Mozarabic churches such as San Miguel de Escalada, San Cebrian de Mazote (fig.127), Santiago de Penalba, Sainta Maria de Vilanova and Santa Maria de Melque where it represented the apse. The introduction of multifoil arches was also carried through into church plans where the square or rectangular plan ends with multifoil arch representing the apses of churches that predominated in much of later Romanesque and Gothic styles. Another connecting feature in plan design is the adoption by the Cistercian order of the T shaped plan, emphasising the importance of the nave and the apses. Muslims developed such schemes in both eighth and ninth centuries as we saw in chapter two, in the Al-Aqsa Mosque, al-Kairawan and the Great Mosque of Cordoba. In this plan, Muslims emphasised the mihrab aisle (nave) and the Qibla wall, a fashion that was also used by the Cistercian monks. This is also a possible explanation for the adoption of one aisled church plan, which replaced the tradition of multi-nave plans. However, according to Male cathedrals of the south of France and Languedoc were the origin of the church of one nave[947]. In the north, churches had more than one aisle. The circumstances of the transfer were as follows: Guillaume de Volpiano, a Lombard who entered the monastery of Cluny at the time of Saint Mayeul, became Abbot of Saint Benigne of Dijon. The Duke Richard II, of Normandy (963-1027), gave him the task of establishing order in the monasteries of Normandy. At Fecamp, he established the Abbey of Bernay in 1017 and was in charge of a number of other churches. It appears that he was behind the plan adopted for the church, which had the characteristic described above, imitating those of the Cluniac order at Saint Mayeul and Bernay, and thus introducing this new plan to Normandy. In his turn, Abbot Wilhelm, the abbot of Hirsau introduced it to Souabe in Germany. It has also been established that the plan was exported to Switzerland as in the old church of Romainmotiers

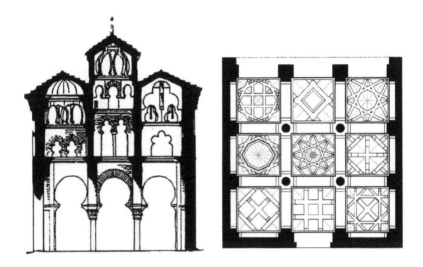

Figure 124 Plan and section of Bab Mardum Mosque.

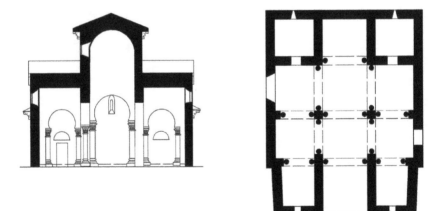

Figure 125 Plan and section of San Maria de Lebana, Spain, clearly show similarities with Bab Mardum Mosque.

321

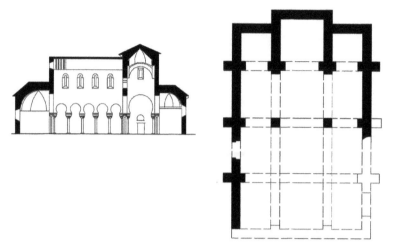

Figure 126 Plan and section San Maria de Wamba, Spain.

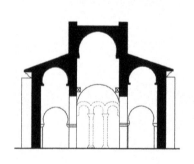

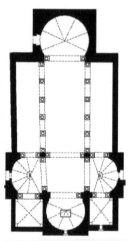

Figure 127 Plan and section of San Cebrian de Mazote, Spain, showing the use of horseshoe arch in the plan.This adoption of the horseshoe plan became fashionable and spread among most Mozarab churches of the 10th and 11th centuries.

(in Switzerland).[948] This Cluniac plan, according to Male, originated from the Muslims due to the contacts described above. In the opinion of Lefevre-Pontalis, this plan first appeared in the ninth century in Saint Philibert de Grandlieu, was adopted later by all the Benedictine traditions[949]. It spread to most parts of French Midi and then to the North. According to Dehio and von Bezold,[950] the Norman feature of the choir was imported from the Cluniac tradition. This is particularly connected to St Mayeul church, built in 981. In their study of the plan of 11th century European churches of the Cluniac tradition, they established that this church had one single nave and low sides, which extended beyond the transept on both sides of the choir creating the apse. It appears that there has been similar influence on the plan of 11th century German churches such as Hirsau (1060) and Saint Aurelius, which display similar plans. However, Western scholars including Braun[951] and Lethaby[952] emphasised the influence of Armenian churches. For them the main development of church plan, after the Romans, were introduced through Armenia. The process of such a transfer is related to Armenian artists and masons who "fled" their country after the fall of their city Ani in 1064 into the hands of the Muslim Suljuks. These Armenian refugees are supposed to have fled to Constantinople where they settled and worked. Others made their way to Europe where they introduced these plans. Such claims leave one wondering how people from such a distant land could exercise such an influence in Europe, yet neighbouring Mozarabs and Muslims are constantly denied any influence. More research on this issue needs to be carried out to settle the controversy of the origin of the medieval church plan.

Walls and the Material of Construction.

Early buildings were made of wood and only a few were of masonry. These consisted of thick blind and short walls reflecting the primitive building techniques and understanding of statics. The use of barrel and groin vault roofing systems necessitated walls with such characteristics to cope with the thrust created by these vaults. Furthermore, the material used in construction, which consisted mainly of rubble and small stones also played a part in causing the thickening of the walls. Graceful walls did not come until large heavy stones were introduced. Such a technique originated in the East and were imitated by crusaders first in their military constructions (castles and towers), and later transmitted into ecclesiastical buildings. It was also due to the Muslim machinery brought by crusaders as part of the spoils of their victory. Harvey confirmed this, at least in England: "*In the earlier period the stones used has been small and such as could be carried singly by hand. Clearly, such hoisting machinery as existed was very*

323

be carried singly by hand. Clearly, such hoisting machinery as existed was very simple and incapable of raising heavy weights. In England it is possible to narrow down to within a few years of 1100 the date of introduction of improved plant. This date is highly suggestive of the direct importation of Saracen machinery brought back by returning Crusaders from victorious campaign...Saracen prisoners are likely to have a leading part in the next stage of stylistic development, and it is reasonable to include mechanical devices, too, as part of the booty."[953]

Another contribution of Muslims is the introduction of brick building into Europe. Brick building, which was already known in Byzantium but not used in the West, first appeared in northern Italy in the 11th century in buildings such as St. Mark Cathedral (1063). This involved an innovation consisting of using bricks in decorative patterns such as dogtooth friezes, arched friezes and crossed arch friezes, which became ornamental themes widely used in 12th century Italy and Europe. The brick building and ornamentation spread to Germany in the second half of the twelfth century. It appears particularly in the Cathedral of Luebeck (1173) and Lehnin (after 1215). Although dogtooth friezes were common in Byzantine brick architecture, the crossed arch friezes were of Muslim origin originating from southern Italy, Sicily and Spain. Such features appear in countries bordering Muslim lands. In southern Italy and Sicily, the crossed arch frieze decorates stone buildings in the form of arcades, which cross each other, such as the Church of St. Michael in Caserta Vecchia, completed in 1153. In Spain, examples of the use of bricks appear at Cordoba, and in the towers of Saragossa and Teruel, in Giralda of Seville (1176-1196). The improvement in forming and firing, which were introduced from the East, had a major influence on the development of brick architecture in Europe and its widespread use.

The Spire and Tower

The other architectural feature adopted by Gothic architecture was the tower, which first appeared in the Romanesque period. Hostile western academics claim that the use of the tower is a Christian tradition that was adopted by Europeans. For them, the tower differs substantially from the minaret, from which Muslims claim it is derived. It is true that the early Syrian Christians, for example, added a small projection to the roof where they hung their bells[954]. Muslims copied this functional device and developed their elaborate minaret. Michell et al. claimed that Muslims borrowed the use of minaret from the Roman lighthouse.[955] Not only did the design reflect this, but the name "*minaret*" is translated as "light house". Briggs thought the idea of tower/minaret was taken from the Christians, but provided another explanation. Muslims imitated the use of sanctuaries where Christian clerics used to retire for meditation and worship. Such usage is manifested in the use of "*Soumaa*" in North Africa, which translates the exclusion room rather than lighthouse.[956]

No matter how the Muslims got the idea of using the minaret/tower, they developed it into a fascinating feature as early as the eighth century in the Great Mosque of Damascus and it became an essential element of Muslim religious architecture. It was later adopted in European Romanesque buildings no earlier than the 10th century. Historians established that the use of a tower at or near the gate was imported from Muslims who used it particularly in their castles.[957] This suggests that the crusaders were the importers. Evidence shows the close resemblance between the Romanesque/Gothic tower and the Muslim minaret in both design and aesthetics. The earliest surviving Muslim tower is Qalaa' of Beni Hammad, which was built in 1007 in Eastern Algeria (fig.128). With its huge size expressing the power of Benu Hammad, the tower was also used as a watchtower. In terms of aesthetics, the tower was richly decorated with a number of openings providing greater light and reducing the weight of the structure. Various types of arches were used on the frames of these windows including the trefoil, cinqfoil, semi-circular and polylobed arches. Such features later became characteristic of the Romanesque and Gothic towers in the West. This can be seen in many examples such as St. Abbondio church in Italy (1063-1095), Abbey aux Hommes at Caen (1066-1160), the Abbey gateway at Bury St.Edmund in England (1120) (fig.129) and many other ecclesiastical buildings as shown in figs.130, 131, 132, and 133. In all cases, the influence of Qalaa' Beni Hammad is unquestionable and one can easily establish that European trade links with North Africa must have been responsible for the transfer of this motif. This is particularly so if one considers the influence of the Qalaa' on the form of the next generations of minarets of North Africa which are locally known as "Soumaa", translated as sanctuary.

Male found that Muslim minarets/towers were a major influence on western Gothic towers.[958] In his opinion, Muslim minarets, in general, illustrate two main characteristics. The lower part of the minaret consists of a strong blind base with little or no decoration. However, the upper part is very graceful and richly decorated as outlined above. According to Warton[959], the spire were never used until the Muslim mode took place, although Muslims used cupolas (domes), the notion of a spire was brought from the East. Pyramidical structures were very common there and spiral ornaments were, and still today, the fashionable decorations of their mosques in areas such as Iran, Anatolia and India. In England, there was no spire before 1200 and the first being of the first church of St. Paul finished in 1221. Meanwhile, Briggs found that Muslim minarets especially the Egyptians exerted a strong influence on European towers[960]. The minarets of Al-Jeyushi Mosque in Cairo were particularly influential in Italy and England. *"Mohammedan minarets of the graceful type found, especially, in Cairene buildings of the 14th and 15th centuries may have influenced the design of the later Renaissance Campanili of Italy, and hence some of Wren's fine city steeples"*[961]. Square shaped minarets continued to influence European towers as seen at Piza la Signora (1299-1314) in Italy (fig.134). Similarly, we find the graceful circular form minaret imitated in Germany as in the Cathedral of the Holy Apostles (1190) at Cologne (fig.135), in Mainz cathedral (1009-1239), and in Worms cathedral (11th-13th centuries) in the Rhineland.

A close examination of minarets such as those of the Kutubia Mosque (1164-1184) (fig.136), Tour Hassan in Morocco, and La Giralda (1184-1196) in Spain (fig.137) reveals common features such as the square shape, the use of brick work and the multifoil arches around window frames although these the minarets are more graceful than the Qalaa'. Jubir, the architect of these three minarets must have seen the Qalaa. We find similar characters in the minaret of al-Mahdiya Mosque at Telemcen (Algeria), built in 1172. We find also close similarities between these four graceful minarets and a generation of towers that appeared in Europe after the second half of the twelfth century. The twin towers of Cefalu Cathedral in Sicily, which Sir Banister Fletcher described them as "of minaret proportions,"[962] were rebuilt around 1400, although the church was dated between 1131 and 1200), are a good example (fig.138). The tower/minarets of Basilica di Sant'Antonio in Padua, built between 1238 and 1310, are another example as well as the church of Erice in Sicily built in 1312 or before (fig.139).

Figure 128 Qalaa beni Hammad, the tower reconstructed by Marcai G. (1954),op.cit., showing the trefoil, cinqfoil, semi-circular and polylobed arches of Qala' shows early Muslim adoption of this type of tower and could be the source of Western towers that was adopted in the Gothic style.

Figure 129 A gateway to the former abbey of St Edmunds, at Suffolk (England, 1120) which is now the bell tower to the Anglican cathedral of St James shown in the right of the picture

327

Figure 130 Tower of Santa María de Tauste, Spain (late 12th- early 13th century).

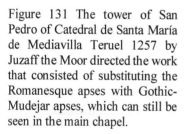

Figure 131 The tower of San Pedro of Catedral de Santa María de Mediavilla Teruel 1257 by Juzaff the Moor directed the work that consisted of substituting the Romanesque apses with Gothic-Mudejar apses, which can still be seen in the main chapel.

132 Tower of St.Martin, Spain

Figure 133 La iglesia de San
Pedro Apóstol built between
1319 and 1392, Aragon,
Spain

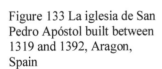

329

Figure 134 Tower of Pisa la Signora, Italy (1299-1314) is one the many campanile that are thought to be derived from Muslim towers/minarets, the corbelling of the tower middle section is a 12th century Eyyubid tradition.

Figure 135 The twin octagonal towers of the Cathedral of the Holy Apostles at Cologne (1190 CE) resembling those of Al-Azhar Mosque.

Figure 135 Al-Azhar Mosque minarets

331

Figure 136 Kutubia Tower, Morocco (1164-1184).

Figure 137 La Giralda (1184-1196), old tower of the Great mosque of Seville, built by Kutubia's architect Jebir

Figure 138 Twin towers of Cefalu Cathedral, Sicily (Italy, 1131-1200)

Figure 139 Medieval church - Medieval town of Erice, Sicily, built in 312 for Frederick II of Aragon (1272-1337), but the tower could be earlier.

Notes

[710] Violet le-Duc (1858) `Dictionnaire Raisonne de l'Architecture Francaise du Onzieme Siecle au Seizieme Siecle', B. Bance, Paris.

[711] Bentham, J. (1808), 'Historical Remarks on the Saxon churches', in T. Warton· J Bentham, Francis, C. Grose and J. Milner (eds.), 'Essays on Gothic Architecture', printed for J. Taylor, at the Architectural Library, London, pp.17-94, at p.18.

[712] Harvey, J. (1973), 'the Master Builders', Thames and Hudson, London, p.10.

[713] Harvey, J. (1972), 'The Mediaeval Architect', Wayland, London.

[714] Such as Porter Arthur Kingsley (1909), 'Medieval Architecture, its Origins and Development/ Vol: 1-2. Vol.1: Origins. Vol.2: Normandy and The Ile de France., The Baker and Taylor N.Y.

[715] They were created by the King Ropthari (636-652) who in the year 643, issued laws organising these guilds and assigning responsibilities. For example article 143 decrees that the magister comacinus, together with his colleagues, is responsible for fatal accidents at the site of the building if he has hired the individual in question; the owner is not responsible. Article 144 adds that even if a comacinus is killed or injured at work the owner is not liable. However, no proof has yet been established connecting these guilds with the rise of Gothic which started five centuries later.

[716] Lombards were descendants of ancient Germanic people whom under the leadership of Albion invaded northern Italy and established a kingdom at Pavia in 568. They expanded into central and southern Italy, but the regions around Ravenna, the Pentapolis (Rimini, Ancona, Fano, Pesaro, and Senigallia), and much of the coast remained under Byzantine rule while Rome and the Patrimony of St. Peter was kept by the papacy. The Lombard kingdom reached its height in the 7th and 8th cent after converting from Paganism and Arianism to Christianity. In 774, it became part of Charlemagne's empire, and in the 11th century it was conquered by the Normans (see The Columbia Encyclopaedia, Sixth Edition. 2001).

[717] Harvey, J. (1972),op cit..

[718] Harvey, J. (1973), op cit. p.95

[719] Harvey, J. (1973), op cit. p.6

[720] Harvey, J. (1973), op cit. p.7

[721] Lethaby, W.R. (1926), 'Medieval Architecture', in Crump, C.G. & Jacob, E.F. (eds.), the Legacy of the Middle Ages, Clarendon Press, Oxford., pp59-91. p. 63.

[722] Harvey, J. (1971), op cit. p.16.

[723] Harvey, J. (1971), op cit. p.14.

[724] Cochrane, L. (1994), `Adelard of Bath, the First English Scientist', British Museum Press, p.66.

[725] Huntington Ellsworth (1977), 'The Character of Races', Ayer Company Publishers, p.264

[726] Harvey, J. (1950), 'The Gothic World :1100-1600, a Survey of Architecture and Art', B.T. Batsford Ltd, London. p.57.

[727] Porter Arthur Kingsley (1909), 'Medieval Architecture, its Origins and Development', Vol.1,The Baker and Taylor N.Y, p.244

[728] Quoted in Scott, S. P. (1904), 'History of the Moorish Empire in Europe', Vol. I, J. B. Lippincott Company, p.178.

[729] Frankl, P.(1960), 'the Gothic', Princeton University Press, Princeton

[730] Florent Le Comte, (1699), 'Cabinet des Singularités d' Architecture, Peinture, Sculpture et Gravure ou Introduction à la Connaissance des Plus Beaux-Arts, Figures Sous les Tableaux, les

Statues, et les Estampes', Paris, cited in Frankl, P.(1960), the Gothic, Princeton University Press, Princeton, p.346.

[731] See Wren, Christopher, (1750), *'Parentalia'* , T. Osborn and R. Dodsley, London, p.297 & appendix 1.

[732] Elmes, James, (1971 ed.), *`Lectures on Architecture'*, B. Blom, New York, pp.375-6.

[733] Elmes, J. (1823), *'Memoires of the life of Sir Christopher Wren'*, Priestley and Weale, London p. 107. Also quoted in Frankl, P. (1960), op cit. p.364.

[734] Elmes, J. (1823), op. cit.p.116.

[735] See Oeuvres de Fénelon, Paris, vol.21, 1824. cited in Frankl, P. (1960), op cit. p.375.

[736] Published in Oeuvres de Fénelon 1824, p.259, quoted in Frankl, P. (1960), op cit. p.375.

[737] Fénelon, (1718), *'Dialogue sur l'Éloquence en Général et Sur Celle de la Chaire en Particulier*, Paris, pp.156, and in Oeuvres de Fénelon 1824, appendix 24b, cited in Franl, P. (1960), op cit. p.376.

[738]Francois Blondel the Younger (1751), *'Encyclopedie'*, vol.1, Paris, p.617, quoted in Frankl, P, (1960), op cit. p.389.

[739] Francois Blondel the Younger (1752), *'Architecture Françoise, ou Recueil des Plans, Élévations, Coupes et Profiles des Églises'*, Charles Antoine Jombert, Paris, p.15.

[740] William Warburton (1760), *`Pope's Moral Essays'*, quoted by Richard Elsam (1805), An Essay on Rural Architecture: illustrated with original and economical designs ... the whole comprising thirty plates, in Aquatinta, 2nd Edition, Printed for Lackington, Allen London, p.13., also quoted in F.C. Grose, (1808), essay without a title, T. Warton et al., op cit. pp.95-124, at p.121.

[741] Schopenhauer, Arthur, (1819), *'Die Welt als Wille und Vorstellung'*, leipzig, Vol. II, Book 3, Chapter 35, quoted in Frankl, P.(1960) op cit. p.472., See also the English edition, Schopenhauer, Arthur, (1884) *'The World as Will and Idea'*, edit. 1884, Routledge & Kegan Paul, London.

[742] Frankl, P.(1960) op cit. p.486.

[743] Quoted in Frankl, P. (1960) op cit. p.485.

[744] Henry Lemonnier (1922), *`Procès-Verbaux de l'Academie Royale d'Architecture'*, VII, Paris, p.129. cited in Frankl, P.(1960) op cit. p.407.

[745] Anderson, J. (1800), *`Thoughts on the Origin, Excellencies, and Defects of the Grecian and Gothic Styles of Architecture'*, in Recreations in Agriculture, Natural-History, Arts and Miscellaneous Literature, Vol.2, London,.p.420.

[746] August Wilhelm Von Schlegel, (1894), *'Asthetische Ansichten'*, Berlin, p.180.quoted in Frankl, P. (1960), op cit. p.456.

[747] Odard, (1847), *'A Sentimental Journey Through Normandy'*, in Charles Dickens , William Harrison Ainsworth and Adam Smith, (eds.), Bentley's Miscellany, Vol.21, Richard Bentley, London, pp.395-p.529.

[748] Gordon, George Hamilton-, fourth earl of Aberdeen (1784–1860), prime minister and scholar,

[749] Richard Payne Knight (1750-1824), classical English scholar and connoisseur renowned for his theories of picturesque beauty and for his interest in ancient phallic imagery.

[750] Ibid., p.530.

[751] Spengler, Oswald (1923),' *Der Untergang des Abendlandes : Umrisse Einer Morphologie der Weltgeschichte: Namen- und Sachverzeuchnis'*, Beck, München,p.291.

[752] Bond Francis (1906), *'Gothic Architecture in England: An Analysis of the Origin and development of English Church'*, B. T. Batsford Publishing, p.22.

[753] Seesselberg Friedrich. (1897), *`Die Früh-Mittelaterliche Kunst der Germanischen Voelker Unter Besonderer Berücksichtigung der Skandinavischen Kunst in Ethnologisch-Anthropologischer Begrundung dargestell,* Berlin, cited in Frankl, P. (1960), op cit. p.657.

335

[754] Worringer, Wilhelm , (1967), '*Abstraction and Empathy,a Contribution to the Psychology of Style*', translated by Michael Bullock, Routledge, London.

[755] Haupt A. (1909) `*Die Alteste Kunst, Insbedondere die Baukunst der Germanen*', Leipzig, cited in Frankl, P. (1960), op cit. p.669.

[756] Mason William, (1827), '*The Works of Thomas Gray: Collated from the Various Editions ; With Memoirs of his Life and Writings,* published by J. F, Dove, London, p.188.

[757] See Mitford Joan (ed.1843), '*The Works of Gray', vol.5, William Pickering*', London, pp.327, also see Frankl, P. (1960), op cit. pp.402-403.

[758] Milner, J. (1808) `*On the Rise and Progress of the Pointed Arch*', in T. Warton et. al (eds.) , op cit. pp.125-133, at.p.129.

[759] Christien Ludwig Stieglitz, C. L (1820), `*Von Altdeutscher Baukunst*', Leipzig, cited in Frankl, P. (1960), op cit. pp465-469.

[760] Ibid., 466.

[761] Johan Wolfgang von Goethe (1896), `*Briefe*', Sophienausgabe, IV, Vol.21, Weimar, Letter 5994, p.294, cited in Frankl, P.(1960), op cit. p.469.

[762] Laborde Alexandre de (1816), `*Les Monuments de la France Classes Chronologiquement et Considérés sous le Rapport des Faits Historiques et de l'Étude des Arts par le Comte Alexandre de Laborde: Les Dessins Faits d'Apres Nature par M.M.Bourgeois et Bauce*', 2 volumes, P.Didot, l'aine, 2nd Edition 1836, Paris.

[763] Saunders, G. (1814), `*Observations on the Origin of Gothic Architecture*', in Archeologia, London, cited in Frankl, p. (1960), p.500.

[764] For more see Frankl, P. (1960), op cit. pp499-502.

[765] Caumont, Arcisse de (1830-1841), `*Cours d'Antiquités Monumentales Professé Caen en 1830: Quatrième Partie, Moyen Age, Architecture Religieuse* ', Paris, p.198-200.

[766] Ibid. p.198-99

[767] Violet-le-Duc (1844), `*De la Construction des Edifices Religieuse en France*', in Annales Archeologiques, Vol. I, p.179, cited in Frankl, P. (1960), op cit. p.565.

[768] Quicherat, J. (1885), `*de l'Ogive et de l'Architecture Ogivale', in Melanges d'Archeologie et d'Histoire*', Paris, p.498, cited in Frankl, P. (1960), op cit. p.574.

[769] Harvey, J. (1950), `*The Gothic World :1100-1600, a Survey of Architecture and Art* ', B.T. Batsford Ltd, London. p.7.

[770] Louis Charles Jean Courajod (1899), '*Lecons Professes a l'École du Louvre* ', publiées sur la Direction de H. Lemonier et A. Michel, Puiblishers A. Picard et fils, Paris, p.443.

[771] Costenoble, J.C. (1812), '*Uber Altdeutsche Architektur Und Deren Ursprung* ', Halle, cited in in Frankl, P. (1960), op cit. p.465.

[772] See Frankl, P. (1960), op cit. pp.275 and 660.

[773] Colish, M.L (1997), '*Medieval Foundations of the Western Intellectual Tradition, 400-1400*', Yale University Press, New Heaven and London, p.59.

[774] Translated from the French text quoted in Frankl, P. (1960), op cit. Appendix 28, pp.869-870.

[775] Let ABC be an arch resting at C against an immovable wall KM, but at A upon a pillar AD, so small as to be unable to be a sufficient abutment to the pressure of the half arch AB: what is then to be done? I cannot add (an abutment against the nave) FG to it to make it a abutment, but I build up E so high, as by addition of weight, to establish it so firm as if I had FG to it to make it a butment: It need not be inquired how much E must be, since it cannot exceed, provided AD be sufficient to bear the weight imposed upon it; and this is the reason why, in all Gothic fabrics of this form, the architects were to

build towers or steeples in the middle, not only for ornament, but to confirm the middle pillars against the thrust of the several rows of arches, which force against them every way." (See Elmes, J. (1823), op cit. p.115, cited in Frankl, P. (1960), op cit. p.367.

[776] See Roshdi Rashed, Régis Morelon (1996), '*Encyclopedia of the History of Arabic Science*', Routledge, p.917

[777] Birkenmajer, A. (1948) '*Robert Grosseteste and Richiard Fournival*', in Medievalia et Humanistica, Vol. 4, pp.37.

[778] Otto von Simson (1956) '*The Gothic Cathedral, Origins of Gothic Architecture and the Medieval Concept of Order*', 3rd ed. 1988, Princeton University Press, USA, pp.50-56.

[779] Ibid, p.10.

[780] Kitschelt, L. (1938), '*Die Fruhchristliche Basilika als Darstellung des Himmlischen Jerusalem*', Munich.

[781] Lambert, E. (1931), '*l'Art Gothic en Espagne*', H. Laurens, Paris.

[782] Yarwood, D. (1974), '*The Architecture of Europe*', Chancellor Press, p.135.

[783] See Ettinghausen, R. (1975), '*Muslim Decorative Arts and Painting, Their Nature and Impact on the Medieval West*', in Stanley Ferber, (ed.1975), Islam and the Medieval West, vol.1, State University of New York at Binghamton, p.5-26, at p.9.

[784] He engaged Hermann the Second (or the Dalmatian) and Robert of Rétines, established in Spain; to translate the Quran into Latin, and in 1143 these same translators made Christendom acquainted with Ptolemy's planisphere. See Palter Robert (1961), '*Toward Modern Science*', Noonday Press, p.147

[785] Otto von Simson (1956), op cit. pp.142-156.

[786] Otto von Simson, (1956), op cit. p.37, 52.

[787] See Asin Palacios, (1943), '*La Escatalogia Rnlrsulrnana en lo Divina Comedia*', 2nd ed. Consejo Superior de Investigaciones Cientificas. Madrid, p.44.

[788] Otto von Simson, (1956), op cit. p.37, 52.

[789] Johnson Art (1999), '*Famous Problems and Their Mathematicians*', By Libraries unlimited, p.120

[790] Karpinski Louis Charles, (1930), '*Robert of Chester's Latin translation of the Algebra of al-Khowarizmi*', Macmillan, New York

[791] Lesser, G. (1957), '*Gothic Cathedrals and Sacred Geometry*', volume I, Alec Tiranti, London p.33.

[792] Bilson (1899), '*The Beginnings of Gothic Architecture: Norman Vaulting in England*', in RIBA Journal, Vol.6, pp.259-269, at p.267.

[793] Bony, J. (1949), '*French Influences on the Origin of English Architecture*', in Journal of the Warburg and Courtauld Institutes 12, pp.1–16.

[794] Male, E (1928), '*Art et Artistes du Moyen Age*', Librairie Armand Colin, Paris.

[795] Scott, S. P. (1904), '*History of the Moorish Empire in Europe*', Vol. III, J. B. Lippincott Company, pp.324-423.

[796] Boas Adrian J (2001), '*Jerusalem in the Time of the Crusades: Society, Landscape, and Art in the Holy City Under Frankish Rule*', Routledge, p.79.

[797] Ibid, p.91

[798] Lambert, E. (1927), '*L'art Hispano Mauresque et l'Art Roman*', Hesperis, vol.7, pp.29-43, at p. 36-7.

[799] Lethaby, W.R. (1926), '*Medieval Architecture*', in Crump, C.G. & Jacob, E.F. (eds.), the legacy of the Middle Ages, Clarendon Press, Oxford., pp59-91.p 63.

[800] Scott, S.P (1904) op cit. vol.II, p.534.

[801] Charlemagne has never been in Jerusalem or Constantinople.

[802] Paris, Gaston. (1880), `La Chanson du Pelerinage de Charlemagne', Romania, Vol9, Paris, pp.1-50.

[803] Diehl, C. (1910), 'Manuel de l'Art Byzantin', A. Picard et fils, Paris. And M. Hattstein and P. Delius (eds.) (2000), 'Islam Art and Architecture', Konemann, Cologne, p.95. See also Jenkins Romilly (1987), 'Byzantium: The Imperial Centuries, AD 610-1071', University of Toronto Press, p.148.

[804] Bargebuhr, F.P. (1968), 'The Alhambra, a Cycle of Studies on the Eleventh Century in Moorish Spain', Walter de Gruyter & Co., Berlin.

[805] See Paris Gaston, (1880), op.cit. p.3.

[806] The Latin version "Descriptio" asserts that Charlemagne brought these relices to Aachen and Charles the Bald transfered them to St. Denys.

[807] Frankl, P. (1960), op cit. p.162.

[808] Otto Söhring, (1900), 'Werke Bildender Kunst in Altfranzösischen Epen', Romanische Forschungen, vol.12, Erlangen, quoted in Frankl, P. (1960), op cit. p.164.

[809] Full description is provided by Frankl, P. (1960), op, cit. p.166.

[810] Ibid, pp.169-170.

[811] Ibid. p.170

[812] Eve is buried in Jedda, near Makka Saudi Arabia. Jedda in Arabic means grande mother, referring to the grave the mother of all humans, Eve.

[813] The great age is supposed to be the work of the Grail which preserves the youth of its guardians.

[814] Rothlisberger Blanca (1917), `Die Architektur des Graltempls im Jungeren Ttiturel', Berne, p.55, cited in Frankl, P. (1960),op cit. 185.

[815] Ibid, pp.177-183, see also Resie Lambert-Élisabeth d'Aubert, comte de (1857), 'Historie et Traite des Sciences Occultes', Louis Vivés, Paris, p.521

[816] Resie Lambert-Élisabeth d'Aubert, comte de (1857), 'Historie et Traite des Sciences Occultes', Louis Vivés, Paris, p.521, Translated from French.

[817] Ibid., p.521, also see Warton Thomas (1840), 'The History of English Poetry: From the Close of the Eleventh Century to the Commencement of the Eighteenth Century', vol.1, Printed for T. Tegg, London,p.57.

[818] Faugère Annie (1979), 'Les Origines Orientales du Graal Chez Wolfram von Eschenbach: Etat des Recherches', Kümmerle, p.211

[819] Weysen Alfred (1972), 'L'île des Veilleurs: Saint Graal et Fabuleux Tresor des Templiers', Editions Arcadie, Paris, p.96

[820] Bezold, G. (1888), `Die Schatzhohle, Nach Syriscehn Texten Nebst Einer Arabischen Version Herausgegeben', Leipzig., cited in Frankl, P. (1960), op cit. p.179.

[821] Warton Thomas (1840), 'The History of English Poetry: From the Close of the Eleventh Century to the Commencement of the Eighteenth century', p.56-57.

[822] Hill, D. (1993), `Islamic Science and Engineering', Edinburgh University Press.

[823] Yonge, Charlotte Mary (1863), 'History of Christian Names', vol.2, Parker Son and Bourn, London, p.151. also Warton Thomas (1824) The history of English poetry: from the close of the eleventh to the commencement of the eighteenth century, Harvard University.

[824] The poem says:
They (the Knights of the Grail) live from a stone of purest kind.
If you do not know it,
It shall here be named to you, it is called lapsit exillis
See Jung Emma and Franz Marie-Louise von (1998) 'The Grail Legend', Princeton University Press, p.148.

[825] Adolf Helen (1954), '*Der Gral in Wolframs Parzival: Entstehung und Ausbildung der Gralsage im Hochmittelalter by Bodo Mergell*', Review, *Speculum*, Vol. 29, No. 2, Part 1. pp. 295-300.

[826] See Wolfram, Wolfram von Eschenbach (1984 ed.) '*Willehalm*', Penguin Classics

[827] Adolf Helen (1954), op.cit. p.296.

[828] Scott, S.P. (1904), op cit. vol. II, p.60.

[829] Trend, J.B. (1931) '*Spain and Portugal*', in T. Arnold et al. (eds.), 1931, The Legacy of Islam, Oxford University Press. pp.1-39.

[830] Ibid..

[831] Lambert, E. (1958) '*Art Musulman et Art Chrétien dans la Péninsule Ibérique*', Éditions Privat, Paris., p.177.

[832] Fau, Jean Claude, (1995), '*A Propos de l'Inscription en Caractères Coufiques sur l'Ange Sonneur d'Olifant au Tympan de Sainte-Foy de Conque*', in Kawa Topor (Hg.) ed. Enfer et Paradis: l'au-delà dans l'art et la litterature en Europe ; Actes du Colloque Organisé par le Centre Européen d'Art et de Civilisation Médiévale', Conference à Conques les 22 et 23 avril 1994, Les cahiers de Conques, Riom, Pierre [Publ.]. - Conques (1995) , pp.67-70.

[833] Ibid., p.67

[834] Bouillet, A. and Servières, L. (1900), '*Sainte Foy Vierge et Martyr*', Rodez, pp. 98,601.

[835] Ibid., p.180)

[836] A mithqal equals approximately 87.48g

[837] Fletcher, R. (1992) '*Moorish Spain*', Weidenfield & Nicholson, London, p.114.

[838] Ibid., p.113.

[839] Hilberry Harry H. (1955), '*Charité-sur-Loire Priory Church*', Speculum, Vol.30, No.1., pp.1-14, at p.1

[840] For more on this see Denomy Alexander Joseph (1953), '*Concerning the Accessibility of Arabic Influences to the Earliest Provencal Troubadours*', Mediaeval Studies, vol.15.,1953, p.147-158.

[841] Trend, J.B. (1931) op cit. p.12.

[842] Buloz, F. (1982), '*La Revue des Deux Mondes*', Au Bureau de la Revue des deux Mondes, Paris, p.312.

[843] Mâle, Emile, (1924), '*Art et Artistes du Moyen Age*', Librairie Armand Colin, Paris.

[844] Zarnecki, G. cited in Harvey, J. (1973), op cit. p 46.

[845] Scott, S.P.(1904), op cit. Vol. II p.70

[846] Kristeller, P.O (1945), '*The School of Salerno: Its Development and its Contribution to the History of Learning*', in Bulletin of the History of Medecine, Vol.17, pp.138-194.

[847] Hulme Edward Maslin (1929), '*The Middle Ages*', H. Holt and company, p.280

[848] Reinaud Joseph Toussaint , (1964), '*Muslim colonies in France, northern Italy, and Switzerland: being the English translation of Reinaud's Invasions des Sarrazins en France, et de France en Savoie, en Piémont et en Suisse*', Sh. Muhammad Ashraf pub., Lahore, p.163

[849] Mann, H.K. (1925), '*The Lives of the Popes in early Middle Ages*', volume 4, 2nd ed., K. Paul, London, p.10.

[850] Pirenne, H. (1948), '*Medieval Cities, their Origins and the Revival of Trade*' 5th Edition, Princeton University Press, Princeton p.89.

[851] Breckeuridge, J.D. (1975), '*The Two Sicilies*", in Ferber (ed.), Islam and the Medieval West, pp.39-66.

[852] Briffault, R. (1919), '*The Making of Humanity*', G. Allen & Unwin ltd., p.212

[853] Kaufmann, J. E. Kaufmann H. W., Robert M. Jurga (2004), '*The Medieval Fortress: Castles, Forts and Walled Cities of the Middle Ages*, Da Capo Press, p.273

[854] Hitt Philip Khuri (1996), *'History of the Arabs'*, Regnery Publishing, p.210

[855] Harvey, J. (1950), *'The Gothic World :1100-1600, a Survey of Architecture and Art'*, B.T. Batsford Ltd, London. p.57.

[856] Scarfiotti Gian Luigi and Lunde Paul (1978), *'Muslim Sicily '*, Saudi Aramco World, vol.29, No.6 (November-December), p.29

[857] Also known by other names such as: Badr al-Jamali, Badr al-Gamali, Mashhad of Badr al Jamali, and Mosque of al-Guyushi

[858] Conant K.J. (1942), *`A Brief Commentary on Medieval Church Architecture '*, John Hopkins Press, Baltimore.

[859] Koehler, W. (1939), *`Medieval Studies Dedicated to A.K. Porter '*, vol.2, Harvard University Press, Cambridge, p.336, and Speculum : A Journal of Medieval Studies, vol. 10, 1935, pp.144-146.

[860] White Lynn Jr. (1971), *`Cultural Climates and Technological Advances in the Middle Ages '*, in Viator, Vol.2, pp.171-201 at p. 183.

[861] This church was destroyed by an earthquake in 1349 and entirely destroyed in second World War by allied bombing.

[862] Hill, D. (1993), *`Islamic Science and Engineering'*, Edinburgh University Press.

[863] Thompson, J.W. (1928), *'Economic and Social History of the Middle Ages (300-1300)'*, Unger, New York p.330.

[864] Camera, Matteo (1836). *'Istoria Della Citta e Costiera di Amalfi '*, Stamperia e Cartiera del Fibreno, Napoli, p.28.

[865] Meyerhof, M. (1931), *`Science and Medecine'*, in Arnold et.al. op, cit.pp.311-355.

[866] Wren Benjamin Lee (2004), *'Teaching World Civilisation with Joy and Enthusiasm '*, University Press of America, p.141.

[867] Bony Jean (1983), *'French Gothic Architecture of the 12th and 13th Centuries '*, University of California Press, p.17

[868] BerschinWalter (1988), *'From the Middle of the Eleven Century to the Latin Conquest of Constantinople'*. Catholic University of America Press, p.211

[869] Ibid. p.215

[870] Newton Francis(1994), *'Constantine the African and Monte Cassino: New Elements and the Text of the Isagoge'*, in C. Burnett and D. Jacquart 1994 eds., Constantine the African and Ali ibn Al-Abbas al-Magusi: The Pantegni and Related Texts' E.J. Brill Publishers, Leiden,pp.16-47, Note 81, p.39

[871] Ibid. note 81, p.39

[872] Walsh James, J. (1911), *'Old Time Makers of Medicine '*, Fordham University Press, New York, p.69

[873] Ibid. p.69

[874] Newton Francis(1994), op cit. note 81, p.39

[875] Ibid., note 81, p.39

[876] Ibid., note 81, p.39

[877] Citarella, A.O. (1986), *'Amalfi and Salerno in the Ninth Century '*, Istituzioni civili e organizzazione ecclesiastica nello stato medieval amalfuano, Amalfi, Centro di cultural e storia amalfitana, vol.1, pp.129-45, especially p.141-144. Also Citarella, A.O. (1993),*'Merchants, Markets and Merchandis in Southern Italy in the High Middle Ages'*, Settimane di studio del Centro Italiano di studi sull' alto medioeve, vol.40, pp.239-284. Cited in Burnett C.and Jacquart, D. (1994),op. cit. p.39

[878] Burnett C.and Jacquart, D. (1994) op. cit. p.39. The text of Amatus is found in a preserved copy of his History of the Normans and provided by Burnett and Jaxquart reads as follows:*"Et pour ce qu'il*

non trova in Ytalie homes de cert art, (Desiderius), manda en Constantinoble et en Alexandre pour homes grex et Sarrazins, our aomer lo pavement de la eglize de marmoire entaillié et diverses paintures; laquelle nous clamons "opera de mosy"; over de pierre de diverses colors", See Burnett C.and Jacquart, D. (1994) op. cit. p.39.

[879] Lynn White Jr (1971), op cit. p.184.

[880] Conant, Kenneth John (1968), `*Cluny: les Églises et la Maison du Chef d'Ordre*', Impr. Protat Frères Mâcon, Paris.

[881] They appear as series of touching semi-circles edging the circular arches of the triforium of the surviving transept. Such semi-circular lobes edging arch or window are a Muslim motif prominent in their great Mosques.

[882]But was unfortunately destroyed in 1810

[883] Willard, H.M. (1937) `*Progress on the Graphic Reconstruction of the Desiderian Abbey at Monte Cassino*', American Journal of Archeology', vol.41, no.1, p.112, and Willard, H. M. (1935), '*Desiderian Basilica at Monte Cassino (1066-1071)*', American Journal of Archeology', vol.39, no.1, p116.

[884] Dance, E.H. (1957), '*Europe and the Old World*', Book 1, 1st published in 1947, Longmans Greeen and Co, London, New York and Toronto,p.115.

[885] Shakespeare William and Fletcher John (1998) '*The Two Noble Kinsmen*', Oxford University Press, p.215

[886] Ibid. page?

[887] Herbermann C.G et al. (1913), '*The Catholic Encyclopedia: an International Work of Reference on the Constitution Doctrine*', the Encylopedia Press New York, p.690

[888] Harvey, J. (1973), '*the Master builders*', Thames and Hudson, London, p.95.

[889] Boase, T.S.R. (1967), `*Castels and Churches of the Crusading Kingdom*', Oxford University Press, London, p.104

[890] See also Enlart Camille (1927), '*L'Église du Wast en Boulonnais et Son Portial Arabe*', Gazette des Beaux Arts, vol.15, pp.1-11.

[891] Harvey, J. (1973), '*the Master Builders*', op.cit. p.96

[892] Nicholas Paul and Suzanne Yeager (eds.) (2012), '*Remembering the Crusades: Myth, Image, and Identity*', The johns Hopkins University press, Baltimore, p.118

[893] Briggs Briggs, , M. S. (1931), `*Architecture*', in T. Arnold et al. (1931 eds), The Legacy of Islam, Oxford University Press. pp.155-179, at.p167..

[894]Ibid., p.168.

[895]Ibid., p.168.

[896] Jairazbhoy, R. A. (Rafique Ali), (1972), `*An outline of Islamic Architecture*', Asia Publishing House, London, p.139.

[897] Toy, S. (1939) `Castles', William Heinemann, London.

[898] Braun, H. (1953), `*Historical Architecture, the Development of Structure and Design*', Faber & Faber Ltd. London.

[899] Scott, S.P.(1904), op cit. vol. II, p.513.

[900] Jairazbhoy, R. A. (Rafique Ali) , (1972), op cit. p.44.

[901] In some instances, as in Cordoba, masons used lower voussoirs of a proportionally larger size than the rest of the arch in order to carry the load, see Braun, H. (1953), `*Historical Architecture, the Development of Structure and Design*', Faber & Faber Ltd. London.

[902]Briggs, M.S. (1924) `*Muhammadan Architecture in Egypt and Palestine*', the Clarendon Press, Oxford.

[903] Urice S.K. (1987), '*Qasr Kharana in the Transjordan*'. American Schools of Oriental Research, Durham

[904] Arce Ignacio (2003), '*From the Diaphragm Arches to the Ribbed Vaults, An Hypothesis for the Birth and Development of a Building Technique*', Proceedings of the First International Congress on Construction History, Madrid, 20th-24th January 2003, ed. S. Huerta, Madrid: I. Juan de Herrera, SEDHC, ETSAM, A. E. Benvenuto, COAM, F. Dragados, 2003.

[905] Reuther, O. (1938), '*Parthian Architecture: A History*', in Pope, A.U. ed., A Survey of Persian Art, Oxford University Press, London and New York, pp.411-444.

[906] Dieulafoy, M. (1884), '*l'Art Antique de la Perse*', Librairie central d'Architecture, Paris, pp. 79-88

[907] Bier, L. (1979), '*The "Sasanian Palace" Near Sarvistan*', New York University, Graduate School

[908] Ibid., pp. 79-81

[909] Ibid., p. 83

[910] Godard, A. (1949), '*Voute Iraniennes*', in Athar-e-Iran, vol.4, pp. 185-256.

[911] Due to the lack of any historic record, it was left to estimations, which suggest dates between Abbasids times (after 750) because of the existence of a Minbar (pulpit), and before 789 because of pointed arches not exclusively used. Others date the building back to the Umayyad dynasty.

[912] Choisy, A (1899), '*Histoire de l'Architecture*', 2 /vols, Gauthier Villars, Paris.

[913] Sabouret, V.(1928), '*Les Voutes d'Arêtes Nerveuses*', in le Genie Civil, paris, p.205, citec in Frankl, P. (1960), op cit. p.802.

[914] Violet-le-Duc (1858), '*Dictionnaire Raisonne de l'Architecture Francaise du Onzieme Siecle au Seizieme Siecle*', B. Bance, Paris

[915] Porter, A. K. (1911), '*The Construction of Lombard and Gothic Vaults*', Yale University Press, New Heaven.

[916] Ibid., p.3.

[917] Ibid.

[918] Lethaby, W.R. (1904), '*Medieval Art from the Peace of the Church to the Eve of the Renaissance*', Duckworth &Co, london, Charles Scribner's Sons, New York, Vol.IV, pp100-111, at p.111.

[919] Lambert, E. (1958), op cit. p.208.

[920] Reinaud, M. (1836), '*Invasion des Sarrazins en France et de France en Savoie, en Piémont et Dans la Suisse, Pendant les 8°, 9° et 10° Siècles de Notre ère, d'Après les Auteurs Chrétiens et mahométans Invasion des Sarazins*', librairie orientale de V° Dondey-Dupré Paris, p.297, 298.

[921] Palgrave Francis (1851), '*The History of Normandy and of England*', vol.1, John W. Parer and Son, London, p.416

[922] Haskins, C.H. (1927), '*Studies in Medieval Science*', Unger, New York, p.290, and 281-339.

[923] Lambert ,E. (1933), '*Les Premieres Voutes Nervees Francaises et les Origines de la Croisee d'Ogives*, in Revue archeologique, Vol.2, p.235.

[924] Creswell ,K.A.C. (1958), '*A Short Account of Early Muslim Architecture*', Penguin Books.

[925] Ibn Idhari (1848) '*Al-bayano Al-Moghrib*', ed. R. Dozy, 2 Volumes, Leyde.

[926] Marcais, G. (1954), '*l'Architecture Musulmane d'Occident*', Arts et Metiers Graphiques, Paris.,p.139)

[927] Velazquez Bosco (1912), '*Medina Azzahra y-Alamiriya*', in 8e, Madrid, pp.23-24, cited in Marcais, G. (1954), op cit. p.140.

[928] Willis Frank Roy (1985), '*Western Civilization*', 4th ed. , vol.1.D.C. Heath, p.384

[929] Creswell , K.A.C. (1958), p.228.

[930] Marcais,G. (1954),op cit. p.150.

[931] Harvey, J. (1948), '*Gothic England, a Survey of National Culture, 1300-1550*', Batsford, London, p.55.

[932] Marcais,G. (1954),op cit.

[933] Lambert, E. (1958), op cit.

[934] Rivoira, G.T. (1918), `Moslem Architecture: its Origin and Development', translated by Rushforth, G. Oxford University Press.

[935] Street, G.E. (1865), `Gothic architecture in Spain', John Murray, London.

[936] The original quote in French: *"Et, chose digne de remarque, les arcs qui dans deux travees portent cette coupolette sont au nombre de deux et se croisent a la clef en se coupant a angle droit, exactement comme le feront plus tard les arcs ogives dans les travees gothiques de plan carre. Les architectes arabes ont donc connu et employe des la fin du 10e siecle, pour renforcer leurs voutes, non seulement le principe meme de la nervure, mais encore le systeme d'arcs en croix qui constituera plus tard en France la croisee d'ogives".*

[937] Lambert, E. (1958), op cit. p.40.

[938] Street, G.E. (1865), op cit.

[939] *"A en juger en tout cas d'apres ces curieuses eglises de san Baudelio de Berlanga et de San Millan de la Cogolla, il n'est pas douteux que, des la fin du 10e ciecle et au cours du 11e, la voute nervee avait du devenir d'un usage courant dans l'art hispano-mauresque, et cela non seulement dans les maosquees, mais encore dans les eglises meme du chemin de Saint Jacques ou passeront alors tant de pelerins et de moines francais."*

[940] Lambert, E. (1958), op cit. p.184.

[941] Bevan, B (1938), `History of Spanish Architecture', B.T. Batsford, Ltd. London, p.44.

[942] Dodds, J.D. (1994), `Architecture and Ideology in Early Medieval Spain', Pennsylvania State University Press, USA.

[943] Harvey, J. (1950), `The Gothic World : 1100-1600, a Survey of Architecture and Art', B.T. Batsford Ltd, London, p.vii.

[944] Morino, M. Gomez (1919),`Iglesias Mozarabes, Arte Espagnole de las Siglo ix a xi', Centro de Estudios Historicos, Madrid., pp.303-305.

[945] Ibid., p.57.

[946] Gailliard, G. (1956), `Cluny et l'Espagne dans l'Art Roman du 11eme Siecle', in Bulletin Hispanique, Vol.63, pp.153-160.

[947] Male, E (1928), `Art et Artistes du Moyen Age', Librairie Armand Colin, Paris, p.169

[948] Ibid. p.170.

[949] Lefevre Pontalis (1912), `Bulletin Monumental', Vol.76. Société Fançaise d'Archéologie, Paris.

[950] Dehio, G. & Bezold, G.von. (1892), `Kirchliche Baukunst des Abendlandes.', J. G. Cotta Stuttgart.

[951] Braun, H. (1953), op cit.

[952] Lethaby, W.R. (1926), op cit.

[953] Harvey, J. (1973),op cit. p.24.

[954] Creswell ,K.A.C. (1958), `A Short Account of Early Muslim Architecture', Penguin Books, London. p.14.

[955] Michell, M. et al. (eds.) (1978), `Architecture of the Islamic World', Thames and Hudson, London, p.143.

[956] Briggs, M.S. (1924), op cit.

[957] See Mason William (1827), ʻThe Works of Thomas Gray: Collated From the Various Editions ; with Memoirs of his Life and Writings, op.cit.p.188

[958] Male, E (1928), `Art et Artistes du Moyen Age', Librairie Armand Colin, Paris.

[959] Warten, T. et al. (1808), `Essays on Gothic Architecture', 3rd edition. London.

[960] Briggs, , M. S. (1931), op cit.

[961] Ibid., p. 174.

[962] Dan Cruickhank (edt.) (1996), `Banister Fletcher's A History of Architecture', 20th Edition, Architectural Press, p.480.

CHAPTER SIX

The Contribution of Muslims to European Art and Architecture in Renaissance Period

Perhaps the major characteristic defining European art in the Renaissance was its freedom from the church domination; consequently one would expect a substantial increase in non-European elements as the new "secular" artists could freely employ popular foreign themes. Indeed, Western historians acknowledge the foreign influence but regrettably, they relate it solely to China denying any Muslim contribution. In a recent book, Sweetman[963] rightly agreed that this is a plain denial of the truth. If one compares the degree and nature of the exposure of the West to Muslim and Chinese motifs and art themes, the situation becomes clear as to which side had the more influential role. Historical sources indicate that European relations with China started after Marco Polo's journey (1275) and reached their peak only in the late 17th to mid-18th centuries. Such connections were limited to trade, and were established by companies such as the European East India Companies, which were trading with China, India and South East Asian ports. Among the long list of their imports was Chinese Porcelain, the influence of which is traceable in the European decorative style of 1750's known as Rococo.

Sweetman argued that with the Muslims, the situation is substantially different as the nature and time span of these connections indicate that the West established an in-depth knowledge of Islam and its intellectual and artistic culture much earlier than that of China[964]. The religious "common grounds' which are connected to worship of the same God, a common ancestor and sometimes the same moral message is another area of meeting between the two despite their frequent enmity. Historically, Christianity was born in Jerusalem that later became the second most important city of Islam.

Islam and the West co- existed long before the West discovered China. As outlined in previous chapters, Muslims and Christians co-existed in Europe in Andalusia for over seven centuries (8th-15th centuries), in Sicily for over two centuries (8th-10th centuries), in the Balkans for over four centuries (from 15th – present), and in neighbouring North Africa for over 13 centuries (from the 7th century until the present). Historical evidence shows that contacts with the Muslim lands had never ceased even during times of war. Medieval contacts have already been discussed in the previous chapter, but by the 15th century, they

344

increased substantially as rising Christian sea power encouraged trade ventures. The accounts of trading centres of Medieval and Renaissance Europe, Florence, Amalfi, Venice and Marseille, reveal substantially more commercial dealing with the Muslim world than with China or any other part of the world[965]. According to Holmes "*Amalfi's prosperity was based on its trade with the Muslim World*"[966]. The crusades and the establishment of the Latin Kingdom in the East cemented further these relations and "*Cities such as Venice, while part of the Latin Kingdom, formed hubs of trade with the East. Marseille rivalled Venice as a coastal port city heavily dependent on trade with Islam. Such cities competed with one another in the Latin Kingdom of the East, and were just as willing to side with the Muslims in the interest of trade as to defend one another out of shared faith.*"[967]

Key imports of these centres were pottery, spices, silk, cotton and gold. The role these centres played in conveying Islamic designs and artistic motifs to Europe was considerable. Muslim textile manufacturing centres such as Mosul, Damascus and Fustat had worldwide trade links and the presence of names such as Damask, Muslin and Fustian is a clear indication of these strong trade links and European acceptance and fascination with Muslim products. This brings to mind the concept used by Brotton "The Renaissance Bazaar" where he rightly argues that: "*modern Europe emerged in this period by competing and exchanging ideas and commodities with the eastern (and predominantly Islamic) neighbours. These east-west transactions laid the bases for the great art and culture that we now associate with the Renaissance.*"[968]

Several documented instances show Europe imported, among other goods, Muslim books. Cosimo de'Medici (1389-1464) is a good example of how important was the collection of Muslim intellectual and artistic objects. This rich Florentine patron and founder of the famous banking Medici family ordered, in 1444, the building of the library at the monastery of Saint Marco, Florence, to store the precious Islamic and Greek books and art works, which he acquired, thus, establishing the Biblioteca Marciana, the first public library in Europe[969]. His grandson Lorenzo de'Medici assumed his role and founded the Bilioteca Medicea Laurenziana at their family palace.

345

Geopolitics also provided opportunities for many friendly treaties and alliances between some Muslim countries and Europeans. The rising powers of Ottoman Turkey and Spain drove many European countries to establish relations with various Muslim parts.[970] Countries such as Britain and France developed good relationships with Turkey in an attempt to avoid confrontation while maintaining their guard against the might of Spain. In 1588, for example, England's Queen Elizabeth 1st proposed the alliance of Protestant England with the Ottomans against Roman Catholic Spain and formerly requested Sultan Murad for naval assistance against the Spanish Armada. These relations were greatly strengthened by the relative peace and general improvement in economic and social structures of the European continent. The British established the Levant Company in 1581, giving trade with the Muslims a great boost. The Company installed agents in Constantinople, Aleppo and many other Muslim cities. Because of this, the import of carpets and other Muslim artefacts was increased substantially. In 1585, five of the Company's ships arrived in London from Syria with a large cargo of Muslim goods including 13 carpets.[971]

The French followed suite and in 1664 they set up the French East India Company to trade and provide continuous contact with the East, especially Persia and India. A few years later, in 1673, the director of this company was sent, by the French Royal court, to the Shah of Persia to obtain trade privileges for his country. This agreement gave great impetus to trade exchange between the two countries, which was maintained through the old route, and the ports of the eastern Mediterranean.

The 17th century was the golden age of Dutch relations with the Muslim world, particularly Indonesia, Mogul India, Ottoman Turkey, Safavid Iran, and Morocco. The Dutch had strong trade relations with these countries, which were translated in good political and cultural interaction, which encouraged the establishment of Arabic studies in their colleges and universities.

From the above, it is difficult to understand Western denial of the role of Muslims at a time when they emphasise the role of China and other cultures. In this concern, Sweetman exclaimed, *"we would expect Islam to make a more complex and insistent disturbance on the Western consciousness, in many level, than China, powerful as the emanation from that country were."*[972]

Cultural Encounters and Sources of Information about Islam in Renaissance Europe

The factors described earlier enabled considerable cultural exchange between the two worlds as each of them developed a good knowledge of the other. During the Renaissance, the Muslim East never ceased to attract the attention and curiosity of the West, partly due to Biblical ties and partly due to the new information coming from travellers and traders, which raised interest in the discoveries of the East. *"The Islamic Orient is, for us, a companion almost as ancient and familiar as the biblical, at times re-teaching us Hebrew through Arabic. It is the Orient most acclaimed in our literary traditions, which have, in every case abandoned other Orients whenever there has been a massive return of the picturesque Musulman whose charm recaptures poets and story tellers through the glamour of the Thousand and One Night."*[973] This was the age of the birth of early "Orientalism" as the interest in Islam and Muslim culture required varied and more accurate information, initiating an unprecedented appeal to the study of the Arabic language, which resulted in the foundation of chairs of Arabic studies in many European universities.[974]

Various accounts about the East reached Europe through a variety of channels. Muslim merchants (especially Turkish) visiting different capitals of the continent, especially Paris and London, have provided detailed information and the goods they imported and sold reached large sections of European populations. Luxury consumer goods, in particular, freely circulated beyond the geographical boundaries of the two worlds. For their part, European traders visiting commercial centres, such as Aleppo, Damascus and Istanbul, in Muslim lands often brought back items and souvenirs and told stories of their encounters to the fascination of many of their audiences. An evidence of this is a considerable amount of artwork, which depicted Muslim themes during this period, did not reflect direct experience of their artists but consisted merely of their imagination of what they thought to be. There is also the literary evidence found in Renaissance work, such as those discussed in the cultural sources of Gothic in the previous chapter.

The second means was the personal visits undertaken by travellers and explorers to various parts of the Muslim World and who published stories of their encounters often containing detailed descriptions and illustrations. Interest in the Muslim world was gaining momentum as the fanaticism of the Middle Ages weakened and the Renaissance curiosity to finding different themes and alternatives to their art became an overwhelming desire. This coincided with increasing interest in geographical discoveries and the rise of foreign travel leading to the appearance of many books and portraits about the East. Key influential events were, in particular, the trips of the Italian Pietro della Valle to Istanbul and Persia in 1614 and 1617 respectively; George Sandys to Istanbul, Cairo and Jerusalem before 1615; Peter Mundy (1596-1667) to Istanbul and India, and Thomas Herbert (1606-1682) to Persia. Visits to the Levant included those undertaken by William Lithgow in 1612, Fynes Moryson in 1617, and Sir Henry Blount in 1634.

The collection of Muslim artwork, especially manuscripts, was a priority of these travellers. Archbishop Laud (1573-1645), founder of chairs of Arabic at universities of Cambridge (1632) and Oxford (1636), worked tirelessly to collect Muslim manuscripts[975]. The order made by King Charles I on 21st February 1634 to the East India Company requesting each of their returning ships to obtain for him Arabic and Persian manuscripts also testifies these ambitions. Edward Pococke (1640-1691), a colleague of Laud, also collected Arabic and Jewish books and treatises. He studied literature and served as chaplain at the consulate in Aleppo then moved to Istanbul where he was employed by the English embassy there. Pococke initiated a truly informed study of Islam and his contribution included teaching Arabic at Oxford and the translation of Arabic manuscripts including the book of collection of Arabic proverbs of Ahmed al-Maydani (13th century) *"Amthal Al-'Arab"*, and *"Specimen"* of the Syrian historian Abu al-Faraj, known as Bar-Hebraeus Gregorius, (1226-86).[976]

In the Netherlands, studies of Arabic also started in earnest soon after the foundation of Leiden University in 1576. Leiden became a very active centre of Arabists, especially after the arrival of Franciscus Raphelengius (1539-1597) from Antwerp in 1585. Raphelengius collaborated with Josef Scaliger (1540-1609) to launch Arabic studies and he made Arabic types cut with which he printed Arabic passages in the revised edition of Scaliger's *De emendatione temporum*[977]. Towards the end of his life, he worked on an Arabic-Latin dictionary, which was printed by his sons in 1613 to become the first of its kind in Europe[978]. Scaliger's pupil Thomas Erpenius (1596-1667) taught Arabic there and had a richer collection of oriental manuscripts than his predecessors had. Shortly before his death in 1624, he finalised his edition of *Ta'rikh al-Muslimin* of al-Makin, Egyptian historian of the thirteenth century. Translated as *Historia saracenica* and published by his pupil Jacob Golius (1596-1667), the work was of revolutionary importance in Europe[979]. In 1622, Golius was sent with an embassy to the Moroccan ruler Mulay Zaydan, after that he travelled to Aleppo with the Dutch consul and subsequently joined the Dutch ambassador in Istanbul.[980] He brought back from these trips an immense collection of manuscripts, most of which entered the Leiden library. He published in 1653 his Arabic Latin dictionary, a considerably improved version of that of Raphelengius. Another Dutch Levinus Warner (d.1665) also succeeded in obtaining an important number of Muslim manuscripts while living in Istanbul, as the Resident General of the Netherlands, for over twenty years.[981]

In Italy, the Medici family made substantial contribution to disseminating knowledge about the Muslim world. In addition to the collections of Cosomo and Lorenzo, their printing press in Rome produced, under the charge of Giambattista Raimondi, a series of important publications in and on Arabic between 1590 and 1610. [982] With his collection of manuscripts, Cardinal Federigo Borromeo set up in 1609 the Milan library, from which Antonio Giggei published an Arabic-Latin lexicon in 1632.

In France, Guillaume Postel issued and held the first chair of Arabic in 1539, in the College de France, on his return from the Levant[983]. He mastered Arabic that he wrote a book on the Arabic grammar, *Grammatica Arabica*, introducing Arabic to the public for the first time. Later, the Arabic linguist, Antoine Galland (1646-1715) visited the Middle East in 1679 and translated *the Arabian Nights.*[984] He also helped Jean Baptiste Colbert[985] with his collection of oriental books and manuscripts. Barthelemy d'Herbelot (1625-1695) published his Bibliotheque Orientale[986] (1679) with a preface by Galland. This encyclopaedic work provided a detailed explanation of a large number of Eastern cultural aspects arranged in alphabetical order, touching generally on Muslim cities, customs, costumes and history as well as architecture and arts, but it lacked illustrations.[987] Jean Baptiste Tavernier (1605-1686) was among the first Europeans to see Taj Mahal at Agra in 1641; just eleven years after Shah Jehan started its construction. Tavernier published his work *Six Voyages* in Paris in 1676 and a year later, it was translated into English[988]. In addition to Taj Mahal, he was fascinated by Constantinople (Istanbul) and Persia. In his footsteps, followed other influential French travellers including Francois Bernier (1620-1688) and Jean de Thevenot (1633-1667), who both toured the Muslim World, including Mughal India. Thevenot published his travels in *Voyages* in Paris in 1684 and in London[989] in 1687, while Bernier published them in *Travels in the Mogul Empire.*[990] John Chardin (1643-1713) explored the East, including Persia and Isfahan, and the works he produced were made available in both French and English, before settling in London to become a member of the Royal Society. The work of the artist traveller, Guillaume Joseph Grelot[991] (b.ca. 1630), *Relation d'un Voyage de Constantinople* published in France in 1680 and later in English in 1683, is in some respect unique as it provided unprecedented detailed illustrations of Turkish life, particularly his descriptions of Istanbul's main mosques, baths, bazaars and public buildings. About this time, an American named Elihu Yale (1649-1721), widely known for his connection with the college of Connecticut, bearing his name, which later became the University of Yale, spent most of his life in India. He worked first in the service of East India Company, then Governor of Madras (between 1687-1692) and later Director of the Company of East India. Yale worked first in the service of East India Company, then as Governor of Madras between 1687 and 1692, and later as Director of the East India Company. He collected Mogul miniatures and among his collection were 23 Indian pieces in glass frames. This collection is thought to have had a strong influence on woven tapestries in Yale and particularly on the appearance of what is known as the 'Indian manner' at Soho in London. This consists of elements such as fishermen, flowering trees, and trabeated buildings by using straight horizontal beams or lintels instead of arches. [992]

The role played by artists and their illustrations in popularising Muslim themes as well as enhancing the knowledge and awareness of Muslim life was decisive. The first contact Renaissance artists made with the Muslim East took place as early as the 15th century when Italian artists developed the interest in Muslim and Turkish costumes. The Sultan Mohammed II, "Al-Fateh" or the Conqueror who entered Constantinople in 1453, employed Italian artists at his court, among them the painter Gentile Bellini and the painter medallist Constanzo de Ferrara, who made portraits of him[993]. John Baptiste Vanmour (1671-1737) settled in Constantinople and became the royal painter for Ahmed III, and recorded the parties, receptions and hunting arties. He also worked for the Dutch and French ambassadors and the consul for the Levant. Another influential artist is the Swiss Jean-Etienne Liotard (1702-1789) who stayed in Constantinople for five years, FROM 1738 to 1742, living and dressing like a native Turkish. His female portraits of sitters *en sultane* helped greatly to diffuse the fashion for portraying Turkish dress throughout Europe, they "*catered to a Turkomania which spread among the aristocracy of eighteenth- century Europe- particularly of France. This was expressed in balls and masquerades costumed a la Turque, while the aristocracy had themselves painted in Turkish dress.*"[994]

Venetian painters were renowned for their use of oriental figures in their paintings. The *Reception of the Ambassadors* (Louvres), by an unknown artist, depicts members of a Venetian embassy with Muslim subjects in an entirely Muslim setting. This unique example demonstrates the respect Europeans had for Muslim and Turkish clothing and lifestyle[995]. However, Raby claims that it was a depiction of Mamluk ceremony in Damascus rather than an Ottoman ceremony in Cairo as had commonly been thought. He dates it between 1495 and 1499[996]. Further additions to the knowledge of Turkish life and costume took place in the 16th century. Two artists having particular impact were Pieter Coecke van Aelst (1502-1550) and Melchior Lorichs of Flensburg (1527-1583) both of whom lived in Constantinople and made woodcuts of people, costumes and buildings, which they published in a book form.[997]

In England, the love of Lady Mary Wortley (1689-1762), the wife of the British ambassador in Constantinople, for Turkish life and dress played a significant role in providing publicity for Turkish elements[998]. Not only did she write about her fascination with Turkish life but also wore Turkish dresses as demonstrated in her portrait `*Sultana Wortley Montago'*. She even spoke of how Islam gave Muslim women greater freedom than women did in the West[999]. Another portrait showed Sir Francis Dashwood, the owner of West Wycombe Park, Buckinghamshire in a Turkish dress with the inscription: `*El-Faquir Dashwood Pasha'*. The attraction to Muslim and eastern dress continued until the late 18th century. For instance, Andrew Geddes (1783-1844) was portrayed in Turkish clothing in 1817.

Another influential work was the work of the Austrian architect of the Baroque style, Johann Bernhard Fischer von Erlach (1656-1737*) A Plan of Civil and Historical Architecture*, which ran to three editions in 1721, 1730, and 1737[1000]. His accurate illustrations of Muslim buildings such as the Suleimaniya Mosque, al-Haram at Makkah, Prophet's Mosque at Medina, and the Maydan of Isfahan (Maydan-i-Shah) had much to offer the architects, particularly in terms of silhouette and mass. In England, these illustrations had considerable influence on Renaissance architects, especially on the design of garden buildings.

Perhaps the most influential artist in the 18th century was William Hodges (1744-1797), an artist and traveller who spent four years in India between 1780-1784 collecting visual evidence of Indian buildings which he published *Select Views in India* (1785-1788)[1001]. Hodges was particularly fascinated by the mosque of Chunar Gur and Taj Mahal of which he wrote: "*The whole together appears like a most perfect pearl on an azure ground. The effect is such as, I confess, I never experienced from any work of art. The fine materials, the beautiful forms, and the symmetry of the whole, with the judicious choice of situation, far surpass anything I ever beheld."*[1002]

The fourth channel was through glittering public events. Historical sources reveal that the French King, Louis XIV (1638- 1715), was renowned for his love and support for arts and the courtly life. He centralised the arts under the control of the crown and its government and it was during his reign that the French Baroque style reached its culmination in late 17th century[1003]. He was particularly an admirer of the Islamic World, about which he accumulated a considerable knowledge through the contemporary travellers Francois de la Boullaye-le-Gouz and Jean Baptiste Tavernier. Naderzad reports that Louis had helped in the publication of "Voyages et Observations" of La Boullaye[1004] in 1653, which was about his trip to the Muslim East[1005]. He also related that la Boullaye arrived at the Royal court wearing Persian dress. Louis also had in his service two renowned Arab linguists, Laurent d'Arvieux and Galland. His reign is also notable for the expansion of royal parties using firework displays, processions and ceremonial tents in similar fashion to that used in Turkey during this time.[1006] Meantime, the increasing number of ambassadorial exchanges between the East and Europe and the numerous appearances of Turkish Embassies in Paris, in his reign, had its impact on many aspects of the Western life, especially the arts. There is at least one evidence of a Turkish ambassadorial delegation recorded by Charles Nicolas Cochin's engraving in the Galerie des Glaces of Versailles of the Royal masked ball[1007], which was organised to celebrate the marriage of the Dauphin, the eldest and only surviving son of King Louis 15th, to Maria Theresa of Spain in 1745. The painting depicted a number of Turkish guests with their turbans present at this ball. Louis's connection with the East and particularly Turkey has positively contributed to the development of the French Baroque art.

The French admiration of Islamic lifestyle and motifs was not unique. English interest in the Muslim World started as early as the 1630s when English universities endowed the first chairs in Arabic language. The Oxford Orientalist Thomas Hyde (1636-1703) worked on Muslim manuscripts and collected a number of them. John Ogilby, publisher and writer of geographical works, published his work *"Asia atlas"* in 1673 where he recounts the use of *Jade*[1008] in medical treatment by the Moors[1009]. Furthermore, the Royal Society for Natural Philosophy, established in 1661, had among its members, Sir John Chardin (1643-1713), an expert on Islamic matters, as well as Sir Christopher Wren

(1632-1723), the founder of the Saracen theory in Gothic architecture. This had a great impact on disseminating information about the Muslim World and its art and architecture in particular. Great interest was also generated by the publication of Simon Ockley of his book *History of the Saracens,*[1010] published between 1708 and 1718. Under King Charles II (1660-1685), who led a similar lifestyle to his French cousin King Louis XIV, courtly life as well as arts considerably blossomed. In addition to his Palace at Winchester, which he built to rival Versailles[1011], he consumed luxurious Eastern and Persian products. It was reported by John Evelyn that in 18 October 1666, he publicly appeared in a Persian vest or waistcoat,,[1012] *"To Court, it being the first time his Majesty put himself solemnly into the Eastern fashion of vest, changing doublet, stiff collar, bands and cloaks, into a comely vest after the Persian fashion, with girdle or straps and shoe strings and buckles of which some were set with precious stones"*[1013]. The vest became so fashionable that portraits of all the men illustrated during this period wore their coats cut wide open on front *"so that the vest of rich brocade dominates*[1014]*"*

Muslim Motifs in the West

The appeal of Muslim motifs is no mystery, *"their obvious aesthetic quality- their harmony, opulence, and often the great richness of their colours. A further asset, especially in the early periods, was the high degree of technical skill evident in the execution, far surpassing anything possible in the West. To this was added their exotic quaintness and, what was particularly important, their true assumed association with the Holy Land and specific saintly figures."*[1015] Muslim art works have common features, which give them a remarkable coherence and unity, regardless of the country or the time in which they were created. The combination of colourful vegetal and abstract geometrical forms presented in a precise mathematical and logical order appeal to any audience. Linda Komaroff, Curator of Islamic Art at the Los Angeles County Museum of Art, observes, *"Islamic art is perhaps the most accessible expression of a complex civilization that often seems enigmatic to outsiders. Through its brilliant use of colour and its superb balance between design and form, Islamic art creates an immediate visual impact. Its strong aesthetic appeal transcends distances in time and space, as well as differences in language, culture, and creed. Islamic art not only invites a closer look but also beckons the viewer to learn more."*[1016]

Neutrality is another quality of the majority of these motifs as objects and designs were prepared free of any distasteful or provocative iconography: *"there was no specifically Muslim iconography or overt religious symbolism, which would have been offensive to the Christian mind."*[1017] Although Arabic writing had a symbolic meaning in the Muslim world, and certain formulae contain religious invocations including the name of ALLAH, the west apparently did not understand it as such. As this writing often occurred on Biblical figures, including the Jewish High Priest, it may have been interpreted as ancient Hebrew script or at least that used by the New Testament figures and by Christian saints.[1018]

Decorative Art and the Arabesque

According to Ward, the fertilisation of European ornament in the 16th century was at the hands of Arabesque[1019]. At first, imitation of Arabesque designs was carried out in individual decorative work, and this became very popular, resulting in the appearance of a large number of collections and published material. One of the earliest books to be published on the subject appeared in 1527, by Giovanni Antonio Tagliente, entitled "Essempi di recammi". It was essentially on embroidery but contained a good number of arabesque designs[1020]. However, the first comprehensive and most popular collection was that of Francesco Pellegrino (1530), a Florentine in the service of King Francis I (1494-1547) of France, entitled *"la fleur de la science de pourtraiture, patrons de broderie, facon arabicque et ytalique*, Paris[1021]. The collection contained a series of arabesque reproductions on woodcut. After this, a large number of collections and works emerged, most of them coming from Venice.[1022]

The geometrical pattern of Arabesque was particularly popular. The ability of these patterns to adapt to different surfaces, whether they were of architectural, ceramic, textile, leather, paper, wood or iron, made them very suitable to architectural décor essentially in ceilings and internal surfaces. There are a few examples of its adaptation in European context. The so-called cosmati flooring, which consists of inlaid geometrical designs, applied on marble and found in many churches around Europe including[1023] the Basilica St. Marco, Venice, or that of Dumo Pisa, Italy or that of Presbytery of Westminster Abbey in London, which is thought to be made by Odericus of Rome in 1286.[1024] An imitation of these patterns is found in pavement of the Presbytery of Norwich cathedral, made in 1878 by Sir Arthur Blomfield. In ceilings, there is the Rotunda of Ballyfin, now a secondary school for boys and girls in Ireland (1822), which was designed by Richard Morrison (1776-1849)[1025] (fig.140). In Westminster Abbey, bands of eight pointed stars and other patterns decorate the retable. These star patterns also decorate the four corners of the glass dome of the gallery Galleria Vittorio Emanuele II in Milan, Italy, built between 1865 and 1878.[1026]

In addition to possessing similar flowing and interlacing characteristics to the plant type of Arabesque, these consist mainly of geometrical "angular" shapes and constructions crossing each other, and sometimes overlapping in a pattern to form stars and polygons. The organisational system is made in way of zooming inward and outward while at the same time incorporating a variety of fascinating visual displays. As one proceeds from the inner star or polygon leading to the outer background where this star develops into a bigger complex star interlacing with others to form the bigger frame before he is drawn back to the inner shape once again. Christie claimed that this geometrical patterning was derived from Roman mosaic patterns used in first century pavement.[1027] It is difficult to accept simple primitive geometrical lines as the source of such complex designs, which obviously required a good knowledge of both mathematics and geometry, sciences firmly established only under Muslim scholars. In relation to the techniques used in the compilation of these shapes, Critchlow provided an explanation suggesting the design was based on the use of the compass, ruler and strings held between points, a technique handed down from generation to generation. Artisans drew these patterns on sheets, which enabled them to carry them from one place to another.[1028] Evidence of this is the collection belonging to Mirza Akbar, a Persian decorator from the 15th century which contained sheets wrapped in a leather scroll. This is now in the Victoria and Albert Museum. The recently discovered Topkapi Scroll is another example endorsing such views. A set of well-preserved scrolls that contains 114 coloured drawings of medieval Muslim architects and compiled by the mathematician Ghiat al-Din al-Kashi (Iran, 1380-1429).[1029] A study of the scrolls was carried out by Necipoğlu revealed astonishing facts connecting much of these patterns to mathematics suggesting that these artists must have had a very good understanding of the developments made in mathematics. She put forward three major connections with mathematics suggesting that artisans were literate and had good training in mathematics, which was accessible to them through Muslim mathematicians. As noted in chapter one started in earnest in the eighth century. The artisans had opportunities to discuss their geometrical concerns with theoretical mathematicians some of whom were themselves involved in developing patterns that are more complex. Finally, the dissemination of these patterns was achieved mainly through the spread of mathematical works especially towards the 11th century.[1030]

Necipoglu's theory was confirmed recently by Harvard University. A recent study of medieval Muslim geometrical patterns revealed some of the patterns use principles established only in the last few decades by modern mathematicians. BBC reported on February 24th 2007 that Researchers in the US, Peter Lu and Paul Steinhard, have found examples in some girih tile designs in Darb-i-Umam shrine in Isfahan, Iran, built in 1453, which use the concept of quasicrystalline geometry. Harvard's graduate Peter Lu said in the BBC interview, "*They (Muslims) made tilings that reflect mathematics that were so sophisticated that we didn't figure it out until the last 20 or 30 years.*" The Islamic designs echo quasicrystalline geometry in that both use symmetrical polygonal shapes to create patterns that can be extended indefinitely. Until now, the conventional view was that the complicated star-and-polygon patterns of Islamic design were conceived as zigzagging lines drafted using straightedge rulers and compasses[1031]. The research indicates that by 1200 an important breakthrough had occurred in Islamic mathematics and design, as illustrated by these geometric designs. Future research may reveal significant clues, which can improve our understanding of how these patterns were drawn and what they mean.

The influence of Arabesque was widespread. Indeed, "*European fascination with Islamic aesthetics from the Middle Ages to nineteenth century orientalism is a commonplace in the history of Western and Islamic art*"[1032]. The famous knot, for example, was used on a wide scale by the Norman king Henry VIII appearing in his portrait on the border of his cloak and on the curtains. The Muslim knot so fascinated Leonardo da Vinci (1452-1518) that he produced two plates of six knots, which were later reproduced in circular copper engravings by one of his followers in Milan around 1483 and 1499.[1033] The German artist, Albrecht Durer (1471-1528) imitated these works between 1505 and 1507.[1034] This motif was made known to Europeans through engravings, pottery, textiles and metalwork, which were mostly imported from Damascus and spread through the agency of Venice and other Italian merchant cities. The spread of the knot and Arabesque designs was later to introduce the Moresque fashion consisting mainly of interlacing arabesque and floral designs, which widely used in most metal, wood-cutting, bookbinding, fabric embroidery, and all sorts of crafts throughout

Europe in the late 1530's. The Muslim influence extended to other art works, glass, woodcarving, metalwork and bookbinding. The prominent role in this area of influence has been the friendly relations between the Mamluk of Egypt and Italy: *"In this context the relationship between Renaissance Italy and the Muslim Mediterranean world occupies a prominent place. Mamluk art is known to have had an impact on Venetian craftsmanship in glass, metalwork, and other media."*[1035]

The second major factor enabling the spread of Arabesque designs was through bookbinding. *"We find geometrical designs on the fifteenth century Italian and French decorated books, knotted orders and patterns, oval centre medallions and Arabesque, all very suggestive of Islamic influence."* [1036] Muslims used both vegetal and geometrical arabesque in their bookbinding industry, particularly in the decoration of the Holy Quran. The numerous manuscripts of various designs, which reached Europe, as mentioned earlier, provided artists with a good exposure to various forms of arabesque. They soon imitated these patterns in their books. They were used by French *"doreurs"* who worked on gilding books such as the work done for Jean Grolier (Vicomte of Aguisiy 1479-1565), the Treasurer General of France (1547 - 1565). The bookbinders of Tudor and Elizabethan England also copied them. The Basel print of the Quran made in 1543, for Thomas Wotton (1527-1587), illustrates the incorporation of both vegetal and geometrical arabesque.[1037] Hans Holbein the younger is also known to have composed arabesque designs in 1537.[1038] Through this means, Arabesque became commonly used in public and private domains appearing in many objects in daily use.

The publication of books of ornamentation containing details of arabesque designs. The book of Thomas Geminus (1548) entitled *Morysse and Damaschin renewed and encreased, very profitable for goldsmythes and embroderars* (London) was particularly influential.[1039] The title also shows the popularity of Muslim arabesque and ornament in Europe, which made it a source of profitable work. Jean de Gourment published another book in 1560, under the title *Livre de moresques* in Paris[1040]. In it, de Gourment presented a variety of arabesque designs with their suggested usage on particular delicate parts of garments, such as on sleeves, collars and on coverlets. The term *Moresque* was used by both authors referred to the Moorish type of arabesque known in Italy, and used by Tagliente, as *moreschi*. The Moresque decoration became a fashion widely used in English silver and in designs for male and female fashions during the Elizabethan period. Sweetman summarised the sphere of influence of Muslim decorative art in the following: "*If we look back from here (1500) to 1660 at the fortunes of Islamic and Islamic-inspired art in France and England, we have an overwhelming impression of the importance of decorative arts. The style had a part to play at the Baroque courts of Europe...In England, under later Stuarts, as under the Tudors, the brilliance of Islamic textiles and the captivating intricacy of the arabesque found a happy correspondence with existing tastes and also made notable contribution to them.*"[1041]

Calligraphy is another form of art that had many admirers and exercised strong influence on European decorative art. The decorative use of letters is not limited to Muslim civilisation it is found in other cultures in Ancient Egypt, China and Japan. Islamic calligraphy was, however, developed independently as the wide difference between the two languages in the way and the direction they are written make the suggestion of any link between them inconceivable. It is true that the ancient Egyptians widely used hieroglyphics on wall paintings, but these had no decorative purpose[1042]. The development of calligraphy as a decorative art was due to a number of factors. The importance Muslims attach to their Holy Book, the Quran, which promises Divine blessings to those who read and write it down, was decisive. The pen, a symbol of knowledge, is given a special significance by the verse: "*Read! Your Lord is the Most Bounteous, Who has taught the use of the pen, taught man what he did not know*"(96:3-5). Calligraphy was not merely to provide decoration but also to worship and remember Allah (or God). The importance of Arabic language in Islam is another factor; its use is compulsory in prayers, the language of the Quran, and believed to be the language of Paradise.[1043] Arabic calligraphy was generally developed from two distinctive script forms[1044]. The *Kufic* script, derived from the city of Kufa where it was invented by scribes of the Quran[1045], has a rectangular form, which made them well suited for architectural and surface use. The other forms were developed from al-*Naskhi* script of generally round and cursive characteristics. They are al-Raqai', al-thuluth, Diwani, Persian and Ottoman, often differentiated by the varying degree of refinement, size, thickness and cursiveness.[1046]

Historical sources show many instances where Muslim calligraphy was either directly copied or modified to develop different styles in a number of European art works. In chapter three, we provided some examples where Arabic quotes or phrases were copied in woodcarvings, textiles, and bronze work. The cases of the door carving of Le Puy and the embroidery of the coronation mantle of King Roger II of Sicily, and the decoration of the Irish 9th century cross are reminders of such influence. In Notre-Dame cathedral of Le Puy, the door

358

carving was no more than the Arabic inscription in pseudo-Kufic script of a typical sacred phrase in Islam "*There is no other God beside Allah*", Emile Mâle commented: "*Here the presence of Islam is evident and any doubts we may have had are hereby dispelled.*"[1047] According to some scholars, carved inscriptions of Gothic work originated from *Kufic* inscriptions of the Mosque of Ibn Tulun (Cairo, built in 879). They were first copied in France imitating Cordoban and Andalusian calligraphy, later spread to the rest of Europe.[1048] In the Renaissance, the inspirational side was the most influential leading to the emergence of many ornamental forms and patterns used for the decoration of a large variety of media. The term used to describe these is, *mock Arabic* or *simulated Arabic[1049]*. Christie studied some of these forms and produced two interesting articles,[1050] which both appeared in the Burlington Magazine for Connoisseurs. His conclusion is that these patterns are "*certainly, the result of a succession of gradual changes, brought about by causes that came into operation as soon as craftsmen began to use Arabic inscriptions on their work. In the process of variation, decorative qualities first appeared as something in the nature of by-products, and, in the perfection of these new found powers, the original information-giving purpose was lost.*"[1051] An example of this "mock-Arabic" calligraphy is found in Gentile da Fabriano's "*Adoration of the Magi,*" painted in 1423. They decorate bands edging a woman's shawl as well as in the embroidery on the sash of a squire from shoulder to waist.[1052]

The Textile and Carpet Industry

The Muslim world produced textiles in a large quantities and varieties as wholesale production of wool and cotton available in most regions Iran, Egypt, North Africa and Spain provided continuous and cheap supply of materials. Cotton, native to India, was first imported into the Levant then spread into Egypt and southern Spain, from which it was transmitted into Europe. Silk was made in Syria and Palestine and other additional supplies were imported from China. Textile industry reached its golden age with the appearance of many textile centres, which excelled in particular products. Shiraz, for example, was famous for its woollen cloths; Baghdad for its baldachin hangings and tabby silks; Khuzestan for fabrics of camel's or goat's hair; Khorasan for its sofa covers; Tyre for its carpets; Bukhara for its prayer rugs; and Herat for its gold brocades. Several Mamluk silks mostly in fragments have survived,[1053] an example of this is the silk cope found in St. Mary's church, at Danzig. Sweetman established that the silk belonged to an Egyptian Mamluk Sultan, which was inscribed with *'the learned Sultan'* dating from the 14th century, *"tapis Sarrasinois was known in the France of Louis IX and in 1277 there were trade privileges for it in Paris. In the fourteenth century, woven Islamic hangings were prized in Arras. Silks too were by then a precious part of church treasures; a cope from Mamluk Egypt inscribed in Arabic with the words 'the learned Sultan' was in St Mary's church, Danzig, early in the same century."*[1054]

The appeal of Muslim textile products, which was well developed in the middle Ages (chapter 4), intensified in the Renaissance. The acquisition of Muslim textile products mainly from Persia, Turkey and India played a complementary role in popularising Muslim art and motifs in the West. The use of contrast, repetition and alternation were the main artistic rules composing the delicate textile design. With their sophisticated patterns and colours, these products became a major attraction competing with this industry in Venice, Lucca and Florence. This popularity reached its peak in the 17th century, the period of great development in the trade relations with England. Historical sources indicate that in 1616 the Shah credited England with 3,000 bales to encourage trade[1055]. Since then, Persian silk was on the top of the list of imports; the ship "Royal Anne" brought in 1619 some 11 bales of Persian silk that were shipped first from Persia to Surat (India) then to England. Between 1603 and 1625, King James I considered establishing the silk industry in England. He acquired the silkworms and made special arrangements for their nursery in his country estates and in his gardens at Whitehall[1056]. He also ordered a French John Bonoeil, who was the manager of the royal silk works to compile a treatise dealing with techniques of silk production, which was published in 1622[1057]. This was a failure because they used the wrong species of mulberry on which the silkworm caterpillars feed.

The East India Company, through its trade links with India, introduced the Indian Chintz to England. This consisted of a painted cotton textile knitted in a combination of Muslim designs and Indian tradition. These imports were so important that they competed with local textile production in both France and Britain that historical sources talked of complaints from local silk weavers in 1685 forcing the British government in 1700 to issue an act prohibiting the import of Indian Chintz as well as Persian and Chinese fabrics and restricting the import of Muslim silk.[1058] The Muslim pattern and motifs in these textiles provided models for European cotton as well as wallpaper production.

Another area where Muslim influence was significant is in carpet industry. Historical sources indicate that the earliest floor covering in Europe consisted of rushes, which were scattered over the floor and renewed from time to time. An illumination in a MS. At Lambeth Palace (*The Dictes and Sayings of the Philosophers*) depicting King Edward IV (1461-83) receiving a copy of it from its translator William Caxton. The King was seated in a room strewn with bright green rushes. Hampton Court is said to have had its rushes changed daily on the orders of Cardinal Wolsey. This practice continued up to the second half of the fifteenth century. It was the Muslims who taught Europeans how to weave carpets as confirmed by Christie: "*European craftsmen learned how to weave pile-carpets from the Muslims, using at first the traditional sleight-of-hand, but in later times purely mechanical means.*"[1059] Birdwood et al. explained in more details how this skill reached Europe: "*The first weavers of tapestries known to modern Europe were the Saracens, who introducing their looms into Spain and Southern France, transmitted to these countries the textile traditions inherited by themselves from Nineveh and Babylon, and Memphis, Thebes, and Akhmim; and it was from France that the weaving of tapestries spread into all the countries of Western and Northern Europe*"[1060] As might have been expected Muslim carpets had been known in France much earlier and were particular popular at the times of Louis IX under the name "*tapis Sarrasinois*" and in 1277 there were trade privileges for this *tapis* in Paris[1061]. The Cordoban Poet al-Shakindi, writing early in the 13th century, revealed that woollen carpets were produced in the 12th century at Chinchilla and Murcia (both in Spain) and were exported all over the world[1062].

There is also another source of credible evidence enabling us to evaluate the extent of use and the position of the Muslim carpet in Europe. The study of paintings made in late medieval period supplied considerable information on how and where these carpets were used and how they were regarded. The earliest occurrences of carpets in European paintings go back to early 1300s, starting with the painting of the Italian Simone Martini (1284-1344). In addition to the depiction of stylised animals[1063], there was also a Turkish element in these carpets consisting of similar knotting technique[1064]. Simone Martini portrayed an oriental carpet in his painting Saint Louis of Toulouse Crowning Robert of Anjou as King of Naples of about 1316-1319.[1065] Glimpses of a large carpet in the narrow spaces in front of and beside the dais of Saint Louis show geometrical patterns and stylised eagles. The painting is kept at the Capodimonte Museum in Naples. More paintings of carpets featuring stylised animal motifs were executed including; "The marriage of the Virgin" of Nicolo of Buonaccorso[1066]

361

(1348-1388), the "Madonna and Child with Saints" of Stefano de Giovanni (ca.1284-1344), or that of Anbrogio Lorenzetti (ca.1290-1328) "Madonna and Child Enthroned with Saints". The origins of the depiction of animals have been traced back to ninth century Egypt as excavations at Fustat (Cairo) revealed the existence of such designs in Cairene carpets. There is also a Turkish element in these carpets, as shown in these paintings, exhibiting similar traditional knotting techniques.[1067] Sometime in the fifteenth century, carpets with animal motifs ceased to exist but so far, no concrete explanation has been established. It might be due to the rise of more religious Ottomans who could have prohibited the depiction of such animals, which was islamically discouraged. Consequently, a return to abstract geometrical forms took place signalling the beginning of the Ottoman art.

Paintings executed during the 15th and 16th centuries indicate a considerable increase in the popularity of Muslim carpets, particularly those made in Turkey and Persia. During this period, growing trade relations and the increasing prosperity of Europe resulted in greater importation of Muslim works of art and luxury goods as European society (especially the wealthy) started to experience a life of comfort. Large quantities of rugs, ceramics and other items formed an essential part of this trade, as confirmed by Mills, "*By 1500 we reach a time when certain Turkish products were being produced and exported to the West in large number, and pieces evidently belonging to the same group are to be found represented by painters both of Italy and Northern Europe.*"[1068] The Ottomans also imported European and Italian products, particularly those relating to the baroque style. Both sides found need for each other as outlined by Rosemond Mack: "*This reciprocal copying occurred quite peacefully because it benefited both parties. Italians and Ottomans recognized the economic importance of trade and industrial development and accepted the cultural and artistic exchange required to become and remain competitive. ... Sixteenth-century East-West trade and artistic exchange softened a clash of civilizations, establishing a historical precedent for cultural coexistence and mutual enrichment.*"[1069] Portraits of dignitaries from Italy, France, Germany, Holland and Belgium illustrated the luxurious usage of these carpets. Examples portrayed in the work of the German painter Hans Holbein, the younger contained this theme, his painting known as the *French Ambassadors* depicts two wealthy men standing in front of a table topped with an Ottoman carpet. There are other instances where Ottoman carpets are present in Christian themes for example depicting the Virgin Mary in a setting with Ottoman textiles.

In Belgium, similar processes took place as carpets were given a similar privileged treatment. Two examples are the works of Van Eyck (ca.1390-1440) and Hans Memlinc (ca.1430-1494). They both two incorporated the Muslim carpet into their drawings of holy and noble themes. Van Eyck's painting of *the Virgin and Child with St. Donatian, St. George and Canon Van der Paele*, painted in 1436, at Bruges, shows Mary (peace be upon her) seated on a carpet with geometrical shapes essentially circles drawn around rosettes combined with lozenges and eight pointed star motifs. Hans Memlinc in his *Mystical Marriage of St. Catherine* (1479) and *The Virgin Enthroned* used Anatolian patterns very closely resembling the carpet of Eshrefoglu at Beysehir.[1070]

In Italian paintings carpets were placed either below the throne of the Madonna, on the floor of sad rites, or hanging from house windows on feast days. By the 15th century, they gained greater popularity as they began to appear in documents showing that they were used as table carpets (*tapedi de tavola*), and desk carpets (*tapedi da desco*). These were both *tapedi damaschini*, Damascus carpets, and *tapedi ciaiarini*, Cairo carpets, which saturated trading markets of Venice.[1071] In other occasions, Muslim carpets formed fashionable diplomatic gifts, especially the stylish Mamluk carpet from Egypt.[1072] The portrait of *Husband and Wife* of Lotto (1480-1556) shows the use of the "S" pattern for inner border combined with a delightful arabesque followed by another wider border made essentially of vine leaves. The painting of the Venetian Cittore Carpaccio, "*St. Ursula taking leave of her father*" shows the popularity of rugs with them appearing on the boat and on the balcony of the tower. It is said that these carpets (in the painting) were made by Turkish craftsmen living in Venice in the "Fondaco dei Turchi" (hotel of Turkey) which sheds further light on how the transformation of the Muslim/Turkish carpet, into the so called "Venetian Carpaccio", took place.[1073] Late 15th century paintings show the "Venetian Carpaccio" being hung from windows and balconies of houses as well as thrown on tables and other places where they can be appreciated. From this time, the representation of carpets in paintings spread to Spain, Germany and France.[1074]

The first arrival of the Muslim carpet in England was in 1255 when Queen Eleanor, the Castilian Bride of King Edward I, brought Andalusian carpets as precious items of her dowry. However, the earliest recorded English contact with Muslim textiles was in the 12th century when Henry of Blois (c.1100-1171), the Grandson of William the Conqueror, who lived in the Abbey of Cluny in the 12th century gave an Islamic (Saracenic) carpet to an English church[1075]. Muslim textiles provided not only material for clothing but also ingredients for home furnishing such as curtains, covers, pillows, carpets and other tapestry.

The Ottoman/Turkish carpet in England arrived in 1518 when Cardinal Wolsey ordered seven from Venice and another 60 Damascene carpets were dispatched to him in 1520.[1076] King Henry VIII is known to have owned over 400 Muslim carpets.[1077] A portrait painted for him by Holbein in 1537 shows him standing on a Turkish carpet with its Ushak star[1078], while an Arabesque borders his grown, and other Muslim interlacing patterns appear on the curtains. Another portrait shows the King and Princess Mary seated at a table on which a Turkish carpet is spread. Records also show that Robert Dudley (1532-1588), the Earl of Leicester, who lived during the reign of Elizabeth I, left a total of 46 Turkish and one Persian carpets[1079]. Turkish carpets were also acquired for Hardwick Hall, built by Elizabeth of Shrewsbury (also known as Bess of Hardwick) in the 1590's. An inventory for Bess's will of 1601 listed 32 carpets.[1080] Records also show that in 1610, the Hall purchased two Turkish carpets for the price of £1315.[1081] Therefore, when they were first introduced to England, aristocratic households used carpets in places of display such as tables, desks, and coffers.

During the Tudor period, Muslim carpets decorated tables, chests, and walls. There is evidence suggesting that some carpets were made specifically for Europeans customers. The presence of round carpets that could only be used for tables and other cross- shaped carpets produced in Egypt are suggestive of a European destination[1082]. In some carpets the figure of the crucifixion was inserted into floral motifs, while others carried the European coat of arms of which some were sent to King Sigismund III (1566–1632) of Poland.

It is quite clear that the Ottoman carpet reached an unprecedented position in European high society as confirmed by Ettinghausen who wrote: "*There is no doubt that carpets exerted a great fascination on would-be buyers and owners, whatever their social position-whether they were Hapsburgs or members of the royal house of Sweden, princes of the church, the nobility, or were just well-to-do members of the bourgeoisie. Their esteem can be gauged by the fact that they served as the setting for coronations and other important festive occasions. They became what is now called a 'status symbol'*"[1083]. In the 17th century, the carpet fashion took off strongly as records reveal the existence of many types of carpets including foot carpet, table carpet, cupboard carpet and window carpet[1084]. Such overwhelming popularity continued until the 20th century when the import of Muslim carpets continued to be strong despite the fierce competition from the oriental (Chinese) carpets.[1085] Ajmar-Wolheim et al. observe, *"Scholars today have a growing awareness of the importance of the Islamic world on developments in Europe, and studies of objects found in Renaissance homes reveal this to be true. The link was so close that you had Ottoman carpets that were designed for Western tables."*[1086]

Ceramics and Pottery

The production of pottery is a very old tradition found in the major civilisations. Sources indicate that Muslim pottery was not firmly established until the 9th century in Mesopotamia, Syria and Persia when it used mainly white tin-glaze[1087]. Information on earlier periods (7th and 8th centuries) is very limited partly due to the limited interest in the study of ceramics of these periods and the lack of any substantial amount of specimens in good condition. Archaeological excavations carried out in Jordan uncovered only a few examples from the Umayyad period, mostly unglazed vessels from Khirbat Al-Mafjar.[1088] During the Abbasid dynasty pottery production gained momentum, largely using tin glazes mostly in the form of opaque white glaze. Lane[1089] and others attribute the rise of this industry to Chinese influence. Early potters first used lead glazes[1090] with relief designs, a technique which came down from the Romans who spread it throughout the countries of the Mediterranean basin including Egypt.[1091] These wares consisted mostly of red earthenware on which the shiny green or yellowish brown glazes were applied.[1092] In a second stage, they introduced tin oxides[1093] to the lead glaze, a development which evolved from attempts to imitate the white Chinese ceramics, giving it a white finish. In a third stage, Muslim potters developed different glaze recipes from the latter method, of which the most successful innovation was the use of 'blue-on-white' decoration technique, which, as we shall see later, was re-exported to China and Europe, instigating the spread of Chinese blue and white ware.

The other innovation was the decoration in lustre. Muslims were eager to develop this type of glaze in an attempt to produce a closer version of the golden and silver vessels of paradise described numerous times in the Quran. In Surah 76, for example, Allah promises His devotees: *"Enter ye the Garden, ye and your wives, in (beauty and) rejoicing. To them will be passed round, dishes and goblets of gold: there will be there all that the souls could desire, all that their eyes could delight in: and ye shall abide therein (for eye). Such will be the Garden of which ye are made heirs for your (good) deeds (in life). Ye shall have therein abundance of fruit, from which ye shall have satisfaction "*.(43:71-3). In Surah 43, the Exalted reminds the believers: *"And amongst them (the Devotees of Allah) will be passed round vessels of silver and goblets of crystal. Crystal-clear, made of silver: they will determine the measure thereof (according to their wishes). And they will be given to drink there of a Cup (of Wine) mixed with Zanjabil, A fountain there, called Salsabil"* (76:15-8).

Lustre provided the right ingredients for producing such vessels in a cheaper and acceptable way since Islam prohibits the use of gold and silver vessels. It was produced by applying a thin glaze prepared from the oxides of silver and copper before the vessel is placed in a reducing furnace. When silver is used, a paler yellow or golden and silvery effect was obtained. In case of copper, the produce is of darker and redder colour. This is not the first time we see Muslim artisans trying to imitate the themes of paradise. A similar approach was adopted in architecture, gardening, and even carpet making.

Muslims excelled in the art of ceramics probably more than in any other type of art, and consequently exercised a considerable influence on Europe in this area. The combination of colour and form and the contrast they create gained their ceramics a worldwide reputation. Two distinctive types of pottery, the Hispano-Moorish (Spanish) and Iznik (blue Turkish pottery) were highly regarded by Europeans, especially the British. Although the two types share common features such as the use of floral and vegetal motifs in the decoration of surfaces, they differ in a number of characteristics. Hispano-Moorish ceramics are characterised by their dense pattern of vegetal motifs obscuring the background. They also make extensive use of metallic lustre, which makes them glossy and shiny. They follow the eastern production technique based on tin glaze, but employ natural and animal motifs especially the renowned sailing ships and raging animals. Iznik pottery, originating from Iznik in northwest Anatolia, reached their peak of production between 1520 and 1560. They employ generally free flow of low-density plant motifs, especially roses, tulips, carnations and hyacinths. Their distinctive background is generally white, commonly in combination with blue. Iznik wall tiles are often organised in a theme, especially with floral motifs, in an arched frame in the form of a window or a door opening on to a garden or paradise.

Muslim ceramics with these features were widely sought by collectors, artists, merchants and wealthy Europeans. A sign of this is the large number of Muslim ceramic vessels and basins decorating (inserted in) the façade and campanile of churches, a fashion, which spread in Italy, between 11th and 13th centuries. This not only shows the trade relations between the Muslims and Italian towns such as Pisa, Genoa and Venice but also provides an interesting insight into the value attached to these vessels. The greatest influence of Muslim ceramics was on the development of the so-called *maiolica* ceramics. Historical sources indicate that sometime before 1154, Muslim pottery making techniques reached Spain where Al-Idrissi confirmed its existence in Aragon. In the 13th century, this production reached its apogee in Malaga (Maliqa in Arabic), which became renowned for its "golden pottery". Some specimens of this pottery dating back to 1303 were found in Sandwich in England. Hurst revealed that some 44 pieces of Moorish lustre, dating back to the late the 13 and 14th centuries, and other 22 pieces from the 15th century were found in Britain[1094]. Tin glazed pottery, from Spain reached Italy between the 13th and 16th centuries where it became widely known as *maiolica* ceramics, a derivation from Malaga. This style and pattern dominated the ceramic industry in Italy to the extent that *maiolica* was used also for metallic lustre in the 1530's. Italian potters learned how to decorate from their Muslim counterparts, using colour from pigments painted on a tin glaze, and gold from metallic stains on a tin glaze. It was only after mastering the Muslim technique that Italian artists produced their famous Renaissance ornamentation, such as narrative scenes, which predominated by about 1520[1095]. Via Italy and Spain, Muslim motifs and the technique of tin-glaze were passed to France where they appeared in the *faience* industry. It was later imported into the 17th century delftware industry in Holland and England.[1096]

The impact of Islamic glass industry is also traceable in European medieval and Renaissance glasswork. Catherine Hess[1097] traces back the origins of fine Italian glass, or *cristallo*, to 10th century Muslim glassmakers who produced first luxury glass since antiquity. For over two centuries, Egyptians and Syrians produced some of the finest and most exquisite enamelled and gilded glass, which reached a worldwide reputation. According to Hess, these skills reached Italy through the influx of a number of Egyptian and Byzantine glassmakers, who arrived in

Venice by 1300. Italians at first emulated Islamic decoration, particularly in areas of dense surface ornamentation composed of scrolling foliage, interlacing geometric patterns, and Arabic calligraphy, before they developed their landscape and classical motifs.

The Dutch industry, famous for its blue and white tiles, based mainly at Deflt, Rotterdam and Amsterdam, adopted the Muslim techniques, especially that of painting in colour on tin-glaze. The production used cobalt, the most stable ingredient in the potter's repertoire, which Muslim potters had introduced into Mesopotamia in the ninth century, centuries before the Chinese adopted it for the decoration of their porcelain[1098]. The Chinese porcelain did not reach European markets until 1657, a fact which strongly rejects claims giving the priority of influence to Chinese porcelain over the Muslim lusterware.

Muslim ceramics were the source of transfer of a number of types of flowers that were previously unknown in Europe, particularly the carnation and tulip. The tulip, for example, has a Persian origin where it was cultivated as early as 11th century. Omar al-Khayyam used it in his poetry as a metaphor for female beauty. It reached Istanbul (Constantinople) where it was planted in large quantities in its Serail gardens. The flower first came to Europe through Count Ogier de Busbecq, ambassador for Ferdinand I of Spain to the Ottoman Sultan Suleiman the Magnificent who brought it to Spain in 1554. Busbecq took the word they used "*dulban*", a term describing the turban, for the name and eventually it became Tulip. The flower later reached Holland about 1560 and to Italy by 1640's when the Duke of Sermoneta, Francisco Caetani collected some 15,147 tulips in his garden.[1099] In France, the gardeners among the Huguenots took the tulip with them as they fled religious persecution and popularised it in their new home countries. In the 1680's an Englishman, Sir George Wheeler brought tulips from the Serail gardens of Constantinople.

In ceramics, the tulip appeared largely in Iznik pottery where it was used as a decorative device. These ceramics reached Europe in early 17th century, it appeared in England before 1600. The Turkish jug found in the Victoria and Albert Museum and dating from the late 16th century is a good specimen of the tulip ceramics that were imported into Europe. However, the adoption of the tulip decoration by Dutch ceramics widened the spread of this motif throughout Europe and by the end of the 17th century; it became widely copied in most

European art works appearing in the decoration of English earthenware, silver, bookbinding and samplers. It is worth noting that the European imitation extended to include the vertical representation of this motif developed in Iznik pottery, a further indication of the influence of this art on European pottery.[1100]

In addition to the tulip, the carnation and the Iris were both popular plant motif in Persian and Turkish ceramics. With its fan shape, the former offered a successful combination with the tulip in Iznik pottery. This combination was also copied in European decoration appearing in a number of Lambeth chargers dating from 1660-1700. Persian potters, particularly under the Safavid dynasties in the 16th and 17th centuries, used the iris in horizontal and circular forms of decoration. Here once again we find the influence of these techniques on European presentation of the iris as seen in Bristol delftware specimens.[1101]

Architectural Motifs

One of the most interesting books about the Muslim architectural influence on Europe just before the flowering of the Renaissance was Debora Howard's book discussed partly in chapter four. In her study of Venice, she revealed astonishing results on how deep the impact of Muslim-Egyptian and Syrian motifs on the architecture and character of the city. On city level, Howard compared Venice with Aleppo, Damascus, and Cairo.[1102] She finds "*characteristics of the emporia of the Islamic world came to be reflected in Venice*"[1103] in both plan and buildings. The organisation of the use and space around Rialto market and its streets followed that of the Islamic suq as seen in Aleppo. Other eastern features included: the existence of a number of *funduq* or fundaco (remodelled from the khans), the use of particular areas or shopping streets in particular type of merchandise, the adoption of covered galleries in arcades along shopping streets, the presence of warehousing utilities above shops, and the use of wooden shutters that could be folded out to form sun blinds and counters, are also eastern characters found in most Muslim markets and shops[1104]. Howard even showed how the clock of Venice's famous tower, Torre dell'Orologio, assembled in 1498, resembles in its zodiac face that of al-Ghazi treatise on robots and the clock of the Great Mosque of Damascus.[1105] The figure, which strikes the hours, was made of bronze in the form of a Moor.

Figure 140 Rotunda of Ballyfin in Ireland (1820) by Richard Morrison (1776-1849)

Figure 141 The basilica of Saint Marco (1071 CE) showing the influence of Muslim architecture; the domes are reputed for their resemblance with their Egyptian prototypes

In religious architecture the basilica Saint Marco (1071 CE) is one example of many showing the influence of Islam, especially Alexandria. Built four centuries later, the domes are reputed for their Islamic character, resembling their Egyptian prototypes in form and structure (fig.141). Not only they had the bulbous form but they were also built in double shell. The decoration of the building was Islamic; almost all the internal mosaic decoration and painting were the inspiration of Muslim miniatures and cityscapes, particularly of Alexandria and Egypt. The resemblance between the stone window grilles, particularly those over the Porta Saint'Alippio, and grilled windows in the great Mosque of Damascus can only testify for a direct imitation (fig. 142 and 143). Traceries of this type may also be seen in the tomb of the Dogaressa Felicitas Michiel (d. 1111) inside the narthex; and the Islamic tree of life motif is incorporated into its decorative stonework. The resemblance between relief panels in Saint Marco, such as the peacock relief on the west facade, and the stylized symmetry of Egyptian woodcarvings of the Fatimid period were also highlighted by Howard. The delicate metalwork lanterns, although probably made in Venice, clearly show the impact of Islamic metalwork.

In secular buildings, the impact goes beyond simple ornamentation to design of roof platforms and terraces (altana), corner stairwells, balconies, porticoed courts, even street facades. The spread use of *funduqs* in Venice is attributed to this influence; among the surviving examples is the Fondaco dei Turchi, built 13th century but restored 1861-9. In many Muslim cities, especially Egypt and Damascus Venetians were privileged with the possession of *funduqs* as early as 1238 when the Mamluk Sultan authorized them to have two funduqs in Alexandria.[1106] Howard drew a comparison of the plan of Fondaco dei Turchi and a house of an Egyptian wealthy at Fouah in Lower Egypt and surveyed by Pascal Coste in 1839. She commented on the close similarity of the plans *"Venetians were certainly visiting Damietta as well as Alexandria in the eleventh and twelfth centuries, and it is not unlikely that a similar type of house was to be found in Alexandria at that time."*[1107] According to Scattolin, the Venetian palace grew from the *funduq* tradition and plan.[1108] Venetian rich merchants, who made their fortunes from the east, built these palaces to provide warehousing space for their imported merchandise and a home for the family. It was here where they monopolised and controlled the prices of goods in European markets.

371

Figure 142 The resemblance between the stone window grilles, particularly those over the Porta Sant Alippio, and grilled windows in the great Mosque of Damascus can only testify for a direct imitation

Figure 143 Window grills of Umayyad mosque, Damascus

372

In decoration the outlining of pointed arched windows in rectangles, mihrab windows as Howard called them, derive from the Islamic practice of enclosing arched niches in frames (*pishtaq*) as found in many Venetians palaces such as in Ca'Arian (14-15th century). In Ca' Priuli at San Savero (14th century). In some cases like Ca' Loredan (c.1200) rectangle framed windows of the frame is bordered with dentil and circular medallions fill the spandrels of the arches, a feature used extensively in Islamic architecture as in mihrab of Sultan Hassan (1356-9) and of Ibn Tulun (879). Another feature is which are stilted (pointed) arches imitating Muslims practices. The distinctive Venetian gothic arches, or ogee arches seem to be inspired by arches of al-Jaferia Palace, although Howard thought they were developed from Muslim woodwork, ivory carving and other minor art works.[1109] An example of this is the minbar of Nûr al-Dîn in 1168 which he made for al-Aqsa mosque and was transported by Salah al-Din and destroyed by a fire, had a gothic arches forming the gallery. In Dodge Palace (1340-1361), most obvious Islamic qualities are the insistent two-dimensionality and openness of the facades, the lozenge pattern on the upper wall (fig.144), the roofline battlements, and the delicate traceries of its principal floor or Piano Nobile. Stefano Cabrini summed it up when he stated, *"The Serenissima seems to have been touched in endless ways by Islamic culture, not only in the visual arts, but also in her structural appearance. ...... major monuments such as the Baislica of San Marco, the Palazzo Ducale, and the Fondaci dei tedeschi and dei Turchi, as well as public and private palaces with Islamic style windows, cernellations, and courtyards, reflect the city's connections to the Islamic Near East."*[1110]

The late Renaissance years were described by art critics as the European "age of despair", expressing the artistic stagnation of European society as it exhausted its talent in Gothic which lost its appeal and was subsequently abandoned.[1111] Once more Europeans looked to Islam for inspiration and subsequently developed new styles including the Baroque and Rococo, which covered most of the 17th century and 18th centuries respectively. Rococo used light and linear rhythms together with natural shapes like shells, corals and ammonites breaking from the formalities of the Baroque style. This distinctive style was developed in France at a time when it had strong contacts with the east, as outlined earlier, during the reign of Louis XIV, a time when the *Turqueries* and Turkish themes were highly appreciated in France. Turkish subjects dominated the Rococo for

Figure 144 Dodge Palace (1340-1361), most obvious Islamic qualities are the insistent two-dimensionality and openness of the facades, the lozenge pattern on the upper wall

Figure 145 the Cathedral of St. Paul (1675 to 1710), the Muslim influence can be traced in the structure of the domes as well as in the use of the combination of dome and tower

considerable time. In literature, it has been revealed that in 1670, on the visit of a Turkish dignitary, King Louis asked Molière (1622-1673) to include an important Turkish sequence in his comedy *Le Bourgeois Gentilhome.*[1112] The popular Italian *Commedia dell'arte*, staged themes involving Turkish subjects.

In paintings, Turkish elements were also present as in *Turc Amoureux* of Nicolas Lancret (1690-1743) painted for the Salon of the Hotel de Boulogne in the Place Vendome, Paris, and in *Mehmet Affendi giving audience* in 1721 of Antoine Coypel (1661-1722). Charles Parrocel (1688 – 1752) made two pictures of the Turkish visit of 1721, which were made into gobelin tapestries. Turkish subjects were also illustrated by Francois Boucher (1703-1770) and by Amedee Vanloo (1719-1795) in his work *Fête Champetre donnée par les Odalisques en presence du Sultan et de la Sultane* in 1775. These tales of the highly civilised Turkish lifestyle and sophistication were adopted in Europe through the imports of various items of this comfort including the carpets, sofas and upholstered seats. Turkish influence on Rococo culture therefore is immense.

In architecture, the Rococo was expressed in plasterwork and stucco where Muslim decor excelled. Muslim ingredients were widely used in temples and gazebos, which appeared in English landscape. Islamic buildings were erected in many celebrated European gardens. The work of William Wright presenting three varieties of mosques in his pattern book *"Grotesque Architecture or Rural Amusement"* (1767)[1113]. The book was particularly influential as it consisted of plans, elevations, and sections for baths, mosques, Moresque pavilions, grotesque and rustic seats and green houses. The Turkish minaret in Carmontelle's Parc Monceau, Paris (Duc de Chartres, 1773), and Nicolas de Pigage's mosque (1778-1795), at Schwetzingen, Mannheim (Elector Palatine) are three examples among many inspirations directly from the influence of Wright's work.

Muslim architecture also gained the respect of the distinguished Christopher Wren (1632 - 1723), famous for his Saracenic theory of Gothic discussed in previous chapter, who adopted numerous Muslim architectural solutions in his designs. In his greatest ever project, the Cathedral of St. Paul (1675 to 1710), the Muslim influence can be traced in the structure of the domes in the aisles as well as in the use of the combination dome and tower[1114] (fig.145). Danby reported that Wren closely studied a number of Ottoman mosques prior to his design[1115]. The structural similarities between St Paul and the Blue Mosque in Istanbul are not entirely coincidental. The use of ribs and squinches to achieve the transition from a square to octagonal plan are reminders of Muslim domes. The aesthetic appeal created by the soaring minarets counter-posing the central dome on the Muslim landscape and skyline was also influential in St. Paul. In the minaret of St. Mary le Bow (London 1671-1683), the influence of the Muslim minaret on Wren's design is clearly visible as he adopted it with little modifications (fig.146). Other European architects, especially the Italians in late renaissance campanili, also adopted the combination of dome and minaret.

The late 17th century saw the rise of Turkish tents in Europe. Symbol of ancient and modern Arabia, the tent has always played an important role in the cultural and social life of the Arabian community. It has remained the main shelter for the Bedouin communities until the Ottoman times when it was given a new impetus making it a royal structure set for the sultan in ceremonial occasions. Tents were elaborately decorated with beautifully coloured silk, crowned at the peak with a raised section adding extra splendour and majesty. They were usually equipped with comfortable seats, canapés and colourful carpets together with a selection of some of the Sultan's favourite weapons and toiletries. The tent followed the sultan in most of his outings, in his march for war, in his hunting trips and during his visits and ceremonies.

Europeans made contact with the tent through ambassadorial exchanges with the "Sublime Port". They used it mainly for royal ceremonies and parties, a fashion which later spread among the nobles and the wealthy. As mentioned previously King Louis XIV, was renowned for the numerous ceremonial tents (à la Turque), extravagant processions, and royal parties using firework displays. By late 17th century, these tents invaded most European courts and gardens. The two most famous Turkish tents in England were built around the 1750s in the Painshill, Surrey garden of the Hon. Charles Hamilton and Stourhead Wiltshire of Henry Colt Hoare. John Parnell (1744-1801) visited it in 1763 and made a watercolour illustration of the tent. At Stourhead, Richard Pococke (1704-1765) reported that the site was first designated for a mosque with a minaret but the idea was later transformed into a tent, which was dismantled in the 1790s[1116]. A third Turkish tent was built at Bellevue, Delgany, Wicklow, in Ireland by David la Tourche, in the late 18th century. In Vauxhall Gardens, the roof of the Rotunda was made in tent form with blue and yellow alternating stripes and thought to be supported by twenty pillars.[1117] It has been described as a Persian Pavilion[1118]. One of the garden tents was built in 1744 consisting of a large shelter and a dining area accommodating up to 14 tables[1119]. Whittock reported another tent which he named "Mamluke pavilion", indicating its resemblance to Egyptian tents at the time of the Mamluke dynasties. The popularity of tents extended to the Royal court that Empress Josephine had a Muslim tent room made for her at Malmaison.[1120] Conner revealed that a German Prince, Puckler Muskau recounted the existence of a number of Turkish tents at Virginia Water,[1121] and that King George IV had often dined in them.[1122] Meanwhile the Marquess of Hertford (nicknamed the Caliph) had a Muslim tent room made for him by Decimus Burton at St. Dunstan's House[1123]. It was burnt, in 1930, in a fire and was rebuilt in a different design. English art historian Sweetman thought more tents were built, but weather conditions and their fragile structure often resulted in their dismantling.

The Romanticism of the 18th century provided greater impetus to the study of the Orient as Europe looked at the East and the Muslim world with romance and admiration filled with memories and glorious landscapes. Many institutions were established to "discover" the East, but the real aim was not always honourable as Edward Said puts it. In his view, orientalism was not really aimed at establishing the truth of what is the East but intended to ascertain the Western supremacy. He accuses it of being "*a Western style for dominating, restructuring and having authority over the Orient and its rule over it.*"[1124]

Whatever the intentions were, these studies disseminated, nevertheless, a great deal of information on oriental art and architecture, giving rise to a number of great works of oriental taste, with Islamic motifs taking the lion's share of the imported features. The work of Fischer Von Erlach (1656–1723), an Austrian architect who built the Karlskirche (1715-1737) and wrote *A Plan of Civil and Historical Architecture* on the history of architecture illustrating buildings of Muslim as well as Chinese and Japanese origins, had considerable influence on architects in England. The book was translated to English into English in 1737, where it was inspirational for many constructions including a Turkish tent erected in 1744 in Vauxhall Gardens.[1125] The English novelist and art and architecture enthusiast, William Beckford (1760-1844) was particularly attracted to Moorish architecture that he visited Spain. He later published Letters from Italy with Sketches of Spain and Portugal (1834), a work that contained some brilliant descriptions of scenes and manners. In 1793, he moved to Portugal, where he settled for a while.[1126] He collected Mughol miniatures and published *Vathek: an Arabian Tale* in 1786.[1127] He built a Turkish Chamber in his house on his Fonthill estate at Wiltshire completed in 1768, and a Turkish Salon in1793 for his house in Lisbon, and a Moorish summer house in his garden at 20 Lansdown Crescent, in Bath (fig.147). Danby thought that Moorish architecture

377

also influenced Beckford's Fonthill Abbey through the work of James Cavanah on Portugal.[1128] The influential Thomas Hope (1769-1831) developed a special admiration of Muslim arts and lifestyle, demonstrated in his portrait made in 1798 where he appears standing in front of a mosque in golden turban and scarlet slippers. In his Duchess Street mansion, he made a number of rooms of eastern themes: an Egyptian, an Indian, and a Greek room. His book *Household Furniture and Interior Design* had Islamic art patterns on its title page using the combination of Muslim crescent and star.[1129]

The views and illustrations William Hodges (1744-1797) produced for various Muslim monuments, discussed in the previous section, have greatly influenced British artists and architects. This has been admitted by the Royal Academy as quoted by Joshua Reynolds in his discourse at The Royal Academy (December 1786) outlined how the works of Hodges on Muslim buildings could: *"furnish an architect not with models to copy, but with hints of composition and general effects which would not otherwise have occurred."*[1130] Such an influence can be seen in the design of the south façade of the Guild Hall in London, which was designed by George Dance the Younger (1741-1825) in its Islamo-Indian manner (fig.148). The similarity between the illustration of Jami Mosque at Jaunpur (1470) and the façade is evident in the relationship of windows to the solid wall, although the absence of the central dominating pointed arch of the mosque produced quite different effect. Stroud, however, related such influence to the Mosque 'Chunar Gur'. She provided more examples on the influence of Hodges's *Select Views* on the architectural works of Dance,[1131] including: the turret-caps at Coleorton at Leicester made between 1804-1806 for Sir George Beaumont, in caps and in the proportions of his gateway at Stratton Park at Hampshire (made around 1807) for Sir Francis Baring, as well as in the turret at Ashburnham in Sussex (1807) and Norman Court at Dorset (1810).

The works of Thomas Daniell (1749-1840) and his nephew William Daniell (1769-1837) are considered among the most influential illustrations of Muslim architecture. They played a great part in the introduction of many Muslim motifs into British art and architecture. Their joint work was, between 1795 and 1808, published in *Oriental Scenery* consisting of six folio-sized parts, with a total of 144 illustrations and plates.[1132] Many reproductions of these plates were made available for individual collections to be hung on the walls of offices, study rooms and lounges, while others printed on earthenware reached English dinner tables. For example, John Davenport of Longport produced a blue printed design

Figure 146 The minaret of St. Mary le Bow,London (1671-1683), the influence of the Muslim minaret on Wren's design is clearly visible in the sectioning

Figure 147 The Moorish summer house at 20 Lansdown Crescent, in Bath

Figure 148 The Guild Hall in London was designed by George Dance the Younger (1741-1825) in its Islamo-Indian manner

illustrating a mosque in an English-looking landscape (c.1820).[1133] The Herculaneum pottery of Liverpool (c.1793-1841) made a number of pottery representations of Muslim Indian motifs including three major designs. The first marked as showing '*Gate of a mosque built by Hafiz Ramut, Philipbeat*', the second marked as '*the Mausoleum of Nawub Assoph Khan, Rajemahal*', while the third was unmarked and representing '*the Mausoleum of Sultan Purveiz near Allahabad.*'[1134] Another successful designs was based on the doomed central pavilion of the Fort, Madura (now Madurai), also depicted by Daniell and published in 1797. This soon became known as the Madura pattern, which became a central theme used in pottery decoration; "The Madura pattern is found on every conceivable earthenware article-tablewares, assorted household items and even a bedpan".[1135] Other companies such as George Rogers of Longport (c.1784-1842), and R. Riley of Burslem (c.1802-1828) and J. Bevington of Swansea (1817-1824) also made representations of Muslim Indian motifs.[1136]

Muslim motifs were also employed for wallpaper and other media of home decoration. Evidence shows that wallpapers based on eastern motifs were very popular along the 17th and 18th centuries. There is a rare statement made by the British diarist Samual Pepys (1633-1703) who revealed that his wife's closet was done up in 'counterfeit damask', most probably because they could not afford the real one.[1137] Sources also indicate that George Wythe House (1726-1806), an American politician and art collector obtained Damask wallpaper for his house, Williamsburg in Virginia, which was thought to be made about 1770. Wythe House is also known to have collected a Damask tablecloth and some Moroccan shoes.[1138] The reason behind this prestigious popularity of this type of wallpaper is its smooth surface, which makes the overall effect somewhat lighter.[1139]

Arabesque pattern was the second most popular theme in wallpaper decoration. This type of wallpaper was produced by the Parisian Jean-Baptiste Reveillon, whose papers are still considered as some of the best produced. His factory produced some of the most exquisite papers that were used all over Europe not only for wall decoration but extended to the embellishment of wooden panelling, doors and shutters.[1140] Muslim environment and landscape also provided artists and manufacturers of panoramic wallpaper, with the right ingredients, themes and colours. This decorative fashion, which appeared in early nineteenth century, consisted of large paintings that were painted *in situ* by artists intended to be block-printed by hand on rolls of wallpaper. Two French manufacturers developed the scenic wallpaper: the Zuber Company of Rxheim and Dufour in

Macon and Paris.[1141] Jean Zuber of Rixheim (near Mulhouse, Haut Rhin) produced in 1806 a wallpaper representing a panoramic view of *Indoustan*, as he called it, based on Daniell's work with Islamo-Indian buildings and Indian flora and fauna.[1142] He also produced wallpaper and fabrics using Muslim motifs from other parts of the world including `Samarqand'. In 1815, Dufour produced two of his most successful papers based on Indian and Turkish scenery, the *Paysage Indien*, which included panorama of the fort of Madura, and *Paysage Turc, which* used scenes from the Ottoman landscape.[1143]

Oriental Scenery made an impact on building design, because its engravings gave rise to a large number of 'eastern" style garden buildings. The most famous of these was the design of Sezincote House (Gloucestershire) made between 1805 and 1810 by Samuel Pepys Cockrell, under the advice of his consultant Thomas Daniell, for his brother Charles Cockrell[1144]. The building had a strong Mughal appearance (fig.149) with its bulbous dome raised on a square base, the cusped arches, corner pavilions (*Chattris*) resembling the "Mausoleum of Sultan Purveiz, near Allahabad" and deep cornices known as *chujjas* resembling the 'Lal Bagh, at Faizabad". Cockrell also designed the farm buildings on the estate in the same style, as well as some cottages at Lower Swell, which had multifoil arched windows.[1145]   In this same spirit, William Porden (c1755-1822) who worked for Cockrell designed a number of buildings of Muslim character. In 1797, he designed a Palace of Amusement at the Royal Academy in Muslim-Indian fashion. The Royal stables[1146] and Riding House at Brighton, which he built between 1803 and 1808, under the commission of the Prince Regent, are of great interest in this area. Here, we find the elements of the rotunda, the *chattris*, the bulbous dome and various types of arches combined together in an English landscape to construct a fascinating romantic scene. In the interior, Porden created a sense of movement through the use of superimposed arcades of multifoil arches. On these arcades, he raised a great dome, which he decorated with corbels at the area where it meets the arcaded wall. The dome itself has a series of narrow and wide ribs meeting at the centre to form a geometrically defined rose (fig.150). Porden followed this building, in 1804, by Eaton Hall in Cheshire, which was in Gothic style, but its domes were of Muslim style raised on projecting columns.[1147]

Figure 149 Sezincote House (Gloucestershire) made between 1805 and 1810 by Samuel Pepys Cockrell, with a strong Mughal appearance

Figure 150 The Royal stables and Riding House at Brighton, now the Dome theatre, which he built between 1803 and 1808, under the commission of the Prince Regent, are of great interest in this area.

Another professional who was greatly affected by Muslim architecture and Hodges' work, especially *Select Views,* was the famous landscape designer, Humphry Repton (1752-1818). In his *Designs for the Pavillon at Brighton* (1808), one can see clearly his admiration as he incorporated the richness of Indian architecture with that of Gothic.[1148] Nevertheless, due to lack of finance, the project was dropped only to be revived eight years later by John Nash. In his design John Nash (1752-1835) accentuated Mughal forms producing a "*total exotic exterior effect*"[1149] which pleased his royal Patrons so the Royal Pavilion was built (1815-1822). Historical sources confirm that Nash had consulted the *Oriental Scenery* of Daniell, as he is known to have borrowed four volumes from the Royal Library at Carlton House on November 14th 1815.[1150] In the Royal Pavilion, Nash combined the bulbous domes with the concave shape of roofs imitating the Turkish Sultan's tents, which covered the banqueting and music rooms of the building. He used minaret-like structures to disguise the chimneys and pierced the façade walls with an arcade of alternating single and double arches (fig.151). The Pavilion gained a wide reputation, John Evans in his book *"Excursion to Brighton, 1822"*[1151] commented on the building: *"England has been reproached by travellers for want of a palace on a scale commensurate with the grandeur of its monarchy…The Pavilion is only a winter residence, but in proportion to its extent it may be said to exceed any other of the palaces in the Kingdom."*[1152]

The good reception of the Royal Pavilion encouraged other British architects to indulge in Muslim and eastern style buildings. In Brighton, a number of edifices with Muslim facades, domes and concave roofs emerged. Resources reveal that the architect Amon Henry Wilds, who designed houses in Sillwood Place and Western Terrace at Brighton reflected in his designs the inspiration of the Pavilion.[1153] Another building echoing this influence was a mausoleum built by Sir Albert Abdullah Sasson (1818-1896), a British Indian philanthropist and merchant born at Bagdad, in Paston Place. Not far from Brighton, the Englefields, an aristocratic family, had a garden building built for them at Whiteknights in Berkshire, by the architect J.B. Papworth between 1815 and 1819.[1154] The influence of the Pavilion extended to Ireland and America, Conner provided greater details about this impact.[1155]

The imitation of Muslim and eastern buildings extended to include mosques and palaces, which appealed especially to the English who adapted them in their garden structures. For example, William Chambers (1723-1796), who had travelled extensively in the East, designed a Mosque for Kew gardens in 1761 for his patron Frederick, Prince of Wales, who was well known for his oriental tastes (fig.152). Although it was demolished later, the mosque was a clever adaptation of Muslim architectural elements to English taste. In 1758, Chambers made another building for the gardens based on the imitation of Alhambra, but was also demolished.[1156] The design was a version of the famous Andalusian building but in Rococo-Gothic style with the final product showing the great flexibility and adaptability of Muslim architecture. This can be seen further in the version of Alhambra by Johann Heinrich Muntz (1727-1798) also designed for Kew gardens in 1750 (fig.153). Here, Muntz showed a great knowledge of Moorish architecture[1157] as he employed a variety of Muslim arcades, thin columns and the polychrome (red, blue and gold). Sweetman thought that the celebrity of the Kew mosque could have influenced the creation of a fashion, which used mosques as garden buildings.[1158] Other mosques were planned for Hartwell House, Buckinghamshire, and a second at the Hoo in Hertfordshire, a third at Stourhead and a fourth at Wroxton.[1159]

There are also instances, which show Europe adopting elements of Muslim lifestyle often resulting in the introduction of particular building types. One of these is the café, which was directly imported from Turkey in the seventeenth century. The European first contacted coffee in the sixteenth century, imported by Venetian merchants trading with North Africa, Egypt and the East. The earliest coffee drink made in Europe was prepared in 1570 in Venetian ports but the first coffee houses appeared about a century later, in 1645, in Venice.[1160] Galland traced the first introduction of coffee into France back to 1644, when some French men from Marseilles brought back from Istanbul, not only quantities of coffee, but also the proper vessels and apparatus for making the beverage.[1161] In 1671, the first coffeehouse was opened in Marseilles in the Exchange District, after that more coffee houses were opened elsewhere in France and in Germany by 1720s.

It was not until 1650 when a Turk named Pasqua Rosée brought coffee to England, and sold it in a coffee house in George-yard, Lombard Street, London.[1162] Eight years later another café was opened "Sultaness Head" in Cornhill[1163] and by 1700; there were about 500 coffee houses in London and 3,000 in England[1164]. They were known as "penny universities" because they

Figure 151 Historical sources confirm that Nash had consulted the Oriental Scenery of Daniell before designing the Royal Pavilion.

Figure 152 Kew Gardens in 1761 for his patron Frederick, Prince of Wales, who was well known for his oriental tastes

Figure 153 Alhambra by Johann Heinrich Muntz (1727-1798), also designed for Kew gardens in 1750

often held intellectual and political debates while paying a penny[1165] for the price of a cup of coffee. Later the coffee beans came to England from Mokah[1166] on the Red Sea (Yemen), imported by the East India Company and from Aleppo by the Levant Company. With the use of coffee came the need for coffee ceramics and silver pots and ewer shapes that had been long established in the Islamic World since the 13th and 14th centuries. The Muslim origin of most of the coffee houses and inns such as the Saracen's Head, The Sultan's Head or the Turk's Head explains the fascination of the population of Europe with Muslims despite their sworn enmity.

Another element that was borrowed from the prosperous Turkish lifestyle was the bath. It is commonly known that the Romans built elaborated baths complete with a medium heated room or *Tepidarium*, a hot steam room or *Caldarium*, and a room with a cold plunge pool or *Frigidarium*. In larger baths, there were other sections with changing rooms called *Apodyterium*, a reading room and sports area. Nevertheless, these treatment centres were for the rich and political elite only. After the collapse of the Romans, these baths went out of use and Europe of the Dar Ages lost contact with them. The Muslims who had been under Roman rule in countries like Syria, Lebanon and North Africa inherited the tradition and gave it greater impetus because of Islam's emphasis on cleanliness, hygiene and good health, *"cleanliness is half the faith"* prophet Muhammed asserted. Muslim baths, or *Hammams* as they are usually known, were very elaborate often with elegant designs, décor and ornamentation. Under the Mamluk and Ottoman rules, they were especially sumptuous buildings in their rich design and luxurious decorations, furnished with beautiful fountains and decorative pools. The Muslim art of bathing is subject to many rules and manners that need to be strictly followed, especially those separating between times of use between males and females and the prohibition of complete nakedness as bathers have always to cover themselves in lower garments. A few books were written about these manners, but the most revered one is the work of Abu Ishaq Ibrahim Ibn Ishaq al-Harbi (9th century): *Hammam and it manners.*

Europe and the Christian world did not rediscover the bath until the Crusades when they encountered them in Jerusalem and Syria[1167]. Towards the 12th century baths became popular for a while but the church banned their use partly because they belonged to "the culture of Muslims, the infidels" and partly because of the improper use of them, leading to widespread adultery and bad sexual habits. In the 1529, Sir John Treffy, in his 'Grete herball', reported, "*many folke that hath bathed them in colde water have dyed.*"[1168] By late seventeenth

388

century, the West rediscovered baths through Turkey. Since then the use of oriental baths became fashionable, especially in England where places such as London, Manchester, and Leeds were renowned for their elegant baths. The first Turkish bath or "Bagnio" built by Turkish Merchants was opened as early as 1679, off Newgate Street, now Bath Street, in London.[1169]

A more remarkable bath was opened by a Muslim Indian migrant, Mohammad Sake, in Brighton on the site of the present Queen's Hotel. The bath was opened in 1786 in the style and functions of a Turkish bath with a medicated steam or vapour bath and a room for massage, which was then, called shampooing, a term which was derived from the Indian treatment of *champi* or therapeutic massage. This bathing and messaging method was behind the inspiration of the so-called shampoo, the hair cleaning foam. With this innovation, Mohammad Sake received the ultimate accolade of being appointed 'Shampooing Surgeon' to both George IV and William IV. Turkish baths were also built in Scotland and in Edinburgh where John Burnet designed the famous Drumsheugh Baths in 1882. The elaborate nature of the bath was still in all its glory incorporating a suite of Turkish baths with a dome supported on a brick and stone structure with geometrical lattice windows in frames of horseshoe arches. The façade was decorated with elegant Moorish arcade with iron grilles in geometric patterns.

Another area of imitation was in the design of kiosks and conservatories. The kiosk, koshk in Turkish, can be defined as an open summerhouse or pavilion usually having its roof supported by pillars with screened or totally open walls. The Suljuks first introduced it as a domed hall with open arched sides attached to the main mosque, gradually evolving into a summerhouse used by Ottoman sultans. There are at least two of the most famous Ottoman kiosks, which still survive including the Cinili koshk and Baghdad Koshk. The first was built in 1473 by Mohammed al-Fatih at the Topkapi Palace, Istanbul, and consists of two-storey building topped with a dome and having open sides overlooking the gardens of the palace. Sultan Murad 4th also built the Baghdad Koshk at the Topkapi Palace in 1638/39. The building is also domed offering direct views onto the Palace gardens and the city of Istanbul.

It was Lady Wortley Montagu (1689-1762), the wife of the English ambassador to Constantinople, who first brought the concept of kiosk into English usage. In a letter she wrote on 1 April 1717 to Anne Thistlethwayte, she mentioned a "*chiosk*": '*In the midst of the garden is the chiosk, that is, a large room, commonly beautiful with fine fountain in the midst of it. It is raised by 9 or 10 steps and enclosed with gilded lattices, round which vines, jessamines and honeysuckles make a sort of green wall. Large tress are planted round this place, which is the scene of their greatest pleasures, and where the ladies spend most of their hours, employed by their music or embroidery."*[1170] However, European monarchs brought it into Europe. The King of Poland Stanislas of Lorraine, who was also the father in law of Louis XV, built several kiosks based on his memories of his residence in Turkey.[1171] Following his defeat against his rival King Augustus II, Stanislas requested the protection of the Ottomans who hosted him, between 1712 to 1714 in cities of Bendery or Bender (in today's Moldova) and Adrianople (Edirne).[1172] From Stanislas' pavilions, kiosks spread into the rest of European capitals where they were used as garden pavilions serving coffee and beverages. More recently, they were converted into bandstands and tourist information stands decorating many European gardens, parks and high streets.

From the kiosk evolved also the so-called conservatory, glass rooms erected in gardens of most European houses. Historical sources indicate that the earliest conservatories were perhaps those made by Humphrey Repton (1752 - 1818) for the Royal Pavilion at Brighton, in the form of corridors connecting the Pavilion to the stables and consisting of a passage of flowers covered with glass and linked with an orangery, a greenhouse, an aviary, a pheasantry and hothouses.[1173] The influence of Muslim and Indian forms on these buildings is overwhelming and particularly in the pheasantry where its higher part was an adaptation of kiosks on the roof of the Palace in the Fort of Allahabad which was illustrated by Daniells. The 19th century witnessed a great upsurge of the gardening fashion in Europe and England and with it, the construction of glass buildings gained popularity. Islamic-Indian forms and motifs provided an aesthetic exoticism and furnished the lightness that these structures needed. The appeal extended even to flowers and plants, which were imported for these conservatories from India.[1174] Today's conservatories still incorporates some of the Muslim elements although modern art forms have shifted from the classical motifs.

Notes

[963] Sweetman, John (1987), '*the Oriental Obsession: Islamic Inspiration in British and American Art and Architecture 1500-1920*', Cambridge University Press, Cambridge.

[964] Ibid.

[965] See for example, Armand, O. Citarella, (1968), '*Patterns in Medieval Trade: The Commerce of Amalfi Before the Crusades*', Journal of Economic History, Vol.28, pp.531-555

[966] Holmes George (ed.) (2002), '*The Oxford History of Medieval Europe*', Oxford University Press, p.211

[967] Battles Dominique (2004), '*The Medieval Tradition of Thebes: History and Narrative in the OF Roman De Thebes, Boccaccio, Chaucer and Lydgate*', Routledge, UK, p.27

[968] Brotton Jerry (2003), '*The Renaissance Bazaar: From the Silk Road to Michelangelo*', Oxford University Press, p.1.

[969] See Wedgeworth Robert (1993), '*World Encyclopaedia of Library and Information Services*', 3rd edition, American Library Association, Chicago, p.577 and Hancock Lee (2005), '*Lorenzo De' Medici: Lorenzo De'medici:Patron of Art* ', the Rosen Publishing Group, p.31.

[970] These complicated relations with the Muslims are fully developed by Chew, Samuel Claggett, (1974), '*The Crescent and the Rose: Islam and England During the Renaissance*', Oxford University Press, New York.

[971] Willan, T.S. (1955) '*English Trade with the Levant in the 16th Century*', in English History Review, vol. LXX, pp.399-410.

[972] Sweetman, J. (1987), op cit. p.3.

[973] Schwab, Raymond, 1884-1956 (1984), '*The Oriental Obsession: Islamic Inspiration in British and American Art and Architecture 1500-1920*', translated by Gene Patterson-Black and Victor Rethinking La Renaissance oriental. English Guildford: Columbia University Press New York, p.5.

[974] See Holt Peter Malcolm (1973), '*Studies in the History of the Near East*', Routledge, pp.27-50

[975] Le Bas Charles Webb (2005), '*The Life of Archbishop Laud*' , Kessinger Publishing, p.250

[976] Nanji Azim et.al.(1997), '*Mapping Islamic Studies: Genealogy, Continuity and Change*', Walter de Gruyter, Berlin and New York p.51

[977] See Grafton T. Anthony (1993), '*Joseph Scaliger: A Study in the History of Classical Scholarship*', Oxford University Press.

[978] Fuks Lajb, R. G. and Fuks-Mansfel (1984), '*Hebrew Typography in the Northern Netherlands, 1585-1815: Historical Evaluation and Descriptive Bibliography*', Brill d Academic Publishers, p.18

[979] Nanji Azim et.al. (1997), '*Mapping Islamic Studies: Genealogy, Continuity and Change*', op.cit. p.69

[980] Hamilton Alastair and Richards Francis (2004), '*Andre´ du Ryer and Oriental Studies*' in Seventeenth-Century France', Oxford: Oxford University Press, p.16

[981] Ibid., p.69

[982] Jones Robert, (1994), 'The Medici Oriental Press (Rome 1584-1614) and the Impact of its Arabic Publications on Northern Europe' in G.A. Russell (ed.), *The 'Arabick' Interests of the Natural Philosophers in Seventeenth-Century England*, E. J. Brill, Leiden, pp.88-108.

[983] Nanji Azim et.al. (1997), op cit. p.33

[984] This translation was widely read.

[985] He was the King's minister and administrator of the collection of Cardinal Mazarin 1624-1661, after his death in 1661, which included many Persian and Turkish art pieces.

[986] The complete title of his work is as follows: Herbelot Barthelemy de. (1697), `Bibliothèque Oriental, ou Dictionnaire Universel Contenant Généralement Tout ce qui Regarde la Connoissance des Peuples de l'Orient'. La Compagnie des Libraires, First Edition, Paris.

[987] Schwab, R. (1984), op cit. p.22.

[988] Tavernier, Jean-Baptiste, 1605-1689 (1678), 'Six Voyages Through Turkey into Persia and the East-Indies', made English by J. Phillips, London.

[989] Thévenot, Jean de, 1633-1667 (1687), 'The Travels of Monsieur de Thévenot into the Levant', In three parts, viz. Into I. Turkey, II. Persia, III. The East Indies, done out of French by A. Lovell, London

[990] Bernier, François, 1620-1688, 'Travels in the Mogul Empire, AD 1656-1668', 3rd ed1972, revised by A. Constable, Chand.

[991] Who was a draughtsman to Chardin, Grelot, Guillaume Joseph (1680), 'Relation Nouvelle d'un Voyage de Constantinople', Paris.

[992] Sweetman, J. (1987), op cit.

[993] Shaw, J.B. (1984) `Gentile Bellini and Constantinople', in Apollo, Volume cxx, pp.56-58.

[994] Scarce M. Jennifer (2014) 'Women's Costume of the Near and Middle East', Routledge', p.40

[995] However, Raby claims that it was a depiction of Mamluk ceremony in Damascus rather than an Ottoman ceremony in Cairo as had commonly been thought. For the dating, he predicts to be made between 1495 and 1499, see Raby, Julian (1982) `Venice, Durer and the Oriental Mode' The Hans Huth Memorial Studies, London.

[996] Raby, Julian (1982) `Venice, Durer and the Oriental Mode' The Hans Huth Memorial Studies, London.

[997] Pieter's book was Moeurs et Fachons de Faire de Turcs, while Melchior 's book was published in 1626, see Sweetman, J. (1987), op cit. note 29, p.259.

[998] Halsband, R. (1965 ed.), 'The complete letters of Lady Mary Wortley Montagu', Clarendon Press, Oxford, pp.308, 328.

[999] She was the one who introduced the inoculation against the smallpox. In her writing, she wrote about the Ottoman practice of deliberately stimulating a mild form of the disease through inoculation, which conferred immunity. She reported having the procedure performed on both her children. She writes : "I am patriot enough to take the pains to bring this useful invention into fashion in England, and I should not fail to write to some of our doctors very particularly about it, if I knew any one of them that I thought had virtue enough to destroy such a considerable branch of their revenue, for the good of mankind" On here return to England she introduced the inoculation which was practised there until the end of the eighteenth century, when the English physician Edward Jenner was able to cultivate a serum in cattle (Jenner used cow pox for inoculation- different and less dangerous), which was used in human vaccination. From Anthony Henricy, (1796), 'Lady Mary Wortley Montagu, Letters of the Right Honourable Lady Mary Wortley Montagu: Written During her Travels in Europe, Asia and Africa. . . , vol. 1 (Aix:), pp. 167-69; letter 36, to Mrs. S. C. from Adrianople, N.D.

[1000]Fischer von Erlach, Johann Bernhard, 1656-1723, (1737), 'A Plan of Civil and Historical Architecture', First published at Leipzig, in German and French and translated into English, with large additional notes; by Thomas Lediard, The second edition, London.

[1001] Hodges, William, 1744-1797, 'Choix de Vues de l'Inde Dessinées sur les Lieux, Pendant les Annees 1780, 1781, 1782, et 1783', ... par W. Hodges, ... Select Views in India, Drawn on the Spot, in the Years 1780, 1781, 1782, and 1783', printed by Joseph Cooper for the author, London.

[1002] quoted by Danby Miles, (1995), op cit. p.154.

[1003] Rabun Julie L., and Blakemore Robbie G. (1996), '*History of Interior Design and Furniture: From Ancient Egypt to Nineteenth-Century Europe*', John Wiley and Sons, p.106

[1004] La Boullaye le Gouz, François de, (1653), '*Les voyages et observations, où sont décrites les religions, gouvernements et situations des états d'Italie, Grèce, Natolie, Syrie, Palestine, etc., Grand Mogol, Bijapour, Indes Orientales*', Gervais Closier, Paris.

[1005] Naderzad , B (1972) '*Louis 14th, La Boullaye et l'Exorisme Persan*', in Gazette des Beaux Arts, Vol.79, pp.29-38.

[1006] Levey, Michael, (1975), '*The World of Ottoman Art*', Thames and Hudson, London, p.55.

[1007] Often referred to as The Yew Tree Ball

[1008] A plant, of yellow flower, known for its cure of a number of diseases.

[1009] Ogilby, John, (1673), '*Asia, the first Part, Being an Accurate Description of Persia, the Vast Empire of the Great Mogol, and Other Parts of India, etc*'. London, See Eerde, Katherine S. van (1976), *John Ogilby and the Tate of His Times*, Dawson, London.

[1010] Ockley, Simon, (1718), '*The History of the Saracens*', printed for Bernard Lintot, London.

[1011] The Palace was designed by Sir Christopher Wren and built on the site of an ancient castle in 1683. See Bryant Arthur (1932), 'King Charles II', Longmans, Green and Co. London, p.338

[1012] Marly Diana de (1974) '*King Charles II's Own Fashion: The Theatrical Origins of the English Vest*', in Journal of the Warburg and Courtauld Institutes, London: Warburg Institute (JWCI), vol. 37, pp.378-382

[1013] Marly Diana de (1974) OP.CIT. pp.378-382O

[1014] Marly Diana de (1974) '*King Charles II's own fashion: The Theatrical Origins of the English Vest*', op.cit. p.379.

[1015] Ettinghausen, R. (1974), '*The Impact of Muslim Decorative Arts and Painting on the Arts of Europe*', Schacht Joseph and Boswoth, C. E. ed., 'The Legacy of Islam', 2nd Edition, The Clarendon Press, Oxford, pp.292-317, p.295.

[1016] Linda Komaroff, Curator of Islamic Art at the Los Angeles Country Museum of Art, http://www.lacma.org/islamic_art/intro.htm, accessed June 23rd 2015.

[1017] Ettinghausen, R. (1974), '*The Impact of Muslim decorative arts and painting on the Arts of Europe*', Schacht Joseph and Boswoth, C. E. ed., 'The Legacy of Islam', 2nd Edition, The Clarendon Press, Oxford, pp.292-317, p.295.

[1018] Ibid.

[1019] Ward, P.J. (1967) '*Some Mainstreams and Tributaries in European Ornament From 1500 to 1750*', Bulletin of the Victoria and Albert Museum, Vol.3, part 1 and 2.

[1020] Giovanni Antonio Tagliente (1527), '*Essempio di Recammi*'. Venedig: Giovan Antonio et fratelli de Sabbio; ab. 1530 u. d. T.: Esemplario nuovo (vor allem Stickmuster).

[1021] Pellegrino, Francesco di (1908 ed.), '*La Fleur de la Science de Pourtraicture. Patrons de Broderie, Facons Arabicque et Ytalique*', par Francisque Pellegrin 1530, Printed by Jacques Nyverd avec introduction par Gaston Migeon, Paris.

[1022] More than 100 according to Sweetman, J.(1987), op cit. p.21.

[1023] Hamlin Dwight Foster (2003), '*A History of Ornament Ancient and Medieval 1916*', 1st published 1916, Kessinger Publishing, p.243

[1024] Christie A.H. (1931), '*Islamic minor Arts and Their Influence Upon European Work*', in T. Arnold and A.Guillaume, eds., The Legacy of Islam, (1st ed), Oxford University Press, pp. 108—154, at p.151.

[1025] McCormack W. J. (1999), '*The Blackwell Companion to Modern Irish Culture*', Blackwell, p.255

[1026] Fontoynont Marc (1999), *'Daylight Performance of Building'*, European Commission Directorate-General XII, Science, Research, and Development, James and James, p.37

[1027] Christie, A.H. (1929) `*Traditional Methods of Pattern Designing'*, revised edition, Clarendon Press, Oxford, and Creswell (1932), *'Early Muslim Architecture'*, Oxford, went for the same claim in his study of window grill of the Umayyad Mosque in Damascus.

[1028] Critchlow, Keith (1976), 'Islamic *Patterns: an Analytical and Cosmological* Approach', Thames and Hudson, London.

[1029] See Necipoglu Gulru (1995), *'The Topkapi Scroll: Geometry and Ornament in Islamic Architecture'*, Getty Centre for the History of Art and the Humanities, Santa Monica, California.

[1030] Ibid.

[1031] BBC.co.uk, News 24/02/2007: http://news.bbc.co.uk/2/hi/middle_east/6389157.stm

[1032] Abouseaf Doris Behrens (2005), *'European Arts and Crafts at the Mamluk Court'*, in Rogers J. Michael et al. ed. Muqarnas Essays in Honor of J.M. Rogers: An Annual on the Visual Culture of the Islamic World, Brill Academic publishers, pp.45-54, at p.45.

[1033] Hind, A.M. (1908), *'Two Unpublished Plates of the Series of Six "Knots" Engraved After Designs by Leonardo de Vinci'*, The Burlington Magazine, vol.12, p.41.

[1034] Ettinghausen, R. (1974), op cit. p.304.

[1035] Abouseaf Doris Behrens (2005), op cit. p.45

[1036] Diehl Edith (1980), *'Bookbinding: its Background and Technique'*, Dover Publications, p. 82

[1037] Ettinghausen, R. (1974), op cit. p.307.

[1038] Hans Holbein (1497-1543) was a 16th-Century English Portraits Painter Best Known for his Portraits of Henry VIII and His Children, in Which Blackwork and the "Double Running Stitch" were used as decoration on shirt collars, ruffs, cuffs, and linens.

[1039] Thomas Geminus (1548), *'Morysse and Damaschin Renewed and Encreased, Very Profitable for Goldsmythes and Embroderars'*, London.

[1040] Jean de Gourment (1560), *'Livre de Moresques ,Très Utile et Nécessaire à Tous Orfèvres,..."'*, Paris.

[1041] Sweetman, J.(1987), op cit. pp.71-72.

[1042] Briggs, M.S. (1924),*'Muhammadan Architecture in Egypt and Palestine'*, Clarendon Press, Oxford., p.179)

[1043] See Al-Faruqi Isma'il R. (1973), *'Islam and Art'*, Studia Islamica, No. 37. (1973), pp. 81-109.

[1044] From these two main styles, a number of other sub-styles emerged as calligraphers introduced new modifications to the original style. The most familiar ones are Thuluth, Al-Rakaa, Al-Diwany, Jali Diwany, and Persain.

[1045] According to Al-Jaburi, after the establishment of Kufa, some Yemeni tribes who knew an early form of this lettering style settled there. This style attained its complete shape under the reign of the fourth Caliph (Ali), between 657 and 661 CE, who was a calligrapher himself, see Al-Jaburi Mahmood Shukre (1974), *'The Birth of Arabic Calligraphy and its Development'*, (in Arabic) Library Al-shark al-Jadid, Baghdad.

[1046] For more see Al-Jaburi Mahmood Shukre (1974), *'The Birth of Arabic Calligraphy and its Development'*, (in Arabic) op, cit.

[1047] Male, E (1923) *'Les Influences arabes dans l'art roman'*, in *Revue des Deux-Mondes*, p. 311-343.

[1048] Christie, A.H. (1922) `*Development of Ornament from Arabic Script'*, Burlington Magazine, XLI, pp.2867-288.

[1049] Christie, A.H. (1922) `*Development of Ornament from Arabic Script'*, Burlington Magazine, Vol. 40, No. 231. (Jun., 1922), pp. 287-288+291-292, at p.287

[1050] Christie, A.H. (1922) `Development of Ornament from Arabic Script', Burlington Magazine, Vol. 40, No. 231. (Jun.1922), pp. 287-288+291-292. and Christie, A.H. (1922), `Development of Ornament from Arabic Script II', the Burlington Magazine for Connoisseurs, Vol. 41, No. 232. (JuL, 1922), pp. 34+37-38+41.

[1051] Christie, A.H. (1922) `Development of Ornament from Arabic Script', Burlington Magazine, Vol. 40, No. 231. (Jun. 1922), pp. 287-288+291-292.

[1052] Friedman Jane M. (1997), `These Stitches Speak', Saudi Aramco, vol.48, No.2, pp.2-11

[1053] Mackie Louise W. (1984), `Toward an Understanding of Mamluk Silks: National and International Considerations', Muqarnas, Vol. 2, The Art of the Mamluks., pp. 127-146.

[1054] Sweetman, J. (1987), op cit. p.5.

[1055] Clair Alexandrine N St (1973), `The Image of the Turk in Europe', Metropolitan Museum of Art, New York.

[1056] Willson, D. H. (1956), `King James VI and I', Jonathan Cape, London, p.331.

[1057] Sweetman, J. (1987), op cit. p.42.

[1058] Irwin John and Katherine B. Brett (1970), `Origins of Chintz: With a Catalogue of Indo-European Cotton-Paintings in the Victoria and Albert Museum', London, and the Royal Ontario Museum, Toronto', H.M.S.O, London.

[1059] Christie A.H. (1931), `Islamic minor Arts and Their Influence Upon European Work', in T. Arnold and A. Guillaume, eds., The Legacy of Islam, (1st ed.), Oxford University Press, pp. 108—154

[1060] Birdwood, George C. M., and Frank Herbert Brown (1915), `Sva', P.L. Warner, London, p.247

[1061] Sweetman,J. (1987), op cit. p.5.

[1062] Dimand M. S. (1964), `Two Fifteenth Century Hispano-Moresque Rugs', The Metropolitan Museum of Art Bulletin, New Series, Vol. 22, No. 10., pp. 341-352.

[1063] The origins of the depiction of animals have been traced back to ninth century Egypt as excavations at Fustat (Cairo) revealed the existence of such designs in Cairene carpets. They became particularly fashionable in Anatolian typology of 14th and 15th centuries.

[1064] Mills, J. (1975), `Carpets in Pictures', Publications Department National Gallery, London. pp.4-5.

[1065] Mack, E. Rosamond (2004), `Oriental Carpets in Italian Renaissance Painting: Art Objects and Status Symbols', Magazine Antiques, Brant Publications.

[1066] Which contains a floor carpet with octagons depicting eagles, now at the National Gallery of London.

[1067] Mills, J. (1975), `Carpets in Pictures', Publications Department National Gallery, London, pp.4-5.

[1068] Ibid. p.16.

[1069] Mack, E. Rosamond (2004), `Oriental Carpets in Italian Renaissance Painting: Art Objects and Status Symbols', Magazine Antiques, Brant Publications. p. 179.

[1070] Gans-Ruedin, E. (1975), `Antique Oriental Carpets, From the Seventeenth to the Early Twentieth Century', translated from, 'le tapis de l'Amateur', by Richard and Elizabeth Bartlett, Thames and Hudson, London.p.20.

[1071] Victoria and Albert Museum (1920) `Guide to the Collection of Carpets', HMSO, London, p.3.

[1072] Erdmann, K. (1962), `Europa und der Orinetteppich', Mainz, Berlin, pp.11-17.

[1073] Mills, J. (1975), op.cit. p.17.

[1074] Victoria and Albert Museum (1920), op cit. p.3.

[1075] Boase, T. S. R. (Thomas Sherrer Ross), (1953), `English Art, 1100-1216', Clarendon Press, Oxford, p. 170.

[1076] Beattie, M. (1964), `Britain and the Oriental Carpet', Leeds Art Calendar 55: 4–15, and Mills, J. (1983), 'the coming of the carpet to the West', in ARTS n ARTS, Exhibition Catalogue, the Eastern Carpet in the Western World, London, pp. 11-23. E

[1077] King, D. (1983) `the Inventories of the Carpets of King Henry 8 ', in Hali 5, pp.287-296.

[1078] The Ushak star consists of eight point indented star motif alternating with lozenge shapes.

[1079] Ettinghausen, (1974), op. cit. p.301.

[1080] Beattie, M.H. (1959) 'Antique Rugs at Hardwick Hall', in Oriental Art, vol. 5, pp.52-61.

[1081] Ibid.

[1082] Ettinghausen, 1974, op.cit. p301.

[1083] Ibid.

[1084] Victoria and Albert Museum, op., cit. p.9.

[1085] See Wirth, E. (1976) 'Der Orientteppich und Europa', Heft 37, Gedruckt in der universitatsbuchdruckerei Junge & Sohn, Erlangen, p.337.

[1086] Ajmar-Wollheim and Flora Dennis (2006), 'At Home in Renaissance Italy: Art and Life in the Italian House 1400-1600', V&A Publications, London, Quoted in Rob Attar(2006),'At Home in Renaissance', BBC History magazine, volume 7, No.10, p.26.

[1087] Glaze: made from chemicals producing glass like coat. It is transparent but coloured when colorants are added. It is usually applied in a liquid form before firing. It gives a glossy coating to the surface of the clay. The technique used consisted of two main methods: For the production of tin glazed pottery, the potted clay was first biscuited (fired), then dipped in slurry of lead- glaze made opaque by the addition of oxide (ashes) of tin. The glaze turned white when the piece is fired once more.
In the production of lustre, the tin glazed product is given a second firing then painted with metal oxide. Later, it is fired again (for the third time) at a lower temperature and in a reducing atmosphere (carbon in the oxygen-less kiln reduces the oxides to thin films of the basic metal). Copper sulphate gives a rich ruby-red, silver nitrate a yellowish brown.

[1088] See Baramki, D.C. (1942), `The Pottery from Khirbet El-Mefjer', The Quarterly of the Department of Antiquities in Palestine (QDAP), vol. 10, pp.65-103., Sauer, J.A. (1975), `Umayyad pottery from sites in East Jordan', Jordan, Vol.4, pp.25-32.

[1089] Lane, A. (1947) `Early Islamic Pottery', Faber and Faber, London., p.3.

[1090] Whereas more lead enhances the optical properties of the glaze, giving a smooth, brilliant surface finish.

[1091] Lane, A. (1947) op. cit. P.12.

[1092] Fehérvári, Géza (2000), 'Ceramics of the Islamic world in the Tareq Rajab Museum', I.B. Tauris, London & New York. p.36.

[1093] Tin causes greater opacity and therefore whiteness.

[1094] Hurst, J.C. (1977) `Spanish pottery imported into Medieval Britain', in Medieval Archaeology, vol.21, pp68-105.

[1095] Hess, Catherine, et al. (eds.) (2004) 'The Arts of Fire: Islamic Influences on Glass and Ceramics of the Italian Renaissance', Getty Publications, Los Angeles

[1096] Sweetman, J. (1987), p.35.

[1097] Hess, Catherine, et al. (eds.) (2004) op,cit.

[1098] Sweetman, J. (1987), op cit. p.50.

[1099] Craf Nora (2002), 'Javelina Candy', in Yavapi gardens, Master Gardener Newsletter, University of Arizona, Yavapai County, County Cooperative Extension, December 2002, pp.3-7

[1100] Archer, M and Morgan, B. (1977) `Fair as China Dishes', International Exhibitions Foundation, Washington DC, cat.21. Also, Archer M. (1982) `the Dating of Delfware Chargers', in Transactions of the English Ceramic Circle, vol.11, pp.112-121. at p.118.

[1101] Mellor Gilbert sir (1934)`Bristol Delftware' in Transactions of the English Ceramic Circle ,vol.1, No.2, plate 10, b, c, &d) .

[1102] Howard Debora (2000),' Venice an d the East', Yale University Press, p.7

[1103] Howard Debora (2000),' Venice an d the East', Yale University Press, p.111

[1104] Howard Debora (2000),' Venice an d the East', Yale University Press, p.115

[1105] Howard Debora (2000),' Venice an d the East', Yale University Press, p.119

[1106] Ibid.p. 122

[1107] Howard Debora (2000), p, cit. p.140

[1108] Scattolin Giorgia (1961), 'Le case fondaco sul Canal Grande', private printing, Venice.

[1109] Howard Debora (2000),' Venice an d the East', Yale University Press, p.144

[1110] Stefano Carboni (2007), 'Venice and the Islamic World, 827-1797', Yale University Press, p.8

[1111] Klingender, Francis Donald (1968), 'Art and the Industrial Revolution', edited and revised by Arthur Elton, Revised ed., Kelley, New York.

[1112] Molière, 1622-1673 (1964 ed.), 'Le bourgeois Gentilhomme', Petits classiques Bordas, Paris.

[1113] Sweetman, J. (1987) op cit. p.68.

[1114] Danby, M (1995), op cit. p.153.

[1115] Ibid.

[1116] Ibid.

[1117] Nathaniel Whittock, (1827) `Decorative Painter's and Glazier's Guide' Isaac Taylor Hinton, London.

[1118] Mackenzie, John, M. (1995), 'Orientalism: History, Theory and the Arts', Manchester University Press, p.76.

[1119] Sweetman, J.(1987), op cit. p.68.

[1120] Sweetman, J.(1987), op cit. p.109.

[1121] Conner, Patrick, (1979),`Oriental Architecture in the West', Thames and Hudson, London.

[1122] Ibid.

[1123] In 1930, it was burnt in a fire and was rebuilt in a different design.

[1124] Said Edward (1978), 'Orientalism', Vintage Books, New York, p.3

[1125] Conner, P. (1979), op cit. p.68.

[1126] Berkeley Alice, Lowndes Susan, Lowndes Marques Susan (1994), 'English Art in Portugal', Edições Inapa, p.100

[1127] Beckford, William, (1786), 'Vathek: An Arabian Tale', printed for J. Johnson London. Vathek is an Oriental tale about a Caliph named Vathek who builds a tall tower so that he can view all seven kingdoms of the world. Beckford here hopelessly attacked Islam and this book is considered worse than the Satanic Verses of Salman Rushdie.

[1128] Danby, M. (1995), op cit. p.153.

[1129] Hope, Thomas, (1970 ed.), 'Household Furniture and Interior Decoration', Tiranti, London.

[1130] Sweetman, J. (1987), op cit. p,98.

[1131] Stroud, Dorothy (1971), 'George Dance, Architect, 1741-1825', Faber and Faber Ltd., London.p.70,

[1132] Daniell, Thomas, (1797), 'Oriental Scenery. : Twenty-Four Views in Hindoostan, Taken in the Year 1792, Drawn by Thomas Daniell, and Engraved by Himself and William Daniell', printed by Robert Bowyer, London.

[1133] Coysh, A. W. (Arthur Wilfred), (1970), 'Blue and White Transfer Ware, 1780-1840', David & Charles, Newton Abbot., p.30, fig.42.

[1134] Hyland Peter (2005), 'The Herculaneum Pottery: Liverpool's Forgotten Glory', Liverpool University Press, Fig.90, p.118, Fig.9, p.119 and p.120.

[1135] Ibid. p.117.

[1136] Sweetman, J. (1987), op cit.

[1137] Ibid. Clark, Gordon Jane, (2004) 'Wallpaper in Decoration', Frances Lincoln Ltd., p.46

[1138] Lyon Gardiner Tyler, (1967), Tyler's Quarterly Historical and Genealogical Magazine, p.189

[1139] Clark, Gordon Jane, (2004), op cit. p.46.

[1140] Ibid., p.21.

[1141] Ibid., p.23.

[1142] Archer, Mildred (1980), 'Early views of India: the Complete Acquatints: the Picturesque Journeys of Thomas and William Daniell 1786-1794', Thames and Hudson, London, p.229.

[1143] Ibid. p.229.

[1144] Danby, M. (1995), op cit. p.155.

[1145] Conner, P. (1979), op cit. plate 125.

[1146] Currently known as the Dome Concert Hall. This was a huge 65 feet high domed rotunda with opening whose character greatly matching those of the Great Mosque of Delhi and illustrated by Daniells (Danby, 1995, p.158).

[1147] Conner, 1979, p.131, plate 185.

[1148] See Stroud, Dorothy (1962), 'Humphry Repton', Country Life, London.

[1149] Danby, M.(1995, p.158.

[1150] Dinkel, J. (1983), 'The Royal Pavilion, Brighton', Philip Wilson Publishers, London, p.53.

[1151] Evans, John, (1821), `Recreation for the Young and the Old. An Excursion to Brighton, With an Account of the Royal Pavilion, a Visit to Tunbridge Wells, and a Trip to Southend,. In a series of letters, etc., Chiswick.

[1152] Sweetman, J. (1987), op cit. p.107.

[1153] Ibid. note 73, p.278.

[1154] Ibid.

[1155] Conner, P. (1979), op cit.

[1156] Mackenzie, John, M. (1995), op cit. p.75.

[1157] According to Danby, M (1995), op. cit. Muntz visited Spain.

[1158] Sweetman, J.(1987), op cit. p.70.

[1159] Ibid. p.70 and Mackenzie, John, M. (1995), op cit. p.75.

[1160] Darby, M. (1983), 'The Islamic Perspective, an Aspect of British Architecture and Design in the 19th Century', Leighton House, Gallery, London.

[1161] Antoine Galland in his 1699 book 'de l'Origine et du Progrez du Café', Éd. originale J. Cavelier Paris, 1992- La Bibliothèque, coll. L'Écrivain Voyageur.

[1162] Pasqua Rosée was a servant of Daniel Edwards, and English merchant who imported coffee from Turkey.

[1163] Darby, M. (1983), op cit.

[1164] Ellis, Aytoun, (1956), 'the Penny Universities : a History of the Coffee-Houses'. - Secker & Warburg, London and Burn, Jacob Henry, (d. 1869), 'A Descriptive Catalogue of the London Traders, Tavern, and Coffee-House Token', 2nd ed., London.

[1165] About 120th of the current Pound Sterling.

[1166] The earliest cup of coffee was made as early as 9th century in Yemen by a group of Sufis, who boiled the beans and drunk it to help them stay awake all night in prayers and remembrance of God (Allah). A group of their students took it to Cairo using it in their study circles at the al-Azhar university. From there the habit of drinking coffee took off in most Middle Eastern countries and by 13th century, it reached Turkey.

[1167] Danby, M. (1995), op. cit.

[1168] Arber Robertson Agnes, Stearn Thomas William (1987), '*Herbals Their Origin and Evolution*', 3rd Edition, Cambridge University Press, p.47.

[1169] Aubrey John (1949) ed. 'Brief *lives; Life of Sir Henry Blount*', edited from the original manuscripts by Oliver Lawson Dick Secker and Warburg, London, pp.25-27, at p.26.

[1170] Lady Mary Wortley Montagu (2005), '*Letters from the Right Honourable Lady Mary Wortley Montagu 1709 to 1762*', republished by Kessinger Publishing, p128.

[1171] Avcioglu Nebahat (2003), '*A Palace of One's Own: Stanislas I's Kiosks and the Idea of Self-Representation*', The Art Bulletin, vol.85, pp. 662-684.

[1172] Ibid.

[1173] Sweetman, J. (1987),op cit. p.108.

[1174] Ibid.

GENERAL CONCLUSION

The argument developed in this work has established the decisive influence of Muslim art and architecture on the development of Medieval European architecture. In contrast to what has long been claimed that the Muslim contribution was insignificant and mainly centred around ornamentation and decor, the analysis has concentrated on providing substantial proof that Muslim structural and formal motifs made a crucial contribution to the European architectural revival of the 12th century. This revival provided Europe with the torch of enlightenment that later produced the great artistic and architectural achievements of the Renaissance.

At the outset we began by briefly analysing the general conditions dominating the period of the Middle Ages with the aim of assessing both the validity of Muslim influence and the motivation for European borrowing. Within this objective our discussion of the Muslim achievement has established the Muslim superiority in the Middle Ages which extended to all intellectual and creative domains whether it was science, technology or architecture. Starting at the end of the 7th century, at a time when Europe was engulfed in the darkness of the Middle Asges under the tyranny of the Barbarians, Muslims began building their civilising mission. First the Quran and the authentic hadith of the prophet established the broad ethical foundations. Seeking knowledge and developing a scientific approach to understanding life and the universe were firmly advocated by the two most important sources of Islamic religion. Succeeding caliphs from the Umayyad, Abbasids and their successors eagerly applied these directives producing some of the greatest achievements of humanity.

Architectural advances made in a number of structural and decorative aspects formed an integral part of this achievment which reached its peack in the eleventh century coinciding with the appearance of the first signs of revival in Europe. The most influential innovations which had a dramatic impact on the architectural revival in Europe were the introduction of the pointed arch, the rib vaulting, and the improvement of the pier. The advances made in military architecture also found their use in Europe.

The task undertaken in Chapter three was an examination of the socio-cultural conditions of Europe during the Medieval period demonstrating that Europe was in a state of scientific, economic and artistic decline and unable to undertake any architectural development. Perhaps the most relevant conclusion drawn is that Europe, during much of this period, had lost contact with classical architecture as the social and cultural life retreated to rural localities based on an agricultural economy with wood providing the main ingredient for its construction industry.

This material assisted the destructive role of the Barbarians who set fire to much of what was standing. It was not until the beginning of the 11th century that Europe saw an unprecedented architectural activity leading to the appearance of large and complex stone and brick buildings. We can only ask how did the European patrons and masons discover this new impetus and at this particular time? The conditions of Europe at the time were not in favour of the development of any artistic or architectural talents and therefore an external origin becomes paramount.

The absence of any evidence to suport the usual claim of slow self development endorses our view that such a revival was due to foreign sources, especially Muslims who were the world leaders at that time. This has not escaped some impartial Western academics who declare their support for the Muslim origin of the development of Medieval European architecture. In cultural terms, we discovered a strange consistent parallel in the development of cultural and philosophical subjects between Muslims and Europeans. Ideas and subjects debated by Muslim scholars in the 10th and 11th centuries, particularly those relating to mystic meaning of beauty and light, were taken over by Europeans in the 12th and 13th centuries and in most cases producing the same arguments and definitions. This parallelism extended also to areas of science and especially art and architecture. This can mean only one simple truth consolidating the influence of Muslims. Such truth was tested also in the literary sources, which might have influenced the medieval architectural development in Europe. Here, once again, we find strong connections to Muslim traditions, life and buildings.

After establishing these theoretical elements, we proceeded with our argument attempting to provide material and historical evidence, which can prove such influence. In both historical and factual terms we discovered three main transfer routes which provided a rational explanation for the movement of artistic and architectural motifs and forms. Contact with the Muslims through the Crusades, pilgrimage, and the Andalusian and Sicilian connections inspired European architects, masons, patrons and clergy with solutions to their building problems.

European patrons, nobles and churchmen travelling as traders, pilgrims, missionaries, embassies or crusaders admired both the design, size and architectural aesthetics of Muslim buildings especially the masterpieces described in earlier chapters. In order to counter Islam and establish the "superiority" of Christianity, the church engaged in building "bigger" and "better" edifices. The time for building was also right because the church was freed from secular domination and established its supreme power and authority. The church also accumulated large wealth from the collections made for Crusades or from pilgrimage. Meanwhile, European masons learnt Muslim skills and building techniques and adapted them to their own environment. The learning process took place through three main ways. The first was through the observation of Muslim buildings, either completed or in the process of construction. The learning could also have taken place through the discussion with local masons who were employed by crusaders in their buildings, and in some cases through taking part in the construction of Muslim buildings as both sides (Muslims and Christians) recruited "enemy" masons in the rebuilding activity at times of peace. Another learning was made through Muslim masons and artists enslaved during the continuous clashes on the Spanish and Sicilian borders, or during crusades played a decisive part in the transfer of Muslim construction techniques and forms to the West. The impact of these masons will be better understood, if we could prove that these slaves ended up as the property of either the church or the noble, the main patrons of the construction industry at that time. The result of all this was the spread of large scale ecclesiastical constructions celebrating both the power of the church and the patrons and establishing first the Romanesque style and from late 12th century, the Gothic style.

This inspiration was subsequently demonstrated in Chapters; five and six, covering in depth all structural aspects from the plan, roofing system and tower to decorative aspects where the role of Muslims has been reluctantly admitted. The contribution of Muslims to Western architecture has taken various forms reflecting the technical and aesthetic needs of the European construction industry and affected by changing technological progress and sophistication of Western tastes. We can group Western borrowings from Muslim architecture into two categories. The first involves technical/structural solutions and forms, which were widely adopted in the West. This was particularly so in medieval times when European masons needed to borrow solutions to a number of technical and structural challenges raised by the ambitious building projects of medieval patrons and clergy. The second category involves artistic motifs that Europeans adopted in their buildings as well as cultural life once they had resolved, with the help of the Muslims, their technical and structural weaknesses. Here, much of the borrowing centred round decorative means and luxury artefacts.

The first solution, the West borrowed from the Muslims, was the replacement of the classical column by the pier, thus allowing greater height, the main handicap of the column. Historical evidence shows that a century before Europeans, Muslims employed the pier in Samarra (9th century) and Ibn Tulun Mosque (later 9th century). The first recorded European use of the pier is 10th century. The claim that Europe borrowed the pier from Byzantine Constantinople cannot be accepted although Byzantine masons are known to have used the pier. If this were true, the pier would have appeared earlier. As we established earlier, European borrowing during this period was from the Muslims.

The next structural element was the arch, which provided numerous solutions particularly those relating to statics and weight. More than any other nation, Muslims understood these characteristics of the arch and subsequently mastered its use and design. This was greatly facilitated by their skills and in depth knowledge of geometry and the laws of statics. The reduction of the thrust on a few points of the arch allowed lighter walls and vaults and enabled huge savings in material. Meanwhile, supports could be provided at either end of the arch extending laterally in the vertical plane of the arch forming what is known as buttresses. The impact of this was the abandonment of thick walls and heavy roofs for lighter and more graceful structures. The arch was first employed for structural and functional purposes but progressively it was used for both structural and decorative means.

The horseshoe type was the first arch form developed by Muslims. This had the advantage of allowing more height than the classical (semi-circular) arch as well as its aesthetic and decorative qualities. This form also had a greater advantage in the centring technique during its construction as the lower parts of the curve could carry the centring. The first appearance of the horseshoe arch was in the Umayyad Great Mosque of Damascus; its adoption in Cordoba (in the Great Mosque 756-796) paved the way for its transmission to Europe via Christian refugees of Asturian Mountains in Northern Spain who used it in their churches. It then reached churches on the pilgrimage road to Santiago Compostella in Spain, then onto French soil, and later to most of Europe.

The introduction of transverse and pointed arches were the two major developments that provided the fundamental structural steps in the process of development of Gothic and Western architecture in general. The transverse arch appeared when semi-circular arches were thrown from each pier of the arcade to the wall of the aisle, and a flat pilaster was added in order to support the connecting point, at which the arch sprang from the pier,. Later these transverse arches were thrown over the nave, providing greater safety and durability for the roof. The Muslims developed this in the 8th century, in the Palace of Ukhaidir (720-800), where the first pointed arch was also made. The first recorded European example is found in the church of St. Felice e Fortunato at Vicenza (985) and therefore the Muslim precedent is historically established and it could be possible that its transmission to the west followed the same route of the pointed arch.

The pointed arch was the second major development that took place in the 11th century when Europe adopted the transverse and later the pointed arch. Its first appearance was traced in the Mosque of Dome of the Rock, but the Palace of Ukhaidir remains the first building where the pointed arch was systematically used in construction. However, the first recorded appearance of the pointed arch in Europe was in France in the third great church of Cluny after 1125, and in Germany, it was mid-12th century. The main advantages of the pointed arch were that it concentrated the thrust of the vault on a narrow vertical line that could be supported by the flying buttresses. It enabled the reduction of the lateral thrust on the foundations and in the Gothic style, it permitted architects to lighten the walls and buttresses which had to be massive in order to support semi-circular arches. The pointed arch resolved the difficulty of achieving level crowns in the arches of the vault allowing the vault to become suitable for any ground plan.

The other fundamental technical and structural borrowing from the Muslims was the use of ribbed vaulting. The ribs provided support to the weakest points of the vault particularly in the groins and the crown areas. They allowed the thinning of the cells, and consequently also of the piers and walls and facilitated the construction of vaults, saving wood as well as providing the builder with security during the hardening of the mortar. The rib became an essential technique in the construction of roofs and floors (in multi storey buildings) until the present time. Evidence shows that the earliest development of such vaulting can be traced to Muslim lands in the Abbasid Palace of Ukhaidar (720-800). Use of the transverse arch and groin vault occurs eight times in the Palace, the vaults of the main hall and the mosque provide convincing arguments. Further proof can be found in the system of vault support provided in the Ribat of Susa (821-822), which greatly resembles the rib vaulting introduced into Europe after the 11th century. in the cross vaults of the nave of St. Philibert at Tournous built at the end of 11th century , St. Foy (1050-1120), Nevers (1083-1097) at St. Etienne, and Cluny (1095-1130), Ste. Mary la Madeleine at Vezelay (1104-1132), and Fontenay Abbey (1139-1147). The suggested route for the transfer in this case is European, particularly French, contacts with North Africa. However, the appearance of these vaults in Andalusia, the closest Muslim neighbour to Europe can also explain the way this technical motif was transferred, since historical sources refer to the use of "Sussa ribs" in Medinat al-Zahra.

Another vaulting system also copied from Muslims is found in the cistern of Ramla (Palestine), built by Harun Al-Rashid in 789. The cistern is composed of pointed arcades carried on cruciform piers of masonry and covered with six-barrel vaults reinforced with walls carried on these arches. Similar arrangements were employed in Sussa, in Abu Fatata Mosque (834-841) and the Great Mosque (850-851). The similarity between this technique and that employed in Notre Dame d'Orcival is striking. In this instance, we suggest both North African and Crusader connections to be the means of transfer.

The third vaulting system, "the Quadripartite vault", which had a strong influence on the vaulted domes in Europe and on the development of the Gothic vaulting system was employed in Cordoba and Toledo, and represents the connecting point acknowledged by a number of impartial Western scholars. The central argument is that the ribs of Cordoba inspired European architects and patrons to adopt them first in the Romanesque style and later in the Gothic. The germ of the quadripartite vault can be seen clearly in the Mosque of Bab Mardum in Toledo, which is a unique example of a well-developed technique consisting of an intersecting form of rib vaulting. Similar vaulting was used in another mosque later transformed into a house named Las Tornerias (built in 980 CE), with its nine ribbed domes combining a variety of ribs and dominated by the central dome. In the three instances, the domes were made of arches intersecting at the centre, forming a cross in exactly the same manner as the quadripartite vaults are constructed. We find these ribbed domes spreading to Christian Northern Spain, in churches on the route of pilgrimage to Santiago de Compostella, such as San Millan de la Cogolla de Suso, San Baudelio de Berlanga of Duoro (984 CE) in Soria, and Almazan church in Castile, Torres del Rio in Navarre. They reached churches in the Pyrenees such as Saint Croix d'Oloron and the hospital of Saint Blaise. They are also found at the Templar church at Segonia and the chapter house at Salamanca (12th. century) The capture of Toledan mosques (in 1060) including Bab Mardun must have provided lessons for European artists and architects, particularly the French who had close connections with this town after its fall.

Other areas of influence include the imitation of Muslim towers and minarets, which were incorporated into Western religious buildings as well as secular ones. Muslims used minarets as early as the 8th century in the Great Umayyad Mosque of Damascus and later developed it into an essential element of religious architecture. The European adoption of the tower did not take place until the 10th century, in Romanesque buildings. The use of a number of superimposed sections in these towers and their use at the main entrance points to Muslim influence rather the Armenian connection, which some Western academics are happy to support.

405

In the arts, the transfer can be easily established as the transportation of Muslim objects and motifs to various European lands can be made without difficulty. Items such as glassware, carpets, and ceramics were essential components of the trade in luxuries between Muslims and Christians, which reached its peak during the Fatimid dynasties (11th century). Muslim artefacts and slaves were the main booty and spoils of the Crusades. In this way, large quantities of rare and valuable items reached Europe and were destined mainly for nobles and the clergy, the main consumers of such luxury items. These objects influenced much of European art for a considerable time, firstly through the direct acquisition and use of these items as in the use of Persian and Syrian ceramics in numerous churches of Northern Italy or the spread of Persian and Turkish carpets in European Royal households. A further proof of this is the accumulation of quantities of rare Muslim artefacts in European and Western Museums and art collectors. Secondly, these items were a source of inspiration for European artists throughout the middle Ages and up to the present day. In some instances, we find direct imitation and copying of motifs as in the case of the Kufic calligraphy found on the door of le Puy cathedral, or that used on the Virgin's robe. Chevrons, Dogtooth friezes, and crossed arch brick décor, which was first adopted in Lombardy then spread to Europe, originated from Muslim Sicily and Spain. In Sicily, such features decorated stone buildings such as in St. Michael in Caserta Vechia (1153) while in Spain they were used in Cordoba Mosque and Giralda (1176-1196). These were spread to England and Normandy through the Normans. We find that Islamic ceramics, were a source of inspiration for the spread of floor decoration adopted from Muslim tiles, appearing first in Northern France in the second half of the 12th century. Meanwhile, faience decor was spread by tile workshops from Manises in Valencia, Spain, a place, which had a strong tradition of tile making established under the Muslims. After its capture by the Christians in 1238, the city became the main exporter of tiles and faience to Europe. This was in addition to the role of the Crusades and the role of ceramic workshops in Syrian cities captured by the French.

However, most important was the adaptation and inclusion of Muslim motifs and themes in European art production. The popularity of exotic Muslim arts inspired the foundation of many workshops, which reproduced these motifs and in some cases incorporated them into local European themes. Elliot Jason wrote in the Guardian (2006): *"The European attraction to Islamic art did not, of course, begin in the 19th century. Throughout the middle ages, highly prized specimens of Islamic artisanship entered the treasuries of churches and aristocratic homes, both through trade and as booty. European monarchs were crowned in robes woven in Sicily, one of the great creative workshops of the Muslim artist; Fatimid rock crystal ewers from North Africa were used to display Christian relics; and Turkish and Persian rugs were favoured as royal wedding presents"*.[1175]

He further continues: "*In today's climate of cultural divisiveness, this sense of interconnection is refreshing. It suggests for Islamic art a global significance, and tells not so much of a clash of civilisations, but of a resounding chorus. Islamic art is, after all, probably the world's greatest artistic success story. Soon after the earliest Islamic conquests of the Middle East in the late seventh century, artists drawing on the existing traditions of the region began to produce art and architecture with its own distinctive personality. Easily differentiated from its Greco-Roman and Hellenistic predecessors, it spread through the burgeoning empire with extraordinary speed. The universal appeal and adaptability of this new artistic mode allowed its themes and principles to be taken up by artists from the Atlantic coast to the Gobi desert, enriching thereby the vast and intervening blocs of culture.*"[1176]

Notes:

[1175] Jason Elliot (2006), 'Beauty and Harmony', Arts and Entertainment, the Guardian, Saturday July 15.
[1176] Ibid.

BIBLIOGRAPHY

Abouseaf Doris Behrens (2005), *'European Arts and Crafts at the Mamluk Court'*, in Rogers J. Michael et al. ed. 'Muqarnas Essays in Honor of J.M. Rogers: An Annual on the Visual Culture of the Islamic World', Brill Academic publishers, pp.45-54p.

Abouseif Doris Behrens- (1989), *'Islamic Architecture in Cairo: an Introduction'*, Brill Publishers.

Abulfeda Isma'il (1273-1331), *'Annales Muslemici Arabice et Latine'*, 5 volumes, edited and Translated by J. J. Reiske, edited by J. G. C. Adler, Hafniae, 1789-1794, Copenhagen.

Ackerman *eds., Survey of Persian Art, vol.II,* reprint Oxford University Press London.

Adolf Helen (1954), *'Der Gral in Wolframs Parzival: Entstehung und Ausbildung der Gralsage* in Aḥmad ibn Muḥammad Ibn Arabshāh, (1936), 'Tamerlane, Or Timur, the Great Amir', translated by J. H. Sanders, Luzac & co., London.

Ajmar-Wollheim and Flora Dennis (2006), *'At Home in Renaissance Italy: Art and Life in the Italian House 1400-1600'*, V&A Publications, London, Quoted in Rob Attar(2006),'At Home in Renaissance', BBC History magazine, volume 7, No.10.

Al- Bakri (1068), **'Description de l'Afrique Septentrionale'***,* translation of de Slane, 1913, Alger, Paris.

Al-Faruqi Isma'il R. (1973), *'Islam and Art'*, StudiaIslamica, No. 37. (1973), pp. 81-109.

Al-Hassani S.T.S., E. Woodcock and R. Saoud (2006), *'Muslim Heritage in Our World'*, Foundation for Science, technology and Civilisation publishing, pp.286-289.

Al-Jaburi Mahmood Shukre (1974), *'The Birth of Arabic Calligraphy and its Development'*, (in Arabic) Library Al-shark al-Jadid, Baghdad.

Amin, S. (1974), '*Accumulation on a World Scale: a critique of the theory of underdevelopment*', 2 vols, Monthly Review Press, New York, and Frank, A.G. (1967), '*Capitalism and Underdevelopment in Latin America*', Pelican, London.

Anderson, J. (1800), `*Thoughts on the Origin, Excellencies, and Defects of the Grecian and Gothic styles of Architecture*', in Recreations in Agriculture, Natural-History, *Arts and Miscellaneous Literature*, Vol.2, London.

Anthony Henricy, (1796), '*Lady Mary Wortley Montagu, Letters of the Right Honourable Lady Mary Wortley Montagu: Written During her Travels in Europe, Asia and Africa. . . , vol. 1* (Aix:), pp. 167-69; letter 36, to Mrs. S. C. from Adrianople.

Antoine Galland (1699), '*de l'Origine et du Progrez du Café*', Éd. originale J. Cavelier Paris, 1992- La Bibliothèque, coll. L'Écrivain Voyageur.

Arber Robertson Agnes, Stearn Thomas William (1987), '*Hmelloerbals Their Origin and Evolution*', 3rd Edition, Cambridge University Press.

Archer M. (1982) `*the Dating of Delfware Chargers*', in Transactions of the English Ceramic Circle ,vol.11, pp.112-121.

Archer, M and Morgan, B. (1977) `*Fair as China Dishes*', International Exhibitions Foundation, Washington DC, cat.21.

Archer, Mildred (1980), '*Early Views of India: the Complete Acquatints: the Picturesque Journeys of Thomas and William Daniell 1786-1794*', Thames and Hudson, London.

Armand, O. Citarella, (1968), '*Patterns in Medieval Trade: The Commerce of Amalfi before the Crusades*', Journal of Economic History, Vol.28, pp.531-555

Arnold T. W. (1965) '*the Preaching of Islam: A History of the Propagation of the Muslim Faith*', Muhammad Ashraf Publications Lahore, Pakistan.

Asin Palacios, (1943), '*La Escatalogia Rnlrsulrnana en lo Divina Comedia*', 2nd ed. Consejo Superior de Investigaciones Cientificas. Madrid.

Association of America Victorian Literature Group (1903), '*Modern Philology*', University of Chicago, vol.1.

Aubrey John (1949) edn. ' *Brief Lives; Life of Sir Henry Blount'*, edited from the original manuscripts by Oliver Lawson Dick Secker and Warburg, London, pp.25-27.

August Wilhelm Von Schlegel, (1894), *'Asthetische Ansichten'*, Berlin

Avcioglu Nebahat (2003), *'A Palace of One's Own: Stanislas I's Kiosks and the Idea of Self-Representation'*, The Art Bulletin, vol.85, pp. 662-684.

Baeck Louis (1994), *'The Mediterranean Tradition in Economic Thought'*, Routledge.

Ballaster Rosalind (2005), *'Fabulous Orients: Fictions of the East in England, 1662-1785'* Oxford University Press. Baltimore.

Banister Fletcher Sir (1975), *'A History of Architecture'*: 18th edition, revised by J. C. Palmes: University of London, The Athlone press, London.

Baramki, D.C. (1942), *'The Pottery from Khirbet El-Mefjer'*, The Quarterly of the Department of Antiquities in Palestine (QDAP), vol. 10, pp.65-103., Sauer, J.A. (1975*), 'Umayyad Pottery from Sites in East Jordan'*, Jordan, Vol.4, pp.25-32.

Bargebuhr, F.P.(1968), *'The Alhambra, a Cycle of Studies on the Eleventh Century in Moorish Spain'*, Walter de Gruyter & Co., Berlin.

Barthold V. V. (1958), ' *Four Studies on the History of Central Asia'*, tr. V. and T. Minorsky, 1958, vol. 2. Leiden .

BBC.co.uk, News 24/02/2007:
http://news.bbc.co.uk/2/hi/middle_east/6389157.stm

Beattie, M. H. (1964), `*Britain and the Oriental Carpet'*, in Leeds Art Calendar 55, PP 4–15.

Beattie, M.H. (1959) *'Antique Rugs at Hardwick Hall'*, in Oriental Art, vol. 5, pp.52-61.

Beckford, William, (1786), *'Vathek: An Arabian Tale'*, printed for J. Johnson London.

Behrens-Abouseif, D. (1989), '*Islamic Architecture in Cairo*', The American University in Cairo Press.

Bentham, J. (1808), 'H*istorical Remarks on the Saxon Churches*', in T. Warton. J Bentham, Francis, C.

Berchem, Max van. (1978), ' *Une mosquée du Temps des Fatimites au Caire. Notes sur le Gami el Goyushi.* Opera Minora I. Editions Slatkine. Geneva, pp.61-75.

Berggren, J. L. (1983), '*The Correspondence of Abu Sahl al-Kuhl and Abu Ishaq al- Sabl: A translation with Commentaries*', Journal of the History of Arabic Science 7, PP.39-124

Berkeley Alice, Lowndes Susan, Lowndes Marques Susan (1994), '*English Art in Portugal*', Edições Inapa.

Bernier, François, 1620-1688, '*Travels in the Mogul Empire, AD 1656-1668*', 3rd ed1972, revised by A. Constable, Chand.

BerschinWalter (1988), '*From the Middle of the Eleven Century to the Latin Conquest of Constantinople*'. Catholic University of America Press.

Bevan, B (1938, *History of Spanish Architecture*', B.T. Batsford, Ltd. London.

Beylié, G. L. de, (1909), 'Le Kalaa des Beni-Hammad, une Capitale Berbére de l'Afrique du Nord au XIe siècle,' Ernest Leroux Paris.

Bezold, Carl (1888), '*Die Schatzhöhle. Nach dem Syrischen Texte der Handschriften zu Berlin, London und Rom nebst einer Arabischen Version nach den Handschriften zu Rom, Paris und Oxford Herausgegeben.* Zweiter Teil: Texte, Leipzig.

The Bible Cyclopedia, or Illustrations of the Civil and Natural History of the Sacred Writings by Reference to the-Manners Customs Rites Traditions Antiquities and Literature of Eastern Nations,John W. Parker West Strand, London volume 1, 1841

Bier, L. (1986), '*Sarvistan: A Study in Esarly Iranian Architecture*', Pennyslevania state university press

Bier, L. (1979), '*The "Sasanian Palace" Near Sarvistan*', New York University, Graduate School

Bilson (1899), `*The Beginnings of Gothic Architecture: Norman Vaulting in England*', in RIBA Journal, Vol.6, pp.259-269.

Birdwood, George C. M., and Frank Herbert Brown (1915), '*Sva*', P.L. Warner, London.

Birkenmajer, A. (1948), `*Robert Grosseteste and Richiard Fournival*', in Medievalia et Humanistica, Vol. 4, pp.37.

Blair Sheila S. and Bloom Jonathon M. (1997), '*Islamic Arts*', Phaidon Press, Hong Kong.

Blair, S. & Bloom, J. (2000), '*Islamic Carpets*', M.Hattstein & P. Delius eds, Islam: Art and Architecture, Konemann, Cologne, pp.530-533.

Blair, S. And Bloom, S. (2000), '*Architecture (of the Safavids)*', in M. Hattstein and p.Delius (eds.), Islam Art and Architecture, Konemann, pp.504-519.

Blair, Sheila S. and Jonathan M. Bloom (1994), '*The Art and Architecture of Islam 1250-1800*', Yale University Press, New Haven.

Blanchet, P. (1889), '*La Kalaa des Beni-Hammad*', Recueil de la Sociéte Archéologique de Constantine', Cezayir, s.97-176.

Blanchet, P. (1904), '*Description des Monuments de la Kalaa des Beni-Hammâd*', Nowelles Notices de Missions Scientifiques, XVII, Paris, pp. 1-21

Bloom M. Jonathan (1985), '*The Origins of Fatimid Art*', Muqarnas, Vol. 3. pp. 20-38.

Bloom, J. & Blair, S. (1998), `*Islamic Arts*', Phaidon Press, London.

Bloom Jonathan M. and Blair Sheila s.(2009), '*The Grove Encyclopedia of Islamic Art and Architecture*', Oxford University.

Boas Adrian J (2001), '*Jerusalem in the Time of the Crusades: Society, Landscape, and Art in the Holy City Under Frankish Rule*', Routledge.

Boase, T. S. R. (Thomas Sherrer Ross), (1953), *'English Art, 1100-1216'*, Clarendon Press, Oxford,

Boase, T.S.R. (1967), `*Castles and Churches of the Crusading Kingdom'*, Oxford University Press, London.

Bond Francis (1906), *'Gothic Architecture in England: An Analysis of the Origin and Development of English Church'*, B. T. Batsford Publishing.

Bony Jean (1983), *'French Gothic Architecture of the 12th and 13th Centuries'*, University of California Press.

Bony, J. (1949), `*French Influences on the Origin of English Architecture'*, in Journal of the *Warburg and Courtauld Institutes* 12, pp.1–16.

Bowman Jeffrey Alan (2004), *'Shifting Landmarks: Property, Proof, and Dispute in Catalonia Around the Year 1000'*, Cornell University Press

Braudel, F. (1987),*'Grammaire des Civilisations'*, Arthaud, Falmmarion, Paris.

Braun, H. (1953), `*Historical Architecture, the Development of Structure and Design'*, Faber & Faber Ltd. London.

Breckenridge J. D. (1975), *'The Two Sicilies'*, in S. Feber (ed.), *Islam and the Medieval West*; A Loan Exhibition at the University Art Gallery; State University of New York.

Breckeuridge, J.D. (1975), `*The Two Sicilies*", in Ferber (ed.), Islam and the Medieval West, pp.39-66.

Briffault Robert (1928), *'The Making of Humanity'*, George Unwin and Allen, London.

Briffault, R. (1919), *'The Making of Humanity'*, G. Allen & Unwin ltd. , London.

Briggs, M.S. (1924) `*Muhammadan Architecture in Egypt and Palestine*', the Clarendon Press, Oxford.

Briggs, M.S. (1931), *'Architecture'*, in T. and A. Guillaume, eds., The Legacy of Islam, Oxford University Press.

Briggs, S. Martin (1920), '*The Fatimite Architecture of Cairo (A.D.969-1171)*, in The Burlington Magazine for Connoisseurs, Vol.37, N0.210, pp.137-139 and 142-147.

Brotton Jerry (2003), '*The Renaissance Bazaar: From the Silk Road to Michelangelo*', Oxford University Press.

Brown, P. (1968), `*Indian Architecture (Islamic Period)*', Taraporevala's Treasure House of Books. Bombay.

Bryant Arthur (1932), '*King Charles II*', Longmans', Green and Co. London.

Bucaille M. (1981), '*The Bible, The Quran and Science*', translated from the French by A.D. Pannell and the Author; 3rd edition, Seghers Publishers, Paris

Buloz, F. (1982), '*Les Revue des Deux Mondes*', Au Bureau de la Revue des deux Mondes, Paris.

Burn, Jacob Henry, (d. 1869), '*A Descriptive Catalogue of the London Traders, Tavern, and Coffee-House Token*', 2nd ed., London.

Burnett Charles (1999), '*The Sons of Averroes with the Emperor Frederick*" and the Transmission of the Philosophical Works by Ibn Rushd', in G. Endress and J. A. Aertsen with the assistance of K. Braun (eds.), *Averroes and the Aristotelian Tradition: Sources, Constitution and Reception of the Philosophy of Ibn Rushd (1126–1198)*, Leiden, 1999, pp. 259–99.

Burnett C. and Jacquart D. 1994 eds., '*Constantine the African and Ali ibn Al-Abbas al-Magusi: The Pantegni and Related Texts*' E.J. Brill Publishers, Leiden,pp.16-47.

Cabaniss Allen (1953), '*Agobard of Lyons: Churchman and Critic*', Syracuse University Press

Cabaniss, A.J. (1951), '*Agobard of Lyons*', Speculum, Vol.26, No1, pp.50-76.

Camera, Matteo (1836). '*Istoria Della Citta e Costiera di Amalfi*', Stamperia e Cartiera del Fibreno, Napoli.

Campbell, D. (1926), '*Arabian Medicine in the Middle Ages*', Cambridge University Press, vol.1.

Caroline Williams, (1983), *"The Cult of the Alid Saints in the Fatimid Monuments of Cairo: Part One: The Mosque of al-Aqmar'*, Muqarnas, vol. 1, pp. 37-54.

Carra de Vaux, Baron, (1931) *"Astronomy and Mathematics,"* in T. Arnold and A. Guillaume, eds., The Legacy of Islam, (1st ed. 1931), Oxford University Press. pp. 376—397.

Caumont, Arcisse de (1830-1841), `Cours d'Antiquités Monumentales Professé Caen en 1830: Quatrieme Partie, Moyen Age, Architecture Religieuse '*, Paris

Chambers Mortimer (1958), *'Greek and Roman History'*, Service Center for Teachers of History, Washington.

Chandè Gérard ed. (1989), *'Le Merveilleux et la Magie dans la Literature: Acte du Colloque de Caen'*, 31August 2nd September, Redopi, Amsterdam and Atlanta.

Chardin Chevalier (1686), *'Journal du Voyage du Chevalier Chardin en Perse et aux Indes Orientales, par la Mer Noire et par la Colchide'*, Vol.7, Moses Pitt, London.

Chew, Samuel Claggett, (1974), *'The Crescent and the Rose: Islam and England During the Renaissance'*, Oxford University Press, New York.

Chisholm Hugh (1910), *'The Encyclopaedia Britannica'*, The Encyclopædia Britannica Co. Vol.1, p.395

Chisholm Hugh (ed.) (1910), *'The Encyclopædia Britannica: A Dictionary of Arts, Sciences, Literature and General Information'*, The Cambridge University Press, Vol.29, p.189

Chmelnizkij, S. (2000), *'Central Asia: The Timurids, the Shaybanids, and the Khan Princedoms'*, in , Hattstein, M. And Delius, P. (eds.), Islam Art and Architecture, Konemann, p.406-451,

Choisy, A (1899) `Histoire de l'Architecture'*, 2 /vols, Gauthier Villars, Paris.

Christie A.H. (1931), *'Islamic minor Arts and their Influence Upon European Work'*, in T. Arnold and A. Guillaume, eds., The Legacy of Islam, (1st ed), Oxford University Press, pp. 108—154.

Christie, A.H. (1922) `Development of Ornament from Arabic Script',
Burlington Magazine, XLI, pp.2867-288.

Christie, A.H. (1922) `Development of Ornament from Arabic Script',
Burlington Magazine,Vol. 40, No. 231. (Jun., 1922), pp. 287-288+291-292

Christie, A.H. (1922) `Development of Ornament from Arabic Script II', the
Burlington Magazine for Connoisseurs, Vol. 41, No. 232. (JuL, 1922), pp.
34+37-38+41.

Christie, A.H. (1929) `Traditional Methods of Pattern Designing', revised
edition, Clarendon Press,

Christien Ludwig Stieglitz, C. L (1820), `Von Altdeutscher Baukunst', Leipzig,

Citarella, A.O. (1986), 'Amalfi and Salerno in the Ninth Century', Istituzioni
Civili e Organizzazione Ecclesiastica Nello Stato Medieval Amalfuano',
Amalfi, Centro di Cultural e Storia Amalfitana, vol.1, pp.129-45.

Citarella, A.O. (1993), 'Merchants, Markets and Merchandis in Southern Italy
in the High Middle Ages', Settimane di Studio del Centro Italiano di Studi Sull'
Alto Medioeve, vol.40, pp.239-284

Clair Alexandrine N St (1973), 'The Image of the Turk in Europe',
Metropolitan Museum of Art, New York.

Clark, Gordon Jane, (2004) 'Wallpaper in Decoration', Frances Lincoln Ltd.
London

Clévenot, Dominique (2000), 'Splendors of Islam: Architecture, Decoration,
and Design'; photographs by Gérard Degeorge, Vendome Press, New York.

Cochrane, L. (1994), `Adelard of Bath, the First English Scientist', British
Museum Press.

Colish, M.L (1997), 'Medieval Foundations of the Western Intellectual
Tradition, 400-1400', Yale University Press, New Heaven and London.

Conant K.J. (1942) `A Brief Commentary on Medieval Church Architecture',
John Hopkins Press,

Conant, Kenneth John (1968), `Cluny: les Eglises et la Maison du Chef d'Ordre', Impr. Protat Frères Mâcon, Paris.

Conder, C.R. (1886), 'Syrian Stone Iore', R.Bentley and Son,

Conner, Patrick, (1979),`Oriental Architecture in the West', Thames and Hudson, London.

Cormack Robin (2000), 'Byzantine Art', Oxford University Press.

Costenoble, J.C. (1812), 'Uber Altdeutsche Architektur und Deren Ursprung', Halle.

Coysh, A. W. (Arthur Wilfred), (1970), 'Blue and White Transfer Ware, 1780-1840', David & Charles, Newton Abbot.

Craf Nora (2002), 'Javelina Candy', in Yavapi gardens, Master Gardener Newsletter, University of Arizona, Yavapai county County Cooperative Extension, December 2002.

Creswell (1932), 'Early Muslim Architecture', Oxford.

Creswell ,K.A.C. (1958) `A Short Account of Early Muslim Architecture', Harmondsworth, Middlesex; Baltimore Penguin Books.

Creswell K. A. C. (1926), 'The Evolution of the Minaret, with Special Reference to Egypt-II', The Burlington Magazine for Connoisseurs, Vol. 48, No. 278, pp. 252+256-259.

Creswell, K.A.C. (1959). 'The Muslim Architecture of Egypt', vol. II. Clarendon Press, Oxford, reprinted by Hacker Art Books, New York, 1978.

Critchlow, Keith (1976),'Islamic Patterns: an Analytical and Cosmological Approach', Thames and Hudson, London.

Dan Cruickhank (edt.) (1996), 'Banister Fletcher's A History of Architecture', 20th Edition, Architectural Press.

Dance, E.H. (1957), 'Europe and the Old World', Book 1, 1st published in 1947, Longmans Greeen and Co, London, New York and Toronto.

Dani, A.H. et al. (1999), '*History of Civilizations of Central Asia*', Motilal Banarsidass Publishing,

Daniell, Thomas, (1797), '*Oriental Scenery. : TwentyFourVviews in Hindoostan, Taken in the Year 1792, Drawn by Thomas Daniell, and Engraved by Himself and William Daniell*', printed by Robert Bowyer, London.

Darby, M. (1983), '*The Islamic Perspective, an Aspect of British Architecture and Design in the 19th century*', Leighton House, Gallery, London.

Davies, J.G. (1982), '*Temples. Churches and Mosques*', Pilgrim Press, New York.

Dearmer, P. (1921) '*Art*', ed. Hearnshaw, F.J.C., Medieval Contributions to Modern Civilisation, Dawson of Pall Mall, London, pp.149-173.

Dehio, G. & Bezold, G.von. (1892), '*Kirchliche Baukunst des Abendlandes.*', J. G. Cotta Stuttgart.

DenomyAlexander Joseph (1953), '*Concerning the Accessibility of Arabic Influences to the Earliest Provencal Troubadours*', Mediaeval Studies, vol.15.,1953, pp.147-158.

Diana de Marly (1974) '*King Charles II's Own Fashion: The Theatrical Origins of the English Vest*', in Journal of the Warburg and Courtauld Institutes, London: Warburg Institute (JWCI), vol. 37, pp.378-382

Diehl Edith (1980), '*Bookbinding: its Background andTtechnique*', Dover Publications.

Diehl, C. (1910) '*Manuel de l'Art Byzantin*', A. Picard et Fils, Paris.

Dieulafoy (1889), '*l'Art Antique de la Perse*', Vol.4, Librairie central d'Architecture, Paris.

Dieulafoy, M. (1884), '*l'Art Antique de la Perse*', Librairie central d'Architecture, Paris.

Dimand M. S. (1964), '*Two Fifteenth Century Hispano-Moresque Rugs*', The Metropolitan Museum of Art Bulletin, New Series, Vol. 22, No. 10., pp. 341-352.

Dinkel, J. (1983), '*The Royal Pavilion, Brighton*', Philip Wilson Publishers, London.

Dodds, J.D. (1994), `*Architecture and Ideology in Early Medieval Spain*', Pennsylvania State University Press, USA.

Dodge B.(1962), '*Muslim Education in Medieval Times*', The Middle East Institute, Washington, D.C.

Donzel, E.J. Van, (1994), ' *Islamic Desk Reference*', Brill Academic Publishers.

Doris Behrens Abouseif, ((1992), '*The Facade of the Aqmar Mosque in the Context of Fatimid Ceremonial*', Muqarnas, vol. 9, pp. 29-38.

Drane Augusta Theodosia (1910), '*Christian Schools and Scholars: Or, Sketches of Education from the Christian Era to the Council of Trent*', G. E. Stechert & co. New York

Duby, Georges, (1981), '*The Age of the Cathedrals: Art and Society, 980-1420*', University of Chicago Press.

Dunlop, D. (1952), '*A Christian Mission to Muslim Spain in the Eleventh Century*', in al-Andalus, Vol.17. pp.259-310

Edward Gibbon (1862), '*History of The Decline And Fall Of The Roman Empire*', John Murray, London, Vol. 2.

Ellis, Aytoun, (1956), '*The Penny Universities : a History of the Coffee-Houses*',Secker & Warburg, London

Elmes, J. (1823), '*Memoires of the Life of Sir Christopher Wren*', Priestley and Weale, London.

Elmes, James, (1971 ed.), `*Lectures on Architecture*', B. Blom, New York.

Elsberg H. A.; Guest R. (1936), '*The Veil of Saint Anne*', The Burlington Magazine for Connoisseurs, Vol. 68, No. 396, pp. 140+ 144-145+ 147.

Encyclopaedia of the History of Arabic Science, Routledge, 3 vols., vol.3.

Endress G. and Aertsen J. A. (eds.) (1999), '*Averroes and the Aristotelian Tradition: Sources, Constitution and Reception of the Philosophy of Ibn Rushd (1126–1198)*', Leiden.

Enlart Camille (1927) '*L'Eglise du Wast en Boulonnais et son Portial Arabe*', Gazette des Beaux Arts, vol.15, pp.1-11.

Erdmann, K. (1962), '*Europa und der Orinetteppich*', Mainz, Berlin, pp.11-17.

Ettinghausen Richard Oleg Grabar (1987), '*The Art and Architecture of Islam: 650-1250*', Yale University Press.

Ettinghausen, R. (1974), '*The Impact of MuslimDecorative Arts and Painting on the Arts of Europe*', in Schacht Joseph and Boswoth, C. E. ed., The Legacy of Islam, 2nd Edition, The Clarendon Press, Oxford, pp.292-317.

Ettinghausen, R. (1975), '*Muslim Decorative Arts and Painting, their Nature and Impact on the Medieval West*', in Stanley Ferber, (ed.1975), Islam and the Medieval West, vol.1, State University of New York at Binghamton, pp.5-26.

Ettinghausen, R. and Grabar, O. (1987). '*The Art and Architecture of Islam 650-1250*', New Haven, Yale University Press, republished in 1994.

Evans, John, (1821), '*Recreation for the Young and the Old. An Excursion to Brighton, with an Account of the Royal Pavilion, a Visit to Tunbridge Wells, and a Trip to Southend*,. In a series of letters, etc., Chiswick.

Farmer, H.G. (1970), '*Historical Facts for the Arabian Musical Influence*', Georg OlmVarlag, Hildesheim, New York.

Faugère Annie (1979), '*Les Origines Orientales du Graal chez Wolfram Von Eschenbach: Etat des Recherches*', Kümmerle.

Fehérvári, Géza (2000), 'Ceramics *of the Islamic World in the Tareq Rajab Museum*', I.B. Tauris, London.

Fénelon, (1718), *Dialogue sur l'Eloquence en Général et sur Celle de la Chaire en Particulier*, Paris.

Ferrier, R.W. and Chardin John (1996), '*A Journey to Persia: Jean Chardin's Portrait of a Seventeenth Century Empire*', I.b. Tauris, New York.

420

Fikret Yegül (1992), `Baths and Bathing in Classical Antiquity' The Architectural History Foundation,. New York.

Fletcher, B (1961) 'A History of Architecture, on the Comparative Method', the Athlone Press, London, 17th edition.

Fletcher, R. (1992), 'Moorish Spain', Weidenfield & Nicholson, London.

Florent Le Comte, (1699), 'Cabinet des Singularitez d' Architecture, Peinture, Sculpture et Gravure ou Introduction a la Connaissance des Plus Beaus Arts, Figures sous les Tableaux, les Statues, et les Estampes, Paris.

Fontoynont Marc (1999), 'Daylight Performance of Building', European Commission Directorate-General XII, Science, Research, and Development, James and James.

Francois Blondel the Younger (1751), 'Encyclopedie', vol.1, Paris.

Francois Blondel the Younger (1752), 'Architecture Francoise, ou Receuil des Plans, Elevations, Coupes et Profiles des Eglises', Charles Antoine Jombert, Paris.

Frankl, P.(1960), 'the Gothic', Princetone University Press, Princeton

Freeman Ann (1957), 'Theodulf of Orleans and the Libri Carolini', Speculum, Vol. 32, No. 4. pp. 663-705.

Freeman Ann (1992), 'Theodulf of Orléans: A Visigoth at Charlemagne's Court', in Jacques Fontaine and Christine Pellistrandi eds., L'Europe héritière de l'Espagne wisigothique, Collection de la Casa de Velázquez n° 35, Madrid, pp.185-193-94

Friedman Jane M. (1997), 'These Stitches Speak', Saudi Aramco, vol.48, No.2, pp.2-11

Fuks Lajb, R. G. and Fuks-Mansfel (1984), 'Hebrew Typography in the Northern Netherlands, 1585-1815: Historical Evaluation and Descriptive Bibliography', Brill d Academic Publishers.

Gailliard, G. (1956) `Cluny et l'Espagne dans l'art Roman du 11eme Siecle', in Bulletin Hispanique, Vol.63, pp.153-160.

Gansho Franðcois-Louis, (1996), '*Feudalism*', University of Torento Press.

Gans-Ruedin, E. (1975), '*Antique Oriental Carpets, From the Seventeenth to the Early Twentieth Century*', Harper & Row; 1st edition London.

Makdisi George (1980), ' *On the Origin and Development of the College in Islam and the West*, in Khalil I. Semaan ed., Islam and the Medieval West, State University of New York Press/Albany.

Marcais Georges, (1954), '*L'Architecture Musulmane d'Occident*', Arts et Metiers Graphiques, Paris.

Ghazanfar S.M. and Lowry S.T (2003), ' *Medieval Islamic Economic Thought: Filling the Great Gap in European Economics*', Routledge.

Gibb H. A. R, et al.(1979), '*Encyclopaedia of Islam*', Brill : Luzac Leiden ; London : Vol.4, pp.29-30.

Giovanni Antonio Tagliente (1527), '*Essempio di Recammi*'. Venedig: Giovan Antonio et fratelli de Sabbio; ab. 1530 u. d. T.: Esemplario nuovo (vor allem Stickmuster).

Glick, F. Thomas, Livesey, J. Steven and Wallis faith (2005), '*Medical Science, Technology and Medicine: An Encyclopaedia*', Routledge.

Glick, T. F. (2005),' *Islamic and Chrsitain Spain in the Early Middle Ages*', Brill Academic Publishers.

Glubb John (1963), '*The Empire of the Arabs*', Hodder & Stoughton, London

Glubb Sir John (1969), '*A Short History of the Arab Peoples*', Hodder and Stoughton,

Godard, A. (1949), '*Voute Iraniennes*', in Athar-e-Iran, vol.4, pp. 185-256.

Godard, A. (1965) `*the Art of Iran*', Allen & Unwin, New York.

Goldstein, T. (1988), `*Dawn of Modern Science*', Houghton Mufflin, Boston.

Golombek, Lisa and Wilber Donald (1988), '*The Timurid Architecture of Iran and Turan*, Vol. 1, Princeton: Princeton University Press.

Golvyn, L. (1971) '*Essai sur l'Architecture Religieuse Musulmane*', Tome 2, l'Art religieux des Umayyades de Syrie', Klioncksiek, Paris.

Goodwin Godfrey (1987), '*A History of Ottoman Architecture*", Thames and Hudson, London.

Gorini, R. (2002), '*Attention and Care to the Madness During the Islamic Middle Age Syria*', JISHIM, vol.2, pp.40-42.

Gorman, M. (1997), '*The Commentary o Genesis of Claudius of Turin and Biblical Studies Under Louis the Pious*', Speculum, Vol.72, No.2, pp.279-329.

Goss, V.P. (1986), `*Western architecture and the World of Islam in the 12th Century*', in V.P. Goss and Borstein (eds.), pp.361-375.

Goulton, G.G. (1930), '*Crusades, Commerce and Adventure*', Nelson, London

Grabar, O. (1959), '*The Umayyad Dome of the Rock in Jerusalem*', Ars Orientalis, vol.3, pp.39-62.

Grabar, Oleg (1978), '*The Alhambra*',: Harvard University Press, Cambridge, Mass.

Graetz Heinrich Hirsch (1949), '*History of the Jews*', Jewish Publication Society of America, Philadelphia, Volume 3, pp.168-169.

Grafton T. Anthony (1993), '*Joseph Scaliger: A Study in the History of Classical Scholarship*', Oxford University Press.

Green N. ed. (2014) '*Writing Travel in Central Asian History*', Indiana University Press,Bloomington and Indianapolis

Grose and J. Milner (eds.), '*Essays on Gothic Architecture*', printed for J. Taylor, at the Architectural Library, London, pp.17-94.

Grose F.C., (1808), '*Essay Without a Title*, T. Warton et al., op cit. pp.95-124.

Guillaume Joseph (1680), '*Relation Nouvelle d'un Voyage de Constantinople*', Paris.

Guy le Strange (ed.1928), '*Clavijo, Embassy to Tamerlane 1403-1406*', Harper New York and London.

Haines Charles Reginald (1889), '*Christianity and Islam in Spain (756-1031)*', Kegan Paul, Trench & Co., London.

Hakim.B. (1986) Hakim, B. (1986) '*Arabic Islamic Cities: Buildings and Planning Principles*', Kegan Paul, London.

Halsband, R. (1965 edn.), '*The Complete Letters of Lady Mary Wortley Montagu*', Clarendon Press, Oxford.

Hamarneh, Sami Khalaf, (1975), '*Catalogue of Arabic Manuscripts on Medicine and Pharmacy at the British Library*', History of Arabic Medicine and Pharmacy ; no.3, The Publishing House of the Egyptian University [Dār al-Nashr lil-Jamiāt al-Misriyah], Cairo.

Hamilton Alastair and Richards Francis (2004), '*Andre´ du Ryer and Oriental Studies in Seventeenth-Century France*', Oxford: Oxford University Press.

Hamlin Dwight Foster (2003), '*A History of Ornament Ancient and Medieval 1916*', 1ˢᵗ published 1916, Kessinger Publishing.

Hancock Lee (2005), '*Lorenzo De' Medici: Lorenzo De'medici:Patron of Art* ', the Rosen Publishing Group.

Hankin E. H. (1925), '*The Drawing of Geometric Patterns in Saracenic Art*', Central Publication Branch, Calcutta, Governement of India.

Hardy Adam (1995), '*Indian Temple Architecture: Form and Transformation: The Karnata Dravida Tradition 7th to 13th.* ', Abhinav Publications.

Harvey J.H. (1992), '*Gardens Plants of Moorish Spain: A Fresh Look*', Garden History, vol.20, No.1., pp.71-82.

Harvey John H. (1975), '*Gardening Books and Plant Lists of Moorish Spain*', Garden History, Vol. 3, No.2, pp. 10-21.

Harvey, J. (1948), '*Gothic England, a survey of National Culture, 1300-1550*', Batsford, London.

Harvey, J. (1950) '*The Gothic World :1100-1600, a Survey of Architecture and Art*', B.T. Batsford Ltd, London.

Harvey, J. (1972), '*The Mediaeval Architect*', Wayland, London.

424

Harvey, J. (1973), '*the Master Builders*', Thames and Hudson, London.

Haskins C.H. (1927), '*Studies in the History of Medieval Science*', Harvard University Press, Cambridge Mass., 2nd Edition.

Haskins, C.H. (1922), '*Science at the Court of the Emperor Frederick II*', The American Historical Review, Vol. 27, N0.4, pp.669-694.

Haskins, C.H. (1927), '*Sudies in Medieval Science*', Unger, New York.

Hastings Rashdall (1936), '*The Universities of Europe in the Middle Ages*', Clarendon Press.

Hattstein Markus and Delius Peter (eds.) (2000), ' *Islam : Art and Architecture*', Konemann, Cologne.

Haupt, A. (1909), '*Die Alteste Kunst, Insbedondere die Baukunst der Germanen*', Leipzig,

Havell, E. B. (Ernest Binfield), (1913), '*Indian Architecture: its Psychology, Structure, and History From the First Muhammadan Invasion to the Present Day*', J. Murray, London.

Heinrich Fichtenau, (1976), '*The Carolingian Empire*', University of Toronto Press,

Henry Lemonnier (1922), '*Proces-Verbaux de l'Academie Royale d'Architecture*', VII, Paris.

Herbelot Barthelemy de. (1697), '*Bibliotheque Oriental, ou Dictionnaire Universel Contenant Generalement tout ce qui Regarde la Connoissance des Peuples de l'Orient*'. La Compagnie des Libraires, First edition, Paris.

Herbermann C.G et al. (1913), '*The Catholic Encycoledia: And International Work of Reference on the Constitution Doctrine*'.

Herbermann Charles George (1913), '*The Catholic Encyclopedia*', The Encyclopedia Press.

Hess, Catherine, et al. (eds.) (2004) '*The Arts of Fire: Islamic Influences on Glass and Ceramics of the Italian Renaissance*', Getty Publications, Los Angeles

Hilberry Harry H. (1955), '*Charité-sur-Loire Priory Church*', Speculum, Vol.30, No.1., pp.1-14.

Hill, D. (1976), '*Islamic Architecture in North Africa*', Faber and Faber, London.

Hill, D.R. (1993),'*Islamic Science and Engineering*', Edinburgh University Press.

Hill, D.R. (1994), '*Arabic Fine Technology*', in, The Arab Influence in Medieval Europe,' ed. D. Agius, and R. Hitchcock, Ithaca Press, Reading.

Hillenbrand, R. (1994), '*Islamic Architecture Form, Function and Meaning*' Edinburgh University Press, Edinburgh.

Hind, A.M. (1908), '*Two Unpublished Plates of the Series of Six "Knots" Engraved After Designs by Leonardo de Vinci*', The Burlington Magazine, vol.12, p.41.

Hitti, P.K. (1996), '*The Arabs: a Short History*', Regnery Gateway publishers, Washington.

Hoag, J.D (1968), '*Western Islamic Architecture*', Studio Vista, London.

Hoag, J.D. (1987) '*Islamic Architecture*', Faber & Faber, London.

Hodges William, 1744-1797, '*Choix de Vues de l'Inde Dessinées sur les Lieux, Pendant les Annees 1780, 1781, 1782, et 1783*', ... par W. Hodges, ... Select Views in India, Drawn on the Spot, in the Years 1780, 1781, 1782, and 1783, printed by Joseph Cooper for the author, London.

Hodges Richard and Whitehouse David (1983), '*Mohammed, Charlemagne and the Origins of Europe: Archaeology and the Pirenne Thesis*', Cornell University Press,

Hodgson Marshall G. S., Burke Edmund (1993), '*Rethinking World History: Essays on Europe, Islam, and World History*', Cambridge University Press, p.119

Holland, T.E. (1891), '*The Origin of the University of Oxford*', The English Historical Review, Vol.6, No.22, pp.238-249

Holmes George (edt.) (2002), '*The Oxford History of Medieval Europe*', Oxford University Press.

Holt Peter Malcolm (1973), '*Studies in the History of the Near East*', Routledge.

Hommon, R. (1947), '*The Philosophy of Alfarabi and its Influence on Medieval Thought*', Hobson Press, New York.

Hope, T. (1835) '*An Historical Essay on Architecture*', John Murray, London.

Hope, Thomas, (1970 ed.), '*Household Furniture and Interior Decoration*', Tiranti, London.

Howard Debora (2000),' *Venice and the East*', Yale University Press.

http://www.bestofsicily.com/mag/art154.htm accessed 14/01/2014

Hulme Edward Maslin (1929), '*The Middle Ages*', H. Holt and company, New York.

Humphreys R. Stephen (1972), '*The Expressive Intent of the Mamluk Architecture of Cairo: A Preliminary Essay*', Studia Islamica, No. 35., pp. 69-119.

Humphreys R. Stephen (1994), '*Women as Patrons of Religious Architecture in Ayyubid Damascus*', Muqarnas, Vol. 11. (1994), pp. 35-54.

Huntington Ellsworth (1977), '*The Character of Races*', Ayer Company Publishers, New York.

Huntington Samuel. P (1996), '*the Clash of Civilisations and the Remaking of World Order*', Simon and Schuster, New York

Hurst, J.C. (1977), `*Spanish Pottery Imported into Medieval Britain*', in Medieval Archaeology, vol.21, pp68-105.

Hutt, A. (1984). '*Arab Architecture: Past and Present. An Exhibition presented by The Arab-British Chamber of Commerce at the Royal Institute of British Architects*". University of Durham, The Centre for Middle Eastern & Islamic Studies, Durham

427

Hyland Peter (2005), '*The Herculaneum Pottery: Liverpool's forgotten Glory*', Liverpool University Press.

Ibn al-Awwam: '*Kitab al-Filaha,*' or '*le Livre de l'Agriculture*' (French), translation J.J. Clement-Mullet, 1 vols, Tunis 1977.

Ibn Bassal (ed. 1955): '*Kitab al-Filaha*', or '*Book of Agriculture*', translation J.M. Millas Vallicrosa and M. Azi- man, Tetuan, Morocco.

Ibn Idhari (1848) `*Al-bayano Al-Moghrib*', ed. R. Dozy, 2 Volumes, Leyde.

Ibn Khaldoun (1967), '*The Muqaddimah: An Introduction to History*' trans. by F. Rosenthal, 2nd edition (1967), Routledge and Kegan Paul, London.

Ibn Khaldun (1967) `*The Muqadimah*', translated from the Arabic by F. Rosenthal, edited by N.J. Dawood, Princeton pub.

Irwin John and Katherine B. Brett (1970), '*Origins of Chintz : with a Catalogue of Indo-European Cotton-Paintings in the Victoria and Albert Museum*', London, and the Royal Ontario Museum, Toronto', H.M.S.O, London.

Jackson P., and Lokhart Laurence (1986), '*The Cambridge History of Iran*', Cambridge University Press.

Jacquart, D. (1996), '*The influence of Arabic Medicine in the Medieval West*', in Roshdi Rashed (ed.), Encyclopaedia of The History of Arabic Science, 3 Vols, Routledge, London-New York.

Jairazbhoy, R.A. (1972), '*An Outline of Islamic Architecture*', Asia Publishing House, Bombay, London and New York.

Jason Elliot (2006), '*Beauty and Harmony*', Arts and Entertainment, the Guardian, Saturday July 15.

Jean de Gourment (1560), '*Livre de Moresques , très utile et nécessaire à tous orfèvres,...*"', Paris.

Jenkins Romilly (1987), '*Byzantium: The Imperial Centuries, AD 610-1071*', University of Toronto Press.

Johan Wolfgang von Goethe (1896) `*Briefe*', Sophienausgabe, IV, Vol.21, Weimar, Letter 5994.

John R. Hayes (ed.) (1983), '*The Genius of Arab Civilization*', MIT Press, USA and Westerham Press, UK.

John Tolan, Henry Laurens and Gilles Veinstein (2012), '*Europe and the Islamic World: A History*,' Princeton University Press, 2012

Johnson Art (1999), '*Famous Problems and Their Mathematicians*', Greenwood publishing, Libraries Unlimited, USA

Jonathan Wolff and M. W. F. Stone (eds.), (2000), '*The Proper Ambition of Science*', Routledge .

Jones Robert, (1994), '*'The Medici Oriental Press (Rome 1584-1614) and the Impact of its Arabic* Publications on Northern Europe' in G.A. Russell (ed.), *The 'Arabick' Interests of the Natural Philosophers in Seventeenth-Century England*, E. J. Brill, Leiden, pp.88-108.

Jung Emma and Franz Marie-Louise von (1998), '*The Grail Legend*', Princeton University Press.

Karpinski Louis Charles, (1930), '*Robert of Chester's Latin Translation of the Algebra of al-Khowarizmi*', Macmillan, New York

Kaufmann, J. E. Kaufmann H. W., Robert M. Jurga (2004), '*The Medieval Fortress: Castles, Forts and Walled Cities of the Middle Ages*, Da Capo Press.

Kenneth Glyn Jones, (1968), '*The Search for the Nebulae, part I*', Journal of the British Astronomical Association, Vol. 78, No. 4, pp. 256-267.

King, D. (1983)'*the Inventories of the Carpets of King Henry 8*', in Hali 5, pp.287-296.

Kirby, R.S., Withington, S., Darling, A.B and Kilgam, F.G. (1956), '*Engineering in History*', Mcgrow Hill, New York, Torento, London, reprinted by Dover Publications in 1990.

Kitschelt, L. (1938)'*Die Fruhchristliche Basilika als Darstellung des Himmlischen Jerusalem*', Miinchener Beitrage zur Kunstgeschichte 3, Munich.

Kitzinger Ernst and Curcic Slobodan (1990), '*The Mosaics of St. Mary's of the Admiral in Palermo*', Dumbarton Oaks Studies 27, Washington, 35 ff.

Kleinhenz Christopher (2004), '*Medieval Italy: An Encyclopedia*', Routledge.

Klingender, Francis Donald (1968), '*Art and the Industrial Revolution*', edited and revised by Arthur Elton, Revised ed., Kelley, New York.

Knight, H.G. (1839), '*The Normans in Sicily*', The Dublin Review, Vol.7, C. Dolman, London.

Koehler, W. (1939), `*Medieval Studies Dedicated to A.K.Porter*', vol.2, Harvard University Press, Cambridge, p.336, and Speculum : A Journal of Medieval Studies, vol. 10, 1935, pp.144-146.

Kostof, S. (1995), '*A History of World Architecture*'', Oxford University Press, Oxford.

Krauss, S. (1996), '*The Jewish-Christian Controversy from the Earliest Times to 1789*', Volume 1, History, edited and revised by William Horbury, Tubingen, Mohr Siebeck.

Kristeller, P.O (1945) `*The School of Salerno: Its Development and its Contribution to the History of Learning*', in Bulletin of the History of Medecine, Vol.17, pp.138-194.

Kritzeck, J. (1964) '*Peter the Venerable and Islam*', Princeton University Press.

Kutlesa Stipe (2004), '*Croatian Philosophers I: Hermann of Dalmatia (1110-1154)*', in Prolegomena vol.3, Number 1, pp.57-70.

La Boullaye le Gouz, François de, (1653), '*Les Voyages et Observations, où sont Décrites les Religions, Gouvernemens et Situations des Estats d'Italie, Grèce, Natolie, Syrie, Palestine, etc., Grand Mogol, Bijapour, Indes Orientales*', Gervais Closier, Paris.

Lacost Pascal (1837), '*Architecture Arabe ou Momnuments du Kaire Mesurés et Dessinés* ', Paris.

Laborde Alexandre de (1816)`*Les Monuments de la France Classes Chronologiquement et Considérés sous le Rapport des Faits Historiques et de l'Etude des Arts par le Comte Alexandre de Laborde: Les Dessins Faits d'Apres Nature par M.M.Bourgeois et Bauce*', 2 volumes, P.Didot, l'aine, 2nd Edition 1836, Paris.

Lady Mary Wortley Montagu (2005), '*Letters from the Right Honourable Lady Mary Wortley Montagu 1709 to 1762*', republished by Kessinger Publishing.

Lambert ,E. (1933), '*Les Premieres Voutes Nervees Francaises et les Origines de la Croisee d'Ogives*, in Revue Archeologique, Vol.2.

Lambert, E. (1927), '*L'art Hispano Mauresque et l'Art Roman*', Hesperis, vol.7, pp.29-43.

Lambert, E. (1931) `*l'Art Gothic en Espagne*', H. Laurens, Paris.

Lambert, E. (1958) `*Art Musulman et Art Chretien dans la Peninsul Iberique*', Editions Privat, Paris.

Lamperez y Romea (1930), '*Historia de la Arquitectura Cristiana en la Edad Media Según el Estudio de los Elementos y los Monuments*', Espasa-Calpe, Madrid, Spain.

Landu Rom (1967), `*Afrique Mauresque*', Albin Michel, Paris.

Lane, A. (1947) `*Early Islamic Pottery*', Faber and Faber, London.

Lavagnini, B. (1987), '*L'Epigramma e il Committente,*', *Dumbarton Oaks Papers* vol.41., pp. 339-50.

Le Bas Charles Webb (2005), '*The Life of Archibishop Laud,*' Kessinger Publishing, USA

Le Bon G. (1884), '*La Civilisation des Arabes*', IMAG, Syracuse, Italy.

Lefevre Pontalis (1912) `*Bulletin Monumental*', Vol.76. Société française d'archéologie, Paris.

Lemay Richard (1978), '*Gerard of Cremona*', Dictionary of Scientific Biography, volume 15, pp. 173-92.

Lesser, G. (1957) `*Gothic Cathedrals and Sacred Geometry*', volume I, Alec Tiranti, London.

Lethaby, W.R. (1904) `*Medieval Art from the Peace of the Church to the Eve of the Renaissance*', Duckworth &Co, London, Charles Scribner's Sons, New York, Vol.4, pp100-111.

Lethaby, W.R. (1904) `Medieval Art From the Peace of the Church to the Eve of the Renaissance', Duckworth &Co, london, Charles Scribner's Sons, New York, Vol.IV.

Lethaby, W.R. (1926) 'Medieval Architecture', in Crump, C.G. & Jacob, E.F. (eds.), the Legacy of the Middle Ages, Clarendon Press, Oxford., pp59-91.

Levey, Michael, (1975), 'The World of Ottoman Art', Thames and Hudson, London.

Lewis, B. (1995), 'Cultures in Conflict: Christians, Muslims, and Jews in the Age of Discovery ', Oxford University press.

Lezine Alexandre (1965), 'Mahdiya: Recherches d'Archlologie Islamique', C. Klinksieck, Paris.

Lezine Alexandre, (1967), 'Notes d'Archeologie Ifriqiyenne, IV: Mahdiya, Quelques Precisions sur la Ville' des Premiers Fatimides,', Revue des Etudes Islamiques, Vol.35, p.90.

Limongelli M. D. (1921), 'La Stabilite de la Coupole au Mausolee de Tamerlan a Samarcande', in Bulletin de I'Institut d' Egypte, vol. IV, pp. 77-92.

Linda Komaroff, Curator of Islamic Art at the Los Angeles Country Museum of Art, http://www.lacma.org/islamic_art/intro.htm, accessed June 23rd 2015.

Lindberg David C. (1980), 'Science in the Middle Ages', University of Chicago Press.

Lombard Maurice (1947), 'L'Or Musluman du VII au XI Siecles, Les Bases Monetaires d'Une Suprematie Economique', Annales, ESC e, pp.143-60.

Lombard, Maurice (1971), 'L'Islam Dans sa Premiere Grandeur, VIIIe-XIe siecle', Flammarion, Paris.

Loudon, J.C. (1822), 'An Encyclopaedia of Gardening', 3rd Edition (1825), Book 1, volume 9,

Louis Charles Jean courajod (1899), 'Lecons Professes a l'Ecole du Louvre', publiees sur la Direction de H. Lemonier et A. Michel, Publishers A. Picard et Fils, Paris.

Lynn Teo Simarski *(1987), 'The Lure of Aleppo'*, ARAMCO, Vol.38, Number 4, pp.34-40

Lyon Gardiner Tyler, (1967), *'Tyler's Quarterly Historical and Genealogical Magazine'*, vol.3., Kraus Reprint, Michigan State University

Hughes M. Albert, O.P (1987), *'Albert the Great,Doctor Universalis'*, Spirituality Today, Autumn 1987, Vol. 39, Supplement chapter 6 and 8..

Mack, E. Rosamond (2004), *'Oriental Carpets in Italian Renaissance Painting: Art Objects and Status Symbols'*, Magazine Antiques, Brant Publications.

Mackenzie, John,M. (1995), *'Orientalism: History, Theory and the Arts'*, Manchester University Press.

Mackie Louise W. (1984), *'Toward an Understanding of Mamluk Silks: National and International Considerations'*, Muqarnas, Vol. 2, The Art of the Mamluks., pp. 127-146.

Mahmoud Raghib (1929), *'Descriptions d'Orgues Donnees par Quelques Anciens Auteurs Turcs'*, Revue de Musicologie, Volume 10, No.30, pp. 99-104.

Male, E (1928) *'Art et Artistes du Moyen Age'*, Librairie Armand Colin, Paris.

Mâle, Emile, (1924), *'Art et Artistes du Moyen Age'*, Librairie Armand Colin, Paris.

Male, E (1923) *'Les Influences Arabes dans l'Art Roman'*, in *Revue des Deux-Mondes*, p. 311-343.

Mann, H.K. (1925), *'The Lives of the Popes in Early Middle Ages'*, volume 4, 2nd ed., K. Paul, London.

Manucci Niccolao (ed.1907), *'Storia do Mogor'*, translated by William Irvine, John Murray, London

Marçais, Georges, (1954), *'L'architecture Musulmane d'Occident : Tunisie, Algérie, Maroc, Espagne et Sicily'*, Arts et Métiers Graphiques, Paris.

Marly Diana de (1974) *'King Charles II's Own Fashion: The Theatrical Origins of the English Vest'*, in Journal of the Warburg and Courtauld Institutes, London: Warburg Institute (JWCI), vol. 37, pp.378-382

Mason William, (1827), '*The Works of Thomas Gray: Collated From the Various Editions; with Memoirs of his Life and Writings,* published by J. F, Dove, London,

Mathe, J. (1980), '*The Civilisation of Islam*', Tr. David Macrae, Crescent Books, New York.

McCormack W. J. (1999), '*The Blackwell Companion to Modern Irish Culture*', Blackwell.

Mellor Gilbert sir (1934)'*Bristol Delftware*' in Transactions of the English Ceramic Circle ,vol.1 No.2, pp.22-28

Meyerhof, M. (1931), '*Science and Medecine*', in T. Arnold et al. (eds.1931), The Legacy of Islam, Oxford University Press.pp.311-355

Michell G. (1978), '*Architecture of the Islamic World*', Thames and Hudson

Michell, George (ed). (1980), '*Architecture of the Islamic World: Its History and Social Meaning*', Thames and Hudson, London.

Michell, M. et al. (eds.) (1978), '*Architecture of the Islamic World*', Thames and Hudson, London.

Michener, James, A. (1955), '*Islam-the Misunderstood Religion*', Readers' Digest, vol. LXVI (May, 1955), pp.67-75

Mills, J. (1983), '*the Coming of the Carpet to the West*', in ARTS, Exhibition Catalogue, the Eastern Carpet in the Western World, London, pp. 11-23.

Mills, J. (1975), '*Carpets in Pictures*', Publications Department National Gallery, London.

Minorsky, V. *(ed.1959), 'Calligraphers and Painters, a Treatise by Qadi Ahmad, Son of Mir-Munshi',* tr. V. Minorsky, Freer Gallery of Art, Washington DC.

Mitford Joan (ed.1843), '*The Works of Gray*', vol.5, William Pickering, London.

Molière, 1622-1673 (1964 ed.), '*Le Bourgeois Gentilhomme*', Petits Classiques Bordas, Paris.

Monthly Review Press, New York, and Frank, A.G. (1967), *'Capitalism and Underdevelopment in Latin America'*, Pelican, London.

Morino, M. Gomez (1919),*'Iglesias Mozarabes, Arte Espagnole de las Siglo ix a xi'*, Centro de Estudios Historicos, Madrid..

Mumford, L.(1966), *'The City in History'* Penguin Books, Harmondsworth, UK.

Musca G. (1963), *'Carlo Magno ed Harun alRashid'*, Dedalo, Bari.

Naderzad , B (1972) ,*'Louis 14th, La boullaye et l'Exorisme Persan'*, in Gazette des Beaux Arts, Vol.79, pp.29-38.

Nanji Azim et.al.(1997), *'Mapping Islamic Studies: Genealogy, Continuity and Change'*, Walter de Gruyter, Berlin and New York .

Nathaniel Whittock, (1827)*'Decorative Painter's and Glazier's Guide'* Isaac Taylor Hinton, London.

Necipoglu Gulru (1995), *'The Topkapi Scroll: Geometry and Ornament in Islamic Architecture'*, Getty Centre for the History of Art and the Humanities, Santa Monica, California.

Newman, A.J. (2006), *'Safavid Iran: Rebirth of a Persian Empire'*, I.B. Tauris, London and New York

Newton Francis(1994), *'Constantine the African and Monte Cassino: New Elements and the Text of the Isagoge'*, in C. Burnett and D. Jacquart eds., Constantine the African and Ali ibn Al-Abbas al-Magusi: The Pantegni and Related Texts' E.J. Brill Publishers, Leiden,pp.16-47.

Nicholas Paul and Suzanne Yeager (eds) (2012), *'Remembering the Crusades: Myth, Image, and Identity'*,The Johns Hopkins University Press, Baltimore

Nikolai Alexandrenko, (1970), *'The Poetry of Theodulf of Orléans: A Translation and Critical Study,'* Ph.D. Dissertation, Tulane University

Nordenstreng Kaarle, Schiller Herbert I.(1993), *'Beyond National Sovereignty: International Communication in the 1990s'*, Praeger/ Greenwood.

O'Callaghan, J.F. (1983), *'A History of Medieval Spain'*, Cornell University Press.

O'Leary de Lacy (1923), '*Islam at the Crossroads: a Brief Survey of the Present Position and Problems*', Kegan Paul, London.

Ockley, Simon, (1718), '*The History of the Saracens*', printed for Bernard Lintot, London.

Odard, (1847), '*A Sentimental Journey through Normandy*', in Charles Dickens , William Harrison Ainsworth and Adam Smith, (eds.), Bentley's Miscellany, Vol.21, Richard Bentley, London, pp.395-p.529.

Ogilby, John, (1673), '*Asia, the First Part, Being an Accurate Description of Persia, the Vast Empire of the Great Mogol, and Other Parts of India, etc*'. London, See Eerde, Katherine S. van (1976),.*John Ogilby and the Tate of His Times*, Dawson, London.

Otto Söhring, (1900), '*Werke Bildender Kunst in Altfranzösischen Epen*', Romanische Forschungen, vol.12, Erlangen.

Otto von Simson (1956) `*The Gothic Cathedral, Origins of Gothic Architecture and the Medieval Concept of Order*', 3rd ed. 1988, Princeton University Press, USA.

Owens, E.,J. (1992), `*The City in the Greek and Roman World*', Routledge, London.

Palgrave Francis (1851), '*The History of Normandy and of England*', vol.1, John W. Parer and Son, London.

Palter Robert (1961), '*Toward Modern Science*', Noonday Press.

Paris, Gaston. (1880), `*La Chanson du Pelerinage de Charlemagne*', Romania, Vol9, Paris, pp.1-50.

Pellegrino, Francesco di (1908 ed.), '*La Fleur de la Science de Pourtraicture. Patrons de Broderie, Facons Arabicque et Ytalique*', par Francisque Pellegrin 1530, Printed by Jacques Nyverd avec introduction par Gaston Migeon, Paris.

Peter Linehan, Janet Laughland Nelson, (2001), '*The Medieval Word*', Routledge.

Pirenne Henri (1939), '*Mohammed and Charlemagne*', Translated by Bernard Miall, George Allen and Unwin Ltd, London.

Pirenne, H. (1948), '*Medieval Cities, their Origins and the Revival of Trade*' 5th Edition, Princeton University Press, Princeton.

Pope, Aurthur Upham (1965), '*Persian Architecture*', George Braziller Inc., New York..

Pope Arthur Upham and Ackerman Phyllis eds., (1967), '*Survey of Persian Art*', vol.II, reprint Oxford University Press London

Porter Arthur Kingsley (1909), '*Medieval Architecture, its Origins and Development*/ Vol:1-2. Vol.1: Origins. Vol.2: Normandy and The Ile de France., The Baker and Taylor, New York.

Porter, A. K. (1911), '*The Construction of Lombard and Gothic Vaults*', Yale University Press, New Heaven.

Prioreschi P. (2001), '*A History of Medicine*', vol.5, Priscilla P. Soucek (2000), '*Monumentalizing Piety: Religious Practices and Mamluk Architecture*', Islamic Area Studies Group 5, Report on the 6th Seminar of Group a Institute of Fine Arts, New York University. http://www.l.u-tokyo.ac.jp/IAS/HP-e2/eventreports/45urbanspaceHY.html, accessed 30/05/2015.

Prisse d'Avennes (1877), '*L'Art Arabe d'Après les Monuments du Kaire; Depuis le VIIe Siècle Jusqu'a la Fin du XVIIIe*', Morel, Paris.

Quicherat, J. (1885), '*de l'Ogive et de l'Architecture Ogivale*', in Melanges d'Archeologie et d'Histoire, Paris.

Rabun Julie L., and Blakemore Robbie G. (1996), '*History of Interior Design and Furniture: From Ancient Egypt to Nineteenth-Century Europe*', John Wiley and Sons.

Raby, Julian (1982), '*Venice, Durer and the Oriental Mode*' The Hans Huth Memorial Studies, London.

Ralph McInern (1963),' *A History of Western Philosophy*', University of Notre Dame Press, Indiana, USA.

Ratiya S. E. (1950), '*The Mechet' Bibi Khanum at Samarcand*', (in Russian), Moscow.

Reinaud Joseph Toussaint , (1964), *'Muslim Colonies in France, Northern Italy, and Switzerland: Being the English Translation of Reinaud's Invasions des Sarrazins en France, et de France en Savoie, en Piémont et en Suisse'*, Sh. Muhammad Ashraf pub., Lahore.

Reinaud, M. (1836), *'Invasion des Sarrazins en France et de France en Savoie, en Piémont et dans la Suisse, Pendant les 8°, 9° et 10° Siècles de Notre Ere, d'Après les Auteurs Chrétiens et Mahométans Invasion des Sarazins'*, Librairie Orientale de V° Dondey-Dupré, Paris.

Resie Lambert-Élisabeth d'Aubert, comte de (1857), *'Historie et Traite des Sciences Occultes'*, Louis Vivés, Paris, p.521

Reuther, O. (1938), *'Parthian Architecture: A History'*, in Pope, A.U. ed., A Survey of Persian Art, Oxford University Press, London and New York, pp.411-444

Reuther, Oscar (1938), *'Sâsânian Architecture. A. History'*, in Arthur Upham Pope and Phyllis Ackerman *eds., Survey of Persian Art, vol.II,* reprint Oxford University Press London, pp. 493-537.

Reynolds Susan (1994), *'Fiefs and Vassals: the Medieval Evidence Reinterpreted',* Oxford University Press, Oxford.

Ribera J. (1928), *' Disertaciones Y Opusculos'*, 2 vols. Imprenta de Estanislao Maestre. Madrid.

Rice, D.T. (1979) *'Islamic Art'*, Thames & Hudson, Norwich, reprinted in 1993.

Richmond, Ernest Tatham (1926), `*Moslem Architecture, 623 to 1516 : Some Causes and Consequences'*, The Royal Asiatic Society, London.

Rivoira G. T. (1919), *'Moslem Architecture',* translated by G. MeN. Rushforth. London.

Rivoira, G. T. (Giovanni Teresio), (1918), *'Moslem Architecture : its Origins and Development'*, translated from the Italian by G. McN. Rushforth, Oxford University Press, London..

Robert (1928), *'the Making of Humanity'*, George Unwin and Allen, London.

Roland Allen (1892), '*Gerbert, Pope Silvester II*', The English Historical Review, Vol. 7, No. 28. (Oct. 1892), pp. 625-668.

Roshdi Rashed, Régis Morelon (1996), '*Encyclopedia of the History of Arabic Science*', 3 Vols Routledge. London-New York.

Rothlisberger Blanca (1917) `*Die Architektur des Graltempls im Jungeren Ttiturel*', Berne.

Ruskin, John (1859), '*The Works of John Ruskin*', ed. E. T. Cook and A. Wedderburn, George Allen, 1903-1912, London

Russell, Bertrand, 1872-1970. '*History of Western Philosophy*' 2nd ed. (2000), Routledge, London.

Sabouret, V.(1928), '*Les Voutes d'Arêtes Nerveuses*', in le Genie Civil, Paris.

Said Edward (1978), '*Orientalism*', Vintage Books, New York.

Saladin, H. (1899) `*La Grande Mosquee de Kairwan*', Paris

Saladin, H. (1905), '*Deuxieme Note sur lea Monuments Arabes de la Kalaa des Beni Hammad*', Bulletin Archeologique. CTHS, pp.185-198

Sarre Fredrick (1924), '*Ardabil, Grabmoschee des Schech Safi*', Berlin Translation Sedigheh Khansari Mousavi and Minorsky, V. *(ed.1959), 'Calligraphers and Painters, a treatise by Qadi Ahmad, Son of Mir-Munshi*', tr. V. Minorsky, Freer Gallery of Art, Washington DC.

Saunders, G. (1814) `*Observations on the Origin of Gothic Architecture*', in Archeologia, vol.17, pp.-29, London.

Savory R. (2007), '*Iran Under the Safavid*', Cambridge University Press.

Sayili, A. (1980), '*the Observatory in Islam*', the International symposium on the Observatories in Islam 19-23 September 1977 (ed. M. Dizer), Istanbul 1980, pp. 53-56.

Scarce M.Jennifer (2014), '*Women's Costume of the Near and Middle East*', Routledge.

Scarfiotti Gian Luigi and Lunde Paul (1978), '*Muslim Sicily*', Saudi Aramco World, vol.29, No.6 (November-December).

Scattolin Giorgia (1961), '*Le Case Fondaco sul Canal Grande*', private printing, Venice.

Scerrato Umberto (1980), '*Islam, Monuments of Civilisation*', The Reader's Digest Association Ltd., London.

Scerrato, U. (1976), '*Islam: Monuments of Civilisation*', the Reader's Digest Association Ltd., London..

Schlesinger, Kathleen (1910), ' *The Instruments of the Modern Orchestra*', Vol. 1 Modern Orchesteral Instruments'; Vol. 2 The Precursors of the Violin Family, Charles Schribner, New York.

Schopenhauer, Arthur, (1819),'*Die Welt als Wille und Vorstellung*', Vol.II, Book 3, Leipzig,.

Schopenhauer, Arthur, (1884) '*The World as Will and Idea*', edit. 1884, Routledge & Kegan Paul, London.

Schwab, Raymond, 1884-1956 (1984), '*The Oriental Renaissance : Europe's Rediscovery of India and the East, 1680-1880*', translated by Gene Patterson-Black and Victor Rethinking La Renaissance oriental. English Guildford : Columbia University Press New York.

Scott S.P. (1904), '*History of the Moorish Empire in Europe*', 3 vols; J.B. Lippincott Company.

Sear, F (1983), '*Roman Architecture*', Cornell University Press.

Seesselberg Friedrich. (1897) '*Die Früh-Mittelaterliche Kunst der Germanischen Voelker Unter Besonderer Berücksichtigung der Skandinavischen Kunst in Ethnologisch-Anthropologischer Begrundung Dargestell*', Berlin

Shakespear, John (1816), '*The History of the Mahometan Empire in Spain*', James Cavanah Murphy., T. Cadell and W. Davies, London

Shakespeare William and Fletcher John (1998) '*The Two Noble Kinsmen*', Oxford University Press.

Shalem Avinoam (2004), '*The Oliphant: Islamic Objects in Historical Context*', Brill.

Shaw, J.B. (1984) `*Gentile Bellini and Copnstantinople*', in Apollo, Volume cxx, pp.56-58.

Silberberg, B. (1910), '*Das Pflanzenbuch des Abu Hanifa Ahmed ibn Da'ud al-Dinawari. Ein Beitrag zur Geschichte der Botanik bei den Arabern*,' dissertation, Breslau, published in part in *Zeitschrift für Assyriologie* 24 (1910): 225-65; 25 (1911): 38-88.

Simpson, F.M. (1913) '*A History of Architectural Development*', Longmans, Green & Co. London.

Smith R.B. (1874), '*Mohammed and Mohammedanism*', Smith Elder, London.

Solomon Joan (2000), '*Chemistry*', Nelson Thornas publishers.

Soudovar Abolala (1992), '*Art of the Persian Courts*', Rizzoli International Publications, New York.

Southern, R.W. (1984), '*From School to University*', in J.I. Catto (ed.), The Early Oxford School, vol.1, of T.H. Aston (ed.), The History of the University of Oxford, Clarendon Press, Oxford, pp.1-36

Spargo John Webster (2004), '*Virgil the Necromancer: Studies in Virgilian Legends*', Kessinger Publishing.

Spengler, Oswald (1923) ' *Der Untergang des Abendlandes : Umrisse einer Morphologie der Weltgeschichte: Namen- und Sachverzeuchnis*', Beck, München.

Spirituality Today Autumn (1987), '*Albert the Great by Sr. M. Albert Hughes, O.P. The Mission of St. Albert and St. Thomas*', Vol. 39 Supplement, chapter 8.

Stanley Lane-Poole (1894), '*Mohammedan Dynasties : Chronological and Genealogical Tables With Historical Introductions*', A. Constable and Company, Westminster.

Stanley- Lane Poole (1898), '*Review of Books*', in Justin Winsor, Samuel Rawson Gardiner, Reginald Lane Poole, John Goronwy Edwards, Mandell Creighton (eds.), English Historical Review, vol.13, Longman: 756-758.

Stanley Lane-Poole (1886), '*Saracenic Art*', J.S. Virtue & Co., London

Stefano Carboni (2007), '*Venice and the Islamic World, 827-1797*', Yale University Press.

Stephenson Carl, (1956), '*Mediaeval Feudalism*', Cornell University Press.

Stevens Roger Sir (1979), '*The Land of the Great Sophy*', Eyre Methuen,

Street, G.E. (1865), '*Gothic Architecture in Spain*', John Murray, London.

Stroud, Dorothy (1962), '*Humphry Repton*', Country Life, London.

Stroud, Dorothy (1971), '*George Dance, Architect, 1741-1825*', Faber and Faber Ltd., London.

Sture Bolin (1952), '*Mohammed, Charklemagne and Ruric*', Scandinavian Economic History Review, Vol.1. pp.5-39

Sweetman, J.W.(1955), '*Islam and Christian Theology*', Lutterworth Press.

Sweetman, John (1987), '*The Oriental Oobsession : Islamic Inspiration in British and American Art and Architecture 1500-1920*', Cambridge University Press, Cambridge.

Symonds John Addington (1910), Sketches and Studies in Italy and Greece', John Murray, London.

Tabaa Yasser (1993), '*Circles of Power: Palace, Citadel, and City in Ayyubid Aleppo*', Ars Orientalis, Vol.23, pp. 181-191.

Tabaa Yasser (2001), '*The Transformation of Islamic Art During the Sunni Revival*', University of Washington Press.

Tabbaa Yasser (1997), ' *Construction of Power and Piety in Medieval Aleppo*', Pennsylvania State University Press.

Tabbaa, Yasser (1982), '*The Architectural Patronage of Nûr al-Dîn*', Thesis (Ph.D), New York University.

Tavernier, Jean-Baptiste, 1605-1689 (1678), '*Six Voyages Through Turkey into Persia and the East-Indies*', made English by J. Phillips, London.

Taylor, W. (1933), '*Arabic Words in English*', Society, Vol.38, the Clarendo Press, pp.567- 599.

Thackston, W. M. (1988), '*The Diwan of Khatai: Pictures for the Poetry of Shah Ismail*', Asian Art, p. 37.

The Encyclopaedia of Islam, (1997), volume 6, Brill, Leyden.

The Metropolitan Museum of Art Bulletin (1988), '*Painting in Rome and Pompeii*', in The Metropolitan Museum of Art Bulletin, New Series, Vo.45, No.3, (Winter, 1987-1988), pp.3-16.

The Society for the Diffusion of Useful Knowledge (1939), '*Library of Useful Knowledge*', Vol.III, Philosophy, Baldwin and Cradock, Paternoster-Row, London.

Thévenot, Jean de, 1633-1667 (1687), '*The Travels of Monsieur de Thévenot into the Levan*t' , In three parts, viz. Into I. Turkey, II. Persia, III. The East Indies, done out of French by A. Lovell, London

Thomas F. Glick, Steven John Livesey, and Faith Wallis (eds.) (2005), '*Medieval Science, Technology, and Medicine: An Encyclopedia*', Routledge.

Thomas Geminus (1548), '*Morysse and Damaschin Renewed and Encreased, Very Profitable for Goldsmythes and Embroderars*', London.

Thompson, J.W. (1928) '*Economic and Social History of the Middle Ages (300-1300)*', Unger, New York .

Tina Stiefel (1989), '*The Intellectual Revolution in Twelfth Century Europe*'; St. Martin's Press, New York.

Toy, S. (1939) `*Castles*', William Heinemann, London.

Trend, J.B. (1931) `*Spain and Portugal*', in T. Arnold et al. (eds), 1931, in T. Arnold and A. Guillaume The Legacy of Islam, Oxford University Press. pp.1-39.

Turner Jane (ed. 1996), '*The Dictionary of Art*', Macmillan Publishers, London.

Tytler Patrick Fraser (1831), '*Lives of Scottish Worthies*', vol.1, John Murray, London.

Udovitch A.L. (1980), '*Islamic Sicily*', in Dictionary of the Middle Ages; Charles Scribners' Son, New York, Vol. 11, p.263.

Urice S.K. (1987), '*Qasr Kharana in the Transjordan*', American School of Oriental Research, Durham, N.C.

Van dyke, J.C (1909), '*A Text Book of the History of Painting*', Longman Greens and Co., London, Calcutta and Bombay.

Velazquez Bosco (1912) `*Medina Azzahra y-Alamiriya*', Junta para Amplicacion de Estudios e Investigaciones Cientificas, Madrid, pp.23-24

Victoria and Albert Museum (1920) '*Guide to the collection of Carpets*', HMSO, London.

Violet le-Duc (1858) `*Dictionnaire raisonne de l'architecture francaise du onzieme siecle au seizieme siecle*', B. Bance, Paris.

Violet-le-Duc (1844) `*De la Construction des Edifices Religieuse en France*', in Annales Archeologiques, Vol.I.pp.179-186

Wack, Mary Frances (1990), '*Lovesickness in the Middle Ages: The Viaticum and its Commentaries*', University of Pennsylvania Press, Philadelphia.

Waddington George (2004), '*A History of the Church, from the Earliest Ages to the Reformation*', 1st published in 1833, Kessinger Publishing.

Walsh James, J. (1911), '*Old Time Makers of Medicine*', Fordham University Press, New York.

Ward, P.J. (1967) `*Some Mainstreams and Tributaries in European Ornament From 1500 to 1750*', Bulletin of the Victoria and Albert Museum, Vol.3, part 1 and 2.

Warten, T. et al. London. Warton T., Bentham J, Francis, C. Grose and J. Milner (eds.1808) `*Essays on Gothic Architecture*', printed for J. Taylor, at the Architectural Library, 3rd edition London,

Warton Thomas (1824) '*The History of English Poetry: From the Vlose of the Eleventh to the Commencement of the Eighteenth Century*', Harvard University.

Warton Thomas (1840) '*The History of English Poetry: From the Close of the Eleventh Century to the Commencement of the Eighteenth Century*', vol.1, Printed for T. Tegg, London.

Watson, A.M (1983), '*Agricultural Innovation in the Early Islamic World*', Cambridge University Press.

Watt W.M. (1972), '*The Influence of Islam on Medieval Europe*, Edinburgh University Press,

Wedgeworth Robert (1993), '*World Encyclopedia of Library and Information Services*', 3rd edition, American Library Association, Chicago.

Weissenborn, H. (1888), '*Gerbert: Beiträge zur Kenntniss der Mathematik des Mittelalters*', Berlin.

Weysen Alfred (1972), '*L'île des Veilleurs: Saint Graal et Fabuleux Tresor des Templiers*', Editions Arcadie, Paris.

White Lynn Jr. (1971) '*Cultural Climates and Technological Advances in the Middle Ages*', in Viator, Vol.2, pp.171-201.

Wickens, G. M. (1976), '*The Middle East as a World Centre of Science and Medicine*', in, Introduction to Islamic Civilisation, edited by R.M. Savory, Cambridge University Press, Cambridge, pp. 111-18.

Wijdan Ali (2000), '*The Arab Contribution to Islamic Art: From the Seventh to the Fifteenth* Centuries', The American University in Cairo Press.

Wilber, Donald N. (1969),'*The Architecture of Islamic Iran*', Greenwood Press, New York.

Wilfrid Blunt, (1973), 'The Golden Road to Samarkand', Hamish Hamilton, London.

Willan, T.S. (1955) '*English Trade With the Levant in the 16th Century*', in English History Review, vol. LXX, pp.399-410.

Willard, H.M. (1937) `*Progress on the Graphic Reconstruction of the Desiderian Abbey at Monte Cassino'*, American Journal of Archeology', vol.41, no.1, p112.

Willard, H. M. (1935), *'Desiderian Basilica at Monte Cassino (1066-1071)'*, American Journal of Archeology', vol.39, no.1, p116.

William Warburton (1760) `*Pope's Moral Essays'*, quoted by Richard Elsam (1805), An Essay on Rural Architecture: illustrated with original and economical designs ... the whole comprising thirty plates, in aquatinta', 2nd Edition, Printed for Lackington, Allen London, p.13.,

Williams Caroline (1985), *'The Cult of 'Alid Saints in the Fatimid Monuments of Cairo'*, Part I: The Mosque of al-Aqmar', Muqarnas, vol. 1, pp. 37-54.

Williams Caroline (1985), *'The Cult of 'Alid Saints in the Fatimid Monuments of Cairo'*, Part II: The Mausolea', in Muqarnas: An Annual on Islamic Art and Architecture', vol.3., pp.39-6o,

Willis Frank Roy (1985), *'Western Civilization'*, 4th ed. , vol.1.D.C. Heath, p.384

Willson, D. H. (1956), *'King James VI and I'*, Jonathan Cape, London.

Wilson Brian C. and Lewis Nancy D.(2002), *'The Pocket Idiot's Guide to Christianity'*, Alpha Books.

Wirth, E. (1976) *'Der Orientteppich und Europa'*, Heft 37, Gedruckt inder universitatsbuchdruckerei Junge & Sohn, Erlangen.

Wolff Philippe (1968), *'The Cultural Awakening'*, Pantheon Books.

Wolfram, Wolfram von Eschenbach (1984 ed.) *'Willehalm'*, Penguin Classics

Worringer, Wilhelm , (1967), *'Abstraction and Empathy a Contribution to the Psychology of Style'*, translated by Michael Bullock, Routledge, London.

Wren Benjamin Lee (2004), *'Teaching World Civilisation With Joy and Enthusiasm'*, University Press of America.

Wren, Christopher, (1750), *'Parentalia'* , T. Osborn and R. Dodsley, London, p.297 & appendix 1.

Yaqut, 1866-70. *'Jacut's Geographisches Worterbuch'*, ed. F. Wustenfeld. 6 vols. Leipzig,

Yarwood, D. (1974), *'The Architecture of Europe'*, Chancellor Press.

Yonge, Charlotte Mary (1863), *'History of Christian Names'*, vol.2, Parker Son and Bourn, London.

Index

A

Aachen, 151, 343
Aaron the Just, 151
abacus, 155, 171, 239, 293
Abbas-Ibn-Ahnaf, 20
Abbasid architecture, 46
Abbasids, 43, 46, 47, 59, 60, 70, 72, 75, 78, 81, 295, 347, 402
Abbey aux Hommes, 61, 330
Abbey of Bernay, 327
Abbey of Malmesbury, 236
Abbey of St. Cuxa, 211
Abbot Desiderius, 162, 276
Abbot Mayeul, 274
Abbot Suger, 261, 280
Abbot Wilhelm, 327
Abd Allah ibn Sahloh, 214
Abd al-Rahman al-Sufi, 24
Abd al-Rahman III, 27, 220
Abd al-Razzak Samarkandi, 103
Abd-al-Rahman I, 17, 52
Abd-al-Rahman II, 17
Abdellah, 162, 308
Abelard of Bath, 165
ablaq, 87
Abraham bar Chiya, 223
Abraham ben Muhajir, 220
Abraham Ibn Ezra, 222
Abu Abdullah al-Bakri, 22
abu al-Abbas, 151
Abu al-Fida, 22
Abu al-Wafa al-Buzjani, 24
Abu Bakr, 13, 20
Abu Dulaf, 48
Abu Fadl ben Hasday, 220
Abu Fatata Mosque, 55, 406
Abu Hanifa al-Dinawari, 27
Abu Huraira, 34
Abu Ubayda ibn al-Jarrah, 16
Abu-Dullaf (mosque), 38
Abu-Laith, 274
Abul-Beka, 20
Abul-Hasan, 20
Abyssinian, 13

acanthus foliage, 143
acitara, 212
Acre, 178, 181, 195, 199, 201, 204, 205, 231
Adalboldus, 156
Adelard of Bath, 160, 173, 185, 186, 187, 204, 227, 228, 230, 233, 254, 255, 339, 419
adufe, 179
Afghanistan, 96, 98, 105, 107, 108
Aghlabid, 70, 316
Agobard of Lyons, 170, 222, 417
Agobardus, 149, 151
Agora, 99
Agra, 109, 354
Ahahr-i-Sabz, 99
Ahmed Ibn Fadlan, 22
Allahvardi Khan, 121
Ain Jalut, 96
Ajanta, 106
Ajlun, 88
Ajmer, 107
Akcha Qala, 80
al Dikka, 87
al- Firdaws, 89
al- Mansura, 86
al- Shammasiyya, 103
al-'Aziz, 64
al-Adhid, 85
al-Andalus, 155, 156, 157, 163, 166, 171, 422
al-Aqmar, 65, 68, 132, 418, 449
al-Aqsa, 38, 39, 47, 49, 65, 375
Al-Aqsa, 39, 85, 130, 256, 324
Alastain Crombie, 187
al-Azhar, 64, 65, 67, 71, 401
al-Aziza, 72, 87, 276
al-Bahr, 61
Al-Bakri, 75
Albert the Great, 160, 171, 172, 436, 444
Albertus Magnus, 160
Albigensian heresy, 220
al-Bitruji, 158
Albrecht Durer, 360
Alcala de Henares, 216, 217
Alcazar, 211, 217
Alcázar, 217

D

E

455

Jaunpur, 108, 110, 135, 381
Jawhar, 59
Jean Baptiste Colbert, 354
Jean Baptiste Tavernier, 354, 356
Jean de Gourment, 361, 397, 431
Jean de Joinville, 188
Jean de Thevenot, 354
Jean Grolier, 361
Jean-Baptiste Reveillon, 384
Jean-Etienne Liotard, 355
Jerusalem, 4, 59, 65, 85, 86, 130, 156,
    178, 187, 188, 195, 196, 199, 200,
    203, 204, 206, 208, 220, 227, 228,
    230, 231, 232, 249, 252, 255, 260,
    264, 285, 286, 342, 349, 352, 392,
    415, 426, 432
Jesus, 3, 114, 139, 168
Jewish, 4, 8, 9, 18, 23, 157, 159, 162,
    168, 170, 352, 358, 426, 433
Jewish Courtiers, 221
Jews, 4, 15, 16, 17, 19, 31, 127, 139,
    151, 158, 160, 165, 168, 170, 176,
    197, 213, 214, 215, 219, 220, 221,
    222, 223, 224, 233, 234, 426, 435
Jizya, 15, 16
joggled voussoirs, 60, 66
Johann Bernhard Fischer von Erlach,
    356
Johannes Afflacius, 185
Johannes Saracenus, 185
John Baptiste Vanmour, 355
John Evelyn, 357
John Mandeville, 188, 229
John Milner, 246
John Nash, 386
John of Salisbury, 254
John of Seville, 158
John of Wurzburg, 188
John Ogilby, 357, 396, 439
Jordan, 38, 39, 40, 42, 88, 293, 295,
    368, 399, 413
Joris Karl Huysmans, 249
Josef Scaliger, 353
Joseph Ferrizuel, 221
Joseph Kaspi, 223
Joseph Quicherat, 248
Juan I of Portugal, 221
Juan II of Castile, 221

Judah ben Saul, 222
Judaism, 15, 129, 151
Judas Levi, 220
Judith Field, 187
Julian of Brioude, 189
Julian Ribera y Tarrago, 163
Jumna River, 112
jurjani, 179
Justinian, 145, 146

K

Kaaba, 2, 20, 39, 130
Kalbid, 70
Kalonymos ben Kalonymos, 223
Karlskirche, 380
Kashan, 115
Kayseri, 80
"keel" arch, 64, 67
Kepler, 24, 172
Kerman, 115
Kew gardens, 388, 389, 390
Khalid Ibn al-Walid, 16, 38
khanqah, 89
Khanqah, 89
Kheyruddin, 124
Khirbat al-Mafjar, 39, 43, 45
Khirbat Hamman Sark, 295
Khoja Ahmed Yassawi, 102
Khoja Mi'mar Sinan, 109, 124, 126
Khorasan, 22, 78, 79, 96, 363
Khurja, 106
Khuzestan, 293, 363
Khwarazm, 96
Kimchi, 222
King Akbar, 108, 109
King Alfonso VIII, 164, 283
King Edward IV, 364
King Hugo, 260
King Louis the Pious, 151
King Offa, 154
King Sigismund III, 115, 368
King's Exchequer, 165
kiosk, 392, 393
Kiosk", 80
Kitab al-Manazir, 59, 131
knighthood, 86
Knights, 178, 256, 343

344, 361, 369, 370, 380, 382, 388,
392, 413, 424, 427, 443
Moors, 38, 213, 214, 224, 233, 239,
242, 260, 357
morabetinos, 164
Moradabad, 106
Morocco,, 4, 22, 53, 316, 336
Morris dance, 284
mortar, 40, 52, 106, 145, 303, 304, 406
mosaic, 4, 43, 117, 143, 147, 279, 359,
374
Moses ibn Tibbon, 222
Moses Sepharadi, 223
Moses-Ben-Maimon, 220
Mosul, 179, 198, 199, 350
motifs, 9, 10, 48, 80, 86, 98, 115, 117,
119, 123, 138, 143, 149, 180, 181,
185, 189, 190, 203, 211, 215, 221,
245, 266, 283, 289, 349, 350, 357,
358, 364, 365, 366, 368, 369, 370,
371, 372, 380, 384, 393, 402, 403,
404, 407, 408
mouldings, 138
Mount Vesuvius, 144
Mozarab, 184, 190, 209, 210, 211,
212, 266, 268, 270, 316, 320, 324
Mozarab churches, 190, 270, 316, 320,
324
Mozarabic, 152, 267, 324
Mozarabic art, 212
Mozarabic castles, 211
Mozarabic churches, 210
Mozarabs, 165, 209, 210, 211, 212,
232, 266, 320, 327
Mu'izz Lidin Allah, 59
Mua'wiya, 34, 39
mudaraba, 180
Mudejar art, 215, 216, 217, 272
Mudejar artisans, 217
Mudejar atesonado, 216
Mudéjar belfry, 216
Mudejar culture, 213
Mudejar style, 215, 216, 217, 276
Mudejars, 203, 213, 214, 215, 217,
218, 233, 272
Mughal architecture, 112, 113
Muhammad al-Riquti, 213
Mujeer al-Din Abaq, 204

Mumtaz Mahal, 112
Muqaddam Ibn Mu'afi Al Oabri, 20
Muqaddimah, 21, 127, 431
muqarnas, 56, 60, 65, 66, 72, 82, 87,
91, 92, 93, 94, 99, 107, 115, 116,
119, 124, 276
Murcia, 164, 213, 365
musk, 179
Muslim architecture, 5, 1, 3, 4, 5, 6, 7,
8, 33, 36, 38, 53, 56, 106, 107, 123,
246, 261, 266, 276, 286, 293, 379,
384, 386, 388, 404
Muslim Architecture in Sicily, 70
Muslim art, 3, 10, 70, 181, 205, 211,
215, 216, 218, 358
Muslim carpet, 365, 366, 367
Muslim gold, 152
Muslim libraries, 19, 174
Muslim miniatures, 374
Muslim Minorities, 213
Muslim motifs, 178, 190, 212, 257,
266, 272, 276, 357, 370, 384, 385,
408
Muslim philosophy, 159
Muslim pottery, 368, 370
Muslim science, 156
Muslim textile, 350, 364
Muslim World, 3, 31, 33, 75, 96, 123,
350, 352, 354, 357
Muslims, 4, 1, 2, 3, 4, 7, 8, 9, 10, 12,
13, 15, 16, 17, 18, 19, 20, 21, 22,
23, 24, 27, 28, 29, 32, 33, 35, 36,
38, 46, 47, 52, 60, 70, 71, 72, 88,
92, 105, 106, 127, 149, 150, 151,
152, 154, 156, 158, 160, 163, 164,
165, 167, 168, 169, 171, 235, 237,
238, 239, 241, 242, 244, 245, 246,
249, 253, 255, 256, 257, 260, 261,
264, 266, 267, 270, 271, 274, 275,
278, 279, 283, 284, 285, 287, 289,
290, 292, 293, 297, 307, 308, 313,
316, 320, 324, 327, 328, 329, 330,
349, 351, 360, 361, 362, 364, 369,
370, 374, 391, 392, 394, 402, 403,
404, 405, 406, 407, 435
Muslin, 179, 350
Musta'arab, 209
Muwashahat, 20

465

N

O

Oxford University, 127, 128, 129, 133, 136, 165, 169, 170, 171, 172, 344, 346, 347, 394, 396, 398, 411, 413, 416, 417, 418, 420, 426, 427, 430, 433, 435, 437, 440, 441, 443, 446

P

Padua, 158, 161, 164, 172, 336
painting, 43, 98, 108, 144, 147, 252, 357, 365, 366, 367, 371, 374, 396, 398, 423, 436
Palace de Grand, 208
Palace of Al-Jafaria, 216
Palace of al-Qastal, 295
Palace of Amusement, 385
Palace of Ardeshir, 145
Palace of Beaumont, 165
Palace of Ukhaidar, 406
Palazzo Reale, 71, 74, 275
Palencia, 210
Palermo, 22, 31, 70, 72, 87, 132, 274, 276, 281, 432
Palermo Cathedral, 64, 276, 281
Palestine, 4, 39, 47, 75, 85, 86, 129, 145, 242, 308, 346, 363, 395, 397, 399, 406, 413, 416, 433
Pamplona, 267
Pantheon, 141, 142, 171, 449
Paradigm, 4
Paradise, 2, 34, 72, 91, 263, 278, 362
Parc Monceau, 377
Paris, 23, 127, 130, 131, 132, 133, 158, 160, 161, 162, 163, 165, 170, 171, 229, 249, 261, 339, 340, 341, 342, 343, 344, 346, 347, 348, 352, 354, 356, 358, 361, 363, 365, 377, 385, 394, 395, 396, 397, 399, 401, 411, 412, 414, 415, 416, 417, 418, 420, 421, 423, 424, 425, 426, 428, 431, 433, 434, 435, 436, 437, 439, 440, 441, 442, 447, 448
Parthian Palace, 293
Pasqua Rosée, 391, 401
Paulus Albarus, 209, 232
pediment, 93, 138, 140, 141
Pedro or Pierre the Cruel, 216
Pedro the Cruel, 216, 221

Pelerinage de Charlemagne, 261
pendentives, 43, 145
Pepin III, 151
perpendicular style, 189, 284
Perpignan, 157
Persia, 3, 5, 12, 15, 34, 46, 60, 66, 75, 78, 79, 82, 96, 102, 105, 107, 108, 115, 116, 121, 129, 244, 278, 284, 293, 313, 351, 352, 354, 364, 366, 368, 395, 396, 423, 439, 446
Persian (architecture), 1, 2, 3, 8, 19, 36, 40, 43, 46, 52, 64, 65, 66, 67, 87, 96, 98, 107, 114, 115, 124, 130, 135, 169, 237, 262, 286, 313, 347, 352, 356, 357, 359, 362, 364, 367, 371, 372, 380, 394, 408, 411, 438, 440, 441, 444
Persian arch, 64, 67
Persian miniature, 114
Peter Abelard, 159
Peter the Venerable, 157, 159, 171, 253, 433
Petrus Alphonsi, 223
Philip August, 199
Philip I, 197
Philipe Chinard, 207
Philippe Chinard, 285
Philippe of Alsace, 208
philosophy, 19, 22, 129, 139, 148, 156, 158, 159, 242, 253, 254, 265, 266, 442
Philosophy, 17, 170, 172, 173, 357, 417, 423, 430, 440, 446
Piedad de San Marina, 215
Pierenne, 152
Pierre le Chambrier, 285
piers, 36, 40, 47, 48, 65, 78, 94, 99, 103, 124, 141, 143, 167, 241, 249, 250, 257, 303, 304, 308, 313, 406
Pietro della Valle, 352
Pietro of Abano, 184
pilgrimage, 9, 22, 78, 129, 151, 155, 156, 166, 174, 187, 188, 189, 190, 195, 257, 270, 279, 316, 403, 404, 405, 407
pilgrimage route, 187, 190, 257, 270, 316
pilgrimage routes, 78, 166

467

252, 257, 263, 278, 283, 303, 304, 313, 320, 324, 329, 404, 407
Romanesque churches, 166
Romanesque style, 166, 167, 206, 218, 238, 247, 253, 263, 283, 304, 404, 407
Romanos, 27
rosette window, 43, 45
Rotunda of Ballyfin, 359
round arches, 53, 243, 246, 248
round towers, 88, 286
rounded arch, 218
Roussillon, 211
Royal Academy, 381, 385
Royal Library, 386
Royal Pavilion, 112, 386, 388, 393, 400, 422, 423
Royal stables, 385, 387
Rufina, 212
Russia, 85, 152

S

Saad ibn al-Waqqas, 34
Sacrobosto, 158
Safavid, 98, 114, 115, 116, 120, 121, 135, 351, 372, 438, 442
Safavid Architecture, 115
saffron, 179
Sahagun, 216
Sahn, 80
Saif al-Din Qutuz, 86
Saint Ambrogio, 306
Saint Aurelius, 327
Saint Benigne, 327
Saint Croix d'Oloron, 316
Saint Eugene, 215
Saint Eustorgio, 289, 292
Saint Gilles, 267
Saint Hugh, 270, 271
Saint James, 189
Saint Lazarus Cathedral, 272
Saint Marco, 240, 350, 372, 373
Saint Martin de Seez, 267
Saint Mayeul, 327
Saint Miquel de Cuxa, 211
Saint Philibert, 295, 296, 327
Saint Ruf d'Avignon, 267

Saint Victor, 267
Sainta Maria de Vilanova, 324
Saint-Benigne, 236
Salah al-Din, 85, 86, 88, 89, 91, 93, 287, 375
Salamanca, 267, 316, 407
Salerno, 31, 160, 162, 163, 164, 274, 278, 279, 344, 345, 419, 433
Salerno medical school, 162
Salerno School, 274
Samanid, 82, 84, 108
Samaniyah, 201
Samara, 38, 47, 48, 271, 286
Samarkand, 18, 80, 87, 96, 98, 102, 103, 104, 108, 116, 134, 448
Samarra, 82, 88, 130, 289, 404
Samuel Ben-Alarif, 220
Samuel Halevi, 216
Samuel Halevi Aboulafia, 216
Samuel Ibn Tibbon, 222
Samuel Levi, 221
Samuel Pepys Cockrell, 385, 387
Samuel the Nagid, 220
San Bartolomé, 216
San Baudelio, 211, 316, 320, 407
San Cataldo, 71, 276, 281
San Cebrian de Mazote, 210, 266, 268, 324
San Esteban, 211, 217
San Esteban de Gormaz, 211
San Facundo of Sahagun, 210
San Giovanni degli Eremiti, 71, 73, 218
San Ildefonso, 216, 217
San Isidore, 217
San Juan de Los Reyes, 216
San Juan of Pena, 210
San Julian, 217
San Lorenzo, 144, 216
San Lorenzo Fuori le Mura, 144
San Marcos, 215, 217
San Martin, 210, 216
San Martin de Castaneda, 210
San Miguel de Celarona, 316
San Miguel de Celnova, 210
San Miguel de Escalada, 210, 212, 266, 268, 324
San Millan de la Cogolla, 348, 407

475

W

Y

Z

Umayyad Great Mosque, Damascus (706 and 715 CE) was inspirational for Castello Sforzesco at Milano, Italy, 15th century (book cover image) and Piazza Ducale at Vigevano, Italy, ca 1492.

CPSIA information can be obtained
at www.ICGtesting.com
Printed in the USA
LVHW031512141221
706184LV00002B/79